NatWest

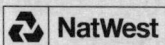

PLAYFAIR CRICKET ANNUAL 2000

53r

EDIT

All sta

PLAYFAIR CRICKET COMPETITION 2000

CRICKET QUIZ

£1500 TO BE WON

PLUS NATWEST FINAL TICKETS AND HOSPITALITY
PLUS 25 CONSOLATION PRIZES

First Prize	£500 +	overnight accommodation (B and B) at the Regents Park Jarvis International (opposite Lord's) on 25 and 26 August + TWO tickets to the 2000 NatWest Trophy Final + NatWest hospitality
Second Prize	£400 +	TWO tickets to the 2000 NatWest Trophy Final
Third Prize	£300 +	TWO tickets to the 2000 NatWest Trophy Final
Fourth Prize	£200	
Fifth Prize	£100	

Consolation prizes

Senders of the next 25 correct entries will each receive a signed copy of

THE WISDEN BOOK OF CRICKET RECORDS

Fourth Edition, published by Headline at £40.00

Compiled and Edited by Bill Frindall

Closing date for entries:
12.00 noon on 21 July 2000

Winning entries will be drawn by the Man of the Match Adjudicator at one of the NatWest semi-finals on 12/13 August.

PLAYFAIR CRICKET COMPETITION 2000

CRICKET QUIZ

ENTRY FORM

Please PRINT your answers in the spaces provided and answer every question

The answers to all ten questions can be found within this Annual

1 In which season was the oldest surviving County Championship partnership record set? ....

2 Who set a record score by an England 'night-watchman' in 1999? ....

3 In which domestic competition is a free hit awarded as a no-ball penalty? ....

4 Which specially registered county cricketer has represented Italy in the European Championships? ....

5 How many counties are in the first division of both the County Championship and the National League in 2000? ....

6 Who, in 1999, became the youngest Englishman to score a triple century in first-class cricket? ....

7 On which ground will a visiting county be the home team in a domestic competition match this season? ....

8 Who returned England's best Limited-Overs International bowling analysis whilst on tour in 1999-00? ....

9 What unique Test match record is Lord's Cricket Ground scheduled to set in June? ....

10 Who, during the 1999-00 season, became the second umpire to officiate in 50 Test matches? ....

Your name and address:

....

....

....

Your daytime telephone number: ....

Post to: PLAYFAIR CRICKET COMPETITION, FAO Andrew Dart, Octagon Event Marketing Ltd, 2nd Floor, Glen House, Stag Place, London, SW1 5AG.

Entries must be received before noon on 21 July 2000. All-correct entries will go into the prize-winning draw on 12/13 August and an announcement detailing all prize-winners will appear in the October edition of *The Cricketer* magazine. A list of winners will be available on request by writing to Andrew Dart at the above address and enclosing a stamped addressed envelope.

Rules: All entries must be on this official form. Proof of posting is not proof of entry. The decision of the editor regarding the answers to this quiz shall be final and binding; no correspondence may be entered into.

1999 PLAYFAIR CRICKET COMPETITION

CRICKET QUIZ ANSWERS

1	Which country will be competing in the NatWest Trophy for the first time this season?	**DENMARK**
2	Who, in 1998, shared a record English fifth-wicket partnership of 401?	Mal **LOYE** and David **RIPLEY**
3	Which bowler took the most wickets in the 1998 County Championship?	Courtney **WALSH**
4	In which season did Durham first award county caps on merit?	**1998**
5	Who scored over 1000 first-class runs in 1998 having appeared in only one previous match?	Matthew **WOOD**
6	Which county has three pairs of brothers currently under contract?	**SURREY**
7	In which town or city is the Asgiriya Stadium situated?	**KANDY**
8	Which first-class team plays its home matches at Riverside?	**DURHAM**
9	Name the newly registered county cricketer who appeared for Holland in the 1995-96 World Cup.	Bas **ZUIDERENT**
10	Which batsman scored the most runs in the 1998 County Championship?	John **CRAWLEY**

There were **929** sets of correct answers from a total of **1304** entries. The winners were drawn by David Gower OBE at the 1999 NatWest Trophy semi-final between Somerset and Surrey at Taunton.

First Prize:	£500 + two nights' accommodation + two tickets to include hospitality at the 1999 NatWest Trophy Final	**T.W.STAINES** (Folkestone)
Second Prize:	£400 + two tickets to the 1999 NatWest Trophy Final	Miss E.A.SCAFF (Bromley)
Third Prize:	£300 + two tickets to the 1999 NatWest Trophy Final	T.HANKS (Binfield)
Fourth Prize:	£200	V.GITTINS (Collompton)
Fifth Prize:	£100	D.E.LITTLE (New Bradwell)

25 Runners-up: each winning a signed copy of ***FROM OUTBACK TO OUTFIELD*** by Justin Langer, published by Headline at £16.99.

D.Aldington	(Alcester)
P.Baker	(Billericay)
I.W.Bedwell	(Northborough)
Mrs L.Billington	(Chesterfield)
T.Bryan	(Ruislip)
A.Burrows	(Belfast)
G.Davies	(Amlwch)
J.A.Eyre	(Ecclesfield)
T.Hammond	(King's Heath)
M.A.Hawker	(Stratford-upon-Avon)
D.R.Jackson	(Edgware)
B.King	(Bedford)
R.Klarik	(Wakefield)
D.Major	(Reading)
S.Morgan	(Pontcanna)
R.A.Pratt	(Bicester)
S.W.Rowell	(Durham)
T.J.W.Saunders	(Whitfield)
V.Shrimpton	(Marton)
C.Skippins	(Dewsbury)
W.Thornhill	(Hadfield)
R.N.Tillard	(West Tytherley)
P.D.Ward	(Wrea Green)
T.S.Warren	(Netherwallop)
R.White	(Tolworth)

SPONSOR'S MESSAGE FROM

NatWest

2000 heralds a new era for NatWest Cricket sponsorship. Earlier this year NatWest announced that it would be sponsoring the new annual, triangular one-day international competition that begins this summer.

The NatWest Series will bring together England and two touring teams for a 9-match 'round robin' international tournament, the top two teams progressing to a showpiece final at Lord's. In this year's NatWest Series, England will play host to the West Indies and Zimbabwe, with the opening match at Bristol on Thursday 6th July, marking the start of a 17-day, cross country, carnival of cricket.

The excitement of one-day cricket continues to capture the public's imagination. The NatWest Series is bound to have some memorable matches and close finishes. This, coupled with the prospect of the first ever day/night full international matches to be held in England, ensures that we will see some great action.

NatWest also announced that after this year it will not be renewing its sponsorship of the NatWest Trophy. NatWest has made a significant investment in cricket over the past two decades and has enjoyed an excellent association with the NatWest Trophy.

As part of the new sponsorship NatWest will also be supporting a new grassroots programme which aims to enhance practice facilities for young cricketers at clubs and schools. The introduction of new mobile non-turf pitches and new 'skill balls' are just two elements of this new ECB programme.

So as we say farewell to two decades of the NatWest Trophy and welcome in the new NatWest Series, we herald the emergence of any exciting new tournament. NatWest is looking forward to what is sure to be an exciting summer of one-day cricket.

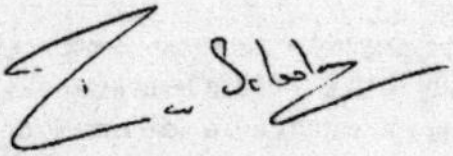

Ian Schoolar
Head of Brand Communication

FOREWORD

by JUSTIN LANGER

Imagine if you were a selector in a county cricket club and you had the luxury of choosing your best first eleven from the following list of players. Your top order could consist of Alec Stewart, Graham Thorpe, Mark Ramprakash, Mark Butcher, Alistair Brown, Owais Shah, Ben Hutton, Adam Hollioake and Paul Weekes. Only six of this very strong, talented and experienced group of batsmen could be selected for any one fixture, and therefore they would all be vying for one of the treasured six batting positions.

After careful deliberation on the batting front the selectors are then faced with the prospect of choosing three, maybe four, fast bowlers from Angus Fraser, Martin Bicknell, Alex Tudor, Richard Johnson, Jamie Hewitt and Tim Bloomfield. On a pitch offering early season assistance, this wouldn't be a bad bowling attack for an opposing batting line-up to come up against.

Phil Tufnell and Ian Salisbury would be competing for one of the spin bowling positions in this dream team, while Alec Stewart, David Nash and Jonathan Batty would be fighting for the role behind the stumps. While the balance of the team would be settled by choosing an all-rounder between Ben Hollioake, Simon Cook or Paul Weekes.

This would be a tough selection meeting, of course, but one any selector would surely dream about, and one which could become common practice if teams in the County Championship were to merge in the future. Add to this a very strong second team at each new county club and the Championship would be in great shape.

Obviously, the example above is purely hypothetical, but one which should be given careful consideration when the decision-makers next peer into the crystal ball to see where English cricket is going. The merging of clubs to reduce the number of people competing for positions as a first-class cricketer could have a profound effect upon the short-and long-term future of the currently disappointing state of English cricket.

Reducing the number of county clubs through merger may seem a drastic move but some people would argue that the success rate of the English team at international level has been so disappointing for so long that drastic measures must be taken. Having been asked for an opinion on the two-division system being employed this summer, I must confess that I cannot see how two divisions are going to change anything at all.

The simple fact is that county cricket will still be played by the same number of players, under the same playing conditions in as many fixtures as have been played in the past. In all of my days as a player I have never witnessed a team-mate or opponent walking on to the playing arena not wanting to do anything but win or at the very least fight out for a draw. This in mind, the two-tiered system may add some extra spice to certain fixtures during the summer, especially towards the business end of the season, but I can't see it having a profound effect on the overall standard or intensity of the county competition. More importantly, I can't see how it is going to improve the attitude, determination, hunger and general skill level of the players involved in the English system.

It seems the administrators have it the wrong way around in worrying about the 'dead game' syndrome of some teams when they may be out of the race for positions in the top half of the table. Surely more emphasis should be placed on how the system can improve the above attributes of its players. Attributes that are so crucial in developing a tough competition and an effective finishing school for the next level of the game – Test cricket.

Fewer teams means fewer players, and fewer players means fewer available places. When there are fewer positions and opportunities, the players in the first eleven must constantly prove they are the best around by being single-minded in their determination always to improve their technique, fitness and mental skills. With fewer positions, the cream of the competition will rise to the top and the standard of the county competition and the Test team will improve dramatically by natural progression.

The other question I have about the two-tiered system is whether the England selectors will pick their best Test team only from players in the first division. If the idea of this new system is to help improve the level and consistency of the Test team it would seem logical for the selectors to pick their side from the players in the first division. Theory would suggest that the toughest competition will be in the first division, and therefore the toughest players will come out of the stronger of the two divisions. Surely then every player wanting to make it at the next level must have at least have played in the first division of county cricket if he is to survive the tough and daunting world of international cricket.

Obviously this is unlikely to happen in the short term, but if it does in the future, an open transfer system will have to be introduced to accommodate every player looking to represent his country. There is no way a player can be deprived the opportunity of playing Test cricket because he is playing in a team struggling to win games. Conversely, it will be difficult to rate the performances of someone playing in the lower division. If, for example, a young batsman scores heavily in the second division, will he be rated less highly than a player scoring the same number of runs in the higher division? This scenario is likely to cause heated debate when the best team is due to be selected for a Test match and, more significantly, is likely to ignite debate on the open transfer of players to counties in the first division.

Obviously, people in England are searching for a solution to the continued disappointments of English cricket. Two divisions may be the answer but I personally don't think so. This new summer will answer the question for itself, but while there are so many first-class cricketers playing enormous amounts of cricket I can't see much changing.

Food for thought as they say . . .

Justin Langer
February 2000

EDITORIAL PREFACE

Whether or not one accepts that the year 2000 marks the start of a new millennium (as opposed to being the final year of the old one), and it is all pretty small beer in relation to the real age of this planet, this season marks a new dawn in the history of English and Welsh professional cricket. ECB contracts, a record seven Test matches, the first triangular limited-overs tournament in England and a two-divisional County Championship will dominate the longest and most congested season ever.

A brave new dawn perhaps but only time will tell if these bewildering changes can improve the quality of our professional cricket. Personally I find it hard to argue with the newly-appointed Middlesex captain's thought provoking rationale on the preceding pages. Far better than two divisions would have been a trial of regional cricket by combining pairs of counties to oppose the touring teams as South Africa did on England's recent tour. The real bugbears of our system, apart from an apparent surfeit of first-class teams and registered players, are the archaic benefit system and the poor quality of many of our pitches.

Chroniclers of the county game have been severely tested by the wholesale reforms of the limited-overs competitions, all three changing substantially last season. Commendably, the Association of Cricket Statisticians and Historians (ACS) has decided to simplify matters by adding the revised NatWest Trophy, the temporarily reduced Benson & Hedges Cup and the new CGU National League to the old records. The latter will have caused considerable debate. Increased to 45 overs, split into two divisions, sometimes played under lights and seldom staged on Sundays, it has little in common with the old Sunday League. With the three competitions now being played under fairly uniform rules, except for the National League with its fewer overs, coloured clothing and white ball, I have combined the individual career bests under a single entry for each player in the county register. Thus *LO HS* replaces *NWT HS*, *BHC HS* and *SL HS* and similarly for the bowling. Philip Bailey, compiler/editor of the *ACS International Cricket Year Book* has checked these entries and contributed a new section giving the limited-overs career records of all currently registered county cricketers.

The hex rather unjustly attributed to *Playfair*'s cover has been extended by Mark Ramprakash's recent fall from favour and no doubt Andrew Caddick's many fans will be quaking when they see this edition. Sadly, his consistently high-class contributions at county and international level made him an automatic selection and his agents failed to provide financial persuasion to exclude him.

Playfair has once again been generously served by the county clubs' administrators, scorers and statisticians, by Alan Fordham and Clare Fathers (ECB), by Clive Hitchcock (ICC), by David Armstrong (MCCA) and by many overseas correspondents. Special thanks to our sponsors NatWest, contributors Philip Bailey and Marion Collin, publishing editor Ian Marshall, new proof-reader David Mitchell, to Chris Leggett and his typesetting experts at Letterpart, and to my wife, Debbie, for much clerical assistance and doughty support.

BILL FRINDALL
Urchfont
10 March 2000

ENGLAND v ZIMBABWE

SERIES RECORDS

HIGHEST INNINGS TOTALS

England	in Zimbabwe	406		Bulawayo	1996-97
Zimbabwe	in Zimbabwe	376		Bulawayo	1996-97

LOWEST INNINGS TOTALS

England	in Zimbabwe	156		Harare	1996-97
Zimbabwe	in Zimbabwe	215		Harare	1996-97

HIGHEST INDIVIDUAL INNINGS

England	in Zimbabwe	113	N.Hussain	Bulawayo	1996-97
Zimbabwe	in Zimbabwe	112	A.Flower	Bulawayo	1996-97

HIGHEST AGGREGATE OF RUNS IN A SERIES

England	in Zimbabwe	241	(av 80.33)	A.J.Stewart	1996-97
Zimbabwe	in Zimbabwe	135	(av 45.00)	A.D.R.Campbell	1996-97

RECORD WICKET PARTNERSHIPS – ENGLAND

1st	48	N.V.Knight (56)/M.A.Atherton (16)	Bulawayo	1996-97
2nd	137	N.V.Knight (96)/A.J.Stewart (73)	Bulawayo	1996-97
3rd	68	A.J.Stewart (48)/N.Hussain (113)	Bulawayo	1996-97
4th	106*	A.J.Stewart (101*)/G.P.Thorpe (50*)	Harare	1996-97
5th	148	N.Hussain (113)/J.P.Crawley (112)	Bulawayo	1996-97
6th	22	N.V.Knight (96)/D.Gough (3*)	Bulawayo	1996-97
7th	34	J.P.Crawley (47*)/R.D.B.Croft (14)	Harare	1996-97
8th	9	J.P.Crawley (112)/C.E.W.Silverwood (0)	Bulawayo	1996-97
9th	25	J.P.Crawley (112)/A.D.Mullally (4)	Bulawayo	1996-97
10th	28	J.P.Crawley (112)/P.C.R.Tufnell (2*)	Bulawayo	1996-97

RECORD WICKET PARTNERSHIPS – ZIMBABWE

1st	6	G.W.Flower (0)/S.V.Carlisle (4)	Bulawayo	1996-97
2nd	127	G.W.Flower (43)/A.D.R.Campbell (84)	Bulawayo	1996-97
3rd	64	G.W.Flower (73)/D.L.Houghton (29)	Harare	1996-97
4th	70	D.L.Houghton (34)/A.Flower (112)	Bulawayo	1996-97
5th	29	A.Flower (112)/A.C.Waller (15)	Bulawayo	1996-97
6th	17	A.Flower (112)/G.J.Whittall (7)	Bulawayo	1996-97
7th	79	A.Flower (112)/P.A.Strang (38)	Bulawayo	1996-97
8th	41	A.Flower (112)/H.H.Streak (19)	Bulawayo	1996-97
9th	24	G.J.Whittall (56)/H.H.Streak (8*)	Bulawayo	1996-97
10th	4	P.A.Strang (47*)/H.K.Olonga (0)	Harare	1996-97

BEST INNINGS BOWLING ANALYSIS

England	in Zimbabwe	4- 40	D.Gough	Harare	1996-97
Zimbabwe	in Zimbabwe	5-123	P.A.Strang	Bulawayo	1996-97

BEST MATCH BOWLING ANALYSIS

England	in Zimbabwe	6-137	P.C.R.Tufnell	Bulawayo	1996-97
Zimbabwe	in Zimbabwe	7-186	P.A.Strang	Bulawayo	1996-97

HIGHEST AGGREGATE OF WICKETS IN A SERIES

England	in Zimbabwe	8	(av 22.25)	R.D.B.Croft	1996-97
Zimbabwe	in Zimbabwe	10	(av 25.90)	P.A.Strang	1996-97

RESULTS SUMMARY
ENGLAND v ZIMBABWE – IN ZIMBABWE

	Series				Bulawayo			Harare		
	Tests	*E*	*Z*	*D*	*E*	*Z*	*D*	*E*	*Z*	*D*
1996-97	2	–	–	2	–	–	1	–	–	1

ENGLAND v WEST INDIES

SERIES RECORDS

1928 to 1997-98

HIGHEST INNINGS TOTALS

England	in England	619-6d	Nottingham	1957
	in West Indies	849	Kingston	1929-30
West Indies	in England	692-8d	The Oval	1995
	in West Indies	681-8d	Port-of-Spain	1953-54

LOWEST INNINGS TOTALS

England	in England	71	Manchester	1976
	in West Indies	46	Port-of-Spain	1993-94
West Indies	in England	86	The Oval	1957
	in West Indies	102	Bridgetown	1934-35

HIGHEST MATCH AGGREGATE	1815 for 34 wickets	Kingston	1929-30
LOWEST MATCH AGGREGATE	309 for 29 wickets	Bridgetown	1934-35

HIGHEST INDIVIDUAL INNINGS

England	in England	285*	P.B.H.May	Birmingham	1957
	in West Indies	325	A.Sandham	Kingston	1929-30
West Indies	in England	291	I.V.A.Richards	The Oval	1976
	in West Indies	375	B.C.Lara	St John's	1993-94

HIGHEST AGGREGATE OF RUNS IN A SERIES

England	in England	506	(av 42.16)	G.P.Thorpe (*6 Tests*)	1995
	in West Indies	693	(av 115.50)	E.H.Hendren	1929-30
West Indies	in England	829	(av 118.42)	I.V.A.Richards	1976
	in West Indies	798	(av 99.75)	B.C.Lara	1993-94

RECORD WICKET PARTNERSHIPS – ENGLAND

1st	212	C.Washbrook (102)/R.T.Simpson (94)	Nottingham	1950
2nd	266	P.E.Richardson (126)/T.W.Graveney (258)	Nottingham	1957
3rd	303	M.A.Atherton (135)/R.A.Smith (175)	St John's	1993-94
4th	411	P.B.H.May (285*)/M.C.Cowdrey (154)	Birmingham	1957
5th	150	A.J.Stewart (143)/G.P.Thorpe (84)	Bridgetown	1993-94
6th	205	M.R.Ramprakash (154)/G.P.Thorpe (103)	Bridgetown	1997-98
7th	197	M.J.K.Smith (96)/J.M.Parks (101*)	Port-of-Spain	1959-60
8th	217	T.W.Graveney (165)/J.T.Murray (112)	The Oval	1966
9th	109	G.A.R.Lock (89)/P.I.Pocock (13)	Georgetown	1967-68
10th	128	K.Higgs (63)/J.A.Snow (59*)	The Oval	1966

RECORD WICKET PARTNERSHIPS – WEST INDIES

1st	298	C.G.Greenidge (149)/D.L.Haynes (167)	St John's	1989-90
2nd	287*	C.G.Greenidge (214*)/H.A.Gomes (92*)	Lord's	1984
3rd	338	E.de C.Weekes (206)/F.M.M.Worrell (167)	Port-of-Spain	1953-54
4th	399	G.St A.Sobers (226)/F.M.M.Worrell (197*)	Bridgetown	1959-60
5th	265	S.M.Nurse (137)/G.St A.Sobers (174)	Leeds	1966
6th	274*	G.St A.Sobers (163*)/D.A.J.Holford (105*)	Lord's	1966
7th	155*	G.St A.Sobers (150*)/B.D.Julien (121)	Lord's	1973
8th	99	C.A.McWatt (54)/J.K.Holt (48*)	Georgetown	1953-54
9th	150	E.A.E.Baptiste (87*)/M.A.Holding (69)	Birmingham	1984
10th	70	I.R.Bishop (44*)/D.Ramnarine (19)	Georgetown	1997-98

BEST INNINGS BOWLING ANALYSIS

England	in England	8-103	I.T.Botham	Lord's	1984
	in West Indies	8- 53	A.R.C.Fraser	Port-of-Spain	1997-98
West Indies	in England	8- 92	M.A.Holding	The Oval	1976
	in West Indies	8- 45	C.E.L.Ambrose	Bridgetown	1989-90

BEST MATCH BOWLING ANALYSIS

England	in England	12-119	F.S.Trueman	Birmingham	1963
	in West Indies	13-156	A.W.Greig	Port-of-Spain	1973-74
West Indies	in England	14-149	M.A.Holding	The Oval	1976
	in West Indies	11- 84	C.E.L.Ambrose	Port-of-Spain	1993-94

HIGHEST AGGREGATE OF WICKETS IN A SERIES

England	in England	34	(av 17.47)	F.S.Trueman	1963
	in West Indies	27	(av 18.66)	J.A.Snow	1967-68
		27	(av 18.22)	A.R.C.Fraser	1997-98
West Indies	in England	35	(av 12.65)	M.D.Marshall	1988
	in West Indies	30	(av 14.26)	C.E.L.Ambrose	1997-98

RESULTS SUMMARY

ENGLAND v WEST INDIES – IN ENGLAND

		Series			Lord's			Manchester			The Oval			Nottingham			Birmingham			Leeds		
	Tests	*E*	*WI*	*D*	*E*	*WI*	*D*	*E*	*WI*	*D*	*E*	*WI*	*D*	*E*	*WI*	*D*	*E*	*WI*	*D*	*E*	*WI*	*D*
1928	3	3	–	–	1	–	–	1	–	–	1	–	–	–	–	–	–	–	–	–	–	–
1933	3	2	–	1	1	–	–	–	–	1	1	–	–	–	–	–	–	–	–	–	–	–
1939	3	1	–	2	1	–	–	–	–	1	–	–	1	–	–	–	–	–	–	–	–	–
1950	4	1	3	–	–	1	–	1	–	–	–	1	–	–	1	–	–	–	–	–	–	–
1957	5	3	–	2	1	–	–	–	–	–	1	–	–	–	–	1	–	–	1	1	–	–
1963	5	1	3	1	–	–	1	–	1	–	–	1	–	–	–	–	1	–	–	–	1	–
1966	5	1	3	1	–	–	1	–	1	–	1	–	–	–	1	–	–	–	–	–	1	–
1969	3	2	–	1	–	–	1	1	–	–	–	–	–	–	–	–	–	–	–	1	–	–
1973	3	–	2	1	–	1	–	–	–	–	–	1	–	–	–	–	–	–	1	–	–	–
1976	5	–	3	2	–	–	1	–	1	–	–	1	–	–	–	1	–	–	–	–	1	–
1980	5	–	1	4	–	–	1	–	–	1	–	–	1	–	1	–	–	–	–	–	–	1
1984	5	–	5	–	–	1	–	–	1	–	–	1	–	–	–	–	–	1	–	–	1	–
1988	5	–	4	1	–	1	–	–	1	–	–	1	–	–	–	1	–	–	–	–	1	–
1991	5	2	2	1	–	–	1	–	–	–	1	–	–	–	1	–	–	1	–	1	–	–
1995	6	2	2	2	1	–	–	1	–	–	–	–	1	–	–	1	–	1	–	–	1	–
	65	18	28	19	5	4	6	4	5	3	5	6	3	–	4	4	1	3	2	3	6	1

ENGLAND v WEST INDIES – IN WEST INDIES

		Series			Bridgetown			Port-of-Spain			Georgetown			Kingston			St John's		
	Tests	*E*	*WI*	*D*	*E*	*WI*	*D*	*E*	*WI*	*D*	*E*	*WI*	*D*	*E*	*WI*	*D*	*E*	*WI*	*D*
1929-30	4	1	1	2	–	–	1	1	–	–	–	1	–	–	–	1	–	–	–
1934-35	4	1	2	1	1	–	–	–	1	–	–	–	1	–	1	–	–	–	–
1947-48	4	–	2	2	–	–	1	–	–	1	–	1	–	–	1	–	–	–	–
1953-54	5	2	2	1	–	1	–	–	–	1	1	–	–	1	1	–	–	–	–
1959-60	5	1	–	4	–	–	1	1	–	1	–	–	1	–	–	1	–	–	–
1967-68	5	1	–	4	–	–	1	1	–	1	–	–	1	–	–	1	–	–	–
1973-74	5	1	1	3	–	–	1	1	1	–	–	–	1	–	–	1	–	–	–
1980-81	4	–	2	2	–	1	–	–	1	–	–	–	–	–	–	1	–	–	1
1985-86	5	–	5	–	–	1	–	–	2	–	–	–	–	–	1	–	–	1	–
1989-90	4	1	2	1	–	1	–	–	–	1	–	–	–	1	–	–	–	1	–
1993-94	5	1	3	1	1	–	–	–	1	–	–	1	–	–	1	–	–	–	1
1997-98	6	1	3	2	–	–	1	1	1	–	–	1	–	–	–	1	–	1	–
	56	10	23	23	2	4	6	5	7	5	1	4	4	2	5	6	–	3	2
Totals	121	28	51	42															

TOURING TEAM REGISTER 2000

ZIMBABWE PROBABLES

Full Names	*Birthdate*	*Birthplace*	*Team*	*Type*	*F-C Debut*
BLIGNAUT, Arnoldus Mauritius	1. 8.78	Salisbury	Mashonaland	LHB/RMF	1997-98
BRENT, Gary Bazil	13. 1.76	Sinoia	Mashonaland	RHB/RMF	1994-95
CAMPBELL, Alistair Douglas Ross	23. 9.72	Salisbury	Mashonaland	LHB/OB	1990-91
CARLISLE, Stuart Vance	10. 5.72	Salisbury	Mashonaland	RHB/RM	1993-94
FLOWER, Andrew	28. 4.68	Cape Town	Mashonaland	LHB/OB/WK	1986-87
FLOWER, Grant William	20.12.70	Salisbury	Mashonaland	RHB/SLA	1989-90
GOODWIN, Murray William	11.12.72	Salisbury	Mashonaland	RHB/LB	1994-95
GRIPPER, Trevor Raymond	28.12.75	Salisbury	Matabeleland	RHB/OB	1996-97
JOHNSON, Neil Clarkson	24. 1.70	Salisbury	Matabeleland	LHB/RMF	1989-90
MBANGWA, Mpumelelo	26. 6.76	Plumtree	Matabeleland	RHB/RFM	1995-96
MURPHY, Brian Andrew	1.12.76	Salisbury	Mashonaland	RHB/LBG	1995-96
NKALA, Mluleki Luke	1. 4.81	Bulawayo	Matabeleland	RHB/RFM	1999-00
OLONGA, Henry Khaaba	3. 7.76	Lusaka	Matabeleland	RHB/RFM	1993-94
STRANG, Bryan Colin	9. 6.72	Bulawayo	Mashonaland	RHB/LMF	1994-95
STRANG, Paul Andrew	28. 7.70	Bulawayo	Mashonaland	RHB/LBG	1992-93
STREAK, Heath Hilton	6. 3.74	Bulawayo	Matabeleland	RHB/RFM	1992-93
VILJOEN, Dirk Peter	11. 3.77	Salisbury	Mashonaland	LHB/SLA	1994-95
WHITTALL, Guy James	5. 9.72	Chipinga	Matabeleland	RHB/RM	1990-91
WISHART, Craig Brian	9. 1.74	Salisbury	Mashonaland	RHB/RM	1992-93

WEST INDIES PROBABLES

Full Names	*Birthdate*	*Birthplace*	*Team*	*Type*	*F-C Debut*
ADAMS, James Clive	9. 1.68	Port Maria	Jamaica	LHB/SLA/WK	1984-85
AMBROSE, Curtly Elconn Lynwall	21. 9.63	Swetes, Antigua	Leeward Is	LHB/RF	1985-86
CAMPBELL, Sherwin Legay	1.11.70	Belleplaine	Barbados	RHB/RM	1990-91
CHANDERPAUL, Shivnarine	18. 8.74	Unity	Guyana	LHB/LB	1991-92
COLLINS, Pedro Tyrone	12. 8.76	Boscobelle	Barbados	RHB/LFM	1996-97
DILLON, Mervyn	5. 6.74	Toco	Trinidad	RHB/RFM	1996-97
GAYLE, Christopher Henry	21. 9.79	Kingston	Jamaica	LHB/OB	1998-99
GRIFFITH, Adrian Frank Gordon	19.11.71	Holders Hill	Barbados	LHB/RM	1992-93
HINDS, Wavell Wayne	7. 9.76	Kingston	Jamaica	LHB/RM	1995-96
JACOBS, Ridley Detamore	26.11.67	Antigua	Leeward Is	LHB/WK	1991-92
KING, Reon Dane	6.10.74	Berbice	Guyana	RHB/RFM	1995-96
LARA, Brian Charles	2. 5.69	Santa Cruz	Trinidad	LHB/LBG	1987-88
McLEAN, Nixon Alexei McNamara	20. 7.73	St Vincent	Windward Is	LHB/RF	1992-93
MORTON, Runako Shaku	22. 7.68	Nevis	Leeward Is	RHB/OB	1996-97
NAGAMOOTOO, Mahendra Veeren	9.10.75	Port Mourant	Guyana	LHB/LBG	1994-95
PERRY, Nehemiah Odulphus	16. 6.68	Kingston	Jamaica	RHB/OB	1986-87
POWELL, Ricardo Lloyd	16.12.78	St Elizabeth	Jamaica	RHB	1997-98
ROSE, Franklyn Albert	1. 2.72	Chalk Hill	Jamaica	RHB/RF	1992-93
WALSH, Courtney Andrew	30.10.62	Kingston	Jamaica	RHB/RF	1981-82

THE FIRST-CLASS COUNTIES REGISTER, RECORDS AND 1999 AVERAGES

Career statistics are to 23 February 2000 and include all England's winter tours

ABBREVIATIONS

General

*	not out/unbroken partnership
b	born
BB	Best innings bowling analysis
Cap	Awarded 1st XI County Cap
f-c	first-class
HS	Highest Score
LOI	Limited-Overs Internationals
Tests	Official Test Matches
Tours	Overseas tours involving first-class appearances

Awards

BHC	Benson and Hedges Cup 'Gold' Award
NWT	NatWest Trophy/Gillette Cup 'Man of the Match' Award
Wisden 1998	One of *Wisden Cricketers' Almanack's* Five Cricketers of 1998
YC 1999	Cricket Writers' Club Young Cricketer of 1999

ECB Competitions

BHC	Benson & Hedges Cup
CC	PPP County Championship
NWT	NatWest Trophy
NL	CGU National League (1999)
SL	Sunday League (1969-98)

Overseas Competitions

BHS	Benson & Hedges Night Series (SA)
FAI	Mercantile Mutual Cup (A)
MM	Federated Automobile Insce Cup (A)
RSB	Red Stripe Bowl (WI)
SBC	Standard Bank Cup (SA)
SST	Shell/Sandals Trophy (WI)
WT	Wills Trophy (I)

Education

BHS	Boys' High School
C	College
CFE	College of Further Education
CHE	College of Higher Education
CS	Comprehensive School
GS	Grammar School
HS	High School
IHE	Institute of Higher Education
RGS	Royal Grammar School
S	School
SFC	Sixth Form College
SM	Secondary Modern School
SS	Secondary School
TC	Technical College
T(H)S	Technical (High) School
U	University
UMIST	University of Manchester Institute of Science and Technology

Playing Categories

LBG	Bowls right-arm leg-breaks and googlies
LF	Bowls left-arm fast
LFM	Bowls left-arm fast-medium
LHB	Bats left-handed
LM	Bowls left-arm medium pace
LMF	Bowls left-arm medium fast
OB	Bowls right-arm off-breaks
RF	Bowls right-arm fast
RFM	Bowls right-arm fast-medium
RHB	Bats right-handed
RM	Bowls right-arm medium pace
RMF	Bowls right-arm medium-fast
RSM	Bowls right-arm slow-medium
SLA	Bowls left-arm leg-breaks
SLC	Bowls left-arm 'Chinamen'
WK	Wicket-keeper

Teams (see also p 113)

B	Bangladesh
CD	Central Districts
DHR	D.H.Robins' XI
EP	Eastern Province
GW	Griqualand West
K	Kenya
NSW	New South Wales
NT	Northern Transvaal
OFS	(Orange) Free State
PIA	Pakistan International Airlines
Q	Queensland
RW	Rest of the World XI
SAB	South African Breweries XI
SAU	South African Universities
WA	Western Australia
WP	Western Province

DERBYSHIRE

Formation of Present Club: 4 November 1870
Colours: Chocolate, Amber and Pale Blue
Badge: Rose and Crown
County Champions: (1) 1936
NatWest Trophy/Gillette Cup Winners: (1) 1981
Benson and Hedges (Super) Cup Winners: (1) 1993
CGU National League (Div 1) Winners: (0); best – 8th (Div 2) 1999
Sunday League Winners: (1) 1990
Match Awards: NWT 44; BHC 67

Secretary/General Manager: J.Smedley, County Cricket Ground, Nottingham Road, Derby DE2 6DA ▲ Tel: 01332 383211 ▲ Fax: 01332 290251 ▲ Email: derby@ecb.co.uk ▲ Web: www.dccc.org.uk

Captain: D.G.Cork. **Vice-Captain:** K.M.Krikken. **Overseas Player:** M.J.Di Venuto. **2000 Beneficiary:** None. **Scorer:** J.M.Brown. ‡ New registration

ALDRED, Paul (Lady Manner's S, Bakewell), b Chellaston 4 Feb 1969. 5'10". RHB, RM. Debut 1995. Cap 1999. Cheshire 1994. HS 83 v Hants (Chesterfield) 1997. 50 wkts (1): 50 (1999). BB 7-101 (13-184 match) v Lancs (Derby) 1999. LO HS 39* v Surrey (Derby) 1999 (NL). LO BB 4-30 v Lincs (Lincoln) 1997 (NWT).

‡BAILEY, Robert John (Biddulph HS), b Biddulph, Staffs 28 Oct 1963. 6'3". RHB, OB. Northamptonshire 1982-99; cap 1985; benefit 1993; captain 1996-97. Staffordshire 1980. YC 1984. **Tests:** 4 (1988 to 1989-90); HS 43 v WI (Oval) 1988. **LOI**: 4 (1984-85 to 1989-90); HS 43* v SL (Oval) 1988. Tours: SA 1991-92 (Nh); WI 1989-90; Z 1994-95 (Nh). 1000 runs (13); most – 1987 (1990). HS 224* Nh v Glam (Swansea) 1986. BB 5-54 Nh v Notts (Northampton) 1993. Awards: NWT 7; BHC 9. LO HS 145 Nh v Staffs (Stone) 1991 (NWT). LO BB 3-23 Nh v Leics (Leicester) 1987 (SL).

CASSAR, Matthew Edward (Sir Joseph Banks HS, Sydney), b Sydney, Australia 16 Oct 1972. Husband of Jane Cassar (England). 6'0". RHB, RFM. Debut 1994. ECB qualified/CC debut 1997. HS 121 v Sussex (Horsham) 1998. BB 5-51 v Essex (Chelmsford) 1999. Award: NWT 1. LO HS 134 v Northants (Northampton) 1998 (SL). LO BB 4-31 v Middx (Derby) 1999 (NL).

CORK, Dominic Gerald (St Joseph's C, Stoke-on-Trent), b Newcastle-under-Lyme, Staffs 7 Aug 1971. 6'2". RHB, RFM. Debut 1990; cap 1993; captain 1998 to date; benefit 2001. *Wisden* 1995. Staffordshire 1989-90. **Tests:** 27 (1995 to 1998-99); HS 59 v NZ (Auckland) 1996-97; BB 7-43 v WI (Lord's) 1995 – on debut (record England analysis by Test match debutant); hat-trick v WI (Manchester) 1995 – the first in Test history to occur in the opening over of a day's play. **LOI:** 25 (1992 to 1996-97); HS 31* v NZ (Napier) 1996-97; BB 3-27 v WI (Lord's) 1995. Tours: A 1992-93 (Eng A), 1998-99; SA 1993-94 (Eng A), 1995-96; WI 1991-92 (Eng A); NZ 1996-97; I 1994-95 (Eng A). HS 104 v Glos (Cheltenham) 1993. 50 wkts (5); most – 90 (1995). BB 9-43 (13-93 match) v Northants (Derby) 1995. Took 8-53 before lunch on his 20th birthday v Essex (Derby) 1991. 2 hat-tricks: 1994 and 1995 (*see Tests*). Awards: NWT 3; BHC 3. LO HS 92* v Lancs (Lord's) 1993 (BHC). LO BB 6-21 v Glam (Chesterfield) 1997 (SL).

DEAN, Kevin James (Leek HS; Leek C), b Derby 16 Oct 1975. 6'5". LHB, LMF. Debut 1996. Cap 1998. HS 27* v SA (Derby) 1998. CC HS 25* v Essex (Derby) 1998. 50 wkts (1): 74 (1998). BB 6-63 (12-133 match) v Somerset (Taunton) 1998. Hat-trick 1998. Award: NWT 1. LO HS 16* v Glam (Cardiff) 1998 (SL). LO BB 5-32 v Glos (Derby) 1996 (SL).

‡Di VENUTO, Michael James (St Virgil's C; Hobart), b Hobart, Australia 12 Dec 1973. 6'0". LHB, RM/LB. Tasmania 1991-92 to date. Sussex 1999; cap 1999. **LOI** (A): 9 (1996-97 to 1997-98); HS 89 v SA (Jo'burg) 1996-97. Tours: Z 1995-96 (Tas); Sc/Ire 1998 (Aus A – captain). 1000 runs (1): 1067 (1999). HS 189 Tas v WA (Perth) 1997-98. CC HS 162 Sx v Glos (Hove) 1999. BB (Sx) 1-3. LO HS 129* Tas v S Aus (Hobart) 1996-97 (MM). LO BB (Tas) 1-10 (MM).

‡DOWMAN, Mathew Peter (St Hugh's CS; Grantham C), b Grantham, Lincs 10 May 1974. 5'10". LHB, RMF. Nottinghamshire 1994-99; cap 1998. Scored 267 for England YC v WI YC (Hove) 1993 – record score in youth 'Tests'. 1000 runs (1): 1091 (1997). HS 149 Nt v Leics (Leicester) 1997. BB 3-10 Nt v Pak A (Nottingham) 1997. CC BB 2-10 Nt v Kent (Canterbury) 1998. LO HS 92 Nt v Northants (Nottingham) 1997 (BHC). LO BB 3-21 Nt v Worcs (Nottingham) 1996 (BHC).

EAGLESON, Ryan Logan, b Carrickfergus, N Ireland 17 Dec 1974. RHB, RFM. Ireland debut 1996. Derbyshire debut 1999. HS 50* and BB 2-50 Ire v Scot (Linlithgow) 1996 – on debut. De HS 0. De BB 1-34. LO HS 15* Ire v Essex (Chelmsford) 1998 (BHC) and 15* Ire v Sussex (Belfast) 1996 (NWT). LO BB 4-59 Ire v Leics (Dublin) 1999 (NWT).

KRIKKEN, Karl Matthew (Rivington & Blackrod HS & SFC), b Bolton, Lancs 9 Apr 1969. Son of B.E. (Lancs and Worcs 1966-69). 5'9". RHB, WK. GW 1988-89. Derbyshire debut 1989; cap 1992. HS 104 v Lancs (Manchester) 1996. BB 1-54. LO HS 55 v Kent (Derby) 1996 (NWT).

LACEY, Simon James (Aldercar CS; Ripley Mill Hill SFC), b Nottingham 9 Mar 1975. 5'11". RHB, OB. Debut 1997. HS 50 v Somerset (Derby) 1997. BB 3-97 v Essex (Southend) 1997. LO HS 15 v Notts (Derby) 1999 (NL). LO BB 3-38 v Notts (Nottingham) 1999 (NL).

‡MUNTON, Timothy Alan (Sarson HS; King Edward VII Upper S), b Melton Mowbray, Leics 30 Jul 1965. 6'6". RHB, RMF. Warwickshire 1985-99; cap 1989; captain 1997 (no appearances – back injury); benefit 1998. *Wisden* 1994. **Tests:** 2 (1992); HS 25* v P (Manchester) 1992; BB 2-22 v P (Leeds) 1992. Tours: SA 1992-93 (Wa); WI 1991-92 (Eng A); P 1990-91 (Eng A), 1995-96 (Eng A – *part*); SL 1990-91 (Eng A); Z 1993-94 (Wa). HS 54* Wa v Worcs (Worcester) 1996. 50 wkts (6); most – 81 (1994). BB 8-89 (11-128 match) Wa v Middx (Birmingham) 1991. Hat-trick (Wa) 1999. Awards: NWT 2; BHC 1. LO HS 17 Wa v Glam (Cardiff) 1999 (NWT). LO BB 5-23 Wa v Glos (Moreton-in-M) 1990 (SL).

PYEMONT, James Patrick (Tonbridge S; Trinity Hall, Cambridge), b Eastbourne, Sussex 10 Apr 1978. Son of C.P. (Cambridge U 1967; cricket and hockey blue). 6'0". RHB, OB. Sussex 1997 – no CC appearances. Cambridge U 1998-99; blue 1998-99). Derbyshire debut 1999 (dismissed first ball in both innings – first instance by Derbyshire player). HS 90* CU v Middx (Cambridge) 1999. De HS 13 v Leics (Leicester) 1999. LO HS 25 Brit U v Somerset (Taunton) 1998 (BHC).

SHAH, Kasir Zamir, b Jhelum, Pakistan 15 Jun 1978. LHB, LMF. Awaiting f-c debut. LO HS 0* (NL). LO BB 2-36 v Middx (Derby) 1999 (NL).

SMITH, Trevor Mark (Friesland S, Sandiacre; Broxtowe C, Chilwell), b Derby 18 Jan 1977. 6'3". LHB, RFM. Debut 1997. HS 29 and BB 6-32 v Essex (Derby) 1998. LO HS 8* (NL). LO BB 4-38 v Somerset (Derby) 1999 (NL).

SPENDLOVE, Benjamin Lee (Trent C), b Belper 4 Nov 1978. 6'1". RHB, OB. Debut 1997. HS 63 v Warwks (Birmingham) 1999. LO HS 58 v Leics (Leicester) 1998 (NWT).

STUBBINGS, Stephen David (Frankston HS; Swinburne U), b Huddersfield, Yorks 31 Mar 1978. 6'3". LHB, OB. Debut 1997. HS 45 v Leics (Leicester) 1999. LO HS 37 v Notts (Nottingham) 1999 (NL) and 37 v Middx (Derby) 1999 (NL).

‡**SUTTON, Luke** David (Millfield S; Durham U), b Keynsham, Somerset 4 Oct 1976. 5'11". RHB, WK. Somerset 1997-98. HS 16* Sm v SL (Taunton) 1998. CC HS (Sm) 5. LO HS 60 Brit U v Kent (Oxford) 1998 (BHC).

TITCHARD, Stephen Paul (Lymm County HS; Priestley C), b Warrington 17 Dec 1967. 6'3". RHB, RM. Lancashire 1990-98; cap 1995. Derbyshire 1999. HS 163 La v Essex (Chelmsford) 1996. De HS 136 v Northants (Derby) 1999. BB 1-11 (La – twice). Award: NWT 1. LO HS 96 La v Essex (Chelmsford) 1994 (SL). LO BB (De) 1-19 (NL).

RELEASED/RETIRED

(Having made a first-class County appearance in 1999)

BASE, Simon John (Fish Hoek HS, Cape Town), b Maidstone, Kent 2 Jan 1960. 6'2". RHB, RMF. W Province 1981-82 to 1983-84. Glamorgan 1986-87. Boland 1987-88 to 1988-89. Border 1989-90 to date. Derbyshire 1988-96 and 1999 (one match); cap 1990. HS 58 v Yorks (Chesterfield) 1990. 50 wkts (1): 60 (1989). BB 7-60 v Yorks (Chesterfield) 1989. LO HS 31 v Kent (Canterbury) 1993 (SL). LO BB 4-14 v Northants (Derby) 1991 (SL) and v Glos (Cheltenham) 1993 (SL).

BLACKWELL, I.D. – *see SOMERSET.*

DEANE, Michael John, b Chesterfield 9 Mar 1977. RHB, RM. Derbyshire 1999. HS 10 v Somerset (Derby) 1999. BB 2-42 v Yorks (Derby) 1999 – on debut. LO HS 1* (NWT). LO BB 3-42 v Surrey (Oval) 1999 (NL).

DeFREITAS, P.A.J. – *see LEICESTERSHIRE.*

GRIFFITHS, Steven Paul (Beechen Cliff S, Bath; Brunel C of Art & Technology, Bristol), b Hereford 31 May 1973. RHB, WK. 5'11". Derbyshire 1995-99. HS 35 v Warwks (Birmingham) 1999. LO HS 9 (NL).

HARRIS, A.J. – *see NOTTINGHAMSHIRE.*

NEWELL, Mark (Hazelwick SS; City of Westminster C), b Crawley 19 Dec 1973. Brother of K. (*see GLAMORGAN*). 6'1½". RHB, OB. Sussex 1996-98. Derbyshire 1999. MCC YC. HS 135* Sx v Derbys (Horsham) 1998. De HS 25 v Durham (Chester-le-St) 1999. LO HS 92 Sx Board v Herts (Hertford) 1999 (NWT).

ROLLINS, A.S. – *see NORTHAMPTONSHIRE.*

SLATER, Michael Jonathon (Wagga Wagga HS), b Wagga Wagga, NSW, Australia 21 Feb 1970. 5'9". RHB, RM. NSW 1991-92 to date. Derbyshire 1998-99; cap 1998. **Tests** (A): 59 (1993 to 1999-00); HS 219 v SL (Perth) 1995-96; BB 1-4. **LOI** (A): 42 (1993-94 to 1997); HS 73 v SA (Melbourne) 1993-94 – on debut. Tours (A): E 1993, 1995 (NSW), 1997; SA 1993-94; WI 1994-95, 1998-99; I 1996-97, 1997-98; P 1994-95, 1998-99; SL 1999-00; Z 1999-00. 1000 runs (1+1); most – 1472 (1994-95). HS 219 (*see Tests*). De HS 185 v SA (Derby) 1998. CC HS 99 v Surrey (Oval) 1998. BB 1-4 (*see Tests*). LO HS 110 v Worcs (Derby) 1998 (SL).

THOMAS, Paul Anthony (Broadway S; Sutton C; Sandwell C), b Perry Barr, Birmingham 3 Jun 1971. 5'11". RHB, RFM. Worcestershire 1995-97. Derbyshire 1999. Shropshire 1992-94. HS 25 Wo v Warwks (Birmingham) 1995. De HS 1. BB 5-70 Wo v WI (Worcester) 1995 – on debut. CC BB 4-78 Wo v Sussex (Eastbourne) 1995. De BB 2-54 v Essex (Chelmsford) 1999. LO HS 12* Salop v Middx (Telford) 1992 (NWT). LO BB 2-30 Wo v Cumberland (Worcester) 1995 (NWT).

TWEATS, Timothy Andrew (Endon HS; Stoke-on-Trent SFC), b Stoke-on-Trent, Staffs 18 Apr 1974. 6'3". RHB, RM. Derbyshire 1992-99. HS 189 v Yorks (Derby) 1997. BB 1-23. Award: BHC 1. LO HS 42* v Scot (Forfar) 1998 (BHC).

WESTON, R.M.C. – *see MIDDLESEX.*

WOOLLEY, Anthony Paul (Spondon S), b Derby 4 Dec 1971. RHB, RM. Derbyshire 1999. HS 8. LO HS 1* (NL). LO BB 4-61 v Notts (Derby) 1999 (NL).

DERBYSHIRE 1999

RESULTS SUMMARY

	Place	Won	Lost	Tied	Drew	No Result
PPP County Championship	**9th**	7	8		2	
All First-Class Matches		7	8		2	
NatWest Trophy	4th Round					
CGU National League (Division 2)	**8th**	4	10	1		1

COUNTY CHAMPIONSHIP AVERAGES

BATTING AND FIELDING

Cap		M	I	NO	HS	Runs	Avge	100	50	Ct/St
1995	A.S.Rollins	15	28	3	113	965	38.60	2	5	9
–	R.M.S.Weston	15	26	2	156	838	34.91	3	2	9
1998	M.J.Slater	10	18	1	171	540	31.76	1	2	9
–	S.P.Titchard	17	31	4	136	752	27.85	1	2	2
1993	D.G.Cork	14	22	2	82	535	26.75	–	4	18
1994	P.A.J.DeFreitas	13	18	1	105	441	25.94	1	2	7
–	S.J.Lacey	6	8	2	42	154	25.66	–	–	5/1
–	I.D.Blackwell	10	16	2	62*	347	24.78	–	2	6
1992	K.M.Krikken	12	19	3	88	389	24.31	–	3	30/1
–	B.L.Spendlove	7	13	–	63	279	21.46	–	2	2
–	S.D.Stubbings	5	10	–	45	213	21.30	–	–	3
–	M.E.Cassar	14	24	3	42	393	18.71	–	–	5
–	S.P.Griffiths	5	7	1	35	108	18.00	–	–	16/1
–	T.M.Smith	8	9	6	20*	52	17.33	–	–	2
1996	A.J.Harris	7	11	7	8*	48	12.00	–	–	4
1999	P.Aldred	12	17	2	29*	122	8.13	–	–	4
–	J.P.Pyemont	3	6	1	13	23	4.60	–	–	3
–	T.A.Tweats	4	7	–	10	21	3.00	–	–	2

Also batted: S.J.Base (1 match – cap 1990) 17, 8*; K.J.Dean (3 – cap 1998) 5, 10* (1 ct); M.J.Deane (2) 1, 0, 10 (1 ct); R.L.Eagleson (1) 0 (1 ct); M.Newell (1) 25, 7 (1 ct); P.A.Thomas (1) 1, 0; A.P.Woolley (1) 8, 1.

BOWLING

	O	M	R	W	Avge	Best	5wI	10wM
K.J.Dean	66.4	14	198	12	16.50	4- 34	–	–
T.M.Smith	183.4	34	646	31	20.83	5- 63	3	1
P.Aldred	362.4	85	1063	50	21.26	7-101	5	1
P.A.J.DeFreitas	477.2	121	1284	59	21.76	6- 41	4	–
D.G.Cork	427.3	91	1229	55	22.34	6-113	4	–
A.J.Harris	229.3	44	752	26	28.92	5- 63	2	–
M.E.Cassar	164	34	562	19	29.57	5- 51	1	–
I.D.Blackwell	250.1	69	595	12	49.58	3- 30	–	–

Also bowled: S.J.Base 10-3-34-0; M.J.Deane 31.4-8-112-2; R.L.Eagleson 10.5-2-34-1; K.M.Krikken 9.2-1-54-1; S.J.Lacey 81-15-238-3; M.J.Slater 4-0-23-0; S.D.Stubbings 5-0-41-0; P.A.Thomas 16-1-74-2; S.P.Titchard 8-3-19-0; R.M.S.Weston 6-1-23-1; A.P.Woolley 11-1-61-0.

The First-Class Averages (pp 113-128) give the records of Derbyshire players in all first-class county matches, with the exception of J.P.Pyemont whose full county figures are as above.

DERBYSHIRE RECORDS

FIRST-CLASS CRICKET

Highest Total	For 645		v	Hampshire	Derby	1898
	V 662		by	Yorkshire	Chesterfield	1898
Lowest Total	For 16		v	Notts	Nottingham	1879
	V 23		by	Hampshire	Burton upon T	1958
Highest Innings	For 274	G.A.Davidson	v	Lancashire	Manchester	1896
	V 343*	P.A.Perrin	for	Essex	Chesterfield	1904

Highest Partnership for each Wicket

1st	322	H.Storer/J.Bowden	v	Essex	Derby	1929
2nd	417	K.J.Barnett/T.A.Tweats	v	Yorkshire	Derby	1997
3rd	316*	A.S.Rollins/K.J.Barnett	v	Leics	Leicester	1997
4th	328	P.Vaulkhard/D.Smith	v	Notts	Nottingham	1946
5th	302*†	J.E.Morris/D.G.Cork	v	Glos	Cheltenham	1993
6th	212	G.M.Lee/T.S.Worthington	v	Essex	Chesterfield	1932
7th	241*	G.H.Pope/A.E.G.Rhodes	v	Hampshire	Portsmouth	1948
8th	198	K.M.Krikken/D.G.Cork	v	Lancashire	Manchester	1996
9th	283	A.Warren/J.Chapman	v	Warwicks	Blackwell	1910
10th	132	A.Hill/M.Jean-Jacques	v	Yorkshire	Sheffield	1986

† *346 runs were added for this wicket in two separate partnerships*

Best Bowling	For	10- 40	W.Bestwick	v	Glamorgan	Cardiff	1921
(Innings)	V	10- 45	R.L.Johnson	for	Middlesex	Derby	1994
Best Bowling	For	17-103	W.Mycroft	v	Hampshire	Southampton	1876
(Match)	V	16-101	G.Giffen	for	Australians	Derby	1886

Most Runs – Season	2165	D.B.Carr	(av 48.11)	1959
Most Runs – Career	23854	K.J.Barnett	(av 41.12)	1979-98
Most 100s – Season	8	P.N.Kirsten		1982
Most 100s – Career	53	K.J.Barnett		1979-98
Most Wkts – Season	168	T.B.Mitchell	(av 19.55)	1935
Most Wkts – Career	1670	H.L.Jackson	(av 17.11)	1947-63

LIMITED-OVERS CRICKET

Highest Total	**NWT**	365-3		v	Cornwall	Derby	1986
	BHC	366-4		v	Combined U	Oxford	1991
	NL	292-9		v	Worcs	Knypersley	1985
Lowest Total	**NWT**	79		v	Surrey	The Oval	1967
	BHC	98		v	Worcs	Derby	1994
	NL	61		v	Hampshire	Portsmouth	1990
Highest Innings	**NWT**	153	A.Hill	v	Cornwall	Derby	1986
	BHC	142	D.M.Jones	v	Minor C	Derby	1996
	NL	141*	C.J.Adams	v	Kent	Chesterfield	1992
Best Bowling	**NWT**	8-21	M.A.Holding	v	Sussex	Hove	1988
	BHC	6-33	E.J.Barlow	v	Glos	Bristol	1978
	NL	6- 7	M.Hendrick	v	Notts	Nottingham	1972

DURHAM

Formation of Present Club: 10 May 1882
Colours: Navy Blue, Yellow and Maroon
Badge: Coat of Arms of the County of Durham
County Champions: (0) 8th 1999
NatWest Trophy/Gillette Cup Winners: (0); best – quarter-finalist 1992
Benson and Hedges Cup Winners: (0); best – quarter-finalist 1998
CGU National League (Div 1) Winners: (0); best – 9th (Div 2) 1999
Sunday League Winners: (0); best – 7th 1993
Match Awards: NWT 20; BHC 13

Director of Cricket: G.Cook, County Ground, Riverside, Chester-le-Street, Co Durham DH3 3QR ▲ Tel: 0191 387 1717 ▲ Fax: 0191 387 1616 ▲ Email: durham@ecb.co.uk ▲ Web: www.durham-ccc.org.uk

Captain: N.J.Speak. **Vice-Captain:** No appointment. **Overseas Player:** S.M.Katich. **2000 Beneficiary:** None. **Scorer:** B.Hunt. ‡ New registration

ALI, Syed **Muazam** (Chigwell S), b Whipps Cross, Essex 23 Oct 1979. 5'7". RHB, LB. Staff 1999 – awaiting f-c debut. MCC YC. LO HS 17 v Northants (Northampton) 1999 (NL).

BETTS, Melvyn Morris (Fyndoune CS, Sacriston), b Sacriston 26 Mar 1975. 5'10". RHB, RFM. Debut 1993; cap 1998. Tour: Z 1998-99. HS 57* v Sussex (Hove) 1996. BB 9-64 (Durham record; 13-143 match) v Northants (Northampton) 1997. LO HS 21 v Hants (Chester-le-St) 1997 (SL). LO BB 4-39 v Somerset (Taunton) 1999 (NL).

BRIDGE, Graeme David (Southmoor S, Sunderland), b Sunderland 4 Sep 1980. 5'8". RHB, SLA. Debut 1999. Eng U-19 to NZ 1998-99. HS 6. BB 1-60. LO HS 15 and LO BB 1-49 Durham Board v Glos (Chester-le-St) 1999 (NWT).

BROWN, Simon John Emmerson (Boldon CS), b Cleadon 29 Jun 1969. 6'3". RHB, LFM. Northamptonshire 1987-90. Durham debut 1992; captain 1996 (part); cap 1998. **Tests**: 1 (1996); HS 10* and BB 1-60 v P (Lord's) 1996. HS 69 v Leics (Durham) 1994. 50 wkts (6); most – 79 (1996). BB 7-70 v A (Durham) 1993. CC BB 7-105 v Kent (Canterbury) 1992. Awards: NWT 1; BHC 1. LO HS 18 v Derbys (Derby) 1996 (SL). LO BB 6-30 v Northants (Chester-le-St) 1997 (BHC).

COLLINGWOOD, Paul David (Blackfyne CS; Derwentside C), b Shotley Bridge 26 May 1976. 5'11". RHB, RMF. Debut 1996 v Northants (Chester-le-St) taking wicket of D.J.Capel with his first ball before scoring 91 and 16; cap 1998. HS 107 v OU (Oxford) 1997. CC HS 106 v Notts (Chester-le-St) 1999. BB 3-7 v Glam (Cardiff) 1999. Award: BHC 1. LO HS 86 v Northants (Northampton) 1999 (NL). LO BB 3-20 v Derbys (Derby) 1998 (SL).

DALEY, James Arthur (Hetton CS), b Sunderland 24 Sep 1973. 5'10". RHB, RM. Debut 1992; cap 1999. MCC YC. HS 159* v Hants (Portsmouth) 1994. BB 1-12. LO HS 98* v Kent (Canterbury) 1994 (SL).

DAVIES, Anthony **Mark** (Northfield CS, Billingham), b Stockton-on-Tees 4 Oct 1980. 6'2". RHB. RM. Non-contracted Durham Academy player awaiting f-c debut. LO HS 0 and BB 2-44 v Surrey (Chester-le-St) 1998 (SL).

GOUGH, Michael Andrew (English Martyrs CS; Hartlepool SFC), b Hartlepool 18 Dec 1979. 6'5". Son of M.P. (Durham 1974-77). RHB, OB. Debut 1998. Tours (Eng A): NZ 1999-00; B 1999-00. HS 123 v CU (Cambridge) 1998. CC HS 67 v Kent (Stockton) 1999. BB 4-49 v Notts (Chester-le-St) 1999. LO HS 16 v Glam (Chester-le-St) 1999 (NL).

HARMISON, Stephen James (Ashington HS), b Ashington, Northumb 23 Oct 1978. 6'4". RHB, RF. Debut 1996; cap 1999. Northumberland 1996. Tours (Eng A): SA 1998-99; Z 1998-99. HS 36 v Kent (Canterbury) 1998. 50 wkts (2); most – 64 (1999). BB 5-70 v Glos (Chester-le-St) 1998. LO HS 2* (NWT). LO BB 2-40 v Northants (Chester-le-St) 1999 (NL).

HATCH, Nicholas Guy (Barnard Castle S; Hull U), b Darlington 21 Apr 1979. 6'7". RHB, RMF. Joined staff on summer contract 1999 during university vacation – awaiting f-c debut.

‡**HUNTER, Ian** David (Fyndoune Community C, Sacriston; New College, Framwellgate Moor), b Durham City 11 Sep 1979. 6'1". RHB, RMF. Staff 2000 – awaiting f-c debut. LO HS 4 (NL). LO BB 2-34 v Glam (Cardiff) 1999 (NL).

‡**KATICH, Simon** Mathew, b Middle Swan, Western Australia 21 Aug 1975. LHB. SLC. W Australia 1996-97 to date. Tour (A): SL 1999-00. 1000 (0+1): 1632 (1998-99). HS 154* WA v Tasmania (Hobart) 1998-99. BB 1-4 (WA). LO HS 74* WA v Q (Perth) 1998-99 (MM).

KILLEEN, Neil (Greencroft CS; Derwentside C; Teesside U), b Shotley Bridge 17 Oct 1975. 6'2". RHB, RFM. Debut 1995; cap 1999. HS 48 v Somerset (Chester-le-St) 1995. 50 wkts (1): 58 (1999). BB 7-85 v Leics (Leicester) 1999. LO HS 32 v Middx (Lord's) 1996 (SL). LO BB 5-26 v Northants (Northampton) 1995 (SL).

LEWIS, Jonathan James Benjamin (King Edward VI S, Chelmsford; Roehampton IHE), b Isleworth, Middx 21 May 1970. 5'9½". RHB, RSM. Essex 1990-96; cap 1994; scored 116* on debut v Surrey (Oval). Durham debut 1997; cap 1998. 1000 runs (2); most – 1252 (1997). HS 210* v OU (Oxford) 1997 – on Du debut. CC HS 160* v Derbys (Chester-le-St) 1997. BB 1-73. Award: BHC 1. LO HS 102 v Glos (Cheltenham) 1997.

PHILLIPS, Nicholas Charles (Wm Parker S, Hastings), b Pembury, Kent 10 May 1974. 5'10½". RHB, OB. Sussex 1993-97. HS 53 Sx v Young A (Hove) 1995. CC HS 52 Sx v Lancs (Lytham) 1995. Du HS 42 v Glos (Cheltenham) 1999. BB 6-97 (12-268 match) v Glam (Cardiff) 1999. Award: NWT 1. LO HS 38* Sx v Essex (Chelmsford) 1996 (SL). LO BB 4-13 v Derbys (Chester-le-St) 1999 (NL).

PRATT, Andrew (Willington Parkside CS; Durham New C), b Helmington Row, Crook 4 Mar 1975. 6'0". LHB, WK. Debut 1997. MCC YC. HS 34 v Lancs (Chester-le-St) 1998. LO HS 26 v Sussex (Hove) 1999 (NL).

ROBINSON, Ryan (Shelley HS & SFC), b Huddersfield, Yorks 19 Oct 1976. 6'0". Cousin of A.Walker (Northamptonshire 1983-93 and Durham 1994-98). RHB, RM. Staff 1999 awaiting f-c debut. LO HS 33 v Middx (Lord's) 1999 (NL). LO BB 2-22 v Derbys (Chester-le-St) 1999 (NL).

SPEAK, Nicholas Jason (Parrs Wood HS, Manchester), b Manchester 21 Nov 1966. 6'0". RHB, LB. Lancashire 1986-87 to 1996; cap 1992. Durham debut 1997; cap 1998; captain 2000. Tours (La): WI 1986-87, 1995-96. 1000 runs (3); most – 1892 (1992). HS 232 La v Leics (Leicester) 1992. Du HS 124* v CU (Cambridge) 1997. BB 1-0. Award: BHC 1. LO HS 102* La v Yorks (Leeds) 1992 (SL).

SPEIGHT, Martin Peter (Hurstpierpoint C; Durham U), b Walsall, Staffs 24 Oct 1967. 5'9". RHB, WK. Sussex 1986-96; cap 1991. Wellington 1989-90 to 1992-93. Durham debut 1997; cap 1998. 1000 runs (3); most – 1375 (1990). HS 184 Sx v Notts (Eastbourne) 1993. Du HS 97* v Hants (Southampton) 1998 and 97* v Glam (Cardiff) 1999. BB 1-2. Awards: BHC 2. LO HS 126 Sx v Somerset (Taunton) 1993 (SL).

SYMINGTON, Marc Joseph (St Michaels, Billingham; Stockton SFC), b Newcastle upon Tyne, Northumb 10 Jan 1980. 5'8". RHB, RM. Debut 1998. HS 8*. CC HS – . BB 3-55 v Derbys (Derby) 1998. LO HS 10 v Northants (Northampton) 1999 (NL). LO BB 1-39 (NL).

WOOD, John (Crofton HS; Wakefield District C; Leeds Poly), b Crofton, Yorks 22 Jul 1970. 6'3". RHB, RFM. GW in Nissan Shield 1990-91. Debut 1992; cap 1998. HS 63* v Notts (Chester-le-St) 1993. 50 wkts (1): 62 (1998). BB 7-58 v Yorks (Leeds) 1999. LO HS 28 v Worcs (Worcester) 1994 (SL). LO BB 4-17 v Kent (Darlington) 1997 (SL).

RELEASED/RETIRED see p 30

DURHAM 1999

RESULTS SUMMARY

	Place	Won	Lost	Tied	Drew	No Result
PPP County Championship	**8th**	6	7		4	
All First-Class Matches		6	7		4	
NatWest Trophy	3rd Round					
CGU National League (Division 2)	**9th**	3	12			1

COUNTY CHAMPIONSHIP AVERAGES

BATTING AND FIELDING

Cap		M	I	NO	HS	Runs	Avge	100	50	Ct/St
1998	J.J.B.Lewis	16	28	–	132	1146	40.92	2	8	7
1998	N.J.Speak	10	17	2	110	561	37.40	2	2	6
1998	D.C.Boon	16	27	2	139	839	33.56	1	7	8
1998	J.E.Morris	15	25	–	119	792	31.68	2	4	7
1999	J.A.Daley	14	24	1	105	609	26.47	1	3	7
1998	M.P.Speight	17	27	5	97*	566	25.72	–	4	48/2
1998	P.D.Collingwood	17	28	–	106	692	24.71	1	4	25
–	S.Chapman	2	4	1	32	67	22.33	–	–	3
–	M.A.Gough	12	20	–	67	424	21.20	–	4	17
1999	N.Killeen	12	19	3	46	251	15.68	–	–	1
–	N.C.Phillips	6	9	–	42	105	11.66	–	–	5
1998	S.J.E.Brown	15	23	8	29*	160	10.66	–	–	3
1998	J.Wood	10	15	1	49*	139	9.92	–	–	4
1998	M.M.Betts	7	11	2	19*	55	6.11	–	–	4
1999	S.J.Harmison	17	24	9	14*	79	5.26	–	–	4

Also batted: G.D.Bridge (1 match) 6, 5 (1 ct).

BOWLING

	O	M	R	W	Avge	Best	5wI	10wM
N.Killeen	411.3	113	1070	58	18.44	7-85	4	–
J.Wood	247.4	57	805	36	22.36	7-58	2	–
S.J.E.Brown	475	112	1448	63	22.98	6-25	5	–
S.J.Harmison	565.5	120	1775	64	27.73	5-76	1	–
M.M.Betts	175.1	41	583	20	29.15	4-34	–	–
N.C.Phillips	212	41	677	18	37.61	6-97	2	1

Also bowled: D.C.Boon 5-1-17-1; G.D.Bridge 44-12-110-1; S.Chapman 14-1-60-1; P.D.Collingwood 91.1-25-238-8; J.A.Daley 11-2-40-0; M.A.Gough 77.4-14-259-4.

The First-Class Averages (pp 113-128) give the records of Durham players in all first-class county matches.

DURHAM RECORDS

FIRST-CLASS CRICKET

Highest Total	For 625-6d		v	Derbyshire	Chesterfield	1994
	V 810-4d		by	Warwicks	Birmingham	1994
Lowest Total	For 67		v	Middlesex	Lord's	1996
	V 73		by	Oxford U	Oxford	1994
Highest Innings	For 210*	J.J.B.Lewis	v	Oxford U	Oxford	1997
	V 501*	B.C.Lara	for	Warwicks	Birmingham	1994

Highest Partnership for each Wicket

1st	334*	S.Hutton/M.A.Roseberry	v	Oxford U	Oxford	1996
2nd	206	W.Larkins/D.M.Jones	v	Glamorgan	Cardiff	1992
3rd	205	G.Fowler/S.Hutton	v	Yorkshire	Leeds	1993
4th	204	J.J.B.Lewis/J.Boiling	v	Derbyshire	Chester-le-St[2]	1997
5th	185	P.W.G.Parker/J.A.Daley	v	Warwicks	Darlington	1993
6th	193	D.C.Boon/P.D.Collingwood	v	Warwicks	Birmingham	1998
7th	119	N.Killeen/M.P.Speight	v	Glamorgan	Cardiff	1999
8th	134	A.C.Cummins/D.A.Graveney	v	Warwicks	Birmingham	1994
9th	127	D.G.C.Ligertwood/S.J.E.Brown	v	Surrey	Stockton	1996
10th	103	M.M.Betts/D.M.Cox	v	Sussex	Hove	1996

Best Bowling	For	9- 64	M.M.Betts	v	Northants	Northampton	1997
(Innings)	V	8- 22	D.Follett	for	Middlesex	Lord's	1996
Best Bowling	For	14-177	A.Walker	v	Essex	Chelmsford	1995
(Match)	V	12- 68	J.N.B.Bovill	for	Hampshire	Stockton	1995

Most Runs – Season	1536	W.Larkins	(av 37.46)	1992
Most Runs – Career	5670	J.E.Morris	(av 32.77)	1994-99
Most 100s – Season	4	D.M.Jones		1992
	4	W.Larkins		1992
	4	J.E.Morris		1994
Most 100s – Career	14	J.E.Morris		1994-99
Most Wkts – Season	77	S.J.E.Brown	(av 25.87)	1996
Most Wkts – Career	446	S.J.E.Brown	(av 29.27)	1992-99

LIMITED-OVERS CRICKET

Highest Total	**NWT**	326-4		v	Herefords	Chester-le-St[2]	1995
	BHC	287-5		v	Leics	Leicester	1996
	NL	281-2		v	Derbyshire	Durham	1993
Lowest Total	**NWT**	82		v	Worcs	Chester-le-St[1]	1968
	BHC	162		v	Derbyshire	Chesterfield	1996
	NL	99		v	Warwicks	Birmingham	1996
Highest Innings	**NWT**	125	S.Hutton	v	Herefords	Chester-le-St[2]	1995
	BHC	145	J.E.Morris	v	Leics	Leicester	1996
	NL	131*	W.Larkins	v	Hampshire	Portsmouth	1994
Best Bowling	**NWT**	7-32	S.P.Davis	v	Lancashire	Chester-le-St[1]	1983
	BHC	6-30	S.J.E.Brown	v	Northants	Chester-le-St[2]	1997
	NL	5-23	J.Boiling	v	Notts	Nottingham	1998

[1] Chester-le-Street CC (Ropery Lane) [2] Riverside Ground

ESSEX

Formation of Present Club: 14 January 1876
Colours: Blue, Gold and Red
Badge: Three Seaxes above Scroll bearing 'Essex'
County Champions: (6) 1979, 1983, 1984, 1986, 1991, 1992
NatWest Trophy/Gillette Cup Winners: (2) 1985, 1997
Benson and Hedges Cup Winners: (2) 1979, 1998
CGU National League (Div 1) Winners: (0); best – 9th 1999
Sunday League Winners: (3) 1981, 1984, 1985
Match Awards: NWT 47; BHC 84

Acting Secretary: M.C.Field, County Ground, New Writtle Street, Chelmsford CM2 0PG ▲ Tel: 01245 252420 ▲ Fax: 01245 254030 ▲ Email: essex@ecb.co.uk ▲ Web: www.essexcricket.org.uk

Captain: R.C.Irani. **Vice-Captain:** No appointment. **Overseas Player:** S.G.Law. **2000 Beneficiary:** Essex Benefit Association Fund. **Scorer:** D.J.Norris. ‡ New registration

ANDERSON, Ricaldo Sherman Glenroy (Alperton HS; Barnet C; North West London C), b Hammersmith, London 22 Sep 1976. 5'10". RHB, RFM. Debut 1999. HS 44 v Kent (Canterbury) 1999. 50 wkts (1): 50 (1999). BB 5-36 v Middx (Southgate) 1999. LO HS 10 v K (Canterbury) 1999 (NL) and 10 v Warwks (Colchester) 1999 (NL). LO BB 3-32 v Glos (Bristol) 1999 (NL).

BISHOP, Justin Edward (Bury St Edmunds County Upper S), b Bury St Edmunds, Suffolk 4 Jan 1982. 6'0". LHB, LMF. Debut 1999. Awaiting CC debut. HS 17 and BB 2-89 v SL A (Chelmsford) 1999. LO HS 1 (NL).

COWAN, Ashley Preston (Framlingham C), b Hitchin, Herts 7 May 1975. 6'4". RHB, RFM. Debut 1995; cap 1997. Cambridgeshire 1993. Tour: WI 1997-98. HS 94 v Leics (Leicester) 1998. 50 wkts (1): 52 (1997). BB 6-47 v Glam (Cardiff) 1999. Hat-trick 1996. Award: BHC 1. LO HS 40* v Notts (Chelmsford) 1998 (SL). LO BB 5-28 v Middx (Lord's) 1998 (BHC).

FLANAGAN, Ian Nicholas (Colne Community S), b Colchester 5 Jun 1980. 6'0". LHB, OB. Debut 1997. HS 61 v Warwks (Birmingham) 1998. BB 1-50 (not CC).

FOSTER, James Savin (Forest S, Snaresbrook; Durham U), b Whipps Cross 15 Apr 1980. 6'0". RHB, WK. Staff 1999 – awaiting f-c debut.

GRAYSON, Adrian **Paul** (Bedale CS), b Ripon, Yorks 31 Mar 1971. 6'1". RHB, SLA. Yorkshire 1990-95. Essex debut/cap 1996. Tour: SA 1991-92 (Y). 1000 runs (3); most – 1083 (1999). HS 159* v Hants (Ilford) 1999. BB 4-16 v Middx (Southgate) 1999. LO HS 82* v Worcs (Chelmsford) 1997 (NWT). LO BB 4-25 Y v Glam (Cardiff) 1994 (SL).

HUSSAIN, Nasser (Forest S, Snaresbrook; Durham U), b Madras, India 28 Mar 1968. Son of J. (Madras 1966-67); brother of M. (Worcs 1985). 5'11". RHB, LB. Debut 1987; cap 1989; captain 1999; benefit 1999. YC 1989. **ECB contract 2000. Tests:** 47 (1989-90 to 1999-00; 8 as captain); HS 207 v A (Birmingham) 1997. **LOI:** 42 (1989-90 to 1999-00, 10 as captain); HS 93 v A (Sydney) 1998-99. Tours: A 1998-99; SA 1999-00 (captain); WI 1989-90, 1991-92 (Eng A), 1993-94, 1997-98; NZ 1996-97; P 1990-91 (Eng A), 1995-96 (Eng A – captain); SL 1990-91 (Eng A); Z 1996-97. 1000 runs (5); most – 1854 (1995). HS 207 (*see Tests*). Ex HS 197 v Surrey (Oval) 1990. BB 1-38. Awards: NWT 3; BHC 3. LO HS 118 Comb U v Somerset (Taunton) 1989 (BHC).

HYAM, Barry James (Havering SFC), b Romford 9 Sep 1975. RHB, WK. Debut 1993; cap 1999. MCC YC. HS 51 v Surrey (Oval) 1999. LO HS 37 v Leics (Leicester) 1999 (NL).

ILOTT, Mark Christopher (Francis Combe S, Garston), b Watford, Herts 27 Aug 1970. 6'0½". LHB, LFM. Debut 1988; cap 1993. Hertfordshire 1987-88 (at 16, the youngest to represent that county). **Tests:** 5 (1993 to 1995-96); HS 15 v A (Oval) 1993; BB 3-48 v SA (Durban) 1995-96. Tours: A 1992-93 (Eng A); SA 1993-94 (Eng A), 1995-96; I 1994-95 (Eng A – part); SL 1990-91 (Eng A). HS 60 Eng A v Warwks (Birmingham) 1995. Ex HS 58 v Worcs (Worcester) 1996. 50 wkts (6); most – 78 (1995). BB 9-19 (14-105 match; inc hat-trick – all lbw) v Northants (Luton) 1995. Hat-trick 1995. Awards: BHC 2. LO HS 56* v Sussex (Hove) 1995 (SL). LO BB 5-21 v Scot (Forfar) 1993 (BHC).

IRANI, Ronald Charles (Smithills CS, Bolton), b Leigh, Lancs 26 Oct 1971. 6'3". RHB, RMF. Lancashire 1990-93. Essex debut/cap 1994; captain 2000. **Tests:** 3 (1996 to 1999); HS 41 v I (Lord's) 1996; BB 1-22. **LOI:** 10 (1996 to 1996-97); HS 45* v P (Birmingham) 1996; BB 1-23. Tours: NZ 1996-97, 1999-00 (Eng A); P 1995-96 (Eng A); Z 1996-97; B 1999-00 (Eng A). 1000 runs (4); most – 1165 (1995). HS 153 v SL A (Chelmsford) 1999. CC HS 127* Somerset (Bath) 1998 and 127* v Kent (Canterbury) 1999. 50 wkts (1): 51 (1999). BB 5-19 Eng A v Comb XI (Karachi) 1995-96. Ex BB 5-27 v Notts (Chelmsford) 1996. Awards: NWT 3; BHC 2. LO HS 124 v Durham (Chelmsford) 1996 (NWT). LO BB 5-33 v Hants (Southampton) 1999 (NL).

JEFFERSON, William Ingleby (Beeston Hall S, Norfolk; Oundle S), b Derby 25 Oct 1979. Son of R.I. (Cambridge U and Surrey 1961-66). 6'8". RHB, RMF. Staff 1999 – awaiting f-c debut.

LAW, Danny Richard (Steyning GS), b Lambeth, London 15 Jul 1975. 6'5". RHB, RFM. Sussex 1993-96; cap 1996. Essex debut 1997. HS 115 Sx v Young A (Hove) 1995. CC HS 97 Sx v Glos (Bristol) 1996. Ex HS 81 v CU (Cambridge) 1997. BB 5-33 Sx v Durham (Hove) 1996. Ex BB 5-46 (inc hat-trick) v Durham (Chester-le-St) 1998. Hat-trick 1998. LO HS 82 v Durham (Chelmsford) 1997 (SL). LO BB 3-26 v Leics (Leicester) 1999 (NL).

LAW, Stuart Grant (Craigslea State HS), b Herston, Brisbane, Australia 18 Oct 1968. 6'2". RHB, RM/LB. Queensland 1988-89 to date; captain 1994-95 to 1996-97. Essex debut/cap 1996. *Wisden* 1997. **Tests** (A): 1 (1995-96); HS 54* v SL (Perth) 1995-96. **LOI** (A): 54 (1994-95 to 1998-99); HS 110 v Z (Hobart) 1994-95; BB 2-22 v P (Sydney) 1996-97. Tours: E 1995 (Young A); Z 1991-92 (Aus B). 1000 runs (3+1); most – 1833 (1999). HS 263 v Somerset (Chelmsford) 1999. BB 5-39 Q v Tasmania (Brisbane) 1995-96. Ex BB 3-27 v Worcs (Chelmsford) 1997. Awards: NWT 4; BHC 1. LO HS 159 Q v Tasmania (Brisbane) 1993-94 (MM). LO BB 4-33 Q v WA (Brisbane) 1993-94 (MM).

McGARRY, Andrew Charles (King Edward VI GS, Chelmsford; Southend C), b Basildon 8 Nov 1981. 6'5". RHB, RFM. Debut 1999. Non-contracted player – awaiting CC debut. HS 0* and BB 2-72 v SL A (Chelmsford) 1999 – on debut.

‡**MASON, Timothy** James (Denstone C), b Leicester 12 Apr 1975. 5'8". RHB, OB. Leicestershire 1994-99. HS 36 Le v Worcs (Worcester) 1999. BB 3-32 Le v Worcs (Worcester) 1999. LO HS 36 Le v Yorks (Leicester) 1997 (NWT). LO BB 4-12 Le v Essex (Leicester) 1998 (SL).

NAPIER, Graham Richard (The Gilberd S, Colchester), b Colchester 6 Jan 1980. 5'9½". RHB, RM. Debut 1997. HS 35* v Notts (Worksop) 1997. BB 2-25 v CU (Cambridge) 1997. CC BB 2-59 v Sussex (Chelmsford) 1998. LO HS 19 v Leics (Leicester) 1999 (NL). LO BB 3-22 v Derbys (Derby) 1998 (SL).

PETERS, Stephen David (Coopers Coborn S), b Harold Wood 10 Dec 1978. 5'9". RHB, occ LB. Debut 1996 scoring 110 and 12* v CU (Cambridge). HS 110 (as above). CC HS 81 v Glam (Cardiff) 1999. BB 1-19 (not CC). LO HS 58* v Middx (Lord's) 1998 (BHC).

‡**PETTINI, Mark** Lewis, Brighton, Sussex 7 Aug 1983. RHB. Staff 2000 – awaiting f-c debut.

PHILLIPS, Timothy James (Felsted S), b Cambridge 13 Mar 1981. 6'1". LHB, SLA. Debut 1999. HS 16 and BB 4-42 v SL A (Chelmsford) 1999 – on debut. CC HS 7. CC BB 1-66. LO HS 0 and BB 2-56 v Hants (Southend) 1999 (NL).

PRICHARD, Paul John (Brentwood HS), b Billericay 7 Jan 1965. 5'10". RHB, RSM. Debut 1984; cap 1986; captain 1995-98; benefit 1996. Tour (Eng A): A 1992-93. 1000 runs (8); most – 1485 (1992). HS 245 v Leics (Chelmsford) 1990. BB 1-28. Awards: NWT 1; BHC 4. LO HS 114 v Somerset (Chelmsford) 1997 (BHC).

ROBINSON, Darren David John (Tabor HS, Braintree; Chelmsford CFE), b Braintree 2 Mar 1973. 5'10½". RHB, RMF. Debut 1993; cap 1997. HS 200 v NZ (Chelmsford) 1999. CC HS 148 v Worcs (Chelmsford) 1997. Awards: BHC 2. LO HS 137* v Sussex (Hove) 1998 (BHC). LO BB 1-7 (SL).

‡SHARIF, Zoheb Khalid, b Leytonstone 22 Feb 1983. LHB, LB. Staff 2000 – awaiting f-c debut.

SUCH, Peter Mark (Harry Carlton CS, Ex Leake, Notts), b Helensburgh, Dunbartonshire 12 Jun 1964. 5'11". RHB, OB. Nottinghamshire 1982-86. Leicestershire 1987-89. Essex debut 1990; cap 1991. **Tests:** 11 (1993 to 1999); HS 14* and BB 6-67 v A (Manchester) 1993 – on debut. Tours: A 1992-93 (Eng A), 1998-99; SA 1993-94 (Eng A). HS 54 v Worcs (Chelmsford) 1993 and 54 v Notts (Chelmsford) 1996. 50 wkts (6); most – 82 (1996). BB 8-93 (11-160 match) v Hants (Colchester) 1995. LO HS 19* v Notts (Ilford) 1994 (SL). LO BB 5-29 v Glam (Cardiff) 1997 (SL).

THOMPSON, David James (Ernest Bevin S, Wandsworth; Westminster C), b Wandsworth, London 11 Mar 1976. 6'3". RHB, RFM. Surrey 1994 (one match). Lancashire staff 1995-96. Essex 1999. HS 22 Sy v OU (Oval) 1994 and 22 v Northants (Northampton) 1999. BB 4-46 v Somerset (Chelmsford) 1999. LO HS 1* and LO BB 2-34 v Worcs (Worcester) 1999 (NL).

RELEASED/RETIRED

(Having made a first-class County appearance in 1999)

GROVE, J.O. – *see SOMERSET.*

HODGSON, Timothy Philip (Wellington C; Durham U), b Guildford, Surrey 27 Mar 1975. Brother of J.S. (Cambridge U 1994); great-nephew of N.A.Knox (Surrey and England 1904-10). 5'10". LHB, RM. Debut 1997. HS 54 v Yorks (Scarborough) 1998. BB 1-34 (not CC). LO HS 113 Brit U v Hants (Oxford) 1997 (BHC).

POWELL, Jonathan Christopher (Chelmsford C), b Harold Wood 13 Jun 1979. 5'10". RHB, OB. Debut 1997. Tour (Eng A): SL 1997-98. HS (Eng A) 6. Ex HS 4*. BB (Ex) 1-109. LO HS 2 (SL). LO BB 2-10 v Northants (Northampton) 1997 (SL).

ROLLINS, Robert John (Little Ilford CS), b Plaistow 30 Jan 1974. 5'9". RHB, RM, WK. Brother of A.S. (*see NORTHAMPTONSHIRE*). Debut 1992; cap 1995. HS 133* v Glam (Swansea) 1995. Award: NWT 1. LO HS 87 v Lancs (Chelmsford) 1999 (NL).

WALTON, Timothy Charles (Leeds GS; Newcastle upon Tyne Poly), b Low Head, Yorks 8 Nov 1972. 6'0½". RHB, RM. Northamptonshire 1994-96. Essex 1999. HS 71 Nh v Somerset (Northampton) 1995 and 71 v Glos (Gloucester) 1999. BB 1-8. CC BB 1-26 (Nh). Award: BHC 1. LO HS 72 Nh v Glos (Bristol) 1994 (SL). LO BB 2-27 Nh v Leics (Leicester) 1992 (SL).

ESSEX 1999

RESULTS SUMMARY

	Place	*Won*	*Lost*	*Tied*	*Drew*	*No Result*
PPP County Championship	**12th**	5	7		5	
All First-Class Matches		6	7		8	
NatWest Trophy	3rd Round					
CGU National League (Division 1)	**9th**	3	12			1

COUNTY CHAMPIONSHIP AVERAGES

BATTING AND FIELDING

Cap		*M*	*I*	*NO*	*HS*	*Runs*	*Avge*	*100*	*50*	*Ct/St*
1996	S.G.Law	17	29	4	263	1833	73.32	8	6	29
1989	N.Hussain	9	15	1	143	824	58.85	2	7	10
1994	R.C.Irani	16	28	4	127*	793	33.04	2	3	8
1986	P.J.Prichard	14	24	–	110	786	32.75	2	5	6
1996	A.P.Grayson	17	29	2	159*	875	32.40	2	5	5
1999	B.J.Hyam	16	24	4	51	470	23.50	–	1	40/1
–	S.D.Peters	7	11	1	81	233	23.30	–	1	7
–	T.C.Walton	4	6	–	71	109	18.16	–	1	4
1993	M.C.Ilott	12	17	1	44	290	18.12	–	–	5
1997	D.D.J.Robinson	14	26	1	112	422	16.88	1	–	13
1997	A.P.Cowan	16	24	3	52*	332	15.80	–	1	10
1991	P.M.Such	16	21	11	22*	114	11.40	–	–	4
–	I.N.Flanagan	4	8	–	36	84	10.50	–	–	2
–	R.S.G.Anderson	13	18	2	44	138	8.62	–	–	5
–	D.J.Thompson	6	9	–	22	47	5.22	–	–	1
–	J.O.Grove	3	5	1	7	17	4.25	–	–	–

Also batted (1 match each): D.R.Law 26; T.J.Phillips 7, 0; R.J.Rollins (cap 1995) 3, 20 (3 ct).

BOWLING

	O	*M*	*R*	*W*	*Avge*	*Best*	*5wI*	*10wM*
R.C.Irani	351.3	83	980	46	21.30	4- 29	–	–
M.C.Ilott	310.4	85	900	38	23.68	6- 38	1	–
R.S.G.Anderson	311.3	70	1072	43	24.93	5- 36	2	–
A.P.Cowan	379.1	59	1250	44	28.40	6- 47	1	–
D.J.Thompson	141	14	579	20	28.95	4- 46	–	–
P.M.Such	545	145	1343	41	32.75	7-136	2	1
A.P.Grayson	293.5	87	786	17	46.23	4- 16	–	–

Also bowled: J.O.Grove 57-11-241-4; D.R.Law 7-0-43-0; S.G.Law 35.4-6-133-3; T.J.Phillips 17-1-71-1.

The First-Class Averages (pp 113-128) give the records of Essex players in all first-class county matches (Essex's other opponents being the New Zealanders, Sri Lanka A, Cambridge University and Oxford University), with the exception of N.Hussain, whose full county figures are as above, and:

R.C.Irani 20-32-5-153-1111-41.14-4-3-10ct. 384.3-96-1046-50-20.92-4/29.

P.M.Such 19-23-11-22*-134-11.16-0-0-4ct. 661-181-1596-51-31.29-7/136-2-1.

ESSEX RECORDS

FIRST-CLASS CRICKET

Highest Total	For 761-6d		v	Leics	Chelmsford	1990
	V 803-4d		by	Kent	Brentwood	1934
Lowest Total	For 30		v	Yorkshire	Leyton	1901
	V 14		by	Surrey	Chelmsford	1983
Highest Innings	For 343*	P.A.Perrin	v	Derbyshire	Chesterfield	1904
	V 332	W.H.Ashdown	for	Kent	Brentwood	1934

Highest Partnership for each Wicket

1st	316	G.A.Gooch/P.J.Prichard	v	Kent	Chelmsford	1994
2nd	403	G.A.Gooch/P.J.Prichard	v	Leics	Chelmsford	1990
3rd	347*	M.E.Waugh/N.Hussain	v	Lancashire	Ilford	1992
4th	314	Salim Malik/N.Hussain	v	Surrey	The Oval	1991
5th	316	N.Hussain/M.A.Garnham	v	Leics	Leicester	1991
6th	206	J.W.H.T.Douglas/J.O'Connor	v	Glos	Cheltenham	1923
	206	B.R.Knight/R.A.G.Luckin	v	Middlesex	Brentwood	1962
7th	261	J.W.H.T.Douglas/J.Freeman	v	Lancashire	Leyton	1914
8th	263	D.R.Wilcox/R.M.Taylor	v	Warwicks	Southend	1946
9th	251	J.W.H.T.Douglas/S.N.Hare	v	Derbyshire	Leyton	1921
10th	218	F.H.Vigar/T.P.B.Smith	v	Derbyshire	Chesterfield	1947

Best Bowling	For	10- 32	H.Pickett	v	Leics	Leyton	1895
(Innings)	V	10- 40	E.G.Dennett	for	Glos	Bristol	1906
Best Bowling	For	17-119	W.Mead	v	Hampshire	Southampton	1895
(Match)	V	17- 56	C.W.L.Parker	for	Glos	Gloucester	1925

Most Runs – Season	2559	G.A.Gooch	(av 67.34)	1984
Most Runs – Career	30701	G.A.Gooch	(av 51.77)	1973-97
Most 100s – Season	9	J.O'Connor		1934
	9	D.J.Insole		1955
Most 100s – Career	94	G.A.Gooch		1973-97
Most Wkts – Season	172	T.P.B.Smith	(av 27.13)	1947
Most Wkts – Career	1610	T.P.B.Smith	(av 26.68)	1929-51

LIMITED-OVERS CRICKET

Highest Total	**NWT**	386-5		v	Wiltshire	Chelmsford	1988
	BHC	388-7		v	Scotland	Chelmsford	1992
	NL	310-5		v	Glamorgan	Southend	1983
Lowest Total	**NWT**	57		v	Lancashire	Lord's	1996
	BHC	61		v	Lancashire	Chelmsford	1992
	NL	69		v	Derbyshire	Chesterfield	1974
Highest Innings	**NWT**	144	G.A.Gooch	v	Hampshire	Chelmsford	1990
	BHC	198*	G.A.Gooch	v	Sussex	Hove	1982
	NL	176	G.A.Gooch	v	Glamorgan	Southend	1983
Best Bowling	**NWT**	5- 8	J.K.Lever	v	Middlesex	Westcliff	1972
		5- 8	G.A.Gooch	v	Cheshire	Chester	1995
	BHC	5-13	J.K.Lever	v	Middlesex	Lord's	1985
	NL	8-26	K.D.Boyce	v	Lancashire	Manchester	1971

GLAMORGAN

Formation of Present Club: 6 July 1888
Colours: Blue and Gold
Badge: Gold Daffodil
County Champions: (3) 1948, 1969, 1997
NatWest Trophy/Gillette Cup Winners: (0); best – finalists 1977
Benson and Hedges Cup Winners: (0); best – semi-finalists 1988
CGU National League (Div 1) Winners: (0); best – 4th (Div 2) 1999
Sunday League Winners: (1) 1993
Match Awards: NWT 41; BHC 51

Cricket Secretary: M.J.Fatkin, Sophia Gardens, Cardiff, CF1 9XR ▲ Tel: (029) 20409380 ▲ Fax: (029) 20409390 ▲ Email: glam@ecb.co.uk ▲ Web: www.glamorganccc.cricket.org

Captain: M.P.Maynard. **Vice-Captain:** S.P.James. **Overseas Player:** M.T.G.Elliott. **2000 Beneficiary:** R.D.B.Croft. **Scorer:** B.T.Denning. ‡ New registration

CHERRY, Daniel David (Tonbridge S; U of Wales, Swansea), b Newport, Gwent 7 Feb 1980. 5'9". LHB, RM. Debut 1998. HS 11 v Derbys (Cardiff) 1998 – on debut.

COSKER, Dean Andrew (Millfield S), b Weymouth, Dorset 7 Jan 1978. 5'11". RHB, SLA. Debut 1996. Tours (Eng A): SA 1998-99, SL 1997-98; Z 1998-99, K 1997-98. HS 49 v Sussex (Cardiff) 1999. BB 6-140 v Lancs (Colwyn Bay) 1998. LO HS 27* v Somerset (Taunton) 1999 (NL). LO BB 3-18 v Warwks (Birmingham) 1998 (SL).

CROFT, Robert Damien Bale (St John Lloyd Catholic CS; W Glam IHE), b Morriston 25 May 1970. 5'10½". RHB, OB. Debut 1989; cap 1992; benefit 2000. **Tests**: 15 (1996 to 1998-99); HS 37* v SA (Manchester) 1998; BB 5-95 v NZ (Christchurch) 1996-97. **LOI:** 44 (1996 to 1999); HS 32 v SL (Perth) 1998-99; BB 3-51 v SA (Oval) 1998. Tours: A 1998-99; SA 1993-94 (Eng A), 1995-96 (Gm); WI 1991-92 (Eng A), 1997-98; NZ 1996-97; Z 1990-91 (Gm), 1994-95 (Gm), 1996-97. HS 143 v Somerset (Taunton) 1995. 50 wkts (5); most – 76 (1996). BB 8-66 (14-169 match) v Warwks (Swansea) 1992. Awards: NWT 1; BHC 1. LO HS 77 v Essex (Cardiff) 1998 (BHC). LO BB 6-20 v Worcs (Cardiff) 1994 (SL).

DALE, Adrian (Chepstow CS; Swansea U), b Germiston, SA 24 Oct 1968 (to UK at 6 mths). 5'11½". RHB, RM. Debut 1989; cap 1992. Tours (Gm): SA 1993-94 (Eng A), 1995-96; Z 1990-91, 1994-95. 1000 runs (3); most – 1472 (1993). HS 214* v Middx (Cardiff) 1993. BB 6-18 v Warwks (Cardiff) 1993. Awards: NWT 2; BHC 2. LO HS 110 v Lincs (Swansea) 1994 (NWT). LO BB 6-22 v Durham (Colwyn Bay) 1993 (SL).

DAVIES, Adam James (Bishop of Llandaff HS, Cardiff), b Cardiff 26 Oct 1980. Son of H.D. (Glamorgan 1955-60). 6'3½". RHB, RFM. Staff 1999 – awaiting f-c debut.

DAVIES, Andrew Philip (Dwr-y-Felin CS; Christ C, Brecon), b Neath 7 Nov 1976. 5'11". LHB, RMF. Debut 1995. Wales (MC). HS 34 v Essex (Chelmsford) 1998. BB 2-22 v Sussex (Hove) 1998. LO HS 18 v Essex (Chelmsford) 1998 (SL). LO BB 2-17 v Warwks (Birmingham) 1998 (SL).

‡ELLIOTT, Matthew Thomas Gray (Kyabram Secondary C; La Trobe U), b Chelsea, Victoria, Australia 28 Sep 1971. LHB, LM/SLC. Victoria 1992-93 to date. **Tests** (A): 20 (1996-97 to 1998-99); HS 199 v E (Leeds) 1997. **LOI** (A): 1 (1997); HS 1. Tours (A): E 1995 (Young A), 1997; SA 1996-97; WI 1998-99. 1000 runs (1+3); most – 1233 (1995-96). HS 203 Vic v Tasmania (Melbourne) 1995-96. UK HS 199 (*see Tests*). BB 1-3 (Vic). LO HS 97* Vic v Q (Melbourne) 1998-99 (MM).

EVANS, Alun Wyn (Fishguard SS; Neath Tertiary C), b Glanamman, Dyfed 20 Aug 1975. 5'8". RHB, RM. Debut 1996 v OU (Oxford), scoring 66* and 71*. MCC YC. HS 125 v CU (Cambridge) 1998. CC HS 88* v Durham (Cardiff) 1999. LO HS 108 v Derbys (Cardiff) 1999 (NL).

HARRISON, David Stuart (W Monmouth CS; Pontypool C), b Newport, Gwent 30 Jul 1981. Son of S.C. (Glamorgan 1971-77). 6'4". RHB, RM. Glamorgan debut 1999. HS 16 and BB 1-15 v OU (Oxford) 1999. CC HS – .

HUGHES, Jonathan (Coed-y-Land CS, Pontypridd), b Pontypridd 30 Jun 1981. 5'10". RHB, RM. Staff 1999 – awaiting f-c debut. MCC YC.

JAMES, Stephen Peter (Monmouth S; Swansea U; Hughes Hall, Cambridge), b Lydney, Glos 7 Sep 1967. 6'0". RHB. Debut 1985; cap 1992. Cambridge U 1989-90; blue 1989-90. Mashonaland 1993-94 to date. **Tests**: 2 (1998); HS 36 v SL (Oval) 1998. Tours: SA 1995-96 (Gm); SL 1997-98; Z 1990-91 (Gm); K 1997-98. 1000 runs (7); most – 1775 (1997). HS 259* v Notts (Colwyn Bay) 1999. Awards: NWT 3; BHC 2. LO HS 135 v Comb U (Cardiff) 1992 (BHC).

JONES, Simon Philip (Coedcae CS; Millfield S), b Swansea 25 Dec 1978. Son of I.J. (Glamorgan and England 1960-68). 6'3½". LHB, RF. Debut 1998. HS 19* v OU (Oxford) 1999. CC HS 13 v Sussex (Cardiff) 1999. BB 5-31 v Sussex (Cardiff) 1999. LO HS 12* and BB 1-39 v Notts (Nottingham) 1999 (NL).

LAW, Wayne Lincoln (Graig CS; Graig SFC, Llanelli), b Swansea 4 Sep 1978. 5'11". RHB, OB. Debut 1997. MCC YC. HS 131 v Lancs (Colwyn Bay) 1998. BB 2-29 v CU (Cambridge) 1998. CC BB 1-31. LO HS 24 v Leics (Pontypridd) 1998 (SL).

MAYNARD, Matthew Peter (David Hughes S, Anglesey), b Oldham, Lancs 21 Mar 1966. 5'10½". RHB, RM. Debut 1985 v Yorks (Swansea), scoring 102 out of 117 in 87 min, reaching 100 with 3 sixes off successive balls; cap 1987; captain 1996 to date; benefit 1996. *Wisden* 1997. N Districts 1990-91 to 1991-92. Otago 1996-97 to 1997-98. YC 1988. **Tests:** 4 (1988 to 1993-94); HS 35 v WI (Kingston) 1993-94. **LOI:** 10 (1993-94 to 1996); HS 41 v P (Manchester) 1996. Tours: SA 1989-90 (Eng XI), 1995-96 (Gm – captain); WI 1993-94; Z 1994-95 (Gm). 1000 runs (11); most – 1803 (1991). HS 243 v Hants (Southampton) 1991. BB 3-21 v OU (Oxford) 1987. CC BB 1-3. Awards: NWT 4; BHC 7. LO HS 151* v Durham (Darlington) 1991 (NWT) and 151* v Middx (Lord's) 1996 (BHC). LO BB 1-13 (NL).

NEWELL, Keith (Ifield Community C), b Crawley, Sussex 25 Mar 1972. Brother of M. (Sussex 1996-98). 6'0". RHB, RM. Sussex 1995-98. Matabeleland 1995-96. Glamorgan debut 1999. HS 135 Sx v WI (Hove) 1995. Gm HS 46 v Northants (Cardiff) 1999. CC HS 112 and BB 4-61 Sx v Kent (Horsham) 1997. Gm BB 2-15 v Worcs (Worcester) 1999. LO HS 97 and BB 5-33 Sx v Worcs (Worcester) 1998 (SL).

PARKIN, Owen Thomas (Bournemouth GS, Bath U), b Coventry, Warwks 24 Sep 1972. 6'2". RHB, RFM. Dorset 1992. Debut 1994. HS 24* v Essex (Chelmsford) 1998. BB 5-24 v Somerset (Cardiff) 1998. LO HS 8 (BHC). LO BB 5-28 v Sussex (Hove) 1996 (SL).

POWELL, Michael John (Crickhowell HS; Pontypool CFE), b Abergavenny 3 Feb 1977. 6'1". RHB, RSM. Debut 1997 scoring 200* v OU (Oxford). 1000 runs (1): 1060 (1999). HS 200* (*see above*). CC HS 164 v Notts (Colwyn Bay) 1999. BB 2-39 v OU (Oxford) 1999. CC BB – . LO HS 55 v Derbys (Cardiff) 1998 (SL).

SHAW, Adrian David (Neath Tertiary C), b Neath 17 Feb 1972. 5'11". RHB, WK. Wales (MC) 1990-92. Debut 1994; cap 1999. HS 140 v OU (Oxford) 1999. CC HS 74 v Surrey (Cardiff) 1996. LO HS 48 v Glos (Swansea) 1997 (SL).

THOMAS, Stuart **Darren** (Graig CS, Llanelli; Neath Tertiary C), b Morriston 25 Jan 1975. 6'0". LHB, RFM. Debut v Derbys (Chesterfield) 1992, taking 5-80 when aged 17yr 217d; cap 1997. Tours (Eng A): SA 1995-96 (Gm), 1998-99; NZ 1999-00; Z 1994-95 (Gm), 1998-99. HS 78* v Glos (Abergavenny) 1995. 50 wkts (3); most – 71 (1998). BB 8-50 Eng A v Zim A (Harare) 1998-99 – record Eng A analysis. CC BB 5-24 v Sussex (Swansea) 1997. Award: BHC 1. LO HS 40 v Hants Board XI (Southampton) 1999 (NWT). LO BB 7-16 v Surrey (Swansea) 1998 (SL).

WALLACE, Mark Alexander (Crickhowell HS), b Abergavenny, Gwent 19 Nov 1981. 5'9". LHB, WK. Debut 1999. Eng U-19 to NZ 1998-99. HS 64* v Yorks (Leeds) 1999. LO HS 2 (NL).

WATKIN, Steven Llewellyn (Cymer Afan CS; S Glamorgan CHE), b Maesteg 15 Sep 1964. 6'3". RHB, RMF. Debut 1986; cap 1989. Benefit 1998. *Wisden* 1993. **Tests:** 3 (1991 to 1993); HS 13 and BB 4-65 v A (Oval) 1993. **LOI:** 4 (1993-94); HS 4; BB 4-49 v WI (Kingston) 1993-94. Tours: SA 1995-96 (Gm); WI 1991-92 (Eng A), 1993-94; P 1990-91 (Eng A); Z 1989-90 (Eng A), 1990-91 (Gm), 1994-95 (Gm). HS 41 v Worcs (Worcester) 1992. 50 wkts (9); most – 94 (1989). BB 8-59 v Warwks (Birmingham) 1988. Awards: NWT 1; BHC 1. LO HS 31* v Derbys (Checkley) 1991 (SL). LO BB 5-23 v Warwks (Birmingham) 1990 (SL).

‡**WHARF, Alexander** George (Buttershaw Upper S), b Bradford, Yorks 4 Jun 1975. 6'5". RHB, RMF. Yorkshire 1994-97. Nottinghamshire 1998-99. HS 78 Nt v Glam (Colwyn Bay) 1999. BB 4-29 Y v Lancs (Manchester) 1996 (not CC). Nt BB 4-30 v Essex (Nottingham) 1999. LO HS 38* Nt v Surrey (Nottingham) 1999 (NL). LO BB 4-29 Y v Notts (Leeds) 1996 (BHC).

RELEASED/RETIRED

(Having made a first-class County appearance in 1999)

DAWOOD, Ismail (Batley GS), b Dewsbury, Yorks 23 Jul 1976. 5'8". RHB, WK. Northamptonshire 1994. Worcestershire 1996-97. Glamorgan 1998-99. HS 102 v Glos (Cardiff) 1999. LO HS 57 v Essex (Chelmsford) 1998 (SL).

KALLIS, Jacques Henry (Wynberg HS), b Pinelands, SA 16 Oct 1975. RHB, RMF. Western Province 1993-94 to date. Middlesex 1997; cap 1997. Glamorgan 1999; cap 1999. **Tests** (SA): 34 (1996-97 to 1999-00); HS 148* v NZ (Christchurch) 1998-99; BB 5-90 v WI (Cape Town) 1998-99. **LOI** (SA): 84 (1995-96 to 1999-00); HS 113* v SL (Dhaka) 1998-99; BB 5-30 v WI (Dhaka) 1998-99. Tours: E 1996 (SA A), 1998; A 1995-96 (WP), 1997-98; NZ 1998-99, I 1999-00, P 1997-98; SL 1995-96 (SA U-24); Z 1999-00. 1000 runs (1): 1034 (1997). HS 186* WP v Queensland (Brisbane) 1995-96. UK HS 172* M v Worcs (Kidderminster) 1997. Gm HS 101 v Notts (Colwyn Bay) 1999. BB 5-54 M v Kent (Lord's) 1997. Gm BB 3-52 v Somerset (Taunton) 1999. Award: NWT 1. LO HS 155* v Surrey (Pontypridd) 1999 (NL). LO BB 5-30 (*see LOI*).

DURHAM – RELEASED/RETIRED (continued from p 20)

(Having made a first-class County appearance in 1999)

BOON, David Clarence (Launceston GS), b Launceston, Australia 29 Dec 1960. 5'7½". RHB, OB. Tasmania 1978-79 to date; captain 1992-93 to date. Durham 1997-99; captain 1997-99; cap 1998. MBE. **Tests** (A): 107, inc 60 in succession (1984-85 to 1995-96); HS 200 v NZ (Perth) 1989-90. **LOI** (A): 181 (1983-84 to 1994-95); HS 122 v SL (Adelaide) 1987-88. Tours: E 1985, 1989, 1993; SA 1993-94; WI 1990-91, 1994-95; NZ 1985-86, 1989-90, 1992-93; I 1986-87; P 1988-89, 1994-95; SL 1992-93; Z 1995-96 (Tas – captain). 1000 runs (4+2); most – 1437 (1993). HS 227 Tasmania v Victoria (Melbourne) 1983-84. Du HS 139* v Yorks (Chester-le-St) 1998. BB 2-18 v Kent (Darlington) 1997. LO HS 122 (*see LOI*). LO BB 2-44 v Derbys (Derby) 1998 (SL).

CHAPMAN, Steven (Willington Parkside CS), b Crook 2 Oct 1971. 6'4". RHB, SLA. Durham 1998-99. Cumberland 1997. HS 32 and BB 1-49 v Glam (Cardiff) 1999. LO HS 30 v Notts (Chester-le-St) 1999 (NL). LO BB 2-57 v Surrey (Chester-le-St) 1998 (SL).

MORRIS, J.E. – *see NOTTINGHAMSHIRE.*

GLAMORGAN 1999

RESULTS SUMMARY

	Place	*Won*	*Lost*	*Tied*	*Drew*	*No Result*
PPP County Championship	**14th**	5	7		5	
All First-Class Matches		5	7		6	
NatWest Trophy	Quarter-Finalist					
CGU National League (Division 2)	**4th**	8	7	1		

COUNTY CHAMPIONSHIP AVERAGES

BATTING AND FIELDING

Cap		*M*	*I*	*NO*	*HS*	*Runs*	*Avge*	*100*	*50*	*Ct/St*
–	M.J.Powell	15	25	4	164	949	45.19	1	5	4
1992	S.P.James	16	25	1	259*	1017	42.37	4	3	9
1987	M.P.Maynard	13	18	1	186	685	40.29	2	2	9
1999	J.H.Kallis	6	9	–	101	362	40.22	1	2	3
–	M.A.Wallace	3	4	1	64*	98	32.66	–	1	12
1992	A.Dale	16	26	–	113	809	31.11	3	1	4
–	W.L.Law	4	7	–	64	204	29.14	–	2	3
–	K.Newell	8	11	–	46	239	21.72	–	–	2
–	A.W.Evans	14	22	2	88*	433	21.65	–	2	9
1992	R.D.B.Croft	15	21	4	58*	322	18.94	–	2	5
–	I.Dawood	6	11	–	102	204	18.54	1	–	16
–	D.A.Cosker	12	17	4	49	197	15.15	–	–	12
1997	S.D.Thomas	17	24	1	54	318	13.82	–	1	8
1999	A.D.Shaw	11	15	1	45	172	12.28	–	–	25/1
1989	S.L.Watkin	15	19	9	16*	86	8.60	–	–	7
–	S.P.Jones	9	12	2	13	58	5.80	–	–	2
–	O.T.Parkin	6	8	3	11	14	2.80	–	–	1

Also played (1 match): D.S.Harrison did not bat.

BOWLING

	O	*M*	*R*	*W*	*Avge*	*Best*	*5wI*	*10wM*
S.D.Thomas	443.2	76	1469	61	24.08	5- 64	1	–
O.T.Parkin	129.2	34	404	16	25.25	4- 38	–	–
S.L.Watkin	421.3	121	1087	43	25.27	6- 75	3	–
A.Dale	136.5	46	407	15	27.13	3- 29	–	–
J.H.Kallis	95	12	345	11	31.36	3- 52	–	–
R.D.B.Croft	521.4	135	1412	45	31.37	7- 70	4	1
S.P.Jones	191	27	702	17	41.29	5- 31	1	–
D.A.Cosker	302	73	820	18	45.55	3-100	–	–

Also bowled: A.W.Evans 1-0-3-0; D.S.Harrison 10-2-33-0; W.L.Law 0.1-0-4-0; M.P.Maynard 2-2-0-0; K.Newell 13-1-38-2; M.J.Powell 6-0-32-0.

The First-Class Averages (pp 113-128) give the records of Glamorgan players in all first-class county matches (Glamorgan's other opponents being Oxford University).

GLAMORGAN RECORDS

FIRST-CLASS CRICKET

Highest Total	For	648-4d		v	Notts	Colwyn Bay	1999
	V	712		by	Northants	Northampton	1998
Lowest Total	For	22		v	Lancashire	Liverpool	1924
	V	33		by	Leics	Ebbw Vale	1965
Highest Innings	For	287*	D.E.Davies	v	Glos	Newport	1939
	V	322*	M.B.Loye	for	Northants	Northampton	1998

Highest Partnership for each Wicket

1st	330	A.Jones/R.C.Fredericks	v	Northants	Swansea	1972
2nd	249	S.P.James/H.Morris	v	Oxford U	Oxford	1987
3rd	313	D.E.Davies/W.E.Jones	v	Essex	Brentwood	1948
4th	425*	A.Dale/I.V.A.Richards	v	Middlesex	Cardiff	1993
5th	264	M.Robinson/S.W.Montgomery	v	Hampshire	Bournemouth	1949
6th	230	W.E.Jones/B.L.Muncer	v	Worcs	Worcester	1953
7th	211	P.A.Cottey/O.D.Gibson	v	Leics	Swansea	1996
8th	202	D.Davies/J.J.Hills	v	Sussex	Eastbourne	1928
9th	203*	J.J.Hills/J.C.Clay	v	Worcs	Swansea	1929
10th	143	T.Davies/S.A.B.Daniels	v	Glos	Swansea	1982

Best Bowling	For	10- 51	J.Mercer	v	Worcs	Worcester	1936
(Innings)	V	10- 18	G.Geary	for	Leics	Pontypridd	1929
Best Bowling	For	17-212	J.C.Clay	v	Worcs	Swansea	1937
(Match)	V	16- 96	G.Geary	for	Leics	Pontypridd	1929

Most Runs – Season	2276	H.Morris	(av 55.51)	1990
Most Runs – Career	34056	A.Jones	(av 33.03)	1957-83
Most 100s – Season	10	H.Morris		1990
Most 100s – Career	52	A.Jones		1957-83
	52	H.Morris		1981-97
Most Wkts – Season	176	J.C.Clay	(av 17.34)	1937
Most Wkts – Career	2174	D.J.Shepherd	(av 20.95)	1950-72

LIMITED-OVERS CRICKET

Highest Total	NWT	373-7		v	Beds	Cardiff	1998
	BHC	318-3		v	Combined U	Cardiff	1995
	NL	294-4		v	Surrey	Pontypridd	1999
Lowest Total	NWT	76		v	Northants	Northampton	1968
	BHC	68		v	Lancashire	Manchester	1973
	NL	42		v	Derbyshire	Swansea	1979
Highest Innings	NWT	162*	I.V.A.Richards	v	Oxfordshire	Swansea	1993
	BHC	151*	M.P.Maynard	v	Middlesex	Lord's	1996
	NL	155*	J.H.Kallis	v	Surrey	Pontypridd	1999
Best Bowling	NWT	5-13	R.J.Shastri	v	Scotland	Edinburgh	1988
	BHC	6-20	S.D.Thomas	v	Combined U	Cardiff	1995
	NL	7-16	S.D.Thomas	v	Surrey	Swansea	1998

GLOUCESTERSHIRE

Formation of Present Club: 1871
Colours: Blue, Gold, Brown, Silver, Green and Red
Badge: Coat of Arms of the City and County of Bristol
County Champions (since 1890): (0); best – 2nd 1930, 1931, 1947, 1959, 1969, 1986
NatWest Trophy/Gillette Cup Winners: (2) 1973, 1999
Benson and Hedges Cup Winners: (2) 1977, 1999
CGU National League (Div 1) Winners: (0); best – 4th 1999
Sunday League Winners: (0); best – 2nd 1988
Match Awards: NWT 48; BHC 59

Chief Executive: C.L.Sextone, County Ground, Nevil Road, Bristol BS7 9EJ ▲ Tel: 0117 910 8000 ▲ Fax: 0117 924 1193 ▲ Email: glos@ecb.co.uk ▲ Web: www.glosccc.co.uk

Captain: M.W.Alleyne. **Vice-Captain:** T.H.C.Hancock. **Overseas Player:** I.J.Harvey. **2000 Testimonial:** D.Bridle (Head Groundsman). **Scorer:** K.T.Gerrish. ‡ New registration

ALLEYNE, Mark Wayne (Harrison C, Barbados; Cardinal Pole S, London E9; Haringey Cricket C), b Tottenham, London 23 May 1968. 5'10". RHB, RM. Debut 1986; cap 1990; captain 1997 to date; benefit 1999. **LOI:** 9 (1998-99 to 1999-00); HS 53 v SA (E London) 1999-00; BB 3-27 v SL (Sydney) 1998-99. Tours (Eng A): NZ 1999-00 (captain); SL 1986-87 (Gs), 1992-93 (Gs); B 1999-00 (captain). 1000 runs (6); most – 1189 (1998). HS 256 v Northants (Northampton) 1990. 50 wkts (1): 54 (1996). BB 6-64 v Surrey (Oval) 1997. Awards: NWT 2; BHC 2. LO HS 134* v Leics (Bristol) 1992 (SL). LO BB 5-27 v Comb U (Bristol) 1988 (BHC).

AVERIS, James Maxwell Michael (Cathedral S, Bristol; Portsmouth U; St Cross C, Oxford), b Bristol 28 May 1974. 5'11". RHB, RMF. Oxford U 1997; blue 1997; rugby blue 1996-97. Gloucestershire debut 1997. HS 42 OU v Durham (Oxford) 1997 – on debut. Gs HS 18* v Middx (Bristol) 1999. BB 5-98 OU v Hants (Oxford) 1997. Gs BB 3-42 v Derbys (Bristol) 1999. LO HS 5* (NL). LO BB 3-17 v Yorks (Leeds) 1999 (NL).

BALL, Martyn Charles John (King Edmund SS; Bath CFE), b Bristol 26 Apr 1970. 5'8". RHB, OB. Debut 1988; cap 1996. Tour (Gs): SL 1992-93. HS 71 v Notts (Bristol) 1993. BB 8-46 (14-169 match) v Somerset (Taunton) 1993. LO HS 36* v Northants (Cheltenham) 1998 (SL). LO BB 5-42 v Yorks (Cheltenham) 1999 (NL).

BARNETT, Kim John (Leek HS), b Stoke-on-Trent, Staffs 17 Jul 1960. 6'1". RHB, RM/LB. Derbyshire 1979-98; cap 1982; captain 1983-95; benefit 1992. Boland 1982-83 to 1987-88. Staffordshire 1976. Gloucestershire debut/cap 1999. *Wisden* 1988. **Tests:** 4 (1988 to 1989); HS 80 v A (Leeds) 1989. **LOI:** 1 (1988); HS 84 v SL (Oval) 1988. Tours: SA 1989-90 (Eng XI); NZ 1979-80 (DHR); SL 1985-86 (Eng B). 1000 runs (15); most – 1734 (1984). HS 239* De v Leics (Leicester) 1988. Gs HS 125 v Kent (Canterbury) 1999. BB 6-28 De v Glam (Chesterfield) 1991. Gs BB 2-52 v Worcs (Cheltenham) 1999. Awards: NWT 5; BHC 11. LO HS 131* De v Essex (Derby) 1984 (SL). LO BB 6-24 De v Cumb (Kendal) 1984 (NWT).

CAWDRON, Michael John (Cheltenham C), b Luton, Beds 7 Oct 1974. 6'2". LHB, RM. Staff 1994; debut 1999. Took 15 wickets in first four innings. HS 42 and BB 5-35 v Hants (Bristol) 1999 – on debut. LO HS 50 v Essex (Cheltenham) 1995 (SL). LO BB 4-17 v Warwks (Cheltenham) 1999 (NL).

COTTERELL, Thomas Paul (King's S, Gloucester; U of Kent), b Hounslow, Middx 9 Mar 1977. 6'2". LHB, SLA. Debut 1999. HS 0 and BB 3-69 v Northants (Northampton) 1999 – on debut.

CUNLIFFE, Robert John (Banbury S; Banbury TC), b Oxford 8 Nov 1973. 5'10". RHB, RM. Debut 1994. Oxfordshire 1991-94. HS 190* v OU (Bristol) 1995. CC HS 108 v Northants (Northampton) 1999. Awards: BHC 2. LO HS 137* v Surrey (Oval) 1996 (BHC).

‡**FORDER, Damian** Joseph (City of Bristol C), b Bristol 11 Mar 1979. RHB, LMF. Staff 2000 – awaiting f-c debut.

GANNON, Benjamin Ward (Dragon S, Oxford; Abingdon S; Cheltenham & Gloucester CHE), b Oxford 5 Sep 1975. 6'3". RHB, RMF. Debut 1999. Herefordshire 1996. HS 18 and BB 6-80 v Glam (Cardiff) 1999 – on debut.

HANCOCK, Timothy Harold Coulter (St Edward's S, Oxford; Henley C), b Reading, Berks 20 Apr 1972. 5'10". RHB, RM. Debut 1991; cap 1998. Oxfordshire 1990. Tour: SL 1992-93 (Gs). 1000 runs (1): 1227 (1998). HS 220* v Notts (Nottingham) 1998. BB 3-5 v Essex (Colchester) 1998. Awards: NWT 2. LO HS 90 v Glam (Cardiff) 1999 (NWT). LO BB 6-58 v Scot (Bristol) 1997 (NWT).

HARDINGES, Mark Andrew (Malvern C; Bath U), b Gloucester 5 Feb 1978. 6'1". RHB, RMF. HS 1 and BB 1-9 v Northants (Northampton) 1999 – on debut.

HARVEY, Ian Joseph, b Wonthaggi, Victoria, Australia 10 Apr 1972. 5'10". RHB, RMF. Victoria 1993-94 to date. Gloucestershire debut/cap 1999. **LOI** (A): 12 (1997-98 to 1999-00); HS 43 v SA (Perth) 1997-98; BB 3-17 v NZ (Sydney) 1997-98. Tour: NZ 1994-95 (Aus Academy). HS 136 Vic v S Aus (Melbourne) 1995-96. Gs HS 123 v Kent (Canterbury) 1999. BB 7-44 Vic v S Aus (Melbourne) 1996-97. Gs BB 5-76 v Notts (Bristol) 1999. Award: NWT 1. LO HS 71 Vic v Q (Melbourne) 1998-99 (MM). LO BB 5-41 v Leics (Bristol) 1999 (NL).

HEWSON, Dominic Robert (Cheltenham C), b Cheltenham 3 Oct 1974. 5'8". RHB, occ RM. Debut 1996. HS 87 v Hants (Southampton) 1996 (on CC debut). BB 1-7. LO HS 45 v Northants (Bristol) 1998 (NWT).

LEWIS, Jonathan (Churchfields S, Swindon; Swindon C), b Aylesbury, Bucks 26 Aug 1975. 6'2". RHB, RMF. Debut 1995; cap 1998. Wiltshire 1993. Northamptonshire staff 1994. HS 62 v Worcs (Cheltenham) 1999. BB 7-56 (10-92 match) v Notts (Bristol) 1999. 50 wkts (2); most – 59 (1998). Award: BHC 1. LO HS 33* v Somerset (Bristol) 1998 (BHC). LO BB 3-27 v Warwks (Birmingham) 1995 (SL) and 3-27 v Somerset (Taunton) 1996 (NWT).

‡**MOHAMMED, Imraan** (St Patrick's HS, Karachi; Karachi GS; Joseph Chamberlain C, Birmingham; St Catharine's C, Cambridge), b Solihull, Warwicks 31 Dec 1976. Son of Sadiq (Karachi, PIA, Essex, Gloucestershire, Tasmania, United Bank and Pakistan 1959-60 to 1986); nephew of Hanif (Bahawalpur, Karachi, PIA and Pakistan 1951-52 to 1975-76), Mushtaq (Karachi, PIA, Northamptonshire and Pakistan 1956-57 and 1984), Raees (Karachi), Wazir (Karachi, Bahawalpur and Pakistan 1949-50 to 1963-64); cousin of Asif (PIA), Shahid (PIA) and Shoaib (Pakistan). 5'10". RHB, OB. Cambridge U 1997-99; blue 1998-99. Brit U 1999. HS 136 and BB 1-13 CU v Yorks (Leeds) 1998.

POPE, Stephen Patrick (Cheltenham Bournside CS), b Cheltenham 25 Jan 1983. 5'8". RHB, WK. Non-contracted player awaiting f-c debut. LO HS (Glos Board) 0 (NWT).

RUSSELL, Robert Charles ('***Jack***') (Archway CS), b Stroud 15 Aug 1963. 5'8½". LHB, WK, occ OB. Debut 1981 – youngest Glos wicket-keeper (17yr 307d), setting record for most match dismissals on f-c debut – 8 v SL (Bristol); cap 1985; benefit 1994; captain 1995. *Wisden* 1989. MBE 1996. **Tests:** 54 (1988 to 1997-98); HS 128* v A (Manchester) 1989; 11 ct v SA (Jo'burg) 1995-96 (Test record); 27 dis 1995-96 series v SA (Eng record). **LOI:** 40 (1987-88 to 1998-99); HS 50 v I (Nottingham) 1990. Tours: A 1990-91, 1992-93 (Eng A); SA 1995-96; WI 1989-90, 1993-94, 1997-98; NZ 1991-92, 1996-97; P 1987-88; SL 1986-87 (Gs). 1000 runs (1): 1049 (1997). HS 129* Eng XI v Boland (Paarl) 1995-96. Gs HS 124 v Notts (Nottingham) 1996. BB 1-4. Awards: NWT 1; BHC 3. LO HS 119* v Brit U (Bristol) 1998 (BHC).

SMITH, Andrew **Michael** (Queen Elizabeth GS, Wakefield; Exeter U), b Dewsbury, Yorks 1 Oct 1967. 5'9". RHB, LMF. Debut 1991; cap 1995. **Tests**: 1 (1997); HS 4*; BB – . Tour: P 1995-96 (Eng A – *part*). HS 61 v Yorks (Gloucester) 1998. 50 wkts (5); most – 83 (1997). BB 8-73 (10-118 match) v Middx (Lord's) 1996. Award: BHC 1. LO HS 26* v Kent (Moreton-in-M) 1996 (SL). LO BB 6-39 v Hants (Southampton) 1995 (BHC).

SNAPE, Jeremy Nicholas (Denstone C; Durham U), b Stoke-on-Trent, Staffs 27 Apr 1973. 5'8½". RHB, OB. Northamptonshire 1992-97. Combined U 1994. Gloucestershire debut/cap 1999. Tour: Z 1994-95 (Nh). HS 98* v Essex (Gloucester) 1999. BB 5-65 Nh v Durham (Northampton) 1995. Gs BB 3-67 v Glam (Cardiff) 1999. Awards: BHC 3. LO HS 77* Nh v Glam (Northampton) 1998. LO BB 5-32 Nh v Leics (Northampton) 1997 (BHC).

‡**TAYLOR, Christopher** Glyn (Colton's Collegiate S), b Bristol 27 Sep 1976. RHB, OB. Staff 2000 – awaiting f-c debut.

WILLIAMS, Richard Charles James ('***Reggie***') (Millfield S), b Southmead, Bristol 8 Aug 1969. 5'8". LHB, WK. Debut 1990; cap 1996. Tour: SL 1992-93 (Gs). HS 90 v OU (Bristol) 1995. CC HS 55* v Derbys (Gloucester) 1991. LO HS 19 v Essex (Cheltenham) 1995 (SL).

WINDOWS, Matthew Guy Newman (Clifton C; Durham U), b Bristol 5 Apr 1973. Son of A.R. (Glos and CU 1960-68). 5'7". RHB, RSM. Debut 1992; cap 1998. Combined U 1995. Tours (Eng A): SA 1998-99; Z 1998-99. 1000 runs (1): 1173 (1998). HS 184 v Warwks (Cheltenham) 1996. BB 1-6 (Comb U). Gs BB – . LO HS 72 v Somerset (Bristol) 1994.

RELEASED/RETIRED
(Having made a first-class County appearance in 1999)

DAWSON, Robert Ian (Millfield S; Newcastle Poly), b Exmouth, Devon 29 Mar 1970. 5'11". RHB, RM. Gloucestershire 1992-99. Devon 1988-91. 1000 runs (1): 1112 (1994). HS 127* v CU (Bristol) 1994. CC HS 101 v Worcs (Gloucester) 1995. BB 3-15 v Lancs (Manchester) 1998. LO HS 85 v Worcs (Worcester) 1996 (SL). LO BB 1-19 (SL).

COUNTY CAPS AWARDED IN 1999

Derbyshire	P.Aldred
Durham	J.A.Daley, S.J.Harmison, N.Killeen
Essex	B.J.Hyam
Glamorgan	J.H.Kallis, A.D.Shaw
Gloucestershire	K.J.Barnett, I.J.Harvey, J.N.Snape
Hampshire	W.S.Kendall
Kent	A.Symonds, J.B.D.Thompson
Lancashire	M.Muralitharan
Leicestershire	M.S.Kasprowicz, J.Ormond
Middlesex	–
Northamptonshire	M.L.Hayden, D.E.Malcolm, D.J.G.Sales, G.P.Swann
Nottinghamshire	V.C.Drakes, P.J.Franks, C.M.W.Read
Somerset	M.Burns, J.Cox, K.A.Parsons, M.E.Trescothick
Surrey	B.C.Hollioake, A.J.Tudor
Sussex	P.A.Cottey, M.J.Di Venuto, R.R.Montgomerie
Warwickshire	T.Frost, M.J.Powell
Worcestershire	–
Yorkshire	G.S.Blewett, R.J.Harden, A.McGrath

GLOUCESTERSHIRE 1999

RESULTS SUMMARY

	Place	*Won*	*Lost*	*Tied*	*Drew*	*No Result*
PPP County Championship	**18th**	2	9		6	
All First-Class Matches		2	9		6	
NatWest Trophy	**Winners**					
Benson & Hedges Super Cup	**Winners**					
CGU National League (Division 1)	**4th**	8	8			

COUNTY CHAMPIONSHIP AVERAGES

BATTING AND FIELDING

Cap		*M*	*I*	*NO*	*HS*	*Runs*	*Avge*	*100*	*50*	*Ct/St*
1998	M.G.N.Windows	17	30	3	118	960	35.55	2	5	5
1985	R.C.Russell	17	30	6	94*	790	32.91	–	5	55/5
–	R.J.Cunliffe	7	13	–	108	421	32.38	1	2	8
1999	K.J.Barnett	15	26	1	125	727	29.08	2	4	15
1998	T.H.C.Hancock	17	30	–	71	858	28.60	–	7	7
1990	M.W.Alleyne	17	29	1	76	672	24.00	–	3	20
1999	I.J.Harvey	12	19	–	123	429	22.57	1	–	6
1999	J.N.Snape	17	29	6	98*	518	22.52	–	3	8
1996	M.C.J.Ball	12	19	4	70*	333	22.20	–	1	11
–	M.J.Cawdron	6	9	2	42	126	18.00	–	–	1
–	D.R.Hewson	5	10	–	40	144	14.40	–	–	3
–	J.M.M.Averis	3	5	2	18*	40	13.33	–	–	–
1998	J.Lewis	14	23	3	62	266	13.30	–	1	2
–	B.W.Gannon	11	12	4	18	70	8.75	–	–	4
1995	A.M.Smith	14	21	5	14	108	6.75	–	–	4

Also batted (1 match each): T.P.Cotterell 0; R.I.Dawson 10, 36 (1 ct); M.A.Hardinges 1.

BOWLING

	O	*M*	*R*	*W*	*Avge*	*Best*	*5wI*	*10wM*
M.J.Cawdron	101.5	30	266	16	16.62	5-35	3	–
A.M.Smith	450.1	127	1168	57	20.49	5-41	2	–
I.J.Harvey	296.1	77	876	31	28.25	5-76	1	–
J.Lewis	492.2	135	1444	49	29.46	7-56	2	1
B.W.Gannon	259.3	47	992	33	30.06	6-80	2	–
M.W.Alleyne	367	109	1000	23	43.47	3-36	–	–
M.C.J.Ball	266	66	723	13	55.61	3-38	–	–
J.N.Snape	277.1	71	804	12	67.00	3-67	–	–

Also bowled: J.M.M.Averis 72.2-16-261-8; K.J.Barnett 40.3-6-134-2; T.P.Cotterell 32-8-81-3; T.H.C.Hancock 53-12-190-4; M.A.Hardinges 23-6-60-1; D.R.Hewson 1-1-0-0; M.G.N.Windows 1-0-7-0.

The First-Class Averages (pp 113-128) give the records of Gloucestershire players in all first-class county matches.

GLOUCESTERSHIRE RECORDS

FIRST-CLASS CRICKET

Highest Total	For	653-6d		v	Glamorgan	Bristol	1928
	V	774-7d		by	Australians	Bristol	1948
Lowest Total	For	17		v	Australians	Cheltenham	1896
	V	12		by	Northants	Gloucester	1907
Highest Innings	For	318 *	W.G.Grace	v	Yorkshire	Cheltenham	1876
	V	296	A.O.Jones	for	Notts	Nottingham	1903

Highest Partnership for each Wicket

1st	395	D.M.Young/R.B.Nicholls	v	Oxford U	Oxford	1962
2nd	256	C.T.M.Pugh/T.W.Graveney	v	Derbyshire	Chesterfield	1960
3rd	336	W.R.Hammond/B.H.Lyon	v	Leics	Leicester	1933
4th	321	W.R.Hammond/W.L.Neale	v	Leics	Gloucester	1937
5th	261	W.G.Grace/W.O.Moberley	v	Yorkshire	Cheltenham	1876
6th	320	G.L.Jessop/J.H.Board	v	Sussex	Hove	1903
7th	248	W.G.Grace/E.L.Thomas	v	Sussex	Hove	1896
8th	239	W.R.Hammond/A.E.Wilson	v	Lancashire	Bristol	1938
9th	193	W.G.Grace/S.A.P.Kitcat	v	Sussex	Bristol	1896
10th	131	W.R.Gouldsworthy/J.G.Bessant	v	Somerset	Bristol	1923

Best Bowling	For	10-40	E.G.Dennett	v	Essex	Bristol	1906
(Innings)	V	10-66	A.A.Mailey	for	Australians	Cheltenham	1921
		10-66	K.Smales	for	Notts	Stroud	1956
Best Bowling	For	17-56	C.W.L.Parker	v	Essex	Gloucester	1925
(Match)	V	15-87	A.J.Conway	for	Worcs	Moreton-in-M	1914

Most Runs – Season	2860	W.R.Hammond	(av 69.75)	1933
Most Runs – Career	33664	W.R.Hammond	(av 57.05)	1920-51
Most 100s – Season	13	W.R.Hammond		1938
Most 100s – Career	113	W.R.Hammond		1920-51
Most Wkts – Season	222	T.W.J.Goddard	(av 16.80)	1937
	222	T.W.J.Goddard	(av 16.37)	1947
Most Wkts – Career	3170	C.W.L.Parker	(av 19.43)	1903-35

LIMITED-OVERS CRICKET

Highest Total	**NWT**	351-2		v	Scotland	Bristol	1997
	BHC	308-3		v	Ireland	Dublin	1996
	NL	284-4		v	Leics	Cheltenham	1996
Lowest Total	**NWT**	82		v	Notts	Bristol	1987
	BHC	62		v	Hampshire	Bristol	1975
	NL	49		v	Middlesex	Bristol	1978
Highest Innings	**NWT**	177	A.J.Wright	v	Scotland	Bristol	1997
	BHC	154*	M.J.Procter	v	Somerset	Taunton	1972
	NL	146*	S. Young	v	Yorkshire	Leeds	1997
Best Bowling	**NWT**	6-21	C.A.Walsh	v	Kent	Bristol	1990
		6-21	C.A.Walsh	v	Cheshire	Bristol	1992
	BHC	6-13	M.J.Procter	v	Hampshire	Southampton	1977
	NL	6-52	J.N.Shepherd	v	Kent	Bristol	1983

HAMPSHIRE

Formation of Present Club: 12 August 1863
Colours: Blue, Gold and White
Badge: Tudor Rose and Crown
County Champions: (2) 1961, 1973
NatWest Trophy/Gillette Cup Winners: (1) 1991
Benson and Hedges Cup Winners: (2) 1988, 1992
CGU National League (Div 1) Winners: (0); best – 4th 1999
Sunday League Winners: (3) 1975, 1978, 1986
Match Awards: NWT 58; BHC 63

Chief Executive: A.F.Baker, County Cricket Ground, Northlands Road, Southampton SO15 2UE ▲ Tel: (023) 80333788 ▲ Fax: (023) 80330121 ▲ Email: hants@ecb.co.uk ▲ Web: www.hampshire.cricket.org

Captain: R.A.Smith. **Vice-Captain:** S.D.Udal. **Overseas Player:** S.K.Warne. **2000 Beneficiary:** A.N.Aymes. **Scorer:** V.H Isaacs. ‡ New registration

‡**ADAMS, James** Henry Kenneth (Sherborne S; University C, London), b Winchester 23 Sep 1980. RHB, RFM. Staff 2000 – awaiting f-c debut.

AYMES, Adrian Nigel (Bellemoor SM, Southampton), b Southampton 4 Jun 1964. 6'0". RHB, WK. Debut 1987; cap 1991; benefit 2000. HS 133 v Leics (Leicester) 1998. BB 2-135 v Northants (Southampton) 1998. Award: NWT 1. LO HS 73* v Middx (Lord's) 1998 (NWT).

‡**BRUNNSCHWEILER, Iain** (King Edward VI S, Southampton), b Southampton 10 Dec 1979. RHB, WK. Staff 1999 – awaiting f-c debut.

FRANCIS, Simon Richard George (Yardley Court, Tonbridge; King Edward VI S, Southampton; Durham U), b Bromley, Kent 15 Aug 1978. 6'2". RHB, RMF. Debut 1997. British U 1998-99. HS 11 v Somerset (Southampton) 1999. BB 2-21 v SL (Southampton) 1998. CC BB 2-94 v Lancs (Southampton) 1999. LO HS 1 and BB 2-28 v Kent (Canterbury) 1999 (NL).

‡**HAMBLIN, James** Rupert Christopher (Charterhouse S; Bristol U), b Pembury, Kent 16 Aug 1978. RHB. Staff 1998 – awaiting f-c debut.

HARTLEY, Peter John (Greenhead GS; Bradford C), b Keighley, Yorks 18 Apr 1960. 6'0". RHB, RMF. Warwickshire 1982. Yorkshire 1985-97; cap 1987; benefit 1996. Hampshire debut/cap 1998. Tours (Y): SA 1991-92; WI 1986-87; Z 1995-96. HS 127* Y v Lancs (Manchester) 1988. H HS 58 v Middx (Lord's) 1999. 50 wkts (7); most – 81 (1995). BB 9-41 (inc hat-trick, 4 wkts in 5 balls and 5 in 9; 11-68 match) Y v Derbys (Chesterfield) 1995. H BB 8-65 (11-117 match) v Yorks (Basingstoke) 1999. Hat-trick 1995. Awards: NWT 1; BHC 2. LO HS 83 Y v Ire (Leeds) 1997 (NWT). LO BB 5-36 Y v Sussex (Scarborough) 1993 (SL).

KENDALL, William Salwey (Bradfield C; Keble C, Oxford), b Wimbledon, Surrey 18 Dec 1973. 5'10". RHB, RM. Oxford U 1994-96; blue 1995-96. Hampshire debut 1996; cap 1999. 1000 runs (2); most – 1186 (1999). HS 201 v Sussex (Southampton) 1999. BB 3-37 OU v Derbys (Oxford) 1995. H BB 2-46 v Notts (Southampton) 1996. LO HS 55 v Essex (Chelmsford) 1997 (SL).

KENWAY, Derek Anthony (St George's S, Southampton; Barton Peveril C, Eastleigh), b Fareham 12 Jun 1978. 5'11". RHB, RM, occ WK. Debut 1997. 1000 runs (1): 1055 (1999). HS 102 v Warwks (Southampton) 1999. BB 1-5. LO HS 58 v Glos (Bristol) 1999 (NL).

LANEY, Jason Scott (Pewsey Vale SS; St John's SFC, Marlborough; Leeds U), b Winchester 27 Apr 1973. 5'10". RHB, OB. Debut 1995; cap 1996. Matabeleland 1995-96. 1000 runs (1): 1163 (1996). HS 112 v OU (Oxford) 1996. CC HS 105 v Kent (Canterbury) 1996. BB 1-24. Award: NWT 1. LO HS 153 v Norfolk (Southampton) 1996 (NWT).

MASCARENHAS, Adrian **Dimitri** (Trinity C, Perth, Australia), b Hammersmith, London 30 Oct 1977. Resident in Australia 1979-96. RHB, RMF. Debut 1996, taking 6-88 v Glamorgan (Southampton); took 16 wickets in first two CC matches; cap 1998. Dorset 1996. HS 89 v Notts (Portsmouth) 1998. BB 6-88 (*see above*). Award: NWT 1. LO HS 79 v Worcs (Southampton) 1999 (NL). LO BB 4-28 v Surrey (Southampton) 1998 (BHC).

MORRIS, Alexander Corfield (Holgate S; Barnsley C), b Barnsley, Yorks 4 Oct 1976. Elder brother of Z.C. 6'3". LHB, RMF. Yorkshire 1995-97. Yorks 2nd XI debut when 16yr 332d. Hampshire debut 1998. Tour: Z 1995-96 (Y). HS 60 Y v Lancs (Manchester) 1996 (not CC). H HS 58* v OU (Oxford) 1999. 50 wkts (1): 50 (1998). BB 5-52 (10-111 match) v Worcs (Southampton) 1999. LO HS 48* Y v Durham (Chester-le-St) 1996 (SL). LO BB 4-49 Y v Leics (Leeds) 1997 (SL).

MORRIS, Zachary Clegg (Holgate S, Barnsley), b Barnsley, Yorks 4 Sep 1978. Younger brother of A.C. 6'1". RHB, SLA. Debut 1998. HS 10 v Glos (Southampton) 1998.

‡**MULLALLY, Alan** David (Cannington HS, Perth, Australia; Wembley TC), b Southend-on-Sea, Essex 12 Jul 1969. 6'5". RHB, LFM. W Australia 1987-88 to 1989-90. Victoria 1990-91. Hampshire (1 match) 1988. Leicestershire 1990-99; cap 1993. **Tests:** 18 (1996 to 1999-00); HS 24 v P (Oval) 1996; BB 5-105 v A (Brisbane) 1998-99. **LOI:** 34 (1996 to 1999-00); HS 20 v Z (Harare) 1996-97; BB 4-18 v A (Brisbane) 1998-99. Tours: A 1998-99; SA 1999-00; NZ 1996-97; Z 1996-97. HS 75 Le v Middx (Leicester) 1996. 50 wkts (4); most – 70 (1996). BB 7-55 (11-89 match) Le v Notts (Worksop) 1998. Award: NWT 1. LO HS 38 Le v Kent (Leicester) 1994 (SL). LO BB 5-15 Le v Warwks (Birmingham) 1996 (SL).

‡**PRITTIPAUL, Lawrence** Roland (St John's C, Southsea; Portsmouth C), b Portsmouth 19 Oct 1979. Cousin of S.Chanderpaul (Guyana and West Indies 1991-92 to date). 6'1". RHB, RM. Staff 1999 – awaiting f-c debut. Two NL appearances 1999. LO HS 30 Hants Board v Salop (Wellington) 1999 (NWT). LO BB 2-53 Hants Board XI v Suffolk (Bury St Edmunds) 1999 (NWT).

RENSHAW, Simon John (Birkenhead S; Leeds U), b Bebington, Cheshire 6 Mar 1974. 6'3". RHB, RMF. Combined U 1995. Hampshire debut 1996. Cheshire 1994-95. HS 56 v Surrey (Guildford) 1997. BB 5-110 v Derbys (Chesterfield) 1997. LO HS 27* v Lancs (Manchester) 1999 (NL). LO BB 6-25 v Surrey (Southampton) 1997 (BHC).

SAVIDENT, Lee (Guernsey GS; Guernsey CFE), b Guernsey 22 Oct 1976. 6'5". RHB, RM. Debut 1997. HS 6 and BB 2-86 v Yorks (Portsmouth) 1997. LO HS 39 v Somerset (Taunton) 1998 (SL). LO BB 3-41 v Middx (Lord's) 1997 (SL).

SMITH, Robin Arnold (Northlands BHS), b Durban, SA 13 Sep 1963. Brother of C.L. (Natal, Glam, Hants and England 1977-78 to 1992) and grandson of Dr V.L.Shearer (Natal). 5'11". RHB, LB. Natal 1980-81 to 1984-85. Hampshire debut 1982; cap 1985; benefit 1996; captain 1998 to date. *Wisden* 1989. **Tests:** 62 (1988 to 1995-96); HS 175 v WI (St John's) 1993-94. **LOI**: 71 (1988 to 1995-96); HS 167* v A (Birmingham) 1993 – Eng record. Tours: A 1990-91; SA 1995-96; WI 1989-90, 1993-94; NZ 1991-92; I/SL 1992-93. 1000 runs (11); most – 1577 (1989). HS 209* v Essex (Southend) 1987. BB 2-11 v Surrey (Southampton) 1985. Awards: NWT 9; BHC 5. LO HS 167* (*see LOI*). LO BB 2-13 v Berks (Southampton) 1985 (NWT).

STEPHENSON, John Patrick (Felsted S; Durham U), b Stebbing, Essex 14 Mar 1965. 6'1". RHB, RM. Essex 1985-94 (cap 1989). Hampshire debut/cap 1995; captain 1996-97. Boland 1988-89. **Tests:** 1 (1989); HS 25 v A (Oval) 1989. Tours: WI 1991-92 (Eng A); Z 1989-90 (Eng A). 1000 runs (5); most – 1887 (1990). HS 202* Ex v Somerset (Bath) 1990. H HS 140 v OU (Oxford) 1997. BB 7-51 v Middx (Lord's) 1995. Awards: BHC 5. LO HS 142 Ex v Warwks (Birmingham) 1991 (BHC). LO BB 6-33 v Worcs (Southampton) 1997 (SL).

UDAL, Shaun David (Cove CS), b Cove, Farnborough 18 Mar 1969. Grandson of G.F.U. (Middx 1932 and Leics 1946); great-great-grandson of J.S. (MCC 1871-75). 6'2". RHB, OB. Debut 1989; cap 1992. **LOI**: 10 (1994 to 1995); HS 11* v Z (Brisbane) 1994-95; BB 2-37 v A (Sydney) 1994-95. Tours: A 1994-95; P 1995-96 (Eng A). HS 117* v Warwks (Southampton) 1997. 50 wkts (5); most – 74 (1993). BB 8-50 v Sussex (Southampton) 1992. Awards: NWT 1; BHC 1. LO HS 78 v Surrey (Guildford) 1997 (SL). LO BB 5-43 v Surrey (Oval) 1998 (SL).

‡**VAN DER GUCHT, Charles** Graham (Radley C), b Hammersmith, London 14 Jan 1980. Grandson of P.I. (Gloucestershire 1932-33). LHB, LM. Staff 2000 – awaiting f-c debut. Award: NWT 1. LO HS 3 and LO BB 3-35 Hants Board XI v Glam (Southampton) 1999 (NWT).

‡**WARNE, Shane** Keith (Hampton HS; Mentone GS), b Upper Ferntree Gully, Melbourne, Australia 13 Sep 1969. 6'0". RHB, LBG. Victoria 1990-91 to date; captain 1997-98 to 1998-99. Joins Hampshire staff 2000. **Tests** (A): 81 (1991-92 to 1999-00); HS 86 v I (Adelaide) 1999-00; BB 8-71 v E (Brisbane) 1994-95; hat-trick v E (Melbourne) 1994-95. **LOI** (A): 137 (1992-93 to 1999-00, 11 as captain); HS 55 v SA (Pt Elizabeth) 1993-94. BB 5-33 v WI (Sydney) 1996-97. Tours (A): E 1993, 1997; SA 1993-94, 1996-97; WI 1994-95, 1998-99; NZ 1992-93; I 1997-98; P 1994-95; SL 1992-93, 1999-00; Z 1991-92 (Aus B), 1999-00. HS 86 (*see Tests*). 50 wkts (2+1); most – 75 (1993). BB 8-71 (*see Tests*). LO HS 55 (*see LOI*). LO BB 5-33 (*see LOI*).

WHITE, Giles William (Millfield S; Loughborough U), b Barnstaple, Devon 23 Mar 1972. 6'0". RHB, LB. Somerset 1991 (one match). Combined U 1994. Hampshire debut 1994; cap 1998. Devon 1988-94. 1000 runs (1): 1211 (1998). HS 156 v SL (Southampton) 1998. CC HS 145 v Yorks (Portsmouth) 1997. BB 3-23 v Notts (Nottingham) 1999. LO HS 76 v Glam (Southampton) 1998 (SL). LO BB 1-45 (Devon – NWT).

RELEASED/RETIRED

(Having made a first-class County appearance in 1999)

GARAWAY, Mark (Sandown HS, IoW), b Swindon, Wilts 20 Jul 1973. 5'8". RHB, WK. Hampshire 1996-99. MCC YC. No CC appearances. HS 55 v NZ (Southampton) 1999. LO HS 4 (NL).

HANSEN, Thomas Munkholt (Norregaard, Falkonergaarden), b Glostrup, Denmark 25 Mar 1976. 6'3". RHB, LFM. Hampshire 1997-99. Denmark 1996 to date. HS 24 v Somerset (Southampton) 1999. BB 3-59 v Sussex (Southampton) 1999.

JAMES, Kevan David (Edmonton County HS), b Lambeth, London 18 Mar 1961. 6'0". LHB, LMF. Middlesex 1980-84. Wellington 1982-83. Hampshire 1985-99; cap 1989; benefit 1999. 1000 runs (2); most – 1274 (1991). HS 162 v Glam (Cardiff) 1989. BB 8-49 (13-93 match) v Somerset (Basingstoke) 1997. Achieved unique double of 4 wkts in 4 balls and a hundred (103) v I (Southampton) 1996. LO HS 66 v Glos (Trowbridge) 1989 (SL). LO BB 6-35 v Notts (Southampton) 1996 (SL).

KEECH, Matthew (Northumberland Park S), b Hampstead 21 Oct 1970. 6'0". RHB, RM. Middlesex 1991-93. Hampshire 1994-99. MCC YC. HS 127 v OU (Oxford) 1997. CC HS 104 v Sussex (Arundel) 1996. BB 2-28 M v Glos (Bristol) 1993. H BB 1-12. Scored 251 (256 balls) v Glam 2nd XI (Usk) – Hants 2nd XI record. LO HS 98 v Worcs (Southampton) 1995 (SL). LO BB 2-16 v Kent Board XI (Canterbury) 1999 (NWT).

LUGSDEN, Steven (St Edmund Campion S, Low Fell), b Gateshead, Co Durham 10 Jul 1976. 6'2". RHB, RFM. Durham 1993-98 (youngest Durham f-c player – 17yr 27d on debut). Hampshire 1999. HS 16 v OU (Oxford) 1999. BB 3-45 Du v Lancs (Chester-le-St) 1996. H BB 3-105 v NZ (Southampton) 1999. LO HS – and BB (Du) 1-55 (SL).

continued on p 75

HAMPSHIRE 1999

RESULTS SUMMARY

	Place	Won	Lost	Tied	Drew	No Result
PPP County Championship	**7th**	5	5		7	
All First-Class Matches		5	5		9	
NatWest Trophy	4th Round					
Benson & Hedges Super Cup	Quarter-Finalist					
CGU National League (Division 1)	**8th**	5	9			2

COUNTY CHAMPIONSHIP AVERAGES

BATTING AND FIELDING

Cap		*M*	*I*	*NO*	*HS*	*Runs*	*Avge*	*100*	*50*	*Ct/St*
1996	J.S.Laney	10	17	1	99	688	43.00	–	6	7
1999	W.S.Kendall	17	29	2	201	1121	41.51	2	7	23
1985	R.A.Smith	17	28	2	96	1065	40.96	–	10	9
–	D.A.Kenway	17	28	5	102	922	40.08	1	6	10
1991	A.N.Aymes	17	26	4	115*	722	32.81	2	4	47/2
–	M.Keech	7	11	1	48	303	30.30	–	–	7
1998	A.D.Mascarenhas	13	19	2	62	460	27.05	–	2	4
1998	G.W.White	14	24	–	92	628	26.16	–	4	10
1998	P.J.Hartley	12	15	6	58	183	20.33	–	1	3
1992	S.D.Udal	13	18	5	40	222	17.07	–	–	1
–	A.C.Morris	5	6	1	22	73	14.60	–	–	–
–	S.J.Renshaw	10	11	5	28	87	14.50	–	–	7
1998	N.A.M.McLean	14	19	3	70	206	12.87	–	1	6
1995	J.P.Stephenson	13	21	1	38	226	11.30	–	–	16
–	T.M.Hansen	3	4	–	24	33	8.25	–	–	–
–	S.R.G.Francis	3	4	1	11	12	4.00	–	–	–

Also batted (1 match each): K.D.James (cap 1989) 5, 0 (1 ct); Z.C.Morris 1, 0.

BOWLING

	O	*M*	*R*	*W*	*Avge*	*Best*	*5wI*	*10wM*
A.C.Morris	152	44	467	24	19.45	5-52	3	1
P.J.Hartley	393	93	1176	54	21.77	8-65	2	1
S.D.Udal	422.3	100	1133	41	27.63	6-47	2	–
J.P.Stephenson	270	43	980	34	28.82	5-60	1	–
N.A.M.McLean	471	105	1489	46	32.36	4-63	–	–
S.J.Renshaw	310.3	68	970	24	40.41	4-43	–	–
A.D.Mascarenhas	291	92	828	13	63.69	2-31	–	–

Also bowled: A.N.Aymes 1-0-1-0; S.R.G.Francis 97-16-332-5; T.M.Hansen 64-17-196-5; K.D.James 29.1-5-99-6; M.Keech 9-1-37-0; W.S.Kendall 4.5-0-17-0; D.A.Kenway 1-0-1-0; J.S.Laney 39-5-126-2; Z.C.Morris 33.1-7-94-0; R.A.Smith 1-0-2-0; G.W.White 35.4-2-148-5.

The First-Class Averages (pp 113-128) give the records of Hampshire players in all first-class county matches (Hampshire's other opponents being the New Zealanders and Oxford University), with the exception of S.R.G.Francis whose full county figures are as above.

HAMPSHIRE RECORDS

FIRST-CLASS CRICKET

Highest Total	For	672-7d		v	Somerset	Taunton	1899
	V	742		by	Surrey	The Oval	1909
Lowest Total	For	15		v	Warwicks	Birmingham	1922
	V	23		by	Yorkshire	Middlesbrough	1965
Highest Innings	For	316	R.H.Moore	v	Warwicks	Bournemouth	1937
	V	303*	G.A.Hick	for	Worcs	Southampton	1997

Highest Partnership for each Wicket

1st	347	V.P.Terry/C.L.Smith	v	Warwicks	Birmingham	1987
2nd	321	G.Brown/E.I.M.Barrett	v	Glos	Southampton	1920
3rd	344	C.P.Mead/G.Brown	v	Yorkshire	Portsmouth	1927
4th	263	R.E.Marshall/D.A.Livingstone	v	Middlesex	Lord's	1970
5th	235	G.Hill/D.F.Walker	v	Sussex	Portsmouth	1937
6th	411	R.M.Poore/E.G.Wynyard	v	Somerset	Taunton	1899
7th	325	G.Brown/C.H.Abercrombie	v	Essex	Leyton	1913
8th	227	K.D.James/T.M.Tremlett	v	Somerset	Taunton	1985
9th	230	D.A.Livingstone/A.T.Castell	v	Surrey	Southampton	1962
10th	192	H.A.W.Bowell/W.H.Livsey	v	Worcs	Bournemouth	1921

Best Bowling	For	9- 25	R.M.H.Cottam	v	Lancashire	Manchester	1965
(Innings)	V	10- 46	W.Hickton	for	Lancashire	Manchester	1870
Best Bowling	For	16- 88	J.A.Newman	v	Somerset	Weston-s-Mare	1927
(Match)	V	17-119	W.Mead	for	Essex	Southampton	1895

Most Runs – Season	2854	C.P.Mead	(av 79.27)	1928
Most Runs – Career	48892	C.P.Mead	(av 48.84)	1905-36
Most 100s – Season	12	C.P.Mead		1928
Most 100s – Career	138	C.P.Mead		1905-36
Most Wkts – Season	190	A.S.Kennedy	(av 15.61)	1922
Most Wkts – Career	2669	D.Shackleton	(av 18.23)	1948-69

LIMITED-OVERS CRICKET

Highest Total	**NWT**	371-4		v	Glamorgan	Southampton	1975
	BHC	321-1		v	Minor C (S)	Amersham	1973
	NL	313-2		v	Sussex	Portsmouth	1993
Lowest Total	**NWT**	98		v	Lancashire	Manchester	1975
	BHC	50		v	Yorkshire	Leeds	1991
	NL	43		v	Essex	Basingstoke	1972
Highest Innings	**NWT**	177	C.G.Greenidge	v	Glamorgan	Southampton	1975
	BHC	173*	C.G.Greenidge	v	Minor C (S)	Amersham	1973
	NL	172	C.G.Greenidge	v	Surrey	Southampton	1987
Best Bowling	**NWT**	7-30	P.J.Sainsbury	v	Norfolk	Southampton	1965
	BHC	6-25	S.J.Renshaw	v	Surrey	Southampton	1997
	NL	6-20	T.E.Jesty	v	Glamorgan	Cardiff	1975

KENT

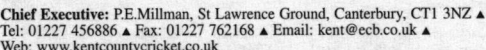

Formation of Present Club: 1 March 1859
Substantial Reorganisation: 6 December 1870
Colours: Maroon and White
Badge: White Horse on a Red Ground
County Champions: (6) 1906, 1909, 1910, 1913, 1970, 1978
Joint Champions: (1) 1977
NatWest Trophy/Gillette Cup Winners: (2) 1967, 1974
Benson and Hedges Cup Winners: (3) 1973, 1976, 1978
CGU National League (Div 1) Winners: (0); best – 3rd 1999
Sunday League Winners: (4) 1972, 1973, 1976, 1995
Match Awards: NWT 49; BHC 90

Chief Executive: P.E.Millman, St Lawrence Ground, Canterbury, CT1 3NZ ▲
Tel: 01227 456886 ▲ Fax: 01227 762168 ▲ Email: kent@ecb.co.uk ▲
Web: www.kentcountycricket.co.uk

Captain: M.V.Fleming. **Vice-Captain:** No appointment. **Overseas Player:** R.Dravid.
2000 Beneficiary: None. **Scorer:** J.C.Foley. ‡ New registration

‡**ADAMS, Kristian**, b Cleethorpes, Lincs 26 Nov 1976. RHB, LMF. Staff 2000 – awaiting f-c debut.

BANES, Matthew John (Tonbridge S; Durham U), b Pembury 10 Dec 1979. 5'9". RHB, OB. Debut 1999. HS 53 v NZ (Canterbury) 1999 – on debut. CC HS 5.

CLINTON, Richard Selvey (Colfes S), b Sidcup 1 Sep 1981. Son of G.S. (Kent and Surrey 1974-90). 6'2". LHB, RM. Staff 1999 – awaiting f-c debut.

‡**DRAVID, Rahul** (St Joseph's HS; Bangalore U), b Indore, India 11 Jan 1973. 5'11½". RHB, OB, WK. Karnataka 1990-91 to date. **Tests** (I): 35 (1996 to 1999-00); HS 190 v NZ (Hamilton) 1998-99 (scored 103* in second innings). **LOI** (I): 116 (1995-96 to 1999-00); HS 153 v NZ (Hyderabad) 1999-00; BB 1-21. Tours (I): E 1996; A 1999-00; SA 1996-97; WI 1996-97; NZ 1998-99; SL 1997-98, 1998-99; Z 1998-99. 1000 runs (0+2); most – 1264 (1997-98). HS 215 Karnataka v Uttar Pradesh (Bangalore) 1997-98. LO HS 153 (*see LOI*). LO BB 1-21 (*see LOI*).

EALHAM, Mark Alan (Stour Valley SS, Chartham), b Willesborough, Ashford 27 Aug 1969. Son of A.G.E. (Kent 1966-82). 5'9". RHB, RMF. Debut 1989; cap 1992. **Tests:** 8 (1996 to 1998); HS 53* v A (Birmingham) 1997; BB 4-21 v I (Nottingham) 1996. **LOI:** 48 (1996 to 1999-00); HS 45 v WI (Bridgetown) 1997-98; BB 5-15 v Z (Kimberley) 1999-00 – Eng record. Tours: A 1996-97 (Eng A); SA 1999-00 (*part*); SL 1997-98; Z 1992-93 (K); K 1997-98. 1000 runs (1): 1055 (1997). HS 139 v Leics (Canterbury) 1997. BB 8-36 (10-74 match) v Warwks (Birmingham) 1996. Awards: NWT 2; BHC 5. LO HS 112 v Derbys (Maidstone) 1995 (off 44 balls – SL record). LO BB 6-53 v Hants (Basingstoke) 1993 (SL).

FLEMING, Matthew Valentine (St Aubyns S, Rottingdean; Eton C), b Macclesfield, Cheshire 12 Dec 1964. 5'11½". RHB, RM. Debut 1989; cap 1990; captain 1999 to date. **LOI:** 11 (1997-98 to 1998); HS 34 v WI (Sharjah) 1997-98; BB 4-45 v I (Sharjah) 1997-98 – on debut. Tour: Z 1992-93 (K). HS 138 v Essex (Canterbury) 1997 and 138 v Worcs (Worcester) 1999. BB 5-51 v Notts (Nottingham) 1997. Awards: NWT 2; BHC 7. LO HS 117* v Cheshire (Bowdon) 1999 (NWT). LO BB 5-27 v Hants (Canterbury) 1997 (BHC).

FULTON, David Paul (The Judd S; Kent U), b Lewisham 15 Nov 1971. 6'2". RHB, SLA, occ WK. Debut 1992; cap 1998. HS 207 v Yorks (Maidstone) 1998. BB 1-37. CC BB – . LO HS 29 v Lancs (Manchester) 1993 (SL).

GOLDING, James Matthew (Kent C, Canterbury; University C, Worcester), b Canterbury 19 Jul 1977. 6'4". RHB, RMF. Debut 1999. Awaiting CC debut. HS 3 and BB 1-74 v NZ (Canterbury) 1999. Award: NWT 1. LO HS 47 Kent Board v Hants (Canterbury) 1999 (NWT).

HEADLEY, Dean Warren (Oldswinford Hospital S; Worcester RGS), b Norton, Stourbridge, Worcs 27 Jan 1970. Son of R.G.A. (Worcs, Jamaica and WI 1958-74); grandson of G.A. (Jamaica and WI 1927-28 to 1953-54). 6'4". RHB, RFM. Middlesex 1991-92; took 5-46 on CC debut, including wicket of A.A.Metcalfe with his first ball. Kent debut 1992-93; cap 1993. Staffordshire 1990. **ECB contract 2000. Tests**: 15 (1997 to 1999); HS 31 v WI (Bridgetown) 1997-98; BB 6-60 v A (Melbourne) 1998-99. **LOI:** 13 (1996 to 1998-99); HS 10* v A (Melbourne) 1998-99; BB 2-38 v I (Sharjah) 1997-98. Tours: A 1996-97 (Eng A), 1998-99; WI 1997-98; P 1995-96 (Eng A); Z 1992-93 (K). HS 91 M v Leics (Leicester) 1992. K HS 81 v Hants (Canterbury) 1998. 50 wkts (2); most – 54 (1998). BB 8-98 (inc hat-trick; 11-165 match) v Derbys (Derby) 1996. 3 hat-tricks (v Derbys, Worcs and Hants) 1996. Awards: BHC 3. LO HS 29* v Glos (Moreton-in-M) 1996 (SL). LO BB 6-42 v Surrey (Canterbury) 1995 (SL).

HOCKLEY, James Bernard (Kelsey Park S, Beckenham), b Beckenham 16 Apr 1979. 6'2". RHB, OB. Debut 1998. HS 34 and BB 1-57 v Glos (Canterbury) 1999. LO HS 19 v Glos (Canterbury) 1999 (NL).

KEY, Robert William Trevor (Colfe's S), b East Dulwich, London 12 May 1979. 6'1". RHB, RM/OB. His mother played for Kent Ladies. Debut 1998. Tours (Eng A): SA 1998-99; Z 1998-99. HS 125 v Somerset (Taunton) 1999. LO HS 76* v York (Canterbury) 1999 (NL).

‡KHAN, Amjad, b Copenhagen, Denmark 14 Oct 1980. RHB, RMF. Staff 2000 – awaiting f-c debut.

McCAGUE, Martin John (Hedland Sr HS; Carine Tafe C), b Larne, N Ireland 24 May 1969. 6'5". RHB, RFM. W Australia 1990-91 to 1991-92. Kent debut 1991; cap 1992. **Tests:** 3 (1993 to 1994-95); HS 11 v A (Leeds) 1993; BB 4-121 v A (Nottingham) 1993. Tours: A 1994-95 (part); SA 1993-94 (Eng A). HS 63* v Surrey (Oval) 1996. 50 wkts (4); most – 76 (1996). BB 9-86 (15-147 match) v Derbys (Derby) 1994. Hat-trick 1996. Award: NWT 1. LO HS 31* v Staffs (Stone) 1995 (NWT). LO BB 5-26 v Middx (Canterbury) 1993 (NWT).

MARSH, Steven Andrew (Walderslade SS; Mid-Kent CFE), b Westminster, London 27 Jan 1961. 5'10". RHB, WK. Debut 1982; cap 1986; benefit 1995; captain 1996-98. Tour: Z 1992-93 (K – captain). HS 142 v Sussex (Horsham) 1997. BB 2-20 v Warwks (Birmingham) 1990. Set world f-c record by holding eight catches in an innings AND scoring a hundred (v Middx at Lord's) 1991. LO HS 71 v Lancs (Manchester) 1991 (BHC). LO BB 1-3 (NWT).

MASTERS, David Daniel (Fort Luton HS; Mid Kent CHE), b Chatham 22 Apr 1978. Son of K.D. (Kent 1981-85, Surrey 1986). 6'4". RHB, RMF. Staff 1998 – awaiting f-c debut.

‡NIXON, Paul Andrew (Ullswater HS, Penrith), b Carlisle, Cumberland 21 Oct 1970. 6'0". LHB, WK. Leicestershire 1989-99; cap 1994. Cumberland 1987. MCC YC. Tours: I 1994-95 (Eng A); SA 1996-97 (Le). 1000 runs (1): 1046 (1994). HS 131 Le v Hants (Leicester) 1994. LO HS 96* Le v Kent (Canterbury) 1999 (NL).

PATEL, Minal Mahesh (Dartford GS; Erith TC), b Bombay, India 7 Jul 1970. 5'9". RHB, SLA. Debut 1989; cap 1994. **Tests:** 2 (1996); HS 27 and BB 1-101 v I (Nottingham) 1996. Tour: I 1994-95 (Eng A). HS 67 v Glos (Canterbury) 1999. 50 wkts (3); most – 90 (1994). BB 8-96 v Lancs (Canterbury) 1994. LO HS 18* v Glam (Canterbury) 1996 (BHC). LO BB 3-22 v Essex (Canterbury) 1999 (NL).

PHILLIPS, Ben James (Langley Park S and SFC, Beckenham), b Lewisham 30 Sep 1974. 6'6". RHB, RFM. Debut 1996. HS 100* v Lancs (Manchester) 1997. BB 5-47 v Sussex (Horsham) 1997. Award: NWT 1. LO HS 29 v Glam (Cardiff) 1996 (SL). LO BB 3-13 v Hants (Southampton) 1998 (BHC).

SAGGERS, Martin John (Springwood HS, King's Lynn; Huddersfield U), b King's Lynn, Norfolk 23 May 1972. 6'2". RHB, RMF. Durham 1996-98. Norfolk 1995-96. Kent debut 1999. HS 18 Du v Somerset (Weston-s-M) 1996. K HS 0. BB 6-65 Du v Glam (Chester-le-St) 1996. K BB 4-26 v CU (Cambridge) 1999. Award: BHC 1. LO HS 34* Minor C v Leics (Jesmond) 1996 (BHC). LO BB 4-35 Du v Essex (Chelmsford) 1997 (SL).

SCOTT, Darren Anthony (Geoffrey Chaucer GS; Christ Church C, Canterbury), b Canterbury 26 Aug 1972. 6'2". LHB, OB. Debut 1998. HS 17* v OU (Canterbury) 1998. CC HS 12* v Lancs (Manchester) 1999. BB 4-151 v NZ (Canterbury) 1999. CC BB 1-48. LO HS – (NL).

SMITH, Edward Thomas (Tonbridge S; Peterhouse, Cambridge), b Pembury 19 Jul 1977. 6'2". RHB, RM. Cambridge U 1996-98, scoring 101 v Glam (Cambridge) on debut; blue 1996-97 (injured 1998). Kent debut 1996. British U 1998. 1000 runs (1): 1163 (1997). HS 190 CU v Leics (Cambridge) 1997. K HS 111 v NZ (Canterbury) 1999. CC HS 102 v Hants (Portsmouth) 1997. LO HS 72* v Hants (Portsmouth) 1997 (SL).

THOMPSON, Dr Julian Barton deCourcy (The Judd S; Guy's Hospital Medical S, London U), b Cape Town, SA 28 Oct 1968. 6'4". RHB, RMF. Debut 1994; cap 1999. HS 65* v OU (Canterbury) 1998. CC HS 59* v Warwks (Tunbridge Wells) 1997. 50 wkts (1): 64 (1999). BB 7-89 v Durham (Stockton) 1999. Awards: BHC 2. LO HS 30 v Glam (Cardiff) 1996 (SL). LO BB 3-16 v Yorks (Scarborough) 1999 (NL).

WALKER, Matthew Jonathan (King's S, Rochester), b Gravesend 2 Jan 1974. Grandson of Jack (Kent 1949). 5'8". LHB, RM. Debut 1992-93 (Z tour). UK debut 1994. Tour: Z 1992-93 (K). HS 275* v Somerset (Canterbury) 1996. Awards: BHC 2. LO HS 117 v Warwks (Canterbury) 1997 (BHC). LO BB 1-33 (NWT).

WATSON, James David (Norton Knathbull S, Ashford; Sutton Valence S), b Willesborough, Ashford 21 Apr 1981. 6'7". RHB, RM. Staff 1999 – awaiting f-c debut.

WELLS, Alan Peter (Tideway CS, Newhaven), b Newhaven, Sussex 2 Oct 1961. Younger brother of C.M. (Sussex, Derbyshire, Border and WP 1979-96). 6'0". RHB, RM. Sussex 1981-96; cap 1986; captain 1992-96; benefit 1996. Border 1981-82. Kent debut/cap 1997. **Tests:** 1 (1995); HS 3*. **LOI:** 1 (1995); HS 15 v WI (Lord's) 1995. Tours (Eng A): SA 1989-90 (Eng XI), 1993-94; I 1994-95 (captain). 1000 runs (11); most – 1784 (1991). 253* Sx v Yorks (Middlesbrough) 1991. K HS 111 v Durham (Stockton) 1999. BB 3-67 Sx v Worcs (Worcester) 1987. Awards: NWT 3; BHC 1. LO HS 127 Sx v Hants (Portsmouth) 1993 (SL). LO BB (Sx) 1-0 (SL).

RELEASED/RETIRED

(Having made a first-class County appearance in 1999)

HOUSE, W.J. – *see SUSSEX.*

SYMONDS, Andrew (All Saints Anglican School, Mudgeeraba, Queensland), b Birmingham 9 Jun 1975. 6'1½". RHB, RMF/OB. Emigrated to Australia when 18 months old. Queensland 1994-95 to date. Australian CA. Gloucestershire 1995-96; cap 1996. Kent 1999; cap 1999. YC 1995. Surrendered England qualification by appearing for Australia A v WI 1996-97. **LOI** (A): 18 (1998-99 to 1999-00); HS 68* v I (Galle) 1999-00; BB 4-11 v I (Sydney) 1999-00. Tours (Aus A): Sc 1998; NZ 1994-95 (Aus Academy). 1000 runs (2); most – 1438 (1995). HS 254* Gs v Glam (Abergavenny) 1995 (including record 16 sixes); hit record 20 sixes in match. K HS 177 v Leics (Canterbury) 1999. BB 4-39 Q v WA (Perth) 1998-99. CC BB 2-21 Gs v Northants (Bristol) 1996. K BB 2-48 v Lancs (Manchester) 1999. Awards: NWT 1; BHC 2. LO HS 95 Gs v Comb Us (Bristol) 1995 (BHC) and 95 v Leics (Canterbury) 1999 (NL). LO BB 3-32 Q v Tasmania (Hobart) 1997-98 (MM).

WARD, T.R. – *see LEICESTERSHIRE.*

WILLIS, Simon Charles (Wilmington GS), b Greenwich, London 19 Mar 1974. 5'8". RHB, WK. Kent 1993-99. Surrey 2nd XI debut when aged 15yr 339d. HS 82 v CU (Folkestone) 1995. CC HS 78 v Northants (Northampton) 1996. LO HS 31* v Worcs (Canterbury) 1996.

KENT 1999

RESULTS SUMMARY

	Place	Won	Lost	Tied	Drew	No Result
PPP County Championship	**5th**	6	4		7	
All First-Class Matches		7	4		8	
NatWest Trophy	Quarter-Finalist					
CGU National League (Division 1)	**3rd**	8	6			2

COUNTY CHAMPIONSHIP AVERAGES

BATTING AND FIELDING

Cap		*M*	*I*	*NO*	*HS*	*Runs*	*Avge*	*100*	*50*	*Ct/St*
1999	A.Symonds	13	23	2	177	829	39.47	2	4	14
1990	M.V.Fleming	16	23	3	138	772	38.60	1	4	4
1997	A.P.Wells	10	15	–	111	490	32.66	2	1	1
–	E.T.Smith	12	21	2	83	615	32.36	–	4	2
1992	M.A.Ealham	12	20	3	88*	542	31.88	–	5	3
1992	M.J.McCague	8	11	2	53	264	29.33	–	1	4
–	R.W.T.Key	17	30	2	125	714	25.50	1	4	17
1998	D.P.Fulton	15	26	2	126*	565	23.54	1	2	16
1986	S.A.Marsh	15	22	2	73*	466	23.30	–	2	28/7
–	M.J.Walker	13	22	1	93	450	21.42	–	3	11
1993	D.W.Headley	12	16	3	72	263	20.23	–	1	9
1999	J.B.D.Thompson	14	19	9	44	176	17.60	–	–	1
1994	M.M.Patel	17	24	3	67	290	13.80	–	1	5
1989	T.R.Ward	7	12	–	42	139	11.58	–	–	8

Also batted: M.J.Banes (1 match) 5, 2 (1 ct); J.B.Hockley (1) 34; M.J.Saggers (1) 0; D.A.Scott (1) 12*, 4*; S.C.Willis (2) 12*, 9, 67 (4 ct).

BOWLING

	O	*M*	*R*	*W*	*Avge*	*Best*	*5wI*	*10wM*
J.B.D.Thompson	434.1	106	1265	64	19.76	7- 89	3	–
M.A.Ealham	308.2	67	892	39	22.87	6- 35	2	–
M.M.Patel	637.4	193	1506	57	26.42	8-115	3	1
M.V.Fleming	242.5	60	654	21	31.14	3- 59	–	–
M.J.McCague	173	30	589	16	36.81	4- 65	–	–
D.W.Headley	399.5	82	1253	33	37.96	4- 74	–	–
A.Symonds	182.1	31	695	12	57.91	2- 48	–	–

Also bowled: J.B.Hockley 12-1-57-1; M.J.Saggers 33.4-6-131-5; D.A.Scott 27.2-2-117-1; E.T.Smith 1-0-3-0; M.J.Walker 19.1-3-64-0.

The First-Class Averages (pp 113-128) give the records of Kent players in all first-class county matches (Kent's other opponents being the New Zealanders and Cambridge University), with the exception of D.W.Headley whose full county figures are as above.

KENT RECORDS

FIRST-CLASS CRICKET

Highest Total	For	803-4d		v	Essex	Brentwood	1934
	V	676		by	Australians	Canterbury	1921
Lowest Total	For	18		v	Sussex	Gravesend	1867
	V	16		by	Warwicks	Tonbridge	1913
Highest Innings	For	332	W.H.Ashdown	v	Essex	Brentwood	1934
	V	344	W.G.Grace	for	MCC	Canterbury	1876

Highest Partnership for each Wicket

1st	300	N.R.Taylor/M.R.Benson	v	Derbyshire	Canterbury	1991
2nd	366	S.G.Hinks/N.R.Taylor	v	Middlesex	Canterbury	1990
3rd	321*	A.Hearne/J.R.Mason	v	Notts	Nottingham	1899
4th	368	P.A.de Silva/G.R.Cowdrey	v	Derbyshire	Maidstone	1995
5th	277	F.E.Woolley/L.E.G.Ames	v	New Zealand	Canterbury	1931
6th	315	P.A.de Silva/M.A.Ealham	v	Notts	Nottingham	1995
7th	248	A.P.Day/E.Humphreys	v	Somerset	Taunton	1908
8th	157	A.L.Hilder/A.C.Wright	v	Essex	Gravesend	1924
9th	171	M.A.Ealham/P.A.Strang	v	Notts	Nottingham	1997
10th	235	F.E.Woolley/A.Fielder	v	Worcs	Stourbridge	1909

Best Bowling	For	10- 30	C.Blythe	v	Northants	Northampton	1907
(Innings)	V	10- 48	C.H.G.Bland	for	Sussex	Tonbridge	1899
Best Bowling	For	17- 48	C.Blythe	v	Northants	Northampton	1907
(Match)	V	17-106	T.W.J.Goddard	for	Glos	Bristol	1939

Most Runs – Season	2894	F.E.Woolley	(av 59.06)	1928
Most Runs – Career	47868	F.E.Woolley	(av 41.77)	1906-38
Most 100s – Season	10	F.E.Woolley		1928
	10	F.E.Woolley		1934
Most 100s – Career	122	F.E.Woolley		1906-38
Most Wkts – Season	262	A.P.Freeman	(av 14.74)	1933
Most Wkts – Career	3340	A.P.Freeman	(av 17.64)	1914-36

LIMITED-OVERS CRICKET

Highest Total	**NWT**	384-6		v	Berkshire	Finchampstead	1994
	BHC	338-6		v	Somerset	Maidstone	1996
	NL	327-6		v	Leics	Canterbury	1993
Lowest Total	**NWT**	60		v	Somerset	Taunton	1979
	BHC	73		v	Middlesex	Canterbury	1979
	NL	83		v	Middlesex	Lord's	1984
Highest Innings	**NWT**	136*	C.L.Hooper	v	Berkshire	Finchampstead	1994
	BHC	143	C.J.Tavaré	v	Somerset	Taunton	1985
	NL	145	C.L.Hooper	v	Leics	Leicester	1996
Best Bowling	**NWT**	8-31	D.L.Underwood	v	Scotland	Edinburgh	1987
	BHC	6-41	T.N.Wren	v	Somerset	Canterbury	1995
	NL	6- 9	R.A.Woolmer	v	Derbyshire	Chesterfield	1979

LANCASHIRE

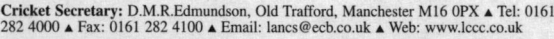

Formation of Present Club: 12 January 1864
Colours: Red, Green and Blue
Badge: Red Rose
County Champions (since 1890): (7) 1897, 1904, 1926, 1927, 1928, 1930, 1934
Joint Champions: (1) 1950
NatWest Trophy/Gillette Cup Winners: (7) 1970, 1971, 1972, 1975, 1990, 1996, 1998
Benson and Hedges Cup Winners: (4) 1984, 1990, 1995, 1996
CGU National League (Div 1) Winners: (1) 1999
Sunday League Winners: (4) 1969, 1970, 1989, 1998
Match Awards: NWT 69; BHC 77

Cricket Secretary: D.M.R.Edmundson, Old Trafford, Manchester M16 0PX ▲ Tel: 0161 282 4000 ▲ Fax: 0161 282 4100 ▲ Email: lancs@ecb.co.uk ▲ Web: www.lccc.co.uk

Captain: J.P.Crawley. **Vice-Captain:** No appointment. **Overseas Player:** S.C.Ganguly. **2000 Beneficiary:** I.D.Austin. **Scorer:** A.West. ‡ New registration

ATHERTON, Michael Andrew (Manchester GS; Downing C, Cambridge), b Failsworth, Manchester 23 Mar 1968. 5'11". RHB, LB. Cambridge U 1987-89; blue 1987-88-89; captain 1988-89. Lancashire debut 1987; cap 1989; benefit 1997. YC 1990. *Wisden* 1990. OBE 1997. **ECB contract 2000. Tests**: 95 (1989 to 1999-00, 52 as captain – England record); HS 185* v SA (Johannesburg) 1995-96; BB 1-20. **LOI**: 54 (1990 to 1998, 43 as captain); HS 127 v WI (Lord's) 1995. Tours (C=captain): A 1990-91, 1994-95C, 1998-99; SA 1995-96C, 1999-00; WI 1993-94C, 1995-96 (La), 1997-98C; NZ 1996-97C; I/SL 1992-93; Z 1989-90 (Eng A), 1996-97C. 1000 runs (6); most – 1924 (1990). Scored 1193 in season of f-c debut. HS 268* v Glam (Blackpool) 1999. BB 6-78 v Notts (Nottingham) 1990. Awards: NWT 4; BHC 3. LO HS 127 (*see LOI*). LO BB 4-42 Comb U v Somerset (Taunton) 1989 (BHC).

AUSTIN, Ian David (Haslingden HS), b Haslingden 30 May 1966. 5'10". LHB, RM. Debut 1987; cap 1990; benefit 2000. *Wisden* 1998. **LOI:** 9 (1998 to 1999); HS 11* v SL (Lord's) 1998; BB 2-25 v SL (Lord's) 1999. Tours (La): WI 1995-96; Z 1988-89. HS 115* v Derbys (Blackpool) 1992. BB 6-43 v SL A (Manchester) 1999. CC BB 5-23 (10-60 match) v Middx (Manchester) 1994. Awards: NWT 2; BHC 2. LO HS 97 v Sussex (Hove) 1997 (NWT). LO BB 5-56 v Derbys (Derby) 1991 (SL).

CHAPPLE, Glen (West Craven HS; Nelson & Colne C), b Skipton, Yorks 23 Jan 1974. 6'1". RHB, RFM. Debut 1992; cap 1994. Tours (Eng A): A 1996-97; WI 1995-96 (La); I 1994-95. HS 109* v Glam (Manchester) 1993 (100 off 27 balls in contrived circumstances). HS (authentic) 83 v Derbys (Derby) 1999. 50 wkts (2); most – 55 (1994). BB 6-48 v Durham (Stockton) 1994. Awards: NWT 1; BHC 1. LO HS 43 v Worcs (Manchester) 1996 (SL). LO BB 6-18 v Essex (Lord's) 1996 (NWT).

CHILTON, Mark James (Manchester GS; Durham U), b Sheffield, Yorks 2 Oct 1976. 6'3". RHB, RM. Debut 1997. British U 1998. HS 106* v CU (Cambridge) 1999 – earliest f-c hundred in Britain (9 Apr). CC HS 102 v Northants (Manchester) 1999. BB 1-1. CC BB – . Awards: BHC 2. LO HS 56 Brit U v Kent (Oxford) 1998 (BHC). LO BB 5-26 Brit U v Sussex (Cambridge) 1997 (BHC).

CRAWLEY, John Paul (Manchester GS; Trinity C, Cambridge), b Maldon, Essex 21 Sep 1971. Brother of M.A. (Oxford U, Lancs and Notts 1987-94) and P.M. (Cambridge U 1992). 6'1". RHB, RM, occ WK. Debut 1990; cap 1994; captain 1999. Cambridge U 1991-93; blue 1991-92-93; captain 1992-93. YC 1994. **Tests:** 29 (1994 to 1998-99); HS 156* v SL (Oval) 1998. **LOI:** 13 (1994-95 to 1998-99); HS 73 v Z (Harare) 1996-97. Tours: A 1994-95,

1998-99; SA 1993-94 (Eng A), 1995-96; WI 1995-96 (La), 1997-98; NZ 1996-97; Z 1996-97. 1000 runs (7); most – 1851 (1998). HS 286 England A v E Province (Port Elizabeth) 1993-94. La HS 281* v Somerset (Southport) 1994. BB 1-90. Award: BHC 1. LO HS 114 v Notts (Manchester) 1995 (BHC).

FAIRBROTHER, Neil Harvey (Lymm GS), b Warrington 9 Sep 1963. 5'8". LHB, LM. Debut 1982; cap 1985; captain 1992-93; benefit 1995. Transvaal 1994-95. **Tests:** 10 (1987 to 1992-93); HS 83 v I (Madras) 1992-93. **LOI**: 75 (1986-87 to 1999); HS 113 v WI (Lord's) 1991. Tours: NZ 1987-88, 1991-92; I/SL 1992-93; P 1987-88, 1990-91 (Eng A); SL 1990-91 (Eng A). 1000 runs (10); most – 1740 (1990). HS 366 v Surrey (Oval) 1990 (ground record), including 311 in a day and 100 or more in each session. BB 2-91 v Notts (Manchester) 1987. Awards: NWT 6; BHC 9. LO HS 123* Transvaal v EP (Johannesburg) 1994-95 (BHS). LO BB 1-17 (BHC).

FLINTOFF, Andrew (Ribbleton Hall HS), b Preston 6 Dec 1977. 6'4". RHB, RM. Debut 1995; cap 1998. **ECB contract 2000. Tests**: 6 (1998 to 1999-00); HS 42 and BB 2-31 v SA (Pt Elizabeth) 1999-00. **LOI**: 9 (1998-99 to 1999); HS 50 v I (Sharjah) 1998-99 – on debut; BB 2-3 v P (Sharjah) 1998-99. Tours (Eng A): SA 1998-99, 1999-00 (Eng); SL 1997-98; Z 1998-99; K 1997-98. HS 160 v Yorks (Manchester) 1999. BB 5-24 v Hants (Southampton) 1999. Award: BHC 1. LO HS 143 (off 66 balls) v Essex (Chelmsford) 1999 (NL). LO BB 4-24 v Hants (Manchester) 1999 (NL).

‡GANGULY, Sourav Chandidas (St Xavier's Collegiate S), b Calcutta, India 8 Jul 1972. Brother of Snehasish C. Ganguly (Bengal 1986-87 to 1996-97). 5'11". RHB, RM. Bengal 1989-90 to date. **Tests** (I): 33 (1996 to 1999-00); HS 173 v SL (Bombay) 1997-98; BB 3-28 v A (Calcutta) 1997-98. **LOI** (I): 133 (1991-92 to 1999-00, 4 as captain); HS 183 v SL (Taunton) 1999. BB 5-16 v P (Toronto) 1997-98. Tours (I): E 1996; A 1991-92, 1999-00; SA 1996-97; WI 1996-97; NZ 1998-99; SL 1997-98, 1998-99; Z 1998-99. HS 200* Bengal v Tripura (Calcutta) 1993-94 and 200* Bengal v Bihar (Calcutta) 1994-95. BB 6-87 Bengal v Delhi (Delhi) 1997-98. LO HS 183 (*see LOI*). LO BB 5-16 (*see LOI*).

GREEN, Richard James (Bridgewater HS, Cheshire; Mid-Cheshire C), b Warrington 13 Mar 1976. 6'1". RHB, RM. Debut 1995. HS 51 v Essex (Manchester) 1997. BB 6-41 v Yorks (Manchester) 1996 (non-CC match). CC BB 4-21 v Yorks (Manchester) 1999. LO HS 14* v Worcs (Manchester) 1999 (NL). LO BB 3-18 v Yorks (Manchester) 1997 (SL).

HARVEY, Mark Edward (Habergham HS; Loughborough U), b Burnley 26 Jun 1974. 5'9". RHB, RM/LB. Debut 1994. Combined U 1995. HS 39 v CU (Cambridge) 1999. CC HS 25 v Glos (Bristol) 1997. Award: NWT 1. LO HS 86 v Berks (Manchester) 1997 (NWT).

HAYNES, Jamie Jonathan (St Edmunds C, Canberra; Canberra U), b Bristol 5 Jul 1974. 5'11". RHB, WK. Debut 1996. Represented Australian Capital Territory at cricket and Australian Rules football. HS 80 v SL A (Manchester) 1999. CC HS 18 v Kent (Manchester) 1997. LO HS – (SL).

HEGG, Warren Kevin (Unsworth HS, Bury; Stand C, Whitefield), b Whitefield 23 Feb 1968. 5'8". RHB, WK. Debut 1986; cap 1989; benefit 1999. **Tests**: 2 (1998-99); HS 15 v A (Sydney) 1998-99. Tours: A 1996-97 (Eng A), 1998-99; WI 1986-87 (La), 1995-96 (La); SL 1990-91 (Eng A); Z 1988-89 (La). HS 134 v Leics (Manchester) 1996. Held 11 catches (equalling world f-c match record) v Derbys (Chesterfield) 1989. Award: BHC 1. LO HS 81 v Yorks (Manchester) 1996 (BHC).

KEEDY, Gary (Garforth CS), b Wakefield, Yorks 27 Nov 1974. 6'0". LHB, SLA. Yorkshire 1994 (one match). Lancashire debut 1995. Tour: WI 1995-96 (La). HS 26 v Essex (Chelmsford) 1996. BB 6-79 (10-173 match) v Surrey (Oval) 1997. LO HS – (SL). LO BB 1-40 (SL).

LLOYD, Graham David (Hollins County HS), b Accrington 1 Jul 1969. Son of D. (Lancs and England 1965-83). 5'9". RHB, RM. Debut 1988; cap 1992. **LOI:** 6 (1996 to 1998-99); HS 22 v A (Oval) 1997. Tours: A 1992-93 (Eng A); WI 1995-96 (La). 1000 runs (5); most – 1389 (1992). HS 241 v Essex (Chelmsford) 1996. BB 1-4. Awards: BHC 2. LO HS 134 v Durham (Manchester) 1997 (SL). LO BB 1-23 (NWT).

McKEOWN, Patrick Christopher (Merchant Taylors S; Rossall S), b Liverpool 1 Jun 1976. 6'3". RHB, OB. Debut 1996. HS 75 v CU (Cambridge) 1999. CC HS 64 v Warwks (Birmingham) 1996. LO HS 69 v Northants (Northampton) 1996 (SL).

MARTIN, Peter James (Danum S, Doncaster), b Accrington 15 Nov 1968. 6'4". RHB, RFM. Debut 1989; cap 1994. **Tests:** 8 (1995 to 1997); HS 29 v WI (Lord's) 1995; BB 4-60 v SA (Durban) 1995-96. **LOI:** 20 (1995 to 1998-99); HS 6; BB 4-44 v WI (Oval) 1995 – on debut. Tour: SA 1995-96. HS 133 v Durham (Gateshead) 1992. 50 wkts (3); most – 58 (1997). BB 8-32 (13-79 match) v Middx (Uxbridge) 1997. Awards: NWT 2. LO HS 35* v Worcs (Manchester) 1996 (SL). LO BB 5-21 v Northants (Manchester) 1997 (SL).

RIDGWAY, Paul Mathew (Settle HS), b Airedale, Yorks 13 Feb 1977. 6'4". RHB, RFM. Debut 1997. HS 35 and BB 3-51 v Durham (Chester-le-St) 1998.

SCHOFIELD, Christopher Paul (Wardle HS), b Birch Hill, Rochdale 6 Oct 1978. 6'2". LHB, LB. Debut 1998. **ECB contract 2000.** Tours (Eng A): NZ 1999-00; B 1999-00. HS 74 Eng A v CD (Palmerston N) 1999-00. La HS 39* v Leics (Leicester) 1999. BB 6-120 Eng A v Bangladesh (Chittagong) 1999-00. La BB 5-66 v Durham (Manchester) 1999. LO HS 28 and LO BB 2-32 v Kent (Manchester) 1999 (NL).

‡SCUDERI, Joseph Charles, b Ingham, Queensland, Australia 24 Dec 1968. RHB, RFM. S Australia 1988-89 to 1997-98. Special ECB registration (holds Italian passport). Italy 1998 to date. HS 125* S Aus v WA (Adelaide) 1991-92. BB 7-79 S Aus v NSW (Adelaide) 1991-92. LO HS 58 S Aus v Vic (Adelaide) 1989-90 (FAI). LO BB 3-36 S Aus v Vic (Melbourne) 1994-95 (MM).

SMETHURST, Michael Paul (Hulme GS, Oldham; Salford U), b Oldham 11 Oct 1976. 6'5". RHB, RM. Debut 1999. BB 4-44 v CU (Cambridge) – on debut. HS 3 and CC BB 4-47 v Leics (Leicester) 1999. Award: NWT 1. LO HS 4* and LO BB 4-46 v Hants (Southampton) 1999 (NWT).

WATKINSON, Michael (Rivington and Blackrod HS, Horwich), b Westhoughton 1 Aug 1961. 6'1". RHB, RMF/OB. Debut 1982; cap 1987; captain 1994-97; benefit 1996. Cheshire 1982. **Tests:** 4 (1995 to 1995-96); HS 82* v WI (Nottingham) 1995; BB 3-64 v WI (Manchester) 1995 – on debut. **LOI:** 1 (1995-96); HS – . Tours: SA 1995-96; WI 1995-96 (La – captain). 1000 runs (1): 1016 (1993). HS 161 v Essex (Manchester) 1995. 50 wkts (7); most – 66 (1992). BB 8-30 (11-87 match) v Hants (Manchester) 1994 – completing match 'double' with 128 runs. Hat-trick 1992. Awards: NWT 3; BHC 3. LO HS 130 v Herts (Radlett) 1999 (NWT). LO BB 5-44 v Derbys (Chesterfield) 1996 (BHC).

WOOD, Nathan Theodore (Wm Hulme's GS), b Thornhill Edge, Yorks 4 Oct 1974. Son of B. (Yorks, Lancs, Derbys and England 1964-83). 5'8". LHB, OB. Debut 1996. HS 155 v Surrey (Oval) 1997. LO HS 23 v Sussex (Hove) 1998 (SL).

YATES, Gary (Manchester GS), b Ashton-under-Lyne 20 Sep 1967. 6'0". RHB, OB. Debut 1990; cap 1994. HS 134* v Northants (Manchester) 1993. BB 6-64 v Kent (Manchester) 1999. LO HS 38 v Essex (Chelmsford) 1996 (SL). LO BB 4-34 v Warwks (Birmingham) 1994 (SL).

RELEASED/RETIRED

(Having made a first-class County appearance in 1999)

MURALITHARAN, Muthiah (St Anthony's C, Kandy), b Kandy, Sri Lanka 17 Apr 1972. 5'5". RHB, OB. Central Province 1989-90 to date. Tamil Union 1991-92 to date. Lancashire 1999 (taking 7-44 and 7-73 v Warwks at Southport on debut); cap 1999. *Wisden* 1998. **Tests** (SL): 48 (1992-93 to 1999-00); HS 39 v I (Colombo) 1997-98; BB 9-65 (16-220 match) v E (Oval) 1998. **LOI** (SL): 132 (1993-94 to 1999-00); HS 18 v E (Lord's) 1998; BB 5-23 v P (Benoni) 1997-98. Tours (SL): E 1991, 1998; A 1995-96; SA 1992-93 (SL U-24), 1994-95, 1997-98; WI 1996-97; NZ 1994-95, 1996-97; I 1993-94, 1997-98; P 1995-96; Z 1994-95. HS 39 (*see Tests*). La HS 10 v Derbys (Derby) 1999. 50 wkts (1+2); most – 66 (1996-97; 1999 – in 7 CC matches). BB 9-65 (*see Tests*). La BB 7-39 (11-61 match) v Derbys (Derby) 1999. LO HS 18 (*see LOI*). LO BB 5-23 (*see LOI*).

LANCASHIRE 1999

RESULTS SUMMARY

	Place	Won	Lost	Tied	Drew	No Result
PPP County Championship	**2nd**	8	4		4	1
All First-Class Matches		9	4		4	1
NatWest Trophy	Quarter-Finalist					
Benson & Hedges Super Cup	Quarter-Finalist					
CGU National League (Division 1)	**1st**	11	2			3

COUNTY CHAMPIONSHIP AVERAGES

BATTING AND FIELDING

Cap		*M*	*I*	*NO*	*HS*	*Runs*	*Avge*	*100*	*50*	*Ct/St*
1989	M.A.Atherton	6	9	2	268*	439	62.71	1	1	3
1992	G.D.Lloyd	15	23	1	144	960	43.63	3	5	7
1998	A.Flintoff	12	19	2	160	716	42.11	2	2	23
1994	J.P.Crawley	15	25	2	158	870	37.82	2	6	10
1989	W.K.Hegg	16	24	3	94	670	31.90	–	3	45/4
1990	I.D.Austin	4	6	2	45*	115	28.75	–	–	2
–	M.J.Chilton	16	26	2	102	680	28.33	1	4	19
1987	M.Watkinson	7	12	–	116	335	27.91	1	–	3
1985	N.H.Fairbrother	11	17	–	83	436	25.64	–	3	17
1994	G.Chapple	12	18	2	83	402	25.12	–	2	2
–	N.T.Wood	5	8	–	82	179	22.37	–	1	1
–	C.P.Schofield	8	11	3	39*	166	20.75	–	–	6
–	R.J.Green	9	10	5	27	96	19.20	–	–	1
1994	P.J.Martin	14	19	5	30*	220	15.71	–	–	2
–	P.C.McKeown	4	6	–	27	67	11.16	–	–	2
1994	G.Yates	4	4	–	21	25	6.25	–	–	4
1999	M.Muralitharan	7	9	1	10	30	3.75	–	–	2
–	G.Keedy	6	7	5	3*	5	2.50	–	–	1

Also batted: P.M.Ridgway (2 matches) 8*, 0, 1*; M.P.Smethurst (3) 2, 3 (1 ct).

BOWLING

	O	*M*	*R*	*W*	*Avge*	*Best*	*5wI*	*10wM*
M.Muralitharan	386.2	122	777	66	11.77	7-39	8	5
P.J.Martin	446.4	134	1028	50	20.56	5-43	4	–
G.Keedy	231.4	62	630	25	25.20	5-67	1	–
A.Flintoff	136.4	28	402	15	26.80	5-24	1	–
C.P.Schofield	230.3	60	662	21	31.52	5-66	1	–
R.J.Green	182.2	33	633	18	35.16	4-21	–	–
G.Chapple	309	81	918	24	38.25	5-92	1	–

Also bowled: I.D.Austin 105-21-364-3; M.J.Chilton 16-8-29-0; J.P.Crawley 6-0-51-0; N.H.Fairbrother 2-0-2-0; G.D.Lloyd 10-0-100-0; P.M.Ridgway 9-1-55-0; M.P.Smethurst 68.1-14-204-6; M.Watkinson 102-20-318-8; N.T.Wood 6-0-36-0; G.Yates 92.1-25-241-9.

The First-Class Averages (pp 113-128) give the records of Lancashire players in all first-class county matches (Lancashire's other opponents being Sri Lanka A and Cambridge University), with the exception of:

M.A.Atherton 7-11-2-268*-445-49.44-1-1-3ct. Did not bowl.

LANCASHIRE RECORDS

FIRST-CLASS CRICKET

Highest Total	For 863		v	Surrey	The Oval	1990
	V 707-9d		by	Surrey	The Oval	1990
Lowest Total	For 25		v	Derbyshire	Manchester	1871
	V 22		by	Glamorgan	Liverpool	1924
Highest Innings	For 424	A.C.MacLaren	v	Somerset	Taunton	1895
	V 315*	T.W.Hayward	for	Surrey	The Oval	1898

Highest Partnership for each Wicket

1st	368	A.C.MacLaren/R.H.Spooner	v	Glos	Liverpool	1903
2nd	371	F.B.Watson/G.E.Tyldesley	v	Surrey	Manchester	1928
3rd	364	M.A.Atherton/N.H.Fairbrother	v	Surrey	The Oval	1990
4th	358	S.P.Titchard/G.D.Lloyd	v	Essex	Chelmsford	1996
5th	249	B.Wood/A.Kennedy	v	Warwicks	Birmingham	1975
6th	278	J.Iddon/H.R.W.Butterworth	v	Sussex	Manchester	1932
7th	248	G.D.Lloyd/I.D.Austin	v	Yorkshire	Leeds	1997
8th	158	J.Lyon/R.M.Ratcliffe	v	Warwicks	Manchester	1979
9th	142	L.O.S.Poidevin/A.Kermode	v	Sussex	Eastbourne	1907
10th	173	J.Briggs/R.Pilling	v	Surrey	Liverpool	1885

Best Bowling	For	10-46	W.Hickton	v	Hampshire	Manchester	1870
(Innings)	V	10-40	G.O.B.Allen	for	Middlesex	Lord's	1929
Best Bowling	For	17-91	H.Dean	v	Yorkshire	Liverpool	1913
(Match)	V	16-65	G.Giffen	for	Australians	Manchester	1886

Most Runs – Season	2633	J.T.Tyldesley	(av 56.02)	1901
Most Runs – Career	34222	G.E.Tyldesley	(av 45.20)	1909-36
Most 100s – Season	11	C.Hallows		1928
Most 100s – Career	90	G.E.Tyldesley		1909-36
Most Wkts – Season	198	E.A.McDonald	(av 18.55)	1925
Most Wkts – Career	1816	J.B.Statham	(av 15.12)	1950-68

LIMITED-OVERS CRICKET

Highest Total	**NWT**	381-3		v	Herts	Radlett	1999
	BHC	353-7		v	Notts	Manchester	1995
	NL	301-6		v	Essex	Chelmsford	1999
Lowest Total	**NWT**	59		v	Worcs	Worcester	1963
	BHC	82		v	Yorkshire	Bradford	1972
	NL	71		v	Essex	Chelmsford	1987
Highest Innings	**NWT**	131	A.Kennedy	v	Middlesex	Manchester	1978
	BHC	136	G.Fowler	v	Sussex	Manchester	1991
	NL	143	A.Flintoff	v	Essex	Chelmsford	1999
Best Bowling	**NWT**	6-18	G.Chapple	v	Essex	Lord's	1996
	BHC	6-10	C.E.H.Croft	v	Scotland	Manchester	1982
	NL	6-25	G.Chapple	v	Yorkshire	Leeds	1998

LEICESTERSHIRE

Formation of Present Club: 25 March 1879
Colours: Dark Green and Scarlet
Badge: Gold Running Fox on Green Ground
County Champions: (3) 1975, 1996, 1998
NatWest Trophy/Gillette Cup Winners: (0); best – finalist 1992
Benson and Hedges Cup Winners: (3) 1972, 1975, 1985
CGU National League (Div 1) Winners: (0); best – 6th 1999
Sunday League Champions: (2) 1974, 1977
Match Awards: NWT 42; BHC 72

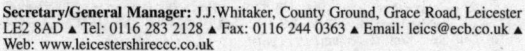

Secretary/General Manager: J.J.Whitaker, County Ground, Grace Road, Leicester LE2 8AD ▲ Tel: 0116 283 2128 ▲ Fax: 0116 244 0363 ▲ Email: leics@ecb.co.uk ▲ Web: www.leicestershireccc.co.uk

Captain: V.J.Wells. **Vice-Captain:** No appointment. **Overseas Player:** A.Kumble. **2000 Beneficiary:** None. **Scorer:** G.A.York. ‡ New registration

‡**ADSHEAD, Stephen** John (Bridley Moor HS, Redditch), b Redditch, Worcs 29 Jan 1980. RHB, WK. Herefordshire 1999. Staff 2000 – awaiting f-c debut. LO HS 22 Herefords v Wilts (Brockhampton) 1999 (NWT).

BOSWELL, Scott Antony John (Pocklington S; Wolverhampton U), b Fulford, Yorks 11 Sep 1974. 6'5". RHB, RFM. Debut (British U) 1996. Northamptonshire 1996-98. Leicestershire debut 1999. HS 35 Nh v Leics (Northampton) 1997. Le HS 15 v NZ (Leicester) 1999 and 15 v Northants (Northampton) 1999. BB 5-94 Nh v Worcs (Northampton) 1997. Le BB 3-71 v NZ (Leicester) 1999. LO HS 14 Brit U v Essex (Chelmsford) 1996 (BHC). LO BB 3-39 Brit U v Kent (Canterbury) 1997 (BHC).

BRIMSON, Matthew Thomas (Chislehurst & Sidcup GS; Durham U), b Plumstead, London 1 Dec 1970. 6'0". RHB, SLA. Kent staff 1991. Leicestershire debut 1993; cap 1998. Tour (Le): SA 1996-97. HS 54* v Warwks (Birmingham) 1998. BB 5-12 v Sussex (Leicester) 1996. LO HS 12* v Glos (Leicester) 1997 (SL). LO BB 3-23 v Glam (Swansea) 1996 (SL) and 3-23 v Northants (Leicester) 1998 (SL).

‡**BURNS, Neil** David (Moulsham HS, Chelmsford), b Chelmsford, Essex 19 Sep 1965. 5'10". LHB, WK, occ SLA. W Province B 1985-86. Essex 1986. Somerset 1987-93; cap 1987. Buckinghamshire 1995-99; Bucks Director of Excellence. HS 166 Sm v Glos (Taunton) 1990. LO HS 58 Sm v Sussex (Hove) 1990 (SL).

CROWE, Carl Daniel (Lutterworth GS), b Leicester 25 Nov 1975. 6'0". RHB, OB. Debut 1995. HS 44* v Northants (Northampton) 1999. BB 3-49 v Durham (Darlington) 1998. LO HS 4* (SL).

DAKIN, Jonathan Michael (King Edward VII S, Johannesburg) b Hitchin, Herts 28 Feb 1973. 6'4". LHB, RM. Debut 1993. Tour (Le): SA 1996-97. HS 190 v Northants (Northampton) 1997. BB 4-27 v Worcester (Worcester) 1999. Award: BHC 1. LO HS 108* v Durham (Leicester) 1996 (BHC). LO BB 5-30 v Kent (Leicester) 1999 (NL).

‡**DeFREITAS, Phillip** Anthony Jason (Willesden HS, London), b Scotts Head, Dominica 18 Feb 1966. 6'0". RHB, RFM. UK resident since 1976. Leicestershire 1985-88; cap 1986. Lancashire 1989-93; cap 1989. Boland 1993-94 and 1995-96. Derbyshire 1994-99; cap 1994; captain 1997 (part). *Wisden* 1991. MCC YC. **Tests:** 44 (1986-87 to 1995-96); HS 88 v A (Adelaide) 1994-95; BB 7-70 v SL (Lord's) 1991. **LOI:** 103 (1986-87 to 1997); HS 67 v SL (Faisalabad) 1995-96; BB 4-35 v A (Adelaide) 1986-87. Tours: A 1986-87, 1990-91,

‡**DeFREITAS, P.A.J.** (*continued*)
1994-95; WI 1989-90; NZ 1987-88, 1991-92; P 1987-88; I 1992-93; Z 1988-89 (La). HS 113 v Notts (Worksop) 1988. 50 wkts (12); most – 94 (1986). Took his 1000th f-c wicket 1999. BB 7-21 La v Middx (Lord's) 1989. Le BB 7-44 (13-86 match) v Essex (Southend) 1986. Hat-trick 1994. Awards: NWT 5; BHC 4. LO HS 75* La v Hants (Manchester) 1990 (BHC). LO BB 5-13 La v Cumb (Kendal) 1989 (NWT).

HABIB, Aftab (Millfield S; Taunton S), b Reading, Berkshire 7 Feb 1972. 5'11". Cousin of Zahid Sadiq (Surrey and Derbys 1988-90). RHB, RMF. Middlesex 1992 (one match). Leicestershire debut 1995; cap 1998. **Tests:** 2 (1999); HS 19 v NZ (Lord's) 1999. Tours (Eng A): NZ 1999-00; B 1999-00. 1000 runs (1): 1055 (1999). HS 215 v Worcs (Leicester) 1996. Award: BHC 1. LO HS 111 v Durham (Chester-le-St) 1997 (BHC). LO BB 2-5 v Ire (Dublin) 1999.

KHAN, Amer Ali (Muslim Modle HS, Lahore; MAO C, Lahore), b Lahore, Pakistan 5 Nov 1969. 5'9½". RHB, LB. Rawalpindi 1987-88 (one match as AAMER ALI). Middlesex 1995. Sussex 1997-98. Leicestershire debut 1999. HS 52 Sx v Hants (Southampton) 1997. Le HS 5. BB 5-137 Sx v Middx (Lord's) 1997. Le BB 1-11. LO HS 22* Sx v Middx (Lord's) 1997 (SL). LO BB 5-40 Sx v Kent (Horsham) 1997 (SL).

‡**KUMBLE, Anil** (National HS; R.V. Engineering C, Bangalore), b Bangalore, India 17 Oct 1970. 6'1½". RHB, LB. Karnataka 1989-90 to date. Northamptonshire 1995 (cap 1995). *Wisden* 1995. **Tests** (I): 59 (1990 to 1999-00); HS 88 v SA (Calcutta) 1996-97; BB 10-74 (14-148 match) v P (Delhi) 1998-99 (second-best innings analysis in Test cricket). **LOI** (I): 191 (1989-90 to 1999-00); HS 26 v A (Perth) 1999-00; BB 6-12 v WI (Calcutta) 1993-94. Tours (I): E 1990, 1996; A 1999-00; SA 1992-93, 1996-97; WI 1996-97; NZ 1993-94, 1998-99; SL 1993-94, 1997-98, 1998-99; Z 1992-93, 1998-99. HS 154* Karnataka v Kerala (Bijapur) 1991-92. CC HS 40* Nh v Glos (Northampton) 1995. 50 wkts (1+1) inc 100 (1): 105 (1995). BB 10-74 (*see Tests*). UK BB 7-82 Nh v Warwks (Birmingham) 1995. LO HS 30* Karnataka v Wills XI (Bangalore) 1994-95 (WT). LO BB 6-12 (*see LOI*).

LEWIS, Clairmonte **Christopher** (Willesden HS, London), b Georgetown, Guyana 14 Feb 1968. 6'2½". RHB, RFM. Leicestershire 1987-91, 1998; cap 1990. Nottinghamshire 1992-94; cap 1994. Surrey 1996-97; cap 1996. **Tests:** 32 (1990 to 1996); HS 117 v I (Madras) 1992-93; BB 6-111 v WI (Birmingham) 1991. **LOI:** 53 (1989-90 to 1998); HS 33 v SA (Melbourne) 1991-92; BB 4-30 v SL (Ballarat) 1991-92. Tours: A 1990-91 (*part*), 1994-95 (*part*); WI 1989-90 (*part*), 1993-94; NZ 1991-92; I/SL 1992-93. HS 247 Nt v Durham (Chester-le-St) 1993. Le HS 189* v Essex (Chelmsford) 1990. 50 wkts (2); most – 56 (1990). BB 6-22 v OU (Oxford) 1988. CC BB 6-55 v Glam (Cardiff) 1990. Award: NWT 1. LO HS 116* v Kent (Canterbury) 1999 (NL). LO BB 5-19 v Staffs (Leicester) 1998 (NWT).

MADDY, Darren Lee (Wreake Valley C), b Leicester 23 May 1974. 5'9". RHB, RM/OB. Debut 1994; cap 1996. **Tests:** 3 (1999 to 1999-00); HS 24 v SA (Durban) 1999-00. **LOI:** 8 (1998 to 1999-00); HS 53 v Z (Harare) 1999-00. Tours (Eng A): SA 1996-97 (Le), 1998-99, 1999-00 (Eng); SL 1997-98; Z 1998-99; K 1997-98. 1000 runs (2); most – 1060 (1999). HS 202 Eng A v Kenya (Nairobi) 1997-98. Le HS 162 v Durham (Darlington) 1998. BB 3-5 v Glos (Leicester) 1999. Awards: NWT 1; BHC 7 (inc 5 in 1998). LO HS 151 v Minor C (Leicester) 1998 (BHC). LO BB 3-11 v Durham (Leicester) 1997 (SL).

ORMOND, James (St Thomas More S, Nuneaton), b Walsgrave, Coventry, Warwks 20 Aug 1977. 6'3". RHB, RFM. Debut 1995; cap 1999. Tours (Eng A): SL 1997-98; K 1997-98. HS 50* v Warwks (Leicester) 1999. 50 wkts (1): 52 (1999). BB 6-33 (9-62 match) v Somerset (Leicester) 1998. LO HS 18 v Notts (Leicester) 1997 (SL). LO BB 4-12 v Middx (Leicester) 1998 (SL).

SACHDEVA, Atul (Lancaster GS), b Preston, Lancs 22 Aug 1980. RHB, LB. Debut 1999. HS 0* and BB 1-32 v Derbys (Leicester) 1999.

SMITH, Benjamin Francis (Kibworth HS), b Corby, Northants 3 Apr 1972. 5'9". RHB, RM. Debut 1990; cap 1995. Tour (Le): SA 1996-97. 1000 runs (2); most – 1243 (1996). HS 204 v Surrey (Oval) 1998. BB 1-5. Award: NWT 1. LO HS 115 v Somerset (Weston-s-M) 1995 (SL).

‡**STELLING, William** Frederik (Michaelhouse; St Stithians; Cape Town U), b Johannesburg, SA 30 Jun 1969. Special ECB registration (holds Dutch passport). RHB, RFM. W Province 1991-92 to 1993-94. Boland 1994-95 to 1996-97. Holland 1995. Berkshire 1999. Award: NWT 1. HS 53 WP B v Natal B (Pietermaritzburg) 1991-92 – off 88 balls on debut. BB 4-12 Boland v Border (Paarl) 1994-95. LO HS 76* Berks v Devon (Torquay) 1999 (NWT). LO BB 3-18 Berks v Warwks (Reading) 1999 (NWT).

STEVENS, Darren Ian (Hinkley C), b Leicester 30 Apr 1976. 5'11". RHB, RM. Debut 1997. HS 130 v Sussex (Arundel) 1999. BB 1-5. LO HS 82 v Warwks (Birmingham) 1999 (NL).

SUTCLIFFE, Iain John (Leeds GS; Queen's C, Oxford), b Leeds, Yorks 20 Dec 1974. 6'2". LHB, occ OB. Oxford U 1994-96; blue 1995-96; boxing blue 1993-94. Leicestershire debut 1995; cap 1997. Tour (Le): SA 1996-97. HS 167 v Middx (Leicester) 1998. BB 2-21 OU v CU (Lord's) 1996. CC BB 1-17. Awards: NWT 1; BHC 1. LO HS 105* v Notts (Nottingham) 1998 (BHC).

‡**WARD, Trevor** Robert (Hextable CS, nr Swanley), b Farningham, Kent 18 Jan 1968. 5'11". RHB, OB. Kent 1986-99; cap 1989; benefit 1999. Tour: Z 1992-93 (K). 1000 runs (6); most – 1648 (1992). HS 235* K v Middx (Canterbury) 1991. BB 2-10 K v Yorks (Canterbury) 1996. Awards: NWT 1; BHC 2. LO HS 131 K v Notts (Nottingham) 1993 (SL). LO BB 3-20 K v Glam (Canterbury) 1989 (SL).

WELLS, Vincent John (Sir William Nottidge S, Whitstable), b Dartford, Kent 6 Aug 1965. 6'0". RHB, RMF. Kent 1988-91. Leicestershire debut 1992; cap 1994; captain 2000; benefit 2001. **LOI:** 9 (1998-99); HS 39 v A (Sydney) 1998-99; BB 3-30 v A (Sydney) 1998-99. Tour (Le): SA 1996-97. 1000 runs (2); most – 1331 (1996). HS 224 v Middx (Lord's) 1997. BB 5-18 v Notts (Worksop) 1998. Hat-trick 1994. Awards: NWT 3; BHC 1. LO HS 201 v Berks (Leicester) 1996 (NWT). LO BB 6-25 v Minor C (Leicester) 1998 (BHC).

WILLIAMSON, Dominic (St Leonard's CS, Durham; Durham SFC), b Durham City 15 Nov 1975. 5'8". RHB, RM. Debut 1996. MCC YC. HS 41* v Hants (Leicester) 1998. BB 3-19 v Glam (Leicester) 1997 – on CC debut. LO HS 39 v Worcs (Leicester) 1999 (NL). LO BB 5-32 v Sussex (Eastbourne) 1997 (SL).

WRIGHT, Ashley Spencer (King Edward VII S, Melton Mowbray), b Grantham, Lincs 21 Oct 1980. 6'0". RHB, RM. Staff 1998 – awaiting f-c debut. LO HS 63 Leics Board v Herts (Radlett) 1999 (NWT).

RELEASED/RETIRED

(Having made a first-class County appearance in 1999)

KASPROWICZ, Michael Scott (Brisbane State HS), b South Brisbane, Australia 10 Feb 1972. 6'4". RHB, RF. Queensland 1989-90 to date. Essex 1994; cap 1994. Leicestershire 1999; cap 1999. **Tests** (A): 16 (1996-97 to 1999-00); HS 25 v I (Calcutta) 1997-98; BB 7-36 v E (Oval) 1997. **LOI** (A): 16 (1995-96 to 1998-99); HS 28* v E (Lord's) 1997; BB 3-50 v I (Cochin) 1997-98. Tours (A): E 1995 (Young A), 1997; I 1997-98; P 1998-99. HS 73 v Hants (Southampton) 1999. 50 wkts (2+2); most: 64 (1995-96). BB 7-36 (*see Tests*). CC BB 7-83 Ex v Somerset (Weston-s-M) 1994. Le BB 5-42 v Middx (Lord's) 1999. LO HS 40 v Warwks (Leicester) 1999 (BHC). LO BB 5-60 Ex v Glam (Cardiff) 1994 (NWT).

MASON, T.J. – *see ESSEX.*

MILLNS, D.J. – *see NOTTINGHAMSHIRE.*

MULLALLY, A.D. – *see HAMPSHIRE.*

NIXON, P.A. – *see KENT.*

WHITAKER, John **James** (Uppingham S), b Skipton, Yorks 5 May 1962. 5'10". RHB, OB. Leicestershire 1983-99; cap 1986; benefit 1993; captain 1996-99. *Wisden* 1986. YC 1986. **Tests:** 1 (1986-87); HS 11 v A (Adelaide) 1986-87. **LOI**: 2 (1986-87); HS 44* v P (Sharjah) 1986-87. Tours: A 1986-87; SA 1996-97 (Le); Z 1989-90 (Eng A). 1000 runs (10); most – 1767 (1990). HS 218 v Yorks (Bradford) 1996. BB 1-29. Awards: NWT 1; BHC 2. LO HS 155 v Wilts (Swindon) 1984 (NWT). Appointed Leicestershire CCC Secretary/General Manager 2000.

LEICESTERSHIRE 1999

RESULTS SUMMARY

	Place	Won	Lost	Tied	Drew	No Result
PPP County Championship	**3rd**	5	3		9	
All First-Class Matches		5	4		9	
NatWest Trophy	4th Round					
Benson & Hedges Super Cup	Quarter-Finalist					
CGU National League (Division 1)	**6th**	6	8			2

COUNTY CHAMPIONSHIP AVERAGES

BATTING AND FIELDING

Cap		*M*	*I*	*NO*	*HS*	*Runs*	*Avge*	*100*	*50*	*Ct/St*
1998	A.Habib	15	24	3	160*	1020	48.57	3	6	2
1990	C.C.Lewis	10	13	2	139	520	47.27	2	2	7
1996	D.L.Maddy	16	26	2	158*	996	41.50	2	4	17
1995	B.F.Smith	13	19	–	154	678	35.68	2	2	9
–	D.I.Stevens	10	18	–	130	553	30.72	1	3	12
–	J.M.Dakin	10	16	2	124	426	30.42	1	3	2
1994	V.J.Wells	12	18	2	109*	483	30.18	1	3	12
1994	P.A.Nixon	17	27	2	121	710	28.40	1	2	45/4
–	C.D.Crowe	4	7	2	44*	135	27.00	–	–	2
1999	M.S.Kasprowicz	16	23	4	73	507	26.68	–	5	3
–	T.J.Mason	2	4	1	36	79	26.33	–	–	–
1997	I.J.Sutcliffe	15	25	–	110	572	22.88	1	2	8
1991	D.J.Millns	6	9	3	47	136	22.66	–	–	5
1986	J.J.Whitaker	5	7	–	44	130	18.57	–	–	1
1999	J.Ormond	12	15	3	50*	177	14.75	–	1	2
–	D.Williamson	2	4	–	19	59	14.75	–	–	2
1998	M.T.Brimson	13	14	4	36*	120	12.00	–	–	1
1993	A.D.Mullally	6	7	4	13	32	10.66	–	–	–

Also batted (1 match each): S.A.J.Boswell 15, 9*; A.A.Khan 5; A.Sachdeva 0*, 0.

BOWLING

	O	*M*	*R*	*W*	*Avge*	*Best*	*5wI*	*10wM*
D.J.Millns	142.3	35	372	23	16.17	5- 62	1	–
D.L.Maddy	79.4	22	223	12	18.58	3- 5	–	–
J.Ormond	374.3	80	1185	47	25.21	5- 85	2	–
J.M.Dakin	198.1	56	495	18	27.50	4- 27	–	–
M.S.Kasprowicz	485.5	112	1458	53	27.50	5- 42	2	–
A.D.Mullally	199	64	471	17	27.70	5-106	1	–
C.D.Crowe	92	14	348	11	31.63	3- 63	–	–
M.T.Brimson	290.5	89	720	22	32.72	5- 51	1	–
C.C.Lewis	191.2	50	585	16	36.56	3- 18	–	–
V.J.Wells	170	47	438	10	43.80	2- 2	–	–

Also bowled: S.A.J.Boswell 21-3-95-2; A.A.Khan 24.2-9-63-1; A.Sachdeva 12-1-54-1; I.J.Sutcliffe 1-1-0-0; T.J.Mason 91-28-182-7; D.Williamson 16-3-33-0.

The First-Class Averages (pp 113-128) give the records of Leicestershire players in all first-class county matches (their other opponents being the New Zealanders), with the exception of A.D.Mullally, whose full county figures are as above, and:

A.Habib 16-26-3-160*-1029-44.73-3-6-2ct. Did not bowl.

D.L.Maddy 17-28-2-158*-1041-40.04-2-4-17ct. 85.4-22-260-12-21.66-3/5.

LEICESTERSHIRE RECORDS

FIRST-CLASS CRICKET

Highest Total	For 701-4d		v	Worcs	Worcester	1906
	V 761-6d		by	Essex	Chelmsford	1990
Lowest Total	For 25		v	Kent	Leicester	1912
	V 24		by	Glamorgan	Leicester	1971
	24		by	Oxford U	Oxford	1985
Highest Innings	For 261	P.V.Simmons	v	Northants	Leicester	1994
	V 341	G.H.Hirst	for	Yorkshire	Leicester	1905

Highest Partnership for each Wicket

1st	390	B.Dudleston/J.F.Steele	v	Derbyshire	Leicester	1979
2nd	289*	J.C.Balderstone/D.I.Gower	v	Essex	Leicester	1981
3rd	316*	W.Watson/A.Wharton	v	Somerset	Taunton	1961
4th	290*	P.Willey/T.J.Boon	v	Warwicks	Leicester	1984
5th	322	B.F.Smith/P.V.Simmons	v	Notts	Worksop	1998
6th	284	P.V.Simmons/P.A.Nixon	v	Durham	Chester-le-St	1996
7th	219*	J.D.R.Benson/P.Whitticase	v	Hampshire	Bournemouth	1991
8th	172	P.A.Nixon/D.J.Millns	v	Lancashire	Manchester	1996
9th	160	W.W.Odell/R.T.Crawford	v	Worcs	Leicester	1902
10th	228	R.Illingworth/K.Higgs	v	Northants	Leicester	1977

Best Bowling	For	10- 18	G.Geary	v	Glamorgan	Pontypridd	1929
(Innings)	V	10- 32	H.Pickett	for	Essex	Leyton	1895
Best Bowling	For	16- 96	G.Geary	v	Glamorgan	Pontypridd	1929
(Match)	V	16-102	C.Blythe	for	Kent	Leicester	1909

Most Runs – Season	2446	L.G.Berry	(av 52.04)	1937
Most Runs – Career	30143	L.G.Berry	(av 30.32)	1924-51
Most 100s – Season	7	L.G.Berry		1937
	7	W.Watson		1959
	7	B.F.Davison		1982
Most 100s – Career	45	L.G.Berry		1924-51
Most Wkts – Season	170	J.E.Walsh	(av 18.96)	1948
Most Wkts – Career	2130	W.E.Astill	(av 23.19)	1906-39

LIMITED-OVERS CRICKET

Highest Total	**NWT**	406-5		v	Berkshire	Leicester	1996
	BHC	382-6		v	Minor C	Leicester	1998
	NL	344-4		v	Durham	Chester-le-St	1996
Lowest Total	**NWT**	56		v	Northants	Leicester	1964
	BHC	56		v	Minor C	Wellington	1982
	NL	36		v	Sussex	Leicester	1973
Highest Innings	**NWT**	201	V.J.Wells	v	Berkshire	Leicester	1996
	BHC	158*	B.F.Davison	v	Warwicks	Coventry	1972
	NL	152	B.Dudleston	v	Lancashire	Manchester	1975
Best Bowling	**NWT**	6-20	K.Higgs	v	Staffs	Longton	1975
	BHC	6-25	V.J.Wells	v	Minor C	Leicester	1998
	NL	6-17	K.Higgs	v	Glamorgan	Leicester	1973

MIDDLESEX

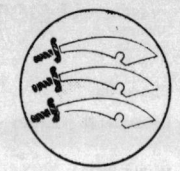

Formation of Present Club: 2 February 1864
Colours: Blue
Badge: Three Seaxes
County Champions (since 1890): (10) 1903, 1920, 1921, 1947, 1976, 1980, 1982, 1985, 1990, 1993
Joint Champions: (2) 1949, 1977
NatWest Trophy/Gillette Cup Winners: (4) 1977, 1980, 1984, 1988
Benson and Hedges Cup Winners: (2) 1983, 1986
CGU National League (Div 1) Winners: (0); best – 7th (Div 2) 1999
Sunday League Winners: (1) 1992
Match Awards: NWT 56; BHC 60

Secretary: V.J.Codrington, Lord's Cricket Ground, London NW8 8QN ▲ Tel: (020) 7289 1300 ▲ Fax: (020) 7289 5831 ▲ Email: Middx@ecb.co.uk ▲ Web: www.middlesexccc.com

Captain/Overseas Player: J.L.Langer. **Vice-Captain:** A.R.C.Fraser.
2000 Beneficiary: M.R.Ramprakash. **Scorer:** M.J.Smith. ‡ New registration

ALLEYNE, David (Enfield GS; Hertford Regional C; City & Islington C), b York 17 Apr 1976. 5'11". RHB, WK. Staff 1999 – awaiting f-c debut. LO HS 13 v Glam (Cardiff) 1999 (NL).

BATT, Christopher James (Cox Green CS), b Taplow, Bucks 22 Sep 1976. 6'4". LHB, LMF. Sussex 1997 – no CC appearances. Middlesex debut 1998. Berkshire 1997. MCC YC. HS 43 v Warwks (Lord's) 1998. BB 6-101 v Notts (Nottingham) 1998. LO HS 8* (NL). LO BB 3-26 v Yorks (Lord's) 1998 (SL).

BLOOMFIELD, Timothy Francis (Halliford S, Shepperton), b Ashford 31 May 1973. 6'2". RHB, RMF. Debut 1997. Berkshire 1996. HS 20* v Sussex (Hove) 1998. BB 5-36 v Glam (Cardiff) 1999. LO HS 15 v Warwks (Lord's) 1998 (SL). LO BB 2-8 v Surrey (Lord's) 1997 (SL).

BROWN, Michael James (Queen Elizabeth GS, Blackburn; Durham U), b Burnley, Lancs 9 Feb 1980. 6'0". RHB, OB. Debut 1999. HS 24* v CU (Cambridge) 1999 – on debut. CC HS 5.

BRYAN, Russell Barnaby (Shebbear C), b Maidstone, Kent 14 Feb 1981. 6'1". RHB, RMF. Staff 1999 – awaiting f-c debut.

COOK, Simon James (Matthew Arnold S), b Oxford 15 Jan 1977. 6'4". RHB, RM. Debut 1999. HS 51 v Hants (Lord's) 1999. BB 4-83 v Yorks (Leeds) 1999. LO HS 20 v Sussex (Arundel) 1999 (NL). LO BB 3-16 v Glam (Cardiff) 1999.

CREESE, Matthew Leonard (Goffs S), b Enfield 13 Feb 1982. LHB, SLA. Debut 1999 (awaiting CC debut). 2nd XI debut when aged 15y 188d. HS 4 and BB 1-37 v CU (Cambridge) 1999 – on debut.

DUTCH, Keith Philip (Nower Hill HS; Weald C), b Harrow 21 Mar 1973. 5'10". RHB, OB. Debut 1993. MCC YC. HS 79 v Glos (Bristol) 1997, BB 3-25 v Somerset (Uxbridge) 1996. LO HS 58 v Kent (Lord's) 1997 (SL). LO BB 5-35 v Somerset (Taunton) 1999 (NL).

‡EDWARDS, Alexander David (Imberhorne CS, E Grinstead; Loughborough U), b Cuckfield, Sussex 2 Aug 1975. 6'0". RHB, RFM. Combined U 1995. Sussex 1995-99. HS 22 Sx v Young A (Hove) 1995 and 22 Sx v Middx (Lord's) 1999. BB 5-34 Sx v Pak A (Hove) 1997. CC BB 4-94 Sx v Surrey (Hove) 1997. LO HS 43 Sx v Essex (Hove) 1998 (BHC). LO BB 3-34 Sx v Notts (Nottingham) 1998 (SL).

FRASER, Angus Robert Charles (Gayton HS, Harrow; Orange Hill HS, Edgware), b Billinge, Lancs 8 Aug 1965. Brother of A.G.J. (Middx and Essex 1986-92). 6'5". RHB, RMF. Debut 1984; cap 1988; benefit 1997. MBE 1999. *Wisden* 1995. **Tests:** 46 (1989 to 1998-99); HS 32 v SL (Oval) 1998; BB 8-53 (11-110 match) v WI (P-of-S) 1997-98 – record England innings analysis v WI. **LOI**: 42 (1989-90 to 1999); HS 38* v A (Melbourne) 1990-91; BB 4-22 v A (Melbourne) 1994-95. Tours: A 1990-91, 1994-95 (part), 1998-99; SA 1995-96; WI 1989-90, 1993-94, 1997-98. HS 92 v Surrey (Oval) 1990. 50 wkts (7); most – 92 (1989). BB 8-53 (*see Tests*). M BB 7-40 v Leics (Lord's) 1993. LO HS 38* (*see LOI*). LO BB 5-32 v Derbys (Lord's) 1995 (SL).

GOODCHILD, David John (Whitmore HS; Weald C; N London U), b Harrow 17 Sep 1976. 6'2". RHB, RM. Debut 1996. HS 105 v SL (Lord's) 1998. CC HS 83* v Yorks (Lord's) 1998. LO HS 38* v Hants (Southampton) 1998 (SL).

HEWITT, James Peter (Teddington S; Richmond C; City of Westminster C), b Southwark, London 26 Feb 1976. 6'2½". LHB, RMF. Debut 1996; cap 1998. HS 75 v Essex (Chelmsford) 1997. 50 wkts (1): 60 (1997). BB 6-14 v Glam (Cardiff) 1997. Took wicket of R.I.Dawson (Glos) with first ball in f-c cricket. LO HS 32* v Glos (Bristol) 1997 (SL). LO BB 4-24 v Worcs (Uxbridge) 1998 (SL).

HUNT, Thomas Aaron '***Thos***' (Acton HS: St Clement Danes S), b Melbourne, Australia 19 Jan 1982. 6'2". Resident in UK since 1985 (English parents). LHB, RMF. Staff 1999 – awaiting f-c debut.

HUTTON, Benjamin Leonard (Radley C; Durham U), b Johannesburg, SA 29 Jan 1977. 6'2". Elder son of R.A. (Yorkshire, Transvaal & England 1962 to 1975-76); grandson of Sir Leonard (Yorkshire and England 1934-60). LHB, RMF. British U 1998-99. Middlesex debut 1999. HS 59 v Notts (Southgate) 1999. BB 2-100 Brit U v NZ (Oxford) 1999. M BB 1-18 (CC). LO HS 24 v Glam (Cardiff) 1999 (NL). LO BB 2-43 Brit U v Surrey (Oval) 1998 (BHC).

JOHNSON, Richard Leonard (Sunbury Manor S; S Pelthorne C), b Chertsey, Surrey 29 Dec 1974. 6'2". RHB, RMF. Debut 1992; cap 1995. Tour: I 1994-95 (Eng A – part). HS 50* v CU (Cambridge) 1994. CC HS 47 v Hants (Southampton) 1994. 50 wkts (2); most – 50 (1997, 1998). BB 10-45 v Derbys (Derby) 1994 (second youngest to take all ten wickets in any f-c match). Award: NWT 1. LO HS 45* v Durham (Southgate) 1998 (NWT). LO BB 5-50 v Kent (Lord's) 1997 (NWT).

JOYCE, Edmund Christopher, b Dublin, Ireland 22 Sep 1978. LHB, RM. Ireland 1997 to date. Middlesex debut 1999. HS 43 v Scot (Dublin) 1997. M HS 9. LO HS 73 Ire v Warwks (Birmingham) 1998 (NWT).

LANGER, Justin Lee (Aquinas C; U of WA), b Perth, Australia 21 Nov 1970. 5'8". LHB, RM. W Australia 1991-92 to date. Middlesex debut/cap 1998; captain 2000. **Tests** (A): 30 (1992-93 to 1999-00); HS 223 v I (Sydney) 1999-00. **LOI**: 8 (1993-94 to 1997); HS 36 v I (Sharjah) 1993-94. Tours (A): E 1995 (Young A), 1997; SA 1996-97; WI 1994-95, 1998-99; NZ 1992-93; P 1994-95, 1998-99; SL 1999-00; Z 1999-00. 1000 runs (2+2); most – 1448 (1998). HS 274* WA v S Australia (Perth) 1996-97. M HS 241* v Kent (Lord's) 1999. BB 2-17 Aus A v SA A (Brisbane) 1997-98. M BB 1-10. Award: NWT 1. LO HS 114* v Herefords (Lord's) 1998 (NWT). LO BB 3-51 v Surrey (Guildford) 1998 (SL).

LARAMAN, Aaron William (Enfield GS), b Enfield 10 Jan 1979. 6'5". RHB, RFM. Debut 1998. Awaiting CC debut. HS – . LO HS 3 (SL).

MAUNDERS, John Kenneth (Ashford HS; Spelthorne C), b Ashford 4 Apr 1981. 5'10". LHB, RM. Debut 1999 (awaiting CC debut). Middx 2nd XI debut aged 16y 19d. HS 9.

NASH, David Charles (Sunbury Manor S; Malvern C), b Chertsey, Surrey 19 Jan 1978. 5'8". RHB, occ LB, WK. Debut 1997. Tour: SL 1997-98 (Eng A). HS 114 v Somerset (Lord's) 1998. BB 1-8. LO HS 43 v Surrey (Oval) 1999 (NL).

RAMPRAKASH, Mark Ravin (Gayton HS; Harrow Weald SFC), b Bushey, Herts 5 Sep 1969. 5'9". RHB, RM. Debut 1987; cap 1990; captain 1997-99. YC 1991. **ECB contract 2000. Tests:** 38 (1991 to 1999); HS 154 v WI (Bridgetown) 1997-98; BB 1-2. **LOI**: 13 (1991 to 1997-98); HS 51 v WI (P-o-S) 1997-98. Tours: A 1994-95 (*part*), 1998-99; SA 1995-96; WI 1991-92 (Eng A), 1993-94, 1997-98; NZ 1991-92; I 1994-95 (Eng A); P 1990-91 (Eng A); SL 1990-91 (Eng A). 1000 runs (9) inc 2000 (1): 2258 (1995). HS 235 v Yorks (Leeds) 1995. BB 3-32 v Glam (Lord's) 1998. Awards: NWT 2; BHC 3. LO HS 147* v Worcs (Lord's) 1990 (SL). LO BB 5-38 v Leics (Lord's) 1993 (SL).

ROSEBERRY, Michael Anthony (Durham S), b Sunderland 28 Nov 1966. Elder brother of A. (Leics and Glam 1992-94). 6'1". RHB, RM. Middlesex 1986-94 and 1999; cap 1990; benefit 2000. Durham 1995-98; captain 1995-96; cap 1998. Tour: A 1992-93 (Eng A). 1000 runs (4) inc 2000 (1): 2044 (1992). HS 185 v Leics (Lord's) 1993. Du HS 145* Du v OU (Oxford) 1996. BB 1-1. Awards: NWT 1; BHC 1. LO HS 121 Du v Herefords (Chester-le-St) 1995 (NWT). LO BB 1-22 (NWT).

SHAH, Owais Alam (Isleworth & Syon S), b Karachi, Pakistan 22 Oct 1978. 6'0". RHB, OB. Debut 1996. Tours (Eng A): A 1996-97; SL 1997-98. HS 140 v Yorks (Lord's) 1998. BB 3-33 v Glos (Bristl) 1999. LO HS 134 v Sussex (Arundel) 1999 (NL). LO BB 2-2 v Glam (Cardiff) 1998 (BHC).

STRAUSS, Andrew John (Radley C; Durham U), b Johannesburg, SA 2 Mar 1977. 5'11". LHB, LM. Debut 1998. Oxfordshire 1996. HS 98 v Surrey (Lord's) 1999. LO HS 29 Brit U v Kent (Oxford) 1998 (BHC).

TUFNELL, Philip Clive Roderick (Highgate S), b Barnet, Herts 29 Apr 1966. 6'0". RHB, SLA. Debut 1986; cap 1990; benefit 1999. MCC YC. **Tests:** 41 (1990-91 to 1999-00); HS 22* v I (Madras) 1992-93; BB 7-47 (11-147 match) v NZ (Christchurch) 1991-92, took 11-93 v A (Oval) 1997. **LOI**: 20 (1990-91 to 1996-97); HS 5*; BB 4-22 v NZ (Christchurch) 1996-97. Tours: A 1990-91, 1994-95; SA 1999-00; WI 1993-94, 1997-98; NZ 1991-92, 1996-97; I/SL 1992-93, Z 1996-97. HS 67* v Worcs (Lord's) 1996. 50 wkts (7); most – 88 (1991). BB 8-29 v Glam (Cardiff) 1993. Award: NWT 1. LO HS 18 v Warwks (Lord's) 1991 (BHC). LO BB 5-28 v Leics (Lord's) 1993 (SL).

WEEKES, Paul Nicholas (Homerton House SS, Hackney), b Hackney, London 8 Jul 1969. 5'10". LHB, OB. Debut 1990; cap 1993. Tour: I 1994-95 (Eng A). MCC YC. 1000 runs (1): 1218 (1996). HS 171* v Somerset (Uxbridge) 1996. BB 8-39 v Glam (Lord's) 1996. Awards: NWT 2; BHC 3. LO HS 143* v Cornwall (St Austell) 1995 (NWT). LO BB 4-29 v Glos (Lord's) 1996 (SL) and 4-29 v Essex (Lord's) 1996 (SL).

‡**WESTON, Robin** Michael Swann (Durham S; Loughborough U), b Durham 7 Jun 1975. Brother of W.P.C. (*see WORCESTERSHIRE*). 5'10". RHB, LB. Durham 1995-97. Derbyshire 1998-99. Scored 72, 129*, 22, 124, 156 in consecutive CC innings 1999. Minor C debut 1991 when aged 15yr 355d (Durham record). HS 156 De v Somerset (Derby) 1999. BB (De) 1-15. LO HS 56 De v Leics (Leicester) 1998 (NWT) and 56 De v Notts (Nottingham) 1999 (NL).

RELEASED/RETIRED

(Having made a first-class County appearance in 1999)

BLANCHETT, Ian Neale (Downham Market SFC; Luton U), b Melbourne, Australia 2 Oct 1975. 6'4". RHB, RMF. Middlesex 1998-99. Norfolk 1993-94. HS 18 v Worcs (Uxbridge) 1998 – on debut. BB 2-38 v Glam (Lord's) 1998. LO HS 9* (SL). LO BB 2-34 v Northants (Northampton) 1999 (NL).

KETTLEBOROUGH, Richard Allan (Worksop C), b Sheffield, Yorks 15 Mar 1973. 6'0". LHB, RM. Yorkshire 1994-97. Middlesex 1998-99. Tour: Z 1995-96 (Y). HS 108 Y v Essex (Leeds) 1996. M HS 93 v Leics (Lord's) 1999. BB 2-26 Y v Notts (Scarborough) 1996. LO HS 58 v Derbys (Derby) 1999 (NL). LO BB 2-43 Y v Surrey (Oval) 1995 (SL).

MIDDLESEX 1999

RESULTS SUMMARY

	Place	Won	Lost	Tied	Drew	No Result
PPP County Championship	**16th**	4	5		7	1
All First-Class Matches		4	6		7	1
NatWest Trophy	3rd Round					
CGU National League (Division 2)	**7th**	5	10	1		

COUNTY CHAMPIONSHIP AVERAGES

BATTING AND FIELDING

Cap		*M*	*I*	*NO*	*HS*	*Runs*	*Avge*	*100*	*50*	*Ct/St*
1998	J.L.Langer	12	22	4	241*	1048	58.22	4	2	12
1990	M.R.Ramprakash	12	22	2	209*	929	46.45	2	6	8
–	D.C.Nash	16	25	8	92	632	37.17	–	4	44/3
1993	P.N.Weekes	16	28	4	140*	828	34.50	1	6	19
–	A.J.Strauss	8	15	1	98	471	33.64	–	4	3
–	O.A.Shah	16	30	2	110*	726	25.92	2	3	6
1990	M.A.Roseberry	12	21	1	116	483	24.15	1	1	7
–	B.L.Hutton	7	13	–	59	307	23.61	–	2	5
–	R.A.Kettleborough	7	14	–	93	300	21.42	–	2	3
–	S.J.Cook	10	16	3	51	237	18.23	–	1	3
1998	J.P.Hewitt	12	19	1	49*	300	16.66	–	–	5
1990	P.C.R.Tufnell	12	15	1	48	184	13.14	–	–	3
1988	A.R.C.Fraser	12	16	5	56*	142	12.90	–	1	–
–	K.P.Dutch	5	8	–	23	103	12.87	–	–	1
1995	R.L.Johnson	6	8	–	39	86	10.75	–	–	1
–	T.F.Bloomfield	11	17	9	17*	80	10.00	–	–	1

Also batted (1 match each): M.J.Brown 5 (1 ct); E.C.Joyce 9 (1 ct).

BOWLING

	O	*M*	*R*	*W*	*Avge*	*Best*	*5wI*	*10wM*
P.C.R.Tufnell	445.1	119	906	34	26.64	5-61	2	–
R.L.Johnson	133.3	30	453	16	28.31	4-50	–	–
A.R.C.Fraser	435.1	113	1093	38	28.76	5-63	1	–
O.A.Shah	84.1	11	294	10	29.40	3-33	–	–
T.F.Bloomfield	266.3	45	1007	33	30.51	5-36	1	–
J.P.Hewitt	272.1	52	948	30	31.60	5-50	1	–
S.J.Cook	276.4	60	954	27	35.33	4-83	–	–
P.N.Weekes	316.1	68	890	23	38.69	4-50	–	–

Also bowled: K.P.Dutch 36-7-119-3; B.L.Hutton 31-5-126-1; J.L.Langer 2-1-3-0; M.R.Ramprakash 9-0-35-0.

The First-Class Averages (pp 113-128) give the records of Middlesex players in all first-class county matches (Middlesex's other opponents being Cambridge University), with the exception of B.L.Hutton, M.R.Ramprakash and P.C.R.Tufnell whose full county figures are as above.

MIDDLESEX RECORDS

FIRST-CLASS CRICKET

Highest Total	For 642-3d		v	Hampshire	Southampton	1923
	V 665		by	W Indians	Lord's	1939
Lowest Total	For 20		v	MCC	Lord's	1864
	V 31		by	Glos	Bristol	1924
Highest Innings	For 331*	J.D.B.Robertson	v	Worcs	Worcester	1949
	V 316*	J.B.Hobbs	for	Surrey	Lord's	1926

Highest Partnership for each Wicket

1st	372	M.W.Gatting/J.L.Langer	v	Essex	Southgate	1998
2nd	380	F.A.Tarrant/J.W.Hearne	v	Lancashire	Lord's	1914
3rd	424*	W.J.Edrich/D.C.S.Compton	v	Somerset	Lord's	1948
4th	325	J.W.Hearne/E.H.Hendren	v	Hampshire	Lord's	1919
5th	338	R.S.Lucas/T.C.O'Brien	v	Sussex	Hove	1895
6th	270	J.D.Carr/P.N.Weekes	v	Glos	Lord's	1994
7th	271*	E.H.Hendren/F.T.Mann	v	Notts	Nottingham	1925
8th	182*	M.H.C.Doll/H.R.Murrell	v	Notts	Lord's	1913
9th	160*	E.H.Hendren/T.J.Durston	v	Essex	Leyton	1927
10th	230	R.W.Nicholls/W.Roche	v	Kent	Lord's	1899

Best Bowling	For	10- 40	G.O.B.Allen	v	Lancashire	Lord's	1929
(Innings)	V	9- 38	R.C.R-Glasgow†	for	Somerset	Lord's	1924
Best Bowling	For	16-114	G.Burton	v	Yorkshire	Sheffield	1888
(Match)		16-114	J.T.Hearne	v	Lancashire	Manchester	1898
	V	16-109	C.W.L.Parker	for	Glos	Cheltenham	1930

Most Runs – Season	2669	E.H.Hendren	(av 83.41)	1923
Most Runs – Career	40302	E.H.Hendren	(av 48.81)	1907-37
Most 100s – Season	13	D.C.S.Compton		1947
Most 100s – Career	119	E.H.Hendren		1907-37
Most Wkts – Season	158	F.J.Titmus	(av 14.63)	1955
Most Wkts – Career	2361	F.J.Titmus	(av 21.27)	1949-82

LIMITED-OVERS CRICKET

Highest Total	**NWT**	304-7		v	Surrey	The Oval	1995
		304-8		v	Cornwall	St Austell	1995
	BHC	325-5		v	Leics	Leicester	1992
	NL	290-6		v	Worcs	Lord's	1990
Lowest Total	**NWT**	41		v	Essex	Westcliff	1972
	BHC	73		v	Essex	Lord's	1985
	NL	23		v	Yorkshire	Leeds	1974
Highest Innings	**NWT**	158	G.D.Barlow	v	Lancashire	Lord's	1984
	BHC	143*	M.W.Gatting	v	Sussex	Hove	1985
	NL	147*	M.R.Ramprakash	v	Worcs	Lord's	1990
Best Bowling	**NWT**	6-15	W.W.Daniel	v	Sussex	Hove	1980
	BHC	7-12	W.W.Daniel	v	Minor C (E)	Ipswich	1978
	NL	6- 6	R.W.Hooker	v	Surrey	Lord's	1969

† R.C.Robertson-Glasgow

NORTHAMPTONSHIRE

Formation of Present Club: 31 July 1878
Colours: Maroon
Badge: Tudor Rose
County Champions: (0); best – 2nd 1912, 1957, 1965, 1976
NatWest Trophy/Gillette Cup Winners: (2) 1976, 1992
Benson and Hedges Cup Winners: (1) 1980
CGU National League Winners: (0); best – 3rd (Div 2) 1999
Sunday League Winners: (0); best – 3rd 1991
Match Awards: NWT 52; BHC 55

Chief Executive: S.P.Coverdale, County Ground, Wantage Road, Northampton, NN1 4TJ ▲ Tel: 01604 32917 ▲ Fax: 01604 514488 ▲ Email: northants@ecb.co.uk ▲ Web: www.nccc.co.uk

Captain/Overseas Player: M.L.Hayden. **Vice-Captain:** D.Ripley.
2000 Beneficiary: J.P.Taylor. **Scorer:** A.C.Kingston. ‡ New registration

BAILEY, Tobin Michael Barnaby (Bedford S; Loughborough U), b Kettering 28 Aug 1976. 5'10". RHB, WK. Debut 1996. British U 1998. Bedfordshire 1994-96. HS 31* v Lancs (Northampton) 1996. LO HS 52 Brit U v Glos (Bristol) 1997.

BLAIN, John Angus Rae (Penicuik HS; Jewel & Esk Valley C), b Edinburgh, Scotland 4 Jan 1979. 6'1". RHB, RMF. Scotland 1996 to date. Northamptonshire debut 1997. HS 0 and BB 1-18 v Worcs (Northampton) 1997. LO HS 10* Scot v Notts (Nottingham) 1996 (BHC). LO BB 5-24 v Derbys (Derby) 1997 (SL).

BROWN, Jason Fred (St Margaret Ward HS & SFC), b Newcastle-under-Lyme, Staffs 10 Oct 1974. 6'0". RHB, OB. Debut 1996. Staffordshire 1994 to date. HS 16* v Durham (Northampton) 1997. BB 6-53 (11-102 match) v Somerset (Taunton) 1998. LO HS – (SL). LO BB 4-26 v Leics (Northampton) 1997 (SL).

COOK, Jeffrey William (James Cook HS, Sydney), b Sydney, Australia 2 Feb 1972. 6'4". LHB, RM. Resident in UK since 1993 – qualifies 2000. Staff 1999 – awaiting f-c debut. NSW U-19. Award: NWT 1. LO HS 130 Northants Board v Wilts (Northampton) 1999 (NWT).

‡COUSINS, Darren Mark (Netherhall CS; Impington Village C), b Cambridge 24 Sep 1971. 6'2". RHB, RMF. Essex 1993-98. Surrey (NL only) 1999. Cambridgeshire 1990, 1999. HS 18* Ex v Durham (Chelmsford) 1995. BB 6-35 Ex v CU (Cambridge) 1994. CC BB 3-73 Ex v Leics (Chelmsford) 1995. LO HS 12* Ex v Glam (Chelmsford) 1995 (BHC). LO BB 3-18 Ex v Warwks (Birmingham) 1994 (SL).

DAVIES, Michael Kenton (Loughborough GS, Loughborough U), b Ashby-de-la-Zouch, Leics 17 Jul 1976. 6'0". RHB, SLA. Debut 1997. British U 1998. Tours (Eng A): NZ 1999-00; B 1999-00. HS 32* v Durham (Northampton) 1999. BB 6-49 v Hants (Northampton) 1999. LO HS 2* (Brit U – BHC). LO BB 3-11 Brit U v Somerset (Taunton) 1998 (BHC).

DOBSON, Martyn Colin, b Scunthorpe, Lincs 28 May 1982. Brother of A.M. (Northants staff 1997-98). RHB, OB. Staff 1999 – awaiting f-c debut.

HAYDEN, Matthew Lawrence (Marist C, Ashgrove; Queensland U of Tech), b Kingaroy, Queensland, Australia 29 Oct 1971. 6'2". LHB, RM. Queensland 1991-92 to date. Hampshire 1997; cap 1997. Northamptonshire debut/cap 1999; captain 1999 to date. **Tests** (A): 7 (1993-94 to 1996-97); HS 125 v WI (Adelaide) 1996-97. **LOI** (A): 13 (1993 to 1993-94); HS 67 v NZ (Sharjah) 1993-94. Tours (A): E 1993, 1995 (Young A); Sc/Ire 1998 (Aus A);

HAYDEN, M.L. (*continued*)
SA 1993-94, 1996-97. 1000 runs (2+3); most – 1446 (1997). HS 235* H v Warwks (Southampton) 1997. Nh HS 170 v Notts (Northampton) 1999. BB 3-10 v Worcs (Northampton) 1999. Awards: NWT 1; BHC 1. LO HS 152* Q v Vic (Melbouurne) 1998-99 (MM). LO BB 2-38 H v Leics (Southampton) 1997 (SL).

INNES, Kevin John (Weston Favell Upper S), b Wellingborough 24 Sep 1975. 5'10". RHB, RM. 2nd XI debut 1990 (aged 14yr 8m – Northamptonshire record). Debut 1994. HS 63 and BB 4-61 v Lancs (Northampton) 1996. LO HS 27 v Middx (Northampton) 1999 (NL). LO BB 4-37 v Derbys (Derby) 1999 (NL).

LOGAN, Richard James (Wolverhampton GS), b Stone, Staffs 28 Jan 1980. 6'1". RHB, RMF. Debut 1999. Awaiting CC debut. HS 1. BB 3-42 v CU (Cambridge) 1999. LO HS 8 (NL). LO BB 2-31 v Somerset (Taunton) 1999 (NL).

LOYE, Malachy Bernhard (Moulton S), b Northampton 27 Sep 1972. 6'2". RHB, OB. Debut 1991; cap 1994. Tours (Eng A): SA 1993-94, 1998-99; Z 1994-95 (Nh), 1998-99. 1000 runs (2); most – 1198 (1998). HS 322* v Glam (Northampton) 1998 – record Northants score. Award: BHC 1. LO HS 122 v Somerset (Luton) 1993 (SL).

MALCOLM, Devon Eugene (St Elizabeth THS; Richmond C, Sheffield; Derby CHE), b Kingston, Jamaica 22 Feb 1963. Qualified for England 1987. 6'2". RHB, RF. Derbyshire 1984-97; cap 1989; benefit 1997. Northamptonshire debut 1998; 1999. *Wisden* 1994. **Tests:** 40 (1989 to 1997); HS 29 v A (Sydney) 1994-95; BB 9-57 v SA (Oval) 1994 – sixth best analysis in Test cricket. **LOI**: 10 (1990 to 1993-94); HS 4; BB 3-40 v I (Gwalior) 1992-93. Tours: A 1990-91, 1994-95; SA 1995-96; WI 1989-90, 1991-92 (Eng A), 1993-94; I 1992-93; SL 1992-93. HS 51 De v Surrey (Derby) 1989. Nh HS 42 v Glam (Northampton) 1998. 50 wkts (7); most – 82 (1996). BB 9-57 (*see Tests*). CC BB 6-23 De v Lancs (Derby) 1997. Nh BB 6-39 v Sussex (Hove) 1999. Awards: NWT 1; BHC 1. LO HS 42 De v Surrey (Oval) 1996 (SL). LO BB 7-35 De v Northants (Derby) 1997 (NWT).

‡**PANESAR,** Mudhsuden Singh '***Monty***' (Bedford Modern S), b Luton, Beds 25 Apr 1982. RHB, SLA. Bedfordshire 1998-99. Staff 2000 – awaiting f-c debut.

PENBERTHY, Anthony Leonard (Camborne CS), b Troon, Cornwall 1 Sep 1969. 6'1". LHB, RM. Debut 1989; cap 1994. Cornwall 1987-89. Tours (Nh): SA 1991-92; Z 1994-95. HS 128 v Warwks (Northampton) 1998. BB 5-37 v Glam (Swansea) 1993. Took wicket of M.A.Taylor (A) with his first ball in f-c cricket. Award: NWT 1. LO HS 81* v Surrey (Northampton) 1997 (SL). LO BB 5-36 v Glos (Northampton) 1993 (SL).

POWELL, Mark John (Campion S, Bugbrooke; Loughborough U), b Northampton 4 Nov 1980. 5'11". RHB, OB. Staff 1999 – awaiting f-c debut.

RIPLEY, David (Royds SS, Leeds), b Leeds, Yorks 13 Sep 1966. 5'9". RHB, WK. Debut 1984; cap 1987; benefit 1997. Tours (Nh): SA 1991-92; Z 1994-95. HS 209 v Glam (Northampton) 1998. BB 2-89 v Essex (Ilford) 1987. Award: BHC 1. LO HS 52* v Surrey (Northampton) 1993 (SL).

ROBERTS, David James (Mullion CS), b Truro, Cornwall 29 Dec 1976. Cousin of C.K.Bullen (Surrey 1982-91). 5'11". RHB, RSM. Debut 1996. HS 117 v Essex (Northampton) 1997.

‡**ROLLINS, Adrian** Stewart (Little Ilford CS), b Barking, Essex 8 Feb 1972. Brother of R.J. (*see ESSEX*). 6'5". RHB, occ WK, occ RM. Derbyshire 1993-99; cap 1995. 1000 runs (3); most – 1142 (1997). HS 210 De v Hants (Chesterfield) 1997. BB (De) 1-19. LO HS 126* De v Surrey (Derby) 1995 (SL).

SALES, David John Grimwood (Caterham S; Cumnor House S), b Carshalton, Surrey 3 Dec 1977. 6'0". RHB, RM. Debut 1996 v Worcs (Kidderminster) scoring 0 and 210* – record Championship score on f-c debut; youngest (18yr 237d) to score 200 in a Championship match; cap 1999. Tours (Eng A): NZ 1999-00; SL 1997-98; K 1997-98; B 1999-00. 1000 runs (1): 1291 (1999). HS 303* v Essex (Northampton) 1999 – youngest Englishman (21y 240d) to score a f-c 300. BB 4-25 v SL A (Northampton) 1999. CC BB 1-5. LO HS 70* (off 56 balls) v Essex (Chelmsford) 1994 (SL), when 16y 289d (youngest to score SL fifty).

‡**STRONG, Michael** Richard (Brighton C; Brunel UC), b Cuckfield, Sussex 28 Jun 1974. 6'1". LHB, RMF. Sussex 1998-99. HS 35* Sx v Leics (Arundel) 1999. LO HS (Sx) 2* (SL).

SUTCLIFFE, Robin Victor (Greenhill C, Harrow), b Hemel Hempstead, Herts 10 Jul 1980. 6'7½". RHB, RFM. Debut 1999 (awaiting CC debut). MCC YC. HS 9* and BB 2-88 v SL A (Northampton) 1999.

SWANN, Alec James (Risade S; Sponne S, Towcester), b Northampton 26 Oct 1976. Son of R. (Northumberland 1969-72; Bedfordshire 1988-95); elder brother of G.P. 6'1". RHB, RM/OB. Debut 1996. Bedfordshire 1994. HS 154 v Notts (Northampton) 1999. BB 1-19. CC BB – . LO HS 74 v Notts (Northampton) 1999 (NWT).

SWANN, Graeme Peter (Sponne SS, Towcester), b Northampton 24 Mar 1979. Son of R. (Northumberland 1969-72; Bedfordshire 1988-95); younger brother of A.J. 6'0". RHB, OB. Debut 1998; cap 1999. Bedfordshire 1996. **LOI**: 1 (1999-00); HS – . Tours (Eng A): SA 1998-99, 1999-00 (Eng); Z 1998-99. HS 130* v SL A (Northampton) 1999. CC HS 111 v Leics (Leicester) 1998. 50 wkts (1): 57 (1999). BB 6-41 (11-126 match) v Leics (Northampton) 1999. LO HS 63 v Glam (Northampton) 1999 (NL). LO BB 5-35 v Durham (Chester-le-St) 1999 (NL).

TAYLOR, Jonathan **Paul** (Pingle S, Swadlincote), b Ashby-de-la-Zouch, Leics 8 Aug 1964. 6'2". LHB, LFM. Derbyshire 1984-86. Northamptonshire debut 1991; cap 1992; benefit 2000. Staffordshire 1989-90. **Tests:** 2 (1992-93 to 1994); HS 17* v I (Calcutta) 1992-93. BB 1-18. **LOI**: 1 (1992-93); HS 1. Tours: SA 1993-94 (Eng A – part); I 1992-93; Z 1994-95 (Nh). HS 86 v Durham (Northampton) 1995. 50 wkts (6); most – 69 (1993). BB 7-23 v Hants (Bournemouth) 1992. Award: BHC 1. LO HS 24 v Worcs (Northampton) 1993 (SL). LO BB 5-45 v Notts (Northampton) 1996 (BHC).

WARREN, Russell John (Kingsthorpe Upper S), b Northampton 10 Sep 1971. 6'1". RHB, OB. Debut 1992; cap 1995. HS 201* v Glam (Northampton) 1996. Award: NWT 1. LO HS 100* v Ire (Northampton) 1994 (NWT).

‡**WHITE, Robert** Allan (Stowe S), b Chelmsford, Essex 15 Oct 1979. RHB, OB. Staff 2000 – awaiting f-c debut.

RELEASED/RETIRED

(Having made a first-class County appearance in 1999)

BAILEY, R.J. – *see DERBYSHIRE.*

CURRAN, Kevin Malcolm (Marandellas HS), b Rusape, S Rhodesia 7 Sep 1959. Son of K.P. (Rhodesia 1947-48 to 1953-54). 6'1". RHB, RMF. Zimbabwe 1980-81 to 1987-88. Qualified for England 1994. Natal 1988-89. Gloucestershire 1985-90; cap 1985. Northamptonshire 1991-99; cap 1992; captain 1998; benefit 1999. Boland 1994-95 and 1997-98. **LOI** (Z): 11 (1983 to 1987-88); HS 73 and BB 3-65 v I (Tunbridge W) 1983. Tours (Z): E 1982; SL 1983-84. 1000 runs (7); most – 1353 (1986). HS 159 v Glam (Abergavenny) 1997. 50 wkts (5); most – 67 (1993). BB 7-47 Natal v Transvaal (Johannesburg) 1988-89 and v Yorks (Harrogate) 1993. Awards: NWT 3; BHC 2. LO HS 119* v Kent (Canterbury) 1990 (SL). LO BB 5-15 Gs v Leics (Gloucester) 1988 (SL).

FOLLETT, David (Moorland Road HS, Burslem; Stoke-on-Trent TC), b Newcastle-under-Lyme, Staffs 14 Oct 1968. 6'2". RHB, RFM. Middlesex 1995-96. Northamptonshire 1997-99. Staffordshire 1994. HS 19 v Surrey (Northampton) 1999. BB 8-22 (10-87 match) M v Durham (Lord's) 1996. Nh BB 3-48 v Glos (Bristol) 1998. LO HS 4 (BHC). LO BB 4-39 v Scot (Northampton) 1997 (BHC).

NORTHAMPTONSHIRE 1999

RESULTS SUMMARY

	Place	Won	Lost	Tied	Drew	No Result
PPP County Championship	**13th**	4	7		6	
All First-Class Matches		5	7		7	
NatWest Trophy	Quarter-Finalist					
CGU National League (Division 2)	**3rd**	9	5			2

COUNTY CHAMPIONSHIP AVERAGES

BATTING AND FIELDING

Cap		*M*	*I*	*NO*	*HS*	*Runs*	*Avge*	*100*	*50*	*Ct/St*
1999	M.L.Hayden	9	15	2	170	745	57.30	4	1	6
1999	D.J.G.Sales	17	27	4	303*	1156	50.26	3	4	13
1987	D.Ripley	14	20	6	107	653	46.64	2	3	36/3
1995	R.J.Warren	17	27	4	110	871	37.86	1	5	11
1985	R.J.Bailey	13	21	1	113*	633	31.65	1	2	9
–	K.J.Innes	6	7	2	47*	157	31.40	–	–	2
1994	A.L.Penberthy	17	24	1	123*	689	29.95	1	4	6
–	A.J.Swann	10	15	–	154	387	25.80	1	2	10
1999	G.P.Swann	16	24	2	78	510	23.18	–	3	13
1994	M.B.Loye	11	18	–	100	302	16.77	1	–	3
1992	J.P.Taylor	17	21	2	71	316	16.63	–	1	5
–	D.Follett	5	5	1	19	44	11.00	–	–	–
–	M.K.Davies	11	16	4	32*	97	8.08	–	–	3
–	D.J.Roberts	4	6	–	17	33	5.50	–	–	3
1999	D.E.Malcolm	15	16	6	10*	32	3.20	–	–	4

Also batted: T.M.B.Bailey (3 matches) 24, 8, 1 (3 ct); J.F.Brown (1) 8; K.M.Curran (cap 1992)(1) 0, 1.

BOWLING

	O	*M*	*R*	*W*	*Avge*	*Best*	*5wI*	*10wM*
M.K.Davies	377.3	126	725	39	18.58	6- 49	3	–
G.P.Swann	519.1	122	1495	53	28.20	6- 41	2	1
D.E.Malcolm	485.1	90	1726	60	28.76	6- 39	3	–
J.P.Taylor	507.2	119	1427	48	29.72	5-105	1	–
A.L.Penberthy	256.5	86	712	19	37.47	3- 13	–	–

Also bowled: R.J.Bailey 9-1-15-1; J.F.Brown 29.5-8-64-2; K.M.Curran 5-1-21-1; D.Follett 120-23-377-8; M.L.Hayden 30-7-92-4; K.J.Innes 93.2-26-304-7; D.J.G.Sales 21.3-4-59-3; A.J.Swann 17-3-61-0.

The First-Class Averages (pp 113-128) give the records of Northamptonshire players in all first-class county matches (Northamptonshire's other opponents being Sri Lanka A and Cambridge University).

NORTHAMPTONSHIRE RECORDS

FIRST-CLASS CRICKET

Highest Total	For 781-7d		v	Notts	Northampton	1995
	V 670-9d		by	Sussex	Hove	1921
Lowest Total	For 12		v	Glos	Gloucester	1907
	V 33		by	Lancashire	Northampton	1977
Highest Innings	For 322	M.B.Loye	v	Glamorgan	Northampton	1998
	V 333	K.S.Duleepsinhji	for	Sussex	Hove	1930

Highest Partnership for each Wicket

1st	372	R.R.Montgomerie/M.B.Loye	v	Yorkshire	Northampton	1996
2nd	344	G.Cook/R.J.Boyd-Moss	v	Lancashire	Northampton	1986
3rd	393	A.Fordham/A.J.Lamb	v	Yorkshire	Leeds	1990
4th	370	R.T.Virgin/P.Willey	v	Somerset	Northampton	1976
5th	401	M.B.Loye/D.Ripley	v	Glamorgan	Northampton	1998
6th	376	R.Subba Row/A.Lightfoot	v	Surrey	The Oval	1958
7th	293	D.J.G.Sales/D.Ripley	v	Essex	Northampton	1999
8th	164	D.Ripley/N.G.B.Cook	v	Lancashire	Manchester	1987
9th	156	R.Subba Row/S.Starkie	v	Lancashire	Northampton	1955
10th	148	B.W.Bellamy/J.V.Murdin	v	Glamorgan	Northampton	1925

Best Bowling	For	10-127	V.W.C.Jupp	v	Kent	Tunbridge W	1932
(Innings)	V	10- 30	C.Blythe	for	Kent	Northampton	1907
Best Bowling	For	15- 31	G.E.Tribe	v	Yorkshire	Northampton	1958
(Match)	V	17- 48	C.Blythe	for	Kent	Northampton	1907

Most Runs – Season	2198	D.Brookes	(av 51.11)	1952
Most Runs – Career	28980	D.Brookes	(av 36.13)	1934-59
Most 100s – Season	8	R.A.Haywood		1921
Most 100s – Career	67	D.Brookes		1934-59
Most Wkts – Season	175	G.E.Tribe	(av 18.70)	1955
Most Wkts – Career	1097	E.W.Clark	(av 21.31)	1922-47

LIMITED-OVERS CRICKET

Highest Total	**NWT**	360-2		v	Staffs	Northampton	1990
	BHC	304-6		v	Scotland	Northampton	1995
	NL	306-2		v	Surrey	Guildford	1985
Lowest Total	**NWT**	62		v	Leics	Leicester	1974
	BHC	85		v	Sussex	Northampton	1978
	NL	41		v	Middlesex	Northampton	1972
Highest Innings	**NWT**	145	R.J.Bailey	v	Staffs	Stone	1991
	BHC	134	R.J.Bailey	v	Glos	Northampton	1987
	NL	172*	W.Larkins	v	Warwicks	Luton	1983
Best Bowling	**NWT**	7-37	N.A.Mallender	v	Worcs	Northampton	1984
	BHC	5-14	F.A.Rose	v	Minor C	Luton	1998
	NL	7-39	A.Hodgson	v	Somerset	Northampton	1976

NOTTINGHAMSHIRE

Formation of Present Club: March/April 1841
Substantial Reorganisation: 11 December 1866
Colours: Green and Gold
Badge: Badge of City of Nottingham
County Champions (since 1890): (4) 1907, 1929, 1981, 1987
NatWest Trophy/Gillette Cup Winners: (1) 1987
Benson and Hedges Cup Winners: (1) 1989
CGU National League (Div 1) Winners: (0); best – 5th (Div 2) 1999
Sunday League Winners: (1) 1991
Match Awards: NWT 42; BHC 67

Chief Executive: D.G.Collier, Trent Bridge, Nottingham NG2 6AG ▲ Tel: 0115 982 1525 ▲ Fax: 0115 945 5730 ▲ Email: trentbridge@btinternet.com ▲ Webs: www.notts.ccc.co.uk and www.trentbridge.co.uk

Captain: J.E.R.Gallian. **Vice-Captain:** No appointment. **Overseas Player:** Shoaib Akhtar. **2000 Beneficiary:** None. **Scorer:** G.Stringfellow. ‡ New registration

AFZAAL, Usman (Manvers Pierrepont CS; S Notts C), b Rawalpindi, Pakistan 9 Jun 1977. 6'0". LHB, SLA. Debut 1995. Tour (Nt): SA 1996-97. HS 109* v Derbys (Derby) 1998. BB 4-101 v Glos (Nottingham) 1998. LO HS 83* v Durham (Nottingham) 1999 (NL). LO BB 2-25 v Yorks (Cleethorpes) 1995 (SL).

‡BICKNELL, Darren John (Robert Haining SS; Guildford TC), b Guildford, Surrey 24 Jun 1967. Elder brother of M.P. 6'4". LHB, SLA. Surrey 1987-99; cap 1990; benefit 1999. Tours (Eng A): WI 1991-92; P 1990-91; SL 1990-91; Z 1989-90. 1000 runs (6); most – 1888 (1991). HS 235* Sy v Notts (Nottingham) 1994. BB 3-7 Sy v Sussex (Guildford) 1996. Awards: NWT 1; BHC 3. LO HS 135* Sy v Yorks (Oval) 1989 (NWT). LO BB (Sy) 1-11 (SL).

BOWEN, Mark Nicholas (Sacred Heart, Redcar; St Mary's C; Tees-side Poly), b Redcar, Yorks 6 Dec 1967. 6'2". RHB, RM. Northamptonshire 1991-92/1994. Nottinghamshire debut 1996; cap 1997. Tours: SA 1991-92 (Nh), 1996-97 (Nt). HS 32 Nh v Northants (Northampton) 1997 and 32 v Durham (Nottingham) 1998. BB 7-73 v Somerset (Taunton) 1998. LO HS 27* Nh v Kent (Northampton) 1994 (SL). LO BB 4-29 v Warwks (Nottingham) 1997 (SL).

FRANKS, Paul John (Southwell Minster CS), b Mansfield 3 Feb 1979. 6'2". LHB, RMF. Debut 1996; cap 1999. Tours (Eng A): SA 1998-99; NZ 1999-00; B 1999-00. HS 66* v Kent (Canterbury) 1998. 50 wkts (2); most – 63 (1999). BB 6-63 v Worcs (Kidderminster) 1998. Hat-trick 1997. Award: NWT 1. LO HS 40 and LO BB 5-27 v Glam (Nottingham) 1999 (NL).

GALLIAN, Jason Edward Riche (Pittwater House S, Sydney; Keble C, Oxford), b Manly, Sydney, Australia 25 Jun 1971. Qualified for England 1994. 6'0". RHB, RM. Lancashire 1990-97, taking wicket of D.A.Hagan (OU) with his first ball; cap 1994. Oxford U 1992-93; blue 1992-93; captain 1993. Nottinghamshire debut/cap 1998; captain 1998 (part) to date. Captained Australia YC v England YC 1989-90, scoring 158* in 1st 'Test'. **Tests:** 3 (1995 to 1995-96); HS 28 v SA (Pt Elizabeth) 1995-96. Tours: A 1996-97 (Eng A); I 1995-96 (La); SA 1995-96 (part); I 1994-95 (Eng A); P 1995-96 (Eng A). 1000 runs (2); most – 1156 (1996). HS 312 La v Derbys (Manchester) 1996 (record score at Old Trafford). Nt HS 120* v Lancs (Manchester) 1999. BB 6-115 La v Surrey (Southport) 1996. Nt BB 2-28 v Warwks (Nottingham) 1999. Awards: NWT 2; BHC 2. LO HS 134 La v Notts (Manchester) 1995 (BHC). LO BB 5-15 La v Minor C (Leek) 1995 (BHC).

‡**HARRIS, Andrew** James (Hadfield CS; Glossopdale Community C), b Ashton-under-Lyne, Lancs 26 Jun 1973. 6'1". RHB, RM. Derbyshire 1994-99; cap 1996. Tour: A 1996-97 (Eng A). HS 36 De v Worcs (Worcester) 1997. BB 6-40 (12-83 match) De v Middx (Derby) 1996. 50 wkts (1): 72 (1996). Award: NWT 1. LO HS 11* De v Kent (Derby) 1996 (NWT). LO BB 4-22 De v Yorks (Derby) 1997 (SL).

‡**HAYWOOD, Giles** Ronald (Lancing C), b Chichester, Sussex 8 Sep 1979. 6'1". LHB, RM. Sussex 1999. HS 14 Sx v Leics (Arundel) 1999 – on debut. LO HS 24 Sx v Northants (Northampton) 1999. LO BB (Sx) 1-18 (NWT).

JOHNSON, Paul (Grove CS, Balderton), b Newark 24 Apr 1965. 5'7". RHB, RM. Debut 1982; cap 1986; benefit 1995; captain 1996-98. Tours: SA 1996-97 (Nt); WI 1991-92 (Eng A). 1000 runs (9); most – 1518 (1990). HS 187 v Lancs (Manchester) 1993. BB 1-9. CC BB 1-14. Awards: NWT 2; BHC 3. LO HS 167* v Kent (Nottingham) 1993 (SL).

LUCAS, David Scott (Djanogoly CTC, Nottingham), b Nottingham 19 Aug 1978. 6'2". RHB, LMF. Debut 1999. HS 24* v Essex (Nottingham) 1999. BB 5-104 v Essex (Nottingham) 1999. LO HS 19* v Sussex (Hove) 1999 (NL). LO BB 3-49 v Derbys (Derby) 1999 (NL).

‡**MILLNS, David** James (Garibaldi CS), b Clipstone, Notts 27 Feb 1965. 6'3". LHB, RF. Nottinghamshire 1988-89. Leicestershire 1990-99; cap 1991; benefit 1999. Boland 1996-97. Tours: A 1992-93 (Eng A); SA 1996-97 (Le). HS 121 Le v Northants (Northampton) 1997. 50 wkts (4); most – 76 (1994). BB 9-37 (12-91 match) Le v Derbys (Derby) 1991. Awards: NWT 1; BHC 1. LO HS 39* Le v Warwks (Birmingham) 1996 (BHC). LO BB 4-26 Le v Durham (Stockton) 1995 (BHC).

‡**MORRIS, John** Edward (Shavington CS; Dane Bank CFE), b Crewe, Cheshire 1 Apr 1964. 5'10". RHB, RM. Derbyshire 1982-93; cap 1986. GW 1988-89 and 1993-94. Durham 1994-99; cap 1998; benefit 1999. **Tests:** 3 (1990); HS 32 v I (Oval) 1990. **LOI:** 8 (1990-91); HS 63* v NZ (Adelaide) 1990-91. Tour: A 1990-91. 1000 runs (11); most – 1739 (1986). HS 229 De v Glos (Cheltenham) 1993. BB 1-6 (De). Awards: NWT 2; BHC 2. LO HS 145 Du v Leics (Leicester) 1996 (BHC). LO BB (GW) 1-44 (NS).

NEWELL, Michael (West Bridgford CS), b Blackburn, Lancs 25 Feb 1965. 5'8". RHB, LB. Nottinghamshire 1984-92; cap 1987; benefit 1999. 2nd XI manager/captain – no f-c appearances since 1992. 1000 runs (1): 1054 (1987). HS 203* v Derbys (Derby) 1987. BB 2-38 v SL (Nottingham) 1988. CC BB 1-0. LO HS 109* v Essex (Southend) 1990 (SL).

NOON, Wayne Michael (Caistor S), b Grimsby, Lincs 5 Feb 1971. 5'9". RHB, WK. Northamptonshire 1989-93. Nottinghamshire debut 1994; cap 1995. Canterbury 1994-95. Worcs 2nd XI debut when aged 15yr 199d. Tours: SA 1991-92 (Nh), 1996-97 (Nt). HS 83 v Northants (Northampton) 1997. LO HS 46 v Warwks (Birmingham) 1998 (BHC).

ORAM, Andrew Richard (Roade CS), b Northampton 7 Mar 1975. 6'2". RHB, RM. Debut 1997. HS 13 and BB 4-37 v Surrey (Nottingham) 1998. LO HS 1* (BHC). LO BB 4-45 v Glam (Colwyn Bay) 1997 (SL).

RANDALL, Stephen John (W Bridgford S), b Nottingham 9 Jun 1980. 5'10". RHB, OB. Debut 1999. HS 20 v Glam (Colwyn Bay) 1999. LO HS (Notts Board) 1 (NWT).

READ, Christopher Mark Wells (Torquay GS; Bath U), b Paignton, Devon 10 Aug 1978. 5'8". RHB, WK. Gloucestershire (L-O) 1997. Nottinghamshire debut 1998; cap 1999. Devon 1995-97. **Tests:** 3 (1999); HS 37 v NZ (Lord's) 1999. **LOI**: 9 (1999-00); HS 26* v SA (Cape Town) 1999-00. Tours (Eng A): SA 1998-99, 1999-00 (Eng); SL 1997-98; Z 1998-99; K 1997-98. HS 160 v Warwks (Nottingham) 1999. LO HS 62 v Somerset (Nottingham) 1999 (NL).

‡**SHOAIB AKHTAR** (Elliott HS; Government C, Rawalpindi), b Rawalpindi, Pakistan 13 Aug 1975. 5'11½". RHB, RF. PIA 1994-95 to 1995-96. Rawalpindi 1994-95 to date. ADBP 1996-97 to date. **Tests** (P): 13 (1997-98 to 1999-00); HS 11 v Z (Lahore) 1998-99; BB 5-43 v SA (Durban) 1997-98. **LOI** (P): 37 (1997-98 to 1999-00); HS 36 v A (Karachi) 1998-99. BB 4-37 v E (Sharjah) 1998-99. Tours (P): E (Pak A) 1997; A 1999-00; SA 1997-98; I 1998-99; Z 1997-98; B 1998-99. HS 23 Rawalpindi v Karachi Whites (Karachi) 1996-97. 50 wkts (0+1): 69 (1996-97). BB 6-69 Rawalpindi B v Lahore City (Lahore) 1994-95. LO HS 36 (*see LOI*). LO BB 4-37 (*see LOI*).

STEMP, Richard David (Britannia HS, Rowley Regis), b Erdington, Birmingham 11 Dec 1967. 6'0". RHB, SLA. Worcestershire 1990-92. Yorkshire 1993-98; cap 1996. Nottinghamshire debut 1999. Tours (Eng A): SA 1992-93 (Y); I 1994-95; P 1995-96. HS 65 Y v Durham (Chester-le-St) 1996. Nt HS 18 v Sussex (Hove) 1999. BB 6-37 Y v Durham (Durham) 1994. Nt BB 4-114 v Lancs (Manchester) 1999. Award: BHC 1. LO HS 29* v Somerset (Nottingham) 1999 (NL). LO BB 4-25 Y v Glos (Bristol) 1996 (SL).

TOLLEY, Christopher Mark (King Edward VI C, Stourbridge; Loughborough U), b Kidderminster, Worcs 30 Dec 1967. 5'9". RHB, LMF. Worcestershire 1989-95; cap 1993. Nottinghamshire debut 1996; cap 1997. Tours (Wo): SA 1996-97 (Nt); Z 1990-91, 1993-94. HS 84 Wo v Derbys (Derby) 1994. Nt HS 78 v Glos (Nottingham) 1998. BB 7-45 v Worcs (Kidderminster) 1998. Hat-trick 1997. Awards: NWT 1; BHC 1. LO HS 77 v Somerset (Nottingham) 1998 (NWT) and 77 Comb U v Lancs (Cambridge) 1990 (BHC). LO BB 5-16 v Hants (Southampton) 1996 (SL).

WELTON, Guy Edward (Healing CS; Grimsby C), b Grimsby, Lincs 4 May 1978. 6'1". RHB, OB. Debut 1997. MCC YC. HS 95 v Sussex (Hove) 1997. LO HS 104* v Durham (Nottingham) 1999 (NL).

WHILEY, Matthew Jeffrey Allen (Harry Carlton CS, Nottingham), b Clifton, Nottingham 6 May 1980. 6'5½". RHB, LMF. Debut 1998. HS 0*. BB 1-44. CC BB 1-66.

RELEASED/RETIRED

(Having made a first-class County appearance in 1999)

ARCHER, Graeme Francis (Heron Brook Middle S; King Edward VI HS, Stafford), b Carlisle, Cumberland 26 Sep 1970. 6'1". RHB, OB. Nottinghamshire 1992-99; cap 1995. Staffordshire 1990. Tour (Nt): SA 1996-97. 1000 runs (1): 1171 (1995). HS 168 v Glam (Worksop) 1994. BB 3-18 v Hants (Southampton) 1996. Awards: BHC 2. LO HS 111* v Durham (Nottingham) 1997 (BHC). LO BB 2-16 v Surrey (Guildford) 1995 (SL).

BATES, Richard Terry (Bourne GS; Stamford CFE), b Stamford, Lincs 17 Jun 1972. 6'1". RHB, OB. Nottinghamshire 1993-99. Lincolnshire 1990-91. HS 34 v Worcs (Worcester) 1996. BB 5-88 v Durham (Chester-le-St) 1995. Award: BHC 1. LO HS 28* v Derbys (Derby) 1998 (SL). LO BB 3-21 v Scot (Nottingham) 1996 (BHC).

DOWMAN, M.P. – *see DERBYSHIRE.*

DRAKES, Vasbert Conneil (St Lucy SS), b St James, Barbados 5 Aug 1969. 6'2". RHB, RFM. Barbados 1991-92 to date. Sussex 1996-97; cap 1996. Border 1996-97 to date. Nottinghamshire 1999; cap 1999. **LOI** (WI): 5 (1994-95); HS 16 v A (P-o-S) 1994-95; BB 1-36. Tour (WI): E 1995. HS 180* Barbados v Leeward Is (Anguilla) 1994-95. CC HS 145* Sx v Essex (Chelmsford) 1996. Nt HS 80 v Kent (Nottingham) 1999. 50 wkts (2+1); most – 80 (1999). BB 8-59 Border v Natal (Durban) 1996-97. Nt BB 6-39 (12-110 match) v Warwks (Nottingham) 1999. LO HS 104 Border v Boland (Paarl) 1996-97 (SBC). LO BB 5-19 v Ire (Hove) 1996 (BHC). Took 4 wkts in 4 balls v Derbys (Nottingham) 1999 (NL).

EVANS, Kevin Paul (Colonel Frank Seely S) b Calverton 10 Sep 1963. Elder brother of R.J. (Notts 1987-90). 6'2". RHB, RMF. Nottinghamshire 1984-99; cap 1990; benefit 1998. HS 104 v Surrey (Nottingham) 1992 and 104 v Sussex (Nottingham) 1994. BB 6-40 v Lancs (Manchester) 1997. Awards: BHC 2. LO HS 55* v Derbys (Derby) 1990 (RAC). LO BB 6-10 v Northumb (Jesmond) 1994 (NWT). Joins Shropshire 2000.

continued on p 75

NOTTINGHAMSHIRE 1999

RESULTS SUMMARY

	Place	*Won*	*Lost*	*Tied*	*Drew*	*No Result*
PPP County Championship	**17th**	4	11		2	
All First-Class Matches		4	11		4	
NatWest Trophy	4th Round					
CGU National League (Division 2)	**5th**	6	8			2

COUNTY CHAMPIONSHIP AVERAGES

BATTING AND FIELDING

Cap		*M*	*I*	*NO*	*HS*	*Runs*	*Avge*	*100*	*50*	*Ct/St*
1986	P.Johnson	15	28	3	126	1090	43.60	1	10	10
1998	J.E.R.Gallian	17	32	2	120*	935	31.16	2	5	18
–	U.Afzaal	14	27	1	104	781	30.03	1	6	4
1998	M.P.Dowman	7	13	3	67*	293	29.30	–	1	5
1983	R.T.Robinson	12	22	1	80	525	25.00	–	4	10
–	N.A.Gie	3	4	1	36	72	24.00	–	–	–
1999	C.M.W.Read	14	25	–	160	572	22.88	1	1	47/1
1995	G.F.Archer	14	27	1	81	503	19.34	–	2	27
–	A.G.Wharf	14	25	3	78	366	16.63	–	2	8
–	G.E.Welton	7	14	–	76	222	15.85	–	1	3
1999	V.C.Drakes	17	30	3	80	427	15.81	–	2	5
1999	P.J.Franks	16	27	3	61	348	14.50	–	1	2
–	D.S.Lucas	4	6	2	24*	55	13.75	–	–	–
1997	C.M.Tolley	4	8	–	51	106	13.25	–	1	–
1997	M.N.Bowen	11	21	8	19	130	10.00	–	–	2
–	S.J.Randall	3	5	1	20	30	7.50	–	–	3
–	R.D.Stemp	11	17	5	18	74	6.16	–	–	1
1995	W.M.Noon	3	5	–	8	22	4.40	–	–	9

Also batted (1 match): R.T.Bates 0.

BOWLING

	O	*M*	*R*	*W*	*Avge*	*Best*	*5wI*	*10wM*
V.C.Drakes	586.2	131	1794	80	22.42	6- 39	5	2
M.N.Bowen	264	53	872	37	23.56	5- 66	1	–
P.J.Franks	513	124	1489	63	23.63	5- 52	1	–
A.G.Wharf	297.3	57	1100	30	36.66	4- 30	–	–
R.D.Stemp	288.5	70	905	15	60.33	4-114	–	–

Also bowled: U.Afzaal 41.1-6-172-3; R.T.Bates 13-0-83-0; M.P.Dowman 30-8-84-0; J.E.R.Gallian 29.4-7-98-5; D.S.Lucas 67.5-9-269-9; S.J.Randall 77-18-237-0; C.M.Tolley 85-20-199-5.

The First-Class Averages (pp 113-128) give the records of Nottinghamshire players in all first-class county matches (Nottinghamshire's other opponents being Cambridge University and Oxford University), with the exception of:

C.M.W.Read 16-27-1-160-615-23.65-1-1-49ct-1st. Did not bowl.

NOTTINGHAMSHIRE RECORDS

FIRST-CLASS CRICKET

Highest Total	For	739-7d		v	Leics	Nottingham	1903
	V	781-7d		by	Northants	Northampton	1995
Lowest Total	For	13		v	Yorkshire	Nottingham	1901
	V	16		by	Derbyshire	Nottingham	1879
		16		by	Surrey	The Oval	1880
Highest Innings	For	312*	W.W.Keeton	v	Middlesex	The Oval	1939
	V	345	C.G.Macartney	for	Australians	Nottingham	1921

Highest Partnership for each Wicket

1st	391	A.O.Jones/A.Shrewsbury	v	Glos	Bristol	1899
2nd	398	A.Shrewsbury/W.Gunn	v	Sussex	Nottingham	1890
3rd	369	W.Gunn/J.R.Gunn	v	Leics	Nottingham	1903
4th	361	A.O.Jones/J.R.Gunn	v	Essex	Leyton	1905
5th	266	A.Shrewsbury/W.Gunn	v	Sussex	Hove	1884
6th	303*	F.H.Winrow/P.F.Harvey	v	Derbyshire	Nottingham	1947
7th	301	C.C.Lewis/B.N.French	v	Durham	Chester-le-St	1993
8th	220	G.F.H.Heane/R.Winrow	v	Somerset	Nottingham	1935
9th	170	J.C.Adams/K.P.Evans	v	Somerset	Taunton	1994
10th	152	E.B.Alletson/W.Riley	v	Sussex	Hove	1911

Best Bowling	For	10-66	K.Smales	v	Glos	Stroud	1956
(Innings)	V	10-10	H.Verity	for	Yorkshire	Leeds	1932
Best Bowling	For	17-89	F.C.Matthews	v	Northants	Nottingham	1923
(Match)	V	17-89	W.G.Grace	for	Glos	Cheltenham	1877

Most Runs – Season	2620	W.W.Whysall	(av 53.46)	1929
Most Runs – Career	31592	G.Gunn	(av 35.69)	1902-32
Most 100s – Season	9	W.W.Whysall		1928
	9	M.J.Harris		1971
	9	B.C.Broad		1990
Most 100s – Career	65	J.Hardstaff jr		1930-55
Most Wkts – Season	181	B.Dooland	(av 14.96)	1954
Most Wkts – Career	1653	T.G.Wass	(av 20.34)	1896-1920

LIMITED-OVERS CRICKET

Highest Total	**NWT**	344-6		v	Northumb	Jesmond	1994
	BHC	296-6		v	Kent	Nottingham	1989
	NL	329-6		v	Derbyshire	Nottingham	1993
Lowest Total	**NWT**	123		v	Yorkshire	Scarborough	1969
	BHC	74		v	Leics	Leicester	1987
	NL	66		v	Yorkshire	Bradford	1969
Highest Innings	**NWT**	149*	D.W.Randall	v	Devon	Torquay	1988
	BHC	130*	C.E.B.Rice	v	Scotland	Glasgow	1982
	NL	167*	P.Johnson	v	Kent	Nottingham	1993
Best Bowling	**NWT**	6-10	K.P.Evans	v	Northumb	Jesmond	1994
	BHC	6-22	M.K.Bore	v	Leics	Leicester	1980
		6-22	C.E.B.Rice	v	Northants	Northampton	1981
	NL	6-12	R.J.Hadlee	v	Lancashire	Nottingham	1980

SOMERSET

Formation of Present Club: 18 August 1875
Colours: Black, White and Maroon
Badge: Somerset Dragon
County Champions: (0); best – 3rd 1892, 1958, 1963, 1966, 1981
NatWest Trophy/Gillette Cup Winners: (2) 1979, 1983
Benson and Hedges Cup Winners: (2) 1981, 1982
CGU National League (Div 1) Winners: (0); best – 2nd (Div 2) 1999
Sunday League Winners: (1) 1979
Match Awards: NWT 55; BHC 65

Chief Executive: P.W.Anderson, The County Ground, Taunton TA1 1JT ▲ Tel: 01823 272946 ▲ Fax: 01823 332395 ▲ Email: Somerset@ecb.co.uk ▲ Web: None.

Captain/Overseas Player: J.Cox. **Vice-Captain:** M.E.Trescothick.
2000 Beneficiary: P.D.Bowler. **Scorer:** G.A.Stickley. ‡ New registration

‡BLACKWELL, Ian David (Brookfield Community S), b Chesterfield, Derbys 10 Jun 1978. HS 62* De v Worcs (Kidderminster) 1999. BB 5-115 De v Surrey (Oval) 1998. LO HS 97 De v Glam (Derby) 1999 (NL). LO BB 3-17 De v Middx (Southgate) 1999 (NL).

BOWLER, Peter Duncan (Educated at Canberra, Australia), b Plymouth, Devon 30 Jul 1963. 6'1". RHB, OB, occ WK. Leicestershire 1986 – first to score hundred on f-c debut for Leics (100* and 62 v Hants). Tasmania 1986-87. Derbyshire 1988-94; cap 1989; scored 155* v CU (Cambridge) on debut – first instance of hundreds on debut for two counties. Somerset debut/cap 1995; captain 1997-98; benefit 2000. 1000 runs (8) inc 2000 (1): 2044 (1992). HS 241* De v Hants (Portsmouth) 1992. Sm HS 207 v Surrey (Taunton) 1996. BB 3-25 v Northants (Taunton) 1998. Awards: BHC 4. LO HS 138* De v Somerset (Derby) 1993 (SL). LO BB 3-31 De v Glos (Cheltenham) 1991 (SL).

BULBECK, Matthew Paul Leonard (Taunton S; Richard Huish C), b Taunton 8 Nov 1979. 6'3½". LHB, LMF. Debut 1998. HS 76* v Durham (Chester-le-St) 1999. 50 wkts (1): 51 (1999). BB 5-45 v Northants (Northampton) 1999. LO HS 5 (NL). LO BB 4-40 v Notts (Nottingham) 1999 (NL).

BURNS, Michael (Walney CS), b Barrow-in-Furness, Lancs 6 Jun 1969. 6'0". RHB, RM, WK. Cumberland 1988-90. Warwickshire 1992-96. Somerset debut 1997; cap 1999. HS 109 v Leics (Taunton) 1999. BB 2-18 v Kent (Taunton) 1997. Award: BHC 1. LO HS 115* v Middx (Taunton) 1997 (SL). LO BB 4-39 v Glos (Taunton) 1997 (SL).

CADDICK, Andrew Richard (Papanui HS), b Christchurch, NZ 21 Nov 1968. Son of English emigrants – qualified for England 1992. 6'5". RHB, RFM. Debut 1991; cap 1992; benefit 1999. Represented NZ in 1987-88 Youth World Cup. **ECB contract 2000. Tests:** 30 (1993 to 1999-00); HS 48 v SA (Jo'burg) 1999-00; BB 7-46 v SA (Durban) 1999-00. **LOI**: 18 (1993 to 1999-00); HS 21* v Z (Harare) 1999-00; BB 4-19 v SA (Jo'burg) 1999-00. Tours: A 1992-93 (Eng A); SA 1999-00; WI 1993-94, 1997-98; NZ 1996-97; Z 1996-97. HS 92 v Worcs (Worcester) 1995. 50 wkts (7) inc 100 (1): 105 (1998). BB 9-32 (12-120 match) v Lancs (Taunton) 1993. Awards: NWT 2. LO HS 39 v Hants (Taunton) 1996 (SL). LO BB 6-30 v Glos (Taunton) 1992 (NWT).

COX, Jamie (Wynyard HS; Deakin U), b Burnie, Tasmania, Australia 15 Oct 1969. 6'0". RHB, OB. Tasmania 1987-88 to date; vice-captain 1996-97 to date. Somerset debut/cap 1999; captain 1999 to date. Tours: Z 1991-92 (Aus B), 1995-96 (Tas). 1000 runs (1+1); most – 1617 (1999). HS 245 Tas v NSW (Hobart) 1999-00. Sm HS 216 v Hants (Southampton) 1999. BB 3-46 v Middx (Taunton) 1999. Awards: NWT 2. LO HS 114 v Surrey (Taunton) 1999 (NWT). LO BB 3-28 v Durham (Taunton) 1999 (NL).

‡**GAZZARD, Carl** Matthew (Mounts Bay S; Richard Huish C), b Penzance, Cornwall 15 Apr 1982. RHB, WK. Cornwall 1998-99. Staff 2000 – awaiting f-c debut. LO HS 16 Cornwall v Cumb (Kendal) 1999 (NWT).

‡**GROVE, Jamie** Oliver (Bury St Edmunds County Upper S), b Bury St Edmunds, Suffolk 3 Jul 1979. 6'1". RHB, RMF. Debut 1998. HS 33 and BB 3-74 v Surrey (Chelmsford) 1998.

HOLLOWAY, Piran Christopher Laity (Millfield S; Taunton S; Loughborough U), b Helston, Cornwall 1 Oct 1970. 5'8". LHB, WK. Warwickshire 1988-93. Somerset debut 1994; cap 1997. Award: NWT 1. HS 168 v Middx (Uxbridge) 1996. LO HS 117 v Glos (Taunton) 1997 (SL).

JARVIS, Paul William (Bydales CS, Marske), b Redcar, Yorks 29 Jun 1965. 5'10". RHB, RFM. Yorkshire 1981-93; cap 1986; youngest Yorkshire debutant at 16yr 75d. Sussex 1994-98; cap 1994. Somerset debut 1999. **Tests:** 9 (1987-88 to 1992-93); HS 29* and BB 4-107 v WI (Lord's) 1988. **LOI:** 16 (1987-88 to 1993); HS 16* v SL (Colombo) 1992-93; BB 5-35 v I (Bangalore) 1992-93. Tours: SA 1989-90 (Eng XI); WI 1986-87 (Y); NZ 1987-88; I/SL 1992-93; P 1987-88. HS 80 Y v Northants (Scarborough) 1992. Sm HS 20 v Sussex (Taunton) 1999. 50 wkts (4); most – 81 (1987). BB 7-55 Y v Surrey (Leeds) 1986. Sm BB 4-76 v Notts (Nottingham) 1999. Hat-trick 1985 (Y). Award: BHC 1. LO HS 63 Sx v Kent (Canterbury) 1997 (BHC). LO BB 6-27 Y v Somerset (Taunton) 1989 (SL).

JONES, Ian (Fyndoune Community C, Sacriston), b Edmonton, Middx 11 Mar 1977. 6'4". RHB, RFM. Debut 1999. HS 35 v Durham (Chester-le-St) 1999. BB 3-81 v NZ (Taunton) 1999. CC BB 2-102 v Kent (Taunton) 1999. LO HS 5* (NL). LO BB 1-53 (NL).

JONES, Philip Steffan (Stradey CS, Llanelli; Neath TC; Loughborough U; Homerton C, Cambridge), b Llanelli, Wales 9 Feb 1974. 6'2". RHB, RMF. Cambridge U 1997; blue 1997. Somerset debut 1997. Wales MC 1992-96. HS 105 v NZ (Taunton) 1999. CC HS 46 v Middx (Taunton) 1999. BB 6-67 CU v OU (Lord's) 1997. Sm BB 4-126 v Essex (Chelmsford) 1999. LO HS 26* Wales MC v Middx (Northop Hall) 1994 (NWT). LO BB 5-23 v Warwks (Taunton) 1998 (SL).

KENNIS, Gregor John (Tiffin S), b Yokohama, Japan 9 Mar 1974. 6'1". RHB, OB. MCC YC. Surrey 1994-97. Scored Surrey 2nd XI record 258 (395 balls, 41 fours) v Leics 2nd XI (Kibworth) 1995. Somerset debut 1998. HS 175 v NZ (Taunton) 1999. CC HS 49 v Derbys (Taunton) 1998. LO HS (Sy) 5 (SL).

KERR, Jason Ian Douglas (Withins HS; Bolton C), b Bolton, Lancs 7 Apr 1974. 6'2". RHB, RMF. Debut 1993. HS 80 v WI (Taunton) 1995. CC HS 68* v Derbys (Taunton) 1996. BB 7-23 v Leics (Taunton) 1999. LO HS 56 v Middx (Southgate) 1999 (NL). LO BB 4-28 v Hants (Basingstoke) 1997 (SL).

LATHWELL, Mark Nicholas (Braunton S, Devon), b Bletchley, Bucks 26 Dec 1971. 5'8". RHB, RM. Debut 1991; cap 1992. YC 1993. MCC YC. **Tests:** 2 (1993); HS 33 v A (Nottingham) 1993. Tours (Eng A): A 1992-93; SA 1993-94. 1000 runs (5); most – 1230 (1994). HS 206 v Surrey (Bath) 1994. BB 2-21 v Sussex (Hove) 1994. Awards: NWT 1; BHC 2. LO HS 121 v Middx (Lord's) 1996 (BHC). LO BB 1-23 (NWT).

PARSONS, Keith Alan (The Castle S, Taunton; Richard Huish C), b Taunton 2 May 1973. Identical twin brother of K.J. (Somerset staff 1992-94). 6'1". RHB, RM. Debut 1992; cap 1999. HS 105 v Young A (Taunton) 1995. CC HS 83* v Middx (Uxbridge) 1996. BB 5-57 v Durham (Chester-le-St) 1999. LO HS 56 v Sussex (Hove) 1996 (SL). LO BB 4-43 v Surrey (Taunton) 1999 (NWT).

PIERSON, Adrian Roger Kirshaw (Kent C, Canterbury; Hatfield Poly), b Enfield, Middx 21 Jul 1963. 6'4". RHB, OB. Warwickshire 1985-91. Leicestershire 1993-97; cap 1995. Somerset debut 1998. Cambridgeshire 1992. MCC YC. Tour (Le): SA 1996-97. HS 108* v Sussex (Hove) 1998. 50 wkts (1): 69 (1995). BB 8-42 Le v Warwks (Birmingham) 1994. Sm BB 5-117 v Glam (Cardiff) 1998. Awards: NWT 1; BHC 1. LO HS 29* Le v Kent (Leicester) 1994 (SL). LO BB 5-36 Le v Derbys (Leicester) 1995 (SL).

ROSE, Graham David (Northumberland Park S, Tottenham), b Tottenham, London 12 Apr 1964. 6'4". RHB, RM. Middlesex 1985-86. Somerset debut 1987; cap 1988; benefit 1997. 1000 runs (1): 1000 (1990). HS 191 v Sussex (Taunton) 1997. 50 wkts (5); most – 63 (1997). BB 7-47 (13-88 match) v Notts (Taunton) 1996. Awards: BHC 4. LO HS 148 v Glam (Neath) 1990 (SL). LO BB 4-21 v Ire (Erlington) 1995 (BHC).

‡**TREGO, Peter** David, b Weston-super-Mare 12 Jun 1981. RHB, RM. Staff 2000 – awaiting f-c debut. LO HS 0 and LO BB 2-42 Somerset Board v Beds (Taunton) 1999 (NWT).

TRESCOTHICK, Marcus Edward (Sir Bernard Lovell S), b Keynsham 25 Dec 1975. 6'2". LHB, RM. Debut 1993; cap 1999. Tours (Eng A): NZ 1999-00; B 1999-00. HS 190 v Middx (Taunton) 1999. BB 4-36 (inc hat-trick) v Young A (Taunton) 1995. CC BB 4-82 v Yorks (Leeds) 1998. Hat-trick 1995. Award: NWT 1. LO HS 122 v Ire (Erlington) 1995 (BHC). LO BB 3-46 v Surrey (Oval) 1998 (BHC).

TUCKER, Joseph Peter (Colston Collegiate S; Richard Huish C), b Bath 14 Sep 1979. 6'3". RHB, RMF. Staff 1998 – awaiting f-c debut. 2nd XI debut 1995 when aged 15y 257d.

TURNER, Robert Julian (Millfield S; Magdalene C, Cambridge), b Malvern, Worcs 25 Nov 1967. 6'1½". RHB, WK. Brother of S.J. (Somerset 1984-85). Cambridge U 1988-91; blue 1988-89-90-91; captain 1991. Somerset debut 1991; cap 1994. Tours (Eng A): NZ 1999-00; B 1999-00. 1000 runs (2); most – 1217 (1999). HS 144 v Kent (Taunton) 1997. Award: BHC 1. LO HS 70 v Glam (Cardiff) 1996 (BHC).

RELEASED/RETIRED

(Having made a first-class County appearance in 1999)

MAHMOOD, Saqib, b Kettering, Northants 24 Aug 1977. RHB, LB. Somerset 1999 (no CC appearances). HS 7*.

HAMPSHIRE – RELEASED/RETIRED (continued from p 40)

McLEAN, Nixon Alexei McNamara (Carapan SS, St Vincent), b Stubbs, St Vincent 20 Jul 1973. 6'4". LHB, RF. Windward Is 1991-92 to date. Hampshire 1998-99; cap 1998. *Tests* (WI): 8 (1997-98 to 1998-99); HS 39 and BB 3-53 v SA (Cape Town) 1998-99. *LOI* (I): 21 (1996-97 to 1999-00); HS 39 v B (Dhaka) 1999-00; BB 3-41 v SA (Cape Town) 1998-99. Tours (WI): A 1996-97; SA 1997-98 (WI A), 1998-99. HS 70 v Surrey (Guildford) 1999. 50 wkts (1): 62 (1998). BB 7-28 WI v Free State (Bloemfontein) 1998-99. H BB 6-101 v Leics (Leicester) 1998. LO HS 41* Windward Is v Barbados (Essequibo) 1996-97 (SST). LO BB 3-21 Windward Is v Jamaica (Kingston) 1997-98 (RSB).

NOTTINGHAMSHIRE – RELEASED/RETIRED (continued from p 70)

GIE, Noel Addison (Trent C), b Pretoria, SA 12 Apr 1977. UK resident since 1984. Son of C.A. (WP and SAU 1970-71 to 1980-81). 6'0". RHB, RM. Nottinghamshire 1995-99. HS 59* v CU (Nottingham) 1999. CC HS 50 v Glos (Nottingham) 1998. Award: BHC 1. LO HS 75* v Kent (Nottingham) 1997 (SL).

ROBINSON, Robert **Timothy** (Dunstable GS; High Pavement SFC; Sheffield U), b Sutton in Ashfield 21 Nov 1958. 6'0". RHB, RM. Nottinghamshire 1978-99; cap 1983; captain 1988-95; benefit 1992. *Wisden* 1985. **Tests:** 29 (1984-85 to 1989); HS 175 v A (Leeds) 1985. **LOI**: 26 (1984-85 to 1988); HS 83 v P (Sharjah) 1986-87. Tours: A 1987-88; SA 1989-90 (Eng XI), 1996-97 (Nt); NZ 1987-88; WI 1985-86; I/SL 1984-85; P 1987-88. 1000 runs (14) inc 2000 (1): 2032 (1984). HS 220* v Yorks (Nottingham) 1990. BB 1-22. Awards: NWT 4; BHC 7. LO HS 139 v Worcs (Worcester) 1985 (NWT).

WHARF, A.G. – *see GLAMORGAN.*

SOMERSET 1999

RESULTS SUMMARY

	Place	Won	Lost	Tied	Drew	No Result
PPP County Championship	**4th**	6	4		7	
All First-Class Matches		6	5		8	
NatWest Trophy	Finalist					
CGU National League (Division 2)	**2nd**	13	3			

COUNTY CHAMPIONSHIP AVERAGES

BATTING AND FIELDING

Cap		*M*	*I*	*NO*	*HS*	*Runs*	*Avge*	*100*	*50*	*Ct/St*
1999	J.Cox	17	29	2	216	1478	54.74	5	6	7
1994	R.J.Turner	17	24	3	138*	1047	49.85	2	8	62/2
1995	P.D.Bowler	16	26	7	149	791	41.63	3	–	8
1999	M.E.Trescothick	13	21	–	190	829	39.47	2	3	26
–	M.P.L.Bulbeck	14	15	8	76*	265	37.85	–	1	1
1999	M.Burns	17	24	1	109	852	37.04	2	5	11
1988	G.D.Rose	8	10	1	123*	294	32.66	1	1	1
1997	P.C.L.Holloway	17	29	4	114*	798	31.92	2	4	9
1999	K.A.Parsons	14	19	3	80	475	29.68	–	3	9
–	P.S.Jones	8	12	3	46	175	19.44	–	–	3
–	J.I.D.Kerr	12	16	–	64	287	17.93	–	2	4
1992	A.R.Caddick	13	17	5	44	205	17.08	–	–	2
–	G.J.Kennis	2	4	–	24	46	11.50	–	–	2
–	P.W.Jarvis	6	8	–	20	73	9.12	–	–	2
–	A.R.K.Pierson	11	11	3	37	63	7.87	–	–	4

Also batted (2 matches): I.Jones 18*, 35.

BOWLING

	O	*M*	*R*	*W*	*Avge*	*Best*	*5wI*	*10wM*
A.R.Caddick	589.4	187	1488	71	20.95	8-113	4	–
M.P.L.Bulbeck	402.4	97	1376	50	27.52	5- 45	3	1
K.A.Parsons	263.2	76	723	24	30.12	5- 57	1	–
P.W.Jarvis	191.5	39	599	18	33.27	4- 76	–	–
J.I.D.Kerr	266.2	58	914	27	33.85	7- 23	1	–
G.D.Rose	206.2	55	636	17	37.41	4- 14	–	–
P.S.Jones	228.2	45	735	19	38.68	4-126	–	–
A.R.K.Pierson	226.2	42	628	11	57.09	4-131	–	–

Also bowled: P.D.Bowler 9.5-2-12-2; M.Burns 76-10-265-4; J.Cox 42-6-152-4; I.Jones 49-3-220-3; M.E.Trescothick 38-8-127-5.

The First-Class Averages (pp 113-128) give the records of Somerset players in all first-class county matches (Somerset's other opponents being the New Zealanders and Cambridge University), with the exception of A.R.Caddick whose full county figures are as above.

SOMERSET RECORDS

FIRST-CLASS CRICKET

Highest Total	For 675-9d		v	Hampshire	Bath	1924
	V 811		by	Surrey	The Oval	1899
Lowest Total	For 25		v	Glos	Bristol	1947
	V 22		by	Glos	Bristol	1920
Highest Innings	For 322	I.V.A.Richards	v	Warwicks	Taunton	1985
	V 424	A.C.MacLaren	for	Lancashire	Taunton	1895

Highest Partnership for each Wicket

1st	346	H.T.Hewett/L.C.H.Palairet	v	Yorkshire	Taunton	1892
2nd	290	J.C.W.MacBryan/M.D.Lyon	v	Derbyshire	Burton upon T	1924
3rd	319	P.M.Roebuck/M.D.Crowe	v	Leics	Taunton	1984
4th	310	P.W.Denning/I.T.Botham	v	Glos	Taunton	1980
5th	235	J.C.White/C.C.C.Case	v	Glos	Taunton	1927
6th	265	W.E.Alley/K.E.Palmer	v	Northants	Northampton	1961
7th	279	R.J.Harden/G.D.Rose	v	Sussex	Taunton	1997
8th	172	I.V.A.Richards/I.T.Botham	v	Leics	Leicester	1983
	172	A.R.K.Pierson/P.S.Jones	v	N Zealanders	Taunton	1999
9th	183	C.H.M.Greetham/H.W.Stephenson	v	Leics	Weston-s-Mare	1963
	183	C.J.Tavaré/N.A.Mallender	v	Sussex	Hove	1990
10th	143	J.J.Bridges/A.H.D.Gibbs	v	Essex	Weston-s-Mare	1919

Best Bowling	For	10- 49	E.J.Tyler	v	Surrey	Taunton	1895
(Innings)	V	10- 35	A.Drake	for	Yorkshire	Weston-s-Mare	1914
Best Bowling	For	16- 83	J.C.White	v	Worcs	Bath	1919
(Match)	V	17-137	W.Brearley	for	Lancashire	Manchester	1905

Most Runs – Season	2761	W.E.Alley	(av 58.74)	1961
Most Runs – Career	21142	H.Gimblett	(av 36.96)	1935-54
Most 100s – Season	11	S.J.Cook		1991
Most 100s – Career	49	H.Gimblett		1935-54
Most Wkts – Season	169	A.W.Wellard	(av 19.24)	1938
Most Wkts – Career	2166	J.C.White	(av 18.02)	1909-37

LIMITED-OVERS CRICKET

Highest Total	**NWT**	413-4		v	Devon	Torquay	1990
	BHC	349-7		v	Ireland	Taunton	1997
	NL	360-3		v	Glamorgan	Neath	1990
Lowest Total	**NWT**	59		v	Middlesex	Lord's	1977
	BHC	98		v	Middlesex	Lord's	1982
	NL	58		v	Essex	Chelmsford	1977
Highest Innings	**NWT**	162*	C.J.Tavaré	v	Devon	Torquay	1990
	BHC	177	S.J.Cook	v	Sussex	Hove	1990
	NL	175*	I.T.Botham	v	Northants	Wellingborough	1986
Best Bowling	**NWT**	7-15	R.P.Lefebvre	v	Devon	Torquay	1990
	BHC	7-24	Mushtaq Ahmed	v	Ireland	Taunton	1997
	NL	6-24	I.V.A.Richards	v	Lancashire	Manchester	1983

SURREY

Formation of Present Club: 22 August 1845
Colours: Chocolate
Badge: Prince of Wales' Feathers
County Champions (since 1890): (16) 1890, 1891, 1892, 1894, 1895, 1899, 1914, 1952, 1953, 1954, 1955, 1956, 1957, 1958, 1971, 1999
Joint Champions: (1) 1950
NatWest Trophy/Gillette Cup Winners: (1) 1982
Benson and Hedges Cup Winners: (2) 1974, 1997
CGU National League (Div 1) Winners: (0); best – 6th (Div 2) 1999
Sunday League Winners: (1) 1996
Match Awards: NWT 50; BHC 67

Chief Executive: P.C.J.Sheldon, Kennington Oval, London, SE11 5SS ▲ Tel: (020) 7582 6660 ▲ Fax: (020) 7735 7769 ▲ Email: enquiries@surreyccc.co.uk ▲ Web: www.surreyccc.co.uk

Captain: A.J.Hollioake. **Vice-Captain:** No appointment. **Overseas Player:** Saqlain Mushtaq. **2000 Beneficiary:** G.P.Thorpe. **Scorer:** K.R.Booth. ‡ New registration

AMIN, Rupesh Mahesh (Riddlesdown HS; John Ruskin C; Croydon C), b Clapham, London 20 Aug 1977. 6'0". RHB, SLA. Debut 1997. HS 12 v Leics (Oval) 1998. BB 4-87 v Somerset (Oval) 1999. LO HS – (SL). LO BB 2-43 v Lancs (Oval) 1997 (SL).

BARRETT, Kevin Andrew Owen (Millfield S; Durham U), b Swansea, Glam 16 Nov 1975. 5'11½". LHB, RM. Devon 1997-98. Staff 1999 – awaiting f-c debut.

BATTY, Gareth Jon (Bingley GS), b Bradford, Yorks 13 Oct 1977. Younger brother of J.D. (Yorkshire and Somerset 1989-96). 5'11". RHB, OB. Yorkshire 1997. Surrey (L-O matches) 1998. Awaiting CC debut. HS 25* and BB 2-45 v SL A (Oval) 1999. LO HS 37 v Derbys (Oval) 1998 (SL). LO BB 1-32 (SL).

BATTY, Jonathan Neil (Wheatley Park S, Oxon; Repton S; Durham U; Keble C, Oxford), b Chesterfield, Derbys 18 Apr 1974. 5'10". RHB, WK. Minor C 1994. Comb U 1995. Oxford U 1996; blue 1996. Surrey debut 1997. Oxfordshire 1993 to date. HS 64 v SL A (Oval) 1999. CC HS 63 v Hants (Southampton) 1998. LO HS 40 v Derbys (Oval) 1998 (SL).

BICKNELL, Martin Paul (Robert Haining SS), b Guildford 14 Jan 1969. Younger brother of D.J. (*see NOTTINGHAMSHIRE*). 6'3". RHB, RFM. Debut 1986; cap 1989; benefit 1997. **Tests:** 2 (1993); HS 14 and BB 3-99 v A (Birmingham) 1993. **LOI:** 7 (1990-91); HS 31* v A (Perth) 1990-91; BB 3-55 v NZ (Christchurch) 1990-91. Tours: A 1990-91; SA 1993-94 (Eng A); Z 1989-90 (Eng A). HS 88 v Hants (Southampton) 1992. 50 wkts (8); most – 71 (1992, 1999). BB 9-45 v CU (Oval) 1988. CC BB 7-52 v Sussex (Oval) 1991. Awards: BHC 3. LO HS 66* v Northants (Oval) 1991 (NWT). LO BB 7-30 v Glam (Oval) 1999 (NL).

BISHOP, Ian Emlyn (Castle S; Somerset C of Art & Tech), b Taunton, Somerset 26 Aug 1977. 6'1". RHB, RMF. Somerset 1996. Surrey debut 1999. HS 7*. BB 2-45 v Derbys (Derby) 1999. LO HS 15* v Middx (Lord's) 1999 (NL). LO BB 4-34 v Durham (Oval) 1999 (NL).

BROWN, Alistair Duncan (Caterham S), b Beckenham, Kent 11 Feb 1970. 5'10". RHB, occ LB. Debut 1992; cap 1994. **LOI:** 13 (1996 to 1998-99); HS 118 v I (Manchester) 1996. 1000 runs (5); most – 1382 (1993). HS 265 v Middx (Lord's) 1999. Awards: BHC 2. LO HS 203 v Hants (Guildford) 1997 (SL). LO BB 1-20 (NL).

BUTCHER, Gary Paul (Trinity S; Riddlesdown S; Heath Clark C), b Clapham, London 11 Mar 1975. Son of A.R. (Surrey, Glam and England 1972-92); brother of M.A. 5'9". RHB, RM. Glamorgan 1994-98. Surrey debut 1999. Tours (Gm): SA 1995-96; Z 1994-95. HS 101* Gm v OU (Oxford) 1997. CC HS 89 Gm v Northants (Northampton) 1996. Sy HS 70 v Warwks (Birmingham) 1999. BB 7-77 v Glos (Bristol) 1996. Sy BB 1-19. LO HS 48 Gm v Beds (Cardiff) 1997 (NWT). LO BB 4-32 Gm v Glos (Bristol) 1996 (SL).

BUTCHER, Mark Alan (Trinity S; Archbishop Tenison's S, Croydon), b Croydon 23 Aug 1972. Son of A.R. (Surrey, Glamorgan and England 1972-92); brother of G.P. 5'11". LHB, RM/OB. Debut 1992; cap 1996. **Tests**: 27 (1997 to 1999-00); HS 116 v SA (Leeds) 1998 and 116 v A (Brisbane) 1998-99; BB 2-32 v SA (Durban) 1999-00. Tours: A 1996-97 (Eng A), 1998-99; SA 1999-00; WI 1997-98. 1000 runs (5); most – 1604 (1996). HS 259 v Leics (Leicester) 1999. BB 4-30 v Lancs (Oval) 1999. Awards: NWT 1; BHC 1. LO HS 91 v Somerset (Oval) 1996 (NWT). LO BB 3-23 v Sussex (Oval) 1992 (SL).

CARBERRY, Michael Alexander (St John Rigby C), b Croydon 29 Sep 1980. 6'0". LHB, OB. Summer contract – awaiting f-c debut. LO HS 19 Surrey Board v Norfolk (Guildford) 1999 (NWT).

GREENIDGE, Carl Gary (Lodge S and St Michael S, Barbados; Heathcote S, Chingford; W Hatch HS; City of Westminster C), b Basingstoke, Hants 20 Apr 1978. Son of C.G. (Hampshire, Barbados and West Indies 1970-92). 5'10". RHB, RMF. MCC YC. Debut 1999. HS 14 v SL A (Oval) 1999. CC HS 2. BB 5-60 (8-124 match) v Yorks (Oval) 1999 – on CC debut. LO HS 2* (NL). LO BB – (NL).

HOLLIOAKE, Adam John (St Joseph's C, Sydney; St Patrick's C, Ballarat; St George's C, Weybridge; Surrey Tutorial C), b Melbourne, Australia 5 Sep 1971. Brother of B.C. 5'11". RHB, RMF. Debut 1993, scoring 13 and 123 v Derbys (Ilkeston); cap 1995; captain 1997 to date. Qualified for England 1992. **Tests**: 4 (1997 to 1997-98); HS 45 and BB 2-31 v A (Nottingham) 1997 – on debut. **LOI:** 35 (1996 to 1999, 14 as captain); HS 83* v SA (Dhaka) 1998-99; BB 4-23 v P (Birmingham) 1996 – on debut. Tours: A 1996-97 (Eng A – captain); WI 1997-98. 1000 runs (2); most – 1522 (1996). HS 182 v Middx (Lord's) 1997. BB 5-62 v Glam (Swansea) 1998. Awards: NWT 1; BHC 1. LO HS 93 v Kent (Canterbury) 1995 (SL). LO BB 5-38 v Kent (Canterbury) 1997 (SL).

HOLLIOAKE, Benjamin Caine (Millfield S), b Melbourne, Australia 11 Nov 1977. Brother of A.J. 6'2". RHB, RFM. Debut 1996; cap 1999. YC 1997. **Tests**: 2 (1997 to 1998); HS 28 v A (Nottingham) 1997 on debut; BB 2-105 v SL (Oval) 1998. **LOI:** 7 (1997 to 1998-99); HS 63 v A (Lord's) 1997 – on debut; BB 2-43 v WI (P-o-S) 1997-98. Tours: A 1998-99; SL (Eng A) 1997-98. HS 163 Eng A v SL A (Moratuwa) 1997-98. Sy 76 v Middx (Lord's) 1997. BB 5-51 v Glam (Oval) 1999. Awards: BHC 2. LO HS 98 v Kent (Lord's) 1997 (BHC). LO BB 5-10 v Derbys (Oval) 1996 (SL).

MURTAGH, Timothy James (John Fisher S), b Lambeth 2 Aug 1981. Nephew of A.J.Murtagh (Hants and E Province 1973-7). 6'0". LHB, RFM. Summer contract. Awaiting f-c debut.

PATTERSON, Mark William (Belfast Royal Academy; Ulster U), b Belfast, N Ireland 2 Feb 1974. Elder brother of A.D. (Ireland 1996). 6'1". RHB, RFM. Debut 1996, taking 6-80 v SA A (Oval). HS 4 and BB 6-80 (*see above*). CC HS 0 and BB 3-25 v Notts (Oval) 1999. LO HS (Ire) 9 (BHC). LO BB 3-48 Ire v Somerset (Eglington) 1995 (BHC).

‡PORTER, Joseph James, b Hammersmith 5 May 1980. LHB, SLA. Staff 2000 – awaiting f-c debut.

RATCLIFFE, Jason David (Sharman's Cross SS; Solihull SFC), b Solihull, Warwks 19 Jun 1969. Son of D.P. (Warwks 1957-68). 6'4". RHB, RM. Warwickshire 1988-94. Surrey debut 1995; cap 1998. Tours (Wa): SA 1991-92, 1992-93; Z 1993-94. HS 135 v Worcs (Worcester) 1997. BB 6-48 v SL A (Oval) 1999. BB 3-28 v Kent (Tunbridge W) 1999. Awards: NWT 2. LO HS 105 Wa v Yorks (Leeds) 1993 (NWT). LO BB 2-11 Wa v Glam (Neath) 1993 (SL).

SALISBURY, Ian David Kenneth (Moulton CS), b Northampton 21 Jan 1970. 5'11". RHB, LBG. Sussex 1989-96; cap 1991. Surrey debut 1997; cap 1998. MCC YC. YC 1992. *Wisden* 1992. **Tests:** 12 (1992 to 1998); HS 50 v P (Manchester) 1992; BB 4-163 v WI (Georgetown) 1993-94. **LOI:** 4 (1992-93 to 1993-94); HS 5; BB 3-41 v WI (P-o-S) 1993-94. Tours: WI 1991-92 (Eng A), 1993-94; I 1992-93; 1994-95 (Eng A); P 1990-91 (Eng A), 1995-96 (Eng A); SL 1990-91 (Eng A). HS 100* v Somerset (Oval) 1999. 50 wkts (5); most – 87 (1992). BB 8-75 (11-169 match) Sx v Essex (Chelmsford) 1996. Sy BB 7-65 v Glam (Swansea) 1998. Awards: NWT 1; BHC 2. LO HS 48* Sx v Glam (Swansea) 1995 (SL). LO BB 5-30 Sx v Leics (Leicester) 1992 (SL).

‡**SAMPSON, Philip** James, b Manchester 6 Sep 1980. RHB, RFM. Staff 2000 – awaiting f-c debut.

SAQLAIN MUSHTAQ (Govt Muslim League HS, M.A.O. College, Lahore), b Lahore, Pakistan 29 Dec 1976. Brother of Sibtain Mushtaq (Lahore 1988-89). 5'11". RHB, OB. Islamabad 1994-95. PIA 1994-95 to date. Surrey debut 1997; cap 1998. **Tests** (P): 24 (1995-96 to 1999-00); HS 79 v Z (Sheikhupura) 1996-97; BB 6-46 v A (Hobart) 1999-00. **LOI** (P): 123 (1995-96 to 1999-00); HS 37* v A (Brisbane) 1999-00; BB 5-29 v A (Adelaide) 1996-97, 2 hat-tricks. Tours (P): E 1996; A 1995-96, 1996-97, 1999-00; SA 1997-98; I 1998-99, SL 1996-97; Z 1997-98; B 1998-99. HS 79 (*see Tests*). Sy HS 45* v Essex (Chelmsford) 1998. 50 wkts (2+1); most – 63 (1998). BB 8-65 (11-107 match) v Derbys (Oval) 1988. Hat-tricks 1997 and 1999. Awards: NWT 2. LO HS 37* (*see LOI*). LO BB 5-29 (*see LOI*).

SHAHID, Nadeem (Ipswich S), b Karachi, Pakistan 23 Apr 1969. 6'0". RHB, LB. Essex 1989-94. Surrey debut 1995; cap 1998. Suffolk 1988. 1000 runs (1): 1003 (1990). HS 139 v Yorks (Oval) 1995. BB 3-91 Ex v Surrey (Oval) 1990. Sy BB 3-93 v SA A (Oval) 1996. LO HS 101 v Derbys (Derby) 1995 (SL). LO BB 3-30 v Bucks (Oval) 1998 (NWT).

STEWART, Alec James (Tiffin S), b Merton 8 Apr 1963. Son of M.J. (Surrey and England 1954-72). 5'11". RHB, WK. Debut 1981; cap 1985; captain 1992-97; benefit 1994. *Wisden* 1992. MBE 1998. **Tests:** 95 (1989-90 to 1999-00, 13 as captain); HS 190 v P (Birmingham) 1992. **LOI**: 125 – shares Eng record (1989-90 to 1999, 30 as captain); HS 116 v I (Sharjah) 1997-98. Tours (C=captain): A 1990-91, 1994-95, 1998-99C; SA 1995-96, 1999-00; WI 1989-90, 1993-94, 1997-98; NZ 1991-92, 1996-97; I 1992-93; SL 1992-93C; Z 1996-97. 1000 runs (8); most – 1665 (1986). HS 271* v Yorks (Oval) 1997. BB 1-7. Held 11 catches (equalling world f-c match record) v Leics (Leicester) 1989. Awards: NWT 5; BHC 5. LO HS 167* v Somerset (Oval) 1994 (BHC).

THORPE, Graham Paul (Weydon CS; Farnham SFC), b Farnham 1 Aug 1969. 5'11". LHB, RM. Debut 1988; cap 1991; benefit 2000. *Wisden* 1997. **Tests:** 57 (1993 to 1999); HS 138 v A (Birmingham) 1997; scored 114* v A (Nottingham) 1993 on debut. **LOI:** 53 (1993 to 1999); HS 89 v Z (Brisbane) 1994-95 and 89 v H (Peshawar) 1995-96; BB 2-15 v I (Manchester) 1996. Tours: A 1992-93 (Eng A), 1994-95, 1998-99 (*part*); SA 1995-96; WI 1991-92 (Eng A), 1993-94, 1997-98; NZ 1996-97; P 1990-91 (Eng A); SL 1990-91 (Eng A); Z 1989-90 (Eng A), 1996-97. 1000 runs (8); most – 1895 (1992). HS 223* Eng XI v S Aus (Adelaide) 1998-99. Sy HS 222 v Glam (Oval) 1997. BB 4-40 v A (Oval) 1993. CC BB 2-14 v Derbys (Oval) 1996. Awards: NWT 3; BHC 1. LO HS 145* v Lancs (Oval) 1994 (NWT). LO BB 3-21 v Somerset (Oval) 1991 (SL).

TUDOR, Alex Jeremy (St Mark's S, Hammersmith; City of Westminster C), b West Brompton, London 23 Oct 1977. 6'5". RHB, RF. Debut 1995; cap 1999. YC 1999. **Tests:** 3 (1998-99 to 1999); HS 99* v NZ (Birmingham) 1999 – record score by an England 'night-watchman'; BB 4-89 v A (Perth) 1998-99 – on debut. Tours: A 1998-99; SA 1999-00. HS 99* (*see Tests*). Sy HS 56 v Leics (Leicester) 1995. BB 7-77 v Leics (Leicester) 1999. LO HS 29* v Essex (Oval) 1995 (SL). LO BB 4-39 v Bucks (Oval) 1998 (NWT).

WARD, Ian James (Millfield S), b Plymouth, Devon 30 Sep 1972. 5'8½". LHB, RM. Surrey 1992, 1996 to date. Tours (Eng A): NZ 1999-00; B 1999-00. 1000 runs (1): 1018 (1999). HS 103 v Derbys (Derby) 1999. LO HS 91 v Middx (Guildford) 1998 (SL).

RELEASED/RETIRED see p 85

SURREY 1999

RESULTS SUMMARY

	Place	*Won*	*Lost*	*Tied*	*Drew*	*No Result*
PPP County Championship	**1st**	12			5	
All First-Class Matches		13			5	
NatWest Trophy	Semi-Finalist					
Benson & Hedges Super Cup	Quarter-Finalist					
CGU National League (Division 2)	**6th**	5	9	1		1

COUNTY CHAMPIONSHIP AVERAGES

BATTING AND FIELDING

Cap		*M*	*I*	*NO*	*HS*	*Runs*	*Avge*	*100*	*50*	*Ct/St*
1994	A.D.Brown	17	26	4	265	1127	51.22	4	2	31/1
1991	G.P.Thorpe	9	13	2	164	561	51.00	2	2	13
1996	M.A.Butcher	13	22	1	259	991	47.19	2	4	12
–	I.J.Ward	17	28	3	103	954	38.16	1	8	6
1995	A.J.Hollioake	12	16	2	116	486	34.71	1	3	6
1990	D.J.Bicknell	10	15	1	115	478	34.14	2	1	2
1989	M.P.Bicknell	15	17	4	69	432	33.23	–	3	5
1985	A.J.Stewart	7	10	1	95	262	29.11	–	1	10/2
1999	B.C.Hollioake	12	18	–	71	468	26.00	–	3	12
–	G.P.Butcher	4	6	–	70	141	23.50	–	1	1
–	J.N.Batty	14	18	5	45*	294	22.61	–	–	43/7
1998	J.D.Ratcliffe	12	18	1	91	380	22.35	–	2	5
1998	I.D.K.Salisbury	17	19	2	100*	353	20.76	1	1	5
1998	Saqlain Mushtaq	7	8	5	25*	46	15.33	–	–	1
1999	A.J.Tudor	9	11	2	33	91	10.11	–	–	3

Also batted: R.M.Amin (3 matches) 2, 3*, 1* (1 ct); J.E.Benjamin (cap 1993)(2) 5, 4 (1 ct); I.E.Bishop (3) 0*, 0*, 7* (2 ct); C.G.Greenidge (1) 2 (1 ct): M.W.Patterson (1) 0; N.Shahid (cap 1998)(2) 12, 23, 1* (2 ct).

BOWLING

	O	*M*	*R*	*W*	*Avge*	*Best*	*5wI*	*10wM*
Saqlain Mushtaq	290.5	90	660	58	11.37	7-19	7	2
M.P.Bicknell	545.4	156	1346	71	18.95	4-32	–	–
A.J.Tudor	281.3	66	836	39	21.43	7-77	3	–
I.D.K.Salisbury	558.2	145	1315	60	21.91	5-44	2	–
M.A.Butcher	168	47	400	16	25.00	4-30	–	–
B.C.Hollioake	234.5	47	754	20	37.70	5-51	1	–

Also bowled: R.M.Amin 101-45-190-9; J.N.Batty 2-1-9-0; I.E.Bishop 44-7-135-3; J.E.Benjamin 17-2-78-1; A.D.Brown 26-3-80-0; G.P.Butcher 13-4-41-1; C.G.Greenidge 46-14-124-8; A.J.Hollioake 45.2-9-177-5; M.W.Patterson 13-2-39-3; J.D.Ratcliffe 75-21-210-8; A.J.Stewart 2-0-6-0; G.P.Thorpe 13-0-42-0; I.J.Ward 4-2-8-0.

The First-Class Averages (pp 113-128) give the records of Surrey players in all first-class county matches (Surrey's other opponents being Sri Lanka A), with the exception of A.R.Butcher, G.P.Thorpe and A.J.Tudor, whose full county figures are as above, and:

A.J.Stewart 8-12-1-95-296-26.90-0-1-11ct-2st. 2-0-6-0.

SURREY RECORDS

FIRST-CLASS CRICKET

Highest Total	For 811		v	Somerset	The Oval	1899
	V 863		by	Lancashire	The Oval	1990
Lowest Total	For 14		v	Essex	Chelmsford	1983
	V 16		by	MCC	Lord's	1872
Highest Innings	For 357*	R.Abel	v	Somerset	The Oval	1899
	V 366	N.H.Fairbrother	for	Lancashire	The Oval	1990

Highest Partnership for each Wicket

1st	428	J.B.Hobbs/A.Sandham	v	Oxford U	The Oval	1926
2nd	371	J.B.Hobbs/E.G.Hayes	v	Hampshire	The Oval	1909
3rd	413	D.J.Bicknell/D.M.Ward	v	Kent	Canterbury	1990
4th	448	R.Abel/T.W.Hayward	v	Yorkshire	The Oval	1899
5th	308	J.N.Crawford/F.C.Holland	v	Somerset	The Oval	1908
6th	298	A.Sandham/H.S.Harrison	v	Sussex	The Oval	1913
7th	262	C.J.Richards/K.T.Medlycott	v	Kent	The Oval	1987
8th	205	I.A.Greig/M.P.Bicknell	v	Lancashire	The Oval	1990
9th	168	E.R.T.Holmes/E.W.J.Brooks	v	Hampshire	The Oval	1936
10th	173	A.Ducat/A.Sandham	v	Essex	Leyton	1921

Best Bowling	For	10-43	T.Rushby	v	Somerset	Taunton	1921
(Innings)	V	10-28	W.P.Howell	for	Australians	The Oval	1899
Best Bowling	For	16-83	G.A.R.Lock	v	Kent	Blackheath	1956
(Match)	V	15-57	W.P.Howell	for	Australians	The Oval	1899

Most Runs – Season	3246	T.W.Hayward	(av 72.13)	1906
Most Runs – Career	43554	J.B.Hobbs	(av 49.72)	1905-34
Most 100s – Season	13	T.W.Hayward		1906
	13	J.B.Hobbs		1925
Most 100s – Career	144	J.B.Hobbs		1905-34
Most Wkts – Season	252	T.Richardson	(av 13.94)	1895
Most Wkts – Career	1775	T.Richardson	(av 17.87)	1892-1904

LIMITED-OVERS CRICKET

Highest Total	**NWT**	350		v	Worcs	The Oval	1994
	BHC	333-6		v	Hampshire	The Oval	1996
	NL	375-4		v	Yorkshire	Scarborough	1994
Lowest Total	**NWT**	74		v	Kent	The Oval	1967
	BHC	89		v	Notts	Nottingham	1984
	NL	64		v	Worcs	Worcester	1978
Highest Innings	**NWT**	146	G.S.Clinton	v	Kent	Canterbury	1985
	BHC	167*	A.J.Stewart	v	Somerset	The Oval	1994
	NL	203	A.D.Brown	v	Hampshire	Guildford	1997
Best Bowling	**NWT**	7-33	R.D.Jackman	v	Yorkshire	Harrogate	1970
	BHC	5-15	S.G.Kenlock	v	Ireland	The Oval	1995
	NL	7-30	M.P.Bicknell	v	Glamorgan	The Oval	1999

SUSSEX

Formation of Present Club: 1 March 1839
Substantial Reorganisation: August 1857
Colours: Dark Blue, Light Blue and Gold
Badge: County Arms of Six Martlets
County Champions: (0); best – 2nd 1902, 1903, 1932, 1933, 1934, 1953, 1981
NatWest Trophy/Gillette Cup Winners: (4) 1963, 1964, 1978, 1986
Benson and Hedges Cup Winners: (0); best – semi-finalists 1982, 1999
CGU National League (Div 1) Winners: (0); best – 1st (Div 2) 1999
Sunday League Winners: (1) 1982
Match Awards: NWT 55; BHC 55

Chief Executive: D.R.Gilbert, County Ground, Eaton Road, Hove BN3 3AN ▲ Tel: 01273 827100 ▲ Fax: 01273 771549 ▲ Email: sccc@mistral.co.uk ▲ Web: www.sussexcricket.co.uk

Captain: C.J.Adams. **Vice-Captain/Overseas Player:** M.G.Bevan. **2000 Beneficiary:** None. **Scorer:** L.V.Chandler. ‡ New registration

ADAMS, Christopher John (Repton S), b Whitwell, Derbyshire 6 May 1970. 6'0". RHB, RM/OB. Derbyshire 1988-97; cap 1992. Sussex debut/cap 1998; captain 1998 to date. **Tests:** 5 (1999-00); HS 31 v SA (Cape Town) 1999-00; BB 1-42. **LOI:** 5 (1998 to 1999-00); HS 42 v SA (Cape Town) 1999-00. Tour: SA 1999-00. 1000 runs (4); most – 1742 (1996). HS 239 De v Hants (Southampton) 1996. Sx HS 170 v Middx (Hove) 1998. BB 4-29 De v Lancs (Derby) 1991. Sx BB 3-37 v Glos (Hove) 1999. Awards: NWT 2; BHC 5. LO HS 163 v Middx (Arundel) 1999 (NL). LO BB 5-16 v Middx (Hove) 1998 (SL).

BATES, Justin Jonathan (Hurstpierpoint C), b Farnborough, Hants 9 Apr 1976. 5'11". RHB, OB. Debut 1997. HS 57 v Hants (Southampton) 1999. BB 5-67 (9-136 match) v Northants (Northampton) 1998. LO HS 8 (SL). LO BB 2-42 v Northants (Northampton) 1998 (SL).

BEVAN, Michael Gwyl (Western Creek HS, Canberra), b Belconnen, ACT, Australia 8 May 1970. 5'11½". LHB, SLC. S Australia 1989-90. NSW 1990-91 to date. Yorkshire 1995-96; cap 1995. Sussex 1998; cap 1998. **Tests** (A): 18 (1994-95 to 1997-98); HS 91 v P (Lahore) 1994-95; BB 6-82 (10-113 match) v WI (Adelaide) 1996-97. **LOI** (A): 132 (1993-94 to 1999-00); HS 108* v E (Oval) 1997; BB 3-36 v P (Melbourne) 1996-97. Tours (A): E 1997; SA 1996-97; I 1996-97; P 1994-95; Z 1991-92 (Aus B). 1000 runs (2); most – 1598 (1995). HS 203* NSW v WA (Sydney) 1993-94. UK HS 160* Y v Surrey (Middlesbrough) 1996. Sx HS 149* v Leics (Leicester) 1998. BB 6-82 (*see Tests*). UK BB 3-36 Y v Warwks (Leeds) 1996 and 3-36 v Kent (Tunbridge W) 1998. Awards: NWT 2; BHC 4. LO HS 108* (*see LOI*). LO BB 5-29 v Sussex (Eastbourne) 1996 (SL).

CARPENTER, James Robert (Birkenhead S), b Birkenhead, Cheshire 20 Oct 1975. 6'1½". LHB, SLA. MCC YC. Debut 1997. HS 65 v Notts (Nottingham) 1998. BB 1-50. LO HS 64* v Notts (Cleethorpes) 1999.

‡CLAPP, Dominic Adrian (Lancing C; Worthing SFC), b Southport, Lancs 25 May 1980. RHB, RM. Staff 2000 – awaiting f-c debut. 2nd XI debut 1997 when aged 16y 347d.

COTTEY, Phillip **Anthony** (Bishopston CS, Swansea), b Swansea, Glamorgan 2 Jun 1966. 5'4". RHB, OB. Glamorgan 1986-98; cap 1992. Sussex debut/cap 1999. E Transvaal 1991-92. Tours (Gm): SA 1995-96; Z 1990-91, 1994-95. 1000 runs (7); most – 1543 (1996). HS 203 and BB 4-49 Gm v Leics (Swansea) 1996. Sx HS 126 v Glos (Arundel) 1999. Sx BB – . LO HS 96 Gm v Sussex (Hove) 1998 (BHC). LO BB 4-56 Gm v Essex (Chelmsford) 1996 (SL).

GREENFIELD, Keith (Falmer HS), b Brighton 6 Dec 1968. 6'0". RHB, RM. Debut 1987; cap 1996. 2nd XI coach/captain – no f-c appearances since 1997. HS 154* v Glam (Hove) 1996. BB 2-40 v Essex (Hove) 1993. Awards: NWT 2. LO HS 129 v Lancs (Hove) 1997 (NWT). LO BB 3-34 v Northants (Hove) 1995 (SL).

HAVELL, Paul Matthew (Warden Park S; Haywards Heath C), b Melbourne, Australia 4 Jul 1980. 6'3". LHB, RFM. Staff 2000 – awaiting f-c debut.

‡HOUSE, William John (Sevenoaks S; Gonville & Caius C, Cambridge), b Sheffield, Yorks 16 Mar 1976. 5'11". LHB, RM. Cambridge U 1996-98, scoring 136 v Derbys on debut; blue 1996-97-98. Kent 1997-99. British U 1998. HS 136 (*see above*). CC HS 5 (K). BB 1-34 (CU). CC BB – . Awards: BHC 2. LO HS 93 Brit U v Surrey (Oval) 1997 (BHC). LO BB 5-58 Brit U v Glos (Bristol) 1998 (BHC).

HUMPHRIES, Shaun (The Weald, Billingshurst; Kingston C, London), b Horsham 11 Jan 1973. 5'9". RHB, WK. Debut 1993. HS 66 v Kent (Tunbridge W) 1998. LO HS 16 v Glam (Hove) 1998 (BHC).

KHAN, Wasim Gulzar (Small Heath CS; Josiah Mason SFC, Erdington), b Birmingham 26 Feb 1971. 6'1". LHB, LB. Warwickshire 1995-97. Sussex debut 1998. HS 181 Wa v Hants (Southampton) 1995. Sx HS 125 v Derbys (Horsham) 1998. LO HS 33 v Glam (Hove) 1998 (BHC) and 33 v Warwks (Hove) 1998 (SL).

KIRTLEY, Robert **James** (Clifton C), b Eastbourne 10 Jan 1975. 6'0". RHB, RFM. Debut 1995; cap 1998. Mashonaland 1996-97. Tours (Eng A): NZ 1999-00; B 1999-00. HS 59 v Durham (Eastbourne) 1998. 50 wkts (2); most – 65 (1999). BB 7-21 v Hants (Southampton) 1999. Took 5-53 (7-88 match) for Mashonaland v Eng XI (Harare) 1996-97. Award: NWT 1. LO HS 17* v Somerset (Hove) 1999 (NL). LO BB 5-39 v Salop (Hove) 1997 (NWT).

LEWRY, Jason David (Durrington HS, Worthing), b Worthing 2 Apr 1971. 6'2". LHB, LFM. Debut 1994; cap 1996. Tour: Z 1998-99 (Eng A). HS 34 v Kent (Hove) 1995. 50 wkts (2); most – 62 (1998). BB 7-38 v Derbys (Derby) 1999. Hat-trick 1998. LO HS 14* v Ire (Hove) 1995 (BHC). LO BB 4-29 v Somerset (Bath) 1995 (SL).

MARTIN-JENKINS, Robin Simon Christopher (Radley C; Durham U), b Guildford, Surrey 28 Oct 1975. Son of C.D.A. (Cricket Correspondent/Commentator). 6'5". RHB, RFM. Debut 1995. British U 1996. HS 78 and BB 7-54 (9-119 match) v Glam (Hove) 1998. Award: BHC 1. LO HS 44 v Yorks (Hove) 1998 (SL). LO BB 4-57 v Glos (Bristol) 1997 (BHC).

MONTGOMERIE, Richard Robert (Rugby S; Worcester C, Oxford), b Rugby, Warwks 3 Jul 1971. 5'10½". RHB, OB. Oxford U 1991-94; blue 1991-92-93-94; captain 1994; half blues for rackets and real tennis. Northamptonshire 1991-98; cap 1995. Sussex debut/cap 1999. Tour: Z 1994-95 (Nh). 1000 runs (2); most – 1178 (1996). HS 192 Nh v Kent (Canterbury) 1995. Sx HS 113* v Northants (Hove) 1999. LO HS 109 Nh v Notts (Nottingham) 1995 (NWT).

PEIRCE, Michael **Toby** Edward (Ardingly C; Durham U), b Maidenhead, Berks 14 Jun 1973. 5'10". LHB, SLA. Combined U 1994. Sussex debut 1995. HS 123 v Glam (Cardiff) 1999. BB 1-16. LO HS 44 Comb U v Middx (Lord's) 1995 (BHC).

RASHID, Umer Bin Abdul (Ealing Green HS; Ealing Tertiary C; Southbank U), b Southampton, Hants 6 Feb 1976. 6'3". LHB, SLA. Middlesex 1996-98. Sussex debut 1999. HS 73 v Kent (Hove) 1999. BB 4-41 v Yorks (Leeds) 1999. LO HS 82 Brit U v Hants (Oxford) 1997. LO BB 5-24 v Glam (Swansea) 1999 (NL).

ROBINSON, Mark Andrew (Hull GS), b Hull, Yorkshire 23 Nov 1966. 6'3". RHB, RFM. Northamptonshire 1987-90; cap 1990. Canterbury 1988-89. Yorkshire 1991-95; cap 1992. Sussex debut/cap 1997. Tours (Y): SA 1991-92, 1992-93. Failed to score in 12 successive f-c innings 1990 – world record. HS 27 v Lancs (Manchester) 1997. 50 wkts (1): 50 (1992). BB 9-37 (12-124 match) Y v Northants (Harrogate) 1993. Sx BB 6-78 v Northants (Hove) 1997 on Sussex debut. Award: BHC 1. LO HS 9* (SL). LO BB 4-23 Y v Northants (Leeds) 1993 (SL).

TAYLOR, Billy Victor (Bitterne Park S, Southampton), b Southampton, Hants 11 Jan 1977. Brother of J.L. (Wiltshire 1998 to date). 6'3". LHB, RMF. Debut 1999. Wiltshire 1996-98. HS 14 and BB 1-54 v Derbys (Derby) 1999 – on debut. LO HS 21* v Notts (Cleethorpes) 1999 (NL). LO BB 3-22 v Surrey (Hove) 1999 (NL).

WILTON, Nicholas James (Beacon Community C and SFC; City of Westminster C), b Pembury, Kent 23 Sep 1978. 5'11". RHB, WK. Debut 1998. MCC YC. HS 55 v Leics (Arundel) 1999. LO HS 7 (NL).

YARDY, Michael Howard (William Parker S, Hastings), b Pembury, Kent 27 Nov 1980. 6'0". LHB, LM. Staff 2000 – awaiting f-c debut. LO HS (Sx Board) 0 (NWT).

ZUIDERENT Bastiaan (***'Bas'***) (Erasmiaans Gymnasium, Rotterdam; Amsterdam U), b Utrecht, Holland 3 Mar 1977. 6'3". RHB, OB. Holland 1994 to date. **LOI** (H): 5 (1995-96 World Cup); HS 54 v E (Peshawar) 1995-96. Awaiting f-c debut. LO HS 99 Holland v Worcs (Worcester) 1997 (NWT).

RELEASED/RETIRED

(Having made a first-class County appearance in 1999)

Di VENUTO, M.J. – *see DERBYSHIRE.*

EDWARDS, A.D. – *see MIDDLESEX.*

HAYWOOD, G.R. – *see NOTTINGHAMSHIRE.*

RAO, Rajesh Krishnakant (Alperton HS; Brighton U), b Park Royal, Middlesex 9 Dec 1974. 5'10". RHB, LBG. Sussex 1996-99. MCC YC. HS 89 v Essex (Hove) 1997. BB 1-1. Award: NWT 1. LO HS 158 v Derbys (Derby) 1997 (NWT). LO BB 3-31 v Worcs (Worcester) 1996 (SL).

STRONG, M.R. – *see NORTHAMPTONSHIRE.*

SURREY – RELEASED/RETIRED (continued from p 80)

(Having made a first-class County appearance in 1999)

BELL, Michael Anthony Vincent (Bishop Milner CS; Dudley TC), b Birmingham 19 Dec 1966. 6'2". RHB, LMF. Warwickshire 1992-97. Surrey 1998 (L-O matches). MCC YC. Tour (Wa): Z 1993-94. HS 30 Wa v Notts (Nottingham) 1997. BB 7-48 Wa v Glos (Birmingham) 1993. LO HS 16 Sy v Derbys (Oval) 1998 (SL). LO BB 5-19 Wa v Leics (Birmingham) 1994 (SL).

BENJAMIN, Joseph Emmanuel (Cayon HS, St Kitts; Mount Pleasant S, Highgate, Birmingham), b Christ Church, St Kitts 2 Feb 1961. 6'2". RHB, RMF. Warwickshire 1988-91. Surrey 1992-99; cap 1993. Staffordshire 1986-88. **Tests:** 1 (1994); HS 0 and BB 4-42 v SA (Oval) 1994. **LOI:** 2 (1994-95); HS 0; BB 1-22. Tour: A 1994-95. HS 49 v Essex (Oval) 1995. 50 wkts (3); most – 80 (1994). BB 6-19 v Notts (Oval) 1993. Awards: NWT 2; BHC 1. LO HS 25 v Worcs (Oval) 1994 (NWT). LO BB 4-19 v Hants (Southampton) 1997 (BHC).

BICKNELL, D.J. – *see NOTTINGHAMSHIRE.*

KNOTT, James Alan (City of Westminster C), b Canterbury, Kent 14 Jun 1975. Son of A.P.E. (Kent, Tasmania and England 1964-85). 5'6". RHB, occ LB, WK. Debut Surrey 1995-98. MCC YC. HS 49* v SA A (Oval) 1996. CC HS 41* v Derbys (Oval) 1988. LO HS 98 v Glos (Cheltenham) 1998 (SL).

SUSSEX 1999

RESULTS SUMMARY

	Place	*Won*	*Lost*	*Tied*	*Drew*	*No Result*
PPP County Championship	**11th**	6	5		6	
All First-Class Matches		6	5		6	
NatWest Trophy	4th Round					
Benson & Hedges Super Cup	Semi-Finalist					
CGU National League (Division 2)	**1st**	13	2			1

COUNTY CHAMPIONSHIP AVERAGES

BATTING AND FIELDING

Cap		*M*	*I*	*NO*	*HS*	*Runs*	*Avge*	*100*	*50*	*Ct/St*
1999	M.J.Di Venuto	16	28	2	162	1067	41.03	3	5	20
1999	R.R.Montgomerie	15	27	1	113*	962	37.00	2	6	19
1998	C.J.Adams	17	31	2	130	956	32.96	1	5	23
–	U.B.A.Rashid	10	18	3	73	454	30.26	–	3	5
–	M.T.E.Peirce	17	31	–	123	919	29.64	1	6	5
1999	P.A.Cottey	17	29	1	126	780	27.85	1	4	11
–	J.J.Bates	6	10	–	57	190	19.00	–	1	2
–	R.S.C.Martin-Jenkins	14	24	2	70	413	18.77	–	2	2
–	W.G.Khan	5	9	–	88	167	18.55	–	2	1
–	R.K.Rao	4	6	1	52*	87	17.40	–	1	1
–	N.J.Wilton	6	10	–	55	156	15.60	–	1	13/2
1996	J.D.Lewry	12	19	7	30*	163	13.58	–	–	2
–	S.Humphries	11	18	2	57	176	11.00	–	1	18/2
1998	R.J.Kirtley	15	23	5	32	194	10.77	–	–	2
1997	M.A.Robinson	17	24	11	10	63	4.84	–	–	1

Also batted: A.D.Edwards (2 matches) 0, 22, 0 (1 ct); G.R.Haywood (1) 14, 1; M.R.Strong (1) 35*, 16 (1 ct); B.V.Taylor (1) 14, 0 (1 ct).

BOWLING

	O	*M*	*R*	*W*	*Avge*	*Best*	*5wI*	*10wM*
R.J.Kirtley	514.3	133	1504	65	23.13	7- 21	3	–
J.D.Lewry	381.4	84	1330	56	23.75	7- 38	4	1
R.S.C.Martin-Jenkins	370.2	99	1074	42	25.57	4- 50	–	–
M.A.Robinson	520.4	140	1438	48	29.95	6- 88	1	–
J.J.Bates	141	46	356	11	32.36	5-154	1	–
C.J.Adams	120	28	333	10	33.30	3- 37	–	–
U.B.A.Rashid	218.3	67	664	15	44.26	4- 41	–	–

Also bowled: P.A.Cottey 2-1-3-0; M.J.Di Venuto 13-2-40-1; A.D.Edwards 48-12-157-3; G.R.Haywood 13.2-1-66-0; R.R.Montgomerie 1-0-6-0; M.T.E.Peirce 6-1-30-1; R.K.Rao 14.5-2-53-1; M.R.Strong 31-5-124-0; B.V.Taylor 25-4-108-2.

The First-Class Averages (pp 113-128) give the records of Sussex players in all first-class county matches.

SUSSEX RECORDS

FIRST-CLASS CRICKET

Highest Total	For	705-8d		v	Surrey	Hastings	1902
	V	726		by	Notts	Nottingham	1895
Lowest Total	For	19		v	Surrey	Godalming	1830
		19		v	Notts	Hove	1873
	V	18		by	Kent	Gravesend	1867
Highest Innings	For	333	K.S.Duleepsinhji	v	Northants	Hove	1930
	V	322	E.Paynter	for	Lancashire	Hove	1937

Highest Partnership for each Wicket

1st	490	E.H.Bowley/J.G.Langridge	v	Middlesex	Hove	1933
2nd	385	E.H.Bowley/M.W.Tate	v	Northants	Hove	1921
3rd	298	K.S.Ranjitsinhji/E.H.Killick	v	Lancashire	Hove	1901
4th	326*	J.Langridge/G.Cox	v	Yorkshire	Leeds	1949
5th	297	J.H.Parks/H.W.Parks	v	Hampshire	Portsmouth	1937
6th	255	K.S.Duleepsinhji/M.W.Tate	v	Northants	Hove	1930
7th	344	K.S.Ranjitsinhji/W.Newham	v	Essex	Leyton	1902
8th	229*	C.L.A.Smith/G.Brann	v	Kent	Hove	1902
9th	178	H.W.Parks/A.F.Wensley	v	Derbyshire	Horsham	1930
10th	156	G.R.Cox/H.R.Butt	v	Cambridge U	Cambridge	1908

Best Bowling	For	10- 48	C.H.G.Bland	v	Kent	Tonbridge	1899
(Innings)	V	9- 11	A.P.Freeman	for	Kent	Hove	1922
Best Bowling	For	17-106	G.R.Cox	v	Warwicks	Horsham	1926
(Match)	V	17- 67	A.P.Freeman	for	Kent	Hove	1922

Most Runs – Season	2850	J.G.Langridge	(av 64.77)	1949
Most Runs – Career	34152	J.G.Langridge	(av 37.69)	1928-55
Most 100s – Season	12	J.G.Langridge		1949
Most 100s – Career	76	J.G.Langridge		1928-55
Most Wkts – Season	198	M.W.Tate	(av 13.47)	1925
Most Wkts – Career	2211	M.W.Tate	(av 17.41)	1912-37

LIMITED-OVERS CRICKET

Highest Total	**NWT**	384-9		v	Ireland	Belfast	1996
	BHC	305-6		v	Kent	Hove	1982
	NL	312-8		v	Hampshire	Portsmouth	1993
Lowest Total	**NWT**	49		v	Derbyshire	Chesterfield	1969
	BHC	61		v	Middlesex	Hove	1978
	NL	59		v	Glamorgan	Hove	1996
Highest Innings	**NWT**	158	R.K.Rao	v	Derbyshire	Derby	1997
	BHC	118	C.W.J.Athey	v	Kent	Hove	1995
	NL	163	C.J.Adams	v	Middlesex	Arundel	1999
Best Bowling	**NWT**	6- 9	A.I.C.Dodemaide	v	Ireland	Downpatrick	1990
	BHC	5- 8	Imran Khan	v	Northants	Northampton	1978
	NL	7-41	A.N.Jones	v	Notts	Nottingham	1986

WARWICKSHIRE

Formation of Present Club: 8 April 1882
Substantial Reorganisation: 19 January 1884
Colours: Dark Blue, Gold and Silver
Badge: Bear and Ragged Staff
County Champions: (5) 1911, 1951, 1972, 1994, 1995
NatWest Trophy/Gillette Cup Winners: (5) 1966, 1968, 1989, 1993, 1995
Benson and Hedges Cup Winners: (1) 1994
CGU National League (Div 1) Winners: (0); best – 7th 1999
Sunday League Winners: (3) 1980, 1994, 1997
Match Awards: NWT 64; BHC 60

Chief Executive: D.L.Amiss MBE, County Ground, Edgbaston, Birmingham, B5 7QU ▲ Tel: 0121 446 4422 ▲ Fax: 0121 446 4544 ▲ Email: Info@warwick.ccc.org.uk ▲ Web: www.thebears.co.uk

Captain: N.M.K.Smith. **Vice-Captain:** N.V.Knight. **Overseas Player:** A.A.Donald. **2000 Beneficiary:** D.P.Ostler. **Scorer:** D.Wainwright. ‡ New registration

ALTREE, Darren Anthony (Ashlawn S, Rugby), b Rugby 30 Sep 1974. 5'11". RHB, LMF. Debut 1996. HS 2*. BB 3-41 v P (Birmingham) 1996. CC BB 2-108 v Hants (Southampton) 1997. LO HS (Warwicks Board) 6 (NWT).

BELL, Ian Ronald (Princethorpe C), b Walsgrave-on-Sowe 11 Apr 1982. 5'9". Debut 1999. HS 0. LO HS 10 Warwks Board v Berks (Reading) 1999 (NWT).

BROWN, Douglas Robert (Alloa Academy; W London IHE), b Stirling, Scotland 29 Oct 1969. 6'2". RHB, RFM. Scotland 1989. Warwickshire debut 1991-92 (SA tour); cap 1995. Wellington 1995-96. **LOI:** 9 (1997-98); HS 21 v WI (Bridgetown) 1997-98; BB 2-28 v WI (Sharjah) 1997-98. Tours (Wa): SA 1991-92, 1994-95; SL 1997-98 (Eng A). HS 142 v Northants (Birmingham) 1999. 50 wkts (2); most – 81 (1997). BB 8-89 (11-154 match) F-C Counties Select XI v Pak A (Chelmsford) 1997. Wa BB 7-66 v Durham (Chester-le-St) 1999. Award: BHC 1. LO HS 78* v Notts (Nottingham) 1995 (SL). LO BB 5-31 v Worcs (Worcester) 1997 (BHC).

DAGNALL, Charles Edward (Bridgewater HS, Worsley; UMIST), b Bury, Lancs 10 Jul 1976. RHB, RFM. Debut 1999 – awaiting CC debut. Cumberland 1997-98. HS 0 and BB 4-20 v OU (Oxford) 1999 – on debut. LO HS 4 and LO BB 1-37 Cumb v Derbys (Derby) 1998 (NWT).

DONALD, Allan Anthony (Grey College HS), b Bloemfontein, SA 20 Oct 1966. 6'2". RHB, RF. OFS 1985-86 to date. Warwickshire 1987-93, 1995, 1997, 1999; cap 1989; benefit 1999. *Wisden* 1991. **Tests** (SA): 60 (1991-92 to 1999-00); HS 34 v WI (Pt Elizabeth) 1998-99; BB 8-71 (11-113 match) v Z (Harare) 1995-96. **LOI** (SA): 121 (1991-92 to 1999); HS 12 v SL (Nottingham) 1998; BB 6-23 v K (Nairobi) 1996-97. Tours (SA): E 1994, 1998; A 1993-94, 1997-98; WI 1991-92; NZ 1994-95, 1998-99; I 1996-97, 1999-00; P 1997-98; SL 1993-94; Z 1995-96, 1999-00. HS 55* SA v Tasmania (Devonport) 1997-98. Wa HS 44 v Essex (Ilford) 1995. 50 wkts (5); most – 89 (1995). BB 8-37 OFS v Transvaal (Johannesburg) 1986-87. Wa BB 7-37 v Durham (Birmingham) 1992. Awards: NWT 3. LO HS 23* v Leics (Leicester) 1989 (BHC). LO BB 6-15 v Yorks (Birmingham) 1995 (SL).

FRANKLIN, Gavin David (Malvern C; Durham U), b Wolverhampton, Staffs 9 Jan 1978. RHB, OB. Staffordshire 1997. Staff 1998 – awaiting f-c debut.

FROST, Tony (James Brinkley HS; Stoke-on-Trent C), b Stoke-on-Trent, Staffs 17 Nov 1975. 5'11". RHB, WK. Debut 1997; cap 1999. HS 111* v OU (Oxford) 1998. CC HS 66 v Sussex (Birmingham) 1999. LO HS 22* v Kent (Birmingham) 1999.

GIDDINS, Edward Simon Hunter (Eastbourne C), b Eastbourne, Sussex 20 Jul 1971. 6'4½". RHB, RFM. Sussex 1991-96; cap 1994. Warwickshire debut/cap 1998. MCC YC. **Tests:** 1 (1999); HS 0* and BB 3-38 v NZ (Oval) 1999. Tour: P 1995-96 (Eng A). HS 34 Sx v Essex (Hove) 1995. Wa HS 18 v Kent (Maidstone) 1999. 50 wkts (4); most – 84 (1998). BB 6-47 Sx v Yorks (Eastbourne) 1996. Wa BB 6-79 (11-164 match) v Glos (Bristol) 1998. Award: BHC 1. LO HS 13 Sx v Essex (Hove) 1994 (NWT). LO BB 5-21 v Leics (Leicester) 1999.

GILES, Ashley Fraser (George Abbot S, Guildford), b Chertsey, Surrey 19 Mar 1973. 6'3". RHB, SLA. Debut 1993; cap 1996. Tour: A 1996-97 (Eng A). **Tests:** 1 (1998): HS 16* and BB 1-106 v SA (Manchester) 1998. **LOI:** 5 (1997 to 1998-99); HS 10* v SL (Sydney) 1998-99; BB 2-37 v SA (Oval) 1998. Tours (Eng A): SL 1997-98; K 1997-98. HS 123* v OU (Oxford) 1999. CC HS 106* v Lancs (Birmingham) 1996. 50 wkts (1): 64 (1996). BB 6-45 v Durham (Birmingham) 1996. Awards: NWT 1; BHC 1. LO HS 69 and LO BB 5-21 v Norfolk (Birmingham) 1997 (NWT).

HEMP, David Lloyd (Olchfa CS; Millfield S; W Glamorgan C), b Bermuda 8 Nov 1970. UK resident since 1976. 6'0". LHB, RM. Glamorgan 1991-96; cap 1994. Warwickshire debut/cap 1997. Wales (MC) 1992-94. Tours: SA 1995-96 (Gm); I 1994-95 (Eng A); Z 1994-95 (Gm). 1000 runs (3); most – 1452 (1994). HS 157 Gm v Glos (Abergavenny) 1995. Wa HS 144 v Worcs (Birmingham) 1999. BB 3-23 Gm v SA A (Cardiff) 1996. CC BB 1-1. Wa BB 2-68 v Ou (Oxford) 1998. Awards: NWT 4; BHC 2. LO HS 121 Gm v Comb U (Cardiff) 1995 (BHC). LO BB 4-32 v Minor C (Lakenham) 1998 (BHC).

KNIGHT, Nicholas Verity (Felsted S; Loughborough U), b Watford, Herts 28 Nov 1969. 6'0". LHB, occ RM. Essex 1991-94; cap 1994. Warwickshire debut 1994-95 (SA tour); cap 1995. **Tests:** 12 (1995 to 1998); HS 113 v P (Leeds) 1996. **LOI:** 53 (1996 to 1999-00); HS 125* v P (Nottingham) 1996. Tours: SA 1994-95 (Wa), 1999-00 (*part*); NZ 1996-97; I 1994-95 (Eng A); SL 1997-98 (Eng A – captain); P 1995-96 (Eng A); Z 1996-97; K 1997-98 (Eng A – captain). 1000 runs (2); most – 1196 (1996). HS 192 v Lancs (Birmingham) 1998. BB 1-61. Awards: NWT 2; BHC 2. LO HS 151 v Somerset (Birmingham) 1995 (NWT). LO BB 1-14 (SL).

O'CONNELL, Brendan William (Tiffin S), b Kingston upon Thames, Surrey 18 Aug 1989. Staff 1998 – awaiting f-c debut.

OSTLER, Dominic Piers (Princethorpe C; Solihull TC), b Solihull 15 Jul 1970. 6'3". RHB, occ RM. Debut 1990; cap 1991; benefit 1999. Tours: SA 1992-93 (Wa); P 1995-96 (Eng A). 1000 runs (4); most – 1284 (1991). HS 208 v Surrey (Birmingham) 1995. Awards: NWT 2; BHC 1. LO HS 104 and LO BB 1-4 v Norfolk (Lakenham) 1993 (NWT).

PENNEY, Trevor Lionel (Prince Edward S, Salisbury), b Salisbury, Rhodesia 12 Jun 1968. 6'0". RHB, RM. Qualified for England 1992. Boland 1991-92. Warwickshire debut 1991-92 (SA tour); UK debut v CU (Cambridge) 1992, scoring 102*; cap 1994. Mashonaland 1993-94 to date. Tours (Wa): SA 1991-92, 1992-93, 1994-95; Z 1993-94. 1000 runs (2); most – 1295 (1996). HS 151 v Middx (Lord's) 1992. BB 3-18 Mashonaland v Mashonaland U-24 (Harare) 1993-94. Wa BB 1-40 (Z tour). CC BB – . Award: NWT 1. LO HS 90 v Cornwall (St Austell) 1996 (NWT). LO BB 1-8 (NWT).

PIPER, Keith John (Haringey Cricket C), b Leicester 18 Dec 1969. 5'6". RHB, WK. Warwickshire debut 1989; cap 1992. Tours (Wa): SA 1991-92, 1992-93, 1994-95; I 1994-95 (Eng A); P 1995-96 (Eng A); Z 1993-94. HS 116* v Durham (Birmingham) 1994. BB 1-57. LO HS 38* v Leics (Birmingham) 1999 (NL).

POWELL, Michael James (Lawrence Sheriff S, Rugby), b Bolton, Lancs 5 Apr 1975. 5'11". RHB, RM. Debut 1996; cap 1999. HS 136 v Glam (Cardiff) 1999. BB 2-16 v OU (Oxford) 1998. CC BB 1-18. LO HS 51 v Yorks (Leeds) 1999 (NL).

RICHARDSON, Alan (Alleyne's HS; Stafford CFE; Durham U), b Newcastle-under-Lyme, Staffs 6 May 1975. 6'2". RHB, RMF. Derbyshire 1995 (one match). Warwickshire debut 1999. Staffordshire 1996-98. HS 4 (De) and 4 (Wa). BB 8-51 (10-107 match) v Glos (Birmingham) 1999. LO HS 11* v Leics (Birmingham) 1999 (NL). LO BB 2-16 v Essex (Colchester) 1999 (NL).

SHEIKH, Mohammad Avez (Broadway S), b Birmingham 2 Jul 1973. 6'0". LHB, RM. Debut 1997. HS 30 v OU (Oxford) 1998. CC HS 25 v Notts (Birmingham) 1998. BB 2-14 v Middx (Birmingham) 1997. LO HS 12* v Bucks (Marlow) 1999 (NWT). LO BB 3-28 v Glam (Birmingham) 1998 (SL).

‡**SIERRA, Ryan** Edward, b Petersburg, SA 8 Sep 1980. LHB, LM. Holds British passport. Staff 2000 – awaiting f-c debut.

SINGH, Anurag (King Edward's, Birmingham; Gonville & Caius C, Cambridge), b Kanpur, India 9 Sep 1975. 5'11½". RHB, OB. Debut 1995. Cambridge U 1996-98; blue 1996-97-98; captain 1997-98. British U 1998 (captain). HS 157 CU v Sussex (Hove) 1996. Wa HS 69 v Worcs (Birmingham) 1999. Award: BHC 1. LO HS 123 Brit U v Somerset (Taunton) 1996 (BHC).

SMITH, Neil Michael Knight (Warwick S), b Birmingham 27 Jul 1967. Son of M.J.K. (Leics, Warwks and England 1951-75). 6'0". RHB, OB. Debut 1987; cap 1993; captain 1999. MCC YC. **LOI:** 7 (1995-96 to 1996); HS 31 v H (Peshawar) 1995-96; BB 3-29 v UAE (Peshawar) 1995-96. Tours (Wa): SA 1991-92, 1994-95; Z 1993-94. 1000 runs (1): 1002 (1998). HS 161 v Yorks (Leeds) 1989. BB 7-42 v Lancs (Birmingham) 1994. Awards: NWT 1; BHC 2. LO HS 125 v Kent (Canterbury) 1997 (BHC). LO BB 6-33 v Sussex (Birmingham) 1995 (SL).

WAGH, Mark Anant (King Edward's S, Birmingham; Keble C, Oxford), b Birmingham 20 Oct 1976. 6'2". RHB, OB. Oxford U 1996-98; blue 1996-97-98; captain 1997. Warwickshire debut 1997. British U 1998. Mashonaland A 1998-99. 1000 runs (1): 1156 (1997). HS 216* v OU (Oxford) 1999. CC HS 124 v Durham (Chester-le-St) 1997. BB 4-11 v Middx (Lord's) 1998. LO HS 27 v Yorks (Birmingham) 1999 (NL). LO BB 1-39 (SL).

‡**WARREN, Nicholas** Alexander (Solihull SFC), b Moseley, Birmingham 26 Jun 1982. RHB, RFM. Staff 2000 – awaiting f-c debut. 2nd XI debut 1998 when aged 16y 76d.

WELCH, Graeme (Hetton CS), b Durham 21 Mar 1972. 5'11½". RHB, RM. Debut 1994; cap 1997. Tour: SA 1994-95 (Wa). HS 84* v Notts (Birmingham) 1994. 50 wkts (1): 65 (1997). BB 6-115 (11-140 match) v Lancs (Blackpool) 1997. LO HS 71 v Kent (Maidstone) 1999 (NL). LO BB 4-31 v Kent (Birmingham) 1998 (NWT).

RELEASED/RETIRED

(Having made a first-class County appearance in 1999)

EDMOND, Michael Denis (Airds HS, Cambelltown, NSW, Australia), b Barrow-in-Furness, Lancs 30 Jul 1969. 6'1". RHB, RMF. Warwickshire 1996-99. Indoor Cricket for Australia. Scored 100 off 48 balls for Warwks 2nd XI II v Somerset 2nd XI (Taunton) 1997. HS 32 v Durham (Birmingham) 1998. BB 2-26 v OU (Oxford) 1997. CC BB 1-6. LO HS 19 v Kent (Tunbridge W) 1997 (SL). LO BB 2-4 v Derbys (Birmingham) 1997 (SL).

MUNTON, T.A. – *see DERBYSHIRE.*

WARWICKSHIRE 1999

RESULTS SUMMARY

	Place	Won	Lost	Tied	Drew	No Result
PPP County Championship	**10th**	6	5		6	
All First-Class Matches		7	5		6	
NatWest Trophy	4th Round					
Benson & Hedges Super Cup	Semi-Finalist					
CGU National League (Division 1)	**7th**	6	8			2

COUNTY CHAMPIONSHIP AVERAGES

BATTING AND FIELDING

Cap		*M*	*I*	*NO*	*HS*	*Runs*	*Avge*	*100*	*50*	*Ct/St*
1999	M.J.Powell	8	12	–	136	467	38.91	2	1	5
1995	N.V.Knight	14	23	2	94	719	34.23	–	6	30
1997	D.L.Hemp	17	28	–	144	920	32.85	2	5	10
1995	D.R.Brown	16	25	1	142	666	27.75	1	3	13
1993	N.M.K.Smith	14	20	–	71	491	24.55	–	3	7
1994	T.L.Penney	14	23	2	73	493	23.47	–	3	5/2
1997	G.Welch	13	20	6	48*	321	22.92	–	–	4
1991	D.P.Ostler	7	11	–	87	250	22.72	–	2	5
1992	K.J.Piper	5	7	–	66	152	21.71	–	1	8/1
–	M.A.Wagh	12	20	–	60	427	21.35	–	1	3
1999	T.Frost	11	17	1	66	331	20.68	–	1	20
–	A.Singh	5	10	–	69	154	15.40	–	2	–
1996	A.F.Giles	15	22	4	30	252	14.00	–	–	5
1998	E.S.H.Giddins	14	18	10	18	76	9.50	–	–	2
1989	A.A.Donald	2	4	2	10	14	7.00	–	–	1
1989	T.A.Munton	13	19	3	24	80	5.00	–	–	5
–	A.Richardson	5	7	2	4	9	1.80	–	–	1

Also batted (1 match each): I.R.Bell 0 (2 ct); M.A.Sheikh 12, 7*.

BOWLING

	O	*M*	*R*	*W*	*Avge*	*Best*	*5wI*	*10wM*
T.A.Munton	409.1	107	1028	52	19.76	7-36	3	–
A.Richardson	156.3	38	434	20	21.70	8-51	1	1
E.S.H.Giddins	355.3	95	1063	48	22.14	6-90	2	–
A.F.Giles	414.4	133	884	34	26.00	5-63	1	–
D.R.Brown	232.5	57	717	26	27.57	7-66	1	–
G.Welch	259.3	44	880	31	28.38	5-47	1	–
N.M.K.Smith	182.3	45	525	16	32.81	4-90	–	–

Also bowled: A.A.Donald 50-15-136-0; D.L.Hemp 9-1-40-0; D.P.Ostler 1-0-2-0; T.L.Penney 2-1-1-0; M.J.Powell 25-6-56-0; M.A.Sheikh 6-0-21-0; M.A.Wagh 9-1-29-1.

The First-Class Averages (pp 113-128) give the records of Warwickshire's players in all first-class county matches (Warwickshire's other opponents being Oxford University), with the exception of E.S.H.Giddins whose full county figures are as above.

WARWICKSHIRE RECORDS

FIRST-CLASS CRICKET

Highest Total	For	810-4d		v	Durham	Birmingham	1994
	V	887		by	Yorkshire	Birmingham	1896
Lowest Total	For	16		v	Kent	Tonbridge	1913
	V	15		by	Hampshire	Birmingham	1922
Highest Innings	For	501*	B.C.Lara	v	Durham	Birmingham	1994
	V	322	I.V.A.Richards	for	Somerset	Taunton	1985

Highest Partnership for each Wicket

1st	377*	N.F.Horner/K.Ibadulla	v	Surrey	The Oval	1960
2nd	465*	J.A.Jameson/R.B.Kanhai	v	Glos	Birmingham	1974
3rd	327	S.P.Kinneir/W.G.Quaife	v	Lancashire	Birmingham	1901
4th	470	A.I.Kallicharran/G.W.Humpage	v	Lancashire	Southport	1982
5th	322*	B.C.Lara/K.J.Piper	v	Durham	Birmingham	1994
6th	220	H.E.Dollery/J.Buckingham	v	Derbyshire	Derby	1938
7th	250	H.E.Dollery/J.S.Ord	v	Kent	Maidstone	1953
8th	228	A.J.W.Croom/R.E.S.Wyatt	v	Worcs	Dudley	1925
9th	154	G.W.Stephens/A.J.W.Croom	v	Derbyshire	Birmingham	1925
10th	141	A.F.Giles/T.A.Munton	v	Worcs	Worcester	1996

Best Bowling	For	10-41	J.D.Bannister	v	Comb Servs	Birmingham	1959
(Innings)	V	10-36	H.Verity	for	Yorkshire	Leeds	1931
Best Bowling	For	15-76	S.Hargreave	v	Surrey	The Oval	1903
(Match)	V	17-92	A.P.Freeman	for	Kent	Folkestone	1932

Most Runs – Season	2417	M.J.K.Smith	(av 60.42)	1959
Most Runs – Career	35146	D.L.Amiss	(av 41.64)	1960-87
Most 100s – Season	9	A.I.Kallicharran		1984
	9	B.C.Lara		1994
Most 100s – Career	78	D.L.Amiss		1960-87
Most Wkts – Season	180	W.E.Hollies	(av 15.13)	1946
Most Wkts – Career	2201	W.E.Hollies	(av 20.45)	1932-57

LIMITED-OVERS CRICKET

Highest Total	**NWT**	392-5		v	Oxfordshire	Birmingham	1984
	BHC	369-8		v	Minor C	Jesmond	1996
	NL	301-6		v	Essex	Colchester	1982
Lowest Total	**NWT**	98		v	Leics	Leicester	1998
	BHC	96		v	Leics	Leicester	1972
	NL	65		v	Kent	Maidstone	1979
Highest Innings	**NWT**	206	A.I.Kallicharran	v	Oxfordshire	Birmingham	1984
	BHC	137*	T.A.Lloyd	v	Lancashire	Birmingham	1985
	NL	134	N.V.Knight	v	Hampshire	Birmingham	1996
Best Bowling	**NWT**	6-32	K.Ibadulla	v	Hampshire	Birmingham	1965
		6-32	A.I.Kallicharran	v	Oxfordshire	Birmingham	1984
	BHC	7-32	R.G.D.Willis	v	Yorkshire	Birmingham	1981
	NL	6-15	A.A.Donald	v	Yorkshire	Birmingham	1995

WORCESTERSHIRE

Formation of Present Club: 11 March 1865
Colours: Dark Green and Black
Badge: Shield Argent a Fess between three Pears Sable
County Championships: (5) 1964, 1965, 1974, 1988, 1989
NatWest Trophy/Gillette Cup Winners: (1) 1994
Benson and Hedges Cup Winners: (1) 1991
CGU National League (Div 1) Winners: (0); best – 2nd 1999
Sunday League Winners: (3) 1971, 1987, 1988
Match Awards: NWT 44; BHC 67

Secretary: Revd M.D.Vockins OBE, County Ground, New Road, Worcester, WR2 4QQ ▲ Tel: 01905 748474 ▲ Fax: 01905 748005 ▲ Email: worcs@ecb.co.uk ▲ Web: www.wccc.co.uk

Captain: G.A.Hick (*tbc*). **Vice-Captain:** No appointment. **Overseas Player:** G.D.McGrath. **2000 Beneficiary:** S.R.Lampitt. **Scorer:** S.S.Hale. ‡ New registration

ALI, Kabir (Moseley SFC), b Moseley, Birmingham 24 Nov 1980. 6'0". RHB, RMF. Debut 1999. HS 11 and BB 2-36 v Middx (Worcester) 1999 – on debut.

ALI, Kadeer (Handsworth GS), b Moseley, Birmingham 7 Mar 1983. 6'1". RHB, LB. Staff 1999 – awaiting f-c debut. LO HS 24 Worcs Board v Kent Board (Maidstone) 1999 (NWT).

CATTERALL, Duncan Neil (Queen Elizabeth's GS, Blackburn; Loughborough U), b Preston, Lancs 19 Sep 1978. 5'11". RHB, RMF. Debut 1998. HS 60 v Essex (Chelmsford) 1999 and 60 v Middx (Worcester) 1999 – in successive innings. BB 2-16 v Essex (Chelmsford) 1999. LO HS 11* v Hants (Worcester) 1998 (SL). LO BB 2-35 v Yorks (Worcester) 1999 (NL).

DRIVER, Ryan Craig (Redruth Community C; Durham U), b Truro, Cornwall 30 Apr 1979. 6'3½". LHB, RM. Debut 1998. Brit U 1999. Cornwall 1996-97. HS 42 v Essex (Chelmsford) 1999. LO HS 3 (NL).

HAYNES, Gavin Richard (High Park S; King Edward VI S, Stourbridge), b Stourbridge 29 Sep 1969. 5'10". RHB, RM. Debut 1991; cap 1994. Tours (Wo): Z 1993-94, 1996-97. 1000 runs (1): 1021 (1994). HS 158 v Kent (Worcester) 1993. BB 6-50 v Hants (Worcester) 1998. Awards: NWT 2; BHC 1. LO HS 116* v Cumb (Worcester) 1995 (NWT). LO BB 4-13 v Surrey (Worcester) 1997 (SL).

HICK, Graeme Ashley (Prince Edward HS, Salisbury), b Salisbury, Rhodesia 23 May 1966. 6'3". RHB, OB. Zimbabwe 1983-84 to 1985-86. Worcestershire debut 1984; cap 1986; benefit 1999; captain 2000. N Districts 1987-88 to 1988-89. Queensland 1990-91. *Wisden* 1986. **ECB contract 2000. Tests:** 54 (1991 to 1999); HS 178 v I (Bombay) 1992-93; BB 4-126 v NZ (Wellington) 1991-92. **LOI:** 105 (1991 to 1999-00); HS 126* v SL (Adelaide) 1998-99; BB 5-33 v Z (Harare) 1999-00. Tours: E 1985 (Z); A 1994-95, 1998-99 (*part*); SA 1995-96, 1999-00 (*part*); WI 1993-94; NZ 1991-92; I 1992-93; SL 1983-84 (Z), 1992-93; Z 1990-91 (Wo), 1996-97 (Wo). 1000 runs (15+1) inc 2000 (3); most – 2713 (1988); youngest to score 2000 (1986). Scored 1019 runs before June 1988, including a record 410 runs in April. Fewest innings for 10,000 runs in county cricket (179). Youngest (24) to score 50 f-c hundreds. Second-youngest (32) to score 100 f-c hundreds. Scored 645 runs without being dismissed (UK record) in 1990. HS 405* (Worcs record and then second highest in UK f-c matches) v Somerset (Taunton) 1988. BB 5-18 v Leics (Worcester) 1995. Awards: NWT 4; BHC 11. LO HS 172* v Devon (Worcester) 1987 (NWT). LO BB 5-35 v Notts (Nottingham) 1991 (RAC).

ILLINGWORTH, Richard Keith (Salts GS), b Bradford, Yorks 23 Aug 1963. 5'11". RHB, SLA. Debut 1982; cap 1986; benefit 1997. Natal 1988-89. **Tests:** 9 (1991 to 1995-96); HS 28 v SA (Pt Elizabeth) 1995-96; BB 4-96 v WI (Nottingham) 1995. Took wicket of P.V.Simmons with his first ball in Tests – v WI (Nottingham) 1991. **LOI:** 25 (1991 to 1995-96); HS 14 v P (Melbourne) 1991-92; BB 3-33 v Z (Albury) 1991-92. Tours: SA

ILLINGWORTH, R.K. (*continued*)
1995-96; NZ 1991-92; P 1990-91 (Eng A); SL 1990-91 (Eng A); Z 1989-90 (Eng A), 1990-91 (Wo), 1993-94 (Wo), 1996-97 (Wo). HS 120* v Warwks (Worcester) 1987 – as night-watchman. Scored 106 for England A v Z (Harare) 1989-90 – also as night-watchman. 50 wkts (5); most – 75 (1990). BB 7-50 v OU (Oxford) 1985. CC BB 7-79 v Hants (Southampton) 1997. LO HS 36* v Kent (Worcester) 1990 (BHC). LO BB 5-24 v Somerset (Worcester) 1983 (SL).

LAMPITT, Stuart Richard (Kingswinford S; Dudley TC), b Wolverhampton, Staffs 29 Jul 1966. 5'11". RHB, RMF. Debut 1985; cap 1989; benefit 1999. Tours (Wo): Z 1990-91, 1993-94, 1996-97. HS 122 v Middx (Lord's) 1994. 50 wkts (6); most – 64 (1994). BB 5-32 v Kent (Worcester) 1989. Awards: NWT 1; BHC 4. LO HS 54 v Scot (Edinburgh) 1998 (NWT). LO BB 6-26 v Derbys (Derby) 1994 (BHC).

LEATHERDALE, David Anthony (Pudsey Grangefield S), b Bradford, Yorks 26 Nov 1967. 5'10½". RHB, RM. Debut 1988; cap 1994. Tours (Wo): Z 1993-94, 1996-97. 1000 runs (1): 1001 (1998). HS 157 v Somerset (Worcester) 1991. BB 5-20 v Glos (Worcester) 1998. LO HS 70* v Yorks (Worcester) 1999 (NL). LO BB 4-13 v Minor C (Worcester) 1997 (BHC).

LIPTROT, Christopher George (The Deanery HS), b Wigan, Lancs 13 Feb 1980. 6'2". LHB, RFM. Debut 1999. HS 61 v Warwks (Birmingham) 1999. BB 5-51 v Surrey (Worcester) 1999.

‡McGRATH, Glenn Donald (Narromine HS), b Dubbo, NSW, Australia 9 Feb 1970. 6'6". RHB, RF. New South Wales 1992-93 to date. *Wisden* 1997. **Tests** (A): 59 (1993-94 to 1999-00); HS 39 v WI (P-o-S) 1998-99; BB 8-38 v E (Lord's) 1997. **LOI** (A): 110 (1993-94 to 1999-00); HS 10 v E (Melbourne) 1994-95; BB 5-14 v WI (Manchester) 1999. Tours (A): E 1997; SA 1993-94, 1996-97; WI 1994-95, 1998-99; I 1996-97; P 1994-95, 1998-99; SL 1999-00; Z 1999-00. HS 39 (*see Tests*). HS UK: 20* A v E (Leeds) 1997. 50 wkts (0+1): 51 (1995-96). BB 8-38 (*see Tests*). LO HS 10 (*see LOI*). LO BB 5-14 (*see LOI*).

MIRZA, Maneer Mohamed (*registered as 'Mohamed MANEER'*)(Sheldon Heath CS; Bournville CHE), b Birmingham 1 Apr 1978. Younger brother of the late Parvaz (Worcestershire 1994-95). 5'10". RHB, RFM. Debut 1997. HS 10* and BB 4-51 v Warwks (Birmingham) 1997. LO HS – (SL). LO BB 1-31 (SL).

PATEL, Depesh Balvant (Moseley Park GS; Bilston Community C), b Wolverhampton, Staffs 23 Sep 1981. 6'3". RHB, RFM. Awaiting f-c debut. LO HS 19* and LO BB 1-36 Worcs Board v Kent Board (Maidstone) 1999 (NWT).

PIPE, David James (Queensbury S, Bradford), b Bradford, Yorks 16 Dec 1977. 5'11". RHB, WK. Debut 1998. Awaiting CC debut. HS 16 v SL A (Worcester) 1999.

POLLARD, Paul Raymond (Gedling CS), b Carlton, Nottingham 24 Sep 1968. 5'11". LHB, RM. Nottinghamshire 1987-98; cap 1992. Worcestershire debut 1999. Tour (Nt): SA 1996-97. 1000 runs (3); most – 1463 (1993). HS 180 Nt v Derbys (Nottingham) 1993. Wo HS 60 v OU (Oxford) 1999. BB 2-79 Nt v Glos (Bristol) 1993. LO HS 132* Nt v Somerset (Nottingham) 1995 (SL).

RAWNSLEY, Matthew James (Shenley Court CS, Birmingham), b Birmingham 8 Jun 1976. 6'2". RHB, SLA. Debut 1996. HS 26 v Essex (Chelmsford) 1997. BB 6-44 (11-116 match) v OU (Oxford) 1998. CC BB 3-84 v Yorks (Leeds) 1999. LO HS 7 (SL). LO BB 5-26 v Kent (Tunbridge W) 1999 (NL).

RHODES, Steven John (Lapage Middle S; Carlton-Bolling S, Bradford), b Bradford, Yorks 17 Jun 1964. Son of W.E. (Notts 1961-64). 5'7". RHB, WK. Yorkshire 1981-84. Worcestershire debut 1985; cap 1986; benefit 1996. *Wisden* 1994. **Tests:** 11 (1994 to 1994-95); HS 65* v SA (Leeds) 1994. **LOI:** 9 (1989 to 1994-95); HS 56 v SA (Manchester) 1994. Tours: A 1994-95; SA 1993-94 (Eng A); WI 1991-92 (Eng A); SL 1985-86 (Eng B), 1990-91 (Eng A); Z 1989-90 (Eng A), 1990-91 (Wo), 1993-94 (Wo), 1996-97 (Wo – captain). 1000 runs (2); most – 1018 (1995). HS 122* v Young A (Worcester) 1995. CC HS 116* v Warwks (Worcester) 1992. Awards: NWT 1; BHC 2. LO HS 105 v Lancs (Manchester) 1991 (RAC).

SHERIYAR, Alamgir (George Dixon S; Joseph Chamberlain SFC; Oxford Poly), b Birmingham 15 Nov 1973. 6'1". RHB, LFM. Leicestershire 1994-95. Worcestershire debut 1996; cap 1997. Tours (Eng A): NZ 1999-00; B 1999-00. HS 21 v Notts (Nottingham) 1997 and 21 v Pak A (Worcester) 1997. 50 wkts (2); most – 92 (1999). BB 7-130 (10-172 match) v Hants (Southampton) 1999. Hat-tricks (2): 1994 (Le), 1999. LO HS 19 v Derbys (Chesterfield) 1996 (SL). LO BB 4-18 v Yorks (Leeds) 1997 (SL).

SOLANKI, Vikram Singh (Regis S, Wolverhampton), b Udaipur, India 1 Apr 1976. 6'0". RHB, OB. Debut 1995; cap 1998. Tours (Eng A): SA 1998-99 (Eng – *part*); NZ 1999-00; Z 1996-97 (Wo), 1998-99; B 1999-00. 1000 runs (1): 1339 (1999). **LOI**: 8 (1999-00); HS 24 v Z (Bulawayo) 1999-00. HS 185 Eng A v Bangladesh (Chittagong) 1999-00. Wo HS 171 v Glos (Cheltenham) 1999. BB 5-69 v Middx (Lord's) 1996. LO HS 120* v Derbys (Derby) 1998 (SL). LO BB 1-9 (SL).

SPIRING, Karl **Reuben** (Monmouth S; Durham U), b Southport, Lancs 13 Nov 1974. 5'11". RHB, OB. Debut 1994; cap 1997. 1000 runs (1): 1084 (1996). HS 150 v Essex (Chelmsford) 1997. LO HS 58* v Sussex (Arundel) 1997 (SL).

WESTON, William **Philip** Christopher (Durham S), b Durham 16 Jun 1973. Son of M.P. (Durham; England RFU); brother of R.M.S. (*see MIDDLESEX*). 6'3". LHB, LM. Debut 1991; cap 1995. Tours (Wo): Z 1993-94, 1996-97. 1000 runs (3); most – 1389 (1996). HS 205 v Northants (Northampton) 1997. BB 2-39 v P (Worcester) 1992. CC BB – . LO HS 125 v Warwks (Birmingham) 1999 (NL). LO BB 1-2 (SL).

WILSON, Elliott James (Felsted S; Durham U), b St Pancras, London 3 Nov 1976. 6'3". RHB, RM. Debut 1998. Brit U 1999. Cambridgeshire 1996. HS 116 v Middx (Worcester) 1999. LO HS 62 v Warwks (Worcester) 1999 (NL).

RELEASED/RETIRED

(Having made a first-class County appearance in 1999)

BATSON, Nathan Evan (Billericay SS; Mayflower County HS), b Basildon, Essex 24 Jul 1978. 6'2". RHB, OB. Worcestershire 1998-99. HS 72 v SL A (Worcester) 1999. CC HS 42 v Warwks (Birmingham) 1999.

De la PENA, Jason Michael (Stowe S; Bournside S), b London 16 Sep 1972. 6'5". RHB, RMF. Gloucestershire 1991-93. Surrey 1995. Kent 1998. Worcestershire 1999. Hertfordshire 1997. HS 7* (Gs). Wo HS 0. CC HS 2* (Sy). BB 6-18 (10-52 match) Wo v OU (Oxford) 1999. CC BB 3-53 Sy v Yorks (Oval) 1995. LO HS (Sy) 2* (SL).

HAFEEZ, Abdul (Handsworth GS; Solihull C), b Moseley, Birmingham 21 Mar 1977. 6'3". RHB, RM. Worcestershire 1998-99. HS 55 v Glos (Worcester) 1998. LO HS 33 v Scot (Edinburgh) 1998 (NWT).

MOODY, Thomas Masson (Guildford GS, WA), b Adelaide, Australia 2 Oct 1965. 6'6½". RHB, RM. W Australia 1985-86 to date; captain 1995-96 to date. Warwickshire 1990; cap 1990. Worcestershire 1991-99; cap 1991; captain 1995 (*part*) to 1999. **Tests** (A): 8 (1989-90 to 1992-93); HS 106 v SL (Brisbane) 1989-90; BB 1-17. **LOI** (A): 76 (1987-88 to 1999-00); HS 89 v P (Brisbane) 1989-90; BB 3-25 v B (Chester-le-St) 1999. Tours (A): E 1989; I 1989-90 (WA); SL 1992-93; Z 1991-92 (Aus B). 1000 runs (5+1); most – 1887 (1991). HS 272 WA v Tasmania (Hobart) 1994-95. Wo HS 212 v Notts (Worcester) 1996. BB 7-38 WA v Tasmania (Hobart) 1995-96. Wo BB 7-92 (13-159 match) v Glos (Worcester) 1996. Awards: NWT 3; BHC 7. LO HS 180* v Surrey (Oval) 1994 (NWT). LO BB 4-24 v Scot (Worcester) 1998 (BHC).

NEWPORT, Philip John (High Wycombe RGS; Portsmouth Poly), b High Wycombe, Bucks 11 Oct 1962. 6'3". RHB, RFM. Worcestershire 1982-99; cap 1986; benefit 1998. Boland 1987-88. N Transvaal 1992-93. Buckinghamshire 1981-82. **Tests:** 3 (1988 to 1990-91); HS 40* v A (Perth) 1990-91; BB 4-87 v SL (Lord's) 1988 – on debut. Tours: A 1990-91 (*part*); P 1990-91 (Eng A); SL 1990-91 (Eng A); Z 1993-94 (Wo), 1996-97 (Wo). HS 98 v NZ (Worcester) 1990. CC HS 96 v Essex (Worcester) 1990. 50 wkts (8); most – 93 (1988). BB 8-52 v Middx (Lord's) 1988. Awards: BHC 2. LO HS 57 Boland v NT (Pretoria) 1987-88 (NS). LO BB 5-22 v Warwks (Birmingham) 1987 (BHC).

WORCESTERSHIRE 1999

RESULTS SUMMARY

	Place	*Won*	*Lost*	*Tied*	*Drew*	*No Result*
PPP County Championship	**15th**	4	6		7	
All First-Class Matches		5	6		8	
NatWest Trophy	4th Round					
CGU National League (Division 1)	**2nd**	10	4			2

COUNTY CHAMPIONSHIP AVERAGES

BATTING AND FIELDING

Cap		*M*	*I*	*NO*	*HS*	*Runs*	*Avge*	*100*	*50*	*Ct/St*
1986	G.A.Hick	12	21	–	150	1051	50.04	4	6	18
1998	V.S.Solanki	17	31	1	171	1147	38.23	3	4	16
1991	T.M.Moody	5	10	2	63*	286	35.75	–	3	5
–	E.J.Wilson	7	13	2	116	382	34.72	1	2	4
1989	S.R.Lampitt	13	18	4	66*	399	28.50	–	2	7
1995	W.P.C.Weston	9	17	–	157	437	25.70	2	–	1
1986	S.J.Rhodes	17	29	5	74	576	24.00	–	1	47/2
1986	R.K.Illingworth	15	25	4	91*	457	21.76	–	1	5
1994	D.A.Leatherdale	17	30	2	85	570	20.35	–	1	9
1986	P.J.Newport	11	19	3	65*	295	18.43	–	1	3
–	P.R.Pollard	9	17	2	58	257	17.13	–	2	1
–	C.G.Liptrot	9	14	5	61	132	14.66	–	1	–
–	N.E.Batson	4	8	–	42	93	11.62	–	–	4
–	M.J.Rawnsley	3	5	1	20	46	11.50	–	–	1
1994	G.R.Haynes	6	9	–	29	98	10.88	–	–	–
1997	A.Sheriyar	17	26	8	18	129	7.16	–	–	3
1997	K.R.Spiring	5	10	–	18	69	6.90	–	–	3
–	A.Hafeez	4	8	–	32	43	5.37	–	–	2

Also batted: D.N.Catterall (2 matches) 12, 60, 60; J.M.de la Pena (2) 0, 0, 0 (1 ct); R.C.Driver (2) 42, 12, 23; Kabir Ali (1) 11.

BOWLING

	O	*M*	*R*	*W*	*Avge*	*Best*	*5wI*	*10wM*
P.J.Newport	274.4	77	747	31	24.09	4- 57	–	–
S.R.Lampitt	270.1	62	851	35	24.31	4- 28	–	–
A.Sheriyar	556.2	106	2128	86	24.74	7-130	4	1
V.S.Solanki	137.4	43	437	13	33.61	4- 62	–	–
C.G.Liptrot	163.4	44	560	16	35.00	5- 51	1	–
R.K.Illingworth	326.4	86	752	15	50.13	3- 58	–	–

Also bowled: D.N.Catterall 46-10-185-5; J.M.de la Pena 35-8-188-3; G.R.Haynes 88.1-18-251-3; G.A.Hick 60-18-155-5; Kabir Ali 20-8-58-3; D.A.Leatherdale 71.4-15-224-8; T.M.Moody 89.5-25-267-6; M.J.Rawnsley 95-23-257-8.

The First-Class Averages (pp 113-128) give the records of Worcestershire's players in all first-class county matches (Worcestershire's other opponents being Sri Lanka A and Oxford University), with the exception of G.A.Hick and R.C.Driver, whose full county figures are as above, and:

E.J.Wilson 8-15-2-116-404-31.07-1-2-5ct. Did not bowl.

WORCESTERSHIRE RECORDS

FIRST-CLASS CRICKET

Highest Total	For 670-7d		v	Somerset	Worcester	1995
	V 701-4d		by	Leics	Worcester	1906
Lowest Total	For 24		v	Yorkshire	Huddersfield	1903
	V 30		by	Hampshire	Worcester	1903
Highest Innings	For 405*	G.A.Hick	v	Somerset	Taunton	1988
	V 331*	J.D.B.Robertson	for	Middlesex	Worcester	1949

Highest Partnership for each Wicket

1st	309	F.L.Bowley/H.K.Foster	v	Derbyshire	Derby	1901
2nd	300	W.P.C.Weston/G.A.Hick	v	Indians	Worcester	1996
3rd	438*	G.A.Hick/T.M.Moody	v	Hampshire	Southampton	1997
4th	281	J.A.Ormrod/Younis Ahmed	v	Notts	Nottingham	1979
5th	393	E.G.Arnold/W.B.Burns	v	Warwicks	Birmingham	1909
6th	265	G.A.Hick/S.J.Rhodes	v	Somerset	Taunton	1988
7th	205	G.A.Hick/P.J.Newport	v	Yorkshire	Worcester	1988
8th	184	S.J.Rhodes/S.R.Lampitt	v	Derbyshire	Kidderminster	1991
9th	181	J.A.Cuffe/R.D.Burrows	v	Glos	Worcester	1907
10th	119	W.B.Burns/G.A.Wilson	v	Somerset	Worcester	1906

Best Bowling	For	9- 23	C.F.Root	v	Lancashire	Worcester	1931
(Innings)	V	10- 51	J.Mercer	for	Glamorgan	Worcester	1936
Best Bowling	For	15- 87	A.J.Conway	v	Glos	Moreton-in-M	1914
(Match)	V	17-212	J.C.Clay	for	Glamorgan	Swansea	1937

Most Runs – Season	2654	H.H.I.Gibbons	(av 52.03)	1934
Most Runs – Career	34490	D.Kenyon	(av 34.18)	1946-67
Most 100s – Season	10	G.M.Turner		1970
	10	G.A.Hick		1988
Most 100s – Career	79	G.A.Hick		1984-99
Most Wkts – Season	207	C.F.Root	(av 17.52)	1925
Most Wkts – Career	2143	R.T.D.Perks	(av 23.73)	1930-55

LIMITED-OVERS CRICKET

Highest Total	**NWT**	404-3		v	Devon	Worcester	1987
	BHC	314-5		v	Lancashire	Manchester	1980
	NL	307-4		v	Derbyshire	Worcester	1975
Lowest Total	**NWT**	98		v	Durham	Chester-le-St	1968
	BHC	81		v	Leics	Worcester	1983
	NL	86		v	Yorkshire	Leeds	1969
Highest Innings	**NWT**	180*	T.M.Moody	v	Surrey	The Oval	1994
	BHC	143*	G.M.Turner	v	Warwicks	Birmingham	1976
	NL	160	T.M.Moody	v	Kent	Worcester	1991
Best Bowling	**NWT**	7-19	N.V.Radford	v	Beds	Bedford	1991
	BHC	6- 8	N.Gifford	v	Minor C (S)	High Wycombe	1979
	NL	6-26	A.P.Pridgeon	v	Surrey	Worcester	1978

YORKSHIRE

Formation of Present Club: 8 January 1863
Substantial Reorganisation: 10 December 1891
Colours: Dark Blue, Light Blue and Gold
Badge: White Rose
County Championships (since 1890): (29) 1893, 1896, 1898, 1900, 1901, 1902, 1905, 1908, 1912, 1919, 1922, 1923, 1924, 1925, 1931, 1932, 1933, 1935, 1937, 1938, 1939, 1946, 1959, 1960, 1962, 1963, 1966, 1967, 1968.
Joint Champions: (1) 1949
NatWest Trophy/Gillette Cup Winners: (2) 1965, 1969
Benson and Hedges Cup Winners: (1) 1987
CGU National League (Div 1) Winners: (0); best – 5th 1999
Sunday League Winners: (1) 1983
Match Awards: NWT 37; BHC 71

Chief Executive: C.D.Hassell, Headingley Cricket Ground, Leeds, LS6 3BU ▲ Tel: 0113 278 7394 ▲ Fax: 0113 278 4099 ▲ Email: cricket@yorkshire-ccc.org.uk ▲ Web: www.yorkshireccc.org.uk

Captain: D.Byas. **Vice-Captain:** No appointment. **Overseas Player:** D.S.Lehmann. **2000 Beneficiary:** D.Byas. **Scorer:** J.T.Potter. ‡ New registration

BLAKEY, Richard John (Rastrick GS), b Huddersfield 15 Jan 1967. 5'9". RHB, WK. Debut 1985; cap 1987; benefit 1998. YC 1987. **Tests:** 2 (1992-93); HS 6. **LOI:** 3 (1992 to 1992-93); HS 25 v P (Lord's) 1992 – on debut. Tours: SA 1991-92 (Y); WI 1986-87 (Y); I 1992-93; P 1990-91 (Eng A); SL 1990-91 (Eng A); Z 1989-90 (Eng A), 1995-96 (Y). 1000 runs (5); most – 1361 (1987). HS 221 Eng A v Z (Bulawayo) 1989-90. Y HS 204* v Glos (Leeds) 1987. BB 1-68. Awards: BHC 2. LO HS 130* v Kent (Scarborough) 1991 (SL).

BYAS, David (Scarborough C), b Kilham 26 Aug 1963. 6'4". LHB, RM. Debut 1986; cap 1991; captain 1996 to date. Tours (Y): SA 1991-92, 1992-93; Z 1995-96. 1000 runs (5); most – 1913 (1995). HS 213 v Worcs (Scarborough) 1995. BB 3-55 v Derbys (Chesterfield) 1990. Awards: BHC 2. LO HS 116* v Surrey (Oval) 1996 (BHC). LO BB 3-19 v Notts (Leeds) 1989 (SL).

‡CRAVEN, Victor John (Harrogate GS), b Harrogate 31 Jul 1980. LHB, RM. Staff 2000 – awaiting f-c debut.

DAWSON, Richard Kevin James (Batley GS; Exeter U), b Doncaster 4 Aug 1980. 6'3". RHB, OB. Staff 1999 – awaiting f-c debut. Devon 1999.

ELLISON, Christopher John (Penrice S, St Austell; St Austell C; Exeter U), b Sheffield 12 Apr 1979. 5'10". RHB, SLA. Staff 1999 – awaiting f-c debut. Cornwall 1998. LO HS 5 and LO BB 3-64 Cornwall v Cumb (Kendal) 1999 (NWT).

FELLOWS, Gary Matthew (N Halifax GS), b Halifax 30 Jul 1978. 5'9". RHB, RM. Matabeleland 1996-97. Yorkshire debut 1998. HS 50 Matabeleland v Mashonaland (Bulawayo) 1996-97. Y HS 34* v Kent (Scarborough) 1999. BB 1-38. LO HS 36 v Kent (Canterbury) 1999 (NL).

FISHER, Ian Douglas (Beckfoot GS, Bingley; Thomas Danby C, Leeds), b Bradford 31 Mar 1976. 5'10½". LHB, SLA. Debut 1995-96 (Y tour). UK debut 1996. Tour: Z 1995-96 (Y). HS 51 v Surrey (Oval) 1999. BB 5-35 v Mashonaland Inv XI (Harare) 1995-96 – on debut. CC BB 5-73 v Essex (Chelmsford) 1999. LO HS 11* v Kent (Canterbury) 1999 (NL). LO BB 3-25 v Essex (Scarborough) 1998 (SL).

GOUGH, Darren (Priory CS, Lundwood), b Barnsley 18 Sep 1970. 5'11". RHB, RF. Debut 1989; cap 1993. *Wisden* 1998. **ECB contract 2000. Tests:** 36 (1994 to 1999-00); HS 65 v NZ (Manchester) 1994 – on debut; BB 6-42 v SA (Leeds) 1998; hat-trick v A (Sydney) 1998-99 – first for E v A since 1899. **LOI:** 74 (1994 to 1999-00); HS 45 v A (Melbourne) 1994-95; BB 5-44 v Z (Sydney) 1994-95 and 5-44 v A (Lord's) 1997. Took wickets with his sixth balls in both Tests and LOIs. Tours: A 1994-95, 1998-99; SA 1991-92 (Y), 1992-93 (Y), 1993-94 (Eng A), 1995-96, 1999-00; NZ 1996-97; Z 1996-97. HS 121 v Warwks (Leeds) 1996. 50 wkts (4); most – 67 (1996). BB 7-28 (10-80 match) v Lancs (Leeds) 1995 (not CC). CC BB 7-42 (10-96 match) v Somerset (Taunton) 1993. 2 hat-tricks (1995, 1998-99); took 4 wkts in 5 balls v Kent (Leeds) 1995. Awards: NWT 2. LO HS 72* v Leics (Leicester) 1991 (SL). LO BB 7-27 v Ire (Leeds) 1997 (NWT).

GUY, Simon Mark (Wickersley CS), b Rotherham 17 Nov 1978. 5'7". RHB, WK. Staff 1999 – awaiting f-c debut.

HAMILTON, Gavin Mark (Hurstmere SS, Kent), b Broxburn, Scotland 16 Sep 1974. 6'1". LHB, RFM. Scotland 1993-94. Yorkshire debut 1994; cap 1998. **Tests:** 1 (1999-00); HS 0 v SA (Jo'burg) 1999-00. **LOI** (Scot): 5 (1999); HS 76 and BB 2-36 v P (Chester-le-St) 1999. Tours: SA 1999-00; Z 1995-96 (Y). HS 94* v Worcs (Leeds) 1999. 50 wkts (1): 59 (1998). BB 7-50 (11-72 match) v Surrey (Leeds) 1998. Match double (79, 70; 5-69, 5-43) v Glam (Cardiff) 1998 – first instance for Yorks since 1964 (R.Illingworth). Award: BHC 1. LO HS 76 (*see LOI*). LO BB 5-16 v Hants (Leeds) 1998 (SL).

HARDEN, Richard John (King's C, Taunton), b Bridgwater, Somerset 16 Aug 1965. 5'11". RHB, SLA. Somerset 1985-98; cap 1989; benefit 1996. Yorkshire debut/cap 1999. C Districts 1987-88. 1000 runs (7); most – 1460 (1990). HS 187 Sm v Notts (Taunton) 1992. Y HS 69 v Leics (Leicester) 1999. BB 2-7 CD v Canterbury (Blenheim) 1987-88. CC BB 2-24 Sm v Hants (Taunton) 1986. Award: NWT 1. LO HS 108* Sm v Scot (Taunton) 1992 (NWT).

HOGGARD, Matthew James (Grangefield S, Pudsey), b Leeds 31 Dec 1976. 6'2". RHB, RFM. Debut 1996. Awaiting CC debut. OFS 1998-99. HS 21 v Somerset (Taunton) 1999. BB 5-47 v Derbys (Derby) 1999. LO HS 2* (NL). LO BB 4-26 Free State v North West (Fochville) 1998-99 (SBC).

HUTCHISON, Paul Michael (Crawshaw HS, Pudsey), b Leeds 9 Jun 1977. 6'3". LHB, LFM. Debut 1995-96 (Y tour); cap 1998. Rest 1996. Tours (Eng A): SI 1997-98; Z 1995-96 (Y); K 1997-98. HS 30 v Essex (Scarborough) 1998. 50 wkts (1): 59 (1998). BB 7-31 v Sussex (Hove) 1998. Award: NWT 1. LO HS 4* (NWT/BHC). LO BB 4-34 v Glos (Gloucester) 1998 (SL).

INGLIS, John William (Ripon GS; St Aiden's S, Harrogate), b Ripon 19 Oct 1979. 6'1". RHB, RM. Staff 1999 – awaiting f-c debut.

LEHMANN, Darren Scott (Gawler HS), b Gawler, S Australia 5 Feb 1970. 5'10. LHB, SLA. S Australia 1987-88 to 1989-90, 1993-94 to date; captain 1998-99. Victoria 1990-91 to 1992-93. Yorkshire 1997-98; cap 1997. **Tests** (A): 5 (1997-98 to 1998-99); HS 98 v P (Rawalpindi) 1998-99; BB 1-6. **LOI** (A): 60 (1996-97 to 1999-00); HS 110* v WI (St George's, Grenada) 1998-99; BB 2-4 v I (Colombo) 1999-00. Tours (A): E 1991 (Vic); I 1997-98; P 1998-99. 1000 runs (1+4); most – 1575 (1997). HS 255 S Aus v Queensland (Adelaide) 1996-97. Y HS 200 v Worcs (Worcester) 1998. BB 4-42 v Kent (Maidstone) 1998. Awards: BHC 2. LO HS 142* S Aus v Tas (Adelaide) 1994-95 (MM). LO BB 3-43 v Northants (Leeds) 1997 (SL).

‡LUMB, Michael, b Johannesburg, SA 12 Feb 1980. Son of R.G. (Yorkshire 1970-84). LHB, RM. Staff 2000 – awaiting f-c debut. Not ECB qualified until 2003.

McGRATH, Anthony (Yorkshire Martyrs Collegiate S), b Bradford 6 Oct 1975. 6'2". RHB, OB. Debut 1995; cap 1999. Tours (Eng A): A 1996-97; P 1995-96; Z 1995-96 (Y). HS 142* v Middx (Leeds) 1999. BB 3-18 v Surrey (Oval) 1999. Awards: NWT 1; BHC 1. LO HS 109* v Minor C (Leeds) 1997 (BHC). LO BB 2-10 v Scot (Leeds) 1996 (BHC).

MIDDLEBROOK, James Daniel (Pudsey Crawshaw S), b Leeds 13 May 1977. 6'1". RHB, OB. Debut 1998. HS 41 v Lancs (Leeds) 1998. BB 3-20 v Worcs (Worcester) 1998. LO HS 5 (SL).

SIDEBOTTOM, Ryan Jay (King James's GS, Almondbury), b Huddersfield 15 Jan 1978. Son of A. (Yorks, OFS and England 1973-91). 6'3". LHB, LFM. Debut 1997. HS 54 v Glam (Cardiff) 1998. BB 3-13 v Durham (Chester-le-St) 1998. LO HS 24* v Hants (Basingstoke) 1999 (NL). LO BB 6-40 v Glam (Cardiff) 1998 (SL).

SILVERWOOD, Christopher Eric Wilfred (Garforth CS), b Pontefract 5 Mar 1975. 6'1". RHB, RFM. Debut 1993; cap 1996. YC 1996. **Tests:** 5 (1996-97 to 1999-00); HS 7*; BB 5-91 v SA (Cape Town) 1999-00. **LOI:** 6 (1996-97 to 1997); HS 12 v NZ (Auckland) 1996-97; BB 2-27 v Z (Bulawayo) 1996-97 – on debut. Tours: SA 1999-00 (*part*); WI 1997-98; NZ 1996-97; Z 1995-96 (Y), 1996-97. HS 58 v Lancs (Manchester) 1997. 50 wkts (2); most – 59 (1999). BB 7-93 (12-148 match) v Kent (Leeds) 1997. Awards: BHC 2. LO HS 14* v Northants (Northampton) 1996 (SL). LO BB 5-28 v Scot (Leeds) 1996 (BHC).

‡**STEAD,** Roger **Alexander** (Hipperholme & Lightcliffe HS; Durham U), b Dewsbury 18 Apr 1980. RHB. Staff 2000 – awaiting f-c debut.

‡**THEWLIS, Matthew** (Wombwell HS), b Barnsley 16 Jul 1981. RHB, WK. Staff 2000 – awaiting f-c debut.

VAUGHAN, Michael Paul (Silverdale CS, Sheffield), b Manchester, Lancs 29 Oct 1974. 6'2". RHB, OB. Debut 1993; cap 1995. **ECB contract 2000. Tests:** 4 (1999-00); HS 69 v SA (Pretoria) 1999-00. Tours (Eng A): A 1996-97; SA 1998-99 (captain), 1999-00 (Eng); I 1994-95; Z 1995-96 (Y), 1998-99 (captain). 1000 runs (4); most – 1244 (1995). HS 183 v Glam (Cardiff) 1996. BB 4-39 v OU (Oxford) 1994. CC BB 4-62 v Surrey (Middlesbrough) 1996. Awards: NWT 1; BHC 1. LO HS 88 v Warwks (Birmingham) 1997 (BHC). LO BB 4-31 v Hants (Basingstoke) 1999 (NL).

WHITE, Craig (Flora Hill HS, Bendigo, Australia; Bendigo HS), b Morley 16 Dec 1969. 6'0". RHB, RFM. Debut 1990; cap 1993. Victoria 1990-91 (2 matches). **ECB contract 2000. Tests:** 8 (1994 to 1996-97); HS 51 v NZ (Lord's) 1994; BB 3-18 v NZ (Manchester) 1994. **LOI:** 23 (1994-95 to 1999-00); HS 38 v NZ (Napier) 1996-97; BB 5-21 v Z (Bulawayo) 1999-00. Tours: A 1994-95, 1996-97 (Eng A); SA 1991-92 (Y), 1992-93 (Y); NZ 1996-97; P 1995-96 (Eng A); Z 1996-97 (*part*). HS 181 v Lancs (Leeds) 1996. BB 8-55 v Glos (Gloucester) 1998 – inc hat-trick. Hat-trick 1998. Awards: NWT 2; BHC 2. LO HS 148 v Leics (Leicester) 1997 (SL). LO BB 4-18 v Durham (Scarborough) 1997 (SL).

WIDDUP, Simon (Ridgewood CS; Danum SFC), b Doncaster 10 Nov 1977. 6'0". RHB, OB. Staff 1999 – awaiting f-c debut.

WOOD, Matthew James (Shelley HS & SFC), b Huddersfield 6 Apr 1977. 5'9". RHB, OB. Debut 1997. 1000 runs (1): 1080 (1998). HS 200* v Warwks (Leeds) 1998. LO HS 65* v Essex (Scarborough) 1998 (SL).

RELEASED/RETIRED

(Having made a first-class County appearance in 1999)

BLEWETT, Gregory Scott (Prince Alfred C), b Adelaide, Australia 28 Oct 1971. Son of R.W. (South Australia 1975-76 to 1978-79). 6'0". RHB, RM. South Australia 1991-92 to date. Yorkshire 1999; cap 1999. **Tests** (A): 44 (1994-95 to 1999-00); HS 214 v SA (Johannesburg) 1996-97; scored 102* v E (Adelaide) on debut; first to score hundreds in his first 3 Ashes Tests; BB 2-9 v WI (St John's) 1998-99. **LOI** (A): 32 (1994-95 to 1998-99); HS 57* v WI (Melbourne) 1996-97; BB 2-6 v SL (Adelaide) 1998-99. Tours (A): E 1997; SA 1996-97; WI 1994-95, 1998-99; I 1997-98; SL 1999-00; Z 1999-00. 1000 runs (0+3); most – 1187 (1998-99). HS 268 S Aus v Vic (Melbourne) 1993-94. Y HS 190 v Northants (Scarborough) 1999. BB 5-29 Aus XI v WI (Hobart) 1996-97. Y BB 2-16 v Durham (Leeds) 1999. LO HS 97 S Aus v ACT (Canberra) 1997-98 (MM). LO BB 4-18 v Lancs (Manchester) 1999 (NWT).

YORKSHIRE 1999

RESULTS SUMMARY

	Place	*Won*	*Lost*	*Tied*	*Drew*	*No Result*
PPP County Championship	**6th**	8	6		3	
All First-Class Matches		8	6		3	
NatWest Trophy	Semi-Finalist					
Benson & Hedges Super Cup	Finalist					
CGU National League (Division 1)	**5th**	8	8			

COUNTY CHAMPIONSHIP AVERAGES

BATTING AND FIELDING

Cap		*M*	*I*	*NO*	*HS*	*Runs*	*Avge*	*100*	*50*	*Ct/St*
1998	G.M.Hamilton	11	20	8	94*	567	47.25	–	4	3
1999	G.S.Blewett	12	23	2	190	655	31.19	1	2	5
1999	A.McGrath	16	30	2	142*	831	29.67	1	6	15
1999	R.J.Harden	10	19	3	69	438	27.37	–	3	2
1991	D.Byas	17	34	2	95	875	27.34	–	8	24
1995	M.P.Vaughan	17	34	1	153	895	27.12	3	3	5
1987	R.J.Blakey	17	31	4	123	684	25.33	1	4	41
–	I.D.Fisher	11	16	5	51	261	23.72	–	1	–
1993	C.White	17	31	2	52	521	17.96	–	1	12
1993	D.Gough	3	5	1	33	66	16.50	–	–	–
–	G.M.Fellows	3	6	1	34*	74	14.80	–	–	1
1996	C.E.W.Silverwood	13	20	2	53*	259	14.38	–	1	3
–	M.J.Wood	17	33	–	53	451	13.66	–	1	10
–	R.J.Sidebottom	12	20	5	48*	146	9.73	–	–	6
–	M.J.Hoggard	8	11	3	21	53	6.62	–	–	2
1998	P.M.Hutchison	3	4	3	4*	6	6.00	–	–	–

BOWLING

	O	*M*	*R*	*W*	*Avge*	*Best*	*5wI*	*10wM*
D.Gough	96.5	20	319	17	18.76	4-27	–	–
G.M.Hamilton	277.1	65	825	43	19.18	5-30	1	–
P.M.Hutchison	65.5	16	263	13	20.23	6-35	1	–
C.E.W.Silverwood	405.2	87	1204	59	20.40	5-28	3	–
M.J.Hoggard	215.1	58	619	28	22.10	5-47	1	–
C.White	354	69	1058	41	25.80	4-32	–	–
R.J.Sidebottom	275.3	70	789	24	32.87	3-16	–	–
I.D.Fisher	162	42	476	14	34.00	5-73	1	–
M.P.Vaughan	137.1	26	424	10	42.40	2-19	–	–

Also bowled: G.S.Blewett 66.4-13-212-5; G.M.Fellows 7-0-38-1; A.McGrath 86-26-204-9.

The First-Class Averages (pp 113-128) give the records of Yorkshire players in all first-class county matches.

YORKSHIRE RECORDS

FIRST-CLASS CRICKET

Highest Total	For	887		v	Warwicks	Birmingham	1896
	V	681-7d		by	Leics	Bradford	1996
Lowest Total	For	23		v	Hampshire	Middlesbrough	1965
	V	13		by	Notts	Nottingham	1901
Highest Innings	For	341	G.H.Hirst	v	Leics	Leicester	1905
	V	318*	W.G.Grace	for	Glos	Cheltenham	1876

Highest Partnership for each Wicket

1st	555	P.Holmes/H.Sutcliffe	v	Essex	Leyton	1932
2nd	346	W.Barber/M.Leyland	v	Middlesex	Sheffield	1932
3rd	323*	H.Sutcliffe/M.Leyland	v	Glamorgan	Huddersfield	1928
4th	312	D.Denton/G.H.Hirst	v	Hampshire	Southampton	1914
5th	340	E.Wainwright/G.H.Hirst	v	Surrey	The Oval	1899
6th	276	M.Leyland/E.Robinson	v	Glamorgan	Swansea	1926
7th	254	W.Rhodes/D.C.F.Burton	v	Hampshire	Dewsbury	1919
8th	292	R.Peel/Lord Hawke	v	Warwicks	Birmingham	1896
9th	192	G.H.Hirst/S.Haigh	v	Surrey	Bradford	1898
10th	149	G.Boycott/G.B.Stevenson	v	Warwicks	Birmingham	1982

Best Bowling	For	10-10	H.Verity	v	Notts	Leeds	1932
(Innings)	V	10-37	C.V.Grimmett	for	Australians	Sheffield	1930
Best Bowling	For	17-91	H.Verity	v	Essex	Leyton	1933
(Match)	V	17-91	H.Dean	for	Lancashire	Liverpool	1913

Most Runs – Season	2883	H.Sutcliffe	(av 80.08)	1932
Most Runs – Career	38561	H.Sutcliffe	(av 50.20)	1919-45
Most 100s – Season	12	H.Sutcliffe		1932
Most 100s – Career	112	H.Sutcliffe		1919-45
Most Wkts – Season	240	W.Rhodes	(av 12.72)	1900
Most Wkts – Career	3608	W.Rhodes	(av 16.00)	1898-1930

LIMITED-OVERS CRICKET

Highest Total	**NWT**	345-5		v	Notts	Leeds	1996
	BHC	317-5		v	Scotland	Leeds	1986
	NL	318-7		v	Leics	Leicester	1993
Lowest Total	**NWT**	76		v	Surrey	Harrogate	1970
	BHC	88		v	Worcs	Leeds	1995
	NL	56		v	Warwicks	Birmingham	1995
Highest Innings	**NWT**	146	G.Boycott	v	Surrey	Lord's	1965
	BHC	142	G.Boycott	v	Worcs	Worcester	1980
	NL	148	C.White	v	Leics	Leicester	1997
Best Bowling	**NWT**	7-27	D.Gough	v	Ireland	Leeds	1997
	BHC	6-27	A.G.Nicholson	v	Minor C (N)	Middlesbrough	1972
	NL	7-15	R.A.Hutton	v	Worcs	Leeds	1969

FIRST-CLASS UMPIRES 2000

BENSON, Mark Richard (Sutton Valence S), b Shoreham, Sussex 6 Jul 1958. LHB, OB. Kent 1980-95; cap 1981; captain 1991-96 (did not play in 1996); benefit 1991. Tests: 1 (1986); HS 30 v I (Birmingham) 1986. LOI: 1 (1986; HS 24). 1000 runs (11); most – 1725 (1987). HS 257 v Hants (Southampton) 1991. BB 2-55 v Surrey (Dartford) 1986. F-c career: 292 matches; 18387 runs @ 40.23, 48 hundreds; 5 wickets @ 98.60; 140 ct. Appointed 2000.

BURGESS, Graham Iefvion (Millfield S), b Glastonbury, Somerset 5 May 1943. RHB, RM. Somerset 1966-79; cap 1968; testimonial 1977. HS 129 v Glos (Taunton) 1973. BB 7-43 (13-75 match) v OU (Oxford) 1975. F-c career: 252 matches; 7129 runs @ 18.90, 2 hundreds; 474 wickets @ 28.57. Appointed 1991.

CLARKSON, Anthony (Harrogate GS), b Killinghall, Harrogate, Yorks 5 Sep 1939. RHB, OB. Yorkshire 1963. Somerset 1966-71; cap 1968. Devon. 1000 runs (2); most – 1246 (1970). HS 131 Sm v Northants (Northampton) 1969. BB 3-51 Sm v Essex (Yeovil) 1967. F-c career: 110 matches; 4458 runs @ 25.18, 2 hundreds; 13 wickets @ 28.23. Appointed 1996.

CONSTANT, David John, b Bradford-on-Avon, Wilts 9 Nov 1941. LHB, SLA. Kent 1961-63. Leicestershire 1965-68. HS 80 Le v Glos (Bristol) 1966. F-c career: 61 matches; 1517 runs @ 19.20; 1 wicket @ 36.00. Appointed 1969. Umpired 36 Tests (1971 to 1988) and 31 LOI (1972 to 1998). Represented Gloucestershire at bowls 1984-86.

COWLEY, Nigel Geoffrey (Dutchy Manor SS, Mere), b Shaftesbury, Dorset 1 Mar 1953. RHB, OB. Dorset 1972. Hampshire 1974-89; cap 1978; benefit 1988. Glamorgan 1990. 1000 runs (1): 1042 (1984). HS 109* H v Somerset (Taunton) 1977. BB 6-48 H v Leics (Southampton) 1982. F-c career: 271 matches; 7309 runs @ 23.35, 2 hundreds; 437 wickets @ 34.04. Appointed 2000.

DUDLESTON, Barry (Stockport S), b Bebington, Cheshire 16 Jul 1945. RHB, SLA. Leicestershire 1966-80; cap 1969; benefit 1980. Gloucestershire 1981-83. Rhodesia 1976-77 to 1979-80. 1000 runs (8); most – 1374 (1970). HS 202 Le v Derbys (Leicester) 1979. BB 4-6 Le v Surrey (Leicester) 1972. F-c career: 295 matches; 14747 runs @ 32.48, 32 hundreds; 47 wickets @ 29.04. Appointed 1984. Umpired 2 Tests (1991 to 1992) and 2 LOI (1992 to 1998).

HAMPSHIRE, John Harry (Oakwood THS, Rotherham), b Thurnscoe, Yorks 10 Feb 1941. RHB, LB. Son of J. (Yorks 1937); brother of A.W. (Yorks 1975). Yorkshire 1961-81; cap 1963; benefit 1976; captain 1979-80. Leicestershire 1980-81 (tour). Derbyshire 1982-84; cap 1982. Tasmania 1967-68 to 1978-79. **Tests:** 8 (1969 to 1975); 403 runs @ 26.86, HS 107 v WI (Lord's) 1969 on debut (only England player to score hundred at Lord's on Test debut). Tours: A 1970-71; SA 1972-73 (DHR), 1974-75 (DHR); WI 1964-65 (Cav); NZ 1970-71; P 1967-68 (Cwlth XI); SL 1969-70; Z 1980-81 (Le XI). 1000 runs (15); most – 1596 (1978). HS 183* Y v Sussex (Hove) 1971. BB 7-52 Y v Glam (Cardiff) 1963. F-c career: 577 matches; 28059 runs @ 34.55, 43 hundreds; 30 wickets @ 54.56; 445 ct. Appointed 1985. Umpired 11 Tests (1989 to 1993) and 8 LOI (1989 to 1998). **Appointed to International Panel 1999.**

HARRIS, John Henry, b Taunton, Somerset 13 Feb 1936. LHB, RFM. Somerset 1952-59. Suffolk 1960-62. Devon 1975. HS 41 v Worcs (Taunton) 1957. BB 3-29 v Worcs (Bristol) 1959. F-c career: 15 matches; 154 runs @ 11.00; 19 wickets @ 32.57. Appointed 1983.

HARRIS, Michael John ('*Pasty*') (Gerrans S, nr Truro), b St Just-in-Roseland, Cornwall 25 May 1944. RHB, LB, WK. Middlesex 1964-68; cap 1967. Nottinghamshire 1969-82; cap 1970; benefit 1977. Eastern Province 1971-72. Wellington 1975-76. 1000 runs (11); most – 2238 (1971). Scored 9 hundreds in 1971 to equal Notts record. HS 201* Nt v Glam (Nottingham) 1973. BB 4-16 Nt v Warwks (Nottingham) 1969. F-c career: 344 matches; 19,196 runs @ 36.70, 41 hundreds; 79 wickets @ 43.78; 302 dismissals (288 ct, 14 st). Appointed 1998.

HOLDER, John Wakefield (Combermere S), b St George, Barbados 19 Mar 1945. RHB, RFM. Hampshire 1968-72. Hat-trick 1972. HS 33 v Sussex (Hove) 1971. BB 7-79 v Glos (Gloucester) 1972. F-c career: 47 matches; 374 runs @ 10.68; 139 wickets @ 24.56.

Appointed 1983. Umpired 10 Tests (1988 to 1991) and 15 LOI (1988 to 1998) including 1989-90 Nehru Cup and one Sharjah tournament.

HOLDER, Vanburn Alonza (Richmond SM), b Deans Village, St Michael, Barbados 8 Oct 1945. RHB, RFM. Barbados 1966-67 to 1977-78. Worcestershire 1968-80; cap 1970; benefit 1979. Shropshire 1981. **Tests** (WI): 40 (1969 to 1978-79); 682 runs @ 14.20, HS 42 v NZ (P-o-S) 1971-72; 109 wkts @ 33.27, BB 6-28 v A (P-o-S) 1977-78. **LOI** (WI): 12. Tours (WI): E 1969, 1973, 1976; A 1975-76; I 1974-75, 1978-79; P 1973-74 (RW), 1974-75; SL 1974-75, 1978-79. HS 122 Barbados v Trinidad (Bridgetown) 1973-74. BB 7-40 Wo v Glam (Cardiff) 1974. F-c career: 311 matches; 3559 runs @ 13.03, 1 hundred; 947 wickets @ 24.48. Appointed 1992.

JESTY, Trevor Edward (Privet County SS, Gosport), b Gosport, Hants 2 Jun 1948. RHB, RM. Hampshire 1966-84; cap 1971; benefit 1982. Surrey 1985-87; cap 1985; captain 1985. Lancashire 1987-88 to 1991; cap 1989. Border 1973-74. GW 1974-75 to 1980-81. Canterbury 1979-80. *Wisden* 1982. **LOI:** 10. Tours: WI 1987-88 (La), 1982-83 (Int); Z 1988-89 (La). 1000 runs (10); most – 1645 (1982). HS 248 H v CU (Cambridge) 1984. Scored 122* La v OU (Oxford) 1991 in his final f-c innings. 50 wkts (2); most – 52 (1981). BB 7-75 H v Worcs (Southampton) 1976. F-c career: 490 matches; 21916 runs @ 32.71, 35 hundreds; 585 wickets @ 27.47. Appointed 1994.

JONES, Allan Arthur (St John's C, Horsham), b Horley, Surrey 9 Dec 1947. RHB, RFM. Sussex 1966-69. Somerset 1970-75; cap 1972. Middlesex 1976-79; cap 1976. Glamorgan 1980-81. Northern Transvaal 1972-73. Orange Free State 1976-77. HS 33 M v Kent (Canterbury) 1978. BB 9-51 Sm v Sussex (Hove) 1972. F-c career: 214 matches; 799 runs @ 5.39; 549 wickets @ 28.07. Appointed 1985. Umpired 1 LOI (1996).

JULIAN, Raymond (Wigston SM), b Cosby, Leics 23 Aug 1936. RHB, WK. Leicestershire 1953-71; cap 1961. HS 51 v Worcs (Worcester) 1962. F-c career: 192 matches; 2581 runs @ 9.73; 421 dismissals (382 ct, 39 st). Appointed 1972. Umpired 3 LOI (1996 to 1998).

KITCHEN, Mervyn John (Backwell SM, Nailsea), b Nailsea, Somerset 1 Aug 1940. LHB, RM. Somerset 1960-79; cap 1966; testimonial 1973. Tour: Rhodesia 1972-73 (Int W). 1000 runs (7); most – 1730 (1968). HS 189 v Pakistanis (Taunton) 1967. BB 1-4. F-c career: 354 matches; 15230 runs @ 26.25, 17 hundreds; 2 wickets @ 54.50. Appointed 1982. Umpired 19 Tests (1990 to 1999) and 25 LOI (1983 to 1998), including tournaments in Sharjah (1) and Nairobi (1). International Panel 1995-99.

LEADBEATER, Barrie (Harehills SS), b Harehills, Leeds, Yorks 14 Aug 1943. RHB, RM. Yorkshire 1966-79; cap 1969; joint benefit with G.A.Cope 1980. Tour: WI 1969-70 (DN). HS 140* v Hants (Portsmouth) 1976. F-c career: 147 matches; 5373 runs @ 25.34, 1 hundred; 1 wicket @ 5.00. Appointed 1981. Umpired 4 LOI (1983).

LLOYDS, Jeremy William (Blundells S), b Penang, Malaya 17 Nov 1954. LHB, OB. Somerset 1979-84; cap 1982. Gloucestershire 1985-91; cap 1985. Orange Free State 1983-84 to 1987-88, Tour (Glos): SL 1986-87. 1000 runs (3); most – 1295 (1986). HS 132* Sm v Northants (Northampton) 1982. BB 7-88 Sm v Essex (Chelmsford) 1982. F-c career: 267 matches; 10,679 runs @ 31.04, 10 hundreds; 333 wickets @ 38.86; 229 ct. Appointed 1998.

MALLENDER, Neil Alan (Beverley GS), b Kirk Sandall, Yorks 13 Aug 1961. RHB, RFM. Northamptonshire 1980-86 and 1995-96; cap 1984. Somerset 1987-94; cap 1987; benefit 1994. Otago 1983-84 to 1992-93; captain 1990-91 to 1992-93. **Tests:** 2 (1992); 8 runs @ 2.66, HS 4; 10 wkts @ 21.50, BB 5-50 v P (Leeds) 1992 – on debut. Tour: Z 1994-95 (Nh). HS 100* Otago v CD (Palmerston N) 1991-92. UK HS 87* Sm v Sussex (Hove) 1990. 50 wkts (6); most – 56 (1983). BB 7-27 Otago v Auckland (Auckland) 1984-85. UK BB 7-41 Nh v Derbys (Northampton) 1982. F-c career: 345 matches; 4,709 runs @ 17.18, 1 hundred; 937 wickets @ 26.31; 111 ct. Appointed 1999.

PALMER, Kenneth Ernest (Southbroom SM, Devizes), b Winchester, Hants 22 Apr 1937. RHB, RFM. Brother of R. (*below*) and father of G.V. (Somerset 1982-88). Somerset 1955-69; cap 1958; testimonial 1968. Tours: WI 1963-64 (Cav); P 1963-64 (Cwlth XI). **Tests:** 1 (1964-65; while coaching in South Africa); 10 runs; 1 wicket. 1000 runs (1): 1036 (1961). 100 wickets (4); most – 139 (1963). HS 125* v Northants (Northampton) 1961. BB

PALMER, K.E. *(continued)*
9-57 v Notts (Nottingham) 1963. F-c career: 314 matches; 7761 runs @ 20.64, 2 hundreds; 866 wickets @ 21.34. Appointed 1972. Umpired 22 Tests (1978 to 1994) and 20 LOI (1977 to 1998). International Panel 1994.

PALMER, Roy (Southbroom SM, Devizes), b Devizes, Wilts 12 Jul 1942. RHB, RFM. Brother of K.E. (*see above*). Somerset 1965-70. HS 84 v Leics (Taunton) 1967. BB 6-45 v Middx (Lord's) 1967. F-c career: 74 matches; 1037 runs @ 13.29; 172 wickets @ 31.62. Appointed 1980. Umpired 2 Tests (1992 to 1993) and 8 LOI (1983 to 1995).

SHARP, George (Elwick Road SS, Hartlepool), b West Hartlepool, Co Durham 12 Mar 1950. RHB, WK, occ LM. Northamptonshire 1968-85; cap 1973; benefit 1982. HS 98 v Yorks (Northampton) 1983. BB 1-47. F-c career: 306 matches; 6254 runs @ 19.85; 1 wicket @ 70.00; 655 dismissals (565 ct, 90 st). Appointed 1992. Umpired 10 Tests (1996 to 1999-2000) and 17 LOI (1995-96 to 1999-2000), including tournaments in Nairobi (1), Sharjah (1) and Singapore (1). **Appointed to International Panel 1996.**

SHEPHERD, David Robert (Barnstaple GS; St Luke's C, Exeter), b Bideford, Devon 27 Dec 1940. RHB, RM. Gloucestershire 1965-79; cap 1969; joint benefit with J.Davey 1978. Scored 108 on debut (v OU). Devon 1959-64. 1000 runs (2); most – 1079 (1970). HS 153 v Middx (Bristol) 1968. F-c career: 282 matches; 10672 runs @ 24.47, 12 hundreds; 2 wickets @ 53.00. Appointed 1981. Umpired 49 Tests (1985 to 1999-2000) and 90 LOI (1983 to 1999-2000), including 1987-88, 1991-92, 1995-96 and 1999 World Cups (2 finals), 1985-86 Asia Cup and tournaments in Dhaka (2), Sharjah (6) and Canada (1). **Appointed to International Panel 1994.**

STEELE, John Frederick (Endon SS), b Brown Edge, Staffs 23 Jul 1946. RHB, SLA. Brother of D.S. (Northants, Derbys and England 1963-84). Leicestershire 1970-83; cap 1971; benefit 1983. Glamorgan 1984-86; cap 1984. Natal 1973-74 to 1977-78. Staffordshire 1965-69. Tour: SA 1974-75 (DHR). 1000 runs (6); most – 1347 (1972). HS 195 Le v Derbys (Leicester) 1971. BB 7-29 Natal B v GW (Umzinto) 1973-74, and Le v Glos (Leicester) 1980. F-c career: 379 matches; 15054 runs @ 28.95, 21 hundreds; 584 wickets @ 27.04; 413 ct. Appointed 1997.

WHITE, Robert Arthur (Chiswick GS), b Fulham, London 6 Oct 1936. LHB, OB. Middlesex 1958-65 (cap 1963). Nottinghamshire 1966-80; cap 1966; benefit 1974. 1000 runs (1): 1355 (1963). HS 116* Nt v Surrey (Oval) 1967. BB 7-41 Nt v Derbys (Ilkeston) 1971. F-c career: 413 matches; 12452 runs @ 23.18, 5 hundreds; 693 wickets @ 30.50. Appointed 1983.

WHITEHEAD, Alan Geoffrey Thomas, b Butleigh, Somerset 28 Oct 1940. LHB, SLA. Somerset 1957-61. HS 15 v Hants (Southampton) 1959 and v Leics (Leicester) 1960. BB 6-74 v Sussex (Eastbourne) 1959. F-c career: 38 matches; 137 runs @ 5.70; 67 wickets @ 34.41. Appointed 1970. Umpired 5 Tests (1982 to 1987) and 13 LOI (1979 to 1996).

WILLEY, Peter (Seaham SS), b Sedgefield, Co Durham 6 Dec 1949. RHB, OB. Northamptonshire 1966-83; cap 1971; benefit 1981. Leicestershire 1984-91; cap 1984; captain 1987. E Province 1982-83 to 1984-85. Northumberland 1992. **Tests:** 26 (1976 to 1986); 1184 runs @ 26.90, HS 102* v WI (St John's) 1980-81; 7 wkts @ 65.14, BB 2-73 v WI (Lord's) 1980. **LOI:** 26. Tours: A 1979-80; SA 1972-73 (DHR), 1981-82 (SAB); WI 1980-81, 1985-86; I 1979-80; SL 1977-78 (DHR). 1000 runs (10); most – 1783 (1982). HS 227 Nh v Somerset (Northampton) 1976. 50 wkts (3); most – 52 (1979). BB 7-37 Nh v OU (Oxford) 1975. F-c career: 559 matches; 24361 runs @ 30.56, 44 hundreds; 756 wickets @ 30.95. Appointed 1993. Umpired 18 Tests (1995-96 to 1999-2000) and 16 LOI (1996 to 1999), including 1999 World Cup and a tournament in Dhaka. **Appointed to International Panel 1996.**

RESERVE FIRST-CLASS LIST: P.Adams, N.L.Bainton, J.H.Evans, C.S.Kelly, N.J.Llong, K.J.Lyons, K.Shuttleworth.

CURRENT INTERNATIONAL PANEL: J.H.Hampshire, G.Sharp, D.R.Shepherd, P.Willey (England); D.B.Hair, D.J.Harper (Australia); A.V.Jayaprakesh, S.Venkataraghavan (India); D.B.Cowie, R.S.Dunne (New Zealand); Athar Zaidi, Riazuddin (Pakistan); R.E.Koertzen, D.L.Orchard (South Africa); B.C.Cooray, P.T.Manuel (Sri Lanka); S.A.Bucknor, E.A.Nicholls (West Indies); I.D.Robinson, R.B.Tiffin (Zimbabwe).

Test Match and LOI statistics to 23 February 2000. See page 13 for key to abbreviations.

TOURING TEAM REGISTER 1999

NEW ZEALAND	Birthdate	Birthplace	Team	Type	F-C Debut
ALLOTT, Geoffrey Ian	24.12.71	Christchurch	Canterbury	RHB/LFM	1994-95
ASTLE, Nathan John	15. 9.71	Christchurch	Canterbury	RHB/RM	1991-92
BELL, Matthew David	25. 2.77	Dunedin	Wellington	RHB/OB	1993-94
CAIRNS, Christopher Lance	13. 6.70	Picton	Canterbury	RHB/RFM	1988
CROY, Martyn Gilbert	23. 1.74	Hamilton	Otago	RHB/WK	1994-95
DOULL, Simon Blair	6. 8.69	Pukekohe	N Districts	RHB/RMF	1989-90
FLEMING, Stephen Paul	1. 4.73	Christchurch	Canterbury	LHB/RSM	1991-92
HARRIS, Chris Zinzan	20.11.69	Christchurch	Canterbury	LHB/RM	1989-90
HORNE, Matthew Jeffery	5.12.70	Auckland	Otago	RHB/RM	1992-93
McMILLAN, Craig Douglas	13. 9.76	Christchurch	Canterbury	RHB/RM	1994-95
NASH, Dion Joseph	20.11.71	Auckland	N Districts	RHB/RFM	1990-91
O'CONNOR, Shayne Barry	15.11.73	Hastings	Otago	LHB/LFM	1994-95
PARORE, Adam Craig	23. 1.71	Auckland	Auckland	RHB/WK	1988-89
PENN, Andrew Jonathan	27. 7.74	Wanganui	N Zealand A	RHB/RFM	1994-95
TWOSE, Roger Graham	17. 4.68	Torquay	Wellington	LHB/RM	1989
VETTORI, Daniel Luca	27. 1.79	Auckland	N Districts	RHB/SLA	1996-97
WALKER, Brooke Graeme Keith	25. 3.77	Auckland	Auckland	RHB/LB	1997-98

SRI LANKA A	Birthdate	Birthplace	Team	Type	F-C Debut
ARNOLD, Russel Premakumaran	25.10.73	Colombo	Nondescripts	LHB/OB	1993-94
BANDARA, Charitha Malinga	31.12.79	Kalutara	Sri Lanka A	RHB/LB	1996-97
BOTEJU, Hemantha	3.11.77	Colombo	Bloomfield	RHB/RM	1995-96
DE SARAM, Samantha Indika	2. 9.73	Matara	Tamil Union	RHB/WK	1990-91
DILSHAN, Tuwan Mohamed	14.10.76	Kalutara	Singha	RHB/RM/WK	1993-94
GALLAGE, Indika Sanjeewa	22.11.75	Panadura	Colombo	RHB/RM	1995-96
GUNAWARDENA, Dihan Avishka	26. 5.77	Colombo	Nondescripts	LHB	1996-97
HERATH, Rangana	19. 3.78	Kurunegala	Kurunegala Y	LHB/SLA	1996-97
HEWAGE, Pradeep Randy	7.12.78	Colombo	Sri Lanka A	RHB/RM	1995-96
JAYANTHA, Saman	26. 1.74	Ambalangoda	Singha	RHB/OB	1992-93
JAYAWARDENA, Hewasandatchige Prasanna Wishvanath	9. 9.79	Colombo	Sri Lanka A	RHB/WK	1997-98
KALAVITIGODA, Shantha	23.12.77	Colombo	Sinhalese	RHB	1997-98
NAWAZ, Mohamed Naveed	20. 9.73	Colombo	Bloomfield	LHB/OB	1993-94
PERERA, Anhettige Suresh Asanka	16. 2.78	Colombo	Sinhalese	RHB/RMF	1995-96
PERERA, Bathia	28. 4.77	Colombo	Colts	RHB	1996-97
PERERA, Nimesh Randika Gayan	5. 9.77	Colombo	Sebastianites	LHB/LB	1995-96
PUSHPAKUMARA, Karuppiahyage Ravindra	21. 7.75	Panadura	Nondescripts	RHB/RFM	1992-93
SILVA, Lidamulage Prageeth Chamara	14.12.79	Panadura	Panadura	RHB	1996-97
VILLAVARAYEN, Mario Suresh	22. 8.73	Colombo	Tamil Union	RHB/RMF	1992-93
WICKREMASINGHE, Prasad Priyankara	12. 5.77	Colombo	Bloomfield	LHB/LB	1996-97

SA ACADEMY XI	Birthdate	Birthplace	Team	Type	F-C Debut
AMLA, Ahmed Mahomed	15. 7.79	Durban	Natal	RHB/LB	1997-98
BODI, Goolam Hussain	4. 1.79	Hathuran, India	Gauteng	LHB/SLC	1996-97
BRYANT, James Douglas Campbell	4. 2.76	Durban	E Province	RHB	1996-97
CREED, Murray	5. 3.79	Port Elizabeth	E Province	RHB/RFM	1997-98
HENDERSON, Tyron	1. 8.74	Durban	Border	RHB/RFM	1998-99
JACOBS, Arno	13. 3.77	Potchefstroom	North West	LHB/WK	1997-98
JENNINGS, Dylan	14. 9.79	Johannesburg	SA Academy	LHB/WK	1999
LOVE, Geoff Terry	19. 9.76	Port Elizabeth	Border	RHB/OB	1995-96
NEL, Andre	15. 7.77	Germiston	Easterns	RHB/RFM	1996-97
ONTONG, Justin Lee	4. 1.80	Paarl	Boland	RHB/OB	1997-98
PRETORIUS, Dewald	6.12.77	Pretoria	Free State	RHB/RF	1997-98
STILL, Quentin Raxham	8. 8.74	Pietermaritzburg	Northerns	RHB/SLA	1993-94
TSOLEKILE, Thami Lungisa	9.10.80	Cape Town	SA Academy	RHB/OB/WK	1999
VAN DEN BERG, Adolf Matthys	9. 3.78	Randfontein	Gauteng	RHB/OB	1999
WINGFIELD, Wade Richard	17.12.77	Scottburgh	Natal	RHB/RM	1997-98

IRELAND REGISTER 1999

Full Names	*Birthdate*	*Birthplace*	*Bat/Bowl*	*F-C Debut*
ARCHER, Barry John	21. 6.77	Dublin	LHB/RSM	1999
CARSON, Neil David	25. 1.73	Banbridge	LHB/RM	1999
COOKE, Gordon	24. 7.75	Londonderry	RHB/RMF	1994
DAVY, John Oliver	1. 7.74	Dublin	RHB/LFM	1997
DAVY, Peter Joseph	1. 7.74	Dublin	RHB	1999
DUNLOP, Angus Richard	17. 3.67	Dublin	RHB/OB	1990
GILLESPIE, Peter Gerard	11. 5.74	Strabane	RHB/RM	1996
McCALLAN, William Kyle	27. 8.75	Carrickfergus	RHB/OB	1996
McCOUBREY, Adrian George Agustus Mathew	3. 4.80	Ballymena	RHB/RFM	1999
McDAID, Richard William	3.11.75	Londonderry	RHB/RM	1999
McGERRIGLE, Robert Dwayne	12. 3.80	Londonderry	RHB/RM	1999
MOLINS, Gregory Leo	19. 3.76	Dublin	RHB/SLA	1996
MOONEY, Paul John Kevin	15.10.76	Dublin	RHB/RM	1998
RHODES, Jonathan Neil ('*Jonty*')	27. 7.69	Pietermaritzburg	RHB/RM	1988-89
RUTHERFORD, Alan Thomas	2. 6.67	Strabane	RHB/WK	1996
SHIELDS, Ian Peter	21.10.79	Comber	RHB/WK	1999
SMYTH, Stephen Gordon	22.12.68	Londonderry	LHB	1991

SCOTLAND REGISTER 1999

Full Names	*Birthdate*	*Birthplace*	*Bat/Bowl*	*F-C Debut*
ALLINGHAM, Michael James de Grey	6. 1.65	Inverness	RHB/RM	1996
ASIM BUTT	24.10.67	Lahore, Pakistan	RHB/LMF	1983-84
AYAZ GUL	19. 4.75	Lyallpur, Pakistan	RHB/OB	1995-96
BRINKLEY, James Edward	13. 3.74	Helensburgh	RHB/RFM	1993
COX, David John	1. 3.73	Coventry	RHB/RMF	1999
DYER, Nicholas Rayner	10. 6.69	Edinburgh	RHB/OB	1997
HAY, Martyn James	24. 5.76	Irvine	RHB/RM	1999
MacRAE, Neil John	25. 3.78	Liverpool	RHB	1999
MAIDEN, Gregor Ian	22. 7.79	Glasgow	RHB/OB	1999
PARSONS, Robert Andrew	26. 7.75	Irvine	LHB/LM	1999
SALMOND, George	1.12.69	Dundee	RHB	1991
SMITH, Colin John Ogilvie	27. 9.72	Aberdeen	RHB/WK	1999
STANGER, Ian Michael	5.10.71	Glasgow	RHB/RFM	1997
STUBBS, Evan Graeme Crowther	23. 4.78	Glasgow	RHB/WK	1999
TENNANT, Andrew McBlain	17. 2.66	Ayr	RHB/SLA	1996
WATTS, David Fraser	5. 6.79	King's Lynn	RHB	1999
WILLIAMSON, John Greig	20.12.68	Glasgow	RHB/RM	1994
WRIGHT, Craig McIntyre	28. 4.74	Paisley	RHB/RFM	1997

MCC REGISTER 1999

Full Names	*Birthdate*	*Birthplace*	*Team*	*Type*	*F-C Debut*
DAVIS, Mark Jeffrey Gronow	10.10.71	Port Elizabeth	Northerns	RHB/OB	1990-91
DAWES, Joseph Henry	29. 8.70	Herston, Aus.	Queensland	RHB/RFM	1997-98
FLOWER, Andrew	28. 4.68	Cape Town	Zimbabwe	LHB/OB/WK	1986-87
GUPTE, Chinmay Madhukar	5. 7.72	Poona, India	Ex Oxford U	RHB/sla	1991
JOHNSON, Neil Clarkson	24. 1.70	Salisbury	Zimbabwe	LHB/RFM	1989-90
KING, Reon Dane	6.10.75	Guyana	Guyana/WI	RHB/RFM	1995-96
LAWSON, Andrew Grant	4. 3.67	Durban	North West	LHB	1991-92
ROBINSON, Jonathan David	3. 8.66	Epsom	Ex Surrey	LHB/RM	1988
STRANG, Paul Andrew	28. 7.70	Bulawayo	Zimbabwe	RHB/LBG	1992-93
WARDEN, Michael John	9.11.67	Herston, Aus.	MCC	RHB/RFM	1999
WILLIAMS, Kelvin Claudius	29. 5.59	Carapichaima	Trinidad	RHB/RFM	1981-82

UNIVERSITY REGISTER 1999

CAMBRIDGE

Full Names	*Birthdate*	*Birthplace*	*College*	*Bat/Bowl*	*F-C Debut*
BIRKS, Malcolm James	29. 7.75	Keighley	Jesus	RHB/WK	1995
COLLINS, Benjamin James	4.11.77	London	Girton	RHB	1998
DANSON, Andrew Richard	25.10.78	Sheffield	Pembroke	RHB/RM	1999
GOODYER, Timothy Edward	21.10.75	Johannesburg	Sidney Sussex	RHB/RM	1999
HALSALL, Richard Grant	1.10.68	Salisbury	Homerton	RHB/RM	1999
HUGHES, Quentin John	17.10.74	Durham City	St Edmund's	LHB/OB	1997
LEWIS, Simon James Ward	9.10.78	Bolton	Jesus	RHB	1998
LOVERIDGE, Greg Riaka	15. 1.75	Palmerston N	St Edmund's	RHB/LBG	1994-95
LOWE, Jonathan Paul	13.11.77	Pontefract	Girton	RHB/RM	1998
McDOWELL, Richard William	29. 6.73	Invercargill	St John's	RHB/LB	1999
MOHAMMED, Imraan	31.12.76	Solihull	St Catharine's	RHB/OB	1997
PIMLOTT, Charles Robert	25. 2.79	Stockport	Downing	RHB/RFM	1999
PYEMONT, James Patrick	10. 4.78	Eastbourne	Trinity	RHB/OB	1997
ROSS, Jonathan Stuart	5. 4.79	Epsom	Emmanuel	RHB/LM	1999
SAJDEH, Rohan Kewal	13. 8.74	Darwin	St John's	RHB/LB	1999
SAYERS, Christopher Allan	19.12.78	Harrow	Trinity Hall	RHB/RMF	1999
SHEIKH, Samir Majid	16.10.78	London	St John's	RHB/RMF	1999
WALKER, Kenneth David Mortimer	28.10.70	Grahamstown	Wolfson	LHB/SLA	1999

OXFORD

Full Names	*Birthdate*	*Birthplace*	*College*	*Bat/Bowl*	*F-C Debut*
ASHLEY, Nathan William	3.10.73	Sydney	University	LHB/RSM	1999
BARNES, Jeremy Paul Blissard	23. 3.70	Orpington	Wycliffe Hall	RHB/WK	1998
BOND, Andrew Nicholas	13. 9.78	Melbourne	St Catherine's	RHB/RM	1999
BULL, James Jonathan	22.12.76	Leicester	Keble	RHB/OB	1996
BYRNE, Byron Walter	15. 2.72	Sydney	Balliol	RHB/OB	1997
CLAUGHTON, John Andrew	28.10.78	Southampton	Keble	RHB/RM	1998
CONWAY, Stephen Lawrence John	15.11.74	Stockton-on-T	Jesus	LHB/RM	1999
EADIE, David John	2. 1.75	Cape Town	St Edmund Hall	RHB/RM	1998
FULTON, James Anthony Gervase	21. 9.77	Plymouth	Brasenose	LHB/RM	1997
GOFTON, Alan Frederick	4.10.79	Chesterfield	Wadham	RHB/RM	1999
HICKS, Thomas Charles	28. 8.79	Farnborough	St Catherine's	RHB/OB	1999
KHAN, Salman Haider	4. 6.71	Rawalpindi	Wadham	RHB/RM	1998
KINO, Dean	15. 4.71	Melbourne	Magdalen	LHB/LMF	1999
LOUW, James Haig	16. 4.71	Dordrecht, SA	Keble	LHB/RM	1999
MATHER, David Peter	20.11.75	Bebington	St Hugh's	LHB/LM	1995
PIRIHI, Nicholas Gordon	19. 4.97	Whangarei	Merton	RHB	1997
SMALLEY, Richard George	20. 3.79	Newcastle-u-T	Keble	LHB/WK	1999

BRITISH UNIVERSITIES

(Excluding players listed either above or in the County Register)

Full Names	*Birthdate*	*Birthplace*	*University*	*Bat/Bowl*	*F-C Debut*
HELLINGS, Christopher James	21. 1.80	Taunton	Loughborough	RHB/WK	1999
LAWRENCE, James Richard Geoffrey	29.11.76	Portsmouth	Durham	RHB/LMF	1999
ROBERTS, Timothy William	4. 3.78	Kettering	Durham	RHB/OB	1999

THE 1999 FIRST-CLASS SEASON STATISTICAL HIGHLIGHTS

HIGHEST INNINGS TOTALS († *County record;* * *Second innings*)

648-4d†	Glamorgan v Nottinghamshire	Colwyn Bay
591-7d	Worcestershire v Gloucestershire	Cheltenham
591	New Zealanders v Kent	Canterbury
585	Surrey v Middlesex	Lord's
579	Northamptonshire v Essex	Northampton
570-6d*	Hampshire v Sussex	Southampton
566-8d	Leicestershire v Sussex	Arundel
558-9d	Surrey v Somerset	The Oval
556-6d	Lancashire v Glamorgan	Blackpool
554	Somerset v New Zealanders	Taunton
552	Durham v Gloucestershire	Cheltenham
544	Glamorgan v Kent	Canterbury
544	Essex v Somerset	Chelmsford
541	Kent v Essex	Canterbury
525-7d*	Sri Lanka A v Essex	Chelmsford
523-3d*	Somerset v Middlesex	Taunton
517-7d	Northamptonshire v Yorkshire	Scarborough
513-6d	New Zealanders v British U	Oxford
509	Northamptonshire v Leicestershire	Northampton
504	Kent v Somerset	Taunton
503-8d	Somerset v Sussex	Taunton
501	Surrey v Leicestershire	Leicester

HIGHEST FOURTH INNINGS TOTALS

455-8	Sussex (set 452) v Gloucestershire	Hove

LOWEST INNINGS TOTALS

52	Yorkshire v Leicestershire	Leicester
67	Yorkshire v Lancashire	Manchester
69	Northamptonshire v Kent (*1st innings*)	Canterbury
71	Kent v Surrey	Tunbridge Wells
76	Nottinghamshire v Warwickshire	Nottingham
76	Hampshire v Sussex	Southampton
81	Oxford U v Worcestershire	Oxford
84	Glamorgan v Surrey	The Oval
86	Warwickshire v Essex	Chelmsford
86	Sri Lanka A v Northamptonshire	Northampton
86	Northamptonshire v Kent (*2nd innings*)	Canterbury
88	Northamptonshire v Middlesex	Lord's
88	Nottinghamshire v Kent	Nottingham
90	Worcestershire v Yorkshire	Leeds
93	Durham v Kent	Stockton
96	Middlesex v Northamptonshire	Lord's
99	Sussex v Warwickshire	Birmingham

VICTORY AFTER FOLLOWING ON

Essex (188 & 432-7d) beat Nottinghamshire (349 & 151)	Nottingham

FIRST TO INDIVIDUAL TARGETS

1000 RUNS	S.G.Law	Essex	July 14
2000 RUNS	–		
100 WICKETS	–		

TRIPLE HUNDRED

D.J.G.Sales	303*	Northamptonshire v Essex	Northampton

Youngest British-born batsman to score 300 (21 years 240 days)

DOUBLE HUNDREDS

M.A.Atherton		268*	Lancashire v Glamorgan	Blackpool
A.D.Brown		265	Surrey v Middlesex	Lord's
M.A.Butcher		259	Surrey v Leicestershire	Leicester
J.Cox		216	Somerset v Hampshire	Southampton
S.P.James		259*	Glamorgan v Nottinghamshire	Colwyn Bay
W.S.Kendall		201	Hampshire v Sussex	Southampton
J.L.Langer		241*	Middlesex v Kent	Lord's
S.G.Law		263	Essex v Somerset	Chelmsford
M.R.Rampra-kash		209*	Middlesex v Surrey	Lord's
D.D.J.Robinson		200	Essex v New Zealanders	Chelmsford
D.J.G.Sales	(2)	303*	Northamptonshire v Essex	Northampton
		205	Northamptonshire v Leicestershire	Northampton
M.A.Wagh		216*	Warwickshire v Oxford U	Oxford

HUNDRED IN EACH INNINGS OF A MATCH

J.Cox	216	129*	Somerset v Hampshire	Southampton
A.Dale	108	113	Glamorgan v Gloucestershire	Cardiff
G.A.Hick	101	150	Worcestershire v Essex	Chelmsford
S.G.Law	159	113*	Essex v Yorkshire	Chelmsford
M.P.Vaughan	100	151	Yorkshire v Essex	Chelmsford

FASTEST HUNDRED (EDS WALTER LAWRENCE TROPHY)

A.Flintoff	61 balls	Lancashire v Gloucestershire	Bristol

HUNDRED BEFORE LUNCH

			Day		
A.Flintoff	(2)	0*-112*	1†	Lancashire v Gloucestershire	Bristol
		45*-156*	2	Lancashire v Yorkshire	Manchester
M.L.Hayden	(2)	13*-139*	3	Northamptonshire v Nottinghamshire	Northampton
		14*-130*	4‡	Northamptonshire v Lancashire	Manchester
J.E.Morris		11*-119	2	Durham v Derbyshire	Chester-le-St

† No play on first two days ‡ In contrived circumstances

HUNDRED ON FIRST-CLASS DEBUT IN BRITAIN

A.M.Amla	107	South African Academy XI v Ireland	Clontarf
J.Cox	139	Somerset v Cambridge U	Cambridge
T.M.Dilshan	115	Sri Lanka A v Northamptonshire	Northampton
M.J.Horne	133	New Zealanders v British U	Oxford

CARRYING BAT THROUGH COMPLETED INNINGS

D.L.Maddy	158*	Leicestershire (297) v Yorkshire	Leicester

AN HOUR BEFORE SCORING FIRST RUN

Min			
72	P.M.Such (0)	England v New Zealand (3rd Test)	Manchester
64	R.W.T.Key (0)	Kent v Worcestershire	Worcester

AN HOUR WITHOUT ADDING TO SCORE

Min			
60	M.J.Horne (10)	New Zealanders v Essex	Chelmsford

FIRST-WICKET PARTNERSHIP OF 100 IN EACH INNINGS

125		T.R.Ward/E.T.Smith	Kent v Cambridge U	Cambridge
	179	E.T.Smith/R.W.T.Key		
100	156	J.Cox/M.E.Trescothick	Somerset v Hampshire	Southampton
117	103	A.J.Strauss/B.L.Hutton	Middlesex v Worcestershire	Worcester

OTHER NOTABLE PARTNERSHIPS († *County record*)

First Wicket

278	J.Cox/P.D.Bowler	Somerset v Cambridge U	Cambridge
256‡	R.J.Bailey/M.L.Hayden	Northamptonshire v Lancashire	Manchester
253	J.Cox/M.E.Trescothick	Somerset v Middlesex	Taunton

‡ *In contrived circumstances*

Second Wicket

296	M.J.Slater/S.P.Titchard	Derbyshire v Northamptonshire	Derby
259	M.A.Wagh/D.L.Hemp	Warwickshire v Oxford U	Oxford

Third Wicket

281	S.P.James/M.J.Powell	Glamorgan v Nottinghamshire	Colwyn Bay

Fourth Wicket

256	M.J.Di Venuto/P.A.Cottey	Sussex v Gloucestershire	Hove

Fifth Wicket

288	A.D.Brown/A.J.Hollioake	Surrey v Middlesex	Lord's
274	S.G.Law/D.D.J.Robinson	Essex v Somerset	Chelmsford

Sixth Wicket

255	D.J.G.Sales/D.Ripley	Northamptonshire v Leicestershire	Northampton
228	P.A.Nixon/C.C.Lewis	Leicestershire v Essex	Chelmsford

Seventh Wicket

293†	D.J.G.Sales/D.Ripley	Northamptonshire v Essex	Northampton
214	A.L.Penberthy/D.Ripley	Northamptonshire v Yorkshire	Scarborough
119†	N.Killeen/M.P.Speight	Durham v Glamorgan	Cardiff

Eighth Wicket

172†	A.R.K.Pierson/P.S.Jones	Somerset v New Zealanders	Taunton

Tenth Wicket

134	P.P.Wickremasinghe/ I.S.Gallage	Sri Lanka A v Lancashire	Manchester
130	M.C.J.Ball/J.Lewis	Gloucestershire v Worcestershire	Cheltenham
123	C.C.Lewis/M.T.Brimson	Leicestershire v Lancashire	Leicester
101	M.V.Fleming/ J.B.D.Thompson	Kent v Worcestershire	Worcester

EIGHT OR MORE WICKETS IN AN INNINGS

A.R.Caddick	8-113	Somerset v Lancashire	Taunton
P.J.Hartley	8- 65	Hampshire v Yorkshire	Basingstoke
M.M.Patel	8-115	Kent v Lancashire	Manchester
A.Richardson	8- 51	Warwickshire v Gloucestershire	Birmingham

TEN OR MORE WICKETS IN A MATCH

P.Aldred	13-184	Derbyshire v Lancashire	Derby
M.P.L.Bulbeck	10-108	Somerset v Northamptonshire	Northampton
C.L.Cairns	10-116	New Zealanders v Kent	Canterbury
R.D.B.Croft	10-238	Glamorgan v Durham	Cardiff
J.M.de la Pena	10- 52	Worcestershire v Oxford U	Oxford
V.C.Drakes (2)	12-110	Nottinghamshire v Warwickshire	Nottingham
	11-113	Nottinghamshire v Middlesex	Southgate
P.J.Hartley	11-117	Hampshire v Yorkshire	Basingstoke
J.Lewis	10- 92	Gloucestershire v Nottinghamshire	Bristol

J.D.Lewry	10-113	Sussex v Derbyshire	Derby
A.C.Morris	10-111	Hampshire v Worcestershire	Southampton
M.Muralitharan (5)	14-117	Lancashire v Warwickshire	Southport
	10-154	Lancashire v Surrey	The Oval
	13-134	Lancashire v Essex	Manchester
	10-176	Lancashire v Glamorgan	Blackpool
	11- 61	Lancashire v Derbyshire	Derby
M.M.Patel	12-235	Kent v Lancashire	Manchester
N.C.Phillips	12-268	Durham v Glamorgan	Cardiff
A.Richardson	10-107	Warwickshire v Gloucestershire	Birmingham
Saqlain Mushtaq (2)	12-110	Surrey v Durham	The Oval
	10- 97	Surrey v Sussex	Hove
A.Sheriyar	10-172	Worcestershire v Hampshire	Southampton
T.M.Smith	10-150	Derbyshire v Leicestershire	Leicester
P.M.Such	13-213	Essex v Lancashire	Manchester
G.P.Swann	11-126	Northamptonshire v Leicestershire	Northampton

HAT-TRICKS

T.A.Munton	Warwickshire v Kent	Maidstone
Saqlain Mushtaq	Surrey v Sussex	Hove
A.Sheriyar	Worcestershire v Kent	Worcester

WICKET WITH FIRST BALL IN FIRST-CLASS CRICKET

K.D.M.Walker	Cambridge U v Lancashire	Cambridge

60 OVERS IN AN INNINGS

J.J.Bates	(2)	60-22-154-5	Sussex v Leicestershire	Arundel
		62-17-166-3	Sussex v Hampshire	Southampton

SIX OR MORE WICKET-KEEPING DISMISSALS IN AN INNINGS

W.M.Noon		7ct	Nottinghamshire v Kent	Nottingham
C.M.W.Read	(2)	6ct	Nottinghamshire v Somerset	Nottingham
		5 ct 1 st	England v New Zealand (1st Test)	Birmingham

NINE OR MORE WICKET-KEEPING DISMISSALS IN A MATCH

D.C.Nash	9ct	Middlesex v Yorkshire	Leeds
C.M.W.Read	9ct	Nottinghamshire v Somerset	Nottingham

NO BYES CONCEDED IN TOTAL OF 500 OR MORE

556-6d	I.Dawood	Glamorgan v Lancashire	Blackpool
504	R.J.Turner	Somerset v Kent	Taunton

SIXTY EXTRAS IN AN INNINGS

	B	LB	W	NB		
98	17	17	16	48	Northamptonshire (579) v Essex	Northampton
73	25	18	24	6	Nottinghamshire (324) v Hampshire	Nottingham
67	8	9	30	20	Oxford U (289) v Glamorgan	Oxford
67	7	38	8	14	Glamorgan (544) v Kent	Canterbury
66	8	31	2	25	Nottinghamshire (417) v Worcestershire	Nottingham
66	9	10	15	32	Somerset (453) v Leicestershire	Taunton
66	5	31	14	16	Somerset (503-8d) v Sussex	Taunton
63	2	17	6	38	Surrey (501) v Leicestershire	Leicester
62	8	12	–	42	Hampshire (402) v Lancashire	Southampton

There were a further 12 instances of 50-59 extras in an innings.

Under ECB first-class regulations for 1999, Test matches excluded, two extras were scored for each no-ball and each wide in addition to any runs scored off that ball.

In Test matches, one extra was scored for each no-ball and each wide in addition to any runs scored off that ball.

1999 FIRST-CLASS AVERAGES

These averages involve the 502 cricketers who appeared in the 187 first-class matches played in the British Isles during the 1999 season.

'Cap' denotes the season in which the player was awarded a 1st XI cap by the county he represented in 1999. Durham, who formerly had awarded caps immediately their players joined the staff, revised their policy in 1998 and now cap players on merit, past 'awards' being nullified.

Team abbreviations: BU – British Universities; CU – Cambridge University; De – Derbyshire; Du – Durham; E – England; Ex – Essex; Gm – Glamorgan; Gs – Gloucestershire; H – Hampshire; Ire – Ireland; K – Kent; La – Lancashire; Le – Leicestershire; M – Middlesex; MCC – Marylebone Cricket Club; Nh – Northamptonshire; Nt – Nottinghamshire; NZ – New Zealand(ers); OU – Oxford University; SAA – South African Academy XI; Sc – Scotland: SL – Sri Lanka A; Sm – Somerset; Sy – Surrey; Sx – Sussex; Wa – Warwickshire; Wo – Worcestershire; Y – Yorkshire.

† Left-handed batsman

BATTING AND FIELDING

	Cap	*M*	*I*	*NO*	*HS*	*Runs*	*Avge*	*100*	*50*	*Ct/St*
Adams, C.J.(Sx)	1998	17	31	2	130	956	32.96	1	5	23
†Afzaal, U.(Nt)	–	16	30	2	104	829	29.60	1	6	4
Aldred, P.(De)	1999	12	17	2	29*	122	8.13	–	–	4
Ali, Kabir (Wo)	–	1	1	–	11	11	11.00	–	–	–
Alleyne, M.W.(Gs)	1990	17	29	1	76	672	24.00	–	3	20
Allingham, M.J.D.(Sc)	–	1	2	1	66*	86	86.00	–	1	–
Allott, G.I.(NZ)	–	6	8	6	13*	23	11.50	–	–	1
Amin, R.M.(Sy)	–	3	3	2	3*	6	6.00	–	–	1
Amla, A.M.(SAA)	–	3	6	1	107	286	57.20	1	2	–
Anderson, R.S.G.(Ex)	–	15	20	2	44	147	8.16	–	–	5
†Archer, B.J.(Ire)	–	3	6	–	27	52	8.66	–	–	3
Archer, G.F.(Nt)	1995	15	28	1	132	635	23.51	1	2	27
†Arnold, R.P.(SL)	–	5	10	1	70	307	34.11	–	2	5
†Ashley, N.W.(OU)	–	5	9	–	96	264	29.33	–	2	4
Asim Butt (Sc)	–	2	3	–	7	9	3.00	–	–	1
Astle, N.J.(NZ)	–	10	15	1	121	617	44.07	3	2	17
Atherton, M.A.(La/E)	1989	9	15	2	268*	578	44.46	1	2	4
†Austin, I.D.(La)	1990	5	8	2	45*	125	20.83	–	–	2
Averis, J.M.M.(Gs)	–	3	5	2	18*	40	13.33	–	–	–
Ayaz Gul (Sc)	–	2	4	1	19	60	20.00	–	–	2
Aymes, A.N.(H)	1991	18	27	5	115*	791	35.95	2	5	51/2
Bailey, R.J.(Nh)	1985	14	23	2	113*	743	35.38	1	3	9
Bailey, T.M.B.(Nh)	–	5	4	–	24	33	8.25	–	–	5/1
Ball, M.C.J.(Gs)	1996	12	19	4	70*	333	22.20	–	1	11
Bandara, C.M.(SL)	–	1	2	–	14	14	7.00	–	–	–
Banes, M.J.(K)	–	2	4	–	53	60	15.00	–	1	1
Barnes, J.P.B.(OU)	–	6	9	–	45	174	19.33	–	–	6
Barnett, K.J.(Gs)	1999	15	26	1	125	727	29.08	2	4	15
Base, S.J.(De)	1990	1	2	1	17	25	25.00	–	–	–
Bates, J.J.(Sx)	–	6	10	–	57	190	19.00	–	1	2
Bates, R.T.(Nt)	–	1	1	–	0	0	0.00	–	–	–
Batson, N.E.(Wo)	–	5	10	1	72	181	20.11	–	1	5
Batty, G.J.(Sy)	–	1	2	1	25*	36	36.00	–	–	–
Batty, J.N.(Sy)	–	15	20	5	64	379	25.26	–	1	49/7
Bell, I.R.(Wa)	–	1	1	–	0	0	0.00	–	–	2
Bell, M.D.(NZ)	–	8	13	1	83	272	22.66	–	1	9
Benjamin, J.E.(Sy)	1993	2	2	–	5	9	4.50	–	–	1
Betts, M.M.(Du)	1998	7	11	2	19*	55	6.11	–	–	4

	Cap	M	I	NO	HS	Runs	Avge	100	50	Ct/St
†Bicknell, D.J.(Sy)	1990	11	17	1	115	504	31.50	2	1	3
Bicknell, M.P.(Sy)	1989	15	17	4	69	432	33.23	–	3	5
Birks, M.J.(CU)	–	7	5	1	18	32	8.00	–	–	8/1
Bishop, I.E.(Sy)	–	4	5	4	7*	7	7.00	–	–	3
†Bishop, J.E.(Ex)	–	2	1	–	17	17	17.00	–	–	–
†Blackwell, I.D.(De)	–	10	16	2	62*	347	24.78	–	2	6
Blakey, R.J.(Y)	1987	17	31	4	123	684	25.33	1	4	41
Blanchett, I.N.(M)	–	1	2	1	6	11	11.00	–	–	1
Blewett, G.S.(Y)	1999	12	23	2	190	655	31.19	1	2	5
Bloomfield, T.F.(M)	–	11	17	9	17*	80	10.00	–	–	1
†Bodi, G.H.(SAA)	–	2	2	1	26*	28	28.00	–	–	–
Bond, A.N.(OU)	–	1	1	–	6	6	6.00	–	–	1
Boon, D.C.(Du)	1998	16	27	2	139	839	33.56	1	7	8
Boswell, S.A.J.(Le)	–	2	4	1	15	39	13.00	–	–	–
Boteju. H.(SL)	–	4	7	–	31	96	13.71	–	–	3
Bowen, M.N.(Nt)	1997	11	21	8	19	130	10.00	–	–	2
Bowler, P.D.(Sm)	1995	17	27	8	149	931	49.00	4	–	8
Bridge, G.D.(Du)	–	1	2	–	6	11	5.50	–	–	1
Brimson, M.T.(Le)	1998	14	16	6	36*	127	12.70	–	–	2
Brinkley, J.E.(Sc)	–	3	4	–	34	57	14.25	–	–	–
Brown, A.D.(Sy)	1994	17	26	4	265	1127	51.22	4	2	31/1
Brown, D.R.(Wa)	1995	16	25	1	142	666	27.75	1	3	13
Brown, J.F.(Nh)	–	1	1	–	8	8	8.00	–	–	–
Brown, M.J.(M)	–	2	3	2	24*	48	48.00	–	–	2
Brown, S.J.E.(Du)	1998	15	23	8	29*	160	10.66	–	–	3
Bryant, J.D.C.(SAA)	–	3	6	2	77	216	54.00	–	3	1
†Bulbeck, M.P.L.(Sm)	–	15	15	8	76*	265	37.85	–	1	1
Bull, J.J.(OU)	–	6	11	–	49	193	17.54	–	–	1
Burns, M.(Sm)	1999	19	27	1	109	915	35.19	2	5	11
Butcher, G.P.(Sy)	–	5	8	–	70	199	24.87	–	2	2
†Butcher, M.A.(Sy/E)	1996	16	28	1	259	1077	39.88	2	4	15
†Byas, D.(Y)	1991	17	34	2	95	875	27.34	–	8	24
Byrne, B.W.(OU)	–	6	11	2	94	374	41.55	–	2	1
Caddick, A.R.(Sm/E)	1992	17	23	5	45	331	18.38	–	–	7
Cairns, C.L.(NZ)	–	7	10	1	80	302	33.55	–	2	1
†Carson, N.D.(Ire)	–	2	4	–	24	30	7.50	–	–	–
Cassar, M.E.(De)	–	14	24	3	42	393	18.71	–	–	5
Catterall, D.N.(Wo)	–	2	3	–	60	132	44.00	–	2	–
†Cawdron, M.J.(Gs)	–	6	9	2	42	126	18.00	–	–	1
Chapman, S.(Du)	–	2	4	1	32	67	22.33	–	–	3
Chapple, G.(La)	1994	13	18	2	83	402	25.12	–	2	2
Chilton, M.J.(La)	–	18	30	3	106*	827	30.62	2	4	21
Claughton, J.A.(OU)	–	7	13	4	85	318	35.33	–	3	3
Collingwood, P.D.(Du)	1998	17	28	–	106	692	24.71	1	4	25
Collins, B.J.(CU)	–	7	11	2	46	141	15.66	–	–	4
†Conway, S.L.J.(OU)	–	1	1	1	0*	0	–	–	–	–
Cook, S.J.(M)	–	10	16	3	51	237	18.23	–	1	3
Cooke, G.(Ire)	–	2	3	2	17	22	22.00	–	–	1
Cork, D.G.(De)	1993	14	22	2	82	535	26.75	–	4	18
Cosker, D.A.(Gm)	–	13	18	4	49	212	15.14	–	–	14
†Cotterell, T.P.(Gs)	–	1	1	–	0	0	0.00	–	–	–
Cottey, P.A.(Sx)	1999	17	29	1	126	780	27.85	1	4	11
Cowan, A.P.(Ex)	1997	17	24	3	52*	332	15.80	–	1	10
Cox, D.J.(Sc)	–	1	1	–	–	–	–	–	–	–
Cox, J.(Sm)	1999	18	30	2	216	1617	57.75	6	6	7
Crawley, J.P.(La)	1994	15	25	2	158	870	37.82	2	6	10
Creed, M.(SAA)	–	3	3	2	21*	35	35.00	–	–	2

	Cap	M	I	NO	HS	Runs	Avge	100	50	Ct/St
†Creese, M.L.(M)	–	1	1	–	4	4	4.00	–	–	–
Croft, R.D.B.(Gm)	1992	15	21	4	58*	322	18.94	–	2	5
Crowe, C.D.(Le)	–	4	7	2	44*	135	27.00	–	–	2
Croy, M.G.(NZ)	–	4	5	1	22	56	14.00	–	–	11/1
Cunliffe, R.J.(Gs)	–	7	13	–	108	421	32.38	1	2	8
Curran, K.M.(Nh)	1992	1	2	–	1	1	0.50	–	–	–
Dagnall, C.E.(Wa)	–	1	1	–	0	0	0.00	–	–	–
†Dakin, J.M.(Le)	–	11	18	2	124	454	28.37	1	3	2
Dale, A.(Gm)	1992	16	26	–	113	809	31.11	3	1	4
Daley, J.A.(Du)	1999	14	24	1	105	609	26.47	1	3	7
Danson, A.R.(CU)	–	6	10	4	31	153	25.50	–	–	2
†Davies, A.P.(Gm)	–	1	1	–	5	5	5.00	–	–	–
Davies, M.K.(Nh)	–	13	18	4	32*	110	7.85	–	–	3
Davis, M.J.G.(MCC)	–	1	1	–	12	12	12.00	–	–	1
Davy, J.O.(Ire)	–	1	1	–	2	2	2.00	–	–	–
Davy, P.J.(Ire)	–	2	4	–	21	29	7.25	–	–	2
Dawes, J.H.(MCC)	–	1	1	1	1*	1	–	–	–	–
Dawood, I.(Gm)	–	7	12	–	102	262	21.83	1	1	20
Dawson, R.I.(Gs)	–	1	2	–	36	46	23.00	–	–	1
†Dean, K.J.(De)	1998	3	2	1	10*	15	15.00	–	–	1
Deane, M.J.(De)	–	2	3	–	10	11	3.66	–	–	1
DeFreitas, P.A.J.(De)	1994	13	18	1	105	441	25.94	1	2	7
De la Pena, J.M.(Wo)	–	3	3	–	0	0	0.00	–	–	1
De Saram, S.I.(SL)	–	3	5	–	89	179	35.80	–	2	1
Dilshan, T.M.(SL)	–	5	10	1	127	562	62.44	2	3	8/1
†Di Venuto, M.J.(Sx)	1999	16	28	2	162	1067	41.03	3	5	20
Donald, A.A.(Wa)	1989	2	4	2	10	14	7.00	–	–	1
Doull, S.B.(NZ)	–	4	5	–	49	128	25.60	–	–	–
†Dowman, M.P.(Nt)	1998	9	15	3	67*	412	34.33	–	3	6
Drakes, V.C.(Nt)	1999	17	30	3	80	427	15.81	–	2	5
†Driver, R.C.(BU/Wo)	–	3	5	–	42	103	20.60	–	–	1
Dunlop, A.R.(Ire)	–	3	6	1	112	263	52.60	1	2	1
Dutch, K.P.(M)	–	6	10	–	23	119	11.90	–	–	2
Dyer, N.R.(Sc)	–	3	4	1	6	12	4.00	–	–	1
Eadie, D.J.(OU)	–	4	8	2	52*	108	18.00	–	1	1
Eagleson, R.L.(De)	–	1	1	–	0	0	0.00	–	–	1
Ealham, M.A.(K)	1992	13	22	3	88*	585	30.78	–	5	3
Edmond, M.D.(Wa)	–	1	1	–	31	31	31.00	–	–	1
Edwards, A.D.(Sx)	–	2	3	–	22	22	7.33	–	–	1
Evans, A.W.(Gm)	–	15	24	3	88*	512	24.38	–	2	10
Evans, K.P.(Nt)	1990	1	–	–	–	–	–	–	–	–
†Fairbrother, N.H.(La)	1985	12	19	–	83	503	26.47	–	4	17
Fellows, G.M.(Y)	–	3	6	1	34*	74	14.80	–	–	1
†Fisher, I.D.(Y)	–	11	16	5	51	261	23.72	–	1	–
†Flanagan, I.N.(Ex)	–	6	10	–	52	165	16.50	–	1	3
Fleming, M.V.(K)	1990	17	25	4	138	830	39.52	1	4	4
†Fleming, S.P.(NZ)	–	9	15	3	127	476	39.66	1	2	20
Flintoff, A.(La)	1998	13	21	2	160	727	38.26	2	2	25
†Flower, A.(MCC)	–	1	2	1	32	40	40.00	–	–	2
Follett, D.(Nh)	–	5	5	1	19	44	11.00	–	–	–
Francis, S.R.G.(BU/H)	–	4	6	2	11	13	3.25	–	–	–
†Franks, P.J.(Nt)	1999	16	27	3	61	348	14.50	–	1	2
Fraser, A.R.C.(M)	1988	12	16	5	56*	142	12.90	–	1	–
†Frost, T.(Wa)	1999	12	18	1	66	348	20.47	–	1	23/1
Fulton, D.P.(K)	1998	17	29	2	126*	722	26.74	1	3	18
†Fulton, J.A.G.(OU)	–	3	5	–	30	48	9.60	–	–	1
Gallage, I.S.(SL)	–	3	6	3	54*	96	32.00	–	1	–

	Cap	M	I	NO	HS	Runs	Avge	100	50	Ct/St
Gallian, J.E.R.(Nt)	1998	19	34	3	120*	985	31.77	2	5	19
Gannon, B.W.(Gs)	–	11	12	4	18	70	8.75	–	–	4
Garaway, M.(H)	–	1	2	–	55	56	28.00	–	1	4/1
Giddins, E.S.H.(Wa/E)	1998	15	20	11	18	76	8.44	–	–	2
Gie, N.A.(Nt)	–	5	6	2	59*	144	36.00	–	1	–
Giles, A.F.(Wa)	–	16	23	5	123*	375	20.83	1	–	6
Gillespie, P.G.(Ire)	–	2	4	–	40	69	17.25	–	–	2
Gofton, A.F.(OU)	–	5	8	1	37*	115	16.42	–	–	–
Golding, J.M.(K)	–	1	2	1	3	3	3.00	–	–	–
Goodchild, D.J.(M)	–	1	2	–	26	26	13.00	–	–	–
Goodyer, T.E.(CU)	–	1	2	–	32	32	16.00	–	–	–
Gough, D.(Y)	1993	3	5	1	33	66	16.50	–	–	–
Gough, M.A.(Du)	–	12	20	–	67	424	21.20	–	4	17
Grayson, A.P.(Ex)	1996	20	32	2	159*	1083	36.10	3	6	8
Green, R.J.(La)	–	10	10	5	27	96	19.20	–	–	1
Greenidge, C.G.(Sy)	–	2	3	–	14	20	6.66	–	–	3
Griffiths, S.P.(De)	–	5	7	1	35	108	18.00	–	–	16/1
Grove, J.O.(Ex)	–	4	5	1	7	17	4.25	–	–	–
†Gunawardena, D.A.(SL)	–	4	8	–	77	257	32.12	–	3	1
Gupte, C.M.(MCC)	–	1	2	–	44	48	24.00	–	–	1
Habib, A.(Le/E)	1998	18	29	3	160*	1055	40.57	3	6	2
Hafeez, A.(Wo)	–	4	8	–	32	43	5.37	–	–	2
Halsall, R.G.(CU)	–	7	9	1	76	157	19.62	–	1	4
†Hamilton, G.M.(Y)	1998	11	20	8	94*	567	47.25	–	4	3
Hancock, T.H.C.(Gs)	1998	17	30	–	71	858	28.60	–	7	7
Hansen, T.M.(H)	–	3	4	–	24	33	8.25	–	–	–
Harden, R.J.(Y)	1999	10	19	3	69	438	27.37	–	3	2
Hardinges, M.A.(Gs)	–	1	1	–	1	1	1.00	–	–	–
Harmison, S.J.(Du)	1999	17	24	9	14*	79	5.26	–	–	4
Harris, A.J.(De)	1996	7	11	7	8*	48	12.00	–	–	4
†Harris, C.Z.(NZ)	–	3	4	–	38	46	11.50	–	–	1
Harrison, D.S.(Gm)	–	2	2	–	16	29	14.50	–	–	–
Hartley, P.J.(H)	1998	12	15	6	58	183	20.33	–	1	3
Harvey, I.J.(Gs)	1999	12	19	–	123	429	22.57	1	–	6
Harvey, M.E.(La)	–	1	1	–	39	39	39.00	–	–	1
Hay, M.J.(Sc)	–	2	3	–	7	10	3.33	–	–	–
†Hayden, M.L.(Nh)	1999	9	15	2	170	745	57.30	4	1	6
Haynes, G.R.(Wo)	1994	8	12	2	60*	177	17.70	–	1	–
Haynes, J.J.(La)	–	2	2	1	80	114	114.00	–	1	8/1
†Haywood, G.R.(Sx)	–	1	2	–	14	15	7.50	–	–	–
Headley, D.W.(K/E)	1993	14	19	3	72	297	18.56	–	1	9
Hegg, W.K.(La)	1989	16	24	3	94	670	31.90	–	3	45/4
Hellings, C.J.(BU)	–	1	2	–	13	26	13.00	–	–	–
†Hemp, D.L.(Wa)	1997	18	29	–	144	1014	34.96	2	6	11
Henderson, T.(SAA)	–	2	2	–	0	0	0.00	–	–	–
†Herath, R.(SL)	–	5	9	4	25	41	8.20	–	–	–
Hewage, P.R.(SL)	–	1	2	–	24	36	18.00	–	–	1
†Hewitt, J.P.(M)	1998	13	21	1	49*	350	17.50	–	–	6
Hewson, D.R.(Gs)	–	5	10	–	40	144	14.40	–	–	3
Hick, G.A.(Wo/E)	1986	13	22	–	150	1063	48.31	4	6	18
Hicks, T.C.(OU/BU)	–	7	10	1	54	178	19.77	–	1	4
Hockley, J.B.(K)	–	1	1	–	34	34	34.00	–	–	–
†Hodgson, T.P.(Ex)	–	1	1	–	24	24	24.00	–	–	–
Hoggard, M.J.(Y)	–	8	11	3	21	53	6.62	–	–	2
Hollioake, A.J.(Sy)	1995	13	18	2	116	534	33.37	1	3	8
Hollioake, B.C.(Sy)	1999	13	20	–	71	538	26.90	–	4	12
†Holloway, P.C.L.(Sm)	1997	19	32	5	114*	869	32.18	2	5	9

	Cap	M	I	NO	HS	Runs	Avge	100	50	Ct/St
Horne, M.J.(NZ)	–	9	15	–	172	670	44.66	3	1	4
†House, W.J.(K)	–	1	1	1	22*	22	–	–	–	–
†Hughes, Q.J.(CU/BU)	–	8	13	2	101	435	39.54	1	3	2
Humphries, S.(Sx)	–	11	18	2	57	176	11.00	–	1	18/2
Hussain, N.(Ex/E)	1989	12	20	1	143	988	52.00	2	8	13
†Hutchison, P.M.(Y)	1998	3	4	3	4*	6	6.00	–	–	–
†Hutton, B.L.(BU/M)	–	8	15	–	59	331	22.06	–	2	5
Hyam, B.J.(Ex)	1999	18	26	4	51	514	23.36	–	1	46/1
Illingworth, R.K.(Wo)	1986	16	26	5	91*	457	21.76	–	1	5
†Ilott, M.C.(Ex)	1993	12	17	1	44	290	18.12	–	–	5
Innes, K.J.(Nh)	–	8	11	3	47*	217	27.12	–	–	4
Irani, R.C.(Ex/E)	1994	21	34	5	153	1121	38.65	4	3	12
†Jacobs, A.(SAA)	–	3	6	3	85	172	57.33	–	1	4
†James, K.D.(H)	1989	2	4	–	18	28	7.00	–	–	2
James, S.P.(Gm)	1992	16	25	1	259*	1017	42.37	4	3	9
Jarvis, P.W.(Sm)	–	7	8	–	20	73	9.12	–	–	2
Jayantha, S.(SL)	–	1	2	–	35	36	18.00	–	–	1
Jayawardena, H.P.W.(SL)	–	4	8	–	89	173	21.62	–	1	14/4
†Jennings, D.(SAA)	–	2	2	2	13*	20	–	–	–	12
†Johnson, N.C.(MCC)	–	1	2	–	29	49	24.50	–	–	1
Johnson, P.(Nt)	1986	16	29	3	126	1104	42.46	1	10	11
Johnson, R.L.(M)	1995	6	8	–	39	86	10.75	–	–	1
Jones, I.(Sm)	–	3	4	1	35	78	26.00	–	–	–
Jones, P.S.(Sm)	–	9	14	3	105	281	25.54	1	–	3
†Jones, S.P.(Gm)	–	10	13	3	19*	77	7.70	–	–	2
†Joyce, E.C.(M)	–	1	1	–	9	9	9.00	–	–	1
Kalavitigoda, S.(SL)	–	6	11	–	73	276	25.09	–	2	10
Kallis, J.H.(Gm)	1999	6	9	–	101	362	40.22	1	2	3
Kasprowicz, M.S.(Le)	1999	16	23	4	73	507	26.68	–	5	3
Keech, M.(H)	–	8	13	1	50	353	29.41	–	1	8
†Keedy, G.(La)	–	7	9	6	9*	17	5.66	–	–	1
Kendall, W.S.(H)	1999	19	32	2	201	1186	39.53	2	7	25
Kennis, G.J.(Sm)	–	3	6	–	175	225	37.50	1	–	2
Kenway, D.A.(H)	–	19	31	6	102	1055	42.20	1	7	13
Kerr, J.I.D.(Sm)	–	14	19	1	64	381	21.16	–	2	5
†Kettleborough, R.A.(M)	–	8	15	–	93	300	20.00	–	2	4
Key, R.W.T.(K)	–	19	33	2	125	836	26.96	1	5	18
Khan, A.A.(Le)	–	1	1	–	5	5	5.00	–	–	–
Khan, S.H.(OU)	–	6	6	–	34	115	19.16	–	–	2
†Khan, W.G.(Sx)	–	5	9	–	88	167	18.55	–	2	1
Killeen, N.(Du)	1999	12	19	3	46	251	15.68	–	–	1
King, R.D.(MCC)	–	1	–	–	–	–	–	–	–	–
†Kino, D.(OU)	–	5	6	2	14*	31	7.75	–	–	–
Kirtley, R.J.(Sx)	1998	15	23	5	32	194	10.77	–	–	2
†Knight, N.V.(Wa)	1995	14	23	2	94	719	34.23	–	6	30
Krikken, K.M.(De)	1992	12	19	3	88	389	24.31	–	3	30/1
Lacey, S.J.(De)	–	6	8	2	42	154	25.66	–	–	5/1
Lampitt, S.R.(Wo)	1989	14	19	5	66*	413	29.50	–	2	7
Laney, J.S.(H)	1996	11	19	1	99	691	38.38	–	6	7
†Langer, J.L.(M)	1998	12	22	4	241*	1048	58.22	4	2	12
Law, D.R.(Ex)	1996	4	4	2	63*	136	68.00	–	1	2
Law, S.G.(Ex)	1996	17	29	4	263	1833	73.32	8	6	29
Law, W.L.(Gm)	–	5	9	–	64	240	26.66	–	2	3
Lawrence, J.R.G.(BU)	–	1	2	–	4	5	2.50	–	–	–
†Lawson, A.G.(MCC)	–	1	2	–	12	15	7.50	–	–	1
Leatherdale, D.A.(Wo)	1994	19	34	3	85	693	22.35	–	3	9
Lewis, C.C.(Le)	1990	10	13	2	139	520	47.27	2	2	7

	Cap	M	I	NO	HS	Runs	Avge	100	50	Ct/St
Lewis, J.(Gs)	1998	14	23	3	62	266	13.30	–	1	2
Lewis, J.J.B.(Du)	1998	16	28	–	132	1146	40.92	2	8	7
Lewis, S.J.W.(CU)	–	4	6	–	17	70	11.66	–	–	3
†Lewry, J.D.(Sx)	1996	12	19	7	30*	163	13.58	–	–	2
†Liptrot, C.G.(Wo)	–	11	16	6	61	142	14.20	–	1	–
Lloyd, G.D.(La)	1992	17	26	1	144	1066	42.64	3	6	7
Logan, R.J.(Nh)	–	2	2	–	1	1	0.50	–	–	1
†Louw, J.H.(OU)	–	7	13	1	82	183	15.25	–	2	5
Love, G.T.(SAA)	–	3	2	–	12	17	8.50	–	–	–
Loveridge, G.R.(CU/BU)	–	7	10	–	126	427	42.70	1	2	7
Lowe, J.P.(CU)	–	2	1	1	0*	0	–	–	–	–
Loye, M.B.(Nh)	1994	13	20	–	102	433	21.65	2	–	4
Lucas, D.S.(Nt)	–	6	7	3	24*	58	14.50	–	–	–
Lugsden, S.(H)	–	2	3	1	16	25	12.50	–	–	–
McCague, M.J.(K)	1992	10	13	2	53	272	24.72	–	1	7
McCallan, W.K.(Ire)	–	2	4	–	24	60	15.00	–	–	1
McCoubrey, A.G.A.M.(Ire)	–	1	1	1	1*	1	–	–	–	–
McDaid, R.W.(Ire)	–	2	1	1	6*	6	–	–	–	2
McDowell, R.W.(CU)	–	1	2	–	2	2	1.00	–	–	–
McGarry, A.C.(Ex)	–	1	1	1	0*	0	–	–	–	–
McGerrigle, R.D.(Ire)	–	1	1	–	0	0	0.00	–	–	–
McGrath, A.(Y)	1999	16	30	2	142*	831	29.67	1	6	15
McKeown, P.C.(La)	–	5	8	1	75	216	30.85	–	2	4
†McLean, N.A.M.(H)	1998	14	19	3	70	206	12.87	–	1	6
McMillan, C.D.(NZ)	–	10	16	2	121	525	37.50	2	1	4
MacRae, N.J.(Sc)	–	3	6	1	51	141	28.20	–	1	1
Maddy, D.L.(Le/E)	1996	18	30	2	158*	1060	37.85	2	4	18
Mahmood, S.(Sm)	–	1	2	1	7*	7	7.00	–	–	1
Maiden, G.I.(Sc)	–	2	2	1	23*	25	25.00	–	–	1
Malcolm, D.E.(Nh)	1999	15	16	6	10*	32	3.20	–	–	4
Marsh, S.A.(K)	1986	15	22	2	73*	466	23.30	–	2	28/7
Martin, P.J.(La)	1994	14	19	5	30*	220	15.71	–	–	2
Martin-Jenkins, R.S.C.(Sx)	–	14	24	2	70	413	18.77	–	2	2
Mascarenhas, A.D.(H)	1998	14	20	2	62	465	25.83	–	2	4
Mason, T.J.(Le)	–	2	4	1	36	79	26.33	–	–	–
†Mather, D.P.(OU)	–	5	6	4	11*	25	12.50	–	–	–
†Maunders, J.K.(M)	–	1	2	–	9	13	6.50	–	–	1
Maynard, M.P.(Gm)	1987	13	18	1	186	685	40.29	2	2	9
†Millns, D.J.(Le)	1991	6	9	3	47	136	22.66	–	–	5
Mohammed, I. (CU/BU)	–	9	16	2	110	520	37.14	1	2	1
Molins, G.L.(Ire)	–	2	2	1	2*	2	2.00	–	–	1
Montgomerie, R.R.(Sx)	1999	15	27	1	113*	962	37.00	2	6	19
Moody, T.M.(Wo)	1991	5	10	2	63*	286	35.75	–	3	5
Mooney, P.J.K.(Ire)	–	3	6	3	20*	66	22.00	–	–	2
†Morris, A.C.(H)	–	6	7	2	58*	131	26.20	–	1	–
Morris, J.E.(Du)	1998	15	25	–	119	792	31.68	2	4	7
Morris, Z.C.(H)	–	1	2	–	1	1	0.50	–	–	–
Mullally, A.D.(Le/E)	1993	9	12	4	13	50	6.25	–	–	2
Munton, T.A.(Wa)	1989	13	19	3	24	80	5.00	–	–	5
Muralitharan, M.(La)	1999	7	9	1	10	30	3.75	–	–	2
Napier, G.R.(Ex)	–	1	1	–	27	27	27.00	–	–	2
Nash, D.C.(M)	–	17	27	8	92	696	36.63	–	4	46/4
Nash, D.J.(NZ)	–	8	11	3	135*	395	49.37	1	2	1
†Nawaz, M.N.(SL)	–	2	3	–	26	50	16.66	–	–	–
Nel, A.(SAA)	–	4	1	–	7	7	7.00	–	–	–
Newell, K.(Gm)	–	8	11	–	46	239	21.72	–	–	2
Newell, M.(De)	–	1	2	–	25	32	16.00	–	–	1

	Cap	M	I	NO	HS	Runs	Avge	100	50	Ct/St
Newport, P.J.(Wo)	1986	11	19	3	65*	295	18.43	–	1	3
†Nixon, P.A.(Le)	1994	18	29	2	121	828	30.66	1	3	46/4
Noon, W.M.(Nt)	1995	3	5	–	8	22	4.40	–	–	9
†O'Connor, S.B.(NZ)	–	5	5	–	13	30	6.00	–	–	1
Ontong, J.L.(SAA)	–	3	5	–	71	155	31.00	–	2	2
Ormond, J.(Le)	1999	13	17	3	50*	183	13.07	–	1	2
Ostler, D.P.(Wa)	1991	7	11	–	87	250	22.72	–	2	5
Parkin, O.T.(Gm)	–	7	9	3	11	21	3.50	–	–	2
Parore, A.C.(NZ)	–	6	8	–	80	193	24.12	–	2	23
Parsons, K.A.(Sm)	1999	15	21	3	80	499	27.72	–	3	12
†Parsons, R.A.(Sc)	–	1	2	–	8	8	4.00	–	–	2
Patel, M.M.(K)	1994	18	24	3	67	290	13.80	–	1	6
Patterson, M.W.(Sy)	–	1	1	–	0	0	0.00	–	–	–
†Peirce, M.T.E.(Sx)	–	17	31	–	123	919	29.64	1	6	5
†Penberthy, A.L.(Nh)	1994	18	25	2	123*	718	31.21	1	4	6
Penn, A.J.(NZ)	–	1	1	1	69*	69	–	–	1	–
Penney, T.L.(Wa)	1994	15	24	3	73	517	24.61	–	3	6/2
Perera, A.S.A.(SL)	–	3	6	1	71*	160	32.00	–	1	–
Perera, B.(SL)	–	1	2	–	47	53	26.50	–	–	–
†Perera, N.R.G.(SL)	–	3	6	–	49	144	24.00	–	–	3
Peters, S.D.(Ex)	–	11	15	2	99	374	28.76	–	2	13
Phillips, N.C.(Du)	–	6	9	–	42	105	11.66	–	–	5
†Phillips, T.J.(Ex)	–	3	4	–	16	27	6.75	–	–	1
Pierson, A.R.K.(Sm)	–	13	13	3	66	129	12.90	–	1	5
Pimlott, C.R.(CU)	–	6	5	4	18*	41	41.00	–	–	–
Pipe, D.J.(Wo)	–	1	2	–	16	21	10.50	–	–	–
Piper, K.J.(Wa)	1992	5	7	–	66	152	21.71	–	1	8/1
Pirihi, N.G.(OU)	–	3	5	–	19	30	6.00	–	–	2
†Pollard, P.R.(Wo)	–	11	21	2	60	377	19.84	–	3	2
Powell, J.C.(Ex)	–	1	–	–	–	–	–	–	–	2
Powell, M.J.(Gm)	–	16	26	4	164	1060	48.18	2	5	5
Powell, M.J.(Wa)	1999	9	14	–	136	494	35.28	2	1	5
Pretorius, D.(SAA)	–	3	1	–	0	0	0.00	–	–	1
Prichard, P.J.(Ex)	1986	16	26	–	110	852	32.76	2	6	6
Pushpakumara, K.R.(SL)	–	4	3	2	8	9	9.00	–	–	–
Pyemont, J.P.(CU/De)	–	11	19	2	90*	398	23.41	–	3	6
Ramprakash, M.R.(M/E)	1990	16	28	3	209*	1056	42.24	2	7	11
Randall, S.J.(Nt)	–	3	5	1	20	30	7.50	–	–	3
Rao, R.K.(Sx)	–	4	6	1	52*	87	17.40	–	1	1
†Rashid, U.B.A.(Sx)	–	10	18	3	73	454	30.26	–	3	5
Ratcliffe, J.D.(Sy)	1998	13	20	1	91	402	21.15	–	2	6
Rawnsley, M.J.(Wo)	–	4	6	1	21	67	13.40	–	–	1
Read, C.M.W.(Nt/E)	1999	19	31	1	160	653	21.76	1	1	59/2
Renshaw, S.J.(H)	–	12	13	6	28	101	14.42	–	–	7
Rhodes, J.N.(Ire)	–	2	4	–	86	199	49.75	–	2	4
Rhodes, S.J.(Wo)	1986	18	30	5	74	591	23.64	–	1	51/2
Richardson, A.(Wa)	–	6	8	3	4	9	1.80	–	–	1
Ridgway, P.M.(La)	–	2	3	2	8*	9	9.00	–	–	–
Ripley, D.(Nh)	1987	15	22	6	107	683	42.68	2	3	40/3
Roberts, D.J.(Nh)	–	5	8	1	34*	73	10.42	–	–	4
Roberts, T.W.(BU)	–	1	2	–	49	88	44.00	–	–	–
Robinson, D.D.J.(Ex)	1997	17	29	1	200	786	28.07	3	1	13
†Robinson, J.D.(MCC)	–	1	2	–	44	77	38.50	–	–	–
Robinson, M.A.(Sx)	1997	17	24	11	10	63	4.84	–	–	1
Robinson, R.T.(Nt)	1983	12	22	1	80	525	25.00	–	4	10
Rollins, A.S.(De)	1995	15	28	3	113	965	38.60	2	5	9
Rollins, R.J.(Ex)	1995	3	4	1	33	65	21.66	–	–	6/1

	Cap	M	I	NO	HS	Runs	Avge	100	50	Ct/St
Rose, G.D.(Sm)	1988	9	11	2	123*	342	38.00	1	1	2
Roseberry, M.A.(M)	1990	12	21	1	116	483	24.15	1	1	7
Ross, J.S.(CU)	–	2	3	1	2*	2	1.00	–	–	–
†Russell, R.C.(Gs)	1985	17	30	6	94*	790	32.91	–	5	55/5
Rutherford, A.T.(Ire)	–	2	3	–	26	47	15.66	–	–	2/1
Sachdeva, A.(Le)	–	1	2	1	0*	0	0.00	–	–	–
Saggers, M.J.(K)	–	2	1	–	0	0	0.00	–	–	–
Sajdeh, R.K.(CU)	–	1	2	–	12	12	6.00	–	–	–
Sales, D.J.G.(Nh)	1999	18	29	4	303*	1291	51.64	3	5	15
Salisbury, I.D.K.(Sy)	1998	17	19	2	100*	353	20.76	1	1	5
Salmond, G.(Sc)	–	3	5	–	46	143	28.60	–	–	3
Saqlain Mushtaq (Sy)	1998	7	8	5	25*	46	15.33	–	–	1
Sayers, C.A.(CU)	–	4	4	3	4*	9	9.00	–	–	1
†Schofield, C.P.(La)	–	10	14	4	39*	205	20.50	–	–	8
†Scott, D.A.(K)	–	3	4	3	12*	16	16.00	–	–	1
Shah, O.A.(M)	–	17	32	2	110*	829	27.63	3	3	9
Shahid, N.(Sy)	1998	2	3	1	23	36	18.00	–	–	2
Shaw, A.D.(Gm)	1999	12	16	1	140	312	20.80	1	–	25/1
†Sheikh, M.A.(Wa)	–	1	2	1	12	19	19.00	–	–	–
Sheikh, S.M.(CU)	–	4	2	1	7*	9	9.00	–	–	1
Sheriyar, A.(Wo)	1997	19	26	8	18	129	7.16	–	–	3
Shields, I.P.(Ire)	–	1	2	–	16	16	8.00	–	–	2
†Sidebottom, R.J.(Y)	–	12	20	5	48*	146	9.73	–	–	6
Silva, L.P.C.(SL)	–	3	5	–	80	141	28.20	–	1	1
Silverwood, C.E.W.(Y)	1996	13	20	2	53*	259	14.38	–	1	3
Singh, A.(Wa)	–	5	10	–	69	154	15.40	–	2	–
Slater, M.J.(De)	1998	10	18	1	171	540	31.76	1	2	9
†Smalley, R.G.(OU)	–	1	–	–	–	–	–	–	–	–
Smethurst, M.P.(La)	–	5	4	–	3	5	1.25	–	–	1
Smith, A.M.(Gs)	1995	14	21	5	14	108	6.75	–	–	4
Smith, B.F.(Le)	1995	14	21	–	154	732	34.85	2	2	10
Smith, C.J.O.(Sc)	–	2	3	–	57	69	23.00	–	1	7/1
Smith, E.T.(K)	–	14	25	2	111	931	40.47	1	6	2
Smith, N.M.K.(Wa)	1993	15	21	–	71	504	24.00	–	3	8
Smith, R.A.(H)	1985	18	29	3	96	1110	42.69	–	10	9
†Smith, T.M.(De)	–	8	9	6	20*	52	17.33	–	–	2
†Smyth, S.G.(Ire)	–	2	4	–	12	30	7.50	–	–	1
Snape, J.N.(Gs)	1999	17	29	6	98*	518	22.52	–	3	8
Solanki, V.S.(Wo)	1998	19	35	2	171	1339	40.57	3	6	21
Speak, N.J.(Du)	1998	10	17	2	110	561	37.40	2	2	6
Speight, M.P.(Du)	1998	17	27	5	97*	566	25.72	–	4	48/2
Spendlove, B.L.(De)	–	7	13	–	63	279	21.46	–	2	2
Spiring, K.R.(Wo)	1997	5	10	–	18	69	6.90	–	–	3
Stanger, I.M.(Sc)	–	1	2	–	18	26	13.00	–	–	–
Stemp, R.D.(Nt)	–	13	17	5	18	74	6.16	–	–	1
Stephenson, J.P.(H)	1995	15	24	2	136	425	19.31	1	1	17
Stevens, D.I.(Le)	–	11	20	–	130	562	28.10	1	3	12
Stewart, A.J.(Sy/E)	1985	12	20	2	95	511	28.38	–	3	15/2
Still, Q.R.(SAA)	–	4	8	1	76	272	38.85	–	2	3
Strang, P.A.(MCC)	–	1	2	1	30	38	38.00	–	–	2
†Strauss, A.J.(M)	–	9	17	1	98	488	30.50	–	4	3
†Strong, M.R.(Sx)	–	1	2	1	35*	51	51.00	–	–	1
†Stubbings, S.D.(De)	–	5	10	–	45	213	21.30	–	–	3
Stubbs, E.G.C.(Sc)	–	1	2	2	14*	21	–	–	–	3
Such, P.M.(Ex/E)	1991	20	24	11	22*	134	10.30	–	–	5
†Sutcliffe, I.J.(Le)	1997	16	27	–	110	590	21.85	1	2	9
Sutcliffe, R.V.(Nh)	–	2	2	1	9*	9	9.00	–	–	–

	Cap	M	I	NO	HS	Runs	Avge	100	50	Ct/St
Swann, A.J.(Nh)	–	12	18	–	154	573	31.83	2	2	11
Swann, G.P.(Nh)	1999	18	27	4	130*	727	31.60	1	4	13
Symonds, A.(K)	1999	14	25	2	177	940	40.86	3	4	15
†Taylor, B.V.(Sx)	–	1	2	–	14	14	7.00	–	–	1
†Taylor, J.P.(Nh)	1992	17	21	2	71	316	16.63	–	1	5
Tennant, A.M.(Sc)	–	1	2	–	0	0	0.00	–	–	1
Thomas, P.A.(De)	–	1	2	–	1	1	0.50	–	–	–
†Thomas, S.D.(Gm)	1997	18	26	2	54	352	14.66	–	1	9
Thompson, D.J.(Ex)	–	8	10	–	22	55	5.50	–	–	1
Thompson, J.B.D.(K)	1999	14	19	9	44	176	17.60	–	–	1
†Thorpe, G.P.(Sy/E)	1991	13	21	4	164	708	41.64	2	2	18
Titchard, S.P.(De)	–	17	31	4	136	752	27.85	1	2	2
Tolley, C.M.(Nt)	1997	4	8	–	51	106	13.25	–	1	–
†Trescothick, M.E.(Sm)	1999	15	24	–	190	898	37.41	2	3	27
Tsolekile, T.L.(SAA)	–	2	2	1	41*	43	43.00	–	–	5
Tudor, A.J.(Sy/E)	1999	10	13	4	99*	222	24.66	–	1	3
Tufnell, P.C.R.(M/E)	1990	16	21	4	48	198	11.64	–	–	3
Turner, R.J.(Sm)	1994	19	27	4	138*	1217	52.91	2	10	67/2
Tweats, T.A.(De)	–	4	7	–	10	21	3.00	–	–	2
†Twose, R.G.(NZ)	–	8	13	–	91	341	26.23	–	3	7
Udal, S.D.(H)	1992	15	21	6	40	261	17.40	–	–	1
Van den Berg, A.M.(SAA)	–	4	6	–	94	126	21.00	–	1	2
Vaughan, M.P.(Y)	1995	17	34	1	153	895	27.12	3	3	5
†Vettori, D.L.(NZ)	–	10	14	2	112	453	37.75	1	4	4
Villavarayen, M.S.(SL)	–	4	6	–	28	54	9.00	–	–	–
Wagh, M.A.(Wa)	–	13	21	1	216*	643	32.15	1	1	3
†Walker, B.G.K.(NZ)	–	2	1	–	5	5	5.00	–	–	1
†Walker, K.D.M.(CU)	–	7	8	–	132	286	35.75	1	1	2
†Walker, M.J.(K)	–	14	23	2	103*	553	26.33	1	3	13
†Wallace, M.A.(Gm)	–	3	4	1	64*	98	32.66	–	1	12
Walton, T.C.(Ex)	–	6	8	–	71	155	19.37	–	1	6
†Ward, I.J.(Sy)	–	18	30	3	103	1018	37.70	1	9	7
Ward, T.R.(K)	1989	8	13	–	101	240	18.46	1	–	9
Warden, M.J.(MCC)	–	1	1	–	2	2	2.00	–	–	1
Warren, R.J.(Nh)	1995	18	29	4	110	935	37.40	1	6	12
Watkin, S.L.(Gm)	1989	15	19	9	16*	86	8.60	–	–	7
Watkinson, M.(La)	1987	8	13	1	116	345	28.75	1	–	4
Watts, D.F.(Sc)	–	2	4	–	28	48	12.00	–	–	–
†Weekes, P.N.(M)	1993	16	28	4	140*	828	34.50	1	6	19
Welch, G.(Wa)	1997	14	21	6	48*	326	21.73	–	–	5
Wells, A.P.(K)	1997	10	15	–	111	490	32.66	2	1	1
Wells, V.J.(Le)	1994	13	20	2	109*	588	32.66	2	3	13
Welton, G.E.(Nt)	–	9	17	1	76	315	19.68	–	1	4
Weston, R.M.S.(De)	–	15	26	2	156	838	34.91	3	2	9
†Weston, W.P.C.(Wo)	1995	11	21	–	157	554	26.38	2	1	3
Wharf, A.G.(Nt)	–	16	26	3	78	370	16.08	–	2	8
Whiley, M.J.A.(Nt)	–	1	–	–	–	–	–	–	–	–
Whitaker, J.J.(Le)	1986	5	7	–	44	130	18.57	–	–	1
White, C.(Y)	1993	17	31	2	52	521	17.96	–	1	12
White, G.W.(H)	1998	16	28	1	121	818	30.29	1	4	11
†Wickremasinghe, P.P.(SL)	–	4	7	2	62	144	28.80	–	1	1
Williams, K.C.(MCC)	–	1	1	1	3*	3	–	–	–	2
Williamson, D.(Le)	–	2	4	–	19	59	14.75	–	–	2
Williamson, J.G.(Sc)	–	1	2	–	18	24	12.00	–	–	–
Willis, S.C.(K)	–	4	6	2	67	117	29.25	–	1	10/1
Wilson, E.J.(Wo/BU)	–	9	17	2	116	536	35.73	1	3	6
Wilton, N.J.(Sx)	–	6	10	–	55	156	15.60	–	1	13/2

	Cap	M	I	NO	HS	Runs	Avge	100	50	Ct/St
Windows, M.G.N.(Gs)	1998	17	30	3	118	960	35.55	2	5	5
Wingfield, W.R.(SAA)	–	3	5	1	61	114	28.50	–	1	3
Wood, J.(Du)	1998	10	15	1	49*	139	9.92	–	–	4
Wood, M.J.(Y)	–	17	33	–	53	451	13.66	–	1	10
†Wood, N.T.(La)	–	6	9	–	82	225	25.00	–	1	1
Woolley, A.P.(De)	–	1	2	–	8	9	4.50	–	–	–
Wright, C.M.(Sc)	–	2	3	1	20	31	15.50	–	–	2
Yates, G.(La)	1994	5	6	–	21	25	4.16	–	–	4

BOWLING

See BATTING and FIELDING section for details of caps and teams

	Cat	O	M	R	W	Avge	Best	5wI	10wM
Adams, C.J.	RM/OB	120	28	333	10	33.30	3- 37	–	–
Afzaal, U.	SLA	49.1	8	198	3	66.00	1- 17	–	–
Aldred, P.	RM	362.4	85	1063	50	21.26	7-101	5	1
Ali, Kabir	RMF	20	8	58	3	19.33	2- 36	–	–
Alleyne, M.W.	RM	367	109	1000	23	43.47	3- 36	–	–
Allingham, M.J.D.	RM	2	0	13	0				
Allott, G.I.	LFM	163.1	32	593	15	39.53	3- 22	–	–
Amin, R.M.	SLA	101	45	190	9	21.11	4- 87	–	–
Amla, A.M.	LB	4	0	16	1	16.00	1- 16	–	–
Anderson, R.S.G.	RMF	378.2	84	1273	50	25.46	5- 36	2	–
Archer, B.J.	RSM	14	5	28	2	14.00	1- 5	–	–
Arnold, R.P.	OB	104	23	279	8	34.87	4- 74	–	–
Asim Butt	LMF	67	13	191	7	27.28	3- 20	–	–
Astle, N.J.	RM	148	65	246	9	27.33	3- 22	–	–
Austin, I.D.	RM	129	29	443	9	49.22	6- 43	1	–
Averis, J.M.M.	RMF	72.2	16	261	8	32.62	3- 42	–	–
Aymes, A.N.	(WK)	1	0	1	0				
Bailey, R.J.	OB	19	1	51	1	51.00	1- 4	–	–
Ball, M.C.J.	OB	266	66	723	13	55.61	3- 38	–	–
Barnett, K.J.	RM/LB	40.3	6	134	2	67.00	2- 52	–	–
Base, S.J.	RMF	10	3	34	0				
Bates, J.J.	OB	141	46	356	11	32.36	5-154	1	–
Bates, R.T.	OB	13	0	83	0				
Batty, G.J.	OB	21	2	58	2	29.00	2- 45	–	–
Batty, J.N.	(WK)	2	1	9	0				
Benjamin, J.E.	RMF	17	2	78	1	78.00	1- 31	–	–
Betts, M.M.	RFM	175.1	41	583	20	29.15	4- 34	–	–
Bicknell, M.P.	RFM	545.4	156	1346	71	18.95	4- 32	–	–
Bishop, I.E.	RMF	79	14	249	5	49.80	2- 45	–	–
Bishop, J.E.	LMF	43	7	180	3	60.00	2- 89	–	–
Blackwell, I.D.	SLA	250.1	69	595	12	49.58	3- 30	–	–
Blanchett, I.N.	RMF	20	1	116	2	58.00	2- 64	–	–
Blewett, G.S.	RM	66.4	13	212	5	42.40	2- 16	–	–
Bloomfield, T.F.	RMF	266.3	45	1007	33	30.51	5- 36	1	–
Bodi, G.H.	SLC	16	4	69	0				
Bond, A.N.	RM	17	3	74	2	37.00	2- 41	–	–
Boon, D.C.	OB	5	1	17	1	17.00	1- 17	–	–
Boswell, S.A.J.	RFM	46	9	214	5	42.80	3- 71	–	–
Boteju, H.	RM	70	10	221	7	31.57	2- 49	–	–
Bowen, M.N.	RM	264	53	872	37	23.56	5- 66	1	–
Bowler, P.D.	OB	9.5	2	12	2	6.00	2- 4	–	–
Bridge, G.D.	SLA	44	12	110	1	110.00	1- 60	–	–
Brimson, M.T.	SLA	316.5	98	784	24	32.66	5- 51	1	–
Brinkley, J.E.	RFM	99	39	167	12	13.91	4- 34	–	–

	Cat	O	M	R	W	Avge	Best	5wI	10wM
Brown, A.D.	LB	26	3	80	0				
Brown, D.R.	RFM	232.5	57	717	26	27.57	7- 66	1	–
Brown, J.F.	OB	29.5	8	64	2	32.00	2- 64	–	–
Brown, S.J.E.	LFM	475	112	1448	63	22.98	6- 25	5	–
Bulbeck, M.P.L.	LMF	425.4	100	1456	51	28.54	5- 45	3	1
Burns, M.	RM	100	18	365	7	52.14	2- 46	–	–
Butcher, G.P.	RM	21	4	77	2	38.50	1- 19	–	–
Butcher, M.A.	RM	180	49	445	17	26.17	4- 30	–	–
Byrne, B.W.	OB	101	18	330	5	66.00	3- 66	–	–
Caddick, A.R.	RFM	763.5	249	1900	91	20.87	8-113	5	–
Cairns, C.L.	RFM	234.2	56	701	32	21.90	7- 46	3	1
Carson, N.D.	RM	21	5	74	4	18.50	3- 39	–	–
Cassar, M.E.	RFM	164	34	562	19	29.57	5- 51	1	–
Catterall, D.N.	RMF	46	10	185	5	37.00	2- 16	–	–
Cawdron, M.J.	RMF	101.5	30	266	16	16.62	5- 35	3	–
Chapman, S.	SLA	14	1	60	1	60.00	1- 49	–	–
Chapple, G.	RFM	338	92	964	24	40.16	5- 92	1	–
Chilton, M.J.	RM	25	9	62	2	31.00	1- 1	–	–
Collingwood, P.D.	RMF	91.1	25	238	8	29.75	3- 7	–	–
Conway, S.L.J.	RM	14	1	56	0				
Cook, S.J.	RM	276.4	60	954	27	35.33	4- 83	–	–
Cooke, G.	RMF	35	8	118	2	59.00	1- 21	–	–
Cork, D.G.	RFM	427.3	91	1229	55	22.34	6-113	4	–
Cosker, D.A.	SLA	321	81	844	19	44.42	3-100	–	–
Cotterell, T.P.	SLA	32	8	81	3	27.00	3- 69	–	–
Cottey, P.A.	OB	2	1	3	0				
Cowan, A.P.	RFM	393.1	66	1267	46	27.54	6- 47	1	–
Cox, D.J.	RMF	25	6	78	1	78.00	1- 33	–	–
Cox, J.	OB	49.3	6	188	4	47.00	3- 46	–	–
Crawley, J.P.	RM	6	0	51	0				
Creed, M.	RFM	35	4	139	2	69.50	1- 27	–	–
Creese, M.L.	SLA	25.3	7	98	1	98.00	1- 37	–	–
Croft, R.D.B.	OB	521.4	135	1412	45	31.37	7- 70	4	1
Crowe, C.D.	OB	92	14	348	11	31.63	3- 63	–	–
Curran, K.M.	RMF	5	1	21	1	21.00	1- 21	–	–
Dagnall, C.E.	RM	26.5	7	88	6	14.66	4- 20	–	–
Dakin, J.M.	RM	219.1	61	575	19	30.26	4- 27	–	–
Dale, A.	RMF	136.5	46	407	15	27.13	3- 29	–	–
Daley, J.A.	RM	11	2	40	0				
Danson, A.R.	RM	42.3	8	166	3	55.33	1- 5	–	–
Davies, A.P.	RMF	21	4	78	1	78.00	1- 48	–	–
Davies, M.K.	SLA	423.3	137	857	40	21.42	6- 49	3	–
Davis, M.J.G.	OB	16.1	6	34	1	34.00	1- 5	–	–
Davy, J.O.	LFM	24.3	7	71	5	14.20	3- 33	–	–
Dawes, J.H.	RFM	36.2	11	102	8	12.75	5- 45	1	–
Dean, K.J.	LMF	66.4	14	198	12	16.50	4- 34	–	–
Deane, M.J.	RM	31.4	8	112	2	56.00	2- 42	–	–
DeFreitas, P.A.J.	RFM	477.2	121	1284	59	21.76	6- 41	4	–
De la Pena, J.M.	RMF	63.5	19	240	13	18.46	6- 18	1	1
Di Venuto, M.J.	RM/LB	13	2	40	1	40.00	1- 3	–	–
Donald, A.A.	RF	50	15	136	0				
Doull, S.B.	RMF	105.3	35	334	8	41.75	2- 30	–	–
Dowman, M.P.	RMF	35	8	109	1	109.00	1- 25	–	–
Drakes, V.C.	RF	586.2	131	1794	80	22.42	6- 39	5	2
Dutch, K.P.	OB	87	17	278	7	39.71	3- 69	–	–
Dyer, N.R.	OB	70.4	20	205	8	25.62	4- 47	–	–
Eadie, D.J.	RM	55	14	168	3	56.00	3- 57	–	–

	Cat	O	M	R	W	Avge	Best	5wI	10wM
Eagleson, R.L.	RFM	10.5	2	34	1	34.00	1-34	–	–
Ealham, M.A.	RMF	339.2	73	981	41	23.92	6-35	2	–
Edmond, M.D.	RMF	8	3	24	0				
Edwards, A.D.	RFM	48	12	157	3	52.33	2-67	–	–
Evans, A.W.	RM	1	0	3	0				
Evans, K.P.	RMF	21	5	70	3	23.33	3-70	–	–
Fairbrother, N.H.	LM	2	0	2	0				
Fellows, G.M.	RM	7	0	38	1	38.00	1-38	–	–
Fisher, I.D.	SLA	162	42	476	14	34.00	5-73	1	–
Flanagan, I.N.	OB	14.3	4	50	1	50.00	1-50	–	–
Fleming, M.V.	RM	266.3	64	726	23	31.56	3-59	–	–
Flintoff, A.	RM	145.4	30	419	15	27.93	5-24	1	–
Follett, D.	RFM	120	23	377	8	47.12	3-64	–	–
Francis, S.R.G.	RMF	118	25	392	6	65.33	2-94	–	–
Franks, P.J.	RMF	513	124	1489	63	23.63	5-52	1	–
Fraser, A.R.C.	RMF	435.1	113	1093	38	28.76	5-63	1	–
Fulton, J.A.G.	RM	1	1	0	0				
Gallage, I.S.	RM	80.5	24	235	10	23.50	3-18	–	–
Gallian, J.E.R.	RM	36.4	11	112	5	22.40	2-28	–	–
Gannon, B.W.	RMF	259.3	47	992	33	30.06	6-80	2	–
Giddins, E.S.H.	RFM	381.3	102	1142	52	21.96	6-90	2	–
Gie, N.A.	RM	5	0	27	0				
Giles, A.F.	SLA	447.4	145	938	39	24.05	5-28	2	–
Gofton, A.F.	RM	84.1	13	302	9	33.55	3-41	–	–
Golding, J.M.	RMF	22	4	74	1	74.00	1-74	–	–
Goodyer, T.E.	RM	3	0	23	0				
Gough, D.	RF	96.5	20	319	17	18.76	4-27	–	–
Gough, M.A.	OB	77.4	14	259	4	64.75	4-49	–	–
Grayson, A.P.	SLA	319.2	98	849	22	38.59	4-16	–	–
Green, R.J.	RM	212.2	46	692	20	34.60	4-21	–	–
Greenidge, C.G.	RFM	76.4	20	231	11	21.00	5-60	1	–
Grove, J.O.	RMF	74	14	304	5	60.80	1-52	–	–
Halsall, R.G.	RM	168	35	491	11	44.63	3-64	–	–
Hamilton, G.M.	RFM	277.1	65	825	43	19.18	5-30	1	–
Hancock, T.H.C.	RM	53	12	190	4	47.50	1- 5	–	–
Hansen, T.M.	LFM	64	17	196	5	39.20	3-59	–	–
Hardinges, M.A.	RMF	23	6	60	1	60.00	1- 9	–	–
Harmison, S.J.	RF	565.5	120	1775	64	27.73	5-76	1	–
Harris, A.J.	RM	229.3	44	752	26	28.92	5-63	2	–
Harris, C.Z.	RM/LB	60	26	105	3	35.00	2-16	–	–
Harrison, D.S.	RFM	22	3	64	1	64.00	1-15	–	–
Hartley, P.J.	RMF	393	93	1176	54	21.77	8-65	2	1
Harvey, I.J.	RM	296.1	77	876	31	28.25	5-76	1	–
Hay, M.J.	RM	19	7	51	0				
Hayden, M.L.	RM	30	7	92	4	23.00	3-10	–	–
Haynes, G.R.	RM	99.1	22	278	3	92.66	2-35	–	–
Haywood, G.R.	RM	13.2	1	66	0				
Headley, D.W.	RFM	457.5	93	1442	37	38.97	4-74	–	–
Hemp, D.L.	RM	21	5	71	1	71.00	1-18	–	–
Henderson, T.	RFM	52.5	19	81	8	10.12	5-44	1	–
Herath, R.	SLA	168	46	448	22	20.36	6-45	1	–
Hewitt, J.P.	RMF	311.1	69	1022	35	29.20	5-50	1	–
Hewson, D.R.	RM	1	1	0	0				
Hick, G.A.	OB	61	18	163	5	32.60	2- 8	–	–
Hicks, T.C.	OB	181.1	29	672	10	67.20	2-61	–	–
Hockley, J.B.	OB	12	1	57	1	57.00	1-57	–	–
Hodgson, T.P.	RM	9	2	34	1	34.00	1-34	–	–

	Cat	O	M	R	W	Avge	Best	5wI	10wM
Hoggard, M.J.	RFM	215.1	58	619	28	22.10	5- 47	1	–
Hollioake, A.J.	RMF	58.1	10	220	6	36.66	1- 7	–	–
Hollioake, B.C.	RFM	249.5	49	801	23	34.82	5- 51	1	–
Horne, M.J.	RM	11.1	5	28	0				
House, W.J.	RM	6	0	12	0				
Hughes, Q.J.	OB	6	1	27	0				
Hutchison, P.M.	LFM	65.5	16	263	13	20.23	6- 35	1	–
Hutton, B.L.	RMF	54	9	226	3	75.33	2-100	–	–
Hyam, B.J.	(WK)	2	0	8	0				
Illingworth, R.K.	SLA	336.4	90	767	15	51.13	3- 58	–	–
Ilott, M.C.	LFM	310.4	85	900	38	23.68	6- 38	1	–
Innes, K.J.	RM	137	37	429	15	28.60	4- 85	–	–
Irani, R.C.	RMF	395.3	99	1084	51	21.25	4- 29	–	–
James, K.D.	LMF	54.1	13	201	6	33.50	3- 38	–	–
Jarvis, P.W.	RFM	201.2	43	619	19	32.57	4- 76	–	–
Jayantha, S.	OB	5	0	29	1	29.00	1- 29	–	–
Johnson, P.	RM	1	0	10	0				
Johnson, R.L.	RMF	133.3	30	453	16	28.31	4- 50	–	–
Jones, I.	RFM	79.2	13	341	6	56.83	3- 81	–	–
Jones, P.S.	RMF	255.2	49	845	21	40.23	4-126	–	–
Jones, S.P.	RF	208	31	776	19	40.84	5- 31	1	–
Kallis, J.H.	RMF	95	12	345	11	31.36	3- 52	–	–
Kasprowicz, M.S.	RF	485.5	112	1458	53	27.50	5- 42	2	–
Keech, M.	RM	9	1	37	0				
Keedy, G.	SLA	265.4	73	711	26	27.34	5- 67	1	–
Kendall, W.S.	RM	4.5	0	17	0				
Kenway, D.A.	RM	1	0	1	0				
Kerr, J.I.D.	RMF	305.2	68	1075	31	34.67	7- 23	1	–
Kettleborough, R.A.	RM	7	6	1	0				
Khan, A.A.	LB	24.2	9	63	1	63.00	1- 11	–	–
Khan, S.H.	RM	151	34	579	9	64.33	3- 70	–	–
Killeen, N.	RFM	411.3	113	1070	58	18.44	7- 85	4	–
King, R.D.	RFM	35	9	84	6	14.00	4- 41	–	–
Kino, D.	LMF	143	24	585	6	97.50	2- 84	–	–
Kirtley, R.J.	RFM	514.3	133	1504	65	23.13	7- 21	3	–
Krikken, K.M.	(WK)	9.2	1	54	1	54.00	1- 54	–	–
Lacey, S.J.	OB	81	15	238	3	79.33	1- 16	–	–
Lampitt, S.R.	RMF	287.1	70	888	39	22.76	4- 28	–	–
Laney, J.S.	OB	39	5	126	2	63.00	1- 24	–	–
Langer, J.L.	RM	2	1	3	0				
Law, D.R.	RFM	105	17	418	9	46.44	4- 32	–	–
Law, S.G.	RM/LB	35.4	6	133	3	44.33	1- 3	–	–
Law, W.L.	OB	0.1	0	4	0				
Lawrence, J.R.G.	LMF	26	5	98	0				
Leatherdale, D.A.	RM	83.4	17	283	8	35.37	2- 14	–	–
Lewis, C.C.	RFM	191.2	50	585	16	36.56	3- 18	–	–
Lewis, J.	RMF	492.2	135	1444	49	29.46	7- 56	2	1
Lewry, J.D.	LFM	381.4	84	1330	56	23.75	7- 38	4	1
Liptrot, C.G.	RFM	194.1	49	665	20	33.25	5- 51	1	–
Lloyd, G.D.	RM	10	0	100	0				
Logan, R.J.	RMF	58	18	178	8	22.25	3- 42	–	–
Love, G.T.	OB	82	23	214	4	53.50	2- 44	–	–
Loveridge, G.R.	LBG	209.4	25	830	11	75.45	2- 59	–	–
Lowe, J.P.	RM	40	9	178	1	178.00	1- 10	–	–
Lucas, D.S.	LFM	103.5	21	394	15	26.26	5-104	1	–
Lugsden, S.	RFM	51	12	161	4	40.25	3-105	–	–
McCague, M.J.	RFM	235	44	754	21	35.90	4- 36	–	–

	Cat	O	M	R	W	Avge	Best	5wI	10wM
McCallan, W.K.	OB	50	9	171	6	28.50	3- 63	–	–
McCoubrey, A.G.A.M.	RFM	27.4	8	78	4	19.50	3- 38	–	–
McDaid, R.W.	RM	42	10	153	2	76.50	1- 34	–	–
McGarry, A.C.	RFM	40	5	149	4	37.25	2- 72	–	–
McGerrigle, R.D.	RM	25	7	70	5	14.00	4- 24	–	–
McGrath, A.	OB	86	26	204	9	22.66	3- 18	–	–
McLean, N.A.M.	RF	471	105	1489	46	32.36	4- 63	–	–
McMillan, C.D.	RM	68.1	15	206	4	51.50	2- 19	–	–
Maddy, D.L.	RM/OB	85.4	22	260	12	21.66	3- 5	–	–
Mahmood, S.	LB	3	0	43	0				
Maiden, G.I.	OB	21	3	61	3	20.33	2- 11	–	–
Malcolm, D.E.	RF	485.1	90	1726	60	28.76	6- 39	3	–
Martin, P.J.	RFM	446.4	134	1028	50	20.56	5- 43	4	–
Martin-Jenkins, R.S.C.	RFM	370.2	99	1074	42	25.57	4- 50	–	–
Mascarenhas, A.D.	RMF	308	98	868	17	51.05	2- 2	–	–
Mason, T.J.	OB	91	28	182	7	26.00	3- 32	–	–
Mather, D.P.	LM	142.2	27	469	12	39.08	3- 44	–	–
Maynard, M.P.	RM	2	2	0	0				
Millns, D.J.	RF	142.3	35	372	23	16.17	5- 62	1	–
Mohammed, I.	OB	41.5	8	134	2	67.00	1- 58	–	–
Molins, G.L.	SLA	42	14	126	2	63.00	2- 61	–	–
Montgomerie, R.R.	OB	1	0	6	0				
Moody, T.M.	RM	89.5	25	267	6	44.50	4- 27	–	–
Mooney, P.J.K.	RM	47.1	14	167	7	23.85	4- 12	–	–
Morris, A.C.	RMF	172	51	497	28	17.75	5- 52	3	1
Morris, Z.C.	SLA	33.1	7	94	0				
Mullally, A.D.	LFM	310.4	93	771	28	27.53	5-106	1	–
Munton, T.A.	RMF	409.1	107	1028	52	19.76	7- 36	3	–
Muralitharan, M.	OB	386.2	122	777	66	11.77	7- 39	8	5
Napier, G.R.	RM	3	0	20	0				
Nash, D.J.	RFM	232	84	548	34	16.11	7- 39	2	–
Nel, A.	RFM	116	42	217	17	12.76	3- 19	–	–
Newell, K.	RM	13	1	38	2	19.00	2- 15	–	–
Newport, P.J.	RFM	274.4	77	747	31	24.09	4- 57	–	–
O'Connor, S.B.	LFM	134.2	32	447	19	23.52	6- 65	2	–
Ontong, J.L.	OB	33	10	70	3	23.33	2- 23	–	–
Ormond, J.	RFM	406.1	88	1283	52	24.67	5- 63	3	–
Ostler, D.P.	RM	1	0	2	0				
Parkin, O.T.	RFM	155.4	39	491	21	23.38	4- 38	–	–
Parsons, K.A.	RM	285.2	80	823	28	29.39	5- 57	1	–
Parsons, R.A.	LM	3	0	10	0				
Patel, M.M.	SLA	674.3	209	1568	63	24.88	8-115	3	1
Patterson, M.W.	RFM	13	2	39	3	13.00	3- 25	–	–
Peirce, M.T.E.	SLA	6	1	30	1	30.00	1- 16	–	–
Penberthy, A.L.	RM	266.5	89	735	19	38.68	3- 13	–	–
Penn, A.J.	RFM	28.3	6	115	8	14.37	6- 51	1	–
Penney, T.L.	RM	2	1	1	0				
Perera, A.S.A.	RMF	66.5	9	253	11	23.00	7- 73	1	–
Perera, N.R.G.	LB	64	12	207	9	23.00	4- 35	–	–
Peters, S.D.	LB	3.5	–	19	1	19.00	1- 19	–	–
Phillips, N.C.	OB	212	41	677	18	37.61	6- 97	2	1
Phillips, T.J.	SLA	76	17	278	8	34.75	4- 42	–	–
Pierson, A.R.K.	OB	271.2	52	789	13	60.69	4-131	–	–
Pimlott, C.R.	RFM	95.2	20	283	5	56.60	3- 10	–	–
Pirihi, N.G.	RSM	1	1	0	1	0.00	1- 0	–	–
Powell, M.J.(Gm)	RSM	20	1	100	2	50.00	2- 39	–	–
Powell, M.J.(Wa)	RM	25	6	56	0				

	Cat	O	M	R	W	Avge	Best	5wI	10wM
Pretorius, D.	RF	103	29	239	15	15.93	4- 39	–	–
Pushpakumara, K.R.	RMF	99	11	445	9	49.44	3- 81	–	–
Ramprakash, M.R.	RM	10	0	36	0				
Randall, S.J.	OB	77	18	237	0				
Rao, R.K.	LBG	14.5	2	53	1	53.00	1- 27	–	–
Rashid, U.B.A.	SLA	218.3	67	664	15	44.26	4- 41	–	–
Ratcliffe, J.D.	RM	99	27	269	15	17.93	6- 48	1	–
Rawnsley, M.J.	SLA	110	28	291	8	36.37	3- 84	–	–
Renshaw, S.J.	RMF	381.3	93	1125	30	37.50	4- 43	–	–
Richardson, A.	RMF	190.3	45	539	23	23.43	8- 51	1	1
Ridgway, P.M.	RFM	9	1	55	0				
Robinson, D.D.J.	RMF	2	1	6	0				
Robinson, M.A.	RFM	520.4	140	1438	48	29.95	6- 88	1	–
Rose, G.D.	RM	219.2	61	657	17	38.64	4- 14	–	–
Ross, J.S.	LMF	40	7	129	0				
Sachdeva, A.	LB	12	1	54	1	54.00	1- 32	–	–
Saggers, M.J.	RMF	59.5	13	192	12	16.00	4- 26	–	–
Sajdeh, R.K.	LB	37	4	130	0				
Sales, D.J.G.	RM	31.3	7	99	8	12.37	4- 25	–	–
Salisbury, I.D.K.	LBG	558.2	145	1315	60	21.91	5- 44	2	–
Saqlain Mushtaq	OB	290.5	90	660	58	11.37	7- 19	7	2
Sayers, C.A.	RMF	83	13	357	2	178.50	2- 21	–	–
Schofield, C.P.	LB	324	82	951	29	32.79	5- 66	1	–
Scott, D.A.	OB	95.2	18	332	8	41.50	4-151	–	–
Shah, O.A.	OB	99.1	14	326	11	29.63	3- 33	–	–
Sheikh, M.A.	RM	6	0	21	0				
Sheikh, S.M.	RMF	96.5	18	338	12	28.16	4- 25	–	–
Sheriyar, A.	LFM	609.2	119	2273	92	24.70	7-130	4	1
Sidebottom, R.J.	LFM	275.3	70	789	24	32.87	3- 16	–	–
Silverwood, C.E.W.	RFM	405.2	87	1204	59	20.40	5- 28	3	–
Slater, M.J.	RM	4	0	23	0				
Smethurst, M.P.	RM	126.1	29	377	13	29.00	4- 44	–	–
Smith, A.M.	LMF	450.1	127	1168	57	20.49	5- 41	2	–
Smith, E.T.	RM	1	0	3	0				
Smith, N.M.K.	OB	190.3	47	540	16	33.75	4- 90	–	–
Smith, R.A.	LB	1	0	2	0				
Smith, T.M.	RFM	183.4	34	646	31	20.83	5- 63	3	1
Snape, J.N.	OB	277.1	71	804	12	67.00	3- 67	–	–
Solanki, V.S.	OB	158.3	47	514	17	30.23	4- 41	–	–
Stanger, I.M.	RMF	15	1	63	1	63.00	1- 40	–	–
Stemp, R.D.	SLA	325.5	88	974	16	60.87	4-114	–	–
Stephenson, J.P.	RM	310	57	1086	37	29.35	5- 60	1	–
Stevens, D.I.	RM	1.1	0	6	0				
Stewart, A.J.	(WK)	2	0	6	0				
Still, Q.R.	SLA	21	2	66	2	33.00	2- 30	–	–
Strang, P.A.	LBG	12	1	31	1	31.00	1- 20	–	–
Strong, M.R.	RMF	31	5	124	0				
Stubbings, S.D.	OB	5	0	41	0				
Such, P.M.	OB	702	192	1710	55	31.09	7-136	2	1
Sutcliffe, I.J.	OB	1	1	0	0				
Sutcliffe, R.V.	RFM	55	14	164	4	41.00	2- 88	–	–
Swann, A.J.	RM/OB	20	3	80	1	80.00	1- 19	–	–
Swann, G.P.	OB	560.1	131	1641	57	28.78	6- 41	2	1
Symonds, A.	OB	207.1	37	761	12	63.41	2- 48	–	–
Taylor, B.V.	RMF	25	4	108	2	54.00	1- 54	–	–
Taylor, J.P.	LFM	507.2	119	1427	48	29.72	5-105	1	–
Tennant, A.M.	SLA	17	5	65	2	32.50	2- 65	–	–

	Cat	O	M	R	W	Avge	Best	5wI	10wM
Thomas, P.A.	RFM	16	1	74	2	37.00	2-54	–	–
Thomas, S.D.	RFM	447.2	78	1480	61	24.26	5-64	1	–
Thompson, D.J.	RFM	184	30	685	24	28.54	4-46	–	–
Thompson, J.B.D.	RMF	434.1	106	1265	64	19.76	7-89	3	–
Thorpe, G.P.	RM	13	0	42	0				
Titchard, S.P.	RM	8	3	19	0				
Tolley, C.M.	LMF	85	20	199	5	39.80	3-15	–	–
Trescothick, M.E.	RM	38	8	127	5	25.40	2-26	–	–
Tudor, A.J.	RF	297.3	70	895	40	22.37	7-77	3	–
Tufnell, P.C.R.	SLA	577.3	155	1223	48	25.47	5-61	2	–
Twose, R.G.	RM	4	1	12	0				
Udal, S.D.	OB	497.3	124	1336	50	26.72	6-47	3	–
Vaughan, M.P.	OB	137.1	26	424	10	42.40	2-19	–	–
Vettori, D.L.	SLA	469	155	1051	32	32.84	5-80	2	–
Villavarayen, M.S.	RMF	85.5	11	314	6	52.33	2-44	–	–
Wagh, M.A.	OB	21.1	4	66	5	13.20	4-33	–	–
Walker, B.G.K.	LB	23	6	69	1	69.00	1-40	–	–
Walker, K.D.M.	SLA	142	31	479	12	39.91	3-65	–	–
Walker, M.J.	RM	19.1	3	64	0				
Walton, T.C.	RM	7.3	2	28	1	28.00	1- 8	–	–
Ward, I.J.	RM	4	2	8	0				
Warden, M.J.	RFM	24	12	48	1	48.00	1-33	–	–
Watkin, S.L.	RMF	421.3	121	1087	43	25.27	6-75	3	–
Watkinson, M.	RMF/OB	137	30	413	12	34.41	3-43	–	–
Weekes, P.N.	OB	316.1	68	890	23	38.69	4-50	–	–
Welch, G.	RM	269.3	45	927	31	29.90	5-47	1	–
Wells, V.J.	RMF	176	47	473	10	47.30	2- 2	–	–
Weston, R.M.S.	LB	6	1	23	1	23.00	1-15	–	–
Wharf, A.G.	RMF	335.3	65	1216	31	39.22	4-30	–	–
Whiley, M.J.A.	LMF	12	3	44	1	44.00	1-44	–	–
White, C.	RFM	354	69	1058	41	25.80	4-32	–	–
White, G.W.	LB	37.4	2	158	5	31.60	3-23	–	–
Wickremasinghe, P.P.	LB	66	18	175	4	43.75	4-56	–	–
Williams, K.C.	RFM	12	2	35	1	35.00	1-18	–	–
Williamson, D.	RM	16	3	33	0				
Windows, M.G.N.	RSM	1	0	7	0				
Wingfield, W.R.	RM	48	13	104	3	34.66	2-22	–	–
Wood, J.	RFM	247.4	57	805	36	22.36	7-58	2	–
Wood, N.T.	OB	6	0	36	0				
Woolley, A.P.	RM	11	1	61	0				
Wright, C.M.	RFM	55	12	158	5	31.60	3-24	–	–
Yates, G.	OB	131.1	42	315	14	22.50	6-64	2	–

COUNTY CHAMPIONSHIP 1999
PPP HEALTHCARE FINAL TABLE

	P	W	L	D	A	Bonus Points Bat	Bonus Points Bowl	Total Points
1 SURREY (5)	17	12	–	5	–	36	64	264
2 Lancashire (2)	16	8	4	4	1	37	55	208
3 Leicestershire (1)	17	5	3	9	–	43	61	200
4 Somerset (9)	17	6	4	7	–	38	56	194
5 Kent (11)	17	6	4	7	–	34	60	194
6 Yorkshire (3)	17	8	6	3	–	21	64	193
7 Hampshire (6)	17	5	5	7	–	45	58	191
8 Durham (14)	17	6	7	4	–	34	66	188
9 Derbyshire (10)	17	7	8	2	–	34	61	187
10 Warwickshire (8)	17	6	5	6	–	35	56	187
11 Sussex (7)	17	6	5	6	–	29	60	185
12 Essex (18)	17	5	7	5	–	38	63	181
13 Northamptonshire (15)	17	4	7	6	–	35	64	171
14 Glamorgan (13)	17	5	7	5	–	26	57	163
15 Worcestershire (12)	17	4	6	7	–	18	65	159
16 Middlesex (17)	16	4	5	7	1	24	52	156
17 Nottinghamshire (16)	17	4	11	2	–	27	57	140
18 Gloucesterhire (4)	17	2	9	6	–	26	62	136

1998 final positions are shown in brackets. The horizontal rule divides the two divisions which will form the 2000 Championship. The match between Middlesex and Lancashire at Lord's on 20-23 April was abandoned without a ball being bowled.

SCORING OF POINTS 1999

(a) For a win, 12 points, plus any points scored in the first innings.

(b) In a tie, each side to score six points, plus any points scored in the first innings.

(c) In a drawn match, each side to score four points, plus any points scored in the first innings (see also paragraph (f) below).

(d) If the scores are equal in a drawn match, the side batting in the fourth innings to score six points plus any points scored in the first innings, and the opposing side to score four points plus any points scored in the first innings.

(e) **First Innings Points** (awarded only for the performances **in the first 120 overs** of each first innings and retained whatever the result of the match).

(i) A maximum of four batting points to be available as under:-

200 to 249 runs	– 1 point
250 to 299 runs	– 2 points
300 to 349 runs	– 3 points
350 runs or over	– 4 points

(ii) A maximum of four bowling points to be available as under:-

3 to 4 wickets taken	– 1 point
5 to 6 wickets taken	– 2 points
7 to 8 wickets taken	– 3 points
9 to 10 wickets taken	– 4 points

(f) If play starts when less than eight hours playing time remains (in which event a one innings match shall be played as provided for in First Class Playing Condition 18), no first innings points shall be scored. The side winning on the one innings to score 12 points. In a tie, each side to score six points. In a drawn match, each side to score four points. If the scores are equal in a drawn match, the side batting in the second innings to score six points and the opposing side to score four points.

(g) If a match is abandoned without a ball being bowled, each side to score four points.

(h) A County which is adjudged to have prepared a pitch which is 'unsuitable for four-day First-Class Cricket' shall be liable to have 25 points deducted from its aggregate of points under the procedure agreed by the Board in December 1988 and revised in December 1993. In addition, a penalty of 10 or 15 points may in certain circumstances be imposed on a County in respect of a 'Poor' pitch under the procedure agreed by the Board in March 1995. There shall be no right of appeal against any points penalty provided for in this Playing Condition.

(i) The side which has the highest aggregate of points gained at the end of the season shall be the Champion County. Should any sides in the Championship table be equal on points, the following tie-breakers will be applied in the order stated: most wins, least losses, team achieving most points in contests between teams level on points, most wickets taken, most runs scored.

COUNTY CHAMPIONS

The English County Championship was not officially constituted until December 1889. Prior to that date there was no generally accepted method of awarding the title; although the 'least matches lost' method existed, it was not consistently applied. Rules governing playing qualifications were not agreed until 1873, and the first unofficial points system was not introduced until 1888.

Research has produced a list of champions dating back to 1826, but at least seven different versions exist for the period from 1864 to 1889 (see *The Wisden Book of Cricket Records*). Only from 1890 can any authorised list of county champions commence.

That first official Championship was contested between eight counties: Gloucestershire, Kent, Lancashire, Middlesex, Nottinghamshire, Surrey, Sussex and Yorkshire. The remaining counties were admitted in the following seasons: 1891 – Somerset, 1895 – Derbyshire, Essex, Hampshire, Leicestershire and Warwickshire, 1899 – Worcestershire, 1905 – Northamptonshire, 1921 – Glamorgan, and 1992 – Durham.

The Championship pennant was introduced by the 1951 champions, Warwickshire, and the Lord's Taverners' Trophy was first presented in 1973. The first sponsors, Schweppes (1977 to 1983), were succeeded by Britannic Assurance (1984 to 1998) and by PPP Healthcare in 1999.

1890	Surrey
1891	Surrey
1892	Surrey
1893	Yorkshire
1894	Surrey
1895	Surrey
1896	Yorkshire
1897	Lancashire
1898	Yorkshire
1899	Surrey
1900	Yorkshire
1901	Yorkshire
1902	Yorkshire
1903	Middlesex
1904	Lancashire
1905	Yorkshire
1906	Kent
1907	Nottinghamshire
1908	Yorkshire
1909	Kent
1910	Kent
1911	Warwickshire
1912	Yorkshire
1913	Kent
1914	Surrey
1919	Yorkshire
1920	Middlesex
1921	Middlesex
1922	Yorkshire
1923	Yorkshire
1924	Yorkshire
1925	Yorkshire
1926	Lancashire
1927	Lancashire
1928	Lancashire
1929	Nottinghamshire
1930	Lancashire
1931	Yorkshire
1932	Yorkshire
1933	Yorkshire
1934	Lancashire
1935	Yorkshire
1936	Derbyshire
1937	Yorkshire
1938	Yorkshire
1939	Yorkshire
1946	Yorkshire
1947	Middlesex
1948	Glamorgan
1949	Middlesex Yorkshire
1950	Lancashire Surrey
1951	Warwickshire
1952	Surrey
1953	Surrey
1954	Surrey
1955	Surrey
1956	Surrey
1957	Surrey
1958	Surrey
1959	Yorkshire
1960	Yorkshire
1961	Hampshire
1962	Yorkshire
1963	Yorkshire
1964	Worcestershire
1965	Worcestershire
1966	Yorkshire
1967	Yorkshire
1968	Yorkshire
1969	Glamorgan
1970	Kent
1971	Surrey
1972	Warwickshire
1973	Hampshire
1974	Worcestershire
1975	Leicestershire
1976	Middlesex
1977	Kent Middlesex
1978	Kent
1979	Essex
1980	Middlesex
1981	Nottinghamshire
1982	Middlesex
1983	Essex
1984	Essex
1985	Middlesex
1986	Essex
1987	Nottinghamshire
1988	Worcestershire
1989	Worcestershire
1990	Middlesex
1991	Essex
1992	Essex
1993	Middlesex
1994	Warwickshire
1995	Warwickshire
1996	Leicestershire
1997	Glamorgan
1998	Leicestershire
1999	Surrey

THE NATWEST TROPHY 1999 RESULTS CHART

THIRD ROUND *23 June*	FOURTH ROUND *7 July*	QUARTER-FINALS *28 July*	SEMI-FINALS *14, 15 August*	FINAL *29 August*
Durham Board†	GLOUCESTERSHIRE†	GLOUCESTERSHIRE	GLOUCESTERSHIRE†	GLOUCESTERSHIRE (£52,000)
GLOUCESTERSHIRE				
Bedfordshire†	Derbyshire			
DERBYSHIRE				
Hampshire Board†	GLAMORGAN†	Glamorgan† (£11,000)		
GLAMORGAN				
Buckinghamshire†	Warwickshire			
WARWICKSHIRE				
Herefordshire†	YORKSHIRE†	YORKSHIRE	Yorkshire (£16,000)	
YORKSHIRE				
Ireland†	Leicestershire			
LEICESTERSHIRE				
Hertfordshire†	LANCASHIRE	Lancashire† (£11,000)		
LANCASHIRE				
Kent Board†	Hampshire†			
HAMPSHIRE				
Essex	NORTHAMPTONSHIRE†	Northamptonshire† (£11,000)	Surrey (£16,000)	Somerset (£26,000)
NORTHAMPTONSHIRE†				
Middlesex	Nottinghamshire			
NOTTINGHAMSHIRE†				
Scotland†	SURREY	SURREY		
SURREY				
Devon†	Worcestershire†			
WORCESTERSHIRE				
Durham	Holland†	Kent (£11,000)	SOMERSET†	
HOLLAND†				
Cheshire†	KENT			
KENT				
Cumberland†	Sussex†	SOMERSET†		
SUSSEX				
Wales Board†	SOMERSET			
SOMERSET				

† *Home team. Winning teams are in capitals. Prize-money shown in brackets.*

1999 NATWEST TROPHY FINAL

GLOUCESTERSHIRE v SOMERSET

At Lord's, London on 29 August.
Result: GLOUCESTERSHIRE won by 50 runs.
Toss: Somerset. Award: R.C.Russell.

GLOUCESTERSHIRE		**Runs**	**Balls**	**4/6**	**Fall**
K.J.Barnett	run out (*Parsons*)	49	66	2	1-125
T.H.C.Hancock	lbw b Jarvis	74	119	8	4-161
R.J.Cunliffe	c Turner b Rose	3	8	–	2-129
* M.W.Alleyne	b Rose	14	30	–	3-161
† R.C.Russell	not out	31	37	1	
M.G.N.Windows	lbw b Jarvis	12	13	2	5-180
I.J.Harvey	c Holloway b Jarvis	7	9	1	6-193
J.N.Snape	st Turner b Jarvis	11	14	–	7-210
M.C.J.Ball	c Burns b Jarvis	5	6	–	8-224
M.J.Cawdron	not out	0	–	–	
A.M.Smith					
Extras	(LB 10, W 10, NB 4)	24			
Total	(50 overs; 8 wickets; 216 minutes)	**230**			

SOMERSET		**Runs**	**Balls**	**4/6**	**Fall**
P.D.Bowler	c Russell b Harvey	1	14	–	1- 5
* J.Cox	lbw b Smith	3	4	–	2- 9
P.C.L.Holloway	c Ball b Smith	13	25	1	3- 37
M.Burns	c Ball b Alleyne	26	39	3	4- 51
M.E.Trescothick	c Russell b Alleyne	5	14	1	5- 52
K.A.Parsons	st Russell b Smith	42	58	3	7-166
† R.J.Turner	c Russell b Alleyne	51	71	3	6-134
G.D.Rose	c Windows b Harvey	24	34	1	10-180
J.I.D.Kerr	run out (*Alleyne*)	2	6	–	8-171
A.R.Caddick	b Harvey	1	2	–	9-174
P.W.Jarvis	not out	3	4	–	
Extras	(LB 4, W 5)	9			
Total	(45.1 overs; 185 minutes)	**180**			

SOMERSET	**O**	**M**	**R**	**W**	**GLOUCESTERSHIRE**	**O**	**M**	**R**	**W**
Caddick	10	1	29	0	Harvey	7.1	0	23	3
Rose	10	3	38	2	Smith	9	0	25	3
Jarvis	10	1	55	5	Alleyne	10	0	37	3
Kerr	10	0	43	0	Cawdron	8	0	38	0
Parsons	10	0	55	0	Ball	7	0	33	0
					Snape	4	0	20	0

Scores after 15 overs: Gloucestershire: 71-0; Somerset 51-4.

Umpires: N.T.Plews and D.R.Shepherd.

NATWEST TROPHY PRINCIPAL RECORDS 1963-99

(Including The Gillette Cup)

Highest Total	413-4	Somerset v Devon	Torquay	1990
Highest Total in a Final	322-5	Warwicks v Sussex	Lord's	1993
Highest Total by a Minor County	323-7	Herts v Leics Board	Radlett	1999
Highest Total Batting Second	350	Surrey v Worcs	The Oval	1994
Highest Total to Win Batting Second	329-5	Sussex v Derbyshire	Derby	1997
Lowest Total	39	Ireland v Sussex	Hove	1985
Lowest Total in a Final	57	Essex v Lancashire	Lord's	1996
Lowest Total to Win Batting First	98	Worcs v Durham	Chester-le-St	1968

Highest Score	206	A.I.Kallicharran	Warwicks v Oxon	Birmingham	1984
HS (Minor County)	138	A.A.Metcalfe	Cumberland v Cornwall	Kendal	1999
Fastest Hundred	36 balls	G.D.Rose	Somerset v Devon	Torquay	1990
Most Hundreds	8	R.A.Smith	Hampshire		1985-99
Most Runs	2547	(av 48.98)	G.A.Gooch	Essex	1973-96

Highest Partnership for each Wicket

1st	311	A.J.Wright/N.J.Trainor	Glos v Scotland	Bristol	1997
2nd	286	I.S.Anderson/A.Hill	Derbys v Cornwall	Derby	1986
3rd	309*	T.S.Curtis/T.M.Moody	Worcs v Surrey	The Oval	1994
4th	234*	D.Lloyd/C.H.Lloyd	Lancashire v Glos	Manchester	1978
5th	166	M.A.Lynch/G.R.J.Roope	Surrey v Durham	The Oval	1982
6th	226	N.J.Long/M.V.Fleming	Kent v Cheshire	Bowden	1999
7th	160*	C.J.Richards/I.R.Payne	Surrey v Lincs	Sleaford	1983
8th	112	A.L.Penberthy/J.E.Emburey	Northants v Lancs	Manchester	1996
9th	87	M.A.Nash/A.E.Cordle	Glamorgan v Lincs	Swansea	1974
10th	81	S.Turner/R.E.East	Essex v Yorkshire	Leeds	1982

Best Bowling	8-21	M.A.Holding	Derbys v Sussex	Hove	1988
	8-31	D.L.Underwood	Kent v Scotland	Edinburgh	1987
Most Wickets	81	(av 14.85)	G.G.Arnold	Surrey	1963-80

Most Wicket-Keeping Dismissals in an Innings

7	(7ct)	A.J.Stewart	Surrey v Glamorgan	Swansea	1994
Most Appearances		67	M.W.Gatting	Middlesex	1975-98

Most Match Wins 76 – Lancashire

Most Cup/Trophy Wins 7 – Lancashire

GILLETTE CUP WINNERS

1963	Sussex	1969	Yorkshire	1975	Lancashire
1964	Sussex	1970	Lancashire	1976	Northamptonshire
1965	Yorkshire	1971	Lancashire	1977	Middlesex
1966	Warwickshire	1972	Lancashire	1978	Sussex
1967	Kent	1973	Gloucestershire	1979	Somerset
1968	Warwickshire	1974	Kent	1980	Middlesex

NATWEST TROPHY WINNERS

1981	Derbyshire	1988	Middlesex	1995	Warwickshire
1982	Surrey	1989	Warwickshire	1996	Lancashire
1983	Somerset	1990	Lancashire	1997	Essex
1984	Middlesex	1991	Hampshire	1998	Lancashire
1985	Essex	1992	Northamptonshire	1999	Gloucestershire
1986	Sussex	1993	Warwickshire		
1987	Nottinghamshire	1994	Worcestershire		

BENSON AND HEDGES CUP PRINCIPAL RECORDS 1972-99

Highest Total		388-7	Essex v Scotland	Chelmsford	1992
Highest Total Batting Second		318-5	Lancashire v Leics	Manchester	1995
Highest Total to Lose Batting Second		303-7	Derbys v Somerset	Taunton	1990
Lowest Total		50	Hampshire v Yorks	Leeds	1991
Highest Score	198*	G.A.Gooch	Essex v Sussex	Hove	1982
Hundreds	316				1972-99
Fastest Hundred	62 min	M.A.Nash	Glamorgan v Hants	Swansea	1976

Highest Partnership for each Wicket

1st	252	V.P.Terry/C.L.Smith	Hants v Combined U	Southampton	1990
2nd	285*	C.G.Greenidge/D.R.Turner	Hants v Minor C (S)	Amersham	1973
3rd	269*	P.M.Roebuck/M.D.Crowe	Somerset v Hants	Southampton	1987
4th	184*	D.Lloyd/B.W.Reidy	Lancashire v Derbys	Chesterfield	1980
5th	160	A.J.Lamb/D.J.Capel	Northants v Leics	Northampton	1986
6th	167*	M.G.Bevan/R.J.Blakey	Yorkshire v Lancs	Manchester	1996
7th	149*	J.D.Love/C.M.Old	Yorks v Scotland	Bradford	1981
8th	109	R.E.East/N.Smith	Essex v Northants	Chelmsford	1977
9th	83	P.G.Newman/M.A.Holding	Derbyshire v Notts	Nottingham	1985
10th	80*	D.L.Bairstow/M.Johnson	Yorkshire v Derbys	Derby	1981

Best Bowling	7-12	W.W.Daniel	Middx v Minor C (E)	Ipswich	1978
	7-22	J.R.Thomson	Middx v Hampshire	Lord's	1981
	7-24	Mushtaq Ahmed	Somerset v Ireland	Taunton	1997
	7-32	R.G.D.Willis	Warwicks v Yorks	Birmingham	1981
Four wickets in Four Balls		S.M. Pollock	Warwicks v Leics	Birmingham	1996
Most Wicket-Keeping Dismissals in an Innings					
8	(8ct)	D.J.S.Taylor	Somerset v Combined U	Taunton	1982
Most Catches in an Innings					
5		V.J.Marks	Combined U v Kent	Oxford	1976
Most Match Awards		22	G.A.Gooch	Essex	1973-97

RESULTS CHART

QUARTER-FINALS	SEMI-FINALS	FINAL
25, 26, 27 June	*10, 11 July*	*1 August*
GLOUCESTERSHIRE† / Surrey (£10,000)	GLOUCESTERSHIRE†	**GLOUCESTERSHIRE** (£50,000)
Lancashire† (£10,000) / SUSSEX	Sussex (£15,000)	
Leicestershire† (£10,000) / WARWICKSHIRE	Warwickshire† (£15,000)	Yorkshire (£25,000)
YORKSHIRE† / Hampshire (£10,000)	YORKSHIRE	

† *Home team. Winning teams are in capitals. Prize-money in brackets.*

BENSON AND HEDGES CUP WINNERS

1972	Leicestershire	1982	Somerset	1992	Hampshire
1973	Kent	1983	Middlesex	1993	Derbyshire
1974	Surrey	1984	Lancashire	1994	Warwickshire
1975	Leicestershire	1985	Leicestershire	1995	Lancashire
1976	Kent	1986	Middlesex	1996	Lancashire
1977	Gloucestershire	1987	Yorkshire	1997	Surrey
1978	Kent	1988	Hampshire	1998	Essex
1979	Essex	1989	Nottinghamshire	1999	Gloucestershire
1980	Northamptonshire	1990	Lancashire		
1981	Somerset	1991	Worcestershire		

1999 B & H SUPER CUP FINAL

GLOUCESTERSHIRE v YORKSHIRE

At Lord's, London on 1 August.
Result: GLOUCESTERSHIRE won by 124 runs.
Toss: Gloucestershire. Award: M.W.Alleyne.

GLOUCESTERSHIRE		**Runs**	**Balls**	**4/6**	**Fall**
K.J.Barnett	b Hutchison	28	39	5	1- 66
T.H.C.Hancock	b White	35	51	6	2- 75
R.J.Cunliffe	b White	61	81	2/1	3-232
* M.W.Alleyne	b White	112	91	11/2	4-255
I.J.Harvey	c Vaughan b Hutchison	13	9	2	5-267
J.N.Snape	c White b Hutchison	3	5	–	6-267
† R.C.Russell	run out (*Harden/Silverwood*)	1	1	–	7-270
M.G.N.Windows	not out	18	15	2	
M.C.J.Ball	b Silverwood	2	4	–	8-283
J.Lewis	b White	2	3	–	9-286
A.M.Smith	not out	1	1	–	
Extras	(LB 7, W 8)	15			
Total	(50 overs; 9 wickets; 207 minutes)	**291**			

YORKSHIRE		**Runs**	**Balls**	**4/6**	**Fall**
C.White	b Lewis	38	53	5	3- 78
G.S.Blewett	c Ball b Harvey	9	13	1	1- 14
* D.Byas	c and b Smith	13	10	–/1	2- 45
M.P.Vaughan	b Ball	24	37	1	4- 99
A.McGrath	run out (*Windows*)	20	26	1	6-122
R.J.Harden	c Cunliffe b Ball	8	19	–	5-115
G.M.Hamilton	st Russell b Lewis	25	43	–/1	8-161
† R.J.Blakey	b Ball	14	19	–	7-156
C.E.W.Silverwood	b Lewis	4	7	–	10-167
R.J.Sidebottom	c and b Snape	0	7	–	9-165
P.M.Hutchison	not out	2	6	–	
Extras	(B 1, LB 5, W 4)	10			
Total	(40 overs; 155 minutes)	**167**			

YORKSHIRE	**O**	**M**	**R**	**W**	**GLOUCESTERSHIRE**	**O**	**M**	**R**	**W**
Silverwood	10	0	47	1	Smith	8	0	28	1
Hamilton	6	0	55	0	Harvey	5	0	25	1
Hutchison	5	0	30	3	Lewis	5	0	32	3
Sidebottom	10	0	54	0	Alleyne	6	1	17	0
White	10	0	51	4	Ball	10	1	39	3
Vaughan	6	0	24	0	Snape	6	0	20	1
Blewett	3	0	23	0					

Scores after 15 overs: Gloucestershire: 72-1; Yorkshire 80-3.

Umpires: R.Julian and P.Willey.

CGU NATIONAL LEAGUE 1999

FIRST DIVISION

	P	*W*	*L*	*T*	*NR*	*Pts*	*NRR*
1 LANCASHIRE	16	11	2	–	3	50	7.49
2 Worcestershire	16	10	4	–	2	44	8.95
3 Kent	16	8	6	–	2	36	4.30
4 Gloucestershire	16	8	8	–	–	32	3.72
5 Yorkshire	16	8	8	–	–	32	–0.60
6 Leicestershire	16	6	8	–	2	28	–1.52
7 Warwickshire	16	6	8	–	2	28	–6.08
8 Hampshire	16	5	9	–	2	24	–9.44
9 Essex	16	3	12	–	1	14	–6.66

SECOND DIVISION

	P	*W*	*L*	*T*	*NR*	*Pts*	*NRR*
1 SUSSEX	16	13	2	–	1	54	11.95
2 Somerset	16	13	3	–	–	52	8.04
3 Northamptonshire	16	9	5	–	2	40	–0.21
4 Glamorgan	16	8	7	1	–	34	–1.34
5 Nottinghamshire	16	6	8	–	2	28	0.41
6 Surrey	16	5	9	1	1	24	0.83
7 Middlesex	16	5	10	1	–	22	–1.70
8 Derbyshire	16	4	10	1	1	20	–7.99
9 Durham	16	3	12	–	1	14	–10.30

Win = 4 points. Tie (T)/No Result (NR) = 2 points. Positions of counties finishing equal on points are decided by most wins or, if equal, by higher net run-rate (NRR – overall run-rate in all matches, i.e. total runs scored x 100 divided by balls received, minus the run-rate of its opponents in those same matches). Horizontal rules segregate the counties relegated and promoted for the 2000 competition.

SUNDAY LEAGUE CHAMPIONS

1969	Lancashire	1979	Somerset	1989	Lancashire
1970	Lancashire	1980	Warwickshire	1990	Derbyshire
1971	Worcestershire	1981	Essex	1991	Nottinghamshire
1972	Kent	1982	Sussex	1992	Middlesex
1973	Kent	1983	Yorkshire	1993	Glamorgan
1974	Leicestershire	1984	Essex	1994	Warwickshire
1975	Hampshire	1985	Essex	1995	Kent
1976	Kent	1986	Hampshire	1996	Surrey
1977	Leicestershire	1987	Worcestershire	1997	Warwickshire
1978	Hampshire	1988	Worcestershire	1998	Lancashire

SUNDAY LEAGUE
PRINCIPAL RECORDS 1969-98

Highest Total			375-4	Surrey v Yorkshire	Scarborough	1994
Highest Total Batting Second			317-6	Surrey v Notts	The Oval	1993
Lowest Total			23	Middlesex v Yorks	Leeds	1974

Highest Score	203	A.D.Brown	Surrey v Hampshire	Guildford	1997
Fastest Hundred	44 balls	M.A.Ealham	Kent v Derbyshire	Maidstone	1995

Highest Partnership for each Wicket

1st	239	G.A.Gooch/B.R.Hardie	Essex v Notts	Nottingham	1985
2nd	273	G.A.Gooch/K.S.McEwan	Essex v Notts	Nottingham	1983
3rd	223	S.J.Cook/G.D.Rose	Somerset v Glam	Neath	1990
4th	219	C.G.Greenidge/C.L.Smith	Hampshire v Surrey	Southampton	1987
5th	190	R.J.Blakey/M.J.Foster	Yorkshire v Leics	Leicester	1993
6th	137	M.P.Speight/I.D.K.Salisbury	Sussex v Surrey	Guildford	1996
7th	132	K.R.Brown/N.F.Williams	Middx v Somerset	Lord's	1988
8th	110*	C.L.Cairns/B.N.French	Notts v Surrey	The Oval	1993
9th	105	D.G.Moir/R.W.Taylor	Derbyshire v Kent	Derby	1984
10th	82	G.Chapple/P.J.Martin	Lancashire v Worcs	Manchester	1996

Best Bowling	8-26	K.D.Boyce	Essex v Lancashire	Manchester	1971
	7-15	R.A.Hutton	Yorkshire v Worcs	Leeds	1969
	7-16	S.D.Thomas	Glamorgan v Surrey	Swansea	1998
	7-39	A.Hodgson	Northants v Somerset	Northampton	1976
	7-41	A.N.Jones	Sussex v Notts	Nottingham	1986

Four Wkts in Four Balls	A.Ward	Derbyshire v Sussex	Derby	1970

Most Wicket-Keeping Dismissals in an Innings

7	(6ct, 1st)	R.W.Taylor	Derbyshire v Lancs	Manchester	1975

Most Catches in an Innings

5	J.M.Rice	Hampshire v Warwicks	Southampton	1978

NATIONAL LEAGUE
PRINCIPAL RECORDS 1999

Highest Total			301-6	Lancashire v Essex	Chelmsford	1999
Highest Total Batting Second			298	Essex v Lancashire	Chelmsford	1999
Lowest Total			44	Glamorgan v Surrey	The Oval	1999

Highest Score	163	C.J.Adams	Sussex v Middlesex	Arundel	1999
Fastest Hundred	50 balls	A.Flintoff	Lancashire v Essex	Chelmsford	1999
Best Bowling	7-30	M.P.Bicknell	Surrey v Glamorgan	The Oval	1999
Four Wkts in Four Balls		V.C.Drakes	Notts v Derbys	Nottingham	1999

MINOR COUNTIES CHAMPIONSHIP

FINAL TABLE 1999

	TWO INNINGS MATCHES				*Bonus Points*		*GRADE RULES*		*Total*
	P	*W*	*L*	*D*	*Bat*	*Bowl*	*P*	*Points*	*Points*
EASTERN DIVISION									
Cumberland	6	3	1	2	13	18	3	28	105(c)
Norfolk	6	3	0	3	7	11	3	25	96(a)
Hertfordshire	6	2	2	2	13	18	3	28	96(b)
Buckinghamshire	6	2	1	3	9	19	3	26	86
Lincolnshire	6	0	2	4	8	15	3	51	79(a)
Suffolk	6	0	1	5	8	10	3	51	72(a/e)
Staffordshire	6	0	1	5	7	12	3	36	65(c)
Bedfordshire	6	1	1	4	9	15	3	17	62(a)
Cambridgeshire	6	1	1	4	4	18	3	23	59(e)
Northumberland	6	0	2	4	4	16	3	38	58
WESTERN DIVISION									
Dorset	6	4	1	1	12	18	3	42	136
Devon	6	3	0	3	14	15	3	51	133(a)
Cheshire	6	2	2	2	11	11	3	40	104(d)
Shropshire	6	1	0	5	8	24	3	49	97
Oxfordshire	6	2	0	4	8	11	3	29	85(a)
Wiltshire	6	1	4	1	13	13	3	29	76(a)
Herefordshire	6	1	2	3	7	12	3	25	60
Cornwall	6	0	4	2	8	14	3	32	59(a)
Berkshire	6	1	0	5	10	15	3	12	58(a)
Wales	6	1	3	2	9	11	3	16	52

(a) Includes 5 points gained in 'No Result' match
(b) Includes 5 points gained in lost match reduced to 1 day
(c) Includes 10 points gained in 2 'No Result' matches
(d) Includes 5 points gained in 'No Result' match plus another 5 gained in lost match reduced to 1 day
(e) 2 points deducted because of slow over rate

Points for 'No Result' Grade Rules matches, and for one day matches originally scheduled to be Grade matches, are included in Grade Rules totals

CHAMPIONSHIP FINAL

At Netherfield on 12, 13, 14 September (*first 3-day final*): **CUMBERLAND beat Dorset by six wickets.** Cumberland 315-7 (80 overs; S.J.O'Shaughnessy 118) and 214-4 (61.4 overs; A.A.Metcalfe 115*). Dorset 130 (59.2 overs) and, following on, 396 (115.5 overs; A.J.Sexton 196, S.A.J.Kippax 4-91, D.B.Pennett 4-106).

ECB 38 COUNTY CUP

At Lord's on 1 September: **BEDFORDSHIRE beat Cumberland by eight wickets.** Cumberland 153 (47.4 overs; R.N.Dalton 5-21). Bedfordshire 154-2 (36.1 overs; A.R.Roberts 80*, D.J.M.Mercer 51*).

MINOR COUNTIES CHAMPIONS

1895	Norfolk Durham Worcestershire
1896	Worcestershire
1897	Worcestershire
1898	Worcestershire
1899	Northamptonshire Buckinghamshire
1900	Glamorgan Durham Northamptonshire
1901	Durham
1902	Wiltshire
1903	Northamptonshire
1904	Northamptonshire
1905	Norfolk
1906	Staffordshire
1907	Lancashire II
1908	Staffordshire
1909	Wiltshire
1910	Norfolk
1911	Staffordshire
1912	*In abeyance*
1913	Norfolk
1920	Staffordshire
1921	Staffordshire
1922	Buckinghamshire
1923	Buckinghamshire
1924	Berkshire
1925	Buckinghamshire
1926	Durham
1927	Staffordshire
1928	Berkshire
1929	Oxfordshire
1930	Durham
1931	Leicestershire II
1932	Buckinghamshire
1933	*Undecided*
1934	Lancashire II
1935	Middlesex II
1936	Hertfordshire
1937	Lancashire II
1938	Buckinghamshire
1939	Surrey II
1946	Suffolk
1947	Yorkshire II
1948	Lancashire II
1949	Lancashire II
1950	Surrey II
1951	Kent II
1952	Buckinghamshire
1953	Berkshire
1954	Surrey II
1955	Surrey II
1956	Kent II
1957	Yorkshire II
1958	Yorkshire II
1959	Warwickshire II
1960	Lancashire II
1961	Somerset II
1962	Warwickshire II
1963	Cambridgeshire
1964	Lancashire II
1965	Somerset II
1966	Lincolnshire
1967	Cheshire
1968	Yorkshire II
1969	Buckinghamshire
1970	Bedfordshire
1971	Yorkshire II
1972	Bedfordshire
1973	Shropshire
1974	Oxfordshire
1975	Hertfordshire
1976	Durham
1977	Suffolk
1978	Devon
1979	Suffolk
1980	Durham
1981	Durham
1982	Oxfordshire
1983	Hertfordshire
1984	Durham
1985	Cheshire
1986	Cumberland
1987	Buckinghamshire
1988	Cheshire
1989	Oxfordshire
1990	Hertfordshire
1991	Staffordshire
1992	Staffordshire
1993	Staffordshire
1994	Devon
1995	Devon
1996	Devon
1997	Devon
1998	Staffordshire
1999	Cumberland

MINOR COUNTIES RECORDS

Highest Total	621		Surrey II v Devon	The Oval	1928
Lowest Total	14		Cheshire v Staffs	Stoke	1909
Highest Score	282	E.Garnett	Berkshire v Wiltshire	Reading	1908
Most Runs – Season	1212	A.F.Brazier	Surrey II		1949
Record Partnership					
2nd	388*	T.H.Clark and A.F.Brazier	Surrey II v Sussex II	The Oval	1949
Best Bowling – Innings	10- 11	S.Turner	Cambs v Cumberland	Penrith	1987
– Match	18-100	N.W.Harding	Kent II v Wiltshire	Swindon	1937
Most Wickets – Season	119	S.F.Barnes	Staffordshire		1906

1999 MINOR COUNTIES CHAMPIONSHIP

LEADING BATTING AVERAGES 1999

(Qualification: 8 completed innings [or 500 runs] average 35.00)

		I	*NO*	*HS*	*Runs*	*Avge*
N.A.Folland	Devon	13	2	249*	838	76.18
C.S. Knightley	Oxfordshire	10	2	118	560	70.00
N.D.Burns	Buckinghamshire	15	4	152*	761	69.18
R.J.Williams	Oxfordshire	11	2	147	608	67.55
J.B.R.Jones	Shropshire	12	1	168*	576	52.36
D.M.Ward	Hertfordshire	13	1	122	627	52.25
O.J.Clayson	Bedfordshire	11	2	166	445	49.44
J.C.Harrison	Lincolnshire	13	1	169	564	47.00
R.D.Hughes	Herefordshire	13	1	226	556	46.33
P.J.Caley	Suffolk	14	2	90	516	43.00
M.A.Fell	Lincolnshire	11	2	90*	386	42.88
C.W.Boroughs	Herefordshire	12	1	87	466	42.36
A.T.Heather	Northumberland	8	–	123	332	41.50
P.J.Deakin	Dorset	13	2	100*	450	40.90
D.W.Randall	Suffolk	12	–	86	479	39.91
G.T.J.Townsend	Devon	13	1	79	475	39.58
M.H.James	Hertfordshire	13	2	74	426	38.72
T.A.Radford	Berkshire	15	3	84	464	38.66
W.Larkins	Bedfordshire	15	2	120	502	38.61
R.P.Harvey	Staffordshire	11	1	153	385	38.50
D.A.Winter	Wiltshire	12	–	108	458	38.16
C.Amos	Norfolk	10	1	78	337	37.44
S.C.Goldsmith	Norfolk	12	2	70	365	36.50
H.M.Hall	Berkshire	9	1	61	289	36.12

LEADING BOWLING AVERAGES

(Qualification: 20 wickets, average 26.00)

		O	*M*	*R*	*W*	*Avge*
P.M.Roebuck	Devon	296.5	79	565	41	13.78
T.J.A.Scriven	Buckinghamshire	134	35	325	23	14.13
D.M.Cousins	Cambridgeshire	247	58	698	48	14.54
V.J.Pike	Dorset	414.3	119	1015	68	14.92
P.J.O'Reilly	Hertfordshire	141.2	37	443	28	15.82
G.M.Kirk	Suffolk	191	69	397	25	15.88
Asif Din	Shropshire	255.5	83	507	30	16.90
D.B.Pennett	Cumberland	222.4	54	681	40	17.02
S.D.Myles	Berkshire	163.4	43	403	23	17.52
K.J.Nash	Wiltshire	123.5	21	493	28	17.60
S.A.Bradford	Lincolnshire	197.1	59	579	31	18.67
A.R.Clarke	Buckinghamshire	282.2	80	786	42	18.71
A.Akhtar	Cambridgeshire	233.4	85	522	27	19.33
K.E.Cooper	Herefordshire	253.2	73	569	29	19.62
P.G.Newman	Norfolk	170.1	47	413	20	20.65
A.Shimmons	Shropshire	174.1	54	431	20	21.55
G.Bulpitt	Staffordshire	167	48	440	20	22.00
D.J.P.Boden	Staffordshire	180.2	48	486	22	22.09
T.C.Hicks	Dorset	210.2	52	589	26	22.65
M.C.Theedom	Devon	153	21	521	22	23.68
S.J.W.Andrew	Hertfordshire	203.5	38	640	27	23.70
K.A.Arnold	Oxfordshire	244.2	50	704	29	24.27
A.R.Roberts	Bedfordshire	254.1	69	715	28	25.53
C.E.Shreck	Cornwall	226.3	49	825	32	25.78
L.J.Crozier	Northumberland	224.5	57	697	27	25.81

SECOND XI CHAMPIONSHIP 1999
FINAL TABLE

	P	W	L	D	*Bonus Points* Bat	*Bonus Points* Bowl	*Total Points*	Avge
1 MIDDLESEX (17)	13	8	1	4	34	48	194	14.92
2 Derbyshire (12)	15	9	2	4	41	47	212	14.13
3 Sussex (2)	13	7	4	2	32	39	163	12.54
4 Lancashire (5)	15	6	4	5	39	53	184	12.27
5 Kent (13)	14	5	4	5	32	49	161	11.50
6 Worcestershire (11)	14	6	3	5	25	42	159	11.36
7 Hampshire (7)	14	4	4	6	34	53	159	11.36
8 Durham (10)	12	4	5	3	28	47	135	11.25
9 Surrey (18)	15	6	7	2	36	49	165	11.00
10 Warwickshire (16)	14	5	5	4	39	38	153	10.93
11 Nottinghamshire (8)	15	6	6	3	29	50	163	10.87
12 Essex (15)	15	6	6	3	33	44	161	10.73
13 Northamptonshire (1)	14	4	4	6	28	45	145	10.36
14 Yorkshire (9)	17	3	8	6	40	59	159	9.35
15 Gloucestershire (4)	15	4	5	6	25	38	135	9.00
16 Leicestershire (6)	13	2	6	5	29	31	104	8.00
17 Glamorgan (14)	14	1	5	8	27	36	107	7.64
18 Somerset (3)	13	–	8	5	21	34	75	5.77

Win = 16 points.
1998 final positions are shown in brackets.

ECB SECOND XI AWARDS 1999

Players of the Month:
G.J.Kennis (Somerset); M.J.Foster (Durham);
C.D.Walsh (Kent); J.R.C.Hamblin (Hampshire)

Player of the Season
K.P.Dutch (Middlesex)

SECOND XI CHAMPIONS

1959	Gloucestershire	1973	Essex	1987	Kent/Yorkshire
1960	Northamptonshire	1974	Middlesex	1988	Surrey
1961	Kent	1975	Surrey	1989	Middlesex
1962	Worcestershire	1976	Kent	1990	Sussex
1963	Worcestershire	1977	Yorkshire	1991	Yorkshire
1964	Lancashire	1978	Sussex	1992	Surrey
1965	Glamorgan	1979	Warwickshire	1993	Middlesex
1966	Surrey	1980	Glamorgan	1994	Somerset
1967	Hampshire	1981	Hampshire	1995	Hampshire
1968	Surrey	1982	Worcestershire	1996	Warwickshire
1969	Kent	1983	Leicestershire	1997	Lancashire
1970	Kent	1984	Yorkshire	1998	Northamptonshire
1971	Hampshire	1985	Nottinghamshire	1999	Middlesex
1972	Nottinghamshire	1986	Lancashire		

FIRST-CLASS CAREER RECORDS

Compiled by Philip Bailey

The following career records are for all players who appeared in first-class or limited-overs cricket during the 1999 season, and are complete to the end of that season. Some players who did not appear in 1999 but may do so in 2000, are also included.

BATTING AND FIELDING

'1000' denotes instances of scoring 1000 runs in a season. Where these have been achieved outside the UK, they are shown after a plus sign.

	M	*I*	*NO*	*HS*	*Runs*	*Avge*	*100*	*50*	*1000*	*Ct/St*
Adams, C.J.	190	313	23	239	10561	36.41	26	48	4	225
Afzaal, U.	64	113	10	109*	2674	25.96	3	17	–	26
Aldred, P.	39	51	9	83	497	11.83	–	1	–	23
Ali, Kabir	1	1	–	11	11	11.00	–	–	–	–
Alleyne, M.W.	254	421	40	256	12100	31.75	16	63	6	213/2
Allingham, M.J.D.	5	9	3	66*	273	45.50	–	2	–	3
Allott, G.I.	31	40	18	13*	107	4.86	–	–	–	6
Altree, D.A.	5	7	3	2*	2	0.50	–	–	–	1
Amin, R.M.	10	13	7	12	31	5.16	–	–	–	3
Amla, A.M.	9	16	1	107	403	26.86	1	3	–	2
Anderson, R.S.G.	15	20	2	44	147	8.16	–	–	–	5
Archer, B.J.	3	6	–	27	52	8.66	–	–	–	3
Archer, G.F.	100	179	14	168	5354	32.44	10	27	1	127
Arnold, R.P.	80	123	15	217*	5465	50.60	16	22	0+1	70
Ashley, N.W.	6	11	1	96	316	31.60	–	2	–	5
Asim Butt	25	33	9	44	371	15.45	–	–	–	12
Astle, N.J.	85	138	12	191	4560	36.19	12	19	–	75
Atherton, M.A.	288	501	44	268*	18927	41.41	48	91	6	222
Athey, C.W.J.	467	784	71	184	25453	35.69	55	126	13	429/2
Austin, I.D.	123	171	37	115*	3778	28.19	2	20	–	35
Averis, J.M.M.	14	22	7	42	322	21.46	–	–	–	2
Ayaz Gul	3	6	1	19	78	15.60	–	–	–	3
Aymes, A.N.	181	266	67	133	6316	31.73	7	31	–	425/35
Bailey, R.J.	347	584	84	224*	20601	41.20	44	104	13	260
Bailey, T.M.B.	9	8	1	31*	81	11.57	–	–	–	11/1
Ball, M.C.J.	133	207	37	71	3156	18.56	–	8	–	155
Bandara, C.M.	19	25	10	24	113	7.53	–	–	–	6
Banes, M.J.	2	4	–	53	60	15.00	–	1	–	1
Barnes, J.P.B.	11	15	3	45	248	20.66	–	–	–	14
Barnett, K.J.	446	728	69	239*	26283	39.88	55	142	15	265
Base, S.J.	134	172	36	58	1551	11.40	–	2	–	60
Bates, J.J.	17	26	2	57	357	14.87	–	1	–	12
Bates, R.T.	33	48	12	34	450	12.50	–	–	–	18
Batson, N.E.	8	16	1	72	231	15.40	–	1	–	5
Batt, C.J.	10	14	2	43	150	12.50	–	–	–	2
Batty, G.J.	2	4	1	25*	54	18.00	–	–	–	–
Batty, J.N.	46	58	12	64	1126	24.47	–	5	–	106/16
Bell, I.R.	1	1	–	0	0	0.00	–	–	–	2
Bell, M.D.	52	87	6	219	2991	36.92	3	22	–	44
Benjamin, J.E.	126	145	43	49	1161	11.38	–	–	–	25
Betts, M.M.	57	87	19	57*	765	11.25	–	1	–	14
Bevan, M.G.	161	269	48	203*	12059	54.56	40	59	2	94
Bicknell, D.J.	211	369	35	235*	13200	39.52	32	60	6	78

	M	I	NO	HS	Runs	Avge	100	50	1000	Ct/St
Bicknell, M.P.	213	253	63	88	3844	20.23	–	14	–	73
Birks, M.J.	16	15	4	23*	113	10.27	–	–	–	16/3
Bishop, I.E.	5	7	4	7*	11	3.66	–	–	–	4
Bishop, J.E.	2	1	–	17	17	17.00	–	–	–	–
Blackwell, I.D.	25	39	2	62*	652	17.62	–	4	–	12
Blain, J.A.R.	3	1	–	0	0	0.00	–	–	–	2
Blakey, R.J.	292	467	71	221	12496	31.55	11	74	5	627/48
Blanchett, I.N.	5	6	1	18	36	7.20	–	–	–	2
Blewett, G.S.	131	229	15	268	9851	46.03	26	48	0+3	98
Bloomfield, T.F.	23	30	16	20*	121	8.64	–	–	–	3
Bodi, G.H.	6	8	3	33	110	22.00	–	–	–	2
Bond, A.N.	1	1	–	6	6	6.00	–	–	–	1
Boon, D.C.	350	585	53	227	23413	44.00	68	114	4+2	283
Boswell, S.A.J.	15	20	6	35	166	11.85	–	–	–	4
Boteju, H.	30	42	8	108	916	26.94	1	6	–	22
Bowen, M.N.	63	86	26	32	734	12.23	–	–	–	15
Bowler, P.D.	247	427	43	241*	15158	39.47	35	78	8	166/1
Bridge, G.D.	1	2	–	6	11	5.50	–	–	–	1
Brimson, M.T.	66	66	27	54*	459	11.76	–	1	–	11
Brinkley, J.E.	18	21	4	34	146	8.58	–	–	–	5
Brown, A.D.	125	198	19	265	7791	43.52	22	31	5	143/1
Brown, D.R.	98	152	16	142	3523	25.90	1	20	–	57
Brown, J.F.	16	21	10	16*	51	4.63	–	–	–	4
Brown, M.J.	2	3	2	24*	48	48.00	–	–	–	2
Brown, S.J.E.	140	195	58	69	1650	12.04	–	2	–	39
Bryant, J.D.C.	15	28	6	104*	862	39.18	1	6	–	9
Bulbeck, M.P.L.	23	26	14	76*	406	33.83	–	1	–	3
Bull, J.J.	11	17	1	49	246	15.37	–	–	–	1
Burns, M.	63	99	4	109	2515	26.47	2	16	–	76/7
Burns, N.D.	156	234	52	166	5349	29.39	5	26	–	316/32
Butcher, G.P.	45	66	10	101*	1556	27.78	1	10	–	18
Butcher, M.A.	126	222	16	259	7753	37.63	14	48	5	127
Byas, D.	235	399	35	213	12949	35.57	24	75	5	291
Byrne, B.W.	25	43	6	94	984	26.59	–	3	–	7
Caddick, A.R.	145	190	36	92	2485	16.13	–	5	–	51
Cairns, C.L.	169	264	30	126	8064	34.49	9	55	1	68
Carpenter, J.R.	12	22	–	65	375	17.04	–	2	–	5
Carson, N.D.	2	4	–	24	30	7.50	–	–	–	–
Cassar, M.E.	41	67	9	121	1462	25.20	1	8	–	13
Catterall, D.N.	3	4	–	60	132	33.00	–	2	–	–
Cawdron, M.J.	6	9	2	42	126	18.00	–	–	–	1
Chapman, S.	3	6	1	32	80	16.00	–	–	–	3
Chapple, G.	101	138	43	109*	2070	21.78	1	6	–	33
Cherry, D.D.	1	1	–	11	11	11.00	–	–	–	–
Chilton, M.J.	22	37	3	106*	994	29.23	2	4	–	21
Claughton, J.A.	12	21	5	85	458	28.62	–	3	–	4
Clough, G.D.	1	2	–	33	34	17.00	–	–	–	1
Collingwood, P.D.	55	94	7	107	2305	26.49	3	12	–	58
Collins, B.J.	10	16	2	46	220	15.71	–	–	–	9
Conway, S.L.J.	1	1	1	0*	0	–	–	–	–	–
Cook, S.J.	10	16	3	51	237	18.23	–	1	–	3
Cooke, G.	5	6	2	17	39	9.75	–	–	–	2
Cork, D.G.	173	260	37	104	5421	24.30	3	32	–	117
Cosker, D.A.	60	66	19	49	489	10.40	–	–	–	36
Cotterell, T.P.	1	1	–	0	0	0.00	–	–	–	–
Cottey, P.A.	220	358	50	203	11399	37.00	22	63	7	153

	M	I	NO	HS	Runs	Avge	100	50	1000	Ct/St
Cousins, D.M.	15	25	5	18*	159	7.95	–	–	–	5
Cowan, A.P.	61	90	17	94	1268	17.36	–	4	–	30
Cox, D.J.	1	1	–	0	0	0.00	–	–	–	–
Cox, J.	131	235	15	216	9526	43.30	28	42	1+1	55
Crawley, J.P.	200	327	31	286	14308	48.33	32	83	7	149
Creed, M.W.	10	15	4	72	269	24.45	–	2	–	5
Creese, M.L.	1	1	–	4	4	4.00	–	–	–	–
Croft, R.D.B.	220	322	63	143	6422	24.79	2	27	–	112
Crowe, C.D.	11	15	3	44*	233	19.41	–	–	–	6
Croy, M.G.	41	64	6	104	1040	17.93	1	2	–	113/8
Cunliffe, R.J.	48	81	5	190*	2051	26.98	3	9	–	37
Curran, K.M.	324	510	83	159	15740	36.86	25	83	7	209
Dagnall, C.E.	1	1	–	0	0	0.00	–	–	–	–
Dakin, J.M.	33	48	5	190	1288	29.95	4	6	–	13
Dale, A.	181	299	24	214*	8966	32.60	17	44	3	68
Daley, J.A.	72	125	11	159*	3467	30.41	3	17	–	38
Danson, A.R.	6	10	4	31	153	25.50	–	–	–	2
Davies, A.P.	9	9	2	34	79	11.28	–	–	–	1
Davies, M.K.	21	30	9	32*	182	8.66	–	–	–	5
Davis, M.J.G.	63	103	16	71	1432	16.45	–	4	–	41
Davy, J.O.	2	3	1	51*	55	27.50	–	1	–	–
Davy, P.J.	2	4	–	21	29	7.25	–	–	–	2
Dawes, J.H.	13	19	8	23*	126	11.45	–	–	–	3
Dawood, I.	17	28	3	102	469	18.76	1	1	–	43/3
Dawson, R.I.	64	115	9	127*	2598	24.50	3	12	1	31
Dean, K.J.	36	43	20	27*	281	12.21	–	–	–	5
Deane, M.J.	2	3	–	10	11	3.66	–	–	–	1
DeFreitas, P.A.J.	300	426	39	113	8500	21.96	7	42	–	109
De la Pena, J.M.	11	11	6	7*	10	2.00	–	–	–	1
De Saram, S.I.	74	110	6	237	4124	39.65	8	24	0+1	92/7
Di Venuto, M.J.	83	145	6	189	5689	40.92	12	34	1	68
Dilshan, T.M.	46	83	4	194	2800	35.44	6	12	0+1	100/14
Donald, A.A.	271	315	120	55*	2386	12.23	–	1	–	102
Doull, S.B.	84	106	24	108	1405	17.13	1	1	–	28
Dowman, M.P.	62	109	7	149	2950	28.92	6	12	1	35
Drakes, V.C.	98	161	19	180*	3138	22.09	4	12	–	30
Dravid, R.	107	170	26	215	8367	58.10	23	47	0+2	111/1
Driver, R.C.	4	7	–	42	108	15.42	–	–	–	1
Dunlop, A.R.	7	13	1	112	443	36.91	1	4	–	3
Dutch, K.P.	22	28	2	79	337	12.96	–	1	–	13
Dyer, N.R.	5	5	2	6	12	4.00	–	–	–	2
Eadie, D.J.	10	14	4	68*	192	19.20	–	2	–	3
Eagleson, R.L.	2	3	2	50*	91	91.00	–	1	–	3
Ealham, M.A.	137	225	37	139	6017	32.00	5	40	1	53
Edmond, M.D.	8	10	3	32	138	19.71	–	–	–	2
Edwards, A.D.	15	23	2	22	156	7.42	–	–	–	11
Elliott, M.T.G.	91	168	12	203	7608	48.76	25	32	1+3	103
Evans, A.W.	32	54	7	125	1335	28.40	1	5	–	23
Evans, K.P.	161	220	44	104	4198	23.85	3	21	–	111
Fairbrother, N.H.	327	519	70	366	18444	41.07	40	100	10	248
Fellows, G.M.	6	11	1	50	161	16.10	–	1	–	1
Fisher, I.D.	17	21	6	51	336	22.40	–	1	–	–
Flanagan, I.N.	14	24	1	61	491	21.34	–	3	–	12
Fleming, M.V.	183	299	35	138	8131	30.79	10	41	–	73
Fleming, S.P.	98	162	15	174*	5936	40.38	11	35	–	133
Flintoff, A.	45	70	6	160	2228	34.81	5	12	–	64

	M	*I*	*NO*	*HS*	*Runs*	*Avge*	*100*	*50*	*1000*	*Ct/St*
Flower, A.	84	138	28	201	5547	50.42	17	28	–	161/15
Follett, D.	18	22	8	19	87	6.21	–	–	–	5
Foster, M.J.	30	50	2	129	1128	23.50	1	6	–	10
Francis, S.R.G.	7	9	3	11	27	4.50	–	–	–	–
Franks, P.J.	44	67	11	66*	1026	18.32	–	4	–	15
Fraser, A.R.C.	260	308	76	92	2522	10.87	–	2	–	46
Frost, T.	29	43	5	111*	895	23.55	1	3	–	72/3
Fulton, D.P.	93	166	11	207	4781	30.84	6	26	–	129
Fulton, J.A.G.	21	36	1	78	679	19.40	–	5	–	11
Gallage, I.S.	52	66	14	54*	772	14.84	–	2	–	12
Gallian, J.E.R.	124	218	19	312	7305	36.70	15	36	2	89
Ganguly, S.C.	97	153	24	200*	6504	50.41	14	39	–	65
Gannon, B.W.	11	12	4	18	70	8.75	–	–	–	4
Garaway, M.	4	5	–	55	124	24.80	–	1	–	13/2
Giddins, E.S.H.	113	139	58	34	440	5.43	–	–	–	18
Gie, N.A.	16	26	2	59*	455	18.95	–	3	–	7
Giles, A.F.	80	110	25	123*	2446	28.77	2	12	–	32
Gillespie, P.G.	3	6	–	53	122	20.33	–	1	–	2
Gofton, A.F.	5	8	1	37*	115	16.42	–	–	–	–
Golding, J.M.	1	2	1	3	3	3.00	–	–	–	–
Goodchild, D.J.	9	18	1	105	354	20.82	1	2	–	1
Goodyer, T.E.	1	2	–	32	32	16.00	–	–	–	–
Gough, D.	157	214	35	121	2871	16.03	1	11	–	37
Gough, M.A.	22	38	–	123	932	24.52	1	6	–	29
Grayson, A.P.	125	201	18	159*	5511	30.11	7	31	3	92
Green, R.J.	28	29	11	51	295	16.38	–	1	–	5
Greenfield, K.	78	135	15	154*	3550	29.58	9	13	–	65
Greenidge, C.G.	2	3	–	14	20	6.66	–	–	–	3
Griffith, F.A.	43	63	9	81	1087	20.12	–	4	–	28
Griffiths, S.P.	12	19	1	35	199	11.05	–	–	–	38/1
Grove, J.O.	8	12	2	33	105	10.50	–	–	–	–
Gunawardena, D.A.	32	47	4	120*	1327	30.86	2	8	–	18
Gupte, C.M.	54	82	10	132	2382	33.08	5	9	–	16
Habib, A.	66	96	17	215	3445	43.60	9	12	1	28
Hafeez, A.	14	26	1	55	346	13.84	–	1	–	8
Halsall, R.G.	8	11	2	76	171	19.00	–	1	–	5
Hamilton, G.M.	51	71	16	94*	1621	29.47	–	11	–	16
Hancock, T.H.C.	129	229	15	220*	6100	28.50	6	38	1	81
Hansen, T.M.	4	6	1	24	64	12.80	–	–	–	–
Harden, R.J.	251	414	63	187	13335	37.99	28	70	7	189
Hardinges, M.A.	1	1	–	1	1	1.00	–	–	–	–
Harmison, S.J.	35	52	15	36	339	9.16	–	–	–	7
Harris, A.J.	46	65	18	36	392	8.34	–	–	–	16
Harris, C.Z.	79	125	28	251*	4222	43.52	8	20	–	56
Harrison, D.S.	2	2	–	16	29	14.50	–	–	–	–
Hartley, P.J.	223	272	61	127*	4218	19.99	2	14	–	68
Harvey, I.J.	55	96	4	136	2421	26.31	3	13	–	36
Harvey, M.E.	7	11	1	39	155	15.50	–	–	–	3
Hay, M.J.	2	3	–	7	10	3.33	–	–	–	–
Hayden, M.L.	142	249	26	235*	11886	53.30	38	51	2+3	117
Haynes, G.R.	100	155	16	158	4173	30.02	3	24	1	39
Haynes, J.J.	5	7	1	80	181	30.16	–	1	–	20/2
Haywood, G.R.	1	2	–	14	15	7.50	–	–	–	–
Headley, D.W.	139	187	44	91	2373	16.59	–	6	–	60
Hegg, W.K.	258	378	72	134	8103	26.48	4	40	–	624/70
Hellings, C.J.	1	2	–	13	26	13.00	–	–	–	–

	M	I	NO	HS	Runs	Avge	100	50	1000	Ct/St
Hemp, D.L.	127	219	17	157	6644	32.89	12	37	3	86
Henderson, T.	12	17	3	45	241	17.21	–	–	–	7
Herath, R.	29	45	17	44	348	12.42	–	–	–	10
Hewage, P.R.	26	40	3	168	1280	34.59	2	3	–	9
Hewitt, J.P.	56	76	11	75	1194	18.36	–	3	–	22
Hewson, D.R.	26	48	4	87	908	20.63	–	6	–	12
Hick, G.A.	382	628	60	405*	31252	55.02	108	118	15+1	474
Hicks, T.C.	7	10	1	54	178	19.77	–	1	–	4
Hockley, J.B.	2	3	–	34	64	21.33	–	–	–	–
Hodgson, T.P.	11	20	–	54	361	18.05	–	1	–	4
Hoggard, M.J.	23	30	9	21	126	6.00	–	–	–	6
Hollioake, A.J.	110	169	16	182	6091	39.81	13	35	2	88
Hollioake, B.C.	53	81	5	163	2066	27.18	2	10	–	42
Holloway, P.C.L.	94	159	26	168	4414	33.18	8	23	–	70/1
Horne, M.J.	53	94	3	241	4166	45.78	13	14	–	44
House, W.J.	27	41	7	136	1201	35.32	2	7	–	16
Hughes, Q.J.	22	32	5	101	849	31.44	1	4	–	7
Humphries, S.	29	43	4	66	514	13.17	–	2	–	52/2
Hussain, N.	251	405	39	207	15939	43.54	41	79	5	296
Hutchison, P.M.	34	34	20	30	175	12.50	–	–	–	6
Hutton, B.L.	9	16	–	59	341	21.31	–	2	–	5
Hyam, B.J.	38	61	9	51	974	18.73	–	1	–	98/4
Illingworth, R.K.	361	415	119	120*	6748	22.79	4	20	–	156
Ilott, M.C.	166	215	44	60	2480	14.50	–	4	–	40
Innes, K.J.	15	21	4	63	370	21.76	–	1	–	9
Irani, R.C.	125	206	23	153	6456	35.27	13	34	4	55
Jacobs, A.	10	15	5	112	460	46.00	1	2	–	14
James, K.D.	225	337	57	162	8526	30.45	10	42	2	78
James, S.P.	204	357	27	259*	13126	39.77	39	49	7	155
Jarvis, P.W.	213	267	67	80	3372	16.86	–	10	–	65
Jayantha, S.	65	112	4	212*	4220	39.07	8	23	0+1	53
Jayawardena, H.P.W.	17	24	4	89	441	22.05	–	2	–	40/10
Jennings, D.	2	2	2	13*	20	–	–	–	–	12
Johnson, N.C.	82	124	16	150	3554	32.90	6	21	–	92
Johnson, P.	332	556	53	187	18835	37.44	37	112	9	213/1
Johnson, R.L.	76	106	11	50*	1333	14.03	–	1	–	29
Jones, I.	3	4	1	35	78	26.00	–	–	–	–
Jones, P.S.	23	32	9	105	454	19.73	1	–	–	7
Jones, S.P.	13	16	6	19*	79	7.90	–	–	–	3
Joyce, E.C.	3	5	–	43	91	18.20	–	–	–	2
Kalavitigoda, S.	27	46	1	135*	1229	27.31	1	8	–	23
Kallis, J.H.	97	151	18	186*	6108	45.92	16	35	1	71
Kasprowicz, M.S.	131	171	33	73	2292	16.60	–	6	–	49
Katich, S.M.	21	39	8	154*	1632	52.64	5	8	0+1	19
Keech, M.	69	111	12	127	2824	28.52	3	15	–	56
Keedy, G.	52	59	38	26	219	10.42	–	–	–	13
Kendall, W.S.	71	111	16	201	3694	38.88	6	19	2	65
Kennis, G.J.	12	23	1	175	436	19.81	1	–	–	13
Kenway, D.A.	23	38	7	102	1195	38.54	1	8	1	15
Kerr, J.I.D.	46	66	10	80	1111	19.83	–	5	–	15
Kettleborough, R.A.	33	56	6	108	1258	25.16	1	7	–	20
Key, R.W.T.	35	61	2	125	1500	25.42	3	6	–	33
Khan, A.A.	24	29	5	52	337	14.04	–	1	–	9
Khan, S.H.	10	8	–	34	116	14.50	–	–	–	2
Khan, W.G.	54	95	8	181	2691	30.93	5	16	–	36
Killeen, N.	30	45	10	48	479	13.68	–	–	–	11

	M	I	NO	HS	Runs	Avge	100	50	1000	Ct/St
King, R.D.	23	34	10	30	132	5.50	–	–	–	4
Kino, D.	5	6	2	14*	31	7.75	–	–	–	–
Kirtley, R.J.	56	80	28	59	590	11.34	–	1	–	15
Knight, N.V.	142	239	25	192	8561	40.00	20	44	2	206
Krikken, K.M.	180	267	54	104	4885	22.93	1	21	–	448/28
Kumble, A.	130	166	35	154*	3547	27.07	6	14	–	69
Lacey, S.J.	15	19	6	50	311	23.92	–	1	–	7/1
Lampitt, S.R.	208	271	61	122	5113	24.34	1	19	–	132
Laney, J.S.	62	110	3	112	3499	32.70	5	21	1	45
Langer, J.L.	139	248	31	274*	11183	51.53	33	43	2+2	115
Laraman, A.W.	1	–	–	–	–	–	–	–	–	–
Lathwell, M.N.	134	237	9	206	7768	34.07	12	48	5	92
Law, D.R.	65	101	2	115	1972	19.91	1	9	–	36
Law, S.G.	181	305	32	263	13367	48.96	41	61	3+1	201
Law, W.L.	15	24	3	131	722	34.38	1	4	–	7
Lawrence, J.R.G.	2	4	1	7*	12	4.00	–	–	–	–
Lawson, A.G.	48	87	8	117*	2293	29.02	4	11	–	22
Leatherdale, D.A.	162	259	29	157	7471	32.48	10	39	1	129
Lehmann, D.S.	143	245	15	255	12210	53.08	37	59	1+4	83
Lewis, C.C.	184	268	34	247	7326	31.30	9	34	–	148
Lewis, J.	60	92	15	62	971	12.61	–	2	–	13
Lewis, J.J.B.	107	189	19	210*	5979	35.17	9	37	2	76
Lewis, S.J.W.	5	8	–	17	73	9.12	–	–	–	3
Lewry, J.D.	57	84	18	34	614	9.02	–	–	–	5
Liptrot, C.G.	11	16	6	61	142	14.20	–	1	–	–
Llong, N.J.	68	108	11	130	3024	31.17	6	16	–	59
Lloyd, G.D.	177	284	26	241	10203	39.54	23	57	5	113
Logan, R.J.	2	2	–	1	1	0.50	–	–	–	1
Louw, J.H.	7	13	1	82	183	15.25	–	2	–	5
Love, G.T.	23	23	5	85*	335	18.61	–	1	–	4
Loveridge, G.R.	23	34	3	126	776	25.03	1	2	–	10
Lowe, J.P.	8	6	3	7*	13	4.33	–	–	–	1
Loye, M.B.	114	182	17	322*	6074	36.81	14	27	2	63
Lucas, D.S.	6	7	3	24*	58	14.50	–	–	–	–
Lugsden, S.	15	21	8	16	70	5.38	–	–	–	2
McCague, M.J.	126	174	45	63*	2129	16.50	–	5	–	73
McCallan, W.K.	5	10	–	65	256	25.60	–	2	–	2
McCoubrey, A.G.A.M.	1	1	1	1*	1	–	–	–	–	–
McDaid, R.W.	2	1	1	6*	6	–	–	–	–	2
McDowell, R.W.	1	2	–	2	2	1.00	–	–	–	–
McGarry, A.C.	1	1	1	0*	0	–	–	–	–	–
McGerrigle, R.D.	1	1	–	0	0	0.00	–	–	–	–
McGrath, A.	82	142	9	142*	3879	29.16	6	18	–	49
McGrath, G.D.	84	89	31	39	328	5.65	–	–	–	20
McKeown, P.C.	16	23	1	75	610	27.72	–	3	–	13
McLean, N.A.M.	66	101	17	70	1402	16.69	–	2	–	18
McMillan, C.D.	57	96	8	159	3657	41.55	8	19	–	29
MacRae, N.J.	3	6	1	51	141	28.20	–	1	–	1
Maddy, D.L.	98	158	9	202	5046	33.86	12	21	2	96
Mahmood, S.	1	2	1	7*	7	7.00	–	–	–	1
Maiden, G.I.	2	2	1	23*	25	25.00	–	–	–	1
Malcolm, D.E.	261	309	97	51	1670	7.87	–	1	–	40
Marsh, S.A.	291	429	69	142	10098	28.05	9	55	–	688/61
Martin, P.J.	162	188	48	133	2690	19.21	1	5	–	39
Martin-Jenkins, R.S.C.	29	46	5	78	913	22.26	–	5	–	7
Mascarenhas, A.D.	39	55	5	89	1184	23.68	–	8	–	15

	M	I	NO	HS	Runs	Avge	100	50	1000	Ct/St
Mason, T.J.	7	6	1	36	86	17.20	–	–	–	4
Mather, D.P.	30	19	8	11*	56	5.09	–	–	–	6
Maunders, J.K.	1	2	–	9	13	6.50	–	–	–	1
Maynard, M.P.	322	527	55	243	20181	42.75	45	109	11	309/5
Middlebrook, J.D.	8	12	2	41	139	13.90	–	–	–	7
Millns, D.J.	162	190	58	121	2880	21.81	3	7	–	73
Mirza, M.M.	6	7	4	10*	17	5.66	–	–	–	1
Mohammed, I.	16	24	3	136	769	36.61	2	2	–	1
Molins, G.L.	4	3	1	2*	3	1.50	–	–	–	1
Montgomerie, R.R.	113	197	20	192	5905	33.36	11	33	2	103
Moody, T.M.	291	487	45	272	20677	46.78	64	92	5+1	289
Mooney, P.J.K.	4	8	3	20*	83	16.60	–	–	–	3
Morris, A.C.	34	45	9	60	712	19.77	–	3	–	18
Morris, J.E.	341	576	33	229	20298	37.38	49	97	11	146
Morris, Z.C.	2	4	–	10	11	2.75	–	–	–	–
Mullally, A.D.	172	192	50	75	1284	9.04	–	2	–	35
Munton, T.A.	227	237	90	54*	1491	10.14	–	2	–	73
Muralitharan, M.	101	122	40	39	912	11.12	–	–	–	59
Napier, G.R.	5	6	2	35*	81	20.25	–	–	–	2
Nash, D.C.	39	57	10	114	1453	30.91	2	6	–	64/5
Nash, D.J.	99	141	30	135*	2807	25.28	3	13	–	41
Nawaz, M.N.	58	86	5	152*	3295	40.67	6	20	–	45
Nel, A.	12	15	7	14*	53	6.62	–	–	–	4
Newell, K.	52	91	11	135	2278	28.47	4	9	–	15
Newell, M. (De)	24	40	2	135*	889	23.39	3	3	–	17
Newell, M. (Nt)	102	178	26	203*	4636	30.50	6	24	1	93/1
Newport, P.J.	290	342	93	98	6010	24.13	–	22	–	79
Nixon, P.A.	181	256	54	131	6269	31.03	11	23	1	469/40
Noon, W.M.	88	138	22	83	2467	21.26	–	12	–	186/20
O'Connor, S.B.	43	61	21	47	536	13.40	–	–	–	19
Ontong, J.L.	12	21	1	71	458	22.90	–	2	–	5
Oram, A.R.	19	28	13	13	53	3.53	–	–	–	6
Ormond, J.	38	38	5	50*	391	11.84	–	1	–	9
Ostler, D.P.	160	267	21	208	8082	32.85	10	52	4	191
Parker, B.	44	71	10	138*	1839	30.14	2	9	–	19
Parkin, O.T.	31	37	17	24*	173	8.65	–	–	–	9
Parore, A.C.	127	199	27	155*	5525	32.12	7	32	–	257/16
Parsons, K.A.	72	118	12	105	2705	25.51	2	18	–	60
Parsons, R.A.	1	2	–	8	8	4.00	–	–	–	2
Patel, M.M.	112	158	33	67	1824	14.59	–	5	–	56
Patterson, M.W.	2	3	–	4	6	2.00	–	–	–	–
Peirce, M.T.E.	55	98	1	123	2482	25.58	2	15	–	27
Penberthy, A.L.	133	197	23	128	4483	25.76	4	25	–	78
Penn, A.J.	28	37	7	90	548	18.26	–	4	–	5
Penney, T.L.	141	226	41	151	7383	39.90	14	34	2	80/2
Perera, A.S.A.	24	28	11	71*	424	24.94	–	1	–	5
Perera, B.	20	21	6	63	418	27.86	–	3	–	22
Perera, N.R.G.	29	42	4	112	1183	31.13	3	6	–	18
Peters, S.D.	31	48	6	110	1135	27.02	2	5	–	28
Phillips, B.J.	27	39	4	100*	584	16.68	1	2	–	8
Phillips, N.C.	42	60	12	53	782	16.29	–	3	–	22
Phillips, T.J.	3	4	–	16	27	6.75	–	–	–	1
Pierson, A.R.K.	173	213	66	108*	2515	17.10	1	5	–	83
Pimlott, C.R.	6	5	4	18*	41	41.00	–	–	–	–
Pipe, D.J.	2	2	–	16	21	10.50	–	–	–	2/1
Piper, K.J.	156	221	34	116*	3632	19.42	2	10	–	409/28

	M	*I*	*NO*	*HS*	*Runs*	*Avge*	*100*	*50*	*1000*	*Ct/St*
Pirihi, N.G.	8	13	1	23	115	9.58	–	–	–	3
Pollard, P.R.	168	296	22	180	8724	31.83	13	43	3	150
Powell, J.C.	3	2	1	6	10	10.00	–	–	–	2
Powell, M.J. (Gm)	37	61	10	200*	2186	42.86	4	10	1	16
Powell, M.J. (Wa)	27	45	1	136	1207	27.43	3	4	–	22
Pratt, A.	3	3	–	34	40	13.33	–	–	–	4
Pretorius, D.	12	11	2	43	131	14.55	–	–	–	2
Prichard, P.J.	306	498	46	245	15858	35.08	31	92	8	191
Pushpakumara, K.R.	65	69	21	27	412	8.58	–	–	–	20
Pyemont, J.P.	18	27	2	90*	525	21.00	–	4	–	11
Ramprakash, M.R.	270	445	58	235	17865	46.16	47	90	9	155
Randall, S.J.	3	5	1	20	30	7.50	–	–	–	3
Rao, R.K.	27	46	4	89	874	20.80	–	6	–	7
Rashid, U.B.A.	12	20	3	73	469	27.58	–	3	–	5
Ratcliffe, J.D.	133	238	13	135	6517	28.96	5	38	–	66
Rawnsley, M.J.	18	19	3	26	190	11.87	–	–	–	9
Read, C.M.W.	41	64	9	160	1269	23.07	1	3	–	116/6
Renshaw, S.J.	35	41	19	56	390	17.72	–	1	–	13
Rhodes, J.N.	130	205	24	156*	6935	38.31	14	37	–	99
Rhodes, S.J.	364	513	136	122*	12428	32.96	10	64	2	915/112
Richardson, A.	7	9	3	4	13	2.16	–	–	–	1
Ridgway, P.M.	5	7	3	35	48	12.00	–	–	–	–
Ripley, D.	279	367	95	209	7737	28.44	9	29	–	595/78
Roberts, D.J.	17	30	1	117	751	25.89	1	2	–	8
Roberts, G.M.	11	17	4	52	334	25.69	–	1	–	8
Roberts, T.W.	1	2	–	49	88	44.00	–	–	–	–
Robinson, D.D.J.	77	136	4	200	3567	27.02	7	15	–	71
Robinson, J.D.	32	51	10	79	975	23.78	–	5	–	12
Robinson, M.A.	205	231	96	27	529	3.91	–	–	–	37
Robinson, P.E.	159	261	35	189	7617	33.70	7	51	–	130
Robinson, R.T.	425	739	85	220*	27571	42.15	63	141	14	257
Rollins, A.S.	101	187	18	210	6021	35.62	11	33	3	81/1
Rollins, R.J.	69	111	10	133*	2258	22.35	1	11	–	158/21
Rose, G.D.	230	321	58	191	8118	30.86	9	40	1	112
Roseberry, M.A.	214	364	38	185	10981	33.68	20	54	4	153
Ross, J.S.	2	3	1	2*	2	1.00	–	–	–	–
Russell, R.C.	409	609	129	129*	14438	30.07	7	77	1	1027/116
Rutherford, A.T.	4	4	–	26	66	16.50	–	–	–	6/1
Sachdeva, A.	1	2	1	0*	0	0.00	–	–	–	–
Saggers, M.J.	12	18	5	18	128	9.84	–	–	–	3
Sajdeh, R.K.	1	2	–	12	12	6.00	–	–	–	–
Sales, D.J.G.	55	86	9	303*	2644	34.33	5	9	1	38
Salisbury, I.D.K.	210	271	54	100*	4002	18.44	1	14	–	144
Salmond, G.	11	19	2	181	852	50.11	2	3	–	8
Saqlain Mushtaq	79	113	34	79	1168	14.78	–	4	–	34
Savident, L.	3	4	1	6	15	5.00	–	–	–	1
Sayers, C.A.	4	4	3	4*	9	9.00	–	–	–	1
Schofield, C.P.	12	17	6	39*	210	19.09	–	–	–	9
Scott, D.A.	5	7	6	17*	38	38.00	–	–	–	1
Scuderi, J.C.	61	100	14	125*	2667	31.01	3	13	–	24
Shadford, D.J.	11	13	5	30	120	15.00	–	–	–	5
Shah, O.A.	51	85	8	140	2462	31.97	6	11	–	35
Shahid, N.	112	179	25	139	4914	31.90	7	26	1	104
Shaw, A.D.	59	78	10	140	1268	18.64	1	5	–	140/10
Sheikh, M.A.	4	6	1	30	99	19.80	–	–	–	–
Sheikh, S.M.	4	2	1	7*	9	9.00	–	–	–	1

	M	I	NO	HS	Runs	Avge	100	50	1000	Ct/St
Sheriyar, A.	77	79	28	21	414	8.11	–	–	–	15
Shields, I.P.	1	2	–	16	16	8.00	–	–	–	2
Shoaib Akhtar	62	77	31	23	377	8.19	–	–	–	22
Sidebottom, R.J.	18	25	8	54	232	13.64	–	1	–	9
Silva, L.P.C.	15	26	3	127*	680	29.56	1	4	–	10
Silverwood, C.E.W.	83	112	24	58	1327	15.07	–	4	–	19
Singh, A.	38	60	3	157	1673	29.35	4	6	–	14
Slater, M.J.	154	273	12	221	11400	43.67	29	54	1+1	84
Small, G.C.	315	404	97	70	4409	14.36	–	7	–	95
Smalley, R.G.	1	–	–	–	–	–	–	–	–	–
Smethurst, M.P.	5	4	–	3	5	1.25	–	–	–	1
Smith, A.M.	124	166	42	61	1536	12.38	–	4	–	24
Smith, B.F.	142	212	29	204	6698	36.60	13	29	2	64
Smith, C.J.O.	2	3	–	57	69	23.00	–	1	–	7/1
Smith, E.T.	50	85	6	190	3092	39.13	5	17	1	11
Smith, N.M.K.	160	232	30	161	5590	27.67	4	27	1	54
Smith, R.A.	368	622	83	209*	23608	43.79	56	119	11	211
Smith, T.M.	16	19	7	29	146	12.16	–	–	–	3
Smyth, S.G.	5	9	1	70	188	23.50	–	1	–	1
Snape, J.N.	56	85	17	98*	1657	24.36	–	10	–	42
Solanki, V.S.	77	130	9	171	4024	33.25	6	20	1	85
Speak, N.J.	160	279	28	232	9045	36.03	15	52	3	105
Speight, M.P.	174	290	27	184	8567	32.57	13	46	3	260/5
Spendlove, B.L.	19	35	2	63	656	19.87	–	2	–	8
Spiring, K.R.	42	74	9	150	2141	32.93	4	13	1	22
Stanger, I.M.	4	6	1	52*	104	20.80	–	1	–	3
Stelling, W.F.	17	28	2	53	475	18.26	–	1	–	8
Stemp, R.D.	149	178	58	65	1499	12.49	–	2	–	60
Stephenson, J.P.	268	453	44	202*	13623	33.30	24	71	5	166
Stevens, D.I.	14	24	–	130	600	25.00	1	3	–	13
Stewart, A.J.	376	626	68	271*	22507	40.33	44	126	8	536/19
Still, Q.R.	30	51	8	129*	1383	32.16	2	9	–	21
Strang, P.A.	84	126	25	106*	2793	27.65	2	14	–	78
Strauss, A.J.	12	23	1	98	634	28.81	–	5	–	6
Strong, M.R.	2	3	2	35*	53	53.00	–	–	–	1
Stubbings, S.D.	6	12	–	45	240	20.00	–	–	–	3
Stubbs, E.G.C.	1	2	2	14*	21	–	–	–	–	3
Such, P.M.	279	294	112	54	1475	8.10	–	2	–	109
Sutcliffe, I.J.	76	115	11	167	3324	31.96	5	17	–	38
Sutcliffe, R.V.	2	2	1	9*	9	9.00	–	–	–	–
Sutton, L.D.	3	6	3	16*	41	13.66	–	–	–	10
Swann, A.J.	28	43	1	154	1085	25.83	3	4	–	18
Swann, G.P.	37	54	7	130*	1451	30.87	2	6	–	28
Symington, M.J.	2	1	1	8*	8	–	–	–	–	1
Symonds, A.	97	165	14	254*	6047	40.04	18	25	2	56
Taylor, B.V.	1	2	–	14	14	7.00	–	–	–	1
Taylor, J.P.	164	186	61	86	1884	15.07	–	8	–	55
Tennant, A.M.	2	2	–	0	0	0.00	–	–	–	1
Thomas, P.A.	22	26	5	25	120	5.71	–	–	–	1
Thomas, S.D.	93	127	27	78*	1838	18.38	–	8	–	36
Thompson, D.J.	9	12	–	22	94	7.83	–	–	–	1
Thompson, J.B.D.	36	48	19	65*	546	18.82	–	2	–	5
Thorpe, G.P.	250	419	61	223*	16111	45.00	35	91	8	208
Titchard, S.P.	93	162	12	163	4697	31.31	5	27	–	54
Tolley, C.M.	100	139	30	84	2443	22.41	–	11	–	40
Trescothick, M.E.	87	146	4	190	4210	29.64	6	24	–	95

	M	I	NO	HS	Runs	Avge	100	50	1000	Ct/St
Tsolekile, T.L.	2	2	1	41*	43	43.00	–	–	–	5
Tudor, A.J.	38	51	14	99*	689	18.62	–	2	–	8
Tufnell, P.C.R.	264	287	108	67*	1809	10.10	–	1	–	99
Turner, R.J.	152	235	46	144	6206	32.83	8	33	2	382/38
Tweats, T.A.	33	62	5	189	1405	24.64	2	4	–	29
Twose, R.G.	173	292	33	277*	9485	36.62	17	51	3	93
Udal, S.D.	155	219	41	117*	4017	22.56	1	17	–	70
Van den Berg, A.M.	4	6	–	94	126	21.00	–	1	–	2
Vaughan, M.P.	121	219	10	183	7071	33.83	16	32	4	46
Vettori, D.L.	48	72	12	112	1294	21.56	1	7	–	22
Villavarayen, M.S.	60	67	17	61	827	16.54	–	2	–	25
Wagh, M.A.	57	90	8	216*	2702	32.95	7	9	1	27
Walker, B.G.K.	16	21	4	52	354	20.82	–	1	–	7
Walker, K.D.M.	7	8	–	132	286	35.75	1	1	–	2
Walker, M.J.	55	92	8	275*	2309	27.48	3	10	–	35
Wallace, M.A.	3	4	1	64*	98	32.66	–	1	–	12
Walton, T.C.	25	37	3	71	808	23.76	–	8	–	11
Ward, I.J.	33	56	5	103	1668	32.70	1	15	1	23
Ward, T.R.	206	355	19	235*	11897	35.40	24	70	6	197
Warden, M.J.	1	1	–	2	2	2.00	–	–	–	1
Warne, S.K.	134	177	25	74*	2429	15.98	–	4	–	91
Warren, R.J.	79	129	16	201*	3678	32.54	4	21	–	94/3
Watkin, S.L.	238	267	96	41	1724	10.08	–	–	–	65
Watkinson, M.	308	459	49	161	10939	26.68	11	50	1	156
Watts, D.F.	2	4	–	28	48	12.00	–	–	–	–
Weekes, P.N.	135	211	24	171*	6156	32.91	10	29	1	123
Welch, G.	71	101	17	84*	1779	21.17	–	7	–	29
Wells, A.P.	364	609	79	253*	20802	39.24	46	99	11	224
Wells, C.M.	318	510	78	203	14289	33.07	24	67	6	111
Wells, V.J.	145	227	18	224	7159	34.25	14	35	2	98
Welton, G.E.	20	37	1	95	762	21.16	–	3	–	8
Weston, R.M.S.	35	62	2	156	1556	25.93	3	6	–	25
Weston, W.P.C.	134	234	23	205	7416	35.14	15	35	3	70
Wharf, A.G.	28	41	5	78	564	15.66	–	3	–	16
Whiley, M.J.A.	2	2	1	0*	0	0.00	–	–	–	–
Whitaker, J.J.	315	497	51	218	17198	38.56	38	80	10	172
White, C.	162	250	35	181	6578	30.59	8	33	–	115
White, G.W.	85	145	11	156	4425	33.02	7	24	1	70
Wickramasinghe, P.P.	35	45	15	121*	849	28.30	1	1	–	31
Wilkinson, R.	1	1	–	9	9	9.00	–	–	–	–
Williams, K.C.	27	44	10	91	834	24.52	–	4	–	12
Williams, R.C.J.	37	47	8	90	712	18.25	–	5	–	97/15
Williamson, D.	6	8	1	41*	157	22.42	–	–	–	5
Williamson, J.G.	5	6	–	55	139	23.16	–	1	–	1
Willis, S.C.	16	21	6	82	506	33.73	–	5	–	37/3
Wilson, E.J.	14	27	2	116	637	25.48	1	3	–	9
Wilton, N.J.	8	14	2	55	202	16.83	–	1	–	18/2
Windows, M.G.N.	77	140	9	184	4414	33.69	8	23	1	56
Wingfield, W.R.	15	26	2	73	524	21.83	–	2	–	7
Wood, J.	78	117	20	63*	1154	11.89	–	2	–	21
Wood, M.J.	37	64	6	200*	1653	28.50	4	6	1	28
Wood, N.T.	29	44	5	155	1152	29.53	1	5	–	5
Woolley, A.P.	1	2	–	8	9	4.50	–	–	–	–
Wright, C.M.	3	4	1	20	31	10.33	–	–	–	2
Yates, G.	75	99	35	134*	1695	26.48	3	4	–	32

BOWLING

'50wS' denotes instances of taking 50 or more wickets in a season. Where these have been achieved outside the UK, they are shown after a plus sign.

	Runs	*Wkts*	*Avge*	*Best*	*5wI*	*10wM*	*50wS*
Adams, C.J.	1530	28	54.64	4- 29	–	–	–
Afzaal, U.	2027	35	57.91	4-101	–	–	–
Aldred, P.	2985	97	30.77	7-101	5	1	1
Ali, Kabir	58	3	19.33	2- 36	–	–	–
Alleyne, M.W.	9825	303	32.42	6- 64	6	–	1
Allingham, M.J.D.	163	4	40.75	3- 53	–	–	–
Allott, G.I.	3097	102	30.36	6- 60	4	1	–
Altree, D.A.	420	8	52.50	3- 41	–	–	–
Amin, R.M.	714	20	35.70	4- 87	–	–	–
Amla, A.M.	32	1	32.00	1- 16	–	–	–
Anderson, R.S.G.	1273	50	25.46	5- 36	2	–	1
Archer, B.J.	28	2	14.00	1- 5	–	–	–
Archer, G.F.	648	14	46.28	3- 18	–	–	–
Arnold, R.P.	3366	131	25.69	7- 84	4	–	–
Asim Butt	1214	45	26.97	5- 53	1	–	–
Astle, N.J.	2791	86	32.45	6- 22	2	–	–
Atherton, M.A.	4733	108	43.82	6- 78	3	–	–
Athey, C.W.J.	2673	48	55.68	3- 3	–	–	–
Austin, I.D.	7922	260	30.46	6- 43	6	1	–
Averis, J.M.M.	1492	26	57.38	5- 98	1	–	–
Aymes, A.N.	318	3	106.00	2-135	–	–	–
Bailey, R.J.	4790	112	42.76	5- 54	2	–	–
Ball, M.C.J.	9233	242	38.15	8- 46	8	1	–
Bandara, C.M.	1093	37	29.54	7- 44	1	1	–
Barnett, K.J.	6999	186	37.62	6- 28	3	–	–
Base, S.J.	11397	388	29.37	7- 60	16	1	1
Bates, J.J.	1154	44	26.22	5- 67	4	–	–
Bates, R.T.	2520	50	50.40	5- 88	1	–	–
Batt, C.J.	946	33	28.66	6-101	2	–	–
Batty, G.J.	128	4	32.00	2- 45	–	–	–
Batty, J.N.	40	0					
Benjamin, J.E.	11588	387	29.94	6- 19	17	1	3
Betts, M.M.	5416	181	29.92	9- 64	9	1	–
Bevan, M.G.	4371	102	42.85	6- 82	1	1	–
Bicknell, D.J.	789	23	34.30	3- 7	–	–	–
Bicknell, M.P.	19091	766	24.92	9- 45	29	2	8
Bishop, I.E.	278	5	55.60	2- 45	–	–	–
Bishop, J.E.	180	3	60.00	2- 89	–	–	–
Blackwell, I.D.	1346	28	48.07	5-115	1	–	–
Blain, J.A.R.	208	2	104.00	1- 18	–	–	–
Blakey, R.J.	68	1	68.00	1- 68	–	–	–
Blanchett, I.N.	423	7	60.42	2- 38	–	–	–
Blewett, G.S.	3615	90	40.16	5- 29	1	–	–
Bloomfield, T.F.	1925	68	28.30	5- 36	4	–	–
Bodi, G.H.	435	11	39.54	6- 82	1	–	–
Bond, A.N.	74	2	37.00	2- 41	–	–	–
Boon, D.C.	696	14	49.71	2- 18	–	–	–
Boswell, S.A.J.	1226	27	45.40	5- 94	1	–	–
Boteju, H.	1603	74	21.66	4- 22	–	–	–
Bowen, M.N.	5717	179	31.93	7- 73	7	1	–
Bowler, P.D.	2009	33	60.87	3- 25	–	–	–

	Runs	Wkts	Avge	Best	5wI	10wM	50wS
Bridge, G.D.	110	1	110.00	1- 60	–	–	–
Brimson, M.T.	4069	124	32.81	5- 12	3	–	–
Brinkley, J.E.	1382	47	29.40	6- 35	2	–	–
Brown, A.D.	258	0					
Brown, D.R.	7135	283	25.21	8- 89	11	3	2
Brown, J.F.	1505	55	27.36	6- 53	4	1	–
Brown, S.J.E.	14194	478	29.69	7- 70	31	2	6
Bryant, J.D.C.	27	1	27.00	1- 22	–	–	–
Bulbeck, M.P.L.	2065	83	24.87	5- 45	3	1	1
Burns, M.	704	12	58.66	2- 18	–	–	–
Burns, N.D.	8	0					
Butcher, G.P.	2187	56	39.05	7- 77	1	–	–
Butcher, M.A.	3302	96	34.39	4- 30	–	–	–
Byas, D.	719	12	59.91	3- 55	–	–	–
Byrne, B.W.	1352	19	71.15	3- 66	–	–	–
Caddick, A.R.	15859	634	25.01	9- 32	42	11	7
Cairns, C.L.	14471	516	28.04	8- 47	23	5	3
Carpenter, J.R.	81	1	81.00	1- 50	–	–	–
Carson, N.D.	74	4	18.50	3- 39	–	–	–
Cassar, M.E.	1585	45	35.22	5- 51	1	–	–
Catterall, D.N.	216	5	43.20	2- 16	–	–	–
Cawdron, M.J.	266	16	16.62	5- 35	3	–	–
Chapman, S.	139	1	139.00	1- 49	–	–	–
Chapple, G.	8376	282	29.70	6- 48	10	–	2
Chilton, M.J.	133	2	66.50	1- 1	–	–	–
Clough, G.D.	11	0					
Collingwood, P.D.	1204	30	40.13	3- 7	–	–	–
Conway, S.L.J.	56	0					
Cook, S.J.	954	27	35.33	4- 83	–	–	–
Cooke, G.	336	8	42.00	2- 49	–	–	–
Cork, D.G.	14790	552	26.79	9- 43	19	2	5
Cosker, D.A.	4857	141	34.44	6-140	2	–	–
Cotterell, T.P.	81	3	27.00	3- 69	–	–	–
Cottey, P.A.	862	16	53.87	4- 49	–	–	–
Cousins, D.M.	1138	27	42.14	6- 35	1	–	–
Cowan, A.P.	5237	159	32.93	6- 47	5	–	1
Cox, D.J.	78	1	78.00	1- 33	–	–	–
Cox, J.	277	4	69.25	3- 46	–	–	–
Crawley, J.P.	180	1	180.00	1- 90	–	–	–
Creed, M.W.	532	12	44.33	4- 30	–	–	–
Creese, M.L.	98	1	98.00	1- 37	–	–	–
Croft, R.D.B.	21570	595	36.25	8- 66	26	4	5
Crowe, C.D.	553	17	32.52	3- 49	–	–	–
Curran, K.M.	16730	605	27.65	7- 47	15	4	5
Dagnall, C.E.	88	6	14.66	4- 20	–	–	–
Dakin, J.M.	1682	44	38.22	4- 27	–	–	–
Dale, A.	6559	178	36.84	6- 18	2	–	–
Daley, J.A.	61	1	61.00	1- 12	–	–	–
Danson, A.R.	166	3	55.33	1- 5	–	–	–
Davies, A.P.	603	16	37.68	2- 22	–	–	–
Davies, M.K.	1723	70	24.61	6- 49	5	–	–
Davis, M.J.G.	4270	128	33.35	8- 37	3	1	–
Davy, J.O.	164	5	32.80	3- 33	–	–	–
Dawes, J.H.	1093	51	21.43	5- 45	1	–	–
Dawson, R.I.	199	8	24.87	3- 15	–	–	–
Dean, K.J.	3052	130	23.47	6- 63	5	1	1

	Runs	Wkts	Avge	Best	5wI	10wM	50wS
Deane, M.J.	112	2	56.00	2- 42	–	–	–
DeFreitas, P.A.J.	28263	1027	27.51	7- 21	54	5	12
De la Pena, J.M.	896	29	30.89	6- 18	1	1	–
De Saram, S.I.	23	0					
Di Venuto, M.J.	201	1	201.00	1- 3	–	–	–
Dilshan, T.M.	12	0					
Donald, A.A.	23970	1073	22.33	8- 37	61	8	5
Doull, S.B.	6376	230	27.72	7- 65	12	1	–
Dowman, M.P.	963	21	45.85	3- 10	–	–	–
Drakes, V.C.	9357	365	25.63	8- 59	18	3	2+1
Dravid, R.	112	0					
Dunlop, A.R.	143	2	71.50	1- 8	–	–	–
Dutch, K.P.	825	21	39.28	3- 25	–	–	–
Dyer, N.R.	392	14	28.00	4- 47	–	–	–
Eadie, D.J.	602	16	37.62	3- 57	–	–	–
Eagleson, R.L.	183	4	45.75	2- 50	–	–	–
Ealham, M.A.	8834	307	28.77	8- 36	13	1	–
Edmond, M.D.	372	7	53.14	2- 26	–	–	–
Edwards, A.D.	1069	26	41.11	5- 34	1	–	–
Elliott, M.T.G.	463	9	51.44	1- 3	–	–	–
Evans, A.W.	3	0					
Evans, K.P.	12097	364	33.23	6- 40	10	–	–
Fairbrother, N.H.	442	5	88.40	2- 91	–	–	–
Fellows, G.M.	64	1	64.00	1- 38	–	–	–
Fisher, I.D.	764	26	29.38	5- 35	2	–	–
Flanagan, I.N.	51	1	51.00	1- 50	–	–	–
Fleming, M.V.	8460	234	36.15	5- 51	2	–	–
Fleming, S.P.	110	0					
Flintoff, A.	1101	25	44.04	5- 24	1	–	–
Flower, A.	163	4	40.75	1- 1	–	–	–
Follett, D.	1509	44	34.29	8- 22	3	1	–
Foster, M.J.	1839	61	30.14	4- 21	–	–	–
Francis, S.R.G.	630	10	63.00	2- 21	–	–	–
Franks, P.J.	4170	148	28.17	6- 63	5	–	2
Fraser, A.R.C.	21772	799	27.24	8- 53	34	5	7
Frost, T.	6	0					
Fulton, D.P.	65	1	65.00	1- 37	–	–	–
Fulton, J.A.G.	18	0					
Gallage, I.S.	3394	154	22.03	7- 62	7	–	0+1
Gallian, J.E.R.	3547	89	39.85	6-115	1	–	–
Ganguly, S.C.	3018	79	38.20	6- 87	1	–	–
Gannon, B.W.	992	33	30.06	6- 80	2	–	–
Giddins, E.S.H.	10575	384	27.53	6- 47	20	2	4
Gie, N.A.	27	0					
Giles, A.F.	5955	227	26.23	6- 45	8	–	1
Gillespie, P.G.	136	5	27.20	3- 93	–	–	–
Gofton, A.F.	302	9	33.55	3- 41	–	–	–
Golding, J.M.	74	1	74.00	1- 74	–	–	–
Goodchild, D.J.	88	0					
Goodyer, T.E.	23	0					
Gough, D.	14884	553	26.91	7- 28	22	3	4
Gough, M.A.	378	6	63.00	4- 49	–	–	–
Grayson, A.P.	4197	100	41.97	4- 16	–	–	–
Green, R.J.	2122	54	39.29	6- 41	1	–	–
Greenfield, K.	524	5	104.80	2- 40	–	–	–
Greenidge, C.G.	231	11	21.00	5- 60	1	–	–

	Runs	Wkts	Avge	Best	5wI	10wM	50wS
Griffith, F.A.	2571	73	35.21	4- 33	–	–	–
Grove, J.O.	651	14	46.50	3- 74	–	–	–
Gupte, C.M.	312	4	78.00	2- 41	–	–	–
Habib, A.	52	0					
Halsall, R.G.	577	13	44.38	3- 64	–	–	–
Hamilton, G.M.	4070	161	25.27	7- 50	7	2	1
Hancock, T.H.C.	1349	35	38.54	3- 5	–	–	–
Hansen, T.M.	271	5	54.20	3- 59	–	–	–
Harden, R.J.	1023	20	51.15	2- 7	–	–	–
Hardinges, M.A.	60	1	60.00	1- 9	–	–	–
Harmison, S.J.	3669	122	30.07	5- 70	2	–	2
Harris, A.J.	4535	137	33.10	6- 40	4	1	1
Harris, C.Z.	3399	81	41.96	4- 22	–	–	–
Harrison, D.S.	64	1	64.00	1- 15	–	–	–
Hartley, P.J.	19938	668	29.84	9- 41	23	3	7
Harvey, I.J.	4077	115	35.45	7- 44	4	–	–
Harvey, M.E.	48	0					
Hay, M.J.	51	0					
Hayden, M.L.	374	8	46.75	3- 10	–	–	–
Haynes, G.R.	3541	96	36.88	6- 50	2	–	–
Haywood, G.R.	66	0					
Headley, D.W.	13293	466	28.52	8- 98	25	2	2
Hegg, W.K.	7	0					
Hemp, D.L.	661	15	44.06	3- 23	–	–	–
Henderson, T.	853	42	20.39	5- 44	2	–	–
Herath, R.	2219	111	19.99	6- 45	7	1	–
Hewage, P.R.	554	21	26.38	4- 56	–	–	–
Hewitt, J.P.	4470	160	27.93	6- 14	5	–	1
Hewson, D.R.	7	1	7.00	1- 7	–	–	–
Hick, G.A.	9649	222	43.46	5- 18	5	1	–
Hicks, T.C.	672	10	67.20	2- 61	–	–	–
Hockley, J.B.	57	1	57.00	1- 57	–	–	–
Hodgson, T.P.	34	1	34.00	1- 34	–	–	–
Hoggard, M.J.	2021	89	22.70	5- 47	3	–	–
Hollioake, A.J.	3875	97	39.94	5- 62	1	–	–
Hollioake, B.C.	3278	106	30.92	5- 51	1	–	–
Holloway, P.C.L.	46	0					
Horne, M.J.	156	0					
House, W.J.	843	3	281.00	1- 34	–	–	–
Hughes, Q.J.	226	4	56.50	2- 73	–	–	–
Hussain, N.	307	2	153.50	1- 38	–	–	–
Hutchison, P.M.	2918	132	22.10	7- 31	7	1	1
Hutton, B.L.	268	3	89.33	2-100	–	–	–
Hyam, B.J.	8	0					
Illingworth, R.K.	25414	808	31.45	7- 50	27	6	5
Ilott, M.C.	15253	564	27.04	9- 19	26	3	6
Innes, K.J.	704	23	30.60	4- 61	–	–	–
Irani, R.C.	7023	227	30.93	5- 19	4	–	1
James, K.D.	12607	395	31.91	8- 49	11	1	–
James, S.P.	3	0					
Jarvis, P.W.	18773	647	29.01	7- 55	22	3	4
Jayantha, S.	2022	64	31.59	3- 24	–	–	–
Johnson, N.C.	4254	141	30.17	5- 79	2	–	–
Johnson, P.	605	6	100.83	1- 9	–	–	–
Johnson, R.L.	6239	224	27.85	10- 45	5	2	2
Jones, I.	341	6	56.83	3- 81	–	–	–

	Runs	Wkts	Avge	Best	5wI	10wM	50wS
Jones, P.S.	1829	48	38.10	6- 67	1	–	–
Jones, S.P.	1121	26	43.11	5- 31	1	–	–
Joyce, E.C.	78	0					
Kalavitigoda, S.	21	0					
Kallis, J.H.	4398	149	29.51	5- 54	3	–	–
Kasprowicz, M.S.	13497	483	27.94	7- 36	26	2	2+2
Katich, S.M.	244	3	81.33	1- 4	–	–	–
Keech, M.	420	8	52.50	2- 28	–	–	–
Keedy, G.	4977	133	37.42	6- 79	3	–	–
Kendall, W.S.	416	10	41.60	3- 37	–	–	–
Kennis, G.J.	4	0					
Kenway, D.A.	76	2	38.00	1- 5	–	–	–
Kerr, J.I.D.	3665	95	38.57	7- 23	2	–	–
Kettleborough, R.A.	243	3	81.00	2- 26	–	–	–
Key, R.W.T.	1	0					
Khan, A.A.	2009	48	41.85	5-137	1	–	–
Khan, S.H.	906	11	82.36	3- 70	–	–	–
Khan, W.G.	31	0					
Killeen, N.	2825	106	26.65	7- 85	6	–	1
King, R.D.	1944	74	26.27	7- 82	5	–	–
Kino, D.	585	6	97.50	2- 84	–	–	–
Kirtley, R.J.	5161	193	26.74	7- 21	10	1	2
Knight, N.V.	191	1	191.00	1- 61	–	–	–
Krikken, K.M.	94	1	94.00	1- 54	–	–	–
Kumble, A.	14221	617	23.04	10- 74	44	11	1+1
Lacey, S.J.	803	14	57.35	3- 97	–	–	–
Lampitt, S.R.	15382	521	29.52	5- 32	17	–	6
Laney, J.S.	224	2	112.00	1- 24	–	–	–
Langer, J.L.	136	3	45.33	2- 17	–	–	–
Lathwell, M.N.	684	13	52.61	2- 21	–	–	–
Law, D.R.	4172	122	34.19	5- 33	4	–	–
Law, S.G.	3565	76	46.90	5- 39	1	–	–
Law, W.L.	89	3	29.66	2- 29	–	–	–
Lawrence, J.R.G.	221	3	73.66	2- 44	–	–	–
Lawson, A.G.	2	0					
Leatherdale, D.A.	2346	76	30.86	5- 20	2	–	–
Lehmann, D.S.	1195	22	54.31	4- 42	–	–	–
Lewis, C.C.	15923	536	29.70	6- 22	20	3	2
Lewis, J.	5347	192	27.84	7- 56	8	1	2
Lewis, J.J.B.	121	1	121.00	1- 73	–	–	–
Lewry, J.D.	5372	218	24.64	7- 38	14	2	2
Liptrot, C.G.	665	20	33.25	5- 51	1	–	–
Llong, N.J.	1259	35	35.97	5- 21	2	–	–
Lloyd, G.D.	440	2	220.00	1- 4	–	–	–
Logan, R.J.	178	8	22.25	3- 42	–	–	–
Love, G.T.	1820	46	39.56	5- 72	1	–	–
Loveridge, G.R.	2260	44	51.36	5- 59	1	–	–
Lowe, J.P.	473	7	67.57	2- 42	–	–	–
Loye, M.B.	43	0					
Lucas, D.S.	394	15	26.26	5-104	1	–	–
Lugsden, S.	1333	29	45.96	3- 45	–	–	–
McCague, M.J.	11881	440	27.00	9- 86	24	2	4
McCallan, W.K.	399	8	49.87	3- 63	–	–	–
McCoubrey, A.G.A.M.	78	4	19.50	3- 38	–	–	–
McDaid, R.W.	153	2	76.50	1- 34	–	–	–
McGarry, A.C.	149	4	37.25	2- 72	–	–	–

	Runs	Wkts	Avge	Best	5wI	10wM	50wS
McGerrigle, R.D.	70	5	14.00	4-24	–	–	–
McGrath, A.	492	14	35.14	3-18	–	–	–
McGrath, G.D.	8283	360	23.00	8-38	20	2	0+1
McLean, N.A.M.	5982	204	29.32	7-28	5	–	1
McMillan, C.D.	1399	41	34.12	6-71	1	–	–
Maddy, D.L.	725	20	36.25	3- 5	–	–	–
Mahmood, S.	43	0					
Maiden, G.I.	61	3	20.33	2-11	–	–	–
Malcolm, D.E.	27304	893	30.57	9-57	36	7	7
Marsh, S.A.	240	2	120.00	2-20	–	–	–
Martin, P.J.	12504	439	28.48	8-32	11	1	3
Martin-Jenkins, R.S.C.	1864	70	26.62	7-54	1	–	–
Mascarenhas, A.D.	2582	71	36.36	6-88	2	–	–
Mason, T.J.	444	10	44.40	3-32	–	–	–
Mather, D.P.	2479	58	42.74	6-74	1	1	–
Maynard, M.P.	829	6	138.16	3-21	–	–	–
Middlebrook, J.D.	422	13	32.46	3-20	–	–	–
Millns, D.J.	14162	522	27.13	9-37	22	4	4
Mirza, M.M.	620	19	32.63	4-51	–	–	–
Mohammed, I.	186	3	62.00	1-13	–	–	–
Molins, G.L.	300	8	37.50	3-62	–	–	–
Montgomerie, R.R.	72	0					
Moody, T.M.	10628	341	31.16	7-38	9	2	–
Mooney, P.J.K.	239	9	26.55	4-12	–	–	–
Morris, A.C.	2017	87	23.18	5-52	3	1	1
Morris, J.E.	913	7	130.42	1- 6	–	–	–
Morris, Z.C.	99	0					
Mullally, A.D.	15016	499	30.09	7-55	18	3	4
Munton, T.A.	17313	683	25.34	8-89	32	6	6
Muralitharan, M.	10233	514	19.90	9-65	44	11	1+2
Napier, G.R.	157	5	31.40	2-25	–	–	–
Nash, D.C.	19	1	19.00	1- 8	–	–	–
Nash, D.J.	6283	228	27.55	7-39	9	1	–
Nawaz, M.N.	377	14	26.92	5-16	1	–	–
Nel, A.	798	38	21.00	5-74	1	–	–
Newell, K.	875	19	46.05	4-61	–	–	–
Newell, M. (De)	15	0					
Newell, M. (Nt)	282	7	40.28	2-38	–	–	–
Newport, P.J.	23737	880	26.97	8-52	35	3	8
Nixon, P.A.	4	0					
Noon, W.M.	34	0					
O'Connor, S.B.	4089	160	25.55	6-31	10	2	–
Ontong, J.L.	373	6	62.16	2-23	–	–	–
Oram, A.R.	1653	57	29.00	4-37	–	–	–
Ormond, J.	3194	132	24.19	6-33	8	–	1
Ostler, D.P.	203	0					
Parker, B.	3	0					
Parkin, O.T.	2278	79	28.83	5-24	2	–	–
Parore, A.C.	55	0					
Parsons, K.A.	2086	51	40.90	5-57	1	–	–
Parsons, R.A.	10	0					
Patel, M.M.	10809	347	31.14	8-96	19	8	3
Patterson, M.W.	163	10	16.30	6-80	1	–	–
Peirce, M.T.E.	235	2	117.50	1-16	–	–	–
Penberthy, A.L.	6787	173	39.23	5-37	3	–	–
Penn, A.J.	2575	115	22.39	6-36	7	1	–

	Runs	Wkts	Avge	Best	5wI	10wM	50wS
Penney, T.L.	184	6	30.66	3- 18	–	–	–
Perera, A.S.A.	1633	78	20.93	7- 73	1	–	–
Perera, B.	962	41	23.46	4- 21	–	–	–
Perera, N.R.G.	2638	86	30.67	7- 66	4	1	–
Peters, S.D.	19	1	19.00	1- 19	–	–	–
Phillips, B.J.	1914	65	29.44	5- 47	2	–	–
Phillips, N.C.	3536	73	48.43	6- 97	3	1	–
Phillips, T.J.	278	8	34.75	4- 42	–	–	–
Pierson, A.R.K.	13446	356	37.76	8- 42	14	–	1
Pimlott, C.R.	283	5	56.60	3- 10	–	–	–
Piper, K.J.	57	1	57.00	1- 57	–	–	–
Pirihi, N.G.	0	1	0.00	1- 0	–	–	–
Pollard, P.R.	268	4	67.00	2- 79	–	–	–
Powell, J.C.	137	1	137.00	1-109	–	–	–
Powell, M.J. (Gm)	111	2	55.50	2- 39	–	–	–
Powell, M.J. (Wa)	120	3	40.00	2- 16	–	–	–
Pretorius, D.	1021	44	23.20	5- 50	1	–	–
Prichard, P.J.	497	2	248.50	1- 28	–	–	–
Pushpakumara, K.R.	5575	192	29.03	7-116	12	3	–
Pyemont, J.P.	20	0					
Ramprakash, M.R.	1778	31	57.35	3- 32	–	–	–
Randall, S.J.	237	0					
Rao, R.K.	296	4	74.00	1- 1	–	–	–
Rashid, U.B.A.	681	15	45.40	4- 41	–	–	–
Ratcliffe, J.D.	851	25	34.04	6- 48	1	–	–
Rawnsley, M.J.	1225	36	34.02	6- 44	2	1	–
Renshaw, S.J.	3361	86	39.08	5-110	1	–	–
Rhodes, J.N.	65	1	65.00	1- 13	–	–	–
Rhodes, S.J.	30	0					
Richardson, A.	599	26	23.03	8- 51	1	1	–
Ridgway, P.M.	301	6	50.16	3- 51	–	–	–
Ripley, D.	103	2	51.50	2- 89	–	–	–
Roberts, G.M.	810	10	81.00	4-105	–	–	–
Robinson, D.D.J.	37	0					
Robinson, J.D.	1152	28	41.14	3- 22	–	–	–
Robinson, M.A.	16049	507	31.65	9- 37	10	2	1
Robinson, P.E.	329	3	109.66	1- 10	–	–	–
Robinson, R.T.	289	4	72.25	1- 22	–	–	–
Rollins, A.S.	122	1	122.00	1- 19	–	–	–
Rose, G.D.	16805	572	29.37	7- 47	14	1	5
Roseberry, M.A.	406	4	101.50	1- 1	–	–	–
Ross, J.S.	129	0					
Russell, R.C.	68	1	68.00	1- 4	–	–	–
Sachdeva, A.	54	1	54.00	1- 32	–	–	–
Saggers, M.J.	961	39	24.64	6- 65	2	–	–
Sajdeh, R.K.	130	0					
Sales, D.J.G.	163	9	18.11	4- 25	–	–	–
Salisbury, I.D.K.	19558	606	32.27	8- 75	30	4	5
Saqlain Mushtaq	7740	370	20.91	8- 65	31	10	2+1
Savident, L.	247	4	61.75	2- 86	–	–	–
Sayers, C.A.	357	2	178.50	2- 21	–	–	–
Schofield, C.P.	1250	39	32.05	5- 66	1	–	–
Scott, D.A.	456	9	50.66	4-151	–	–	–
Scuderi, J.C.	5422	156	34.75	7- 79	8	1	–
Shadford, D.J.	983	23	42.73	5- 80	1	–	–
Shah, O.A.	448	13	34.46	3- 33	–	–	–

	Runs	Wkts	Avge	Best	5wI	10wM	50wS
Shahid, N.	1993	43	46.34	3- 91	–	–	–
Shaw, A.D.	7	0					
Sheikh, M.A.	119	6	19.83	2- 14	–	–	–
Sheikh, S.M.	338	12	28.16	4- 25	–	–	–
Sheriyar, A.	7670	255	30.07	7-130	11	3	2
Shoaib Akhtar	5995	208	28.82	6- 69	15	–	0+1
Sidebottom, R.J.	1250	36	34.72	3- 13	–	–	–
Silva, L.P.C.	204	5	40.80	3- 67	–	–	–
Silverwood, C.E.W.	7331	278	26.37	7- 93	14	1	2
Singh, A.	45	0					
Slater, M.J.	57	1	57.00	1- 4	–	–	–
Small, G.C.	24392	852	28.62	7- 15	29	2	6
Smethurst, M.P.	377	13	29.00	4- 44	–	–	–
Smith, A.M.	10524	424	24.82	8- 73	19	5	5
Smith, B.F.	205	2	102.50	1- 5	–	–	–
Smith, E.T.	25	0					
Smith, N.M.K.	11461	305	37.57	7- 42	16	–	–
Smith, R.A.	967	14	69.07	2- 11	–	–	–
Smith, T.M.	1181	53	22.28	6- 32	5	1	–
Smyth, S.G.	21	0					
Snape, J.N.	3735	77	48.50	5- 65	1	–	–
Solanki, V.S.	2450	57	42.98	5- 69	3	1	–
Speak, N.J.	191	2	95.50	1- 0	–	–	–
Speight, M.P.	32	2	16.00	1- 2	–	–	–
Spiring, K.R.	10	0					
Stanger, I.M.	291	5	58.20	3- 57	–	–	–
Stelling, W.F.	980	28	35.00	4- 12	–	–	–
Stemp, R.D.	11842	335	35.34	6- 37	13	1	–
Stephenson, J.P.	10627	315	33.73	7- 51	10	–	–
Stevens, D.I.	11	1	11.00	1- 5	–	–	–
Stewart, A.J.	423	3	141.00	1- 7	–	–	–
Still, Q.R.	1558	44	35.40	5- 53	2	–	–
Strang, P.A.	8514	268	31.76	7- 75	16	2	1
Strong, M.R.	165	0					
Stubbings, S.D.	41	0					
Such, P.M.	23519	789	29.80	8- 93	44	8	6
Sutcliffe, I.J.	200	5	40.00	2- 21	–	–	–
Sutcliffe, R.V.	164	4	41.00	2- 88	–	–	–
Swann, A.J.	154	1	154.00	1- 19	–	–	–
Swann, G.P.	2845	100	28.45	6- 41	4	1	1
Symington, M.J.	148	6	24.66	3- 55	–	–	–
Symonds, A.	2612	71	36.78	4- 39	–	–	–
Taylor, B.V.	108	2	54.00	1- 54	–	–	–
Taylor, J.P.	14733	506	29.11	7- 23	17	3	6
Tennant, A.M.	187	5	37.40	3- 28	–	–	–
Thomas, P.A.	2369	51	46.45	5- 70	1	–	–
Thomas, S.D.	8812	299	29.47	8- 50	13	–	3
Thompson, D.J.	808	27	29.92	4- 46	–	–	–
Thompson, J.B.D.	3103	122	25.43	7- 89	5	–	1
Thorpe, G.P.	1290	25	51.60	4- 40	–	–	–
Titchard, S.P.	190	4	47.50	1- 11	–	–	–
Tolley, C.M.	6516	185	35.22	7- 45	5	–	–
Trescothick, M.E.	1090	28	38.92	4- 36	–	–	–
Tudor, A.J.	2912	108	26.96	7- 77	6	–	–
Tufnell, P.C.R.	25796	876	29.44	8- 29	43	5	7
Turner, R.J.	29	0					

	Runs	Wkts	Avge	Best	5wI	10wM	50wS
Tweats, T.A.	237	4	59.25	1- 23	–	–	–
Twose, R.G.	4233	133	31.82	6- 28	2	–	–
Udal, S.D.	14819	422	35.11	8- 50	23	4	5
Vaughan, M.P.	3989	80	49.86	4- 39	–	–	–
Vettori, D.L.	4877	161	30.29	6- 64	9	–	–
Villavarayen, M.S.	4280	182	23.51	9- 15	6	1	–
Wagh, M.A.	1671	30	55.70	4- 11	–	–	–
Walker, B.G.K.	859	28	30.67	8-107	1	–	–
Walker, K.D.M.	479	12	39.91	3- 65	–	–	–
Walker, M.J.	134	0					–
Walton, T.C.	310	5	62.00	1- 8	–	–	–
Ward, I.J.	92	0					–
Ward, T.R.	647	8	80.87	2- 10	–	–	–
Warden, M.J.	48	1	48.00	1- 33	–	–	–
Warne, S.K.	14773	551	26.81	8- 71	24	4	2+1
Watkin, S.L.	22724	811	28.01	8- 59	28	4	9
Watkinson, M.	24960	739	33.77	8- 30	27	3	7
Weekes, P.N.	6497	156	41.64	8- 39	3	–	–
Welch, G.	5672	181	31.33	6-115	4	1	1
Wells, A.P.	820	10	82.00	3- 67	–	–	–
Wells, C.M.	14748	428	34.45	7- 42	7	–	–
Wells, V.J.	5838	220	26.53	5- 18	3	–	–
Weston, R.M.S.	104	2	52.00	1- 15	–	–	–
Weston, W.P.C.	599	4	149.75	2- 39	–	–	–
Wharf, A.G.	2003	51	39.27	4- 29	–	–	–
Whiley, M.J.A.	168	2	84.00	1- 44	–	–	–
Whitaker, J.J.	268	2	134.00	1- 29	–	–	–
White, C.	7351	271	27.12	8- 55	7	–	–
White, G.W.	398	7	56.85	3- 23	–	–	–
Wickramasinghe, P.P.	2019	120	16.82	8- 47	6	1	0+1
Wilkinson, R.	35	1	35.00	1- 35	–	–	–
Williams, K.C.	1748	59	29.62	5- 29	2	–	–
Williamson, D.	351	9	39.00	3- 19	–	–	–
Williamson, J.G.	357	5	71.40	2- 51	–	–	–
Windows, M.G.N.	111	2	55.50	1- 6	–	–	–
Wingfield, W.R.	587	12	48.91	2- 18	–	–	–
Wood, J.	7601	227	33.48	7- 58	8	–	1
Wood, N.T.	154	0					
Woolley, A.P.	61	0					
Wright, C.M.	247	8	30.87	3- 24	–	–	–
Yates, G.	6568	169	38.86	6- 64	5	–	–

LEADING CURRENT PLAYERS

The leading career batting/bowling averages and wicket-keeping/fielding aggregates among players currently registered for first-class county cricket. All figures are to the end of the 1999 English season.

BATTING

(Qualification: 100 innings)

	Runs	*Avge*
R.Dravid	8367	58.10
G.A.Hick	31252	55.02
M.G.Bevan	12059	54.56
M.L.Hayden	11886	53.30
D.S.Lehmann	12210	53.08
J.L.Langer	11183	51.53
S.C.Ganguly	6504	50.41
S.G.Law	13367	48.96
M.T.G.Elliott	7608	48.76
J.P.Crawley	14308	48.33
M.R.Ramprakash	17865	46.16
G.P.Thorpe	16111	45.00
R.A.Smith	23608	43.79
N.Hussain	15939	43.54
A.D.Brown	7791	43.52
J.Cox	9526	43.30
M.P.Maynard	20181	42.75
M.A.Atherton	18927	41.41
R.J.Bailey	20601	41.20
N.H.Fairbrother	18444	41.07
M.J.Di Venuto	5689	40.92
A.J.Stewart	22507	40.33
N.V.Knight	8561	40.00
T.L.Penney	7383	39.90
K.J.Barnett	26283	39.88
A.J.Hollioake	6091	39.81
S.P.James	13126	39.77
G.D.Lloyd	10203	39.54
D.J.Bicknell	13200	39.52
P.D.Bowler	15158	39.47
A.P.Wells	20802	39.24

BOWLING

(Qualification: 100 wickets)

	Wkts	*Avge*
Saqlain Mushtaq	370	20.91
P.M.Hutchison	132	22.10
A.A.Donald	1073	22.33
G.D.McGrath	360	23.00
A.Kumble	617	23.04
K.J.Dean	130	23.47
J.Ormond	132	24.19
J.D.Lewry	218	24.64
A.M.Smith	424	24.82
M.P.Bicknell	766	24.92
A.R.Caddick	634	25.01
D.R.Brown	283	25.21
G.M.Hamilton	161	25.27
T.A.Munton	683	25.34
J.B.D.Thompson	122	25.43
A.F.Giles	227	26.23
C.E.W.Silverwood	278	26.37
V.J.Wells	220	26.53
N.Killeen	106	26.65
R.J.Kirtley	193	26.74
D.G.Cork	552	26.79
S.K.Warne	551	26.81
D.Gough	553	26.91
A.J.Tudor	108	26.96
M.J.McCague	440	27.00
M.C.Ilott	564	27.04
C.White	271	27.12
D.J.Millns	522	27.13
A.R.C.Fraser	799	27.24
P.A.J.DeFreitas	1027	27.51
E.S.H.Giddins	384	27.53
J.Lewis	192	27.84
R.L.Johnson	224	27.85
J.P.Hewitt	160	27.93

WICKET-KEEPING

	Total	*Ct*	*St*
R.C.Russell	1143	1027	116
S.J.Rhodes	1027	915	112
S.A.Marsh	749	688	61
W.K.Hegg	694	624	70
R.J.Blakey	675	627	48
D.Ripley	673	595	78
A.J.Stewart	555	536	19
P.A.Nixon	509	469	4

FIELDING

	Ct
G.A.Hick	474
M.P.Maynard	309
N.Hussain	296
D.Byas	291
K.J.Barnett	265
R.J.Bailey	260

LIMITED-OVERS CAREER RECORDS

Compiled by Philip Bailey

The following career records are for all players who appeared in first-class or limited-overs cricket during the 1999 season, and are complete to the end of that season. Some players who did not appear in 1999 but may do so in 2000, are also included. These records are restricted to performances in major domestic competitions and official limited-overs internationals.

	M	*Runs*	*Avge*	*HS*	*100*	*50*	*Wkts*	*Avge*	*Best*	*Ct/St*
Adams, C.J.	214	6857	41.05	163	13	44	27	29.55	5-16	103
Adshead, S.J.	2	41	20.50	22	–	–	–	–	–	2/2
Afzaal, U.	2	401	36.45	83*	–	4	8	31.00	2-25	6
Aldred, P.	56	226	13.29	39*	–	–	49	37.06	4-30	7
Ali, Kadeer	1	24	24.00	24	–	–	–	–	–	–
Ali, S.M.	2	19	9.50	17	–	–	–	–	–	–
Alleyne, D.	1	13	13.00	13	–	–	–	–	–	2/1
Alleyne, M.W.	296	5868	27.94	134*	4	21	269	29.88	5-27	117
Allingham, M.J.D.	11	153	17.00	54	–	1	3	64.66	2-43	2
Allott, G.I.	46	20	4.00	7*	–	–	74	19.83	4-35	12
Altree, D.A.	1	6	6.00	6	–	–	0	–	–	–
Amin, R.M.	2	–	–	–	–	–	2	21.50	2-43	1
Anderson, R.S.G.	7	25	6.25	10	–	–	4	60.25	3-32	–
Archer, G.F.	100	1936	25.14	111*	2	8	11	33.45	2-16	37
Arnold, R.P.	4	15	5.00	11	–	–	0	–	–	2
Asim Butt	11	34	6.80	11	–	–	10	36.00	3-42	1
Astle, N.J.	165	4843	35.09	131	9	28	134	27.97	4-14	69
Atherton, M.A.	240	7926	36.35	127	11	49	20	31.50	4-42	89
Athey, C.W.J.	439	12785	34.18	142*	12	85	47	29.76	5-35	169/1
Austin, I.D.	284	2166	18.83	97	–	4	326	28.57	5-56	49
Averis, J.M.M.	7	6	3.00	5*	–	–	13	30.38	3-17	1
Aymes, A.N.	197	2000	24.09	73*	–	5	–	–	–	194/44
Bailey, R.J.	350	10733	39.17	145	9	70	58	34.72	3-23	98
Bailey, T.M.B.	16	107	13.37	52	–	1	–	–	–	11/8
Ball, M.C.J.	157	879	11.72	36*	–	–	125	37.49	5-42	59
Barnett, K.J.	445	13129	35.38	131*	12	78	96	25.50	6-24	153
Base, S.J.	155	348	6.00	31	–	–	207	25.00	4-14	32
Bates, J.J.	7	22	4.40	8	–	–	3	67.00	2-42	5
Bates, R.T.	70	239	8.53	28*	–	–	63	34.07	3-21	29
Batt, C.J.	5	8	8.00	8*	–	–	7	21.14	3-26	–
Batty, G.J.	8	87	14.50	37	–	–	4	67.75	1-32	2
Batty, J.N.	38	320	14.54	40	–	–	–	–	–	32/6
Bell, I.R.	1	10	10.00	10	–	–	0	–	–	–
Bell, M.D.	38	945	27.00	121*	2	2	0	–	–	8
Benjamin, J.E.	167	327	9.90	25	–	–	173	31.80	4-19	29
Betts, M.M.	58	258	11.21	21	–	–	70	30.95	4-39	9
Bevan, M.G.	211	7693	61.05	108*	5	62	74	31.36	5-29	63
Bicknell, D.J.	156	5180	39.54	135*	7	32	2	19.50	1-11	37
Bicknell, M.P.	250	1159	17.04	66*	–	2	326	25.64	7-30	60
Bishop, I.E.	10	24	24.00	15*	–	–	11	27.54	4-34	–
Bishop, J.E.	1	1	1.00	1	–	–	0	–	–	–
Blackwell, I.D.	29	510	23.18	97	–	3	20	25.95	3-17	7
Blain, J.A.R.	12	29	5.80	10	–	–	22	23.90	5-24	3
Blakey, R.J.	274	5942	33.19	130*	3	32	–	–	–	256/37
Blanchett, I.N.	12	19	6.33	9*	–	–	5	70.00	2-34	4

L-O	M	Runs	Avge	HS	100	50	Wkts	Avge	Best	Ct/St
Blewett, G.S.	82	2066	27.91	97	–	13	56	35.76	4-18	27
Bloomfield, T.F.	24	34	8.50	15	–	–	20	41.30	2- 8	4
Boon, D.C.	287	9154	36.03	122	7	63	2	107.00	2-44	77
Boswell, S.A.J.	16	26	4.33	14	–	–	11	58.72	3-39	1
Boteju, H.	2	3	3.00	2	–	–	0	–	–	1
Bowen, M.N.	65	228	15.20	27*	–	–	71	31.81	4-29	13
Bowler, P.D.	260	7493	32.15	138*	5	58	13	40.84	3-31	102/2
Bridge, G.D.	3	24	24.00	15	–	–	1	123.00	1-49	1
Brimson, M.T.	41	36	7.20	12*	–	–	43	27.34	3-23	8
Brinkley, J.E.	22	105	9.54	30*	–	–	17	39.70	2-26	2
Brown, A.D.	210	6098	32.09	203	11	24	3	48.66	1-20	60
Brown, D.R.	139	2215	22.15	78*	–	12	125	30.35	5-31	34
Brown, J.F.	1	–	–	–	–	–	4	6.50	4-26	–
Brown, S.J.E.	107	214	6.68	18	–	–	128	30.14	6-30	22
Bryant, J.D.C.	9	210	30.00	59	–	1	–	–	–	3
Bulbeck, M.P.L.	7	6	3.00	5	–	–	4	48.75	4-40	1
Burns, M.	106	2107	23.94	115*	1	13	33	24.84	4-39	54/11
Burns, N.D.	155	1721	19.55	58	–	5	–	–	–	154/30
Butcher, G.P.	57	571	16.79	48	–	–	24	45.00	4-32	5
Butcher, M.A.	111	1963	26.52	91	–	8	49	44.14	3-23	39
Byas, D.	263	6801	31.19	116*	5	38	25	25.64	3-19	98
Caddick, A.R.	138	446	12.38	39	–	–	195	24.04	6-30	24
Cairns, C.L.	248	6241	32.67	143	7	33	296	25.69	6-37	68
Carberry, M.A.	2	23	11.50	19	–	–	–	–	–	–
Carpenter, J.R.	38	575	25.00	64*	–	4	0	–	–	20
Cassar, M.E.	35	935	31.16	134	3	5	15	33.13	4-31	11
Catterall, D.N.	7	16	8.00	11*	–	–	3	58.33	2-35	1
Cawdron, M.J.	32	184	20.44	50	–	1	32	30.06	4-17	4
Chapman, S.	3	47	15.66	30	–	–	3	38.00	2-57	2
Chapple, G.	113	236	9.07	43	–	–	130	29.03	6-18	27
Chilton, M.J.	27	601	24.04	56	–	3	23	22.95	5-26	8
Collingwood, P.D.	70	1359	23.03	86	–	6	25	35.72	3-20	27
Cook, J.W.	1	130	130.00	130	1	–	0	–	–	–
Cook, S.J.	18	111	9.25	20	–	–	25	27.48	3-16	2
Cooke, G.	11	76	15.20	38*	–	–	10	51.30	2-33	1
Cork, D.G.	151	1995	19.75	92*	–	9	189	28.85	6-21	55
Cosker, D.A.	45	142	9.46	27*	–	–	48	31.72	3-18	11
Cottey, P.A.	212	3953	26.53	96	–	24	19	35.36	4-56	73
Cousins, D.M.	49	56	4.66	12*	–	–	55	29.01	3-18	5
Cowan, A.P.	73	399	13.75	40*	–	–	81	30.79	5-28	29
Cox, J.	58	1799	32.12	114	2	12	3	9.33	3-28	13
Crawley, J.P.	154	4382	31.07	114	3	28	0	–	–	42/4
Creed, M.W.	7	43	10.75	30	–	–	4	38.00	2-22	1
Croft, R.D.B.	221	2832	22.29	77	–	13	225	32.20	6-20	55
Crowe, C.D.	2	4	–	4*	–	–	–	–	–	–
Croy, M.G.	36	485	18.65	74	–	3	–	–	–	36/7
Cunliffe, R.J.	56	1422	31.60	137*	3	8	–	–	–	15
Curran, K.M.	369	8706	31.09	119*	1	52	325	30.03	5-15	95
Dagnall, C.E.	1	4	4.00	4	–	–	1	37.00	1-37	–
Dakin, J.M.	98	1290	17.43	108*	1	–	80	27.23	5-30	22
Dale, A.	206	4740	28.90	110	2	23	182	30.96	6-22	49
Daley, J.A.	45	954	29.81	98*	–	5	0	–	–	10
Davies, A.M.	1	0	0.00	0	–	–	2	22.00	2-44	1
Davies, A.P.	10	27	6.75	18	–	–	12	23.41	2-17	1
Davies, M.K.	6	4	4.00	2*	–	–	5	47.60	3-11	–

L-O	M	Runs	Avge	HS	100	50	Wkts	Avge	Best	Ct/St
Davis, M.J.G.	58	220	11.57	35	–	–	48	40.43	4-35	17
Davy, J.O.	1	2	–	2*	–	–	0	–	–	1
Dawes, J.H.	1	–	–	–	–	–	1	62.00	1-62	–
Dawood, I.	17	178	14.83	57	–	1	–	–	–	13/4
Dawson, R.I.	114	2258	23.76	85	–	9	2	54.00	1-19	20
De la Pena, J.M.	2	2	–	2*	–	–	0	–	–	–
Dean, K.J.	53	83	13.83	16*	–	–	63	28.17	5-32	12
Deane, M.J.	2	1	–	1*	–	–	3	19.66	3-42	–
DeFreitas, P.A.J.	387	4078	19.05	75*	–	11	456	27.38	5-13	84
Di Venuto, M.J.	61	1938	38.00	129*	1	14	3	28.66	1-10	17
Donald, A.A.	357	443	8.20	23*	–	–	554	21.20	6-15	55
Doull, S.B.	90	383	8.70	22	–	–	87	33.97	4-15	30
Dowman, M.P.	81	1576	21.88	92	–	7	28	39.10	3-21	23
Drakes, V.C.	124	1257	17.45	104	1	1	176	23.18	5-19	25
Dravid, R.S.	126	4256	40.92	145	7	31	1	206.00	1-21	52/3
Driver, R.C.	2	3	1.50	3	–	–	–	–	–	–
Dunlop, A.R.	20	283	18.86	59*	–	–	3	24.66	3-45	5
Dutch, K.P.	67	604	14.38	58	–	2	75	23.54	5-35	21
Dyer, N.R.	9	3	3.00	2*	–	–	9	25.88	2-26	2
Eagleson, R.L.	15	96	9.60	15*	–	–	15	46.13	4-59	5
Ealham, M.A.	226	3603	25.19	112	1	17	245	28.62	6-53	56
Edmond, M.D.	11	58	14.50	19	–	–	14	21.71	2- 4	2
Edwards, A.D.	30	168	9.33	43	–	–	23	43.73	3-34	9
Elliott, M.T.G.	32	692	25.62	97*	–	4	–	–	–	15
Ellison, C.J.	1	5	5.00	5	–	–	3	21.33	3-64	1
Evans, A.W.	38	647	23.10	108	1	3	–	–	–	11
Evans, K.P.	208	1299	15.65	55*	–	1	244	29.63	6-10	45
Fairbrother, N.H.	427	13015	43.52	123*	7	96	3	55.33	1-17	157
Fellows, G.M.	18	209	19.00	36	–	–	0	–	–	2
Fisher, I.D.	19	39	9.75	11*	–	–	18	25.05	3-25	6
Fleming, M.V.	251	4691	23.57	117*	3	18	312	25.40	5-27	65
Fleming, S.P.	148	4138	32.84	116*	5	23	1	28.00	1- 8	68
Flintoff, A.	59	1285	25.70	143	1	7	32	25.15	4-24	21
Flower, A.	114	3409	32.46	115*	1	28	0	–	–	80/25
Follett, D.	24	13	3.25	4	–	–	34	24.35	4-39	6
Foster, M.J.	63	962	20.91	118	1	6	42	43.52	3-26	9
Francis, S.R.G.	5	1	1.00	1	–	–	5	24.80	2-28	–
Franks, P.J.	39	321	14.59	40	–	–	55	23.89	5-27	5
Fraser, A.R.C.	291	778	12.15	38*	–	–	329	27.60	5-32	49
Frost, T.	26	86	10.75	22*	–	–	–	–	–	22/4
Fulton, D.P.	21	207	9.85	29	–	–	0	–	–	8
Gallian, J.E.R.	117	3560	34.56	134	7	21	44	32.31	5-15	42
Ganguly, S.C.	148	5431	43.44	183	11	32	70	32.54	5-16	43
Garaway, M.	1	4	4.00	4	–	–	–	–	–	1
Gazzard, C.M.	1	16	16.00	16	–	–	–	–	–	2
Giddins, E.S.H.	119	70	2.69	13	–	–	141	29.64	5-21	17
Gie, N.A.	21	413	24.29	75*	–	3	–	–	–	5
Giles, A.F.	96	873	18.97	69	–	2	126	20.87	5-21	28
Gillespie, P.G.	5	29	7.25	20	–	–	2	59.00	2-27	2
Golding, J.M.	3	52	26.00	47	–	–	0	–	–	2
Goodchild, D.J.	8	91	22.75	38*	–	–	–	–	–	6
Gough, D.	214	1322	13.08	72*	–	1	311	23.89	7-27	42
Gough, M.A.	3	16	8.00	16	–	–	0	–	–	1
Grayson, A.P.	156	2005	19.27	82*	–	7	137	32.92	4-25	42
Green, R.J.	26	41	10.25	14*	–	–	32	29.93	3-18	3

L-O	M	Runs	Avge	HS	100	50	Wkts	Avge	Best	Ct/St
Greenfield, K.	157	3793	27.88	129	2	22	27	60.55	3-34	49
Greenidge, C.G.	3	2	–	2*	–	–	0	–	–	1
Griffith, F.A.	65	366	9.38	31	–	–	68	31.88	4-48	14
Griffiths, S.P.	8	18	9.00	9	–	–	–	–	–	5/3
Gunawardena, D.A.	11	243	22.09	75	–	2	–	–	–	1
Gupte, C.M.	5	97	24.25	54*	–	1	–	–	–	–
Habib, A.	71	1321	26.95	111	1	6	2	4.50	2- 5	27
Hafeez, A.	8	50	12.50	33	–	–	0	–	–	3
Hamilton, G.M.	69	693	21.65	76	–	2	79	27.56	5-16	12
Hancock, T.H.C.	141	2598	21.12	90	–	13	42	23.54	6-58	47
Harden, R.J.	277	6859	30.48	108*	4	41	0	–	–	85
Harmison, S.J.	10	5	5.00	2*	–	–	4	89.50	2-40	3
Harris, A.J.	58	74	7.40	11*	–	–	83	25.00	4-22	14
Harris, C.Z.	198	4135	34.74	130	2	18	196	30.48	5-42	78
Hartley, P.J.	255	1714	16.16	83	–	4	330	26.24	5-36	45
Harvey, I.J.	67	1029	19.41	71	–	3	90	23.50	5-41	17
Harvey, M.E.	9	157	19.62	86	–	1	–	–	–	8
Hay, M.J.	2	–	–	–	–	–	2	37.00	1-32	–
Hayden, M.L.	79	3040	44.70	152*	8	16	4	30.75	2-38	34
Haynes, G.R.	120	2237	25.42	116*	1	7	95	27.22	4-13	34
Haynes, J.J.	1	–	–	–	–	–	–	–	–	1
Haywood, G.R.	13	88	8.80	24	–	–	7	46.28	1-18	4
Headley, D.W.	156	290	10.74	29*	–	–	197	26.74	6-42	28
Hegg, W.K.	288	2212	22.12	81	–	3	–	–	–	328/40
Hemp, D.L.	127	2749	26.95	121	4	15	8	20.87	4-32	49
Henderson, T.	12	33	11.00	12	–	–	22	12.81	5- 5	2
Hewitt, J.P.	62	272	12.95	32*	–	–	59	30.86	4-24	20
Hewson, D.R.	9	86	14.33	45	–	–	–	–	–	1
Hick, G.A.	414	15446	45.42	172*	28	103	153	30.91	5-35	178
Hockley, J.B.	2	27	13.50	19	–	–	–	–	–	2
Hodgson, T.P.	12	286	26.00	113	1	1	–	–	–	1
Hoggard, M.J.	18	10	2.00	2*	–	–	22	25.22	4-26	1
Hollioake, A.J.	181	3622	26.82	93	–	19	216	26.14	5-38	52
Hollioake, B.C.	79	1384	21.62	98	–	6	82	29.54	5-10	24
Holloway, P.C.L.	99	2236	31.94	117	2	14	–	–	–	47/8
Horne, M.J.	73	1362	19.45	74	–	5	9	43.22	2-33	15
House, W.J.	33	650	23.21	93	–	2	6	28.83	5-58	5
Humphries, S.	31	85	7.08	16	–	–	–	–	–	21/13
Hunter, I.D.	4	7	3.50	4	–	–	4	33.00	2-34	–
Hussain, N.	245	6734	35.25	118	5	45	–	–	–	116
Hutchison, P.M.	24	17	5.66	4*	–	–	31	19.38	4-34	1
Hutton, B.L.	12	79	11.28	24	–	–	5	32.60	2-43	8
Hyam, B.J.	22	150	13.63	37	–	–	–	–	–	20/1
Illingworth, R.K.	335	1153	14.59	36*	–	–	368	26.63	5-24	81
Ilott, M.C.	165	705	11.37	56*	–	2	206	26.02	5-21	25
Innes, K.J.	28	172	19.11	27	–	–	23	33.26	4-37	9
Irani, R.C.	148	3294	28.89	124	2	20	170	25.89	5-33	30
Jacobs, A.	18	386	22.70	81	–	2	–	–	–	14/2
James, K.D.	251	2439	19.99	66	–	7	246	31.01	6-35	66
James, S.P.	172	5451	35.86	135	7	37	–	–	–	41
Jarvis, P.W.	251	1267	13.19	63	–	1	369	23.63	6-27	47
Johnson, N.C.	102	2658	31.27	146*	6	14	85	30.75	4-19	48
Johnson, P.	328	8975	32.87	167*	13	51	0	–	–	103
Johnson, R.L.	97	667	15.88	45*	–	–	102	35.22	5-50	11
Jones, I.	1	5	–	5*	–	–	1	53.00	1-53	–

L-O	M	Runs	Avge	HS	100	50	Wkts	Avge	Best	Ct/St
Jones, P.S.	40	93	10.33	26*	–	–	57	25.14	5-23	12
Jones, S.P.	2	12	–	12*	–	–	1	69.00	1-39	–
Joyce, E.C.	8	263	37.57	73	–	1	–	–	–	2
Kallis, J.H.	133	4406	39.69	155*	10	27	96	29.18	5-30	45
Kasprowicz, M.S.	81	479	12.94	40	–	–	98	30.32	5-60	16
Katich, S.M.	13	272	27.20	74*	–	2	–	–	–	3
Keech, M.	101	1814	22.39	98	–	5	12	41.91	2-16	27
Keedy, G.	5	–	–	–	–	–	1	175.00	1-40	–
Kendall, W.S.	54	790	17.55	55	–	1	0	–	–	24
Kennis, G.J.	2	5	5.00	5	–	–	–	–	–	–
Kenway, D.A.	22	455	25.27	58	–	3	–	–	–	6
Kerr, J.I.D.	73	435	12.42	56	–	1	82	29.03	4-28	11
Kettleborough, R.A.	18	206	22.88	58	–	1	3	43.00	2-43	5
Key, R.W.T.	26	716	37.68	76*	–	7	–	–	–	2
Khan, A.A.	22	67	6.70	22*	–	–	25	35.48	5-40	5
Khan, W.G.	20	178	10.47	33	–	–	–	–	–	5
Killeen, N.	75	266	8.06	32	–	–	81	33.97	5-26	12
King, R.D.	30	48	12.00	12*	–	–	37	28.05	3-27	3
Kirtley, R.J.	54	101	10.10	17*	–	–	85	22.02	5-39	16
Knight, N.V.	196	5560	34.32	151	10	24	2	44.50	1-14	77
Krikken, K.M.	158	1299	19.38	55	–	1	–	–	–	162/24
Kumble, A.	233	956	12.91	30*	–	–	328	25.82	6-12	90
Lacey, S.J.	7	28	7.00	15	–	–	5	46.60	3-38	1
Lampitt, S.R.	229	1733	19.25	54	–	1	288	24.00	6-26	67
Laney, J.S.	72	1955	27.53	153	2	8	0	–	–	24
Langer, J.L.	79	2521	37.07	114*	1	20	7	30.71	3-51	28/1
Laraman, A.W.	2	3	3.00	3	–	–	0	–	–	2
Lathwell, M.N.	143	3931	29.11	121	4	24	1	158.00	1-23	39
Law, D.R.	92	1452	22.68	82	–	5	32	35.06	3-26	19
Law, S.G.	186	5946	36.70	159	15	22	70	38.05	4-33	78
Law, W.L.	10	104	13.00	24	–	–	0	–	–	3
Lawrence, J.R.G.	2	4	–	4*	–	–	0	–	–	1
Lawson, A.G.	31	812	30.07	99*	–	6	–	–	–	8
Leatherdale, D.A.	194	2563	19.12	70*	–	9	67	21.11	4-13	83
Lehmann, D.S.	144	4695	38.17	142*	8	29	23	39.04	3-43	34
Lewis, C.C.	240	3572	25.15	116*	1	12	286	26.14	5-19	92
Lewis, J.	67	250	10.00	33*	–	–	75	31.13	3-27	12
Lewis, J.J.B.	111	2089	26.11	102	1	10	0	–	–	18
Lewry, J.D.	43	103	7.35	14*	–	–	59	26.96	4-29	5
Llong, N.J.	132	2209	25.39	123	2	8	39	28.51	4-24	41
Lloyd, G.D.	230	5184	30.67	134	3	27	1	103.00	1-23	52
Logan, R.J.	4	8	8.00	8	–	–	3	33.66	2-31	2
Love, G.T.	5	10	10.00	5*	–	–	1	76.00	1-19	–
Loveridge, G.R.	18	251	19.30	50*	–	1	21	29.00	4-25	5
Loye, M.B.	120	3056	30.56	122	2	16	–	–	–	29
Lucas, D.S.	5	33	–	19*	–	–	4	39.25	3-49	1
Lugsden, S.	1	–	–	–	–	–	1	55.00	1-55	–
McCague, M.J.	145	603	11.16	31*	–	–	189	26.41	5-26	27
McCallan, W.K.	10	167	16.70	41	–	–	3	48.66	2-45	2
McGerrigle, R.D.	3	11	11.00	9*	–	–	7	22.71	5-66	1
MacGill, S.C.G.	10	25	8.33	18	–	–	21	14.38	5-40	3
McGrath, A.	95	2247	29.96	109*	1	14	9	23.44	2-10	29
McGrath, G.D.	106	49	3.76	10	–	–	155	24.15	5-14	14
McKeown, P.C.	19	315	16.57	69	–	1	0	–	–	5
McLean, N.A.M.	77	665	13.30	41*	–	–	84	31.20	3-21	14

L-O	M	Runs	Avge	HS	100	50	Wkts	Avge	Best	Ct/St
McMillan, C.D.	88	2311	29.62	125	3	10	24	30.33	5-38	31
Maddy, D.L.	123	3295	32.30	151	5	21	44	28.90	3-11	46
Maiden, G.I.	2	–	–	–	–	–	3	18.33	2-27	1
Malcolm, D.E.	151	281	5.97	42	–	–	217	26.68	7-35	15
Marsh, S.A.	299	2794	18.50	71	–	6	1	14.00	1- 3	310/34
Martin, P.J.	177	334	7.42	35*	–	–	243	23.32	5-21	31
Martin-Jenkins, R.S.C.	46	309	10.30	44	–	–	42	33.73	4-57	8
Mascarenhas, A.D.	52	924	23.10	79	–	8	48	27.16	4-28	15
Mason, T.J.	54	269	12.80	36	–	–	40	38.40	4-12	12
Maynard, M.P.	325	9967	34.72	151*	11	60	3	94.66	1-13	132/1
Middlebrook, J.D.	1	5	5.00	5	–	–	0	–	–	–
Millns, D.J.	90	348	15.13	39*	–	–	84	36.67	4-26	17
Mirza, M.M.	4	–	–	–	–	–	1	113.00	1-31	1
Molins, G.L.	4	10	3.33	10	–	–	3	48.66	2-44	3
Montgomerie, R.R.	75	2228	34.27	109	1	18	0	–	–	18
Moody, T.M.	313	10107	39.32	180*	17	71	219	30.91	4-24	104
Mooney, P.J.K.	1	2	2.00	2	–	–	2	28.00	2-56	–
Morris, A.C.	29	217	16.69	48*	–	–	20	26.60	4-49	5
Morris, J.E.	321	7722	27.28	145	9	36	1	66.00	1-44	76
Mullally, A.D.	186	337	7.32	38	–	–	217	28.50	5-15	26
Munton, T.A.	223	230	9.58	17	–	–	227	29.30	5-23	44
Muralitharan, M.	126	195	6.50	18	–	–	169	27.94	5-23	59
Napier, G.R.	15	88	11.00	19	–	–	6	31.66	3-22	2
Nash, D.C.	40	440	18.33	43	–	–	–	–	–	35/5
Nash, D.J.	120	1307	18.40	88	–	3	121	32.41	5-44	37
Nawaz, M.N.	1	5	5.00	5	–	–	–	–	–	–
Nel, A.	13	23	23.00	17*	–	–	14	30.42	3-36	4
Newell, K.	70	1189	22.43	97	–	4	22	46.90	5-33	14
Newell, M. (De)	41	1124	33.05	92	–	9	–	–	–	9
Newell, M. (Nt)	40	962	30.62	109*	1	4	0	–	–	13
Newport, P.J.	273	955	11.64	57	–	1	321	25.20	5-22	55
Nixon, P.A.	189	2771	21.99	96*	–	12	–	–	–	183/36
Noon, W.M.	117	734	13.84	46	–	–	–	–	–	87/26
O'Connor, S.B.	50	136	8.00	22	–	–	72	26.79	5-39	11
Ontong, J.L.	8	98	14.00	26*	–	–	4	48.75	2-31	1
Oram, A.R.	20	1	1.00	1*	–	–	23	31.17	4-45	5
Ormond, J.	31	122	13.55	18	–	–	46	20.32	4-12	6
Ostler, D.P.	201	5339	32.35	104	1	40	1	14.00	1- 4	67
Parker, B.	72	964	18.53	69	–	2	0	–	–	11
Parkin, O.T.	50	38	2.92	8	–	–	67	23.67	5-28	10
Parore, A.C.	163	3612	28.44	108	1	19	–	–	–	96/20
Parsons, K.A.	101	1490	24.03	56	–	5	59	35.74	4-43	45
Parsons, R.A.	7	120	20.00	33	–	–	0	–	–	2
Patel, D.B.	1	19	–	19*	–	–	1	36.00	1-36	–
Patel, M.M.	39	90	10.00	18*	–	–	37	34.05	3-22	12
Patterson, M.W.	9	25	5.00	9	–	–	14	34.57	3-48	–
Peirce, M.T.E.	16	245	16.33	44	–	–	–	–	–	4
Penberthy, A.L.	176	2843	25.38	81*	–	15	168	30.64	5-36	44
Penn, A.J.	23	203	13.53	63	–	1	29	33.55	6-49	7
Penney, T.L.	177	3066	27.62	90	–	13	1	18.00	1- 8	68/1
Perera, A.S.A.	6	17	17.00	17	–	–	8	28.87	2-25	–
Peters, S.D.	36	306	11.76	58*	–	2	–	–	–	11
Phillips, B.J.	23	59	8.42	29	–	–	25	23.52	3-13	9
Phillips, N.C.	57	334	9.54	38*	–	–	50	35.90	4-13	13
Phillips, T.J.	1	0	0.00	0	–	–	2	28.00	2-56	1

L-O	M	Runs	Avge	HS	100	50	Wkts	Avge	Best	Ct/St
Pierson, A.R.K.	110	318	9.63	29*	–	–	92	35.36	5-36	42
Piper, K.J.	148	667	15.15	38*	–	–	–	–	–	168/24
Pollard, P.R.	157	4394	33.28	132*	5	26	0	–	–	58
Pope, S.P.	1	0	0.00	0	–	–	–	–	–	4
Powell, J.C.	6	4	2.00	2	–	–	4	31.25	2-10	1
Powell, M.J. (Gm)	34	551	19.00	55	–	1	–	–	–	9
Powell, M.J. (Wa)	7	157	52.33	51	–	1	0	–	–	1
Pratt, A.	3	34	17.00	26	–	–	–	–	–	3
Pretorius, D.	5	11	11.00	7*	–	–	5	31.40	2-26	1
Prichard, P.J.	279	6932	29.87	114	6	38	–	–	–	80
Prittipaul, L.R.	5	66	22.00	30	–	–	4	31.25	2-53	4
Pushpakumara, K.R.	29	36	12.00	14*	–	–	24	46.20	3-25	8
Pyemont, J.P.	13	129	10.75	25	–	–	–	–	–	5
Ramprakash, M.R.	233	7115	38.25	147*	7	44	33	23.21	5-38	80
Randall, S.J.	1	1	1.00	1	–	–	0	–	–	–
Rao, R.K.	40	961	25.28	158	1	7	5	25.40	3-31	12
Rashid, U.B.A.	39	307	16.15	82	–	1	47	29.95	5-24	14
Ratcliffe, J.D.	84	1528	21.82	105	1	8	14	40.78	2-11	23
Rawnsley, M.J.	24	27	2.70	7	–	–	21	29.28	5-26	7
Read, C.M.W.	34	544	23.65	62	–	1	–	–	–	36/5
Renshaw, S.J.	52	210	16.15	27*	–	–	67	28.07	6-25	5
Rhodes, J.N.	235	5419	30.78	121	1	26	2	19.00	1- 2	106
Rhodes, S.J.	351	3091	18.07	105	1	4	0	–	–	393/93
Richardson, A.	9	16	4.00	11*	–	–	5	49.80	2-16	–
Ripley, D.	237	1492	18.19	52*	–	1	–	–	–	199/24
Roberts, G.M.	37	122	10.16	27	–	–	43	28.90	4-23	9
Robinson, D.D.J.	98	2282	28.17	137*	3	9	1	26.00	1- 7	27
Robinson, J.D.	51	678	19.37	67	–	3	24	49.62	3-46	15
Robinson, M.A.	195	105	2.69	9*	–	–	198	31.87	4-23	22
Robinson, P.E.	196	4217	25.55	104	1	21	–	–	–	76
Robinson, R.	9	52	6.50	33	–	–	4	53.50	2-22	2
Robinson, R.T.	391	11729	34.29	139	9	74	–	–	–	117
Rollins, A.S.	86	1553	20.98	126*	1	6	0	–	–	36
Rollins, R.J.	103	1052	16.96	87	–	5	–	–	–	84/25
Rose, G.D.	270	4818	24.83	148	2	23	285	29.38	4-21	64
Roseberry, M.A.	192	5253	32.22	121	6	36	1	51.00	1-22	64
Russell, R.C.	380	5357	24.46	119*	2	20	–	–	–	357/68
Rutherford, A.T.	7	66	16.50	26	–	–	–	–	–	9
Saggers, M.J.	20	89	17.80	34*	–	–	24	29.66	4-35	5
Sales, D.J.G.	58	1057	21.57	70*	–	4	–	–	–	21
Salisbury, I.D.K.	185	1086	12.62	48*	–	–	185	33.31	5-30	58
Salmond, G.	29	305	11.29	52	–	1	–	–	–	9
Saqlain Mushtaq	141	626	12.27	30*	–	–	257	19.59	5-29	35
Savident, L.	5	60	30.00	39	–	–	6	17.33	3-41	–
Schofield, C.P.	2	33	16.50	28	–	–	2	16.00	2-32	–
Scott, D.A.	2	–	–	–	–	–	0	–	–	–
Scuderi, J.C.	37	577	24.04	58	–	3	32	42.40	3-36	3
Shadford, D.J.	12	3	3.00	2	–	–	11	31.63	3-30	4
Shah, K.Z.	3	0	–	0*	–	–	3	37.66	2-36	1
Shah, O.A.	68	1504	27.85	134	2	6	4	31.00	2- 2	20
Shahid, N.	122	1991	24.28	101	1	7	5	46.60	3-30	36
Shaw, A.D.	57	542	16.42	48	–	–	–	–	–	41/11
Sheikh, M.A.	14	31	5.16	12*	–	–	20	17.95	3-28	6
Sheriyar, A.	64	90	9.00	19	–	–	68	27.94	4-18	5
Shoaib Akhtar	32	66	16.50	36	–	–	47	25.29	4-37	6

L-O	*M*	*Runs*	*Avge*	*HS*	*100*	*50*	*Wkts*	*Avge*	*Best*	*Ct/St*
Sidebottom, R.J.	39	55	6.87	24*	–	–	46	27.50	6-40	5
Silverwood, C.E.W.	108	223	7.96	14*	–	–	144	23.59	5-28	14
Singh, A.	35	826	25.03	123	1	6	–	–	–	8
Slater, M.J.	89	2373	26.96	110	1	21	0	–	–	22
Small, G.C.	381	1042	8.54	40*	–	–	457	26.47	5-18	72
Smethurst, M.P.	5	5	2.50	4*	–	–	9	17.44	4-46	–
Smith, A.M.	179	444	11.68	26*	–	–	202	28.59	6-39	33
Smith, B.F.	167	4017	27.32	115	1	21	0	–	–	52
Smith, C.J.O.	3	71	71.00	48*	–	–	–	–	–	1
Smith, E.T.	24	381	20.05	72*	–	2	–	–	–	5
Smith, N.M.K.	247	4163	22.87	125	2	24	233	26.79	6-33	79
Smith, R.A.	373	13308	42.65	167*	27	71	3	5.00	2-13	145
Smith, T.M.	7	19	9.50	8*	–	–	11	26.36	4-38	3
Smyth, S.G.	10	258	25.80	61	–	1	–	–	–	3
Snape, J.N.	106	1254	22.80	77*	–	5	104	27.25	5-32	39
Solanki, V.S.	88	1506	23.53	120*	1	6	7	43.85	1- 9	29
Speak, N.J.	132	3130	28.98	102*	1	18	0	–	–	24
Speight, M.P.	214	5084	26.89	126	3	25	–	–	–	118/14
Spendlove, B.L.	20	286	15.88	58	–	1	–	–	–	5
Spiring, K.R.	50	1039	31.48	58*	–	4	–	–	–	16
Stanger, I.M.	27	225	15.00	44	–	–	11	78.63	3-34	12
Stelling, W.F.	33	478	36.76	76*	–	2	32	33.40	3-18	12
Stemp, R.D.	115	183	8.31	29*	–	–	122	31.51	4-25	21
Stephenson, J.P.	257	6395	31.50	142	7	37	231	26.16	6-33	97
Stevens, D.I.	19	369	20.50	82	–	2	–	–	–	3
Stewart, A.J.	410	12103	34.97	167*	16	74	0	–	–	347/39
Still, Q.R.	2	24	24.00	20	–	–	0	–	–	2
Strang, P.A.	127	1519	21.09	47	–	–	139	30.10	6-32	43
Strauss, A.J.	14	112	11.20	29	–	–	–	–	–	3
Strong, M.R.	3	4	2.00	2*	–	–	0	–	–	–
Stubbings, S.D.	9	110	12.22	37	–	–	–	–	–	1
Such, P.M.	202	275	8.08	19*	–	–	201	31.43	5-29	48
Sutcliffe, I.J.	44	1145	28.62	105*	2	6	–	–	–	9
Sutton, L.D.	4	105	35.00	60	–	1	–	–	–	–
Swann, A.J.	10	289	28.90	74	–	2	–	–	–	3
Swann, G.P.	28	416	24.47	63	–	2	31	25.54	5-35	5
Symington, M.J.	5	20	6.66	10	–	–	3	71.33	1-39	1
Symonds, A.	88	2144	26.80	95	–	11	28	29.92	3-32	42
Taylor, B.V.	10	22	–	21*	–	–	11	32.27	3-22	1
Taylor, J.P.	184	332	9.48	24	–	–	217	29.12	5-45	39
Tendulkar, S.R.	277	10497	44.29	143	30	55	117	42.29	5-32	94
Tennant, A.M.	2	2	–	2*	–	–	2	26.00	2-29	3
Thomas, P.A.	6	15	15.00	12*	–	–	4	61.75	2-30	–
Thomas, S.D.	68	568	13.52	40	–	–	93	25.13	7-16	13
Thompson, D.J.	3	2	2.00	1*	–	–	2	33.50	2-34	–
Thompson, J.B.D.	50	95	11.87	30	–	–	47	27.63	3-16	6
Thorpe, G.P.	246	7947	39.73	145*	6	61	14	38.92	3-21	112
Titchard, S.P.	52	1188	25.82	96	–	5	1	48.00	1-19	7
Tolley, C.M.	116	1186	19.44	77	–	4	113	29.20	5-16	29
Trego, P.D.	1	0	0.00	0	–	–	2	21.00	2-42	–
Trescothick, M.E.	90	1848	26.78	122	3	5	25	28.80	3-46	32
Tsolekile, T.L.	1	–	–	–	–	–	–	–	–	2
Tudor, A.J.	18	104	9.45	29*	–	–	25	22.88	4-39	5
Tufnell, P.C.R.	81	115	9.58	18	–	–	89	32.15	5-28	15
Turner, R.J.	132	1975	25.00	70	–	7	–	–	–	138/14

L-O	M	Runs	Avge	HS	100	50	Wkts	Avge	Best	Ct/St
Tweats, T.A.	32	303	14.42	42*	–	–	0	–	–	10
Twose, R.G.	255	6793	33.96	121*	8	45	147	27.63	5-30	85
Udal, S.D.	212	1380	15.00	78	–	5	246	30.15	5-43	68
Van den Berg, A.M.	3	3	3.00	3	–	–	0	–	–	–
Van der Gucht, C.G.	3	4	2.00	3	–	–	5	19.00	3-35	–
Vaughan, M.P.	119	2900	26.36	88	–	17	40	30.35	4-31	33
Vettori, D.L.	54	253	11.50	26	–	–	39	42.97	4-49	16
Wagh, M.A.	6	74	14.80	27	–	–	3	39.66	1-39	–
Walker, B.G.K.	11	56	9.33	18	–	–	12	27.50	4-39	7
Walker, M.J.	98	2097	26.21	117	1	13	1	59.00	1-33	25
Wallace, M.A.	3	3	1.50	2	–	–	–	–	–	4/2
Walton, T.C.	88	1441	23.24	72	–	7	7	32.00	2-27	24
Ward, I.J.	49	887	23.34	91	–	4	0	–	–	8
Ward, T.R.	245	7409	32.21	131	7	50	10	35.10	3-20	52
Warne, S.K.	134	758	13.06	55	–	1	221	23.87	5-33	48
Warren, R.J.	105	1742	22.33	100*	1	5	–	–	–	96/10
Watkin, S.L.	219	408	6.80	31*	–	–	275	26.55	5-23	34
Watkinson, M.	358	5217	23.08	130	2	20	362	32.06	5-44	95
Weekes, P.N.	186	3642	26.77	143*	3	17	196	29.26	4-29	70
Welch, G.	103	1042	21.26	71	–	3	82	37.65	4-31	13
Wells, A.P.	351	8841	31.24	127	8	55	7	20.28	1- 0	103
Wells, C.M.	319	6161	25.88	117	4	28	228	31.30	4-15	76
Wells, V.J.	185	4007	26.53	201	4	15	175	27.52	6-25	47
Welton, G.E.	15	299	21.35	104*	1	1	–	–	–	4
Weston, R.M.S.	28	511	21.29	56	–	3	–	–	–	5
Weston, W.P.C.	191	1579	20.24	125	1	5	1	2.00	1- 2	24
Wharf, A.G.	28	257	21.41	38*	–	–	24	42.25	4-29	6
Whitaker, J.J.	274	6650	28.66	155	6	47	0	–	–	65
White, C.	183	3547	26.08	148	2	14	172	27.09	4-18	58
White, G.W.	83	1682	22.42	76	–	11	1	59.00	1-45	27
Williams, K.C.	15	139	19.85	28	–	–	13	34.53	3-37	3
Williams, R.C.J.	20	76	15.20	19	–	–	–	–	–	21/4
Williamson, D.	54	353	14.12	39	–	–	59	24.50	5-32	13
Williamson, J.G.	23	240	11.42	51*	–	1	12	50.00	2-45	2
Willis, S.C.	12	105	17.50	31*	–	–	–	–	–	15/1
Wilson, E.J.	12	255	23.18	62	–	2	–	–	–	6
Wilton, N.J.	3	10	5.00	7	–	–	–	–	–	5
Windows, M.G.N.	82	1453	22.01	72	–	3	0	–	–	28
Wingfield, W.R.	13	328	41.00	83	–	2	8	34.75	2-19	2
Wood, J.	79	315	9.84	28	–	–	75	38.33	4-17	11
Wood, M.J.	17	259	28.77	65*	–	2	–	–	–	4
Wood, N.T.	1	23	23.00	23	–	–	–	–	–	–
Woolley, A.P.	5	2	1.00	1*	–	–	5	36.20	4-61	–
Wright, A.S.	1	63	63.00	63	–	1	–	–	–	–
Wright, C.M.	9	69	11.50	39	–	–	18	13.88	5-23	1
Yardy, M.H.	1	0	0.00	0	–	–	0	–	–	–
Yates, G.	145	555	15.41	38	–	–	143	31.48	4-34	30
Zuiderent, B.	12	249	22.63	99	–	1	0	–	–	8

LOI CAREER RECORDS

These records, complete to the start of LOI No. 1566 (up to 23 February 2000 but excluding the New Zealand v Australia series), include all players registered for county cricket in 2000 at the time of going to press, plus those who have appeared in LOI matches since 25 September 1998 (No. 1354 onwards).

ENGLAND – BATTING AND FIELDING

	M	*I*	*NO*	*HS*	*Runs*	*Avge*	*100*	*50*	*Ct/St*
C.J.Adams	5	4	–	42	71	17.75	–	–	3
M.W.Alleyne	9	8	1	53	151	21.57	–	1	2
M.A.Atherton	54	54	3	127	1791	35.11	2	12	15
I.D.Austin	9	6	1	11*	34	6.80	–	–	–
R.J.Bailey	4	4	2	43*	137	68.50	–	–	1
K.J.Barnett	1	1	–	84	84	84.00	–	1	–
M.P.Bicknell	7	6	2	31*	96	24.00	–	–	2
R.J.Blakey	3	2	–	25	25	12.50	–	–	2/1
A.D.Brown	13	13	–	118	333	25.61	1	1	6
D.R.Brown	9	8	4	21	99	24.75	–	–	1
A.R.Caddick	18	10	6	21*	67	16.75	–	–	5
D.G.Cork	25	15	2	31*	132	10.15	–	–	6
J.P.Crawley	13	12	1	73	235	21.36	–	2	1/1
R.D.B.Croft	44	31	11	32	299	14.95	–	–	9
P.A.J.DeFreitas	103	66	23	67	690	16.04	–	1	26
M.A.Ealham	48	35	3	45	574	17.93	–	–	7
N.H.Fairbrother	75	71	18	113	2092	39.47	1	16	33
M.V.Fleming	11	10	1	34	140	15.55	–	–	1
A.Flintoff	9	6	–	50	100	16.66	–	1	–
A.R.C.Fraser	42	20	9	38*	141	12.81	–	–	5
A.F.Giles	5	3	2	10*	17	17.00	–	–	1
D.Gough	74	47	16	45	340	10.96	–	–	12
D.W.Headley	13	6	4	10*	22	11.00	–	–	3
G.A.Hick	105	104	13	126*	3513	38.60	5	24	58
A.J.Hollioake	35	30	6	83*	606	25.25	–	3	13
B.C.Hollioake	7	6	–	63	122	20.33	–	1	1
N.Hussain	42	42	7	93	932	26.62	–	6	23
R.K.Illingworth	25	11	5	14	68	11.33	–	–	8
R.C.Irani	10	10	2	45*	78	9.75	–	–	2
P.W.Jarvis	16	8	2	16*	31	5.16	–	–	1
N.V.Knight	53	53	5	125*	1924	40.08	3	12	20
C.C.Lewis	53	40	14	33	374	14.38	–	–	20
G.D.Lloyd	6	5	1	22	39	9.75	–	–	2
D.L.Maddy	8	6	–	53	113	18.83	–	1	1
D.E.Malcolm	10	5	2	4	9	3.00	–	–	1
P.J.Martin	20	13	7	6	38	6.33	–	–	1
M.P.Maynard	10	10	1	41	153	17.00	–	–	3
J.E.Morris	8	8	1	63*	167	23.85	–	1	2
A.D.Mullally	34	15	7	20	65	8.12	–	–	7
M.R.Ramprakash	13	13	3	51	265	26.50	–	1	6
C.M.W.Read	9	6	2	26*	70	17.50	–	–	11/2
S.J.Rhodes	9	8	2	56	107	17.83	–	1	9/2
R.C.Russell	40	31	7	50	423	17.62	–	1	41/6
I.D.K.Salisbury	4	2	1	5	7	7.00	–	–	1
C.E.W.Silverwood	6	4	–	12	17	4.25	–	–	–
N.M.K.Smith	7	6	1	31	100	20.00	–	–	1
R.A.Smith	71	70	8	167*	2419	39.01	4	15	26
V.S.Solanki	8	7	1	24	96	16.00	–	–	2
A.J.Stewart	125	120	8	116	3378	30.16	2	19	111/11
G.P.Swann	1	–	–	–	–	–	–	–	–
J.P.Taylor	1	1	–	1	1	1.00	–	–	–
G.P.Thorpe	53	52	8	89	1786	40.59	–	17	31
P.C.R.Tufnell	20	10	9	5*	15	15.00	–	–	4
S.D.Udal	10	6	4	11*	35	17.50	–	–	1

ENGLAND – BATTING AND FIELDING (continued)

	M	I	NO	HS	Runs	Avge	100	50	Ct/St
S.L.Watkin	4	2	–	4	4	2.00	–	–	–
M.Watkinson	1	–	–	–	–	–	–	–	–
A.P.Wells	1	1	–	15	15	15.00	–	–	–
V.J.Wells	9	7	–	39	141	20.14	–	–	7
C.White	23	19	1	38	280	15.55	–	–	4

ENGLAND – BOWLING

	O	R	W	Avge	Best	4wI	R/Over
M.W.Alleyne	58	254	10	25.40	3-27	–	4.37
I.D.Austin	79.1	360	6	60.00	2-25	–	4.54
R.J.Bailey	6	25	0	–	–	–	4.16
M.P.Bicknell	68.5	347	13	26.69	3-55	–	5.04
A.D.Brown	1	5	0	–	–	–	5.00
D.R.Brown	54	305	7	43.57	2-28	–	5.64
A.R.Caddick	174	637	26	24.50	4-19	1	3.66
D.G.Cork	240	1071	35	30.60	3-27	–	4.46
R.D.B.Croft	374	1567	41	38.21	3-51	–	4.18
P.A.J.DeFreitas	952	3775	115	32.82	4-35	1	3.96
M.A.Ealham	406.3	1671	56	29.83	5-15	3	4.11
N.H.Fairbrother	1	9	0	–	–	–	9.00
M.V.Fleming	87.1	434	17	25.52	4-45	1	4.97
A.Flintoff	40.2	228	7	32.57	2- 3	–	5.65
A.R.C.Fraser	398.4	1412	47	30.04	4-22	1	3.54
A.F.Giles	38	197	5	39.40	2-37	–	5.18
D.Gough	690	2870	124	23.14	5-44	8	4.15
D.W.Headley	99	520	11	47.27	2-38	–	5.25
G.A.Hick	186.1	919	28	32.82	5-33	1	4.93
A.J.Hollioake	201.2	1019	32	31.84	4-23	2	5.06
B.C.Hollioake	25	122	2	61.00	2-43	–	4.88
R.K.Illingworth	250.1	1059	30	35.30	3-33	–	4.23
R.C.Irani	54.5	246	4	61.50	1-23	–	4.48
P.W.Jarvis	146.3	672	24	28.00	5-35	2	4.58
C.C.Lewis	437.3	1942	66	29.42	4-30	4	4.43
D.E.Malcolm	87.4	404	16	25.25	3-40	–	4.60
P.J.Martin	174.4	806	27	29.85	4-44	1	4.61
A.D.Mullally	313.3	1198	45	26.62	4-18	2	3.82
M.R.Ramprakash	2	14	0	–	–	–	7.00
I.D.K.Salisbury	31	177	5	35.40	3-41	–	5.70
C.E.W.Silverwood	42	201	3	67.00	2-27	–	4.78
N.M.K.Smith	43.3	190	6	31.66	3-29	–	4.36
G.P.Swann	5	24	0	–	–	–	4.80
J.P.Taylor	3	20	0	–	–	–	6.66
G.P.Thorpe	20	97	2	48.50	2-15	–	4.85
P.C.R.Tufnell	170	699	19	36.78	4-22	1	4.11
S.D.Udal	95	371	8	46.37	2-37	–	3.90
S.L.Watkin	36.5	193	7	27.57	4-49	1	5.24
M.Watkinson	9	43	0	–	–	–	4.77
V.J.Wells	36.4	189	8	23.62	3-30	–	5.15
C.White	172	738	29	25.44	5-21	2	4.29

AUSTRALIA – BATTING AND FIELDING

	M	I	NO	HS	Runs	Avge	100	50	Ct/St
M.G.Bevan	132	117	44	108*	4310	59.04	3	31	45
G.S.Blewett	32	30	3	57*	550	20.37	–	2	7
A.C.Dale	30	12	8	15*	78	19.50	–	–	11
M.J.Di Venuto	9	9	–	89	241	26.77	–	2	1
M.T.G.Elliott	1	1	–	1	1	1.00	–	–	–
D.W.Fleming	72	25	15	14*	72	7.20	–	–	11
A.C.Gilchrist	86	84	4	154	2648	33.10	5	12	111/18
J.N.Gillespie	18	11	3	26	81	10.12	–	–	–
I.J.Harvey	12	10	2	43	101	12.62	–	–	6

	M	I	NO	HS	Runs	Avge	100	50	Ct/St
M.L.Hayden	13	12	1	67	286	26.00	–	2	4
B.P.Julian	25	17	–	35	224	13.17	–	–	8
M.S.Kasprowicz	16	8	6	28*	60	30.00	–	–	3
J.L.Langer	8	7	2	36	160	32.00	–	–	2/1
S.G.Law	54	51	5	110	1237	26.89	1	7	12
B.Lee	9	2	–	2	3	1.50	–	–	–
S.Lee	34	27	6	47	394	18.76	–	–	17
D.S.Lehmann	60	55	8	110*	1531	32.57	2	8	9
S.C.G.MacGill	3	2	1	1	1	1.00	–	–	2
G.D.McGrath	110	33	18	10	52	3.46	–	–	13
D.R.Martyn	48	43	13	59*	926	30.86	–	5	16
T.M.Moody	76	64	12	89	1211	23.28	–	10	21
R.T.Ponting	101	101	12	145	3612	40.58	6	20	32
P.R.Reiffel	92	57	21	58	503	13.97	–	1	25
A.Symonds	18	13	3	68*	342	34.20	–	1	5
S.K.Warne	137	80	24	55	702	12.53	–	1	46
M.E.Waugh	208	203	15	130	7275	38.69	14	45	87
S.R.Waugh	286	257	50	120*	6516	31.47	2	38	102
B.E.Young	6	3	1	18	31	15.50	–	–	2

AUSTRALIA – BOWLING

	O	R	W	Avge	Best	4wI	R/Over
M.G.Bevan	292.2	1446	33	43.81	3-36	–	4.94
G.S.Blewett	124.5	646	14	46.14	2- 6	–	5.17
A.C.Dale	266	979	32	30.59	3-18	–	3.68
D.W.Fleming	627.5	2704	109	24.80	5-36	4	4.30
J.N.Gillespie	158.1	726	23	31.56	4-26	1	4.58
I.J.Harvey	77.3	364	7	52.00	3-17	–	4.69
B.P.Julian	191	997	22	45.31	3-40	–	5.21
M.S.Kasprowicz	136.1	709	22	32.22	3-50	–	5.20
S.G.Law	134.3	635	12	52.91	2-22	–	4.72
B.Lee	81.1	320	16	20.00	5-27	1	3.94
S.Lee	220.2	964	38	25.36	5-33	2	4.37
D.S.Lehmann	77.4	417	11	37.90	2- 4	–	5.36
S.C.G.MacGill	30	105	6	17.50	4-19	1	3.50
G.D.McGrath	987.4	3936	166	23.71	5-14	10	3.98
D.R.Martyn	57.4	274	5	54.80	2-21	–	4.75
T.M.Moody	466.1	2013	52	38.71	3-25	–	4.31
R.T.Ponting	15	64	1	64.00	1-41	–	4.26
P.R.Reiffel	788.4	3096	106	29.20	4-13	5	3.92
A.Symonds	95.2	437	19	23.00	4-11	1	4.58
S.K.Warne	1264.4	5316	216	24.61	5-33	12	4.20
M.E.Waugh	570.3	2714	82	33.09	5-24	2	4.75
S.R.Waugh	1451.3	6596	191	34.53	4-33	3	4.54
B.E.Young	39	251	1	251.00	1-26	–	6.43

SOUTH AFRICA – BATTING AND FIELDING

	M	I	NO	HS	Runs	Avge	100	50	Ct/St
P.R.Adams	13	6	3	15*	25	8.33	–	–	2
D.M.Benkenstein	16	14	3	69	245	22.27	–	1	1
N.Boje	23	9	3	28	76	12.66	–	–	9
M.V.Boucher	50	38	9	51	397	13.68	–	1	70/3
W.J.Cronje	179	167	29	112	5210	37.75	2	36	68
D.N.Crookes	27	19	4	54	276	18.40	–	1	18
D.J.Cullinan	122	118	13	124	3630	34.57	3	23	58
A.C.Dawson	3	1	–	6	6	6.00	–	–	–
H.H.Dippenaar	2	2	–	26	43	21.50	–	–	–
A.A.Donald	121	30	13	12	83	4.88	–	–	16
S.Elworthy	27	10	5	23	59	11.80	–	–	4
H.H.Gibbs	46	46	2	125	1237	28.11	2	5	16
A.J.Hall	1	1	1	9*	9	–	–	–	1
M.Hayward	5	–	–	–	–	–	–	–	1

SOUTH AFRICA – BATTING AND FIELDING (continued)

	M	I	NO	HS	Runs	Avge	100	50	Ct/St
J.H.Kallis	84	82	13	113*	2840	41.15	5	19	34
G.Kirsten	115	115	11	188*	4066	39.09	8	23	39/1
L.Klusener	73	63	22	103*	1943	47.39	2	11	14
L.J.Koen	5	5	–	28	82	16.40	–	–	2
N.D.McKenzie	4	4	–	37	54	13.50	–	–	1
P.V.Mpitsang	2	1	1	1*	1	–	–	–	–
S.M.Pollock	90	66	22	75	1228	27.90	–	5	27
J.N.Rhodes	169	153	30	121	3856	31.34	1	16	81
M.J.R.Rindel	22	22	1	106	575	27.38	1	2	8
P.C.Strydom	5	4	1	34	46	15.33	–	–	2
P.L.Symcox	80	54	13	61	694	16.92	–	3	23
D.J.Terbrugge	1	1	–	5	5	5.00	–	–	–
H.S.Williams	5	2	1	7	8	8.00	–	–	–

SOUTH AFRICA – BOWLING

	O	R	W	Avge	Best	4wI	R/Over
P.R.Adams	101.4	477	19	25.10	3-26	–	4.69
D.M.Benkenstein	2	13	0	–	–	–	6.50
N.Boje	163.4	743	18	41.27	3-33	–	4.53
W.J.Cronje	850.5	3704	110	33.67	5-32	2	4.35
D.N.Crookes	166.3	819	21	39.00	3-30	–	4.91
D.J.Cullinan	28	120	5	24.00	2-30	–	4.28
A.C.Dawson	28	130	5	26.00	3-36	–	4.64
A.A.Donald	1073	4336	206	21.04	6-23	11	4.04
S.Elworthy	196.4	838	30	27.93	3-21	–	4.26
A.J.Hall	7	38	0	–	–	–	5.42
M.Hayward	42	217	5	43.40	2-39	–	5.16
J.H.Kallis	430.5	1958	64	30.59	5-30	1	4.54
G.Kirsten	5	23	0	–	–	–	4.60
L.Klusener	574.3	2746	104	26.40	6-49	5	4.77
P.V.Mpitsang	10	63	2	31.50	2-49	–	6.30
S.M.Pollock	789.2	2978	132	22.56	6-35	7	3.77
M.J.R.Rindel	45	242	6	40.33	2-15	–	5.37
P.C.Strydom	7	25	1	25.00	1-18	–	3.57
P.L.Symcox	665.1	2762	72	38.36	4-28	1	4.15
D.J.Terbrugge	6	23	0	–	–	–	3.83
H.S.Williams	44	177	8	22.12	3-38	–	4.02

WEST INDIES – BATTING AND FIELDING

	M	I	NO	HS	Runs	Avge	100	50	Ct/St
J.C.Adams	104	84	25	82	1797	30.45	–	12	62/5
C.E.L.Ambrose	170	92	34	31*	624	10.75	–	–	44
K.L.T.Arthurton	105	93	20	84	1904	26.08	–	9	27
H.R.Bryan	15	8	2	11	43	7.16	–	–	4
S.L.Campbell	70	68	–	86	1740	25.58	–	12	16
S.Chanderpaul	92	86	9	150	2645	34.35	2	15	26
P.T.Collins	2	2	2	10*	10	–	–	–	–
C.D.Collymore	3	2	1	13*	16	16.00	–	–	–
M.Dillon	40	20	7	21*	112	8.61	–	–	5
D.Ganga	2	2	–	1	1	0.50	–	–	1
C.H.Gayle	7	7	–	22	58	8.28	–	–	–
A.F.G.Griffith	8	7	1	47	89	14.83	–	–	5
W.W.Hinds	12	12	–	65	302	25.16	–	2	4
C.L.Hooper	182	166	36	113*	4612	35.47	6	26	87
R.D.Jacobs	49	41	6	80*	770	22.00	–	5	68/12
R.D.King	31	18	10	12*	59	7.37	–	–	3
C.B.Lambert	11	11	–	119	368	33.45	1	2	–
B.C.Lara	167	164	15	169	6316	42.38	13	39	75
R.N.Lewis	16	12	3	49	157	17.44	–	–	5
N.C.McGarrell	5	3	1	19	25	12.50	–	–	4
N.A.M.McLean	21	15	1	39	134	9.57	–	–	4

	M	I	NO	HS	Runs	Avge	100	50	Ct/St
J.R.Murray	55	36	6	86	678	22.60	–	5	46/7
N.O.Perry	20	16	8	52*	212	26.50	–	1	4
R.L.Powell	22	21	1	124	556	27.80	1	2	9
D.Ramnarine	2	1	–	2	2	2.00	–	–	–
F.L.Reifer	2	2	–	22	31	15.50	–	–	1
F.A.Rose	15	13	3	24	106	10.60	–	–	3
K.F.Semple	7	6	–	23	64	10.66	–	–	3
P.V.Simmons	143	138	11	122	3675	28.93	5	18	55
P.A.Wallace	26	26	–	103	554	21.30	1	2	8
C.A.Walsh	205	79	33	30	321	6.97	–	–	28
S.C.Williams	57	55	6	105*	1586	32.36	1	12	18

WEST INDIES – BOWLING

	O	R	W	Avge	Best	4wI	R/Over
J.C.Adams	234.2	1149	32	35.90	5-37	1	4.90
C.E.L.Ambrose	1506.5	5307	221	24.01	5-17	10	3.52
K.L.T.Arthurton	230.4	1161	42	27.64	4-31	3	5.03
H.R.Bryan	120.2	518	12	43.16	4-24	1	4.30
S.L.Campbell	31.4	163	8	20.37	4-30	1	5.14
S.Chanderpaul	116	600	14	42.85	3-18	–	5.17
P.T.Collins	15.3	95	0	–	–	–	6.12
C.D.Collymore	28	92	2	46.00	1-27	–	3.28
M.Dillon	342.1	1511	53	28.50	5-51	3	4.41
C.H.Gayle	41.5	187	3	62.33	2-18	–	4.47
W.W.Hinds	13	77	2	38.50	1- 6	–	5.92
C.L.Hooper	1266.1	5548	163	34.03	4-34	3	4.38
R.D.King	265.4	1100	45	24.44	3-24	–	4.14
C.B.Lambert	2	8	0	–	–	–	4.00
B.C.Lara	7.1	46	4	11.50	2- 5	–	6.41
R.N.Lewis	119.1	614	12	51.16	2-40	–	5.15
N.C.McGarrell	34	211	3	70.33	2-43	–	6.20
N.A.M.McLean	155.2	778	23	33.82	3-41	–	5.00
N.O.Perry	147.4	729	18	40.50	3-45	–	4.93
R.L.Powell	14.3	108	0	–	–	–	7.44
D.Ramnarine	16.2	75	2	37.50	2-52	–	4.59
F.A.Rose	116	625	14	44.64	3-25	–	5.38
K.F.Semple	22	121	3	40.33	2-35	–	5.50
P.V.Simmons	646.4	2876	83	34.65	4- 3	2	4.44
C.A.Walsh	1803.4	6917	227	30.47	5- 1	7	3.83
S.C.Williams	4	30	1	30.00	1-30	–	7.50

NEW ZEALAND – BATTING AND FIELDING

	M	I	NO	HS	Runs	Avge	100	50	Ct/St
G.I.Allott	22	7	4	7*	14	4.66	–	–	5
N.J.Astle	101	100	4	120	3401	35.42	7	22	41
M.D.Bailey	1	–	–	–	–	–	–	–	–
M.D.Bell	3	3	–	37	55	18.33	–	–	–
C.E.Bulfin	4	2	1	7*	9	9.00	–	–	1
C.L.Cairns	120	110	10	115	2822	28.22	2	15	36
S.B.Doull	40	26	12	22	172	12.28	–	–	10
C.J.Drum	5	2	2	7*	9	–	–	–	1
S.P.Fleming	119	116	12	116*	3275	31.49	3	19	52
C.Z.Harris	146	123	41	130	2588	31.56	1	9	52
M.N.Hart	12	7	–	16	49	7.00	–	–	7
M.J.Horne	44	42	–	74	840	20.00	–	4	10
G.R.Larsen	121	70	27	37	629	14.62	–	–	23
C.D.McMillan	53	50	1	86	1107	22.59	–	5	16
D.J.Nash	72	45	13	40*	490	15.31	–	–	21
S.B.O'Connor	27	10	5	8	22	4.40	–	–	7
A.C.Parore	133	121	22	108	2823	28.51	1	13	78/21
A.J.Penn	4	2	1	7*	8	8.00	–	–	1
C.M.Spearman	41	41	–	78	746	18.19	–	3	11

NEW ZEALAND – BATTING AND FIELDING (continued)

	M	*I*	*NO*	*HS*	*Runs*	*Avge*	*100*	*50*	*Ct/St*
S.B.Styris	8	5	–	43	74	14.80	–	–	1
A.R.Tait	5	5	2	13*	35	11.66	–	–	–
R.G.Twose	55	52	8	97	1643	37.34	–	13	22
D.L.Vettori	48	29	10	25*	208	10.94	–	–	13
P.J.Wiseman	6	2	1	16	23	23.00	–	–	1
B.A.Young	74	73	5	74	1668	24.52	–	9	28

NEW ZEALAND – BOWLING

	O	*R*	*W*	*Avge*	*Best*	*4wI*	*R/Over*
G.I.Allott	184.4	810	43	18.83	4-35	4	4.38
N.J.Astle	513.1	2328	68	34.23	4-43	1	4.53
C.E.Bulfin	17	109	0	–	–	–	6.41
C.L.Cairns	814.3	3747	115	32.58	5-42	3	4.60
S.B.Doull	278.5	1397	34	41.08	4-25	1	5.01
C.J.Drum	36	261	4	65.25	2-31	–	7.25
S.P.Fleming	4.5	28	1	28.00	1- 8	–	5.79
C.Z.Harris	1114.2	4755	140	33.96	5-42	3	4.26
M.N.Hart	91.2	347	13	26.69	5-22	1	3.79
G.R.Larsen	1061.2	4000	113	35.39	4-24	1	3.76
C.D.McMillan	99.5	501	16	31.31	2-17	–	5.01
D.J.Nash	517.4	2395	54	44.35	4-38	1	4.62
S.B.O'Connor	173.1	998	33	30.24	5-39	2	5.76
A.J.Penn	22.3	172	1	172.00	1-50	–	7.64
C.M.Spearman	0.3	6	0	–	–	–	12.00
S.B.Styris	75.2	345	13	26.53	4-57	1	4.57
A.R.Tait	20	88	3	29.33	2-37	–	4.40
R.G.Twose	45.2	237	4	59.25	2-31	–	5.22
D.L.Vettori	327.3	1510	42	35.95	4-24	2	4.61
P.J.Wiseman	19	95	2	47.50	1-21	–	5.00

INDIA – BATTING AND FIELDING

	M	*I*	*NO*	*HS*	*Runs*	*Avge*	*100*	*50*	*Ct/St*
A.B.Agarkar	45	23	4	30	227	11.94	–	–	16
M.Azharuddin	323	297	53	153*	9110	37.33	7	57	153
R.V.Bharadwaj	9	8	4	41*	136	34.00	–	–	3
N.Chopra	36	23	5	61	301	16.72	–	1	16
S.S.Dighe	8	8	3	36*	85	17.00	–	–	7/1
R.Dravid	116	109	9	153	3737	37.37	7	23	65/1
D.J.Gandhi	3	3	–	30	49	16.33	–	–	–
S.C.Ganguly	133	128	10	183	5061	42.88	11	30	36
Harbhajan Singh	13	5	2	4	9	3.00	–	–	2
A.Jadeja	185	168	33	119	5041	37.34	6	28	56
S.B.Joshi	52	30	10	61*	389	19.45	–	1	16
V.G.Kambli	95	88	20	106	2305	33.89	2	13	14
H.H.Kanitkar	34	27	8	57	340	17.89	–	1	14
S.S.Karim	27	21	2	55	313	16.47	–	1	25/2
A.R.Khurasiya	10	9	–	57	137	15.22	–	1	1
T.Kumaran	2	1	–	8	8	8.00	–	–	1
A.Kumble	191	93	32	26	628	10.29	–	–	69
V.V.S.Laxman	13	12	1	23*	86	7.81	–	–	8
J.J.Martin	8	7	1	39	122	20.33	–	–	5
D.S.Mohanty	41	10	5	4*	10	2.00	–	–	10
N.R.Mongia	139	95	33	69	1268	20.45	–	2	110/43
G.K.Pandey	2	2	1	4*	4	4.00	–	–	–
B.K.V.Prasad	142	57	26	19	201	6.48	–	–	34
M.S.K.Prasad	17	11	2	63	131	14.55	–	1	14/7
S.Ramesh	24	24	1	82	646	28.08	–	6	3
R.Sanghvi	10	2	–	8	8	4.00	–	–	4
V.Shewag	1	1	–	1	1	1.00	–	–	–
L.R.Shukla	3	2	–	13	18	9.00	–	–	1
R.R.Singh	114	94	21	100	2008	27.50	1	9	27

	M	I	NO	HS	Runs	Avge	100	50	Ct/St
J.Srinath	184	97	29	53	767	11.27	–	1	30
S.R.Tendulkar	237	230	22	186*	8768	42.15	24	45	82

INDIA – BOWLING

	O	R	W	Avge	Best	4wI	R/Over
A.B.Agarkar	399.5	2113	77	27.44	4-35	3	5.28
M.Azharuddin	92	479	12	39.91	3-19	–	5.20
R.V.Bharadwaj	58	274	15	18.26	3-34	–	4.72
N.Chopra	277.5	1144	43	26.60	5-21	2	4.11
R.Dravid	19	102	1	102.00	1-21	–	5.36
S.C.Ganguly	360.4	1774	50	35.48	5-16	2	4.91
Harbhajan Singh	115	491	18	27.27	3-36	–	4.26
A.Jadeja	207.4	1090	20	54.50	3- 3	–	5.24
S.B.Joshi	420.4	1806	52	34.73	5- 6	1	4.29
V.G.Kambli	0.4	7	1	7.00	1- 7	–	10.50
H.H.Kanitkar	167.4	803	17	47.23	2-22	–	4.78
T.Kumaran	17	53	4	13.25	3-24	–	3.11
A.Kumble	1705.1	7138	254	28.10	6-12	9	4.18
V.V.S.Laxman	6	32	0	–	–	–	5.33
D.S.Mohanty	302.4	1536	53	28.98	4-56	1	5.07
G.K.Pandey	13	60	0	–	–	–	4.61
B.K.V.Prasad	1195.5	5515	169	32.63	5-27	4	4.61
S.Ramesh	6	38	1	38.00	1-23	–	6.33
R.Sanghvi	83	398	10	39.80	3-29	–	4.79
V.Shewag	3	35	–	–	–	–	11.66
L.R.Shukla	19	94	1	94.00	1-25	–	4.94
R.R.Singh	554.4	2657	67	39.65	5-22	2	4.79
J.Srinath	1610.1	7073	251	28.17	5-23	7	4.39
S.R.Tendulkar	767	3804	79	48.15	5-32	3	4.95

PAKISTAN – BATTING AND FIELDING

	M	I	NO	HS	Runs	Avge	100	50	Ct/St
Aamir Sohail	156	155	5	134	4784	31.89	5	31	50
Abdur Razzaq	42	37	8	70*	752	25.93	–	6	5
Akhtar Sarfraz	4	4	–	25	66	16.50	–	–	–
Aqib Javed	163	51	26	45*	267	10.68	–	–	24
Arshad Khan	24	15	9	20	80	13.33	–	–	4
Asif Mahmood	2	2	–	14	14	7.00	–	–	–
Azam Khan	6	5	–	72	116	23.20	–	1	2
Azhar Mahmood	84	65	14	67	937	18.37	–	3	25
Faisal Iqbal	1	1	–	4	4	4.00	–	–	–
Hasan Raja	16	13	–	77	242	18.61	–	1	1
Ijaz Ahmed	245	228	29	139*	6427	32.29	10	36	90
Imran Abbas	2	2	–	28	29	14.50	–	–	1
Imran Nazir	2	2	–	4	6	3.00	–	–	2
Inzamam-ul-Haq	209	198	25	137*	6572	37.98	6	47	61
Kabir Khan	7	3	2	5	7	7.00	–	–	1
Mohammad Akram	15	8	6	7*	13	6.50	–	–	5
Mohammad Wasim	23	23	2	76	499	23.76	–	3	8
Moin Khan	160	136	32	69*	2454	23.59	–	7	159/58
Mushtaq Ahmed	131	69	31	26	343	9.02	–	–	28
Saeed Anwar	200	197	15	194	7080	38.90	17	33	39
Salim Elahi	18	18	1	102*	509	29.94	1	3	4
Salim Malik	283	256	38	102	7171	32.89	5	47	82
Saqlain Mushtaq	123	74	26	37*	611	12.72	–	–	32
Shabbir Ahmed	3	–	–	–	–	–	–	–	2
Shahid Afridi	100	96	2	109	2194	23.34	2	11	36
Shahid Nazir	17	8	6	8	27	135.00	–	–	3
Shoaib Akhtar	37	17	14	36	65	21.66	–	–	7
Shoaib Malik	6	4	1	12	20	6.66	–	–	3
Wajahatullah Wasti	14	14	–	84	339	24.21	–	1	4
Waqar Younis	182	93	35	37	650	11.20	–	–	21

PAKISTAN – BATTING AND FIELDING (continued)

	M	I	NO	HS	Runs	Avge	100	50	Ct/St
Wasim Akram	294	234	40	86	3120	16.08	–	6	82
Yasir Arafat	1	1	–	6	6	6.00	–	–	–
Younis Khan	3	3	–	46	85	28.33	–	–	1
Yousuf Youhana	45	41	6	104*	1372	39.20	2	9	14

PAKISTAN – BOWLING

	O	R	W	Avge	Best	4wI	R/Over
Aamir Sohail	806	3702	85	43.55	4-22	1	4.59
Abdur Razzaq	315	1373	58	23.67	5-31	4	4.35
Aqib Javed	1335.3	5721	182	31.43	7-37	6	4.28
Arshad Khan	194	803	19	42.26	3-22	–	4.13
Azhar Mahmood	636.3	2801	82	34.15	6-18	4	4.40
Faisal Iqbal	2	16	0	–	–	–	8.00
Ijaz Ahmed	106.1	476	5	95.20	2-31	–	4.48
Inzamam-ul-Haq	6.4	52	2	26.00	1- 4	–	7.80
Kabir Khan	39.5	197	7	28.14	2-23	–	4.94
Mohammad Akram	100	478	13	36.76	2-28	–	4.78
Mushtaq Ahmed	1129.5	4873	147	33.14	5-36	3	4.31
Saeed Anwar	36.2	176	5	35.20	2- 9	–	4.84
Salim Malik	584.1	2959	89	33.24	5-35	2	5.06
Saqlain Mushtaq	1076.3	4593	225	20.41	5-29	14	4.26
Shabbir Ahmed	20	90	5	18.00	3-52	–	4.50
Shahid Afridi	652.2	3094	64	48.34	3-33	–	4.74
Shahid Nazir	135	649	19	34.15	3-14	–	4.80
Shoaib Akhtar	307.2	1386	61	22.72	4-37	1	4.50
Shoaib Malik	32.4	142	7	20.28	2-30	–	4.34
Wajahatullah Wasti	5.1	40	3	13.33	3-36	–	7.73
Waqar Younis	1495.4	6882	292	23.56	6-26	20	4.60
Wasim Akram	2524.1	9749	414	23.54	5-15	21	3.86
Yasir Arafat	5	28	1	28.00	1-28	–	5.60

SRI LANKA – BATTING AND FIELDING

	M	I	NO	HS	Runs	Avge	100	50	Ct/St
R.P.Arnold	20	19	4	103	561	37.40	1	2	5
M.S.Atapattu	92	90	10	132*	2790	34.87	3	21	33
H.Boteju	2	2	1	2	3	3.00	–	–	1
U.D.U.Chandana	69	53	7	50	725	15.76	–	1	39
S.I.de Saram	7	6	1	24*	73	14.60	–	–	4
K.S.C.de Silva	37	18	12	13*	38	6.33	–	–	12
P.A.de Silva	264	256	25	145	8193	35.46	11	56	82
H.D.P.K.Dharmasena	94	57	25	69*	849	26.53	–	4	26
T.M.Dilshan	8	8	2	53	192	32.00	–	1	3
I.S.Gallage	1	1	–	14	14	14.00	–	–	–
D.A.Gunawardena	13	13	–	75	258	19.84	–	2	1
U.C.Hathurusinghe	35	33	1	66	669	20.90	–	4	6
S.T.Jayasuriya	201	193	8	151*	5252	28.38	7	35	68
D.P.M.deS.Jayawardena	42	40	2	120	921	24.23	2	4	13
R.S.Kalpage	86	69	28	51	844	20.58	–	1	33
R.S.Kaluwitharana	135	130	9	100*	2572	21.25	1	17	93/61
R.S.Mahanama	213	198	23	119*	5162	29.49	4	35	109
M.Muralitharan	132	62	27	18	185	5.28	–	–	61
A.S.A.Perera	11	6	1	26	53	10.60	–	–	–
R.L.Perera	2	2	–	3	3	1.50	–	–	–
K.R.Pushpakumara	31	9	5	14*	36	9.00	–	–	8
A.Ranatunga	269	255	47	131*	7454	35.83	4	49	63
T.T.Samaraweera	6	4	–	20	39	9.75	–	–	–
L.P.C.Silva	7	5	–	55	85	17.00	–	1	1
H.P.Tillekeratne	181	154	38	104	3439	29.64	2	12	79/6
K.E.A.Upashantha	8	6	1	15	44	8.80	–	–	2
W.P.U.C.J.Vaas	129	82	27	34	696	12.65	–	–	22

	M	I	NO	HS	Runs	Avge	100	50	Ct/St
G.P.Wickremasinghe	126	59	23	21*	305	8.47	–	–	22
D.N.T.Zoysa	19	11	5	22	45	7.50	–	–	1

SRI LANKA – BOWLING

LOI	O	R	W	Avge	Best	4wI	R/Over
R.P.Arnold	83.4	400	9	44.44	2-32	–	4.78
M.S.Atapattu	8.3	41	0	–	–	–	4.82
H.Boteju	17	113	0	–	–	–	6.64
U.D.U.Chandana	434.1	2060	69	29.85	4-31	2	4.74
K.S.C.de Silva	263.5	1289	50	25.78	3-18	–	4.88
P.A.de Silva	691.5	3382	85	39.78	4-45	1	4.88
H.D.P.K.Dharmasena	783	3498	92	38.02	4-37	1	4.46
I.S.Gallage	8	36	0	–	–	–	4.50
U.C.Hathurusinghe	159	709	14	50.64	4-57	1	4.45
S.T.Jayasuriya	1242.1	6039	178	33.92	6-29	8	4.86
D.P.M.deS.Jayawardena	77	425	6	70.83	2-56	–	5.51
R.S.Kalpage	660	2975	73	40.75	4-36	2	4.50
R.S.Mahanama	0.2	7	0	–	–	–	21.21
M.Muralitharan	1191.1	4964	183	27.12	5-23	6	4.16
A.S.A.Perera	72.3	388	10	38.80	2-25	–	5.35
R.L.Perera	20	126	3	42.00	3-55	–	6.30
K.R.Pushpakumara	238.2	1182	24	49.25	3-25	–	4.95
A.Ranatunga	785	3757	79	47.55	4-14	1	4.78
T.T.Samaraweera	56	265	6	44.16	3-34	–	4.73
H.P.Tillekeratne	30	141	6	23.50	1- 3	–	4.70
K.E.A.Upashantha	67	343	7	49.00	2-24	–	5.11
W.P.U.C.J.Vaas	1043.4	4433	158	28.05	4-20	3	4.24
G.P.Wickremasinghe	909	4049	103	39.31	4-48	1	4.45
D.N.T.Zoysa	149.2	615	19	32.36	2-22	–	4.11

ZIMBABWE – BATTING AND FIELDING

	M	I	NO	HS	Runs	Avge	100	50	Ct/St
A.M.Blignaut	6	6	1	27	50	10.00	–	–	1
E.A.Brandes	59	41	10	55	404	13.03	–	2	11
G.B.Brent	15	12	4	24	62	7.75	–	–	4
A.D.R.Campbell	126	122	11	131*	3106	27.98	3	17	47
S.V.Carlisle	34	33	4	121*	620	21.37	1	–	13
C.N.Evans	49	43	5	96*	667	17.55	–	1	11
A.Flower	134	131	9	115*	3963	32.48	1	34	99/28
G.W.Flower	121	119	5	140	3783	33.18	3	25	42
M.W.Goodwin	60	59	2	111	1505	26.40	1	7	20
A.G.Huckle	19	8	4	5*	9	2.25	–	–	7
N.C.Johnson	38	38	1	132*	1380	37.29	4	8	16
T.N.Madondo	6	6	1	29	51	10.20	–	–	–
M.Mbangwa	21	9	3	11	24	4.00	–	–	2
D.T.Mutendera	5	4	2	10	20	10.00	–	–	1
M.Nkala	1	–	–	–	–	–	–	–	–
H.K.Olonga	28	15	7	11	36	4.50	–	–	6
G.J.Rennie	25	22	4	76	404	22.44	–	2	11
J.A.Rennie	43	27	12	27	201	13.40	–	–	12
B.C.Strang	20	12	4	15	51	6.37	–	–	11
P.A.Strang	81	67	22	47	1015	22.55	–	–	24
H.H.Streak	89	76	29	59	998	21.23	–	1	20
D.P.Viljoen	16	15	3	36	159	13.25	–	–	4
A.R.Whittall	63	35	13	29	168	7.63	–	–	21
G.J.Whittall	94	92	14	83	1806	23.15	–	9	22
C.B.Wishart	43	38	2	102	668	18.55	1	1	14

ZIMBABWE – BOWLING

	O	R	W	Avge	Best	4wI	R/Over
A.M.Blignaut	32.4	175	4	43.75	2-35	–	5.35
E.A.Brandes	471.2	2265	70	32.35	5-28	3	4.80

ZIMBABWE – BOWLING (continued)

	O	R	W	Avge	Best	4wI	R/Over
G.B.Brent	121.2	626	19	32.94	4-53	1	5.15
A.D.R.Campbell	63.3	295	10	29.50	2-20	–	4.64
C.N.Evans	154.4	795	19	41.84	3-11	–	5.14
A.Flower	5	23	0	–	–	–	4.60
G.W.Flower	397.4	1862	48	38.79	4-32	1	4.68
M.W.Goodwin	39.2	201	4	50.25	1-12	–	5.11
A.G.Huckle	143	662	7	94.57	2-27	–	4.62
N.C.Johnson	207.3	1030	29	35.51	4-42	1	4.96
M.Mbangwa	165.1	850	9	94.44	2-24	–	5.14
D.T.Mutendera	33	170	2	85.00	1-42	–	5.15
M.Nkala	5	32	1	32.00	1-32	–	6.40
H.K.Olonga	201.1	1149	41	28.02	6-19	3	5.71
J.A.Rennie	317.3	1517	34	44.61	3-27	–	4.77
B.C.Strang	154.2	646	26	24.84	6-20	2	4.18
P.A.Strang	627.3	2657	83	32.01	5-21	4	4.23
H.H.Streak	741.5	3262	108	30.20	5-32	4	4.39
D.P.Viljoen	62	261	10	26.10	3-20	–	4.20
A.R.Whittall	514.1	2250	45	50.00	3-23	–	4.37
G.J.Whittall	506.3	2545	74	34.39	4-35	1	5.02
C.B.Wishart	2	12	0	–	–	–	6.00

BANGLADESH – BATTING AND FIELDING

	M	I	NO	HS	Runs	Avge	100	50	Ct/St
Ahmed Kamal	1	1	–	11	11	11.00	–	–	–
Akram Khan	31	31	2	65	680	23.44	–	4	6
Al Shahriar	4	4	1	62*	99	33.00	–	1	–
Aminul Islam	33	33	5	70	677	24.17	–	3	12
Aminul Islam Bhola	1	1	1	1*	1	–	–	–	–
Enamul Huq	22	19	4	23	167	11.13	–	–	5
Faruque Ahmed	7	7	–	57	105	15.00	–	1	2
Habibul Bashar	10	10	–	70	138	13.80	–	1	4
Hasibul Hussain	25	20	2	21*	145	8.05	–	–	6
Jahangir Alam	3	3	–	3	4	1.33	–	–	–/1
Javed Omer	7	7	–	25	95	13.57	–	–	–
Khaled Mahmud	18	17	–	47	241	14.17	–	–	2
Khaled Masud	27	25	6	53*	253	13.31	–	1	20/4
Mahbubur Rahman	1	1	–	3	3	3.00	–	–	–
Mehrab Hossain	10	10	–	101	327	32.70	1	2	3
Minhazul Abedin	27	26	2	68*	453	18.87	–	2	2
Mohammed Rafique	18	18	–	77	243	13.50	–	1	3
Monjurul Islam	7	5	5	6*	14	–	–	–	2
Naimur Rahman	17	16	1	47	281	18.73	–	–	6
Neeyamur Rashid	2	2	1	4*	5	5.00	–	–	1
Shafiuddin Ahmed	10	9	5	11	29	7.25	–	–	–
Shahriar Hossain	15	15	–	95	347	23.13	–	2	5

BANGLADESH – BOWLING

	O	R	W	Avge	Best	4wI	R/Over
Ahmed Kamal	5	39	1	39.00	1-39	–	7.80
Akram Khan	19.3	138	0	–	–	–	7.07
Aminul Islam	65.4	389	7	55.57	3-57	–	5.92
Aminul Islam Bhola	5	33	1	33.00	1-33	–	6.60
Enamul Huq	148.2	755	12	62.91	2-40	–	5.09
Habibul Bashar	16	57	1	57.00	1-31	–	3.56
Hasibul Hussain	188.1	1062	27	39.33	4-56	1	5.64
Khaled Mahmud	142.3	649	19	34.15	3-31	–	4.55
Minhazul Abedin	91	511	13	39.30	2-39	–	5.61
Mohammed Rafique	145.1	729	17	42.88	3-55	–	5.02
Monjurul Islam	47	238	6	39.66	2-33	–	5.06
Naimur Rahman	98.4	472	7	67.42	2-51	–	4.78

	O	R	W	Avge	Best	4wI	R/Over
Neeyamur Rashid	13	66	1	66.00	1-46	–	5.07
Shafiuddin Ahmed	73.3	361	11	32.81	3-42	–	4.91

KENYA – BATTING AND FIELDING

LOIs	M	I	NO	HS	Runs	Avge	100	50	Ct/St
J.Ababu	2	1	–	11	11	11.00	–	–	1
J.O.Angara	7	3	1	6	12	6.00	–	–	–
D.N.Chudasama	20	19	–	122	435	22.89	1	1	5
S.K.Gupta	9	9	–	41	120	13.33	–	–	–
J.K.Kamande	3	1	1	2*	2	–	–	–	–
A.Y.Karim	30	22	4	53	229	12.72	–	1	5
H.S.Modi	31	26	2	78*	596	24.83	–	4	7
P.Ochieng	1	1	1	0*	–	–	–	–	1
T.M.Odoyo	32	29	4	41	474	18.96	–	–	9
M.O.Odumbe	33	31	2	83	742	25.58	–	6	6
K.O.Otieno	33	32	1	144	857	27.64	2	3	13/8
R.D.Shah	16	16	–	71	539	33.68	–	5	6
M.Sheikh	20	14	4	15*	68	6.80	–	–	7
A.O.Suji	18	16	2	67	185	13.21	–	1	7
M.A.Suji	31	23	15	15	66	8.25	–	–	8
S.O.Tikolo	33	31	1	106*	963	32.10	1	8	16
A.V.Vadher	18	16	6	73*	278	27.80	–	2	6

KENYA – BOWLING

	O	R	W	Avge	Best	4wI	R/Over
J.Ababu	10	41	1	41.00	1-26	–	4.10
J.Angara	47	287	5	57.40	2-50	–	6.10
J.K.Kamande	17	84	1	84.00	1-46	–	4.94
A.Y.Karim	237.5	1043	24	43.45	5-33	1	4.38
H.S.Modi	2	14	0	–	–	–	7.00
P.Ochieng	4	10	1	10.00	1-10	–	2.50
T.M.Odoyo	234.2	1139	30	37.96	3-25	–	4.86
M.O.Odumbe	210.5	999	26	38.42	3-14	–	4.73
R.D.Shah	8	62	0	–	–	–	7.75
M.Sheikh	125.4	596	19	31.36	4-36	1	4.74
A.O.Suji	84.2	394	7	56.28	2-24	–	4.67
M.A.Suji	235	1078	22	49.00	4-24	1	4.58
S.O.Tikolo	151.2	766	21	36.47	3-22	–	5.06

SCOTLAND – BATTING AND FIELDING

	M	I	NO	HS	Runs	Avge	100	50	Ct/St
M.J.D.Allingham	3	3	–	6	11	3.66	–	–	1
Asim Butt	5	4	–	11	23	5.75	–	–	–
J.A.R.Blain	5	5	1	9	15	3.75	–	–	1
J.E.Brinkley	5	5	–	23	52	10.40	–	–	1
A.G.Davies	5	5	1	32	83	20.75	–	–	2/1
N.R.Dyer	5	4	3	2*	3	3.00	–	–	2
G.M.Hamilton	5	5	1	76	217	54.25	–	2	1
B.M.W.Patterson	3	3	–	10	10	3.33	–	–	–
I.L.Philip	3	3	–	17	20	6.66	–	–	4
G.Salmond	5	5	–	31	57	11.40	–	–	1
M.J.Smith	5	5	–	13	19	3.80	–	–	–
I.M.Stanger	4	4	–	27	47	11.75	–	–	2
J.G.Williamson	2	2	–	10	11	5.50	–	–	–

SCOTLAND – BOWLING

	O	R	W	Avge	Best	4wI	R/Over
Asim Butt	37	148	4	37.00	2-24	–	4.00
J.A.R.Blain	37.1	210	10	21.00	4-37	1	5.64
J.E.Brinkley	28	117	2	58.50	1-29	–	4.17
N.R.Dyer	26	117	5	23.40	2-26	–	4.50
G.M.Hamilton	35.4	149	3	49.66	2-36	–	4.17
I.M.Stanger	9	56	0	–	–	–	6.22

TEST CAREER RECORDS

These records, complete to 24 February 2000 prior to the start of Test No. 1484, include all players registered for county cricket in 2000 at the time of going to press, plus those who have played Test cricket after 1 October 1998.

ENGLAND – BATTING AND FIELDING

	M	*I*	*NO*	*HS*	*Runs*	*Avge*	*100*	*50*	*Ct/St*
C.J.Adams	5	8	–	31	104	13.00	–	–	6
M.A.Atherton	95	175	6	185*	6403	37.88	13	39	62
R.J.Bailey	4	8	–	43	119	14.87	–	–	–
K.J.Barnett	4	7	–	80	207	29.57	–	2	1
M.P.Bicknell	2	4	–	14	26	6.50	–	–	–
R.J.Blakey	2	4	–	6	7	1.75	–	–	2
S.J.E.Brown	1	2	1	10*	11	11.00	–	–	1
M.A.Butcher	27	51	1	116	1253	25.06	2	4	21
A.R.Caddick	30	47	5	48	522	12.42	–	–	14
D.G.Cork	27	42	6	59	634	17.61	–	2	13
J.P.Crawley	29	47	5	156*	1329	31.64	3	7	26
R.D.B.Croft	15	24	6	37*	295	16.38	–	–	8
P.A.J.DeFreitas	44	68	5	88	934	14.82	–	4	14
M.A.Ealham	8	13	3	53*	210	21.00	–	2	4
N.H.Fairbrother	10	15	1	83	219	15.64	–	1	4
A.Flintoff	6	9	–	42	172	19.11	–	–	3
A.R.C.Fraser	46	67	15	32	388	7.46	–	–	9
J.E.R.Gallian	3	6	–	28	74	12.33	–	–	1
E.S.H.Giddins	1	2	1	0*	0	0.00	–	–	–
A.F.Giles	1	2	1	16*	17	17.00	–	–	–
D.Gough	36	54	9	65	532	11.82	–	2	9
A.Habib	2	3	–	19	26	8.66	–	–	–
G.M.Hamilton	1	2	–	0	0	0.00	–	–	–
D.W.Headley	15	26	4	31	186	8.45	–	–	7
W.K.Hegg	2	4	–	15	30	7.50	–	–	8
G.A.Hick	54	94	6	178	3005	34.14	5	17	76
A.J.Hollioake	4	6	–	45	65	10.83	–	–	4
B.C.Hollioake	2	4	–	28	44	11.00	–	–	2
N.Hussain	47	84	8	207	2974	39.13	8	13	36
R.K.Illingworth	9	14	7	28	128	18.28	–	–	5
M.C.Ilott	5	6	2	15	28	7.00	–	–	–
R.C.Irani	3	5	–	41	86	17.20	–	–	2
S.P.James	2	4	–	36	71	17.75	–	–	–
P.W.Jarvis	9	15	2	29*	132	10.15	–	–	2
N.V.Knight	12	21	–	113	585	27.85	1	4	21
M.N.Lathwell	2	4	–	33	78	19.50	–	–	–
C.C.Lewis	32	51	3	117	1105	23.02	1	4	25
M.J.McCague	3	5	–	11	21	4.20	–	–	1
D.L.Maddy	3	4	–	24	46	11.50	–	–	4
D.E.Malcolm	40	58	19	29	236	6.05	–	–	7
P.J.Martin	8	13	–	29	115	8.84	–	–	6
M.P.Maynard	4	8	–	35	87	10.87	–	–	3
J.E.Morris	3	5	2	32	71	23.66	–	–	3
A.D.Mullally	18	26	4	24	127	5.77	–	–	6
T.A.Munton	2	2	1	25*	25	25.00	–	–	–
M.M.Patel	2	2	–	27	45	22.50	–	–	2
M.R.Ramprakash	38	67	6	154	1701	27.88	1	10	28
C.M.W.Read	3	4	–	37	38	9.50	–	–	10/1
S.J.Rhodes	11	17	5	65*	294	24.50	–	1	46/3
R.C.Russell	54	86	16	128*	1897	27.10	2	6	153/12
I.D.K.Salisbury	12	22	2	50	284	14.20	–	1	5

ENGLAND – BATTING AND FIELDING (continued)

	M	I	NO	HS	Runs	Avge	100	50	Ct/St
C.E.W.Silverwood	5	6	3	7*	19	6.33	–	–	2
A.M.Smith	1	2	1	4*	4	4.00	–	–	–
R.A.Smith	62	112	15	175	4236	43.67	9	28	39
J.P.Stephenson	1	2	–	25	36	18.00	–	–	–
A.J.Stewart	95	172	12	190	6525	40.78	12	35	172/8
P.M.Such	11	16	5	14*	67	6.09	–	–	4
J.P.Taylor	2	4	2	17*	34	17.00	–	–	–
G.P.Thorpe	57	105	13	138	3599	39.11	6	24	53
A.J.Tudor	3	6	3	99*	166	55.33	–	1	–
P.C.R.Tufnell	41	57	28	22*	146	5.03	–	–	12
M.P.Vaughan	4	7	–	69	204	29.14	–	1	6
S.L.Watkin	3	5	–	13	25	5.00	–	–	1
M.Watkinson	4	6	1	82*	167	33.40	–	1	1
A.P.Wells	1	2	1	3*	3	3.00	–	–	–
C.White	8	12	–	51	166	13.83	–	1	3

ENGLAND – BOWLING

	O	R	W	Avge	Best	5wI	10wM
C.J.Adams	20	59	1	59.00	1- 42	–	–
M.A.Atherton	68	302	2	151.00	1- 20	–	–
K.J.Barnett	6	32	0				
M.P.Bicknell	87	263	4	65.75	3- 99	–	–
S.J.E.Brown	33	138	2	69.00	1- 60	–	–
M.A.Butcher	55.2	169	3	56.33	2- 32	–	–
A.R.Caddick	1127.3	3274	110	29.76	7- 46	7	–
D.G.Cork	993.5	3118	98	31.81	7- 43	5	–
R.D.B.Croft	579.5	1380	36	38.33	5- 95	1	–
P.A.J.DeFreitas	1639.4	4700	140	33.57	7- 70	4	–
M.A.Ealham	176.4	488	17	28.70	4- 21	–	–
N.H.Fairbrother	2	9	0				
A.Flintoff	101.5	302	6	50.33	2- 31	–	–
A.R.C.Fraser	1812.4	4836	177	27.32	8- 53	13	2
J.E.R.Gallian	14	62	0				
E.S.H.Giddins	26	79	4	19.75	3- 38	–	–
A.F.Giles	36	106	1	106.00	1-106	–	–
D.Gough	1287	4105	139	29.53	6- 42	6	–
G.M.Hamilton	15	63	0				
D.W.Headley	504.2	1671	60	27.85	6- 60	1	–
G.A.Hick	497.3	1256	22	57.09	4-126	–	–
A.J.Hollioake	24	67	2	33.50	2- 31	–	–
B.C.Hollioake	42	199	4	49.75	2-105	–	–
N.Hussain	5	15	0				
R.K.Illingworth	247.3	615	19	32.36	4- 96	–	–
M.C.Ilott	173.4	542	12	45.16	3- 48	–	–
R.C.Irani	32	112	3	37.33	1- 22	–	–
P.W.Jarvis	318.4	965	21	45.95	4-107	–	–
C.C.Lewis	1142	3490	93	37.52	6-111	3	–
M.J.McCague	98.5	390	6	65.00	4-121	–	–
D.L.Maddy	14	40	0				
D.E.Malcolm	1413.2	4748	128	37.09	9- 57	5	2
P.J.Martin	242	580	17	34.11	4- 60	–	–
A.D.Mullally	723.4	1713	56	30.58	5-105	1	–
T.A.Munton	67.3	200	4	50.00	2- 22	–	–
M.M.Patel	46	180	1	180.00	1-101	–	–
M.R.Ramprakash	140.1	445	4	111.25	1- 2	–	–
I.D.K.Salisbury	346.2	1346	19	70.84	4-163	–	–
C.E.W.Silverwood	134	415	11	37.72	5- 91	1	–

ENGLAND – BOWLING (continued)

	O	R	W	Avge	Best	5wI	10wM
A.M.Smith	23	89	0				
R.A.Smith	4	6	0				
A.J.Stewart	3.2	13	0				
P.M.Such	520.4	1242	37	33.56	6-67	2	–
J.P.Taylor	48	156	3	52.00	1-18	–	–
G.P.Thorpe	23	37	0				
A.J.Tudor	58.2	239	8	29.87	4-89	–	–
P.C.R.Tufnell	1842.2	4386	120	36.55	7-47	5	2
M.P.Vaughan	18	73	0				
S.L.Watkin	89	305	11	27.72	4-65	–	–
M.Watkinson	112	348	10	34.80	3-64	–	–
C.White	135.1	452	11	41.09	3-18	–	–

AUSTRALIA – BATTING AND FIELDING

	M	I	NO	HS	Runs	Avge	100	50	Ct/St
M.G.Bevan	18	30	3	91	785	29.07	–	6	8
G.S.Blewett	44	75	4	214	2502	35.23	4	15	42
A.C.Dale	2	3	–	5	6	2.00	–	–	–
M.T.G.Elliott	20	34	1	199	1171	35.48	3	4	13
D.W.Fleming	19	18	3	71*	299	19.93	–	2	9
A.C.Gilchrist	6	9	2	149*	485	69.28	1	3	21/2
J.N.Gillespie	14	22	9	41	233	17.92	–	–	4
M.L.Hayden	7	12	0	125	261	21.75	1	–	8
I.A.Healy	119	182	23	161*	4356	27.39	4	22	366/29
M.S.Kasprowicz	16	21	4	25	214	12.58	–	–	6
J.L.Langer	30	49	1	223	1925	40.10	6	9	20
S.G.Law	1	1	1	54*	54	–	–	1	1
B.Lee	2	1	–	27	27	27.00	–	–	–
D.S.Lehmann	5	8	–	98	228	28.50	–	2	3
S.C.G.MacGill	12	18	1	43	164	9.64	–	–	8
G.D.McGrath	59	72	23	39	286	5.83	–	–	19
C.R.Miller	11	14	2	43	80	6.66	–	–	4
S.A.Muller	2	2	2	6*	6	–	–	–	2
M.J.Nicholson	1	2	–	9	14	7.00	–	–	–
R.T.Ponting	34	53	6	197	2233	47.51	7	10	35
G.R.Robertson	4	7	–	57	140	20.00	–	1	1
M.J.Slater	59	104	5	219	4426	44.70	13	16	28
M.A.Taylor	104	186	13	334*	7525	43.49	19	40	157
S.K.Warne	81	113	12	86	1577	15.61	–	4	60
M.E.Waugh	100	165	11	153*	6403	41.57	17	37	129
S.R.Waugh	125	198	36	200	8159	50.36	21	42	88

AUSTRALIA – BOWLING

	O	R	W	Avge	Best	5wI	10wM
M.G.Bevan	214.1	703	29	24.24	6- 82	1	1
G.S.Blewett	228.2	681	13	52.38	2- 9	–	–
A.C.Dale	58	187	6	31.16	3- 71	–	–
M.T.G.Elliott	2	4	0				
D.W.Fleming	658.1	1843	74	24.90	5- 30	3	–
J.N.Gillespie	371	1108	50	22.16	7- 37	3	–
M.S.Kasprowicz	508.2	1561	45	34.68	7- 36	2	–
S.G.Law	3	9	0				
B.Lee	69	184	13	14.15	5- 47	1	–
D.S.Lehmann	17	45	2	22.50	1- 6	–	–
S.C.G.MacGill	468.3	1376	59	23.32	7- 50	3	1
G.D.McGrath	2361.5	6189	276	22.42	8- 38	17	2
C.R.Miller	371.3	928	31	29.93	4- 62	–	–

AUSTRALIA – BOWLING (continued)

	O	R	W	Avge	Best	5wI	10wM
S.A.Muller	58	258	7	36.85	3- 68	–	–
M.J.Nicholson	25	115	4	28.75	3- 56	–	–
R.T.Ponting	36.5	89	4	22.25	1- 0	–	–
G.R.Robertson	149.4	515	13	39.61	4- 72	–	–
M.J.Slater	2.1	6	1	6.00	1- 4	–	–
M.A.Taylor	7	26	1	26.00	1- 11	–	–
S.K.Warne	3787.3	9091	351	25.90	8- 71	16	4
M.E.Waugh	677	1984	50	39.68	5- 40	1	–
S.R.Waugh	1188.5	3161	89	35.51	5- 28	3	–

SOUTH AFRICA – BATTING AND FIELDING

	M	I	NO	HS	Runs	Avge	100	50	Ct/St
P.R.Adams	30	33	10	29	146	6.34	–	–	20
A.M.Bacher	19	33	1	96	833	26.03	–	5	10
M.V.Boucher	26	32	4	125	902	32.21	3	4	107/2
W.J.Cronje	66	108	9	135	3689	37.26	6	23	32
D.J.Cullinan	55	89	8	275*	3520	43.45	10	16	47
H.H.Dippenaar	2	2	–	33	53	26.50	–	–	1
A.A.Donald	60	76	27	34	539	11.00	–	–	16
S.Elworthy	2	3	1	48	61	30.50	–	–	–
H.H.Gibbs	19	32	1	211*	1001	32.29	2	3	11
M.Hayward	3	2	2	10*	10	–	–	–	–
J.H.Kallis	34	53	6	148*	1979	42.10	6	10	28
G.Kirsten	58	102	9	275	3872	41.63	10	19	46
L.Klusener	27	35	6	174	1018	35.10	2	4	16
S.M.Pollock	40	58	12	92	1438	31.26	–	8	21
J.N.Rhodes	49	74	8	117	2337	35.40	3	15	30
P.C.Strydom	1	1	–	30	30	30.00	–	–	–
P.L.Symcox	20	27	1	108	741	28.50	1	4	5
D.J.Terbrugge	4	5	5	4*	14	–	–	–	2

SOUTH AFRICA – BOWLING

	O	R	W	Avge	Best	5wI	10wM
P.R.Adams	990.1	2640	90	29.33	6- 55	1	–
A.M.Bacher	1	4	0				
W.J.Cronje	599.2	1205	37	32.56	3- 14	–	–
D.J.Cullinan	16	54	1	54.00	1- 32	–	–
A.A.Donald	2202.4	6282	290	21.66	8- 71	20	3
S.Elworthy	86	238	9	26.44	4- 66	–	–
M.Hayward	85.2	265	10	26.50	4- 75	–	–
J.H.Kallis	675.2	1632	56	29.14	5- 90	1	–
G.Kirsten	54.1	135	2	67.50	1- 0	–	–
L.Klusener	750.1	2084	57	36.56	8- 64	1	–
S.M.Pollock	1472.4	3425	166	20.63	7- 87	10	–
J.N.Rhodes	2	5	0				
P.C.Strydom	6	27	0				
P.L.Symcox	593.3	1603	37	43.32	4- 69	–	–
D.J.Terbrugge	100	253	9	28.11	3- 27	–	–

WEST INDIES – BATTING AND FIELDING

	M	I	NO	HS	Runs	Avge	100	50	Ct/St
J.C.Adams	39	63	12	208*	2326	45.60	5	11	36
C.E.L.Ambrose	88	129	27	53	1297	12.71	–	1	16
S.L.Campbell	36	63	3	208	2184	36.40	4	12	24
S.Chanderpaul	37	62	7	137*	2234	40.61	2	18	15
P.T.Collins	3	5	–	13	14	2.80	–	–	–
C.D.Collymore	1	2	1	11*	17	17.00	–	–	–

WEST INDIES – BATTING AND FIELDING (continued)

	M	I	NO	HS	Runs	Avge	100	50	Ct/St
M.Dillon	7	13	1	36	84	7.00	–	–	2
D.Ganga	4	6	–	28	75	12.50	–	–	3
O.D.Gibson	2	4	–	37	93	23.25	–	–	–
A.F.G.Griffith	5	10	–	114	358	35.80	1	2	1
R.I.C.Holder	11	17	2	91	380	25.33	–	2	9
C.L.Hooper	80	136	13	178*	4153	33.76	9	18	94
R.D.Jacobs	11	21	4	78	506	29.76	–	3	39/2
D.R.E.Joseph	4	7	–	50	141	20.14	–	1	10
R.D.King	3	6	2	4*	7	1.75	–	–	1
C.B.Lambert	5	9	–	104	284	31.55	1	1	8
B.C.Lara	65	112	4	375	5573	51.60	13	29	86
R.N.Lewis	3	6	–	12	26	4.33	–	–	–
N.A.M.McLean	8	12	1	39	187	17.00	–	–	3
J.R.Murray	31	42	4	101*	917	24.13	1	3	96/3
N.O.Perry	4	7	1	26	74	12.33	–	–	1
R.L.Powell	1	2	–	30	30	15.00	–	–	1
S.Ragoonath	2	4	1	9	13	4.33	–	–	–
D.Ramnarine	3	4	–	19	27	6.75	–	–	3
F.L.Reifer	4	8	–	29	63	7.87	–	–	4
L.A.Roberts	1	1	–	0	0	0.00	–	–	–
F.A.Rose	13	18	2	34	142	8.87	–	–	2
P.A.Wallace	7	13	–	92	279	21.46	–	2	9
C.A.Walsh	112	153	52	30*	834	8.25	–	–	26
S.C.Williams	28	47	2	128	1092	24.26	1	3	26

WEST INDIES – BOWLING

	O	R	W	Avge	Best	5wI	10wM
J.C.Adams	290.5	845	19	44.47	5- 17	1	–
C.E.L.Ambrose	3307.1	7865	369	21.31	8- 45	22	3
S.Chanderpaul	225	669	6	111.50	1- 2	–	–
P.T.Collins	113	362	8	45.25	3- 79	–	–
C.D.Collymore	41	109	1	109.00	1- 49	–	–
M.Dillon	235	742	21	35.33	5-111	1	–
O.D.Gibson	78.4	275	3	91.66	2- 81	–	–
C.L.Hooper	1732.1	4372	93	47.01	5- 26	4	–
R.D.King	90.2	307	8	38.37	4- 81	–	–
C.B.Lambert	1.4	5	1	5.00	1- 4	–	–
B.C.Lara	10	28	0				
R.N.Lewis	97.3	318	1	318.00	1- 67	–	–
N.A.M.McLean	207.2	660	17	38.82	3- 53	–	–
N.O.Perry	134	446	10	44.60	5- 70	1	–
R.L.Powell	5	13	0				
D.Ramnarine	128	234	12	19.50	4- 29	–	–
F.A.Rose	347.4	1097	37	29.64	7- 84	2	–
C.A.Walsh	4116	10853	426	25.47	7- 37	17	2
S.C.Williams	3	19	0				

NEW ZEALAND – BATTING AND FIELDING

	M	I	NO	HS	Runs	Avge	100	50	Ct/St
G.I.Allott	10	15	7	8*	27	3.37	–	–	2
N.J.Astle	34	60	5	125	2020	36.72	5	9	33
M.D.Bell	8	15	1	83	221	15.78	–	1	9
C.L.Cairns	44	74	3	126	2055	28.94	2	17	13
S.B.Doull	30	46	10	46	501	13.91	–	–	16
S.P.Fleming	48	84	6	174*	2984	38.25	2	23	80
C.Z.Harris	19	34	4	71	582	19.40	–	4	12
M.J.Horne	24	45	2	157	1453	33.79	3	5	12

NEW ZEALAND – BATTING AND FIELDING (continued)

	M	*I*	*NO*	*HS*	*Runs*	*Avge*	*100*	*50*	*Ct/St*
C.D.McMillan	19	32	3	142	1256	43.31	3	7	5
D.J.Nash	30	43	13	89*	642	21.40	–	3	13
S.B.O'Connor	10	15	6	7	39	4.33	–	–	5
A.C.Parore	58	98	10	100*	2249	25.55	1	13	131/4
M.S.Sinclair	1	1	–	214	214	214.00	1	–	–
C.M.Spearman	13	25	2	112	759	33.00	1	3	12
G.R.Stead	5	8	–	78	278	34.75	–	2	2
R.G.Twose	16	27	2	94	628	25.12	–	6	5
D.L.Vettori	28	42	7	90	603	17.22	–	4	11
P.J.Wiseman	8	12	3	23	48	5.33	–	–	2
B.A.Young	35	68	4	267*	2034	31.78	2	12	54

NEW ZEALAND – BOWLING

	O	*R*	*W*	*Avge*	*Best*	*5wI*	*10wM*
G.I.Allott	337.1	1111	19	58.47	4- 74	–	–
N.J.Astle	405	1013	22	46.04	2- 26	–	–
C.L.Cairns	1376.4	4395	150	29.30	7- 27	9	1
S.B.Doull	960.5	2730	97	28.14	7- 65	6	–
C.Z.Harris	373.4	1004	15	66.93	2- 16	–	–
M.J.Horne	11	26	0				
C.D.McMillan	124.3	386	8	48.25	2- 27	–	–
D.J.Nash	968.1	2503	92	27.20	6- 27	3	1
S.B.O'Connor	307.2	965	24	40.20	4- 52	–	–
G.R.Stead	1	1	0				
R.G.Twose	35.1	130	3	43.33	2- 36	–	–
D.L.Vettori	1247.3	3161	91	34.73	6- 64	3	–
P.J.Wiseman	238.5	763	15	50.86	5- 82	1	–

INDIA – BATTING AND FIELDING

	M	*I*	*NO*	*HS*	*Runs*	*Avge*	*100*	*50*	*Ct/St*
A.B.Agarkar	4	8	–	19	28	3.50	–	–	1
M.Azharuddin	98	145	9	199	6104	44.88	21	21	105
R.V.Bharadwaj	3	3	–	22	28	9.33	–	–	3
R.Dravid	35	60	4	190	2727	48.69	6	16	39
D.J.Gandhi	4	7	1	88	204	34.00	–	2	3
S.C.Ganguly	33	56	5	173	2458	48.19	7	12	18
Harbhajan Singh	8	11	6	15*	31	6.20	–	–	2
A.Jadeja	14	22	2	96	563	28.15	–	4	4
S.B.Joshi	12	17	2	43	233	15.53	–	–	4
H.H.Kanitkar	2	4	–	45	74	18.50	–	–	–
A.Kumble	59	77	14	88	1120	17.77	–	3	29
V.V.S.Laxman	17	30	2	167	800	28.57	1	5	19
N.R.Mongia	40	61	6	152	1343	24.41	1	6	92/7
A.Nehra	1	–	–	–	–	–	–	–	–
B.K.V.Prasad	29	41	16	30*	161	6.44	–	–	6
M.S.K.Prasad	6	10	1	19	106	11.77	–	–	15
S.Ramesh	9	18	1	143	843	49.58	2	5	7
N.S.Sidhu	51	78	2	201	3202	42.13	9	15	9
R.Singh	1	1	–	0	0	0.00	–	–	1
R.R.Singh	1	2	–	15	27	13.50	–	–	5
J.Srinath	44	64	17	76	789	16.78	–	4	18
S.R.Tendulkar	74	117	12	217	5890	56.09	22	23	50

INDIA – BOWLING

	O	*R*	*W*	*Avge*	*Best*	*5wI*	*10wM*
A.B.Agarkar	142	451	13	34.69	3-43	–	–
M.Azharuddin	2.1	16	0				

INDIA – BOWLING (continued)

	O	R	W	Avge	Best	5wI	10wM
R.V.Bharadwaj	41.1	107	1	107.00	1- 26	–	–
R.Dravid	4	6	0				
S.C.Ganguly	204.3	674	20	33.70	3- 28	–	–
Harbhajan Singh	285.4	810	21	38.57	3- 30	–	–
S.B.Joshi	374.4	901	27	33.37	4- 43	–	–
H.H.Kanitkar	1	2	0				
A.Kumble	3069.1	7471	264	28.29	10- 74	15	3
V.V.S.Laxman	24	67	0				
A.Nehra	28	94	1	94.00	1- 94	–	–
B.K.V.Prasad	1043.3	2950	85	34.70	6- 33	6	1
S.Ramesh	1	5	0				
N.S.Sidhu	1	9	0				
R.Singh	40	176	3	58.66	2- 74	–	–
R.R.Singh	10	32	0				
J.Srinath	1724	4993	164	30.44	8- 86	6	1
S.R.Tendulkar	164	520	14	37.14	2- 7	–	–

PAKISTAN – BATTING AND FIELDING

	M	I	NO	HS	Runs	Avge	100	50	Ct/St
Aamir Sohail	45	79	3	205	2777	36.53	5	13	34
Abdul Razzak	1	2	–	11	13	6.50	–	–	1
Aqib Javed	22	27	7	28*	101	5.05	–	–	2
Arshad Khan	3	3	–	7	14	4.66	–	–	–
Azhar Mahmood	18	29	4	136	811	32.44	3	1	13
Fazal-e-Akber	2	3	2	15*	15	15.00	–	–	1
Hasan Raza	2	2	–	27	30	15.00	–	–	–
Ijaz Ahmed	57	87	4	211	3272	39.42	12	12	44
Imran Nazir	1	2	–	64	77	38.50	–	1	–
Inzamam-ul-Haq	58	97	11	200*	3717	43.22	8	23	50
Mohammad Akram	7	11	4	10*	18	2.57	–	–	4
Mohammad Hussain	2	3	–	17	18	6.00	–	–	1
Mohammad Wasim	13	20	2	192	592	32.88	2	1	15/2
Mohammad Zahid	4	4	1	6*	7	2.33	–	–	–
Moin Khan	50	77	6	117*	2049	28.85	3	13	88/15
Mushtaq Ahmed	43	63	13	59	606	12.12	–	2	19
Nadeem Khan	2	3	1	25	34	17.00	–	–	–
Naved Ashraf	1	1	–	32	32	32.00	–	–	–
Saeed Anwar	44	75	2	188*	3366	46.10	9	21	15
Salim Malik	103	154	22	237	5768	43.69	15	29	65
Saqlain Mushtaq	24	38	7	79	402	12.96	–	2	10
Shahid Afridi	6	11	–	141	354	32.18	1	1	4
Shahid Nazir	8	9	2	18	55	7.85	–	–	3
Shakeel Ahmed	1	1	–	1	1	1.00	–	–	1
Shoaib Akhtar	13	18	6	11	70	5.83	–	–	4
Wajahatullah Wasti	4	7	1	133	303	50.50	2	–	5
Waqar Younis	58	78	18	45	611	10.18	–	–	8
Wasim Akram	91	130	16	257*	2424	21.26	2	5	36
Yousuf Youhana	15	27	1	120*	897	34.50	1	9	17

PAKISTAN – BOWLING

	O	R	W	Avge	Best	5wI	10wM
Aamir Sohail	354.5	950	20	47.50	4-54	–	–
Abdul Razzak	17	66	0				
Aqib Javed	653	1874	54	34.70	5-84	1	–
Arshad Khan	139	324	11	29.45	5-38	1	–
Azhar Mahmood	442	1233	31	39.77	4-53	–	–
Fazal-e-Akber	40	151	4	37.75	2-16	–	–

PAKISTAN – BOWLING (continued)

	O	R	W	Avge	Best	5wI	10wM
Ijaz Ahmed	30	77	2	38.50	1- 9	–	–
Inzamam-ul-Haq	1.3	8	0				
Mohammad Akram	200	660	15	44.00	5-138	1	–
Mohammad Hussain	30	87	3	29.00	2- 66	–	–
Mohammad Zahid	107	394	13	30.30	7- 66	1	1
Mushtaq Ahmed	1798.4	5152	172	29.95	7- 56	10	3
Nadeem Khan	72	230	2	115.00	2-147	–	–
Saeed Anwar	8	23	0				
Salim Malik	122.2	415	5	83.00	1- 3	–	–
Saqlain Mushtaq	1159.4	3118	107	29.14	6- 46	9	2
Shahid Afridi	111.4	327	11	29.72	5- 52	1	–
Shahid Nazir	173.2	566	17	33.29	5- 53	1	–
Shakeel Ahmed	54.1	139	4	34.75	4- 91	–	–
Shoaib Akhtar	404.5	1375	34	40.44	5- 43	1	–
Wajahatullah Wasti	2	8	0				
Waqar Younis	1921.1	6164	279	22.09	7- 76	21	5
Wasim Akram	3389.3	8849	383	23.10	7-119	22	4

SRI LANKA – BATTING AND FIELDING

	M	I	NO	HS	Runs	Avge	100	50	Ct/St
R.P.Arnold	12	19	3	123	635	39.68	2	3	15
M.S.Atapattu	29	51	5	223	1447	31.45	3	3	23
M.R.C.N.Bandaratilake	4	6	–	20	52	8.66	–	–	–
U.D.U.Chandana	2	3	–	28	55	18.33	–	–	1
S.I.de Saram	3	3	–	39	94	31.33	–	–	–
K.S.C.de Silva	8	12	5	27	65	9.28	–	–	5
P.A.de Silva	79	135	11	267	5422	43.72	17	21	40
T.M.Dilshan	3	4	1	163*	209	69.66	1	–	6
I.S.Gallage	1	1	–	3	3	3.00	–	–	–
D.A.Gunawardena	2	4	–	43	84	21.00	–	–	1
U.C.Hathurusinghe	26	44	1	83	1274	29.62	–	8	7
R.Herath	2	1	–	3	3	3.00	–	–	–
S.T.Jayasuriya	44	74	9	340	2751	42.32	5	14	36
D.P.M.deS.Jayawardena	15	22	1	242	933	44.42	2	5	19
R.S.Kalpage	11	18	2	63	294	18.37	–	2	10
R.S.Kaluwitharana	33	50	3	132*	1432	30.46	3	7	57/17
M.Muralitharan	48	62	25	39	481	13.00	–	–	25
R.L.Perera	1	1	1	1*	1	–	–	–	–
K.R.Pushpakumara	19	25	11	23	100	7.14	–	–	8
A.Ranatunga	86	143	10	135*	4695	35.30	4	34	41
H.P.Tillekeratne	56	91	14	126*	2972	38.59	6	16	87/2
K.E.A.Upashanta	1	1	–	6	6	6.00	–	–	–
W.P.U.C.J.Vaas	34	47	7	57	680	17.00	–	2	13
G.P.Wickremasinghe	36	56	5	51	528	10.35	–	1	11
D.N.T.Zoysa	8	10	1	16*	70	7.77	–	–	1

SRI LANKA – BOWLING

	O	R	W	Avge	Best	5wI	10wM
R.P.Arnold	119.5	292	6	48.66	2- 80	–	–
M.S.Atapattu	8	24	1	24.00	1- 9	–	–
M.R.C.N.Bandaratilake	216	483	19	25.42	5- 36	1	–
U.D.U.Chandana	58.1	227	7	32.42	6-179	1	–
K.S.C.de Silva	264.1	889	16	55.56	5- 85	1	–
P.A.de Silva	347.1	1012	26	38.92	3- 30	–	–
I.S.Gallage	25	77	0				
U.C.Hathurusinghe	327	789	17	46.41	4- 66	–	–
R.Herath	69.3	195	6	32.50	4- 97	–	–

SRI LANKA – BOWLING (continued)

	O	R	W	Avge	Best	5wI	10wM
S.T.Jayasuriya	474.4	1256	29	43.31	4- 40	–	–
D.P.M.deS.Jayawardena	60	176	1	176.00	1- 35	–	–
R.S.Kalpage	262.4	774	12	64.50	2- 27	–	–
M.Muralitharan	2480.3	6140	227	27.04	9- 65	17	2
R.L.Perera	44	185	1	185.00	1-125	–	–
K.R.Pushpakumara	530.1	1932	52	37.15	7-116	4	–
A.Ranatunga	393.3	1027	16	64.18	2- 17	–	–
H.P.Tillekeratne	6.4	14	0				
K.E.A.Upashanta	43	135	3	45.00	2- 41	–	–
W.P.U.C.J.Vaas	1225.1	3166	108	29.31	6- 87	4	1
G.P.Wickremasinghe	1091.4	3202	75	42.69	6- 60	3	–
D.N.T.Zoysa	167.4	451	15	30.06	3- 22	–	–

ZIMBABWE – BATTING AND FIELDING

	M	I	NO	HS	Runs	Avge	100	50	Ct/St
E.A.Brandes	10	15	3	39	121	10.08	–	–	4
G.B.Brent	2	3	–	3	3	1.00	–	–	–
A.D.R.Campbell	39	70	2	99	1773	26.07	–	11	39
C.N.Evans	2	4	–	11	25	6.25	–	–	1
A.Flower	39	70	12	156	2580	44.48	6	16	99/5
G.W.Flower	38	70	3	201*	2230	33.28	5	8	22
M.W.Goodwin	15	29	2	166*	1086	40.22	1	8	10
T.R.Gripper	4	8	–	60	114	14.25	–	1	4
A.G.Huckle	8	14	3	28*	74	6.72	–	–	3
N.C.Johnson	9	16	1	107	426	28.40	1	3	9
E.Z.Matambanadzo	3	5	1	7	17	4.25	–	–	–
M.Mbangwa	11	19	6	4	20	1.53	–	–	2
H.K.Olonga	16	23	7	24	73	4.56	–	–	8
R.W.Price	1	2	–	4	6	3.00	–	–	–
G.J.Rennie	14	28	1	84	627	23.22	–	5	9
B.C.Strang	19	33	7	53	336	12.92	–	1	9
H.H.Streak	27	43	7	53	536	14.88	–	2	7
A.R.Whittall	10	18	3	17	114	7.60	–	–	8
G.J.Whittall	31	54	4	203*	1368	27.36	2	7	12
C.B.Wishart	12	22	1	63	302	14.38	–	2	5

ZIMBABWE – BOWLING

	O	R	W	Avge	Best	5wI	10wM
E.A.Brandes	332.4	951	26	36.57	3- 45	–	–
G.B.Brent	61.2	144	5	28.80	3- 21	–	–
A.D.R.Campbell	7	20	0				
C.N.Evans	9	35	0				
A.Flower	0.1	0	0				
G.W.Flower	198.3	525	6	87.50	1- 4	–	–
M.W.Goodwin	19.5	69	0				
T.R.Gripper	12	53	1	53.00	1- 28	–	–
A.G.Huckle	261.2	872	25	34.88	6-109	2	1
N.C.Johnson	84.5	287	7	41.00	3- 41	–	–
E.Z.Matambanadzo	64	250	4	62.50	2- 62	–	–
M.Mbangwa	321.2	756	28	27.00	3- 23	–	–
H.K.Olonga	399.3	1302	41	31.75	5- 70	1	–
R.W.Price	8	22	0				
B.C.Strang	643.2	1511	45	33.57	5-101	1	–
H.H.Streak	1027.3	2726	111	24.55	6- 90	4	–
A.R.Whittall	260.2	736	7	105.14	3- 73	–	–
G.J.Whittall	635.2	1706	42	40.61	4- 18	–	–

FIRST-CLASS CRICKET RECORDS

To 19 September 1999

TEAM RECORDS

HIGHEST INNINGS TOTALS

1107	Victoria v New South Wales	Melbourne	1926-27
1059	Victoria v Tasmania	Melbourne	1922-23
952-6d	Sri Lanka v India	Colombo	1997-98
951-7d	Sind v Baluchistan	Karachi	1973-74
944-6d	Hyderabad v Andhra	Secunderabad	1993-94
918	New South Wales v South Australia	Sydney	1900-01
912-8d	Holkar v Mysore	Indore	1945-46
910-6d	Railways v Dera Ismail Khan	Lahore	1964-65
903-7d	England v Australia	The Oval	1938
887	Yorkshire v Warwickshire	Birmingham	1896
863	Lancashire v Surrey	The Oval	1990
860-6d	Tamil Nadu v Goa	Panjim	1988-89

Excluding penalty runs in India, there have been 30 innings totals of 800 runs or more in first-class cricket. Tamil Nadu's total of 860-6d was boosted to 912 by 52 penalty runs.

HIGHEST SECOND INNINGS TOTAL

770	New South Wales v South Australia	Adelaide	1920-21

HIGHEST FOURTH INNINGS TOTAL

654-5	England v South Africa	Durban	1938-39

HIGHEST MATCH AGGREGATE

2376	Maharashtra v Bombay	Poona	1948-49

RECORD MARGIN OF VICTORY

Innings and 851 runs: Railways v Dera Ismail Khan	Lahore	1964-65

MOST RUNS IN A DAY

721	Australians v Essex	Southend	1948

MOST HUNDREDS IN AN INNINGS

6	Holkar v Mysore	Indore	1945-46

LOWEST INNINGS TOTALS

12	†Oxford University v MCC and Ground	Oxford	1877
12	Northamptonshire v Gloucestershire	Gloucester	1907
13	Auckland v Canterbury	Auckland	1877-78
13	Nottinghamshire v Yorkshire	Nottingham	1901
14	Surrey v Essex	Chelmsford	1983
15	MCC v Surrey	Lord's	1839
15	†Victoria v MCC	Melbourne	1903-04
15	†Northamptonshire v Yorkshire	Northampton	1908
15	Hampshire v Warwickshire	Birmingham	1922

† *Batted one man short*

There have been 26 instances of a team being dismissed for under 20.

LOWEST MATCH AGGREGATE BY ONE TEAM

34 (16 and 18)	Border v Natal	East London	1959-60

LOWEST COMPLETED MATCH AGGREGATE BY BOTH TEAMS

105	MCC v Australians	Lord's	1878

FEWEST RUNS IN AN UNINTERRUPTED DAY'S PLAY

95	Australia (80) v Pakistan (15-2)	Karachi	1956-57

TIED MATCHES

Before 1949 a match was considered to be tied if the scores were level after the fourth innings, even if the side batting last had wickets in hand when play ended. Law 22 was amended in 1948 and since then a match has been tied only when the scores are level after the fourth innings has been completed. There have been 53 tied first-class matches, five of which would not have qualified under the current law. The most recent is:

Worcestershire (203/325-8d) v Nottinghamshire (233/295)	Nottingham	1993

BATTING RECORDS
HIGHEST INDIVIDUAL INNINGS

501*	B.C.Lara	Warwickshire v Durham	Birmingham	1994
499	Hanif Mohammad	Karachi v Bahawalpur	Karachi	1958-59
452*	D.G.Bradman	New South Wales v Queensland	Sydney	1929-30
443*	B.B.Nimbalkar	Maharashtra v Kathiawar	Poona	1948-49
437	W.H.Ponsford	Victoria v Queensland	Melbourne	1927-28
429	W.H.Ponsford	Victoria v Tasmania	Melbourne	1922-23
428	Aftab Baloch	Sind v Baluchistan	Karachi	1973-74
424	A.C.MacLaren	Lancashire v Somerset	Taunton	1895
405*	G.A.Hick	Worcestershire v Somerset	Taunton	1988
385	B.Sutcliffe	Otago v Canterbury	Christchurch	1952-53
383	C.W.Gregory	New South Wales v Queensland	Brisbane	1906-07
377	S.V.Manjrekar	Bombay v Hyderabad	Bombay	1990-91
375	B.C.Lara	West Indies v England	St John's	1993-94
369	D.G.Bradman	South Australia v Tasmania	Adelaide	1935-36
366	N.H.Fairbrother	Lancashire v Surrey	The Oval	1990
366	M.V.Sridhar	Hyderabad v Andhra	Secunderabad	1993-94
365*	C.Hill	South Australia v NSW	Adelaide	1900-01
365*	G.St A.Sobers	West Indies v Pakistan	Kingston	1957-58
364	L.Hutton	England v Australia	The Oval	1938
359*	V.M.Merchant	Bombay v Maharashtra	Bombay	1943-44
359	R.B.Simpson	New South Wales v Queensland	Brisbane	1963-64
357*	R.Abel	Surrey v Somerset	The Oval	1899
357	D.G.Bradman	South Australia v Victoria	Melbourne	1935-36
356	B.A.Richards	South Australia v W Australia	Perth	1970-71
355*	G.R.Marsh	W Australia v S Australia	Perth	1989-90
355	B.Sutcliffe	Otago v Auckland	Dunedin	1949-50
352	W.H.Ponsford	Victoria v New South Wales	Melbourne	1926-27
350	Rashid Israr	Habib Bank v National Bank	Lahore	1976-77

There have been 124 triple hundreds in first-class cricket, W.V.Raman (313) and Arjan Kripal Singh (302*) for Tamil Nadu v Goa at Panjim in 1988-89 providing the only instance of two batsmen scoring 300 in the same innings.

MOST HUNDREDS IN SUCCESSIVE INNINGS

6	C.B.Fry	Sussex and Rest of England	1901
6	D.G.Bradman	South Australia and D.G.Bradman's XI	1938-39
6	M.J.Procter	Rhodesia	1970-71

TWO DOUBLE HUNDREDS IN A MATCH

244	202*	A.E.Fagg	Kent v Essex	Colchester	1938

TRIPLE HUNDRED AND HUNDRED IN A MATCH

333	123	G.A.Gooch	England v India	Lord's	1990

DOUBLE HUNDRED AND HUNDRED IN A MATCH MOST TIMES

4	Zaheer Abbas	Gloucestershire	1976-81

TWO HUNDREDS IN A MATCH MOST TIMES

8	Zaheer Abbas	Gloucestershire and PIA	1976-82
7	W.R.Hammond	Gloucestershire, England and MCC	1927-45

MOST HUNDREDS IN A SEASON

18	D.C.S.Compton	1947	16	J.B.Hobbs	1925

100 HUNDREDS IN A CAREER

	Total		*100th Hundred*	
	Hundreds	*Inns*	*Season*	*Inns*
J.B.Hobbs	197	1315	1923	821
E.H.Hendren	170	1300	1928-29	740
W.R.Hammond	167	1005	1935	679
C.P.Mead	153	1340	1927	892
G.Boycott	151	1014	1977	645
H.Sutcliffe	149	1088	1932	700
F.E.Woolley	145	1532	1929	1031
L.Hutton	129	814	1951	619
G.A.Gooch	128	988	1992-93	820
W.G Grace	126	1493	1895	1113
D.C.S.Compton	123	839	1952	552
T.W.Graveney	122	1223	1964	940
D.G.Bradman	117	338	1947-48	295
I.V.A.Richards	114	796	1988-89	658
G.A.Hick	108	628	1998	574
Zaheer Abbas	108	768	1982-83	658
A.Sandham	107	1000	1935	871
M.C.Cowdrey	107	1130	1973	1035
T.W.Hayward	104	1138	1913	1076
G.M.Turner	103	792	1982	779
J.H.Edrich	103	979	1977	945
L.E.G.Ames	102	951	1950	915
G.E.Tyldesley	102	961	1934	919
D.L.Amiss	102	1139	1986	1081

MOST 400s: 2 – W.H.Ponsford
MOST 300s or more: 6 – D.G.Bradman; 4 – W.R.Hammond
MOST 200s or more: 37 – D.G.Bradman; 36 – W.R.Hammond; 22 – E.H.Hendren

MOST RUNS IN A MONTH

1294 (avge 92.42)	L.Hutton	Yorkshire	June 1949

MOST RUNS IN A SEASON

Runs			*I*	*NO*	*HS*	*Avge*	*100*	*Season*
3816	D.C.S.Compton	Middlesex	50	8	246	90.85	18	1947
3539	W.J.Edrich	Middlesex	52	8	267*	80.43	12	1947
3518	T.W.Hayward	Surrey	61	8	219	66.37	13	1906

The feat of scoring 3000 runs in a season has been achieved 28 times, the most recent instance being by W.E.Alley (3019) in 1961. The highest aggregate in a season since 1969 is 2755 by S.J.Cook in 1991.

1000 RUNS IN A SEASON MOST TIMES

28 W.G.Grace (Gloucestershire), F.E.Woolley (Kent)

HIGHEST BATTING AVERAGE IN A SEASON

(Qualification: 12 innings)

Avge			*I*	*NO*	*HS*	*Runs*	*100*	*Season*
115.66	D.G.Bradman	Australians	26	5	278	2429	13	1938
102.53	G.Boycott	Yorkshire	20	5	175*	1538	6	1979
102.00	W.A.Johnston	Australians	17	16	28*	102	–	1953
101.70	G.A.Gooch	Essex	30	3	333	2746	12	1990
100.12	G.Boycott	Yorkshire	30	5	233	2503	13	1971

FASTEST HUNDRED AGAINST AUTHENTIC BOWLING

35 min	P.G.H.Fender	Surrey v Northamptonshire	Northampton	1920

FASTEST DOUBLE HUNDRED

113 min	R.J.Shastri	Bombay v Baroda	Bombay	1984-85

FASTEST TRIPLE HUNDRED

181 min	D.C.S.Compton	MCC v NE Transvaal	Benoni	1948-49

MOST SIXES IN AN INNINGS

16	A.Symonds	Gloucestershire v Glamorgan	Abergavenny	1995

MOST SIXES IN A MATCH

20	A.Symonds	Gloucestershire v Glamorgan	Abergavenny	1995

MOST SIXES IN A SEASON

80	I.T.Botham	Somerset and England		1985

MOST FOURS IN AN INNINGS

72	B.C.Lara	Warwickshire v Durham	Birmingham	1994

MOST RUNS OFF ONE OVER

36	G.St A.Sobers	Nottinghamshire v Glamorgan	Swansea	1968
36	R.J.Shastri	Bombay v Baroda	Bombay	1984-85

Both batsmen hit for six all six balls of overs bowled by M.A.Nash and Tilak Raj respectively.

MOST RUNS IN A DAY

390*	B.C.Lara	Warwickshire v Durham	Birmingham	1994

There have been 19 instances of a batsman scoring 300 or more runs in a day.

HIGHEST PARTNERSHIPS FOR EACH WICKET

First Wicket

561	Waheed Mirza/Mansoor Akhtar	Karachi W v Quetta	Karachi	1976-77
555	P.Holmes/H.Sutcliffe	Yorkshire v Essex	Leyton	1932
554	J.T.Brown/J.Tunnicliffe	Yorkshire v Derbys	Chesterfield	1898

Second Wicket

576	S.T.Jayasuriya/R.S.Mahanama	Sri Lanka v India	Colombo (RPS)	1997-98
475	Zahir Alam/L.S.Rajput	Assam v Tripura	Gauhati	1991-92
465*	J.A.Jameson/R.B.Kanhai	Warwickshire v Glos	Birmingham	1974

Third Wicket

467	A.H.Jones/M.D.Crowe	N Zealand v Sri Lanka	Wellington	1990-91
456	Khalid Irtiza/Aslam Ali	United Bank v Multan	Karachi	1975-76
451	Mudassar Nazar/Javed Miandad	Pakistan v India	Hyderabad	1982-83
445	P.E.Whitelaw/W.N.Carson	Auckland v Otago	Dunedin	1936-37
438	G.A.Hick/T.M.Moody	Worcestershire v Hants	Southampton	1997

Fourth Wicket

577	V.S.Hazare/Gul Mahomed	Baroda v Holkar	Baroda	1946-47
574*	C.L.Walcott/F.M.M.Worrell	Barbados v Trinidad	Port-of-Spain	1945-46
502*	F.M.M.Worrell/J.D.C.Goddard	Barbados v Trinidad	Bridgetown	1943-44
470	A.I.Kallicharran/G.W.Humpage	Warwickshire v Lancs	Southport	1982

Fifth Wicket

464*	M.E.Waugh/S.R.Waugh	NSW v W Australia	Perth	1990-91
405	S.G.Barnes/D.G.Bradman	Australia v England	Sydney	1946-47
401	M.B.Loye/D.Ripley	Northants v Glamorgan	Northampton	1998

Sixth Wicket

487*	G.A.Headley/C.C.Passailaigue	Jamaica v Tennyson's	Kingston	1931-32
428	W.W.Armstrong/M.A.Noble	Australians v Sussex	Hove	1902
411	R.M.Poore/E.G.Wynyard	Hampshire v Somerset	Taunton	1899

Seventh Wicket

460	Bhupinder Singh jr/P.Dharmani	Punjab v Delhi	Delhi	1994-95
347	D.St E.Atkinson/C.C.Depeiza	W Indies v Australia	Bridgetown	1954-55
344	K.S.Ranjitsinhji/W.Newham	Sussex v Essex	Leyton	1902

Eighth Wicket

433	V.T.Trumper/A.Sims	Australians v C'bury	Christchurch	1913-14
313	Wasim Akram/Saqlain Mushtaq	Pakistan v Zimbabwe	Sheikhupura	1996-97
292	R.Peel/Lord Hawke	Yorkshire v Warwicks	Birmingham	1896

Ninth Wicket

283	J.Chapman/A.Warren	Derbys v Warwicks	Blackwell	1910
268	J.B.Commins/N.Boje	SA 'A' v Mashonaland	Harare	1994-95
251	J.W.H.T.Douglas/S.N.Hare	Essex v Derbyshire	Leyton	1921

Tenth Wicket

307	A.F.Kippax/J.E.H.Hooker	NSW v Victoria	Melbourne	1928-29
249	C.T.Sarwate/S.N.Banerjee	Indians v Surrey	The Oval	1946
235	F.E.Woolley/A.Fielder	Kent v Worcs	Stourbridge	1909

35000 RUNS IN A CAREER

	Career	*I*	*NO*	*HS*	***Runs***	*Avge*	*100*
J.B.Hobbs	1905-34	1315	106	316*	**61237**	50.65	197
F.E.Woolley	1906-38	1532	85	305*	**58969**	40.75	145
E.H.Hendren	1907-38	1300	166	301*	**57611**	50.80	170
C.P.Mead	1905-36	1340	185	280*	**55061**	47.67	153
W.G.Grace	1865-1908	1493	105	344	**54896**	39.55	126
W.R.Hammond	1920-51	1005	104	336*	**50551**	56.10	167
H.Sutcliffe	1919-45	1088	123	313	**50138**	51.95	149
G.Boycott	1962-86	1014	162	261*	**48426**	56.83	151
T.W.Graveney	1948-71/72	1223	159	258	**47793**	44.91	122
G.A.Gooch	1973-97	988	75	333	**44841**	49.11	128
T.W.Hayward	1893-1914	1138	96	315*	**43551**	41.79	104
D.L.Amiss	1960-87	1139	126	262*	**43423**	42.86	102
M.C.Cowdrey	1950-76	1130	134	307	**42719**	42.89	107
A.Sandham	1911-37/38	1000	79	325	**41284**	44.82	107
L.Hutton	1934-60	814	91	364	**40140**	55.51	129
M.J.K.Smith	1951-75	1091	139	204	**39832**	41.84	69
W.Rhodes	1898-1930	1528	237	267*	**39802**	30.83	58
J.H.Edrich	1956-78	979	104	310*	**39790**	45.47	103
R.E.S.Wyatt	1923-57	1141	157	232	**39405**	40.04	85
D.C.S.Compton	1936-64	839	88	300	**38942**	51.85	123
G.E.Tyldesley	1909-36	961	106	256*	**38874**	45.46	102
J.T.Tyldesley	1895-1923	994	62	295*	**37897**	40.60	86
K.W.R.Fletcher	1962-88	1167	170	228*	**37665**	37.77	63
C.G.Greenidge	1970-92	889	75	273*	**37354**	45.88	92
J.W.Hearne	1909-36	1025	116	285*	**37252**	40.98	96
L.E.G.Ames	1926-51	951	95	295	**37248**	43.51	102
D.Kenyon	1946-67	1159	59	259	**37002**	33.63	74
W.J.Edrich	1934-58	964	92	267*	**36965**	42.39	86
J.M.Parks	1949-76	1227	172	205*	**36673**	34.76	51
M.W.Gatting	1975-98	861	123	258	**36549**	49.52	94
D.Denton	1894-1920	1163	70	221	**36479**	33.37	69
G.H.Hirst	1891-1929	1215	151	341	**36323**	34.13	60
I.V.A.Richards	1971/72-93	796	63	322	**36212**	49.40	114
A.Jones	1957-83	1168	72	204*	**36049**	32.89	56
W.G.Quaife	1894-1928	1203	185	255*	**36012**	35.37	72
R.E.Marshall	1945/46-72	1053	59	228*	**35725**	35.94	68
G.Gunn	1902-32	1061	82	220	**35208**	35.96	62

BOWLING RECORDS

ALL TEN WICKETS IN AN INNINGS

This feat has been achieved 77 times in first-class matches (excluding 12-a-side fixtures).
Three Times: A.P.Freeman (1929, 1930, 1931)
Twice: V.E.Walker (1859, 1865); H.Verity (1931, 1932); J.C.Laker (1956)

Instances since 1945:

W.E.Hollies	Warwickshire v Notts	Birmingham	1946
J.M.Sims	East v West	Kingston on Thames	1948
J.K.R.Graveney	Gloucestershire v Derbyshire	Chesterfield	1949
T.E.Bailey	Essex v Lancashire	Clacton	1949
R.Berry	Lancashire v Worcestershire	Blackpool	1953
S.P.Gupte	President's XI v Combined XI	Bombay	1954-55
J.C.Laker	Surrey v Australians	The Oval	1956
K.Smales	Nottinghamshire v Glos	Stroud	1956

G.A.R.Lock	Surrey v Kent	Blackheath	1956
J.C.Laker	England v Australia	Manchester	1956
P.M.Chatterjee	Bengal v Assam	Jorhat	1956-57
J.D.Bannister	Warwicks v Combined Services	Birmingham (M & B)	1959
A.J.G.Pearson	Cambridge U v Leicestershire	Loughborough	1961
N.I.Thomson	Sussex v Warwickshire	Worthing	1964
P.J.Allan	Queensland v Victoria	Melbourne	1965-66
I.J.Brayshaw	Western Australia v Victoria	Perth	1967-68
Shahid Mahmood	Karachi Whites v Khairpur	Karachi	1969-70
E.E.Hemmings	International XI v W Indians	Kingston	1982-83
P.Sunderam	Rajasthan v Vidarbha	Jodhpur	1985-86
S.T.Jefferies	Western Province v OFS	Cape Town	1987-88
Imran Adil	Bahawalpur v Faisalabad	Faisalabad	1989-90
G.P.Wickremasinghe	Sinhalese v Kalutara	Colombo	1991-92
R.L.Johnson	Middlesex v Derbyshire	Derby	1994
Naeem Akhtar	Rawalpindi B v Peshawar	Peshawar	1995-96
A.Kumble	India v Pakistan	Delhi	1998-99

MOST WICKETS IN A MATCH

19	J.C.Laker	England v Australia	Manchester	1956

MOST WICKETS IN A SEASON

Wkts		*Season*	*Matches*	*Overs*	*Mdns*	*Runs*	*Avge*
304	A.P.Freeman	1928	37	1976.1	423	5489	18.05
298	A.P.Freeman	1933	33	2039	651	4549	15.26

The feat of taking 250 wickets in a season has been achieved on 12 occasions, the last instance being by A.P.Freeman in 1933. 200 or more wickets in a season have been taken on 59 occasions, the last being by G.A.R.Lock (212 wickets, average 12.02) in 1957.

The highest aggregates of wickets taken in a season since the reduction of County Championship matches in 1969 are as follows:

Wkts		*Season*	*Matches*	*Overs*	*Mdns*	*Runs*	*Avge*
134	M.D.Marshall	1982	22	822	225	2108	15.73
131	L.R.Gibbs	1971	23	1024.1	295	2475	18.89
125	F.D.Stephenson	1988	22	819.1	196	2289	18.31
121	R.D.Jackman	1980	23	746.2	220	1864	15.40

Since 1969 there have been 49 instances of bowlers taking 100 wickets in a season.

MOST HAT-TRICKS IN A CAREER

7	D.V.P.Wright
6	T.W.J.Goddard, C.W.L.Parker
5	S.Haigh, V.W.C.Jupp, A.E.G.Rhodes, F.A.Tarrant

2000 WICKETS IN A CAREER

	Career	*Runs*	*Wkts*	*Avge*	*100w*
W.Rhodes	1898-1930	69993	**4187**	16.71	23
A.P.Freeman	1914-36	69577	**3776**	18.42	17
C.W.L.Parker	1903-35	63817	**3278**	19.46	16
J.T.Hearne	1888-1923	54352	**3061**	17.75	15
T.W.J.Goddard	1922-52	59116	**2979**	19.84	16
W.G.Grace	1865-1908	51545	**2876**	17.92	10
A.S.Kennedy	1907-36	61034	**2874**	21.23	15
D.Shackleton	1948-69	53303	**2857**	18.65	20
G.A.R.Lock	1946-70/71	54709	**2844**	19.23	14
F.J.Titmus	1949-82	63313	**2830**	22.37	16
M.W.Tate	1912-37	50571	**2784**	18.16	13+1
G.H.Hirst	1891-1929	51282	**2739**	18.72	15

	Career	Runs	Wkts	Avge	100w
C.Blythe	1899-1914	42136	**2506**	16.81	14
D.L.Underwood	1963-87	49993	**2465**	20.28	10
W.E.Astill	1906-39	57783	**2431**	23.76	9
J.C.White	1909-37	43759	**2356**	18.57	14
W.E.Hollies	1932-57	48656	**2323**	20.94	14
F.S.Trueman	1949-69	42154	**2304**	18.29	12
J.B.Statham	1950-68	36999	**2260**	16.37	13
R.T.D.Perks	1930-55	53771	**2233**	24.07	16
J.Briggs	1879-1900	35431	**2221**	15.95	12
D.J.Shepherd	1950-72	47302	**2218**	21.32	12
E.G.Dennett	1903-26	42571	**2147**	19.82	12
T.Richardson	1892-1905	38794	**2104**	18.43	10
T.E.Bailey	1945-67	48170	**2082**	23.13	9
R.Illingworth	1951-83	42023	**2072**	20.28	10
F.E.Woolley	1906-38	41066	**2068**	19.85	8
N.Gifford	1960-88	48731	**2068**	23.56	4
G.Geary	1912-38	41339	**2063**	20.03	11
D.V.P.Wright	1932-57	49307	**2056**	23.98	10
J.A.Newman	1906-30	51111	**2032**	25.15	9
A.Shaw	1864-97	24580	**2026**+1	12.12	9
S.Haigh	1895-1913	32091	**2012**	15.94	11

ALL-ROUND RECORDS

THE 'DOUBLE'

3000 runs and 100 wickets: J.H.Parks (1937)
2000 runs and 200 wickets: G.H.Hirst (1906)
2000 runs and 100 wickets: F.E.Woolley (4), J.W.Hearne (3), W.G.Grace (2), G.H.Hirst (2), W.Rhodes (2), T.E.Bailey, D.E.Davies, G.L.Jessop, V.W.C.Jupp, J.Langridge, F.A.Tarrant, C.L.Townsend, L.F.Townsend
1000 runs and 200 wickets: M.W.Tate (3), A.E.Trott (2), A.S.Kennedy

Most Doubles: 16 – W.Rhodes; 14 – G.H.Hirst; 10 – V.W.C.Jupp

Double in Debut Season: D.B.Close (1949) – the youngest (18) to achieve this feat.

The feat of scoring 1000 runs and taking 100 wickets in a season has been achieved on 305 occasions, R.J.Hadlee (1984) and F.D.Stephenson (1988) being the only players to complete the 'double' since the reduction of County Championship matches in 1969.

WICKET-KEEPING RECORDS

EIGHT DISMISSALS IN AN INNINGS

9	(8ct, 1st)	Tahir Rashid	Habib Bank v PACO	Gujranwala	1992-93
9	(7ct, 2st)	W.R.James	Matabeleland v Mashonaland CD	Bulawayo	1995-96
8	(8ct)	A.T.W.Grout	Queensland v W Australia	Brisbane	1959-60
8	(8ct)	D.E.East	Essex v Somerset	Taunton	1985
8	(8ct)	S.A.Marsh	Kent v Middlesex	Lord's	1991
8	(6ct, 2st)	T.J.Zoehrer	Australians v Surrey	The Oval	1993
8	(7ct, 1st)	D.S.Berry	Victoria v South Australia	Melbourne	1996-97

TWELVE DISMISSALS IN A MATCH

13	(11ct, 2st)	W.R.James	Matabeleland v Mashonaland CD	Bulawayo	1995-96
12	(8ct, 4st)	E.Pooley	Surrey v Sussex	The Oval	1868
12	(9ct, 3st)	D.Tallon	Queensland v NSW	Sydney	1938-39
12	(9ct, 3st)	H.B.Taber	NSW v South Australia	Adelaide	1968-69

MOST DISMISSALS IN A SEASON

128 (79ct, 49st) L.E.G.Ames 1929

1000 DISMISSALS IN A CAREER

	Career	*Dismissals*	*Ct*	*St*
R.W.Taylor	1960-88	**1649**	1473	176
J.T.Murray	1952-75	**1527**	1270	257
H.Strudwick	1902-27	**1497**	1242	255
A.P.E.Knott	1964-85	**1344**	1211	133
F.H.Huish	1895-1914	**1310**	933	377
B.Taylor	1949-73	**1294**	1083	211
D.Hunter	1889-1909	**1253**	906	347
H.R.Butt	1890-1912	**1228**	953	275
J.H.Board	1891-1914/15	**1207**	852	355
H.Elliott	1920-47	**1206**	904	302
J.M.Parks	1949-76	**1181**	1088	93
R.C.Russell	1981-99	**1143**	1027	116
R.Booth	1951-70	**1126**	948	178
L.E.G.Ames	1926-51	**1121**	703	418
D.L.Bairstow	1970-90	**1099**	961	138
G.Duckworth	1923-47	**1096**	753	343
H.W.Stephenson	1948-64	**1082**	748	334
J.G.Binks	1955-75	**1071**	895	176
T.G.Evans	1939-69	**1066**	816	250
A.Long	1960-80	**1046**	922	124
G.O.Dawkes	1937-61	**1043**	895	148
R.W.Tolchard	1965-83	**1037**	912	125
S.J.Rhodes	1981-99	**1027**	915	112
W.L.Cornford	1921-47	**1017**	675	342

FIELDING RECORDS

MOST CATCHES IN AN INNINGS

7	M.J.Stewart	Surrey v Northamptonshire	Northampton	1957
7	A.S.Brown	Gloucestershire v Nottinghamshire	Nottingham	1966

MOST CATCHES IN A MATCH

10	W.R.Hammond	Gloucestershire v Surrey	Cheltenham	1928

MOST CATCHES IN A SEASON

78	W.R.Hammond	1928	77	M.J.Stewart	1957

750 CATCHES IN A CAREER

1018	F.E.Woolley	1906-38	784	J.G.Langridge	1928-55
887	W.G.Grace	1865-1908	764	W.Rhodes	1898-1930
830	G.A.R.Lock	1946-70/71	758	C.A.Milton	1948-74
819	W.R.Hammond	1920-51	754	E.H.Hendren	1907-38
813	D.B.Close	1949-86			

LIMITED-OVERS INTERNATIONALS RESULTS SUMMARY

1970-71 to 23 February 2000

	Opponents	*Matches*								*Won*								*Tied*	*NR*
			E	*A*	*SA*	*WI*	*NZ*	*I*	*P*	*SL*	*Z*	*B*	*C*	*EA*	*H*	*K*	*SC*	*UAE*		
England	Australia	**67**	31	34	–	–	–	–	–	–	–	–	–	–	–	–	–	–	1	1
	South Africa	**22**	7	–	15	–	–	–	–	–	–	–	–	–	–	–	–	–	–	–
	West Indies	**58**	25	–	–	31	–	–	–	–	–	–	–	–	–	–	–	–	–	2
	New Zealand	**47**	23	–	–	–	20	–	–	–	–	–	–	–	–	–	–	–	1	3
	India	**36**	19	–	–	–	–	16	–	–	–	–	–	–	–	–	–	–	–	1
	Pakistan	**43**	27	–	–	–	–	–	15	–	–	–	–	–	–	–	–	–	–	1
	Sri Lanka	**20**	13	–	–	–	–	–	–	7	–	–	–	–	–	–	–	–	–	–
	Zimbabwe	**12**	6	–	–	–	–	–	–	–	6	–	–	–	–	–	–	–	–	–
	Canada	**1**	1	–	–	–	–	–	–	–	–	–	0	–	–	–	–	–	–	–
	East Africa	**1**	1	–	–	–	–	–	–	–	–	–	–	0	–	–	–	–	–	–
	Holland	**1**	1	–	–	–	–	–	–	–	–	–	–	–	0	–	–	–	–	–
	Kenya	**1**	1	–	–	–	–	–	–	–	–	–	–	–	–	0	–	–	–	–
	U A Emirates	**1**	1	–	–	–	–	–	–	–	–	–	–	–	–	–	–	0	–	–
Australia	South Africa	**39**	–	19	19	–	–	–	–	–	–	–	–	–	–	–	–	–	1	–
	West Indies	**92**	–	37	–	52	–	–	–	–	–	–	–	–	–	–	–	–	2	1
	New Zealand	**74**	–	51	–	–	21	–	–	–	–	–	–	–	–	–	–	–	–	2
	India	**61**	–	36	–	–	–	22	–	–	–	–	–	–	–	–	–	–	–	3
	Pakistan	**57**	–	31	–	–	–	–	23	–	–	–	–	–	–	–	–	–	1	2
	Sri Lanka	**43**	–	28	–	–	–	–	–	13	–	–	–	–	–	–	–	–	–	2
	Zimbabwe	**15**	–	14	–	–	–	–	–	–	1	–	–	–	–	–	–	–	–	–
	Bangladesh	**2**	–	2	–	–	–	–	–	–	–	0	–	–	–	–	–	–	–	–
	Canada	**1**	–	1	–	–	–	–	–	–	–	–	0	–	–	–	–	–	–	–
	Kenya	**1**	–	1	–	–	–	–	–	–	–	–	–	–	–	0	–	–	–	–
	Scotland	**1**	–	1	–	–	–	–	–	–	–	–	–	–	–	–	0	–	–	–
S Africa	West Indies	**18**	–	–	12	6	–	–	–	–	–	–	–	–	–	–	–	–	–	–
	New Zealand	**20**	–	–	11	–	7	–	–	–	–	–	–	–	–	–	–	–	–	2
	India	**30**	–	–	20	–	–	9	–	–	–	–	–	–	–	–	–	–	–	1
	Pakistan	**22**	–	–	15	–	–	–	7	–	–	–	–	–	–	–	–	–	–	–
	Sri Lanka	**16**	–	–	9	–	–	–	–	6	–	–	–	–	–	–	–	–	1	–
	Zimbabwe	**12**	–	–	9	–	–	–	–	–	2	–	–	–	–	–	–	–	–	1
	Holland	**1**	–	–	1	–	–	–	–	–	–	–	–	–	0	–	–	–	–	–
	Kenya	**3**	–	–	3	–	–	–	–	–	–	–	–	–	–	0	–	–	–	–
	U A Emirates	**1**	–	–	1	–	–	–	–	–	–	–	–	–	–	–	–	0	–	–
W Indies	New Zealand	**30**	–	–	–	19	9	–	–	–	–	–	–	–	–	–	–	–	–	2
	India	**63**	–	–	–	40	–	21	–	–	–	–	–	–	–	–	–	–	1	1
	Pakistan	**90**	–	–	–	56	–	–	32	–	–	–	–	–	–	–	–	–	2	–
	Sri Lanka	**31**	–	–	–	21	–	–	–	9	–	–	–	–	–	–	–	–	–	1
	Zimbabwe	**6**	–	–	–	6	–	–	–	–	0	–	–	–	–	–	–	–	–	–
	Bangladesh	**3**	–	–	–	3	–	–	–	–	–	0	–	–	–	–	–	–	–	–
	Kenya	**1**	–	–	–	0	–	–	–	–	–	–	–	–	–	1	–	–	–	–
	Scotland	**1**	–	–	–	1	–	–	–	–	–	–	–	–	–	–	0	–	–	–
N Zealand	India	**57**	–	–	–	–	24	30	–	–	–	–	–	–	–	–	–	–	–	3
	Pakistan	**50**	–	–	–	–	18	–	30	–	–	–	–	–	–	–	–	–	1	1
	Sri Lanka	**40**	–	–	–	–	24	–	–	13	–	–	–	–	–	–	–	–	1	2
	Zimbabwe	**18**	–	–	–	–	13	–	–	–	3	–	–	–	–	–	–	–	1	1
	Bangladesh	**2**	–	–	–	–	2	–	–	–	–	0	–	–	–	–	–	–	–	–
	East Africa	**1**	–	–	–	–	1	–	–	–	–	–	–	0	–	–	–	–	–	–
	Holland	**1**	–	–	–	–	1	–	–	–	–	–	–	–	0	–	–	–	–	–
	Scotland	**1**	–	–	–	–	1	–	–	–	–	–	–	–	–	–	0	–	–	–
	U A Emirates	**1**	–	–	–	–	1	–	–	–	–	–	–	–	–	–	–	0	–	–
India	Pakistan	**82**	–	–	–	–	–	28	50	–	–	–	–	–	–	–	–	–	–	4
	Sri Lanka	**62**	–	–	–	–	–	34	–	23	–	–	–	–	–	–	–	–	–	5
	Zimbabwe	**27**	–	–	–	–	–	20	–	–	5	–	–	–	–	–	–	–	2	–
	Bangladesh	**7**	–	–	–	–	–	7	–	–	–	0	–	–	–	–	–	–	–	–
	East Africa	**1**	–	–	–	–	–	1	–	–	–	–	–	0	–	–	–	–	–	–
	Kenya	**6**	–	–	–	–	–	5	–	–	–	–	–	–	–	1	–	–	–	–
	U A Emirates	**1**	–	–	–	–	–	1	–	–	–	–	–	–	–	–	–	0	–	–
Pakistan	Sri Lanka	**79**	–	–	–	–	–	–	49	27	–	–	–	–	–	–	–	–	1	2
	Zimbabwe	**20**	–	–	–	–	–	–	17	–	2	–	–	–	–	–	–	–	1	–
	Bangladesh	**7**	–	–	–	–	–	–	6	–	–	1	–	–	–	–	–	–	–	–
	Canada	**1**	–	–	–	–	–	–	1	–	–	–	0	–	–	–	–	–	–	–

	Opponents	Matches	Won																Tied	NR
			E	A	SA	WI	NZ	I	P	SL	Z	B	C	EA	H	K	SC	UAE		
	Holland	**1**	–	–	–	–	–	–	1	–	–	–	–	–	0	–	–	–	–	–
	Kenya	**1**	–	–	–	–	–	–	1	–	–	–	–	–	–	0	–	–	–	–
	Scotland	**1**	–	–	–	–	–	–	1	–	–	–	–	–	–	–	0	–	–	–
	U A Emirates	**2**	–	–	–	–	–	–	2	–	–	–	–	–	–	–	–	0	–	–
Sri Lanka	Zimbabwe	**21**	–	–	–	–	–	–	–	15	5	–	–	–	–	–	–	–	–	1
	Bangladesh	**5**	–	–	–	–	–	–	–	5	–	0	–	–	–	–	–	–	–	–
	Kenya	**3**	–	–	–	–	–	–	–	3	–	–	–	–	–	0	–	–	–	–
Zimbabwe	Bangladesh	**4**	–	–	–	–	–	–	–	–	4	0	–	–	–	–	–	–	–	–
	Kenya	**11**	–	–	–	–	–	–	–	–	10	–	–	–	–	0	–	–	–	1
Bangladesh	Kenya	**6**	–	–	–	–	–	–	–	–	–	1	–	–	–	5	–	–	–	–
	Scotland	**1**	–	–	–	–	–	–	–	–	–	1	–	–	–	–	0	–	–	–
Holland	U A Emirates	**1**	–	–	–	–	–	–	–	–	–	–	–	–	0	–	–	1	–	–
		1565	156	255	115	235	142	194	235	121	38	3	0	0	0	7	0	1	16	47

MERIT TABLE OF ALL L-O INTERNATIONALS

1970-71 to 23 February 2000

	Matches	*Won*	*Lost*	*Tied*	*No Result*	*% Won (exc NR)*
South Africa	184	115	63	1	5	64.24
West Indies	393	235	146	5	7	60.88
Australia	453	255	182	5	11	57.69
Pakistan	456	235	205	6	10	52.69
England	310	156	144	2	8	51.65
India	433	194	218	3	18	46.74
New Zealand	342	142	180	4	16	43.55
Sri Lanka	320	121	183	2	14	39.54
Zimbabwe	146	38	100	4	4	26.76
Kenya	33	7	25	–	1	21.87
United Arab Emirates	7	1	6	–	–	14.28
Bangladesh	37	3	34	–	–	8.10
Canada	3	–	3	–	–	–
East Africa	3	–	3	–	–	–
Holland	5	–	5	–	–	–
Scotland	5	–	5	–	–	–

LOI RECORDS

To 23 February 2000

TEAM RECORDS

HIGHEST TOTALS

398-5	(50 overs)	Sri Lanka v Kenya	Kandy	1995-96
376-2	(50 overs)	India v New Zealand	Hyderabad, India	1999-00
373-6	(50 overs)	India v Sri Lanka	Taunton	1999
371-9	(50 overs)	Pakistan v Sri Lanka	Nairobi	1996-97
363-7	(55 overs)	England v Pakistan	Nottingham	1992
360-4	(50 overs)	West Indies v Sri Lanka	Karachi	1987-88
349-9	(50 overs)	Sri Lanka v Pakistan	Singapore	1995-96
349-9	(50 overs)	New Zealand v India	Rajkot	1999-00
348-8	(50 overs)	New Zealand v India	Nagpur	1995-96
347-3	(50 overs)	Kenya v Bangladesh	Nairobi	1997-98
339-4	(50 overs)	Sri Lanka v Pakistan	Chandigarh	1996-97
338-4	(50 overs)	New Zealand v Bangladesh	Sharjah	1989-90
338-5	(60 overs)	Pakistan v Sri Lanka	Swansea	1983
337-7	(50 overs)	Australia v Pakistan	Sydney	1999-00

The highest for South Africa is 328-3 (v Holland, Rawalpindi, 1995-96); for Zimbabwe 325-6 (v Kenya, Dhaka, 1998-99); and for Bangladesh 257 (v Zimbabwe, Nairobi, 1997-98) and 257-5 (v Zimbabwe, Dhaka, 1998-99).

HIGHEST TOTALS BATTING SECOND

WINNING:	316-4	(48.5 overs)	Australia v Pakistan	Lahore	1998-99
	316-7	(47.5 overs)	India v Pakistan	Dhaka	1997-98
LOSING:	329	(49.3 overs)	Sri Lanka v West Indies	Sharjah	1995-96

HIGHEST MATCH AGGREGATE

664-19	(99.4 overs)	Pakistan v Sri Lanka	Singapore	1995-96

LARGEST RUNS MARGINS OF VICTORY

232 runs	Australia beat Sri Lanka	Adelaide	1984-85
206 runs	New Zealand beat Australia	Adelaide	1985-86
202 runs	England beat India	Lord's	1975
202 runs	Zimbabwe beat Kenya	Dhaka	1998-99

LOWEST TOTALS (Excluding reduced innings)

43	(19.5 overs)	Pakistan v West Indies	Cape Town	1992-93
45	(40.3 overs)	Canada v England	Manchester	1979
55	(28.3 overs)	Sri Lanka v West Indies	Sharjah	1986-87
63	(25.5 overs)	India v Australia	Sydney	1980-81
64	(35.5 overs)	New Zealand v Pakistan	Sharjah	1985-86
68	(31.3 overs)	Scotland v West Indies	Leicester	1999
69	(28 overs)	South Africa v Australia	Sydney	1993-94
70	(25.2 overs)	Australia v England	Birmingham	1977
70	(26.3 overs)	Australia v New Zealand	Adelaide	1985-86

The lowest for England is 93 (v Australia, Leeds, 1975); for West Indies 87 (v Australia, Sydney, 1992-93); for Zimbabwe 94 (v Pakistan, Sharjah, 1996-97); for Bangladesh 92 (v Zimbabwe, Nairobi, 1997-98); and for Kenya 103 (v South Africa, Nairobi, 1996-97).

LOWEST MATCH AGGREGATE

88-13	(32.2 overs)	West Indies v Pakistan	Cape Town	1992-93

BATTING RECORDS
HIGHEST INDIVIDUAL INNINGS

194	Saeed Anwar	Pakistan v India	Madras	1996-97
189*	I.V.A.Richards	West Indies v England	Manchester	1984
188*	G.Kirsten	South Africa v UAE	Rawalpindi	1995-96
186*	S.R.Tendulkar	India v New Zealand	Hyderabad	1999-00
183	S.C.Ganguly	India v Sri Lanka	Taunton	1999
181	I.V.A.Richards	West Indies v Sri Lanka	Karachi	1987-88
175*	Kapil Dev	India v Zimbabwe	Tunbridge Wells	1983
171*	G.M.Turner	New Zealand v East Africa	Birmingham	1975
169*	D.J.Callaghan	South Africa v New Zealand	Pretoria	1994-95
169	B.C.Lara	West Indies v Sri Lanka	Sharjah	1995-96
167*	R.A.Smith	England v Australia	Birmingham	1993
161	A.C.Hudson	South Africa v Holland	Rawalpindi	1995-96
158	D.I.Gower	England v New Zealand	Brisbane	1982-83
154	A.C.Gilchrist	Australia v Sri Lanka	Melbourne	1998-99
153*	I.V.A.Richards	West Indies v Australia	Melbourne	1979-80
153*	M.Azharuddin	India v Zimbabwe	Cuttack	1997-98
153*	S.C.Ganguly	India v New Zealand	Gwalior	1999-00
153	B.C.Lara	West Indies v Pakistan	Sharjah	1993-94
153	R.Dravid	India v New Zealand	Hyderabad	1999-00
152*	D.L.Haynes	West Indies v India	Georgetown	1988-89
151*	S.T.Jayasuriya	Sri Lanka v India	Bombay	1996-97
150	S.Chanderpaul	West Indies v South Africa	East London	1998-99

The highest for Zimbabwe is 142 by D.L.Houghton (v New Zealand, Hyderabad, India, 1987-88); for Bangladesh 101 by Mehrab Hossain (v Zimbabwe, Dhaka, 1998-99); and for Kenya 144 by K.Otieno (v Bangladesh, Nairobi, 1997-98).

HUNDRED ON DEBUT

D.L.Amiss	103	England v Australia	Manchester	1972
D.L.Haynes	148	West Indies v Australia	St John's	1977-78
A.Flower	115*	Zimbabwe v Sri Lanka	New Plymouth	1991-92
Salim Elahi	102*	Pakistan v Sri Lanka	Gujranwala	1995-96
N.V.Knight	113	England v Pakistan	Birmingham	1996

Fastest 100	37 balls	Shahid Afridi (102)	P v SL	Nairobi	1996-97
Fastest 50	17 balls	S.T.Jayasuriya (76)	SL v P	Singapore	1995-96

CARRYING BAT THROUGH COMPLETED INNINGS

G.W.Flower	84*	Zimbabwe (205) v England	Sydney	1994-95
Saeed Anwar	103*	Pakistan (219) v Zimbabwe	Harare	1994-95
N.V.Knight	125*	England (246) v Pakistan	Nottingham	1996
R.D.Jacobs	49*	West Indies (110) v Australia	Manchester	1999

HIGHEST PARTNERSHIP FOR EACH WICKET

1st	252	S.C.Ganguly/S.R.Tendulkar	India v Sri Lanka	Colombo (RPS)	1997-98
2nd	331	S.R.Tendulkar/R.Dravid	India v New Zealand	Hyderabad (Ind)	1999-00
3rd	237*	R.Dravid/S.R.Tendulkar	India v Kenya	Bristol	1999
4th	275*	M.Azharuddin/A.Jadeja	India v Zimbabwe	Cuttack	1997-98
5th	223	M.Azharuddin/A.Jadeja	India v Sri Lanka	Colombo (RPS)	1997-98
6th	161	M.O.Odumbe/A.V.Vadher	Kenya v Sri Lanka	Southampton	1999
7th	119	T.M.Odoyo/A.O.Suji	Kenya v Zimbabwe	Nairobi	1997-98
8th	119	P.R.Reiffel/S.K.Warne	Australia v South Africa	Port Elizabeth	1993-94
9th	126*	Kapil Dev/S.M.H.Kirmani	India v Zimbabwe	Tunbridge Wells	1983
10th	106*	I.V.A.Richards/M.A.Holding	West Indies v England	Manchester	1984

5000 RUNS IN A CAREER

		LOI	*I*	*NO*	*HS*	***Runs***	Avge	*100*	*50*
M.Azharuddin	I	323	297	53	153*	**9110**	37.33	7	57
S.R.Tendulkar	I	237	230	22	186*	**8768**	42.15	24	45
D.L.Haynes	WI	238	237	28	152*	**8648**	41.37	17	57
P.A.de Silva	SL	264	256	25	145	**8193**	35.46	11	56
A.Ranatunga	SL	269	255	47	131*	**7454**	35.83	4	49
Javed Miandad	P	233	218	41	119*	**7381**	41.70	8	50
M.E.Waugh	A	208	203	15	130	**7275**	38.69	14	45
Salim Malik	P	283	256	38	102	**7171**	32.89	5	47
Saeed Anwar	P	200	197	15	194	**7080**	38.90	17	33
I.V.A.Richards	WI	187	167	24	189*	**6721**	47.00	11	45
Inzamam-ul-Haq	P	209	198	25	137*	**6572**	37.98	6	47
A.R.Border	A	273	252	39	127*	**6524**	30.62	3	39
S.R.Waugh	A	286	257	50	120*	**6516**	31.47	2	38
Ijaz Ahmed	P	245	228	29	139*	**6427**	32.29	10	36
B.C.Lara	WI	167	164	15	169	**6316**	42.38	13	39
R.B.Richardson	WI	224	217	30	122	**6248**	33.41	5	44
D.M.Jones	A	164	161	25	145	**6068**	44.61	7	46
D.C.Boon	A	181	177	16	122	**5964**	37.04	5	37
Ramiz Raja	P	198	197	15	119*	**5841**	32.09	9	31
S.T.Jayasuriya	SL	201	193	8	151*	**5252**	28.38	7	35
W.J.Cronje	SA	179	167	29	112	**5210**	37.75	2	36
R.S.Mahanama	SL	213	198	23	119*	**5162**	29.49	4	35
C.G.Greenidge	WI	128	127	13	133*	**5134**	45.03	11	31
S.C.Ganguly	I	133	128	10	183	**5061**	42.88	11	30
A.Jadeja	I	185	168	33	119	**5041**	37.34	6	28

The most for England is 4290 in 122 innings by G.A.Gooch; for New Zealand 4704 in 141 innings by M.D.Crowe; for Zimbabwe 3963 in 131 innings by A.Flower; for Bangladesh 680 in 31 innings by Akram Khan; and for Kenya 963 in 31 innings by S.O.Tikolo.

13 HUNDREDS IN A CAREER

		LOI	100	E	A	SA	WI	NZ	I	P	SL	Z	K
S.R.Tendulkar	I	237	**24**	–	5	1	1	2	–	2	4	4	2
Saeed Anwar	P	200	**17**	–	1	–	2	2	3	–	6	1	–
D.L.Haynes	WI	238	**17**	2	6	–	–	2	2	4	1	–	–
M.E.Waugh	A	208	**14**	1	–	2	1	3	1	1	1	–	1
B.C.Lara	WI	164	**13**	1	2	2	–	2	–	4	1	–	–

The most for England is 8 by G.A.Gooch; for South Africa 8 by G.Kirsten; for New Zealand 7 by N.J.Astle; for Sri Lanka 11 by P.A.de Silva; for Zimbabwe 4 by N.C.Johnson; for Bangladesh 1 by Mehrab Hossein; and for Kenya 2 by K.O.Otieno.

BOWLING RECORDS

BEST ANALYSES

7-37	Aqib Javed	Pakistan v India	Sharjah	1991-92
7-51	W.W.Davis	West Indies v Australia	Leeds	1983
6-12	A.Kumble	India v West Indies	Calcutta	1993-94
6-14	G.J.Gilmour	Australia v England	Leeds	1975
6-14	Imran Khan	Pakistan v India	Sharjah	1984-85
6-15	C.E.H.Croft	West Indies v England	Kingstown	1980-81
6-18	Azhar Mahmood	Pakistan v West Indies	Sharjah	1999-00
6-19	H.K.Olonga	Zimbabwe v England	Cape Town	1999-00
6-20	B.C.Strang	Zimbabwe v Bangladesh	Nairobi	1997-98
6-23	A.A.Donald	South Africa v Kenya	Nairobi	1996-97
6-26	Waqar Younis	Pakistan v Sri Lanka	Sharjah	1989-90
6-29	B.P.Patterson	West Indies v India	Nagpur	1987-88
6-29	S.T.Jayasuriya	Sri Lanka v England	Moratuwa	1992-93
6-30	Waqar Younis	Pakistan v New Zealand	Auckland	1993-94
6-35	S.M.Pollock	South Africa v West Indies	East London	1998-99
6-39	K.H.MacLeay	Australia v India	Nottingham	1983
6-41	I.V.A.Richards	West Indies v India	Delhi	1989-90
6-44	Waqar Younis	Pakistan v New Zealand	Sharjah	1996-97
6-49	L.Klusener	South Africa v Sri Lanka	Lahore	1997-98
6-50	A.H.Gray	West Indies v Australia	Port-of-Spain	1990-91

The best for England is 5-15 by M.A.Ealham (v Zimbabwe, Kimberley, 1999-00); for New Zealand 5-22 by M.N.Hart (v West Indies, Margao, 1994-95); for Bangladesh 4-36 by Saiful Islam (v Sri Lanka, Sharjah, 1994-95); and for Kenya 5-33 by A.Y.Karim (v Bangladesh, Nairobi, 1997-98).

150 WICKETS IN A CAREER

		LOI	O	R	W	Avge	Best	4w	R/Over
Wasim Akram	P	294	2524.1	9749	**414**	23.54	5-15	21	3.86
Waqar Younis	P	182	1495.4	6882	**292**	23.56	6-26	20	4.60
A.Kumble	I	191	1705.1	7138	**254**	28.10	6-12	9	4.18
Kapil Dev	I	224	1867	6945	**253**	27.45	5-43	4	3.71
J.Srinath	I	184	1610.1	7073	**251**	28.17	5-23	7	4.39
C.A.Walsh	WI	205	1803.4	6917	**227**	30.47	5- 1	7	3.83
Saqlain Mushtaq	P	123	1076.3	4593	**225**	20.41	5-29	14	4.26
C.E.L.Ambrose	WI	170	1506.5	5307	**221**	24.01	5-17	10	3.52
S.K.Warne	A	137	1264.4	5316	**216**	24.61	5-33	12	4.20
A.A.Donald	SA	121	1073	4336	**206**	21.04	6-23	11	4.04
C.J.McDermott	A	138	1243.3	5018	**203**	24.71	5-44	5	4.03
S.R.Waugh	A	286	1451.3	6596	**191**	34.53	4-33	3	4.54
M.Muralitharan	SL	132	1191.1	4964	**183**	27.12	5-23	6	4.16
Aqib Javed	P	163	1335.3	5721	**182**	31.43	7-37	6	4.28
Imran Khan	P	175	1243.3	4845	**182**	26.62	6-14	4	3.89
S.T.Jayasuriya	SL	201	1242.1	6039	**178**	33.92	6-29	8	4.86
B.K.V.Prasad	I	142	1195.5	5515	**169**	32.63	5-27	4	4.61
G.D.McGrath	A	110	987.4	3936	**166**	23.71	5-14	10	3.98
C.L.Hooper	WI	182	1266.1	5548	**163**	34.03	4-34	3	4.38

		LOI	*O*	*R*	*W*	Avge	*Best*	*4w*	*R/Over*
R.J.Hadlee	NZ	115	1030.2	3407	**158**	21.56	5-25	6	3.30
W.P.U.C.J.Vaas	SL	129	1043.4	4433	**158**	28.05	4-20	3	4.24
M.Prabhakar	I	129	1060	4534	**157**	28.87	5-33	6	4.27
M.D.Marshall	WI	136	1195.5	4233	**157**	26.96	4-18	6	3.53

The most for England is 145 in 116 matches by I.T.Botham; for Zimbabwe 108 in 89 matches by H.H.Streak; for Bangladesh 27 in 25 matches by Hasibul Hussain; and for Kenya 30 in 32 matches by T.M.Odoyo.

HAT-TRICKS

Jalaluddin	Pakistan v Australia	Hyderabad	1982-83
B.A.Reid	Australia v New Zealand	Sydney	1985-86
C.Sharma	India v New Zealand	Nagpur	1987-88
Wasim Akram	Pakistan v West Indies	Sharjah	1989-90
Wasim Akram	Pakistan v Australia	Sharjah	1989-90
Kapil Dev	India v Sri Lanka	Calcutta	1990-91
Aqib Javed	Pakistan v India	Sharjah	1991-92
D.K.Morrison	New Zealand v India	Napier	1993-94
Waqar Younis	Pakistan v New Zealand	East London	1994-95
Saqlain Mushtaq	Pakistan v Zimbabwe	Peshawar	1996-97
E.A.Brandes	Zimbabwe v England	Harare	1996-97
A.M.Stuart	Australia v Pakistan	Melbourne	1996-97
Saqlain Mushtaq	Pakistan v Zimbabwe	The Oval	1999

WICKET-KEEPING RECORDS
FIVE DISMISSALS IN AN INNINGS

5 – R.W.Marsh (*Australia*); D.J.Richardson (2), M.V.Boucher (*South Africa*); C.O.Browne, J.C.Adams, R.D.Jacobs (3) (*West Indies*); A.C.Parore (*New Zealand*); S.M.H.Kirmani, S.Viswanath, K.S.More, N.R.Mongia (2), M.S.K.Prasad (*India*); Moin Khan (2), Rashid Latif (*Pakistan*); R.G.de Alwis, H.P.Tillekeratne, R.S.Kaluwitharana (*Sri Lanka*); A.Flower (2) (*Zimbabwe*).

100 DISMISSALS IN A CAREER
(Including catches taken in the field)

		LOI	*Ct*	*St*	*Dis*
I.A.Healy	Australia	168	195	39	**234**
Moin Khan	Pakistan	160	159	58	**217**
P.J.L.Dujon	West Indies	169	183	21	**204**
D.J.Richardson	South Africa	122	149	16	**165**
R.S.Kaluwitharana	Sri Lanka	135	93	61	**154**
N.R.Mongia	India	139	110	43	**153**
A.C.Gilchrist	Australia	86	111	18	**129**
A.Flower	Zimbabwe	121	99	28	**127**
R.W.Marsh	Australia	92	120	4	**124**
Rashid Latif	Pakistan	101	94	28	**122**
A.J.Stewart	England	125	111	11	**122**
Salim Yousuf	Pakistan	86	80	22	**102**

FIELDING RECORDS
FIVE CATCHES IN AN INNINGS

5	J.N.Rhodes	South Africa v West Indies	Bombay	1993-94

100 CATCHES IN A CAREER
(Excluding catches taken while keeping wicket)

		LOI	*Ct*
M.Azharuddin	India	323	**153**
A.R.Border	Australia	273	**127**
R.S.Mahanama	Sri Lanka	213	**109**
S.R.Waugh	Australia	286	**102**
I.V.A.Richards	West Indies	187	**101**

The most for England is 58 in 105 matches by G.A.Hick; for South Africa 81 in 169 matches by J.N.Rhodes; for New Zealand 66 in 143 matches by M.D.Crowe; for Pakistan 90 in 245 matches by Ijaz Ahmed; and for Zimbabwe 47 in 126 matches by A.D.R.Campbell.

ALL-ROUND RECORDS
50 RUNS AND 5 WICKETS IN A MATCH

I.V.A.Richards	119	5-41	West Indies v New Zealand	Dunedin	1986-87
K.Srikkanth	70	5-27	India v New Zealand	Vishakhapatnam	1988-89
M.E.Waugh	57	5-24	Australia v West Indies	Melbourne	1992-93
Abdur Razzaq	70*	5-48	Pakistan v India	Hobart	1999-00
G.A.Hick	80	5-33	England v Zimbabwe	Harare	1999-00

1000 RUNS AND 100 WICKETS

		LOI	*Runs*	*Wkts*
I.T.Botham	England	116	2113	145
C.L.Cairns	New Zealand	120	2822	115
W.J.Cronje	South Africa	179	5210	110
R.J.Hadlee	New Zealand	115	1751	158
C.Z.Harris	New Zealand	146	2588	140
C.L.Hooper	West Indies	182	4612	163
Imran Khan	Pakistan	175	3709	182
S.T.Jayasuriya	Sri Lanka	201	5252	178
Kapil Dev	India	225	3783	253
L.Klusener	South Africa	73	1943	104
Mudassar Nazar	Pakistan	122	2653	111
S.P.O'Donnell	Australia	87	1242	108
S.M.Pollock	South Africa	90	1228	132
M.Prabhakar	India	130	1858	157
I.V.A.Richards	West Indies	187	6721	118
R.J.Shastri	India	150	3108	129
Wasim Akram	Pakistan	294	3120	414
S.R.Waugh	Australia	286	6516	191

1000 RUNS AND 100 DISMISSALS

		LOI	*Runs*	*Dis*
P.J.L.Dujon	West Indies	169	1945	204
A.Flower	Zimbabwe	134	3963	127
A.C.Gilchrist	Australia	86	2648	129
I.A.Healy	Australia	168	1764	234
R.S.Kaluwitharana	Sri Lanka	135	2572	154
R.W.Marsh	Australia	92	1225	124
N.R.Mongia	India	139	1268	153
Moin Khan	Pakistan	160	2454	217
A.J.Stewart	England	125	3378	122

INDIVIDUAL RECORDS – GENERAL
250 APPEARANCES

323	M.Azharuddin	India	273	A.R.Border	Australia
294	Wasim Akram	Pakistan	269	A.Ranatunga	Sri Lanka
286	S.R.Waugh	Australia	264	P.A.de Silva	Sri Lanka
283	Salim Malik	Pakistan			

The most for England is 125 by G.A.Gooch and A.J.Stewart; for South Africa 179 by W.J.Cronje; for New Zealand 149 by J.G.Wright; and for Zimbabwe 134 by A.Flower.

100 MATCHES AS CAPTAIN

193	A.Ranatunga	Sri Lanka	129	W.J.Cronje	South Africa
178	A.R.Border	Australia	109	Wasim Akram	Pakistan
174	M.Azharuddin	India	108	I.V.A.Richards	West Indies
139	Imran Khan	Pakistan			

The most for England is 50 by G.A.Gooch; for New Zealand 60 by G.P.Howarth; and for Zimbabwe 76 by A.D.R.Campbell.

WOMEN'S TEST CRICKET RECORDS

1934 to 1 January 2000

Compiled by Marion Collin

RESULTS SUMMARY

	Opponents	*Tests*	*Won by*								*Drawn*
			E	*A*	*SA*	*WI*	*NZ*	*I*	*P*	*SL*	
England	Australia	36	6	7	–	–	–	–	–	–	23
	South Africa	4	1	–	0	–	–	–	–	–	3
	West Indies	3	2	–	–	0	–	–	–	–	1
	New Zealand	22	6	–	–	–	0	–	–	–	16
	India	7	1	–	–	–	–	0	–	–	6
Australia	West Indies	2	–	0	–	0	–	–	–	–	2
	New Zealand	13	–	4	–	–	1	–	–	–	8
	India	8	–	3	–	–	–	0	–	–	5
South Africa	New Zealand	3	–	–	0	–	1	–	–	–	2
New Zealand	India	5	–	–	–	–	0	0	–	–	5
Pakistan	Sri Lanka	1	–	–	–	–	–	–	0	1	–
		104	16	14	0	0	2	0	0	1	71

	Tests	*Won*	*Lost*	*Drawn*	*Toss Won*
England	72	16	7	49	45
Australia	59	14	7	38	18
South Africa	7	–	2	5	4
West Indies	5	–	2	3	4
New Zealand	43	2	10	31	21
India	20	–	4	16	11
Pakistan	1	–	1	–	–
Sri Lanka	1	1	–	–	1

TEAM RECORDS

HIGHEST INNINGS TOTALS

569-6d	Australia v England	Guildford	1998
525	Australia v India	Ahmedabad	1983-84
517-8d	New Zealand v England	Scarborough	1996
503-5d	England v New Zealand	Christchurch	1934-35
427-4d	Australia v England	Worcester	1998
426-9d	India v England	Blackpool	1986
414	England v New Zealand	Scarborough	1996
414	England v Australia	Guildford	1998
403-8d	New Zealand v India	Nelson	1994-95

LOWEST INNINGS TOTALS

35	England v Australia	Melbourne	1957-58
38	Australia v England	Melbourne	1957-58
44	New Zealand v England	Christchurch	1934-35
47	Australia v England	Brisbane	1934-35

BATTING RECORDS

HIGHEST INDIVIDUAL INNINGS

204	K.E.Flavell	NZ v E	Scarborough	1996
200	J.Broadbent	A v E	Guildford	1998
193	D.A.Annetts	A v E	Collingham	1987
190	S.Agarwal	I v E	Worcester	1986
189	E.A.Snowball	E v NZ	Christchurch	1934-35
179	R.Heyhoe-Flint	E v A	The Oval	1976
176*	K.L.Rolton	A v E	Worcester	1998
167	J.A.Brittin	E v A	Harrogate	1998
161*	E.C.Drumm	E v A	Christchurch	1994-95
160	B.A.Daniels	E v NZ	Scarborough	1996
158*	C.A.Hodges	E v NZ	Canterbury	1984
155*	P.F.McKelvey	NZ v E	Wellington	1968-69

HIGHEST PARTNERSHIP FOR EACH WICKET

1st	178	B.J.Haggett/B.J.Clark	A v I	Sydney	1990-91
2nd	235	E.A.Snowball/M.E.Hide	E v NZ	Christchurch	1934-35
3rd	309	L.A.Reeler/D.A.Annetts	A v E	Collingham	1987
4th	222	D.A.Annetts/L.A.Larsen	A v E	Sydney	1991-92
5th	135	E.R.Wilson/V.Batty	A v E	Adelaide	1957-58
6th	132	B.A.Daniels/K.M.Leng	E v NZ	Scarborough	1996
7th	110	K.Smithies/J.M.Chamberlain	E v A	Hove	1987
8th	181	S.J.Griffiths/D.L.Wilson	A v NZ	Auckland	1989-90
9th	107	B.Botha/M.Payne	SA v NZ	Cape Town	1971-72
10th	78	E.Barker/H.Hegarty	E v A	Adelaide	1957-58
	78	S.Gupta/S.Chakraborty	I v A	Lucknow	1983-84

1000 RUNS IN TESTS

Runs			*M*	*I*	*NO*	*HS*	*Avge*	*100*
1935	J.A.Brittin	England	27	44	5	167	49.61	5
1594	R.Heyhoe-Flint	England	22	38	3	179	45.54	3
1301	D.A.Hockley	New Zealand	19	29	4	126*	52.04	4
1164	C.A.Hodges	England	18	31	2	158*	40.13	2
1110	S.Agarwal	India	13	23	1	190	50.45	4
1078	E.Bakewell	England	12	22	4	124	59.88	4
1007	M.E.Maclagan	England	14	25	1	119	41.95	2

5 HUNDREDS

		M	*I*	*Opponents*							
				E	*A*	*SA*	*WI*	*NZ*	*I*	*P*	*SL*
5	J.A.Brittin (E)	27	44	–	3	–	–	1	1	–	–

BOWLING RECORDS

SEVEN WICKETS IN AN INNINGS

8-53	N.David	I v E	Jamshedpur	1995-96
7- 6	M.B.Duggan	E v A	Melbourne	1957-58
7- 7	E.R.Wilson	A v E	Melbourne	1957-58
7-10	M.E.Maclagan	E v A	Brisbane	1934-35
7-18	A.Palmer	A v E	Brisbane	1934-35
7-24	L.Johnston	A v NZ	Melbourne	1971-72
7-34	G.E.McConway	E v I	Worcester	1986
7-41	J.Burley	NZ v E	The Oval	1966
7-61	E.Bakewell	E v WI	Birmingham	1979

TEN WICKETS IN A TEST

11- 16	E.R.Wilson	A v E	Melbourne	1957-58
11- 63	J.Greenwood	E v WI	Canterbury	1979
10- 65	E.R.Wilson	A v NZ	Wellington	1947-48
10- 75	E.Bakewell	E v WI	Birmingham	1979
10-107	K.Price	A v I	Lucknow	1983-84
10-118	D.A.Gordon	A v E	Melbourne	1968-69
10-137	J.Lord	NZ v A	Melbourne	1978-79

50 WICKETS IN TESTS

Wkts			*M*	*Balls*	*Runs*	*Avge*	*Best*
77	M.B.Duggan	E	17	3734	1039	13.49	7- 6
68	E.R.Wilson	A	11	2885	803	11.80	7- 7
60	M.E.Maclagan	E	14	3432	935	15.58	7- 10
57	R.H.Thompson	A	16	4304	1040	18.24	5- 33
55	J.Lord	NZ	15	3108	1049	19.07	6-119
50	E.Bakewell	E	12	2697	831	16.62	7- 61

HAT-TRICK

E.R.Wilson	Australia v England	Melbourne	1957-58

WICKET-KEEPING AND FIELDING RECORDS

SIX DISMISSALS IN AN INNINGS

8 (6ct, 2st)	L.Nye	E v NZ	New Plymouth	1991-92
6 (2ct, 4st)	B.Brentnall	NZ v SA	Johannesburg	1971-72

EIGHT DISMISSALS IN A TEST

9 (8ct, 1 st)	C.Matthews	A v I	Adelaide	1990-91
8 (6ct, 2st)	L.Nye	E v NZ	New Plymouth	1991-92

25 DISMISSALS IN TESTS

Total			*Tests*	*Ct*	*St*
58	C.Matthews	Australia	20	46	12
36	S.A.Hodges	England	11	19	17
28	B.Brentnall	New Zealand	10	16	12

20 CATCHES IN THE FIELD IN TESTS

Total			*Tests*
25	C.A.Hodges	England	18
20	L.A.Fullston	Australia	12

APPEARANCE RECORDS

25 TEST MATCH APPEARANCES

27	J.A.Brittin	England	1979-98

TEST MATCH RESULTS SUMMARY

To 23 February 2000

	Opponents	*Tests*	*Won by* E	A	SA	WI	NZ	I	P	SL	Z	*Tied*	*Drawn*
England	Australia	296	93	117	–	–	–	–	–	–	–	–	86
	South Africa	120	50	–	23	–	–	–	–	–	–	–	47
	West Indies	121	28	–	–	51	–	–	–	–	–	–	42
	New Zealand	82	37	–	–	–	6	–	–	–	–	–	39
	India	84	32	–	–	–	–	14	–	–	–	–	38
	Pakistan	55	14	–	–	–	–	–	9	–	–	–	32
	Sri Lanka	6	3	–	–	–	–	–	–	2	–	–	1
	Zimbabwe	2	0	–	–	–	–	–	–	–	0	–	2
Australia	South Africa	65	–	34	14	–	–	–	–	–	–	–	17
	West Indies	90	–	37	–	31	–	–	–	–	–	1	21
	New Zealand	35	–	15	–	–	7	–	–	–	–	–	13
	India	57	–	28	–	–	–	11	–	–	–	1	17
	Pakistan	46	–	18	–	–	–	–	11	–	–	–	17
	Sri Lanka	13	–	7	–	–	–	–	–	1	–	–	5
	Zimbabwe	1	–	1	–	–	–	–	–	–	0	–	–
South Africa	West Indies	6	–	–	5	1	–	–	–	–	–	–	–
	New Zealand	24	–	–	13	–	3	–	–	–	–	–	8
	India	10	–	–	4	–	–	2	–	–	–	–	4
	Pakistan	7	–	–	3	–	–	–	1	–	–	–	3
	Sri Lanka	5	–	–	3	–	–	–	–	0	–	–	2
	Zimbabwe	3	–	–	3	–	–	–	–	–	0	–	–
West Indies	New Zealand	30	–	–	–	10	6	–	–	–	–	–	14
	India	70	–	–	–	28	–	7	–	–	–	–	35
	Pakistan	34	–	–	–	12	–	–	10	–	–	–	12
	Sri Lanka	3	–	–	–	1	–	–	–	0	–	–	2
New Zealand	India	40	–	–	–	–	7	14	–	–	–	–	19
	Pakistan	39	–	–	–	–	5	–	18	–	–	–	16
	Sri Lanka	18	–	–	–	–	7	–	–	4	–	–	7
	Zimbabwe	8	–	–	–	–	3	–	–	–	0	–	5
India	Pakistan	47	–	–	–	–	–	5	9	–	–	–	33
	Sri Lanka	20	–	–	–	–	–	7	–	1	–	–	12
	Zimbabwe	3	–	–	–	–	–	1	–	–	1	–	1
Pakistan	Sri Lanka	21	–	–	–	–	–	–	10	3	–	–	8
	Zimbabwe	12	–	–	–	–	–	–	6	–	2	–	4
Sri Lanka	Zimbabwe	10	–	–	–	–	–	–	–	5	0	–	5
		1483	257	257	68	134	44	61	74	16	3	2	567

	Tests	*Won*	*Lost*	*Drawn*	*Tied*	*Toss Won*
England	766	257	222	287	–	375
Australia	603	257	168	176	2	305
South Africa	240	68	91	81	–	114
West Indies	354	134	93	126	1	184
New Zealand	276	44	111	121	–	139
India	331	61	110	159	1	171
Pakistan	261	74	62	125	–	126
Sri Lanka	96	16	38	42	–	48
Zimbabwe	39	3	19	17	–	21

TEST CRICKET RECORDS

To 23 February 2000

TEAM RECORDS

HIGHEST INNINGS TOTALS

952-6d	Sri Lanka v India	Colombo (RPS)	1997-98
903-7d	England v Australia	The Oval	1938
849	England v West Indies	Kingston	1929-30
790-3d	West Indies v Pakistan	Kingston	1957-58
758-8d	Australia v West Indies	Kingston	1954-55
729-6d	Australia v England	Lord's	1930
708	Pakistan v England	The Oval	1987
701	Australia v England	The Oval	1934
699-5	Pakistan v India	Lahore	1989-90
695	Australia v England	The Oval	1930
692-8d	West Indies v England	The Oval	1995
687-8d	West Indies v England	The Oval	1976
681-8d	West Indies v England	Port-of-Spain	1953-54
676-7	India v Sri Lanka	Kanpur	1986-87
674-6	Pakistan v India	Faisalabad	1984-85
674	Australia v India	Adelaide	1947-48
671-4	New Zealand v Sri Lanka	Wellington	1990-91
668	Australia v West Indies	Bridgetown	1954-55
660-5d	West Indies v New Zealand	Wellington	1994-95
659-8d	Australia v England	Sydney	1946-47
658-8d	England v Australia	Nottingham	1938
657-8d	Pakistan v West Indies	Bridgetown	1957-58
656-8d	Australia v England	Manchester	1964
654-5	England v South Africa	Durban	1938-39
653-4d	England v India	Lord's	1990
653-4d	Australia v England	Leeds	1993
652-7d	England v India	Madras	1984-85
652-8d	West Indies v England	Lord's	1973
652	Pakistan v India	Faisalabad	1982-83
650-6d	Australia v West Indies	Bridgetown	1964-65

The highest for South Africa is 622-9d (v A, Durban, 1969-70) and for Zimbabwe 544-4d (v P, Harare, 1994-95).

LOWEST INNINGS TOTALS

26	New Zealand v England	Auckland	1954-55
30	South Africa v England	Port Elizabeth	1895-96
30	South Africa v England	Birmingham	1924
35	South Africa v England	Cape Town	1898-99
36	Australia v England	Birmingham	1902
36	South Africa v Australia	Melbourne	1931-32
42	Australia v England	Sydney	1887-88
42	New Zealand v Australia	Wellington	1945-46
42	India v England	Lord's	1974
43	South Africa v England	Cape Town	1888-89
44	Australia v England	The Oval	1896
45	England v Australia	Sydney	1886-87
45	South Africa v Australia	Melbourne	1931-32
46	England v West Indies	Port-of-Spain	1993-94
47	South Africa v England	Cape Town	1888-89
47	New Zealand v England	Lord's	1958

The lowest for West Indies is 51 (v A, Port-of-Spain, 1998-99); for Pakistan 62 (v A, Perth, 1981-82); for Sri Lanka 71 (v P, Kandy, 1994-95); and for Zimbabwe 102 (v SA, Harare, 1999-00).

BATTING RECORDS
HIGHEST INDIVIDUAL INNINGS

375	B.C.Lara	WI v E	St John's	1993-94
365*	G.St A.Sobers	WI v P	Kingston	1957-58
364	L.Hutton	E v A	The Oval	1938
340	S.T.Jayasuriya	SL v I	Colombo (RPS)	1997-98
337	Hanif Mohammed	P v WI	Bridgetown	1957-58
336*	W.R.Hammond	E v NZ	Auckland	1932-33
334*	M.A.Taylor	A v P	Peshawar	1998-99
334	D.G.Bradman	A v E	Leeds	1930
333	G.A.Gooch	E v I	Lord's	1990
325	A.Sandham	E v WI	Kingston	1929-30
311	R.B.Simpson	A v E	Manchester	1964
310*	J.H.Edrich	E v NZ	Leeds	1965
307	R.M.Cowper	A v E	Melbourne	1965-66
304	D.G.Bradman	A v E	Leeds	1934
302	L.G.Rowe	WI v E	Bridgetown	1973-74
299*	D.G.Bradman	A v SA	Adelaide	1931-32
299	M.D.Crowe	NZ v SL	Wellington	1990-91
291	I.V.A.Richards	WI v E	The Oval	1976
287	R.E.Foster	E v A	Sydney	1903-04
285*	P.B.H.May	E v WI	Birmingham	1957
280*	Javed Miandad	P v I	Hyderabad	1982-83
278	D.C.S.Compton	E v P	Nottingham	1954
277	B.C.Lara	WI v A	Sydney	1992-93
275*	D.J.Cullinan	SA v NZ	Auckland	1998-99
275	G.Kirsten	SA v E	Durban	1999-00
274	R.G.Pollock	SA v A	Durban	1969-70
274	Zaheer Abbas	P v E	Birmingham	1971
271	Javed Miandad	P v NZ	Auckland	1988-89
270*	G.A.Headley	WI v E	Kingston	1934-35
270	D.G.Bradman	A v E	Melbourne	1936-37
268	G.N.Yallop	A v P	Melbourne	1983-84
267*	B.A.Young	NZ v SL	Dunedin	1996-97
267	P.A.de Silva	SL v NZ	Wellington	1990-91
266	W.H.Ponsford	A v E	The Oval	1934
266	D.L.Houghton	Z v SL	Bulawayo	1994-95
262*	D.L.Amiss	E v WI	Kingston	1973-74
261	F.M.M.Worrell	WI v E	Nottingham	1950
260	C.C.Hunte	WI v P	Kingston	1957-58
260	Javed Miandad	P v E	The Oval	1987
259	G.M.Turner	NZ v WI	Georgetown	1971-72
258	T.W.Graveney	E v WI	Nottingham	1957
258	S.M.Nurse	WI v NZ	Christchurch	1968-69
257*	Wasim Akram	P v Z	Sheikhupura	1996-97
256	R.B.Kanhai	WI v I	Calcutta	1958-59
256	K.F.Barrington	E v A	Manchester	1964
255*	D.J.McGlew	SA v NZ	Wellington	1952-53
254	D.G.Bradman	A v E	Lord's	1930
251	W.R.Hammond	E v A	Sydney	1928-29
250	K.D.Walters	A v NZ	Christchurch	1976-77
250	S.F.A.F.Bacchus	WI v I	Kanpur	1978-79

The highest for India is 236* by S.M.Gavaskar (v WI, Madras, 1983-84).

750 RUNS IN A SERIES

Runs			*Series*	*M*	*I*	*NO*	*HS*	*Avge*	*100*	*50*
974	D.G.Bradman	A v E	1930	5	7	–	334	139.14	4	–
905	W.R.Hammond	E v A	1928-29	5	9	1	251	113.12	4	–
839	M.A.Taylor	A v E	1989	6	11	1	219	83.90	2	5
834	R.N.Harvey	A v SA	1952-53	5	9	–	205	92.66	4	3
829	I.V.A.Richards	WI v E	1976	4	7	–	291	118.42	3	2
827	C.L.Walcott	WI v A	1954-55	5	10	–	155	82.70	5	2
824	G.St A.Sobers	WI v P	1957-58	5	8	2	365*	137.33	3	3
810	D.G.Bradman	A v E	1936-37	5	9	–	270	90.00	3	1
806	D.G.Bradman	A v SA	1931-32	5	5	1	299*	201.50	4	–
798	B.C.Lara	WI v E	1993-94	5	8	–	375	99.75	2	2
779	E.de C.Weekes	WI v I	1948-49	5	7	–	194	111.28	4	2
774	S.M.Gavaskar	I v WI	1970-71	4	8	3	220	154.80	4	3
765	B.C.Lara	WI v E	1995	6	10	1	179	85.00	3	3
761	Mudassar Nazar	P v I	1982-83	6	8	2	231	126.83	4	1
758	D.G.Bradman	A v E	1934	5	8	–	304	94.75	2	1
753	D.C.S.Compton	E v SA	1947	5	8	–	208	94.12	4	2
752	G.A.Gooch	E v I	1990	3	6	–	333	125.33	3	2

4000 RUNS IN A TEST CAREER

Runs			*M*	*I*	*NO*	*HS*	*Avge*	*100*	*50*
11174	A.R.Border	A	156	265	44	205	50.56	27	63
10122	S.M.Gavaskar	I	125	214	16	236*	51.12	34	45
8900	G.A.Gooch	E	118	215	6	333	42.58	20	46
8832	Javed Miandad	P	124	189	21	280*	52.57	23	43
8540	I.V.A.Richards	WI	121	182	12	291	50.23	24	45
8231	D.I.Gower	E	117	204	18	215	44.25	18	39
8159	S.R.Waugh	A	125	198	36	200	50.36	21	42
8114	G.Boycott	E	108	193	23	246*	47.72	22	42
8032	G.St A.Sobers	WI	93	160	21	365*	57.78	26	30
7624	M.C.Cowdrey	E	114	188	15	182	44.06	22	38
7558	C.G.Greenidge	WI	108	185	16	226	44.72	19	34
7525	M.A.Taylor	A	104	186	13	334*	43.49	19	40
7515	C.H.Lloyd	WI	110	175	14	242*	46.67	19	39
7487	D.L.Haynes	WI	116	202	25	184	42.29	18	39
7422	D.C.Boon	A	107	190	20	200	43.65	21	32
7249	W.R.Hammond	E	85	140	16	336*	58.45	22	24
7110	G.S.Chappell	A	87	151	19	247*	53.86	24	31
6996	D.G.Bradman	A	52	80	10	334	99.94	29	13
6971	L.Hutton	E	79	138	15	364	56.67	19	33
6868	D.B.Vengsarkar	I	116	185	22	166	42.13	17	35
6806	K.F.Barrington	E	82	131	15	256	58.67	20	35
6525	A.J.Stewart	E	95	172	12	190	40.78	12	35
6403	M.E.Waugh	A	100	165	11	153*	41.57	17	37
6403	M.A.Atherton	E	95	175	6	185*	37.88	13	39
6227	R.B.Kanhai	WI	79	137	6	256	47.53	15	28
6149	R.N.Harvey	A	79	137	10	205	48.41	21	24
6104	M.Azharuddin	I	98	145	9	199	44.88	21	21
6080	G.R.Viswanath	I	91	155	10	222	41.93	14	35
5949	R.B.Richardson	WI	86	146	12	194	44.39	16	27
5890	S.R.Tendulkar	I	74	117	12	217	56.09	22	23
5807	D.C.S.Compton	E	78	131	15	278	50.06	17	28
5768	Salim Malik	P	103	154	22	237	43.69	15	29
5573	B.C.Lara	WI	65	112	4	375	51.60	13	29
5444	M.D.Crowe	NZ	77	131	11	299	45.36	17	18

Runs			M	I	NO	HS	Avge	100	50
5422	P.A.de Silva	SL	79	135	11	267	43.72	17	21
5410	J.B.Hobbs	E	61	102	7	211	56.94	15	28
5357	K.D.Walters	A	74	125	14	250	48.26	15	33
5345	I.M.Chappell	A	75	136	10	196	42.42	14	26
5334	J.G.Wright	NZ	82	148	7	185	37.82	12	23
5248	Kapil Dev	I	131	184	15	163	31.05	8	27
5234	W.M.Lawry	A	67	123	12	210	47.15	13	27
5200	I.T.Botham	E	102	161	6	208	33.54	14	22
5138	J.H.Edrich	E	77	127	9	310*	43.54	12	24
5062	Zaheer Abbas	P	78	124	11	274	44.79	12	20
4882	T.W.Graveney	E	79	123	13	258	44.38	11	20
4869	R.B.Simpson	A	62	111	7	311	46.81	10	27
4737	I.R.Redpath	A	66	120	11	171	43.45	8	31
4695	A.Ranatunga	SL	86	143	10	135*	35.30	4	34
4656	A.J.Lamb	E	79	139	10	142	36.09	14	18
4555	H.Sutcliffe	E	54	84	9	194	60.73	16	23
4537	P.B.H.May	E	66	106	9	285*	46.77	13	22
4502	E.R.Dexter	E	62	102	8	205	47.89	9	27
4455	E.de C.Weekes	WI	48	81	5	207	58.61	15	19
4426	M.J.Slater	A	59	104	5	219	44.70	13	16
4415	K.J.Hughes	A	70	124	6	213	37.41	9	22
4409	M.W.Gatting	E	79	138	14	207	35.55	10	21
4399	A.I.Kallicharran	WI	66	109	10	187	44.43	12	21
4389	A.P.E.Knott	E	95	149	15	135	32.75	5	30
4378	M.Amarnath	I	69	113	10	138	42.50	11	24
4356	I.A.Healy	A	119	182	23	161*	27.39	4	22
4334	R.C.Fredericks	WI	59	109	7	169	42.49	8	26
4236	R.A.Smith	E	62	112	15	175	43.67	9	28
4153	C.L.Hooper	WI	80	136	13	178*	33.76	9	18
4114	Mudassar Nazar	P	76	116	8	231	38.09	10	17

The most for South Africa is 3872 by G.Kirsten (102 innings) and for Zimbabwe 2580 by A.Flower (70).

18 HUNDREDS

					Opponents								
			200	I	E	A	SA	WI	NZ	I	P	SL	Z
34	S.M.Gavaskar	I	4	214	4	8	–	13	2	–	5	2	–
29	D.G.Bradman	A	12	80	19	–	4	2	–	4	–	–	–
27	A.R.Border	A	2	265	8	–	–	3	5	4	6	1	–
26	G.St A.Sobers	WI	2	160	10	4	–	–	1	8	3	–	–
24	G.S.Chappell	A	4	151	9	–	–	5	3	1	6	–	–
24	I.V.A.Richards	WI	3	182	8	5	–	–	1	8	2	–	–
23	Javed Miandad	P	6	189	2	6	–	2	7	5	–	1	–
22	S.R.Tendulkar	I	1	117	4	5	2	1	3	–	1	6	–
22	W.R.Hammond	E	7	140	–	9	6	1	4	2	–	–	–
22	M.C.Cowdrey	E	–	188	–	5	3	6	2	3	3	–	–
22	G.Boycott	E	1	193	–	7	1	5	2	4	3	–	–
21	R.N.Harvey	A	2	137	6	–	8	3	–	4	–	–	–
21	M.Azharuddin	I	–	145	6	2	3	–	2	–	3	5	–
21	D.C.Boon	A	1	190	7	–	–	3	3	6	1	1	–
21	S.R.Waugh	A	1	198	7	–	2	4	1	1	2	3	1
20	K.F.Barrington	E	1	131	–	5	2	3	3	3	4	–	–
20	G.A.Gooch	E	2	215	–	4	–	5	4	5	1	1	–
19	L.Hutton	E	4	138	–	5	4	5	3	2	–	–	–
19	C.H.Lloyd	WI	1	175	5	6	–	–	–	7	1	–	–
19	C.G.Greenidge	WI	4	185	7	4	–	–	2	5	1	–	–

										Opponents				
			200	*I*	*E*	*A*	*SA*	*WI*	*NZ*	*I*	*P*	*SL*	*Z*
19	M.A.Taylor	A	2	186	6	–	2	1	2	2	4	2	–
18	D.L.Haynes	WI	–	202	5	5	–	–	3	2	3	–	–
18	D.I.Gower	E	2	204	–	9	–	1	4	2	2	–	–

The most for South Africa is 10 by D.J.Cullinan (89 innings) and G.Kirsten (102); for New Zealand 17 by M.D.Crowe (131); for Sri Lanka 17 by P.A.de Silva (135); for Zimbabwe 6 by A.Flower (70). The most double hundreds by batsmen not included above is 4 by Zaheer Abbas (12 hundreds for Pakistan) and 3 by R.B.Simpson (10 for Australia).

HIGHEST PARTNERSHIP FOR EACH WICKET

1st	413	V.Mankad/Pankaj Roy	I v NZ	Madras	1955-56
2nd	576	S.T.Jayasuriya/R.S.Mahanama	SL v I	Colombo (RPS)	1997-98
3rd	467	A.H.Jones/M.D.Crowe	NZ v SL	Wellington	1990-91
4th	411	P.B.H.May/M.C.Cowdrey	E v WI	Birmingham	1957
5th	405	S.G.Barnes/D.G.Bradman	A v E	Sydney	1946-47
6th	346	J.H.W.Fingleton/D.G.Bradman	A v E	Melbourne	1936-37
7th	347	D.St E.Atkinson/C.C.Depeiza	WI v A	Bridgetown	1954-55
8th	313	Wasim Akram/Saqlain Mushtaq	P v Z	Sheikhupura	1996-97
9th	195	M.V. Boucher/P.L.Symcox	SA v P	Johannesburg	1997-98
10th	151	B.F.Hastings/R.O.Collinge	NZ v P	Auckland	1972-73
	151	Azhar Mahmood/Mushtaq Ahmed	P v SA	Rawalpindi	1997-98

BOWLING RECORDS

NINE WICKETS IN AN INNINGS

10- 53	J.C.Laker	E v A	Manchester	1956
10- 74	A.Kumble	I v P	Delhi	1998-99
9- 28	G.A.Lohmann	E v SA	Johannesburg	1895-96
9- 37	J.C.Laker	E v A	Manchester	1956
9- 52	R.J.Hadlee	NZ v A	Brisbane	1985-86
9- 56	Abdul Qadir	P v E	Lahore	1987-88
9- 57	D.E.Malcolm	E v SA	The Oval	1994
9- 65	M.Muralitharan	SL v E	The Oval	1998
9- 69	J.M.Patel	I v A	Kanpur	1959-60
9- 83	Kapil Dev	I v WI	Ahmedabad	1983-84
9- 86	Sarfraz Nawaz	P v A	Melbourne	1978-79
9- 95	J.M.Noreiga	WI v I	Port-of-Spain	1970-71
9-102	S.P.Gupte	I v WI	Kanpur	1958-59
9-103	S.F.Barnes	E v SA	Johannesburg	1913-14
9-113	H.J.Tayfield	SA v E	Johannesburg	1956-57
9-121	A.A.Mailey	A v E	Melbourne	1920-21

The best analysis for Zimbabwe is 6-90 by H.H.Streak (v P, Harare, 1994-95).

15 WICKETS IN A TEST († *On debut*)

19- 90	J.C.Laker	E v A	Manchester	1956
17-159	S.F.Barnes	E v SA	Johannesburg	1913-14
16-136†	N.D.Hirwani	I v WI	Madras	1987-88
16-137†	R.A.L.Massie	A v E	Lord's	1972
16-220	M.Muralitharan	SL v E	The Oval	1998
15- 28	J.Briggs	E v SA	Cape Town	1888-89
15- 45	G.A.Lohmann	E v SA	Port Elizabeth	1895-96
15- 99	C.Blythe	E v SA	Leeds	1907
15-104	H.Verity	E v A	Lord's	1934
15-123	R.J.Hadlee	NZ v A	Brisbane	1985-86
15-124	W.Rhodes	E v A	Melbourne	1903-04

The best analysis for South Africa is 13-165 by H.J.Tayfield (v A, Melbourne, 1952-53); for West Indies 14-149 by M.A.Holding (v E, The Oval, 1976); for Pakistan 14-116 by Imran Khan (v SL, Lahore, 1981-82); and for Zimbabwe 11-255 by A.G. Huckle (v NZ, Bulawayo, 1997-98).

35 WICKETS IN A SERIES

Wkts			*Series*	*M*	*Balls*	*Runs*	*Avge*	*5 wI*	*10 wM*
49	S.F.Barnes	E v SA	1913-14	4	1356	536	10.93	7	3
46	J.C.Laker	E v A	1956	5	1703	442	9.60	4	2
44	C.V.Grimmett	A v SA	1935-36	5	2077	642	14.59	5	3
42	T.M.Alderman	A v E	1981	6	1950	893	21.26	4	–
41	R.M.Hogg	A v E	1978-79	6	1740	527	12.85	5	2
41	T.M.Alderman	A v E	1989	6	1616	712	17.36	6	1
40	Imran Khan	P v I	1982-83	6	1339	558	13.95	4	2
39	A.V.Bedser	E v A	1953	5	1591	682	17.48	5	1
39	D.K.Lillee	A v E	1981	6	1870	870	22.30	2	1
38	M.W.Tate	E v A	1924-25	5	2528	881	23.18	5	1
37	W.J.Whitty	A v SA	1910-11	5	1395	632	17.08	2	–
37	H.J.Tayfield	SA v E	1956-57	5	2280	636	17.18	4	1
36	A.E.E.Vogler	SA v E	1909-10	5	1349	783	21.75	4	1
36	A.A.Mailey	A v E	1920-21	5	1465	946	26.27	4	2
36	G.D.McGrath	A v E	1997	6	1499	701	19.47	2	–
35	G.A.Lohmann	E v SA	1895-96	3	520	203	5.80	4	2
35	B.S.Chandrasekhar	I v E	1972-73	5	1747	662	18.91	4	–
35	M.D.Marshall	WI v E	1988	5	1219	443	12.65	3	1

The most for New Zealand is 33 by R.J.Hadlee (v A, 1985-86); for Sri Lanka 20 by R.J.Ratnayake (v I, 1985-86); and for Zimbabwe 22 by H.H.Streak (v P, 1994-95).

200 WICKETS IN TESTS

Wkts			*M*	*Balls*	*Runs*	*Avge*	*5 wI*	*10 wM*
434	Kapil Dev	I	131	27740	12867	29.64	23	2
431	R.J.Hadlee	NZ	86	21918	9612	22.29	36	9
426	C.A.Walsh	WI	112	24696	10853	25.47	17	2
383	Wasim Akram	P	91	20337	8849	23.10	22	4
383	I.T.Botham	E	102	21815	10878	28.40	27	4
376	M.D.Marshall	WI	81	17584	7876	20.94	22	4
369	C.E.L.Ambrose	WI	88	19843	7865	21.31	22	3
362	Imran Khan	P	88	19458	8258	22.81	23	6
355	D.K.Lillee	A	70	18467	8493	23.92	23	7
351	S.K.Warne	A	81	22725	9091	25.90	16	4
325	R.G.D.Willis	E	90	17357	8190	25.20	16	–
309	L.R.Gibbs	WI	79	27115	8989	29.09	18	2
307	F.S.Trueman	E	67	15178	6625	21.57	17	3
297	D.L.Underwood	E	86	21862	7674	25.83	17	6
291	C.J.McDermott	A	71	16586	8332	28.63	14	2
290	A.A.Donald	SA	60	13216	6282	21.66	20	3
279	Waqar Younis	P	58	11527	6164	22.09	21	5
276	G.D.McGrath	A	59	14171	6189	22.42	17	2
266	B.S.Bedi	I	67	21364	7637	28.71	14	1
264	A.Kumble	I	59	18415	7471	28.29	15	3
259	J.Garner	WI	58	13169	5433	20.97	7	–
252	J.B.Statham	E	70	16056	6261	24.84	9	1
249	M.A.Holding	WI	60	12680	5898	23.68	13	2
248	R.Benaud	A	63	19108	6704	27.03	16	1

Wkts			M	Balls	Runs	Avge	5 wI	10 wM
246	G.D.McKenzie	A	60	17681	7328	29.78	16	3
242	B.S.Chandrasekhar	I	58	15963	7199	29.74	16	2
236	A.V.Bedser	E	51	15918	5876	24.89	15	5
236	Abdul Qadir	P	67	17126	7742	32.80	15	5
235	G.St A.Sobers	WI	93	21599	7999	34.03	6	–
228	R.R.Lindwall	A	61	13650	5251	23.03	12	–
227	M.Muralitharan	SL	48	14883	6140	27.04	17	2
216	C.V.Grimmett	A	37	14513	5231	24.21	21	7
212	M.G.Hughes	A	53	12285	6017	28.38	7	1
202	A.M.E.Roberts	WI	47	11136	5174	25.61	11	2
202	J.A.Snow	E	49	12021	5387	26.66	8	1
200	J.R.Thomson	A	51	10535	5601	28.00	8	–

The most for Zimbabwe is 111 in 27 Tests by H.H.Streak.

HAT-TRICKS

F.R.Spofforth	Australia v England	Melbourne	1878-79
W.Bates	England v Australia	Melbourne	1882-83
J.Briggs	England v Australia	Sydney	1891-92
G.A.Lohmann	England v South Africa	Port Elizabeth	1895-96
J.T.Hearne	England v Australia	Leeds	1899
H.Trumble	Australia v England	Melbourne	1901-02
H.Trumble	Australia v England	Melbourne	1903-04
T.J.Matthews (2)[2]	Australia v South Africa	Manchester	1912
M.J.C.Allom[1]	England v New Zealand	Christchurch	1929-30
T.W.J.Goddard	England v South Africa	Johannesburg	1938-39
P.J.Loader	England v West Indies	Leeds	1957
L.F.Kline	Australia v South Africa	Cape Town	1957-58
W.W.Hall	West Indies v Pakistan	Lahore	1958-59
G.M.Griffin	South Africa v England	Lord's	1960
L.R.Gibbs	West Indies v Australia	Adelaide	1960-61
P.J.Petherick[1]	New Zealand v Pakistan	Lahore	1976-77
C.A.Walsh[3]	West Indies v Australia	Brisbane	1988-89
M.G.Hughes[3]	Australia v West Indies	Perth	1988-89
D.W.Fleming[1]	Australia v Pakistan	Rawalpindi	1994-95
S.K.Warne	Australia v England	Melbourne	1994-95
D.G.Cork	England v West Indies	Manchester	1995
D.Gough	England v Australia	Sydney	1998-99
Wasim Akram[4]	Pakistan v Sri Lanka	Lahore	1998-99
Wasim Akram[4]	Pakistan v Sri Lanka	Dhaka	1998-99
D.N.T.Zoysa[5]	Sri Lanka v Zimbabwe	Harare	1999-00

[1] *On debut.* [2] *Hat-trick in each innings.* [3] *Involving both innings.* [4] *In successive Tests.* [5] *His first 3 balls (second over of the match).*

WICKET-KEEPING RECORDS

SEVEN DISMISSALS IN AN INNINGS

7	Wasim Bari	Pakistan v New Zealand	Auckland	1978-79
7	R.W.Taylor	England v India	Bombay	1979-80
7	I.D.S.Smith	New Zealand v Sri Lanka	Hamilton	1990-91

FIVE STUMPINGS IN AN INNINGS

5	K.S.More	India v West Indies	Madras	1987-88

TEN DISMISSALS IN A TEST

11	R.C.Russell	England v South Africa	Johannesburg	1995-96
10	R.W.Taylor	England v India	Bombay	1979-80

25 DISMISSALS IN A SERIES

28	R.W.Marsh	Australia v England	1982-83
27 (inc 2st)	R.C.Russell	England v South Africa	1995-96
27 (inc 2st)	I.A.Healy	Australia v England (6 Tests)	1997
26 (inc 3st)	J.H.B.Waite	South Africa v New Zealand	1961-62
26	R.W.Marsh	Australia v West Indies (6 Tests)	1975-76
26 (inc 5st)	I.A.Healy	Australia v England (6 Tests)	1993
26 (inc 1st)	M.V.Boucher	South Africa v England	1998
25 (inc 2st)	I.A.Healy	Australia v England	1994-95

100 DISMISSALS IN TESTS

Total			*Tests*	*Ct*	*St*
395	I.A.Healy	Australia	119	366	29
355	R.W.Marsh	Australia	96	343	12
272†	P.J.L.Dujon	West Indies	81	267	5
269	A.P.E.Knott	England	95	250	19
228	Wasim Bari	Pakistan	81	201	27
219	T.G.Evans	England	91	173	46
198	S.M.H.Kirmani	India	88	160	38
189	D.L.Murray	West Indies	62	181	8
187	A.T.W.Grout	Australia	51	163	24
180†	A.J.Stewart	England	95	172	8
176	I.D.S.Smith	New Zealand	63	168	8
174	R.W.Taylor	England	57	167	7
165	R.C.Russell	England	54	153	12
152	D.J.Richardson	South Africa	42	150	2
141	J.H.B.Waite	South Africa	50	124	17
135†	A.C.Parore	New Zealand	58	131	4
130	K.S.More	India	49	110	20
130	W.A.S.Oldfield	Australia	54	78	52
114†	J.M.Parks	England	46	103	11
109	M.V.Boucher	South Africa	26	107	2
104	Salim Yousuf	Pakistan	32	91	13
104†	A.Flower	Zimbabwe	39	99	5
103	Moin Khan	Pakistan	50	88	15

The most for Sri Lanka is 74 by R.S.Kaluwitharana (33 Tests).

† *Including catches taken in the field*

FIELDING RECORDS

FIVE CATCHES IN AN INNINGS

5	V.Y.Richardson	Australia v South Africa	Durban	1935-36
5	Yajurvindra Singh	India v England	Bangalore	1976-77
5	M.Azharuddin	India v Pakistan	Karachi	1989-90
5	K.Srikkanth	India v Australia	Perth	1991-92
5	S.P.Fleming	New Zealand v Zimbabwe	Harare	1997-98

SEVEN CATCHES IN A TEST

7	G.S.Chappell	Australia v England	Perth	1974-75
7	Yajurvindra Singh	India v England	Bangalore	1976-77
7	H.P.Tillekeratne	Sri Lanka v New Zealand	Colombo (SSC)	1992-93
7	S.P.Fleming	New Zealand v Zimbabwe	Harare	1997-98

15 CATCHES IN A SERIES

15	J.M.Gregory	Australia v England	1920-21

100 CATCHES IN TESTS

Total			*Tests*	*Total*			*Tests*
157	M.A.Taylor	Australia	104	110	R.B.Simpson	Australia	62
156	A.R.Border	Australia	156	110	W.R.Hammond	England	85
129	M.E.Waugh	Australia	100	109	G.St A.Sobers	West Indies	93
122	G.S.Chappell	Australia	87	108	S.M.Gavaskar	India	125
122	I.V.A.Richards	West Indies	121	105	I.M.Chappell	Australia	75
120	I.T.Botham	England	102	105	M.Azharuddin	India	98
120	M.C.Cowdrey	England	114	103	G.A.Gooch	England	118

The most for South Africa is 56 by B.Mitchell (42 Tests); for New Zealand 80 by S.P.Fleming (48 Tests); for Pakistan 93 by Javed Miandad (124 Tests); for Sri Lanka 56 by R.S.Mahanama (52 Tests); and for Zimbabwe 39 by A.D.R.Campbell (39 Tests).

APPEARANCE RECORDS

100 TEST MATCH APPEARANCES

156	A.R.Border	Australia	114	M.C.Cowdrey	England
131	Kapil Dev	India	112	C.A.Walsh	West Indies
125	S.M.Gavaskar	India	110	C.H.Lloyd	West Indies
125	S.R.Waugh	Australia	108	G.Boycott	England
124	Javed Miandad	Pakistan	108	C.G.Greenidge	West Indies
121	I.V.A.Richards	West Indies	107	D.C.Boon	Australia
119	I.A.Healy	Australia	104	M.A.Taylor	Australia
118	G.A.Gooch	England	103	Salim Malik	Pakistan
117	D.I.Gower	England	102	I.T.Botham	England
116	D.L.Haynes	West Indies	100	M.E.Waugh	Australia
116	D.B.Vengsarkar	India			

The most for South Africa is 66 by W.J.Cronje; for New Zealand 86 by R.J.Hadlee; for Sri Lanka 86 by A.Ranatunga; and for Zimbabwe 39 by A.D.R.Campbell and A.Flower.

100 CONSECUTIVE TEST APPEARANCES

153	A.R.Border	Australia	March 1979 to March 1994
106	S.M.Gavaskar	India	January 1975 to February 1987

75 TESTS AS CAPTAIN

93	A.R.Border	Australia	December 1984 to March 1994

50 TEST UMPIRING APPEARANCES

66	H.D.Bird	July 1973 to June 1996

D.R.Shepherd (August 1985 to February 2000) stood in his 50th Test after the deadline for these records.

INDIA v PAKISTAN (1st Test)

At M.A.Chidambaram Stadium, Madras (Chennai), on 28, 29, 30, 31 January 1999.
Toss: Pakistan. Result: **PAKISTAN** won by 12 runs.
Debuts: India – S.Ramesh.

PAKISTAN

Saeed Anwar	lbw b Srinath	24	lbw b Prasad	7
Shahid Afridi	c Ganguly b Srinath	11	b Prasad	141
Ijaz Ahmed	lbw b Kumble	13	c and b Kumble	11
Inzamam-ul-Haq	c and b Kumble	10	c Laxman b Tendulkar	51
Yousuf Youhana	lbw b Tendulkar	53	b Tendulkar	26
Salim Malik	b Srinath	8	c Dravid b Joshi	32
†Moin Khan	c Ganguly b Kumble	60	c Mongia b Prasad	3
*Wasim Akram	c Laxman b Kumble	38	c Joshi b Prasad	1
Saqlain Mushtaq	lbw b Kumble	2	lbw b Prasad	0
Nadeem Khan	c Dravid b Kumble	8	not out	1
Waqar Younis	not out	0	c Ramesh b Prasad	5
Extras	(LB 5, NB 6)	11	(B 1, LB 4, NB 3)	8
Total		**238**		**286**

INDIA

S.Ramesh	lbw b Wasim	43		c Inzamam b Waqar	5
V.V.S.Laxman	lbw b Wasim	23		lbw b Waqar	0
R.Dravid	lbw b Saqlain	53		b Wasim	10
S.R.Tendulkar	c Salim b Saqlain	0		c Wasim b Saqlain	136
*M.Azharuddin	c Inzamam b Saqlain	11		lbw b Saqlain	7
S.C.Ganguly	c Ijaz b Afridi	54		c Moin b Saqlain	2
†N.R.Mongia	st Moin b Saqlain	5		c Waqar b Wasim	52
A.Kumble	c Yousuf b Saqlain	4	(8)	lbw b Wasim	1
S.B.Joshi	not out	25	(7)	c and b Saqlain	8
J.Srinath	c Ijaz b Afridi	10		b Saqlain	1
B.K.V.Prasad	st Moin b Afridi	4		not out	0
Extras	(B 2, LB 2, NB 18)	22		(B 8, LB 10, NB 18)	36
Total		**254**			**258**

INDIA	O	M	R	W		O	M	R	W
Srinath	15	3	63	3		16	1	68	0
Prasad	16	1	54	0		10.2	5	33	6
Kumble	24.5	7	70	6		22	4	93	1
Joshi	21	8	36	0		14	3	42	1
Tendulkar	3	0	10	1		7	1	35	2
Laxman						2	0	10	0
PAKISTAN									
Wasim Akram	20	4	60	2		22	4	80	3
Waqar Younis	12	2	48	0		12	6	26	2
Saqlain Mushtaq	35	8	94	5	(4)	32.2	8	93	5
Shahid Afridi	7.1	0	31	3	(3)	16	7	23	0
Nadeem Khan	7	0	17	0		13	5	18	0

FALL OF WICKETS

	P	I	P	I
Wkt	*1st*	*1st*	*2nd*	*2nd*
1st	32	67	11	5
2nd	41	71	42	6
3rd	61	72	139	50
4th	66	103	169	73
5th	91	156	275	82
6th	154	166	278	218
7th	214	188	279	254
8th	227	229	279	256
9th	237	246	280	256
10th	238	254	286	258

Umpires: R.S.Dunne (*New Zealand*) (31) and V.K.Ramaswamy (25).
Referee: C.W.Smith (*West Indies*) (20). **Test No. 1442/45 (I322/P254)**

INDIA v PAKISTAN (2nd Test)

At Feroz Shah Kotla, Delhi, on 4, 5, 6, 7 February 1999.
Toss: India. Result: **INDIA** won by 212 runs.
Debuts: None.

INDIA

S.Ramesh	b Saqlain	60		c and b Mushtaq Ahmed	96
V.V.S.Laxman	b Wasim	35		b Wasim	8
R.Dravid	lbw b Saqlain	33		c Ijaz b Saqlain	29
S.R.Tendulkar	lbw b Saqlain	6		c Wasim b Mushtaq Ahmed	29
*M.Azharuddin	c Ijaz b Mushtaq Ahmed	67		b Wasim	14
S.C.Ganguly	lbw b Mushtaq Ahmed	13		not out	62
†N.R.Mongia	run out	10		lbw b Wasim	0
A.Kumble	c Yousuf b Saqlain	0		c Ijaz b Saqlain	15
J.Srinath	lbw b Saqlain	0		c Ijaz b Saqlain	49
B.K.V.Prasad	not out	1		b Saqlain	6
Harbhajan Singh	run out	1		b Saqlain	0
Extras	(B 11, LB 9, NB 6)	26		(B 13, LB 9, NB 9)	31
Total		**252**			**339**

PAKISTAN

Saeed Anwar	c Mongia b Prasad	1		c Laxman b Kumble	69
Shahid Afridi	b Harbhajan	32		c Mongia b Kumble	41
Ijaz Ahmed	c Dravid b Kumble	17		lbw b Kumble	0
Inzamam-ul-Haq	b Kumble	26		b Kumble	6
Yousuf Youhana	c and b Kumble	3		lbw b Kumble	0
Salim Malik	c Azharuddin b Prasad	31	(7)	b Kumble	15
†Moin Khan	lbw b Srinath	14	(6)	c Ganguly b Kumble	3
*Wasim Akram	lbw b Harbhajan	15		c Laxman b Kumble	37
Mushtaq Ahmed	c Laxman b Harbhajan	12		c Dravid b Kumble	1
Saqlain Mushtaq	lbw b Kumble	2		lbw b Kumble	0
Waqar Younis	not out	1		not out	6
Extras	(B 1, LB 8, NB 9)	18		(B 15, LB 2, W 2, NB 10)	29
Total		**172**			**207**

PAKISTAN	O	M	R	W		O	M	R	W
Wasim Akram	13	3	23	1		21	3	43	3
Waqar Younis	13	5	37	0		12	2	42	0
Mushtaq Ahmed	26	5	64	2	(4)	26	4	86	2
Saqlain Mushtaq	33.5	9	94	5	(3)	46.4	12	122	5
Shahid Afridi	4	1	14	0		8	1	24	0
INDIA									
Srinath	12	1	38	1		12	2	50	0
Prasad	11	2	20	2		4	1	15	0
Harbhajan Singh	17	5	30	3	(4)	18	5	51	0
Kumble	24.3	4	75	4	(3)	26.3	9	74	10

FALL OF WICKETS

	I	P	I	P
Wkt	*1st*	*1st*	*2nd*	*2nd*
1st	88	1	15	101
2nd	113	54	100	101
3rd	122	54	168	115
4th	191	60	183	115
5th	231	114	199	127
6th	240	130	199	128
7th	243	139	231	186
8th	247	167	331	198
9th	248	168	339	198
10th	252	172	339	207

Umpires: S.A.Bucknor (*West Indies*) (41) and A.V.Jayaprakash (2).
Referee: C.W.Smith (*West Indies*) (21). **Test No. 1443/46 (I323/P255)**

INDIA v PAKISTAN 1998-99

INDIA – BATTING AND FIELDING

	M	I	NO	HS	Runs	Avge	100	50	Ct/St
S.Ramesh	2	4	–	96	204	51.00	–	2	1
S.C.Ganguly	2	4	1	62*	131	43.66	–	2	3
S.R.Tendulkar	2	4	–	136	171	42.75	1	–	–
R.Dravid	2	4	–	53	125	31.25	–	1	4
M.Azharuddin	2	4	–	67	99	24.75	–	1	1
N.R.Mongia	2	4	–	52	67	16.75	–	1	3
V.V.S.Laxman	2	4	–	35	66	16.50	–	–	5
J.Srinath	2	4	–	49	60	15.00	–	–	–
B.K.V.Prasad	2	4	2	6	11	5.50	–	–	–
A.Kumble	2	4	–	15	20	5.00	–	–	3

Played in one Test: Harbhajan Singh 1, 0; S.B.Joshi 25*, 8 (1 ct).

INDIA – BOWLING

	O	M	R	W	Avge	Best	5wI	10wM
A.Kumble	97.5	24	312	21	14.85	10-74	2	1
S.R.Tendulkar	10	1	45	3	15.00	2-35	–	–
B.K.V.Prasad	41.2	9	122	8	15.25	6-33	1	–
Harbhajan Singh	35	10	81	3	27.00	3-30	–	–
J.Srinath	55	7	219	4	54.75	3-63	–	–

Also bowled: S.B.Joshi 35-11-78-1; V.V.S.Laxman 2-0-10-0.

PAKISTAN – BATTING AND FIELDING

	M	I	NO	HS	Runs	Avge	100	50	Ct/St
Shahid Afridi	2	4	–	141	225	56.25	1	–	–
Saeed Anwar	2	4	–	69	101	25.25	–	1	–
Inzamam-ul-Haq	2	4	–	51	93	23.25	–	1	2
Wasim Akram	2	4	–	38	91	22.75	–	–	2
Salim Malik	2	4	–	32	86	21.50	–	–	1
Yousuf Youhana	2	4	–	53	82	20.50	–	1	2
Moin Khan	2	4	–	60	80	20.00	–	1	1/2
Waqar Younis	2	4	3	6*	12	12.00	–	–	1
Ijaz Ahmed	2	4	–	17	41	10.25	–	–	6
Saqlain Mushtaq	2	4	–	2	4	1.00	–	–	1

Played in one Test: Mushtaq Ahmed 12, 1 (1 ct); Nadeem Khan 8, 1*.

PAKISTAN – BOWLING

	O	M	R	W	Avge	Best	5wI	10wM
Saqlain Mushtaq	149.5	37	403	20	20.15	5-93	4	2
Wasim Akram	76	14	206	9	22.88	3-43	–	–
Shahid Afridi	35.1	9	92	3	30.66	3-31	–	–
Mushtaq Ahmed	52	9	150	4	37.50	2-64	–	–

Also bowled: Nadeem Khan 20-5-35-0; Waqar Younis 49-15-153-2.

PAKISTAN v INDIA
(Asian Test Championship – 1st Match)

At Eden Gardens, Calcutta, India, on 16, 17, 18, 19, 20 February 1999.
Toss: Pakistan. Result: **PAKISTAN** won by 46 runs (*Pakistan 17 points, India 5*).
Debuts: Pakistan – Wajahatullah Wasti.

PAKISTAN

Saeed Anwar	b Prasad	0		not out	188
Shahid Afridi	c Mongia b Srinath	8	(6)	c Laxman b Srinath	0
Ijaz Ahmed	lbw b Srinath	1	(4)	c Mongia b Srinath	11
Wajahatullah Wasti	c Mongia b Prasad	6	(2)	c Mongia b Srinath	9
Yousuf Youhana	c Azharuddin b Srinath	2		c Dravid b Srinath	56
Salim Malik	c Mongia b Srinath	32	(7)	lbw b Srinath	9
Azhar Mahmood	b Srinath	0	(9)	lbw b Srinath	0
†Moin Khan	c Laxman b Tendulkar	70		c Mongia b Prasad	8
*Wasim Akram	c sub (H.H.Kanitkar) b Harbhajan	38	(10)	c Mongia b Srinath	1
Shoaib Akhtar	lbw b Kumble	4	(11)	b Srinath	1
Saqlain Mushtaq	not out	4	(3)	c Mongia b Harbhajan	21
Extras	(LB 11, W 1, NB 8)	20		(LB 3, W 5, NB 4)	12
Total		**185**			**316**

INDIA

S.Ramesh	lbw b Wasim	79		lbw b Saqlain	40
V.V.S.Laxman	b Shoaib	5		c Yousuf b Saqlain	67
A.Kumble	c Moin b Azhar	18	(8)	c Afridi b Shoaib	16
R.Dravid	b Shoaib	24	(3)	c Moin b Shoaib	13
S.R.Tendulkar	b Shoaib	0	(4)	run out	9
*M.Azharuddin	c Saqlain b Wasim	23	(5)	c Yousuf b Saqlain	20
S.C.Ganguly	c Wasim b Saqlain	17	(6)	c Azhar b Wasim	24
†N.R.Mongia	run out	5	(7)	lbw b Shoaib	1
J.Srinath	c Moin b Wasim	3		c Moin b Wasim	3
B.K.V.Prasad	b Shoaib	0		b Shoaib	2
Harbhajan Singh	not out	8		not out	0
Extras	(LB 9, NB 32)	41		(B 10, LB 9, NB 18)	37
Total		**223**			**232**

INDIA	O	M	R	W		O	M	R	W
Srinath	19	4	46	5		27	6	86	8
Prasad	18	6	27	2		24	5	61	1
Ganguly	5	2	9	0					
Kumble	19.2	8	48	1	(3)	27	4	91	0
Harbhajan Singh	12	2	36	1	(4)	16	1	56	1
Tendulkar	3	1	8	1	(7)	2	0	10	0
Laxman					(5)	2	0	4	0
Ramesh					(6)	1	0	5	0
PAKISTAN									
Wasim Akram	24	5	65	3	(2)	24	4	64	2
Shoaib Akhtar	19.2	1	71	4	(1)	20.1	5	47	4
Azhar Mahmood	18	5	40	1		6	0	23	0
Saqlain Mushtaq	13	4	31	1		25	5	69	3
Shahid Afridi	2	0	7	0		4	1	10	0

FALL OF WICKETS

	P	I	P	I
Wkt	*1st*	*1st*	*2nd*	*2nd*
1st	15	26	26	108
2nd	17	91	94	134
3rd	19	147	147	145
4th	23	147	262	149
5th	25	164	262	183
6th	26	205	284	190
7th	110	205	301	219
8th	173	211	302	224
9th	177	212	304	231
10th	185	223	316	232

Umpires: S.A.Bucknor (*West Indies*) (42) and D.L.Orchard (*South Africa*) (11).
Referee: C.W.Smith (*West Indies*) (22). **Test No. 1444/47 (I324/P256)**

SRI LANKA v INDIA
(Asian Test Championship – 2nd Match)

At Sinhalese Sports Club, Colombo, Sri Lanka, on 24, 25, 26, 27, 28 February 1999.
Toss: Sri Lanka. Result: **MATCH DRAWN** (*India 5 points, Sri Lanka 3*).
Debuts: Sri Lanka – K.E.A.Upashantha, R.L.Perera; India – A.Nehra.

INDIA

S.Ramesh	c Ranatunga b Jayawardena	143		c Tillekeratne b Upashantha	30
V.V.S.Laxman	c De Silva b Perera	11		lbw b Upashantha	25
R.Dravid	c Ranatunga b Hathurusinghe	107			
S.R.Tendulkar	c Kaluwitharana b Vaas	53		not out	124
*M.Azharuddin	c Hathurusinghe b Arnold	87		c Arnold b De Silva	15
S.C.Ganguly	c sub (R.S.Kalpage) b Upashantha	56	(3)	st Kaluwitharana b De Silva	78
†N.R.Mongia	c De Silva b Arnold	25			
A.Kumble	not out	10	(6)	c Vaas b Arnold	10
B.K.V.Prasad			(7)	not out	9
Harbhajan Singh					
A.Nehra					
Extras	(B 5, LB 6, W 3, NB 12)	26		(B 1, LB 3, W 2, NB 9)	15
Total	(7 wickets declared)	**518**		(5 wickets)	**306**

SRI LANKA

R.P.Arnold	run out	34
M.S.Atapattu	lbw b Nehra	6
D.P.M.deS.Jayawardena	c and b Kumble	242
U.C.Hathurusinghe	lbw b Prasad	14
P.A.de Silva	b Harbhajan	23
*A.Ranatunga	c sub (H.H.Kanitkar) b Kumble	66
H.P.Tillekeratne	st Mongia b Harbhajan	14
†R.S.Kaluwitharana	b Harbhajan	23
W.P.U.C.J.Vaas	c Laxman b Kumble	23
K.E.A.Upashantha	lbw b Kumble	6
R.L.Perera	not out	1
Extras	(B 1, LB 19, W 4, NB 9)	33
Total		**485**

SRI LANKA	O	M	R	W		O	M	R	W
Vaas	31	5	108	1		18	3	58	0
Perera	30	4	125	1		14	2	60	0
Upashantha	28	3	94	1		15	2	41	2
Hathurusinghe	18	3	51	1					
Arnold	24.5	2	94	2	(4)	23.4	4	54	1
Jayawardena	11	3	35	1		14	1	30	0
De Silva					(5)	18.2	2	59	2
Tillekeratne					(7)	1	1	0	0
INDIA									
Prasad	31	6	94	1					
Nehra	28	5	94	1					
Kumble	54.1	10	134	4					
Harbhajan Singh	40	9	127	3					
Tendulkar	5	0	16	0					
Ganguly	1	1	0	0					

FALL OF WICKETS

	I	SL	I
Wkt	*1st*	*1st*	*2nd*
1st	20	18	50
2nd	252	93	74
3rd	288	129	213
4th	351	178	253
5th	463	354	283
6th	491	390	–
7th	518	466	–
8th	–	466	–
9th	–	484	–
10th	–	485	–

Umpires: R.E.Koertzen (*South Africa*) (12) and R.B.Tiffin (*Zimbabwe*) (9).
Referee: C.W.Smith (*West Indies*) (23). **Test No. 1445/20 (SL88/I325)**

PAKISTAN v SRI LANKA
(Asian Test Championship – 3rd Match)

At Gadaffi Stadium, Lahore, Pakistan, on 4, 5, 6, 7, 8 March 1999.
Toss: Pakistan. Result: **MATCH DRAWN** (*Pakistan 8 points, Sri Lanka 7*).
Debuts: Pakistan – Imran Nazir; Sri Lanka – D.A.Gunawardena.

PAKISTAN

Saeed Anwar	b Wickremasinghe	0	(4)	run out	45
Wajahatullah Wasti	run out	133	(1)	not out	121
Imran Nazir	c De Silva b Wickremasinghe	64	(5)	b Bandaratilake	13
Inzamam-ul-Haq	b Wickremasinghe	0	(3)	lbw b De Silva	4
Yousuf Youhana	c and b Kalpage	83	(6)	st Kaluwitharana b Bandaratilake	0
Shahid Afridi	c Gunawardena b Kalpage	0	(2)	c Kaluwitharana b De Silva	84
†Moin Khan	lbw b Wickremasinghe	57	(8)	run out	2
Saqlain Mushtaq	c De Silva b Bandaratilake	15	(9)	st Kaluwitharana b Kalpage	9
*Wasim Akram	c Arnold b Wickremasinghe	4	(7)	b Kalpage	17
Shahid Nazir	c Atapattu b Wickremasinghe	10			
Fazal-e-Akber	not out	15			
Extras	(B 2, LB 11, NB 4)	17		(B 3, LB 7, NB 9)	19
Total		**398**		(8 wickets declared)	**314**

SRI LANKA

R.P.Arnold	b Saqlain	123	not out	56
D.A.Gunawardena	c Shahid Nazir b Fazal	43	lbw b Shahid Nazir	37
D.P.M.deS.Jayawardena	b Saqlain	4	c Moin b Wasim	50
M.S.Atapattu	c Yousuf b Saqlain	23	not out	6
*H.P.Tillekeratne	b Saqlain	9		
†R.S.Kaluwitharana	c Moin b Wasim	100		
U.C.Hathurusinghe	lbw b Afridi	0		
R.S.Kalpage	not out	2		
M.R.C.N.Bandaratilake	b Wasim	0		
G.P.Wickremasinghe	b Wasim	0		
K.S.C.de Silva	b Wasim	8		
Extras	(LB 8, NB 8)	16	(LB 10, NB 5)	15
Total		**328**	(2 wickets)	**164**

SRI LANKA	O	M	R	W		O	M	R	W
Wickremasinghe	29.1	7	103	6		9	1	27	0
De Silva	14	0	88	0		29	4	90	2
Hathurusinghe	12	3	29	0	(5)	13	2	41	0
Bandaratilake	31	8	90	1	(3)	25	12	54	2
Kalpage	16	2	75	2	(4)	20.5	3	92	2
PAKISTAN									
Wasim Akram	9.2	2	30	4		13	2	39	1
Fazal-e-Akber	19	4	92	1		8	1	27	0
Shahid Nazir	11	1	45	0	(4)	8	0	27	1
Saqlain Mushtaq	25	6	82	4	(3)	21.1	8	53	0
Shahid Afridi	20	4	71	1					
Wajahatullah Wasti					(5)	1	0	8	0

FALL OF WICKETS

Wkt	P *1st*	SL *1st*	P *2nd*	SL *2nd*
1st	0	84	156	64
2nd	105	91	161	158
3rd	105	146	227	–
4th	283	156	250	–
5th	283	299	254	–
6th	302	308	288	–
7th	323	320	296	–
8th	339	320	314	–
9th	373	320	–	–
10th	398	328	–	–

Umpires: R.E.Koertzen (*South Africa*) (13) and D.R.Shepherd (*England*) (45).
Referee: C.W.Smith (*West Indies*) (24). **Test No. 1446/20 P257/SL89)**

PAKISTAN v SRI LANKA
(Asian Test Championship – Final)

At Bangabandhu National Stadium, Dhaka, Bangladesh, on 12, 13, 14, 15 March 1999.
Toss: Sri Lanka. Result: **PAKISTAN** won by an innings and 175 runs.
Debuts: Sri Lanka – U.D.U.Chandana.

SRI LANKA

R.P.Arnold	b Shoaib	10		c Wasim b Arshad	30
D.A.Gunawardena	c Wasti b Wasim	4		c Afridi b Wasim	0
D.P.M.deS.Jayawardena	lbw b Wasim	0	(4)	c Wasti b Wasim	1
M.S.Atapattu	lbw b Saqlain	36	(5)	run out	22
*P.A.de Silva	lbw b Arshad	72	(6)	c Wasti b Saqlain	6
H.P.Tillekeratne	c Wasti b Arshad	15	(7)	not out	55
†R.S.Kaluwitharana	c Yousuf b Arshad	9	(8)	c and b Saqlain	0
U.D.U.Chandana	c Moin b Shoaib	15	(9)	lbw b Afridi	28
W.P.U.C.J.Vaas	not out	20	(3)	b Wasim	0
G.P.Wickremasinghe	c Wasti b Arshad	2		b Afridi	7
K.S.C.de Silva	c Moin b Arshad	11		b Saqlain	27
Extras	(B 12, LB 9, NB 16)	37		(B 4, LB 7, NB 1)	12
Total		**231**			**188**

PAKISTAN

Saeed Anwar	c and b Arnold	57
Wajahatullah Wasti	c Jayawardena b K.S.C.de Silva	22
Ijaz Ahmed	st Tillekeratne b Chandana	211
Inzamam-ul-Haq	not out	200
Yousuf Youhana	c sub‡ b Chandana	19
Shahid Afridi	c and b Chandana	21
†Moin Khan	c K.S.C.de Silva b Arnold	10
*Wasim Akram	c Vaas b Chandana	8
Saqlain Mushtaq	run out	4
Arshad Khan	c Tillekeratne b Chandana	3
Shoaib Akhtar	st Tillekeratne b Chandana	4
Extras	(B 13, LB 14, NB 8)	35
Total		**594**

PAKISTAN	O	M	R	W		O	M	R	W
Wasim Akram	14	2	45	2		7	0	33	3
Shoaib Akhtar	13	3	36	2		10.4	3	26	0
Saqlain Mushtaq	29	7	76	1		28.5	15	46	3
Shahid Afridi	2	0	15	0	(5)	7	1	31	2
Arshad Khan	20	5	38	5	(4)	12	3	41	1
SRI LANKA									
Vaas	32	4	101	0					
Wickremasinghe	20	3	53	0					
K.S.C.de Silva	25.4	3	75	1					
Chandana	47.5	7	179	6					
P.A.de Silva	12	0	44	0					
Arnold	37.2	7	80	2					
Jayawardena	10	1	35	0					

FALL OF WICKETS

	SL	P	SL
Wkt	*1st*	*1st*	*2nd*
1st	16	75	5
2nd	16	117	5
3rd	19	483	9
4th	84	515	48
5th	119	518	59
6th	135	532	59
7th	177	540	61
8th	201	555	101
9th	208	560	115
10th	231	594	188

‡ (U.C.Hathurusinghe)

Umpires: D.B.Cowie (*New Zealand*) (16) and D.R.Shepherd (*England*) (46).
Referee: C.W.Smith (*West Indies*) (25). **Test No. 1447/21 (P258/SL90)**

ASIAN TEST CHAMPIONSHIP 1998-99

INDIA – BATTING	*M*	*I*	*NO*	*HS*	*Runs*	*Avge*	*100*	*50*	*Ct/St*
S.Ramesh	2	4	–	143	292	73.00	1	1	–
S.R.Tendulkar	2	4	1	124*	186	62.00	1	1	–
R.Dravid	2	3	–	107	144	48.00	1	–	1
S.C.Ganguly	2	4	–	78	175	43.75	–	2	–
M.Azharuddin	2	4	–	87	145	36.25	–	1	1
V.V.S.Laxman	2	4	–	67	108	27.00	–	1	3
A.Kumble	2	4	1	18	54	18.00	–	–	1
N.R.Mongia	2	3	–	25	31	10.33	–	–	8/1
B.K.V.Prasad	2	3	1	9*	11	5.50	–	–	–
Harbhajan Singh	2	2	2	8*	8	–	–	–	–

Played in one Test: A.Nehra did not bat; J.Srinath 3, 3.

INDIA – BOWLING	*O*	*M*	*R*	*W*	*Avge*	*Best*	*5wI*	*10wM*
J.Srinath	46	10	132	13	10.15	8- 86	2	1
Harbhajan Singh	68	12	219	5	43.80	3-127	–	–
A.Kumble	100.3	22	273	5	54.60	4-134	–	–

Also bowled: S.C.Ganguly 6-3-9-0; V.V.S.Laxman 2-0-4-0; A.Nehra 28-5-94-1; B.K.V.Prasad 73-17-182-4; S.Ramesh 1-0-5-0; S.R.Tendulkar 10-1-34-1.

PAKISTAN – BATTING	*M*	*I*	*NO*	*HS*	*Runs*	*Avge*	*100*	*50*	*Ct/St*
Inzamam-ul-Haq	2	3	1	200*	204	102.00	1	–	–
Ijaz Ahmed	2	3	–	211	223	74.33	1	–	–
Wajahatullah Wasti	3	5	1	133	291	72.75	2	–	5
Saeed Anwar	3	5	1	188*	290	72.50	1	1	–
Yousuf Youhana	3	5	–	83	160	32.00	–	2	4
Moin Khan	3	5	–	70	147	29.40	–	2	8
Shahid Afridi	3	5	–	84	113	22.60	–	1	2
Wasim Akram	3	5	–	38	68	13.60	–	–	2
Saqlain Mushtaq	3	5	1	21	53	13.25	–	–	2
Shoaib Akhtar	2	3	–	4	9	3.00	–	–	–

Played in one Test: Arshad Khan 3; Azhar Mahmood 0, 0 (1 ct); Fazal-e-Akber 15*; Imran Nazir 64, 13; Salim Malik 32, 9; Shahid Nazir 10 (1 ct).

PAKISTAN – BOWLING	*O*	*M*	*R*	*W*	*Avge*	*Best*	*5wI*	*10wM*
Arshad Khan	32	8	79	6	13.16	5-38	1	–
Shoaib Akhtar	63.1	12	180	10	18.00	4-47	–	–
Wasim Akram	91.2	15	276	15	18.40	4-30	–	–
Saqlain Mushtaq	142	45	357	12	29.75	4-82	–	–

Also bowled: Azhar Mahmood 24-5-63-1; Fazal-e-Akber 27-5-119-1; Shahid Afridi 35-6-134-3; Shahid Nazir 19-1-72-1; Wajahatullah Wasti 1-0-8-0.

SRI LANKA – BATTING	*M*	*I*	*NO*	*HS*	*Runs*	*Avge*	*100*	*50*	*Ct/St*
R.P.Arnold	3	5	1	123	253	63.25	1	1	3
D.P.M.deS.Jayawardena	3	5	–	242	297	59.40	1	1	1
P.A.de Silva	2	3	–	72	101	33.66	–	1	2
R.S.Kaluwitharana	3	4	–	100	132	33.00	1	–	2/3
H.P.Tillekeratne	3	4	1	55*	93	31.00	–	1	2/2
M.S.Atapattu	3	5	1	36	93	23.25	–	–	1
W.P.U.C.J.Vaas	2	3	1	23	43	21.50	–	–	2
A.Gunawardena	2	4	–	43	84	21.00	–	–	1
K.S.C.de Silva	2	3	–	27	46	15.33	–	–	3
U.C.Hathurusinghe	2	2	–	14	14	7.00	–	–	1
G.P.Wickremasinghe	2	3	–	7	9	3.00	–	–	–

Played in one Test: M.R.C.N.Bandaratilake 0; U.D.U.Chandana 15, 28 (1 ct); R.S.Kalpage 2* (1 ct); R.L.Perera 1*; A.Ranatunga 66 (2 ct); K.E.A.Upashanta 6.

SRI LANKA – BOWLING	*O*	*M*	*R*	*W*	*Avge*	*Best*	*5wI*	*10wM*
U.D.U.Chandana	47.5	7	179	6	29.83	6-179	1	–
G.P.Wickremasinghe	58.1	11	183	6	30.50	6-103	1	–
R.P.Arnold	85.5	13	228	5	45.60	2- 80	–	–

Also bowled: M.R.C.N.Bandaratilake 56-20-144-3; K.S.C.de Silva 68.4-7-253-3; P.A.de Silva 30.2-2-103-2; U.C.Hathurusinghe 43-8-121-1; D.P.M.deS.Jayawardena 35-5-100-1; R.S.Kalpage 36.5-5-167-4; R.L.Perera 44-6-185-1; H.P.Tillekeratne 1-1-0-0; K.E.A.Upashanta 43-5-135-3; W.P.U.C.J.Vaas 81-12-267-1.

NEW ZEALAND v SOUTH AFRICA (1st Test)

At Eden Park, Auckland on 27, 28 February, 1, 2, 3 March 1999.
Toss: New Zealand. Result: **MATCH DRAWN**.
Debuts: None.

SOUTH AFRICA

G.Kirsten	c Astle b Allott	128
H.H.Gibbs	b Vettori	34
J.H.Kallis	lbw b Doull	7
D.J.Cullinan	not out	275
*W.J.Cronje	c Allott b Harris	30
J.N.Rhodes	c Twose b Harris	63
S.M.Pollock	not out	69
†M.V.Boucher		
L.Klusener		
A.A.Donald		
P.R.Adams		
Extras	(B 6, LB 7, NB 2)	15
Total	(5 wickets declared)	**621**

NEW ZEALAND

R.G.Twose	c Boucher b Donald	31	(3)	c Cullinan b Klusener	65
M.J.Horne	b Adams	93	(1)	b Adams	60
N.J.Astle	c Boucher b Donald	41	(4)	not out	69
C.D.McMillan	c Boucher b Cronje	25	(5)	not out	22
C.Z.Harris	not out	68			
†A.C.Parore	b Pollock	9			
M.D.Bell	b Klusener	6	(2)	c Donald b Pollock	6
*D.J.Nash	c Boucher b Klusener	1			
D.L.Vettori	c Cronje b Adams	32			
S.B.Doull	c Gibbs b Adams	17			
G.Allott	c Pollock b Kallis	0			
Extras	(LB 21, W 2, NB 6)	29		(B 13, LB 2, W 2, NB 5)	22
Total		**352**		(3 wickets)	**244**

NEW ZEALAND	O	M	R	W		O	M	R	W
Doull	33	7	90	1					
Allott	38	5	153	1					
Nash	28	2	97	0					
Vettori	42	8	120	1					
Harris	45	10	94	2					
McMillan	5.1	0	24	0					
Astle	9	1	30	0					
SOUTH AFRICA									
Donald	27	16	40	2	(3)	9	2	20	0
Pollock	28	11	51	1		13	5	21	1
Klusener	27	8	60	2		13	6	26	1
Adams	46	18	103	3		30	11	96	1
Kallis	21.4	10	44	1	(1)	13	0	61	0
Cullinan	2	1	8	0					
Cronje	9	2	25	1		6	4	5	0

FALL OF WICKETS

	SA	NZ	NZ
Wkt	*1st*	*1st*	*2nd*
1st	76	80	15
2nd	97	170	104
3rd	280	210	193
4th	354	210	–
5th	495	224	–
6th	–	242	–
7th	–	251	–
8th	–	294	–
9th	–	320	–
10th	–	352	–

Umpires: D.B.Cowie (12) and D.J.Harper (*Australia*) (3).
Referee: A.C.Smith (*England*) (2). **Test No. 1448/22 (NZ265/SA231)**

NEW ZEALAND v SOUTH AFRICA (2nd Test)

At Lancaster Park, Christchurch on 11, 12, 13, 14, 15 March 1999.
Toss: New Zealand. Result: **MATCH DRAWN**.
Debuts: New Zealand – G.R.Stead.

NEW ZEALAND

M.J.Horne	c Kirsten b Kallis	36	(2) run out	56
B.A.Young	b Donald	5	(1) not out	55
R.G.Twose	c Cullinan b Pollock	0	not out	6
N.J.Astle	c Klusener b Donald	44		
G.R.Stead	c Boucher b Donald	27		
C.Z.Harris	c Adams b Pollock	0		
†A.C.Parore	c sub (D.M.Benkenstein) b Pollock	14		
*D.J.Nash	lbw b Adams	14		
D.L.Vettori	lbw b Adams	18		
S.B.Doull	c Boucher b Pollock	0		
G.I.Allott	not out	1		
Extras	(LB 4, NB 5)	9	(LB 5, NB 5)	10
Total		**168**	(1 wicket)	**127**

SOUTH AFRICA

G.Kirsten	c Astle b Vettori	65
H.H.Gibbs	not out	211
J.H.Kallis	not out	148
D.J.Cullinan		
*W.J.Cronje		
J.N.Rhodes		
S.M.Pollock		
†M.V.Boucher		
L.Klusener		
P.R.Adams		
A.A.Donald		
Extras	(LB 12, NB 6)	18
Total	(1 wicket declared)	**442**

SOUTH AFRICA	O	M	R	W		O	M	R	W
Donald	17.5	4	54	3					
Pollock	17	5	34	4	(1)	12	4	23	0
Klusener	12	3	37	0	(2)	17	4	33	0
Kallis	5	1	21	1		6	2	13	0
Cronje	6.1	4	9	0		4	3	1	0
Adams	5.4	2	9	2	(3)	15	0	52	0
NEW ZEALAND									
Doull	25.5	9	48	0					
Allott	43	11	109	0					
Nash	22	5	46	0					
Astle	18.1	2	76	0					
Vettori	24	6	73	1					
Stead	1	0	1	0					
Harris	28	9	77	0					

FALL OF WICKETS

	NZ	SA	NZ
Wkt	*1st*	*1st*	*2nd*
1st	13	127	107
2nd	18	–	–
3rd	60	–	–
4th	112	–	–
5th	115	–	–
6th	115	–	–
7th	138	–	–
8th	157	–	–
9th	157	–	–
10th	168	–	–

Umpires: K.T.Francis (*Sri Lanka*) (24) and D.M.Quested (3).
Referee: A.C.Smith (*England*) (3). **Test No. 1449/23 (NZ266/SA232)**

NEW ZEALAND v SOUTH AFRICA (3rd Test)

At Basin Reserve, Wellington, on 18, 19, 20, 21, 22 March 1999.
Toss: New Zealand. Result: **SOUTH AFRICA** won by eight wickets.
Debuts: None.

NEW ZEALAND

M.J.Horne	c Cullinan b Pollock	2	(2)	lbw b Elworthy	27
B.A.Young	c Rhodes b Kallis	18	(1)	c Boucher b Pollock	2
R.G.Twose	c Boucher b Elworthy	12		c Pollock b Elworthy	5
N.J.Astle	b Elworthy	20		b Elworthy	62
G.R.Stead	c Pollock b Elworthy	68		lbw b Elworthy	33
C.Z.Harris	c Rhodes b Pollock	68		b Adams	41
D.L.Vettori	c Kallis b Elworthy	4	(9)	b Pollock	16
†A.C.Parore	c Cullinan b Pollock	5	(7)	c Rhodes b Adams	19
*D.J.Nash	c Adams b Pollock	2	(8)	c Boucher b Adams	27
S.B.Doull	c Boucher b Pollock	0		not out	38
S.B.O'Connor	not out	2		c Rhodes b Adams	2
Extras	(LB 18, NB 3)	21		(B 9, LB 7, NB 3)	19
Total		**222**			**291**

SOUTH AFRICA

G.Kirsten	b O'Connor	40	not out	12
H.H.Gibbs	c O'Connor b Vettori	120	run out	0
J.H.Kallis	c Horne b Nash	17	b Vettori	4
D.J.Cullinan	c and b Astle	152	not out	0
*W.J.Cronje	c Nash b Vettori	72		
J.N.Rhodes	c Young b Vettori	3		
S.M.Pollock	not out	43		
†M.V.Boucher	b Vettori	8		
L.Klusener	c Parore b Nash	19		
S.Elworthy	not out	3		
P.R.Adams				
Extras	(B 10, LB 6, NB 5)	21		
Total	(8 wickets declared)	**498**	(2 wickets)	**16**

SOUTH AFRICA	O	M	R	W		O	M	R	W
Pollock	28.3	14	33	5		25	8	54	2
Elworthy	27	10	66	4		28	5	93	4
Kallis	20	5	44	1		19	7	50	0
Klusener	15	7	33	0		11	7	15	0
Adams	7	2	12	0		22.3	6	63	4
Cronje	5	3	16	0					
NEW ZEALAND									
Doull	24	4	77	0					
O'Connor	24	4	89	1	(1)	4.1	0	9	0
Nash	25	7	76	2					
Vettori	54	16	153	4	(2)	4	0	7	1
Harris	22	0	66	0					
Astle	16	8	21	1					

FALL OF WICKETS

	NZ	SA	NZ	SA
Wkt	*1st*	*1st*	*2nd*	*2nd*
1st	7	73	8	6
2nd	32	105	35	14
3rd	57	258	35	–
4th	58	403	100	–
5th	203	415	152	–
6th	207	420	196	–
7th	218	440	199	–
8th	219	489	233	–
9th	219	–	281	–
10th	222	–	291	–

Umpires: R.S.Dunne (32) and S.Venkataraghavan (*India*) (30).
Referee: A.C.Smith (*England*) (4). **Test No. 1450/24 (NZ267/SA233)**

NEW ZEALAND v SOUTH AFRICA 1998-99

NEW ZEALAND – BATTING AND FIELDING

	M	I	NO	HS	Runs	Avge	100	50	Ct/St
C.Z.Harris	3	4	1	68*	177	59.00	–	2	–
N.J.Astle	3	5	1	69*	236	59.00	–	2	3
M.J.Horne	3	6	–	93	274	45.66	–	3	1
G.R.Stead	2	3	–	68	128	42.66	–	1	–
B.A.Young	2	4	1	55*	80	26.66	–	1	1
R.G.Twose	3	6	1	65	119	23.80	–	1	1
S.B.Doull	3	4	1	38*	55	18.33	–	–	–
D.L.Vettori	3	4	–	32	70	17.50	–	–	–
A.C.Parore	3	4	–	19	47	11.75	–	–	1
D.J.Nash	3	4	–	27	44	11.00	–	–	1
G.I.Allott	2	2	1	1*	1	1.00	–	–	1

Played in one Test: M.D.Bell 6,6; C.D.McMillan 25, 22*; S.B.O'Connor 2*, 2 (1 ct).

NEW ZEALAND – BOWLING

	O	M	R	W	Avge	Best	5wI	10wM
D.L.Vettori	124	30	353	7	50.42	4-153	–	–
D.J.Nash	75	14	219	2	109.50	2- 76	–	–
C.Z.Harris	95	19	237	2	118.50	2- 94	–	–

Also bowled: G.I.Allott 81-16-262-1; N.J.Astle 43.1-11-127-1; S.B.Doull 82.5-20-215-1; C.D.McMillan 5.1-0-24-0; S.B.O'Connor 28.1-4-98-1; G.R.Stead 1-0-1-0.

SOUTH AFRICA – BATTING AND FIELDING

	M	I	NO	HS	Runs	Avge	100	50	Ct/St
D.J.Cullinan	3	3	2	275*	427	427.00	2	–	4
H.H.Gibbs	3	4	1	211*	365	121.66	2	–	1
S.M.Pollock	3	2	2	69*	112	–	–	1	3
G.Kirsten	3	4	1	128	245	81.66	1	1	1
J.H.Kallis	3	4	1	148*	176	58.66	1	–	1
W.J.Cronje	3	2	–	72	102	51.00	–	1	1
J.N.Rhodes	3	2	–	63	66	33.00	–	1	4
L.Klusener	3	1	–	19	19	19.00	–	–	1
M.V.Boucher	3	1	–	8	8	8.00	–	–	10
P.R.Adams	3	–	–	–	–	–	–	–	2
A.A.Donald	2	–	–	–	–	–	–	–	1

Played in one Test: S.Elworthy 3*.

SOUTH AFRICA – BOWLING

	O	M	R	W	Avge	Best	5wI	10wM
S.M.Pollock	123.3	47	216	13	16.61	5-33	1	–
S.Elworthy	55	15	159	8	19.87	4-66	–	–
A.A.Donald	53.5	22	114	5	22.80	3-54	–	–
P.R.Adams	126.1	39	335	10	33.50	4-63	–	–
L.Klusener	95	35	204	3	68.00	2-60	–	–
J.H.Kallis	84.4	25	233	3	77.66	1-21	–	–

Also bowled: W.J.Cronje 30.1-16-56-1; D.J.Cullinan 2-1-8-0.

WEST INDIES v AUSTRALIA (1st Test)

At Queen's Park Oval, Port-of-Spain, Trinidad, on 5, 6, 7, 8 March 1999.
Toss: Australia. Result: **AUSTRALIA** won by 312 runs.
Debuts: West Indies – P.T.Collins, D.R.E.Joseph, S.Ragoonath.

AUSTRALIA

M.J.Slater	c Dillon b Collins	23	(2)	st Jacobs b Adams	106
M.T.G.Elliott	lbw b Collins	44	(1)	c Joseph b Walsh	0
J.L.Langer	c Jacobs b Walsh	5		c Jacobs b Dillon	24
M.E.Waugh	lbw b Walsh	2		lbw b Ambrose	33
*S.R.Waugh	c Jacobs b Dillon	14		c Jacobs b Collins	0
G.S.Blewett	lbw b Ambrose	58		st Jacobs b Adams	28
†I.A.Healy	lbw b Walsh	12		lbw b Walsh	0
S.K.Warne	c Campbell b Ambrose	21		b Walsh	25
J.N.Gillespie	not out	28		c Lara b Ambrose	22
S.C.G.McGill	b Ambrose	0		b Walsh	0
G.D.McGrath	c Jacobs b Dillon	39		not out	4
Extras	(LB 18, NB 5)	23		(LB 7, W 1, NB 11)	19
Total		**269**			**261**

WEST INDIES

S.L.Campbell	lbw b McGrath	9		c M.E.Waugh b Gillespie	0
S.Ragoonath	run out	9		lbw b Gillespie	2
D.R.E.Joseph	lbw b McGrath	50		c Warne b McGrath	5
*B.C.Lara	run out	62		c M.E.Waugh b Gillespie	3
J.C.Adams	b MacGill	13		lbw b McGrath	5
†R.D.Jacobs	lbw b MacGill	6		lbw b McGrath	19
P.T.Collins	lbw b McGrath	1	(10)	b Gillespie	0
R.I.C.Holder	lbw b MacGill	0	(7)	c M.E.Waugh b McGrath	4
C.E.L.Ambrose	c Slater b McGrath	0	(8)	lbw b McGrath	6
M.Dillon	b McGrath	0	(9)	run out	0
C.A.Walsh	not out	0		not out	2
Extras	(B 4, LB 2, NB 11)	17		(B 4, LB 1)	5
Total		**167**			**51**

WEST INDIES	O	M	R	W	O	M	R	W
Walsh	31	9	60	3	25.2	2	71	4
Ambrose	27	15	35	3	18	8	25	2
Collins	23	8	46	2	21	2	72	1
Dillon	26.3	4	69	2	14	1	57	1
Adams	14	2	41	0	8	1	29	2
AUSTRALIA								
McGrath	14	3	50	5	10	3	28	5
Gillespie	12	3	34	0	9.1	4	18	4
MacGill	16	5	41	3				
Warne	14	4	35	0				
Blewett	1	0	1	0				

FALL OF WICKETS

	A	WI	A	WI
Wkt	*1st*	*1st*	*2nd*	*2nd*
1st	42	16	7	3
2nd	51	28	45	8
3rd	53	116	126	11
4th	74	149	127	16
5th	118	156	193	16
6th	153	163	194	31
7th	186	163	227	47
8th	203	163	257	47
9th	203	167	257	49
10th	269	167	261	51

Umpires: E.A.Nicholls (6) and P.Willey (*England*) (13).
Referee: R.Subba Row (*England*) (27). **Test No. 1451/87 (WI349/A590)**

WEST INDIES v AUSTRALIA (2nd Test)

At Sabina Park, Kingston, Jamaica, on 13, 14, 15, 16 March 1999.
Toss: Australia. Result: **WEST INDIES** won by ten wickets.
Debuts: West Indies – N.O.Perry, L.A.Roberts.

AUSTRALIA

M.J.Slater	c Jacobs b Walsh	22	(2) b Walsh	0
M.T.G.Elliott	c Lara b Walsh	0	(1) lbw b Perry	16
J.L.Langer	c Jacobs b Walsh	8	c Jacobs b Perry	24
M.E.Waugh	b Perry	67	c Walsh b Ambrose	21
*S.R.Waugh	c Joseph b Collins	100	c Jacobs b Perry	9
G.S.Blewett	lbw b Walsh	5	c Lara b Perry	30
†I.A.Healy	run out	6	run out	10
S.K.Warne	c Joseph b Collins	24	c Joseph b Walsh	23
J.N.Gillespie	b Ambrose	1	c Jacobs b Walsh	7
S.C.G.MacGill	c Joseph b Collins	0	c Joseph b Perry	7
G.D.McGrath	not out	2	not out	11
Extras	(B 1, LB 3, NB 17)	21	(LB 3, NB 16)	19
Total		**256**		**177**

WEST INDIES

S.L.Campbell	b McGrath	12	not out	1
S.Ragoonath	lbw b Gillespie	0	not out	2
L.A.Roberts	c Warne b McGrath	0		
*B.C.Lara	c Healy b McGrath	213		
D.R.E.Joseph	c Blewett b McGrath	14		
P.T.Collins	c M.E.Waugh b MacGill	13		
J.C.Adams	c Elliott b McGrath	94		
†R.D.Jacobs	c Gillespie b Warne	25		
N.O.Perry	not out	15		
C.E.L.Ambrose	b MacGill	3		
C.A.Walsh	b MacGill	0		
Extras	(B 12, LB 8, NB 22)	42		
Total		**431**	(0 wickets)	**3**

WEST INDIES	O	M	R	W		O	M	R	W
Ambrose	17	9	33	1		14	4	28	1
Walsh	20	6	55	4		18	3	52	3
Collins	16.3	2	79	3	(4)	8	0	24	0
Perry	17	1	79	1	(3)	26	8	70	5
Adams	1	0	6	0					
AUSTRALIA									
McGrath	35	11	93	5		0.3	0	3	0
Gillespie	33	7	79	1					
Warne	30	8	94	1					
MacGill	22.3	3	84	3					
Blewett	10	1	48	0					
M.E.Waugh	2	0	13	0					

FALL OF WICKETS

	A	WI	A	WI
Wkt	*1st*	*1st*	*2nd*	*2nd*
1st	8	4	4	–
2nd	28	5	36	–
3rd	46	17	51	–
4th	158	34	63	–
5th	171	378	86	–
6th	179	398	107	–
7th	227	420	137	–
8th	242	427	157	–
9th	248	431	159	–
10th	256	431	177	–

Umpires: S.A.Bucknor (43) and P.Willey (*England*) (14).
Referee: R.Subba Row (*England*) (28). **Test No. 1452/88 (WI350/A591)**

WEST INDIES v AUSTRALIA (3rd Test)

At Kensington Oval, Bridgetown, Barbados, on 26, 27, 28, 29, 30 March 1999.
Toss: Australia. Result: **WEST INDIES** won by one wicket.
Debuts: None.

AUSTRALIA

M.J.Slater	c Lara b Ambrose	23	(2)	run out	26
M.T.G.Elliott	c Jacobs b Walsh	9	(1)	c Jacobs b Walsh	0
J.L.Langer	b Hooper	51		lbw b Ambrose	1
M.E.Waugh	b Ambrose	0	(5)	lbw b Walsh	3
*S.R.Waugh	lbw b Perry	199	(6)	b Collins	11
R.T.Ponting	c Hooper b Perry	104	(7)	c Griffith b Walsh	22
†I.A.Healy	lbw b Walsh	0	(8)	c Jacobs b Collins	3
S.K.Warne	c Lara b Perry	13	(9)	lbw b Walsh	32
J.N.Gillespie	not out	23	(4)	b Ambrose	14
S.C.G.McGill	run out	17		c Campbell b Walsh	1
G.D.McGrath	c Joseph b Hooper	3		not out	8
Extras	(B 4, LB 10, NB 34)	48		(LB 5, W 1, NB 19)	25
Total		**490**			**146**

WEST INDIES

S.L.Campbell	c S.R.Waugh b Gillespie	105	lbw b McGrath	33
A.F.G.Griffith	run out	0	lbw b Gillespie	35
D.R.E.Joseph	lbw b McGrath	26	lbw b MacGill	1
P.T.Collins	lbw b McGrath	0	lbw b McGrath	0
*B.C.Lara	c Healy b Gillespie	8	not out	153
C.L.Hooper	c Warne b McGrath	25	c Healy b Gillespie	6
J.C.Adams	c M.E.Waugh b McGrath	0	b McGrath	38
†R.D.Jacobs	c M.E.Waugh b Ponting	68	lbw b McGrath	5
N.O.Perry	lbw b Gillespie	24	lbw b McGrath	0
C.E.L.Ambrose	not out	28	c Elliott b Gillespie	12
C.A.Walsh	c Slater b Warne	12	not out	0
Extras	(B 10, LB 3, NB 20)	33	(B 8, LB 13, W 2, NB 5)	28
Total		**329**	(9 wickets)	**311**

WEST INDIES	O	M	R	W		O	M	R	W
Ambrose	31.3	7	93	2	(2)	20	2	60	2
Walsh	38	8	121	2	(1)	17.1	3	39	5
Perry	33	5	102	3	(4)	4	0	11	0
Collins	35.3	7	110	0	(3)	9	0	31	2
Hooper	15.4	4	50	2					
AUSTRALIA									
McGrath	33	5	128	4		44	13	92	5
Gillespie	28	14	48	3		26.1	8	62	3
Warne	15.5	2	70	1		24	4	69	0
MacGill	20	5	47	0		21	6	48	1
Ponting	4	1	12	1					
M.E.Waugh	3	0	11	0					
S.R.Waugh					(5)	5	0	19	0

FALL OF WICKETS

	A	WI	A	WI
Wkt	*1st*	*1st*	*2nd*	*2nd*
1st	31	1	0	72
2nd	36	50	12	77
3rd	36	50	35	78
4th	144	64	46	91
5th	425	98	48	105
6th	427	98	73	238
7th	429	251	81	248
8th	446	265	134	248
9th	483	291	137	302
10th	490	329	146	–

Umpires: E.A.Nicholls (7) and D.L.Orchard (*South Africa*) (12).
Referee: R.Subba Row (*England*) (29). **Test No. 1453/89 (WI351/A592)**

WEST INDIES v AUSTRALIA (4th Test)

At Recreation Ground, St John's, Antigua, on 3, 4, 5, 6, 7 April 1999.
Toss: Australia. Result: **AUSTRALIA** won by 176 runs.
Debuts: West Indies – C.D.Collymore.

AUSTRALIA

M.J.Slater	c Joseph b Perry	33	(2)	b Walsh	44
G.S.Blewett	c Jacobs b Collymore	32	(1)	lbw b Ambrose	7
J.L.Langer	run out	51		b Hooper	127
M.E.Waugh	c Hooper b Walsh	11		c Jacobs b Ambrose	65
*S.R.Waugh	not out	72		c Jacobs b Ambrose	4
R.T.Ponting	lbw b Ambrose	21		not out	21
†I.A.Healy	c Hooper b Ambrose	6		c Adams b Hooper	16
A.C.Dale	c Hooper b Ambrose	1	(9)	c Hooper b Walsh	0
S.C.G.McGill	c Joseph b Ambrose	4	(10)	c Perry b Hooper	2
C.R.Miller	c Joseph b Adams	43	(8)	c Lara b Walsh	1
G.D.McGrath	c Jacobs b Ambrose	5		b Walsh	2
Extras	(LB 5, NB 19)	24		(B 2, LB 1, W 3, NB 11)	17
Total		**303**			**306**

WEST INDIES

S.L.Campbell	c M.E.Waugh b Miller	8	c Healy b McGrath	29
A.F.G.Griffith	c Healy b Miller	9	lbw b MacGill	56
D.R.E.Joseph	lbw b Dale	28	c Miller b Dale	17
*B.C.Lara	c Healy b McGrath	100	lbw b McGrath	7
C.L.Hooper	run out	47	lbw b Blewett	12
J.C.Adams	c Healy b Dale	0	st Healy b Miller	18
†R.D.Jacobs	lbw b MacGill	4	lbw b Blewett	16
N.O.Perry	b McGrath	6	c Slater b MacGill	26
C.E.L.Ambrose	c Ponting b MacGill	0	b MacGill	4
C.D.Collymore	not out	11	c MacGill b McGrath	6
C.A.Walsh	lbw b McGrath	3	not out	0
Extras	(NB 6)	6	(B 5, LB 12, NB 3)	20
Total		**222**		**211**

WEST INDIES	O	M	R	W		O	M	R	W
Ambrose	29.5	6	94	5		27	10	55	3
Walsh	26	1	67	1		32.4	6	78	4
Collymore	25	6	49	1	(5)	16	1	60	0
Perry	15	5	36	1	(6)	7	0	28	0
Adams	6	1	18	1	(4)	8.2	2	13	0
Hooper	10	1	34	0	(3)	30.4	7	69	3
AUSTRALIA									
McGrath	27.2	9	64	3		35.5	15	50	3
Dale	18	7	67	2		12	5	28	1
Miller	17	5	39	2	(4)	21	10	27	1
MacGill	14	3	52	2	(3)	26	8	80	3
Blewett						8	3	9	2

FALL OF WICKETS

	A	WI	A	WI
Wkt	*1st*	*1st*	*2nd*	*2nd*
1st	60	19	15	56
2nd	76	20	76	58
3rd	96	136	223	69
4th	155	176	241	87
5th	211	178	265	105
6th	226	192	287	145
7th	232	205	288	184
8th	242	206	288	190
9th	295	213	296	209
10th	303	222	306	211

Umpires: S.A.Bucknor (44) and D.L.Orchard (*South Africa*) (13).
Referee: R.Subba Row (*England*) (30). **Test No. 1454/90 (WI352/A593)**

WEST INDIES v AUSTRALIA 1998-99

WEST INDIES – BATTING AND FIELDING

	M	I	NO	HS	Runs	Avge	100	50	Ct/St
B.C.Lara	4	7	1	213	546	91.00	3	1	6
S.L.Campbell	4	8	1	105	197	28.14	1	–	2
A.F.G.Griffith	2	4	–	56	100	25.00	–	1	1
J.C.Adams	4	7	–	94	168	24.00	–	1	1
C.L.Hooper	2	4	–	47	90	22.50	–	–	5
R.D.Jacobs	4	7	–	68	143	20.42	–	1	17/2
D.R.E.Joseph	4	7	–	50	141	20.14	–	1	10
N.O.Perry	3	5	1	26	71	17.75	–	–	1
C.E.L.Ambrose	4	7	1	28*	53	8.83	–	–	–
C.A.Walsh	4	7	4	12	17	5.66	–	–	1
S.Ragoonath	2	4	1	9	13	4.33	–	–	–
P.T.Collins	3	5	–	13	14	2.80	–	–	–

Played in one Test: C.D.Collymore 11*, 6; M.Dillon 0, 0 (1 ct); R.I.C.Holder 0, 4; L.A.Roberts 0.

WEST INDIES – BOWLING

	O	M	R	W	Avge	Best	5wI	10wM
C.A.Walsh	208.1	38	543	26	20.88	5-39	1	–
C.E.L.Ambrose	184.2	61	423	19	22.26	5-94	1	–
C.L.Hooper	56.2	12	153	5	30.60	3-69	–	–
N.O.Perry	102	19	326	10	32.60	5-70	1	–
P.T.Collins	113	19	362	8	45.25	3-79	–	–

Also bowled: J.C.Adams 37.2-6-107-3; C.D.Collymore 41-7-109-1; M.Dillon 40.3-5-126-3.

AUSTRALIA – BATTING AND FIELDING

	M	I	NO	HS	Runs	Avge	100	50	Ct/St
S.R.Waugh	4	8	1	199	409	58.42	2	1	1
R.T.Ponting	2	4	1	104	168	56.00	1	–	1
J.L.Langer	4	8	–	127	291	36.37	1	2	–
M.J.Slater	4	8	–	106	277	34.62	1	–	3
G.S.Blewett	3	6	–	58	160	26.66	–	1	1
M.E.Waugh	4	8	–	67	202	25.25	–	2	7
J.N.Gillespie	3	6	2	28*	95	23.75	–	–	1
S.K.Warne	3	6	–	32	138	23.00	–	–	3
G.D.McGrath	4	8	4	39	74	18.50	–	–	–
M.T.G.Elliott	3	6	–	44	69	11.50	–	–	2
I.A.Healy	4	8	–	16	53	6.62	–	–	7/1
S.C.G.MacGill	4	8	–	17	31	3.87	–	–	1

Played in one Test: A.C.Dale 1, 0; C.R.Miller 43, 1 (1 ct).

AUSTRALIA – BOWLING

	O	M	R	W	Avge	Best	5wI	10wM
G.D.McGrath	199.4	59	508	30	16.93	5-28	4	1
J.N.Gillespie	108.2	36	241	11	21.90	4-18	–	–
S.C.G.MacGill	119.3	30	352	12	29.33	3-41	–	–

Also bowled: G.S.Blewett 19-4-58-2; A.C.Dale 30-12-95-3; C.R.Miller 38-15-66-3; R.T.Ponting 4-1-12-1; S.K.Warne 83.5-18-268-2; M.E.Waugh 5-0-24-0; S.R.Waugh 5-0-19-0.

ENGLAND v NEW ZEALAND (1st Test)

At Edgbaston, Birmingham, on 1, 2, 3 July 1999.
Toss: New Zealand. Result: **ENGLAND** won by seven wickets.
Debuts: England – A.Habib, C.M.W.Read.

NEW ZEALAND

R.G.Twose	c Thorpe b Mullally	0		lbw b Caddick	0
M.J.Horne	lbw b Caddick	12		c Read b Mullally	1
*S.P.Fleming	c Thorpe b Tudor	27		c Read b Tufnell	25
N.J.Astle	c Read b Butcher	26		c Read b Mullally	9
C.D.McMillan	c Thorpe b Caddick	18		c Butcher b Mullally	15
C.L.Cairns	c and b Caddick	17		c Read b Caddick	3
†A.C.Parore	c Read b Mullally	73		c Stewart b Caddick	0
D.J.Nash	c Hussain b Tufnell	21		c Read b Caddick	0
D.L.Vettori	c Hussain b Tufnell	1		b Caddick	0
S.B.Doull	c Butcher b Tufnell	11		st Read b Tufnell	46
G.I.Allott	not out	7		not out	0
Extras	(B 1, LB 5, W 1, NB 6)	13		(B 1, LB 4, W 1, NB 2)	8
Total		**226**			**107**

ENGLAND

M.A.Butcher	run out	11		c Parore b Nash	33
A.J.Stewart	lbw b Allott	1		b Allott	0
*N.Hussain	b Doull	10	(4)	b Allott	44
G.P.Thorpe	c Astle b Allott	6	(5)	not out	21
M.R.Ramprakash	c Parore b Cairns	0			
A.Habib	b Cairns	1			
†C.M.W.Read	c sub (C.Z.Harris) b Nash	1			
A.R.Caddick	c Parore b Nash	33			
A.J.Tudor	not out	32	(3)	not out	99
A.D.Mullally	c Parore b Nash	0			
P.C.R.Tufnell	c Fleming b Cairns	6			
Extras	(B 8, LB 11, NB 6)	25		(B 7, LB 2, NB 5)	14
Total		**126**		(3 wickets)	**211**

ENGLAND	O	M	R	W		O	M	R	W
Mullally	26.4	5	72	2	(2)	16	3	48	3
Caddick	27	12	57	3	(1)	14	3	32	5
Tudor	11	2	44	1		5	2	15	0
Butcher	7	2	25	1					
Tufnell	17	9	22	3	(4)	2.1	0	7	2
NEW ZEALAND									
Allott	14	3	38	2		15	0	71	2
Doull	12	6	17	1		7	0	48	0
Cairns	9.4	3	35	3	(5)	4	0	18	0
Nash	11	6	17	3		7	0	29	1
Vettori					(3)	6	1	22	0
Astle						1	1	0	0
McMillan						3.4	0	14	0

FALL OF WICKETS

	NZ	E	NZ	E
Wkt	*1st*	*1st*	*2nd*	*2nd*
1st	0	5	0	3
2nd	19	26	5	76
3rd	55	28	17	174
4th	73	33	39	–
5th	103	38	46	–
6th	104	40	46	–
7th	189	45	52	–
8th	191	115	52	–
9th	211	115	106	–
10th	226	126	107	–

Umpires: S.A.Bucknor (*West Indies*) (45) and P.Willey (15).
Referee: P.L.van der Merwe (*South Africa*) (26). **Test No. 1455/79 (E758/NZ268)**

ENGLAND v NEW ZEALAND (2nd Test)

At Lord's, London, on 22, 23, 24, 25 July 1999.
Toss: England. Result: **NEW ZEALAND** won by nine wickets.
Debuts: None.

ENGLAND

M.A.Butcher	c Parore b Cairns	8		c Astle b Vettori	20
A.J.Stewart	c Fleming b Nash	50		b Vettori	35
*N.Hussain	c Parore b Cairns	61		absent hurt	–
G.P.Thorpe	c Astle b Cairns	7		b Cairns	7
M.R.Ramprakash	lbw b Nash	4	(3)	c Parore b Astle	24
A.Habib	b Nash	6	(5)	c Astle b Allott	19
†C.M.W.Read	b Cairns	0		lbw b Nash	37
A.R.Caddick	run out	18		c Fleming b Allott	45
D.W.Headley	lbw b Cairns	4	(6)	c Fleming b Allott	12
A.D.Mullally	c Astle b Cairns	0	(9)	c Twose b Cairns	10
P.C.R.Tufnell	not out	1	(10)	not out	5
Extras	(B 5, LB 8, NB 14)	27		(B 5, LB 3, NB 7)	15
Total		**186**			**229**

NEW ZEALAND

M.J.Horne	c Hussain b Headley	100	lbw b Caddick	26
M.D.Bell	lbw b Headley	15	not out	26
*S.P.Fleming	c Read b Mullally	1	not out	5
N.J.Astle	c Read b Mullally	43		
R.G.Twose	c Caddick b Headley	52		
C.D.McMillan	c Read b Caddick	3		
D.L.Vettori	c Thorpe b Tufnell	54		
†A.C.Parore	b Caddick	12		
C.L.Cairns	b Caddick	31		
D.J.Nash	c Mullally b Tufnell	6		
G.I.Allott	not out	1		
Extras	(B 1, LB 24, W 2, NB 13)	40	(B 2, NB 1)	3
Total		**358**	(1 wicket)	**60**

NEW ZEALAND	O	M	R	W		O	M	R	W
Allott	10	1	37	0		16.4	6	36	3
Cairns	21.1	1	77	6		25	6	67	2
Nash	23	11	50	3	(4)	25	9	50	1
Astle	7	3	9	0	(5)	4	2	6	1
Vettori					(3)	31	12	62	2
ENGLAND									
Mullally	27	7	98	2		5	0	21	0
Caddick	34	11	92	3		10	4	18	1
Headley	27	7	74	3					
Tufnell	27.1	7	61	2	(3)	8	2	19	0
Butcher	3	0	7	0					
Ramprakash	1	0	1	0					

FALL OF WICKETS

	E	NZ	E	NZ
Wkt	*1st*	*1st*	*2nd*	*2nd*
1st	35	43	55	37
2nd	79	45	71	–
3rd	102	112	78	–
4th	112	232	97	–
5th	123	239	123	–
6th	125	242	127	–
7th	150	275	205	–
8th	165	345	216	–
9th	170	351	229	–
10th	186	358	–	–

Umpires: M.J.Kitchen (19) and R.E.Koertzen (*South Africa*) (14).
Referee: P.L.van der Merwe (*South Africa*) (27). **Test No. 1456/80 (E759/NZ269)**

ENGLAND v NEW ZEALAND (3rd Test)

At Old Trafford, Manchester, on 5, 6, 7, 8, 9 August 1999.
Toss: England. Result: **MATCH DRAWN**.
Debuts: None.

ENGLAND

*M.A.Butcher	c Fleming b Cairns	5	lbw b Nash	9
M.A.Atherton	c Parore b Cairns	11	c Astle b Vettori	48
A.J.Stewart	c Parore b Nash	23	not out	83
G.P.Thorpe	c Bell b Vettori	27	not out	25
G.A.Hick	lbw b Nash	12		
M.R.Ramprakash	not out	69		
D.W.Headley	c Fleming b Harris	18		
†C.M.W.Read	b Harris	0		
A.R.Caddick	run out	12		
P.M.Such	c Bell b Vettori	0		
P.C.R.Tufnell	c Astle b Nash	1		
Extras	(B 9, LB 7, W 5)	21	(B 9, LB 7)	16
Total		**199**	(2 wickets)	**181**

NEW ZEALAND

M.J.Horne	b Caddick	39
M.D.Bell	c Atherton b Headley	83
*S.P.Fleming	lbw b Such	38
N.J.Astle	c Such b Caddick	101
R.G.Twose	lbw b Such	20
C.D.McMillan	not out	107
†A.C.Parore	c Butcher b Such	10
C.L.Cairns	c Caddick b Tufnell	41
D.J.Nash	c Caddick b Such	26
C.Z.Harris	b Tufnell	3
D.L.Vettori	not out	2
Extras	(B 6, LB 17, NB 3)	26
Total	(9 wickets declared)	**496**

NEW ZEALAND	O	M	R	W	O	M	R	W
Cairns	34	12	72	2	11	1	54	0
Nash	31.1	15	46	3	10	3	26	1
Astle	11	5	14	0	3	1	7	0
Vettori	25	7	35	2	26	12	48	1
Harris	8	4	16	2	18	6	30	0
ENGLAND								
Caddick	39	11	112	2				
Headley	31	4	115	1				
Tufnell	46	12	111	2				
Such	41	11	114	4				
Hick	1	0	8	0				
Butcher	2	0	13	0				

FALL OF WICKETS

	E	NZ	E
Wkt	*1st*	*1st*	*2nd*
1st	13	46	19
2nd	54	110	118
3rd	60	263	–
4th	83	280	–
5th	104	321	–
6th	133	331	–
7th	133	425	–
8th	152	476	–
9th	183	487	–
10th	199	–	–

Umpires: D.R.Shepherd (47) and R.B.Tiffin (*Zimbabwe*) (10).
Referee: P.L.van der Merwe (*South Africa*) (28). **Test No. 1457/81 (E760/NZ270)**

ENGLAND v NEW ZEALAND (4th Test)

At Kennington Oval, London, on 19, 20, 21, 22 August 1999.
Toss: England. Result: **NEW ZEALAND** won by 83 runs.
Debuts: England – E.S.H.Giddins, D.L.Maddy.

NEW ZEALAND

M.J.Horne	c Caddick b Irani	15	lbw b Giddins	10
M.D.Bell	c Stewart b Mullally	23	c Irani b Caddick	4
*S.P.Fleming	not out	66	c Thorpe b Caddick	4
N.J.Astle	c Stewart b Caddick	9	c Irani b Giddins	5
R.G.Twose	c Maddy b Giddins	1	c Stewart b Giddins	0
C.D.McMillan	b Tufnell	19	lbw b Mullally	26
†A.C.Parore	c Ramprakash b Tufnell	0	b Caddick	1
C.L.Cairns	b Mullally	11	c and b Mullally	80
D.J.Nash	c Ramprakash b Caddick	18	not out	10
D.L.Vettori	lbw b Tufnell	51	c Ramprakash b Tufnell	6
S.B.O'Connor	lbw b Caddick	1	b Tufnell	6
Extras	(B 9, LB 9, W 2, NB 2)	22	(LB 4, W 1, NB 5)	10
Total		**236**		**162**

ENGLAND

M.A.Atherton	c Fleming b Nash	10	c Parore b Nash	64
D.L.Maddy	b Vettori	14	c Fleming b Nash	5
*N.Hussain	c Bell b Cairns	40	c Parore b O'Connor	9
G.P.Thorpe	c Fleming b Cairns	10	c Fleming b O'Connor	44
†A.J.Stewart	b Vettori	11	c Bell b Nash	12
M.R.Ramprakash	c Parore b Cairns	30	c Parore b Nash	0
R.C.Irani	lbw b Cairns	1	c Parore b Vettori	9
A.R.Caddick	b O'Connor	15	c Bell b Vettori	3
A.D.Mullally	c Bell b Vettori	5	c Twose b Cairns	3
P.C.R.Tufnell	not out	0	run out	1
E.S.H.Giddins	lbw b Cairns	0	not out	0
Extras	(B 1, LB 5, W 5, NB 6)	17	(B 2, LB 3, NB 7)	12
Total		**153**		**162**

ENGLAND	O	M	R	W		O	M	R	W
Caddick	33.1	17	66	3		17	4	35	3
Mullally	26	12	34	2		11	2	27	2
Giddins	16	4	41	1		10	3	38	3
Tufnell	16	3	39	3		16	3	58	2
Irani	11	3	38	1					
NEW ZEALAND									
Cairns	19	8	31	5		15.1	3	50	1
Nash	14	5	40	1		14	3	39	4
O'Connor	13	3	30	1	(4)	11	3	32	2
Vettori	33	12	46	3	(3)	16	6	36	2
Astle	1	1	0	0					

FALL OF WICKETS

	NZ	E	NZ	E
Wkt	*1st*	*1st*	*2nd*	*2nd*
1st	39	25	15	23
2nd	45	29	15	45
3rd	54	46	22	123
4th	62	87	22	143
5th	87	91	37	143
6th	87	94	39	148
7th	104	141	79	157
8th	157	153	149	160
9th	235	153	156	161
10th	236	153	162	162

Umpires: G.Sharp (9) and S.Venkataraghavan (*India*) (31).
Referee: P.L.van der Merwe (*South Africa*) (29). **Test No. 1458/82 (E761/NZ271)**

ENGLAND v NEW ZEALAND 1999

ENGLAND – BATTING AND FIELDING

	M	*I*	*NO*	*HS*	*Runs*	*Avge*	*100*	*50*	*Ct/St*
M.A.Atherton	2	4	–	64	133	33.25	–	1	1
N.Hussain	3	5	–	61	164	32.80	–	1	3
A.J.Stewart	4	8	1	83*	215	30.71	–	2	4
M.R.Ramprakash	4	6	1	69*	127	25.40	–	1	3
G.P.Thorpe	4	8	2	44	147	24.50	–	–	5
A.R.Caddick	4	6	–	45	126	21.00	–	–	5
M.A.Butcher	3	6	–	33	86	14.33	–	–	3
D.W.Headley	2	3	–	18	34	11.33	–	–	–
C.M.W.Read	3	4	–	37	38	9.50	–	–	10/1
A.Habib	2	3	–	19	26	8.66	–	–	–
P.C.R.Tufnell	4	6	3	6	14	4.66	–	–	–
A.D.Mullally	3	5	–	10	18	3.60	–	–	2

Played in one Test: E.S.H.Giddins 0, 0*; G.A.Hick 12; R.C.Irani 1, 9 (2 ct); D.L.Maddy 14, 5 (1 ct); P.M.Such 0 (1 ct); A.J.Tudor 32*, 99*.

ENGLAND – BOWLING

	O	*M*	*R*	*W*	*Avge*	*Best*	*5wI*	*10wM*
E.S.H.Giddins	26	7	79	4	19.75	3- 38	–	–
A.R.Caddick	174.1	62	412	20	20.60	5- 32	1	–
P.C.R.Tufnell	132.2	36	317	14	22.64	3- 22	–	–
A.D.Mullally	111.4	29	300	11	27.27	3- 48	–	–
P.M.Such	41	11	114	4	28.50	4-114	–	–
D.W.Headley	58	11	189	4	47.25	3- 74	–	–

Also bowled: M.A.Butcher 12-2-45-1; G.A.Hick 1-0-8-0; R.C.Irani 11-3-38-1; M.R.Ramprakash 1-0-1-0; A.J.Tudor 16-4-59-1.

NEW ZEALAND – BATTING AND FIELDING

	M	*I*	*NO*	*HS*	*Runs*	*Avge*	*100*	*50*	*Ct/St*
M.D.Bell	3	5	1	83	151	37.75	–	1	6
C.D.McMillan	4	6	1	107*	188	37.60	1	–	–
S.P.Fleming	4	7	2	66*	166	33.20	–	1	10
N.J.Astle	4	6	–	101	193	32.16	1	–	7
C.L.Cairns	4	6	–	80	183	30.50	–	1	–
M.J.Horne	4	7	–	100	203	29.00	1	–	–
D.L.Vettori	4	6	1	54	114	22.80	–	2	–
D.J.Nash	4	6	1	26	81	16.20	–	–	–
A.C.Parore	4	6	–	73	96	16.00	–	1	14
R.G.Twose	4	6	–	52	73	12.16	–	1	2
G.I.Allott	2	3	3	7*	8	–	–	–	–

Played in one Test: S.B.Doull 11, 46; C.Z.Harris 3; S.B.O'Connor 1, 6.

NEW ZEALAND – BOWLING

	O	*M*	*R*	*W*	*Avge*	*Best*	*5wI*	*10wM*
D.J.Nash	135.1	52	297	17	17.47	4-39	–	–
C.L.Cairns	139	34	404	19	21.26	6-77	2	–
D.L.Vettori	137	50	249	10	24.90	3-46	–	–
G.I.Allott	55.4	10	182	7	26.00	3-36	–	–

Also bowled: N.J.Astle 27-13-36-1; S.B.Doull 19-6-65-1; C.Z.Harris 26-10-46-2; C.D.McMillan 3.4-0-14-0; S.B.O'Connor 24-6-62-3.

SRI LANKA v AUSTRALIA (1st Test)

At Asgiriya Stadium, Kandy, on 9, 10, 11 September 1999.
Toss: Australia. Result: **SRI LANKA** won by six wickets.
Debuts: None.

AUSTRALIA

M.J.Slater	lbw b Vaas	0	(2)	lbw b Muralitharan	27
G.S.Blewett	lbw b Zoysa	0	(1)	c Atapattu b Muralitharan	14
J.L.Langer	c De Silva b Vaas	7		lbw b Vaas	5
M.E.Waugh	c and b Vaas	6		b Vaas	0
*S.R.Waugh	c De Silva b Zoysa	19		absent hurt	–
R.T.Ponting	c and b Muralitharan	96	(5)	c Jayasuriya b Chandana	51
†I.A.Healy	st Kaluwitharana b Muralitharan	11	(6)	b Muralitharan	3
S.K.Warne	c Atapattu b Zoysa	0	(7)	run out	6
J.N.Gillespie	lbw b Muralitharan	41		absent hurt	–
C.R.Miller	c Atapattu b Muralitharan	0	(8)	b Vaas	8
G.D.McGrath	not out	4	(9)	not out	10
Extras	(NB 4)	4		(B 6, LB 5, W 1, NB 4)	16
Total		**188**			**140**

SRI LANKA

*S.T.Jayasuriya	lbw b McGrath	18		c sub (M.L.Hayden) b Miller	18
M.S.Atapattu	c Langer b Miller	25		c Blewett b McGrath	0
R.P.Arnold	lbw b Miller	19			
P.A.de Silva	c Ponting b Warne	78		not out	31
D.P.M.deS.Jayawardena	c Ponting b Warne	46		c Slater b Miller	9
A.Ranatunga	c Healy b Warne	4		not out	19
†R.S.Kaluwitharana	b Miller	9	(3)	b Miller	5
U.D.U.Chandana	c sub (M.L.Hayden) b Warne	12			
W.P.U.C.J.Vaas	not out	2			
D.N.T.Zoysa	c Miller b Warne	7			
M.Muralitharan	c McGrath b Miller	0			
Extras	(B 4, LB 7, NB 3)	14		(B 8, LB 2, NB 3)	13
Total		**234**		(4 wickets)	**95**

SRI LANKA	O	M	R	W		O	M	R	W
Vaas	16	2	43	3		15	7	15	3
Zoysa	13	2	38	3		10	3	28	0
Muralitharan	25.1	4	63	4	(4)	26	5	65	3
Jayasuriya	5	0	5	0	(5)	4	1	7	0
Chandana	8	1	39	0	(6)	2.2	0	9	1
De Silva					(3)	3	0	5	0
AUSTRALIA									
McGrath	18	5	66	1		7	2	19	1
Gillespie	12	2	43	0					
Miller	20.3	6	62	4	(2)	13	2	48	3
Warne	16	4	52	5	(3)	6.5	3	18	0

FALL OF WICKETS

	A	SL	A	SL
Wkt	*1st*	*1st*	*2nd*	*2nd*
1st	0	22	37	12
2nd	4	69	49	24
3rd	9	70	49	39
4th	16	177	49	60
5th	40	181	58	–
6th	59	197	75	–
7th	60	223	99	–
8th	167	226	140	–
9th	171	234	–	–
10th	188	234	–	–

Umpires: P.T.Manuel (4) and S.Venkataraghavan (*India*) (32).
Referee: C.W.Smith (*West Indies*) (26). **Test No. 1459/11 (SL91/A594)**

SRI LANKA v AUSTRALIA (2nd Test)

At Galle International Stadium on 22, 23, 24, 25 (*no play*), 26 September 1999.
Toss: Sri Lanka. Result: **MATCH DRAWN**.
Debuts: Sri Lanka – R.Herath.

SRI LANKA

*S.T.Jayasuriya	c M.E.Waugh b McGrath	0	not out	21
M.S.Atapattu	c Healy b Warne	29	not out	28
R.P.Arnold	c Warne b Miller	50		
P.A.de Silva	c S.R.Waugh b Fleming	64		
D.P.M.deS.Jayawardena	c Blewett b Warne	46		
A.Ranatunga	c Miller b Warne	10		
†R.S.Kaluwitharana	b McGrath	25		
W.P.U.C.J.Vaas	c Ponting b Fleming	41		
R.Herath	run out	3		
D.N.T.Zoysa	c M.E.Waugh b McGrath	1		
M.Muralitharan	not out	7		
Extras	(B 4, LB 8, NB 8)	20	(LB 3, NB 3)	6
Total		**296**	(0 wickets)	**55**

AUSTRALIA

M.J.Slater	st Kaluwitharana b Muralitharan	96
G.S.Blewett	b Muralitharan	62
J.L.Langer	c Ranatunga b Muralitharan	7
M.E.Waugh	c Ranatunga b Muralitharan	10
*S.R.Waugh	c Kaluwitharana b Herath	19
†I.A.Healy	c Jayawardena b Muralitharan	4
R.T.Ponting	c Ranatunga b Herath	1
S.K.Warne	c Atapattu b Herath	0
D.W.Fleming	b Herath	16
C.R.Miller	run out	6
G.D.McGrath	not out	0
Extras	(B 1, LB 4, NB 2)	7
Total		**228**

AUSTRALIA	O	M	R	W	O	M	R	W
McGrath	26.5	7	81	3	7	2	23	0
Fleming	23	6	74	2	4	0	15	0
Miller	23	1	72	1	3	1	9	0
Warne	25	11	29	3	3.2	1	5	0
Ponting	4	1	7	0				
M.E.Waugh	2	1	9	0				
Blewett	3	0	12	0				
SRI LANKA								
Vaas	9	3	31	0				
Zoysa	6	1	9	0				
Herath	34.3	6	97	4				
Muralitharan	38	10	71	5				
Jayasuriya	9	1	15	0				

FALL OF WICKETS

	SL	A	SL
Wkt	*1st*	*1st*	*2nd*
1st	0	138	–
2nd	80	160	–
3rd	100	179	–
4th	193	182	–
5th	206	188	–
6th	226	189	–
7th	262	189	–
8th	288	215	–
9th	288	228	–
10th	296	228	–

Umpires: B.C.Cooray (16) and D.B.Cowie (*New Zealand*) (13).
Referee: C.W.Smith (*West Indies*) (27). **Test No. 1460/12 (SL92/A595)**

SRI LANKA v AUSTRALIA (3rd Test)

At Sinhalese Sports Club, Colombo, on 30 September, 1, 2, 3, 4 (*no play*) October 1999.
Toss: Australia. Result: **MATCH DRAWN**.
Debuts: None.

AUSTRALIA

G.S.Blewett	c Atapattu b Herath	70
M.J.Slater	st Kaluwitharana b Arnold	59
J.L.Langer	c Ranatunga b Muralitharan	32
M.E.Waugh	c Arnold b Muralitharan	13
*S.R.Waugh	c Kaluwitharana b Herath	14
R.T.Ponting	not out	105
†I.A.Healy	c Jayawardena b Vaas	7
S.K.Warne	lbw b Vaas	0
D.W.Fleming	c Atapattu b Muralitharan	32
C.R.Miller	lbw b Vaas	0
G.D.McGrath	c Atapattu b Vaas	0
Extras	(NB 10)	10
Total		**342**

SRI LANKA

*S.T.Jayasuriya	c Warne b McGrath	0
M.S.Atapattu	c Healy b Fleming	2
R.P.Arnold	lbw b Fleming	0
P.A.de Silva	not out	19
D.P.M.deS.Jayawardena	c Healy b Fleming	21
A.Ranatunga	not out	1
†R.S.Kaluwitharana		
W.P.U.C.J.Vaas		
R.Herath		
D.N.T.Zoysa		
M.Muralitharan		
Extras	(B 8, LB 1, W 5, NB 4)	18
Total	(4 wickets)	**61**

SRI LANKA	O	M	R	W
Vaas	23.4	5	54	4
Zoysa	10	4	23	0
Herath	35	10	98	2
Muralitharan	52	5	150	3
Jayasuriya	9	2	14	0
Arnold	7	4	3	1
AUSTRALIA				
McGrath	10	3	25	1
Fleming	5.5	0	14	3
Warne	5	1	11	0
Miller	1	0	2	0

FALL OF WICKETS

	A	SL
Wkt	*1st*	*1st*
1st	126	0
2nd	147	7
3rd	182	10
4th	183	60
5th	221	–
6th	253	–
7th	255	–
8th	335	–
9th	342	–
10th	342	–

Umpires: K.T.Francis (25) and P.Willey (*England*) (16).
Referee: C.W.Smith (*West Indies*) (28).

Test No. 1461/13 (SL93/A596)

SRI LANKA v AUSTRALIA 1999-2000

SRI LANKA – BATTING AND FIELDING

	M	*I*	*NO*	*HS*	*Runs*	*Avge*	*100*	*50*	*Ct/St*
P.A.de Silva	3	4	2	78	192	96.00	–	2	2
W.P.U.C.J.Vaas	3	2	1	41	43	43.00	–	–	1
D.P.M.deS.Jayawardena	3	4	–	46	122	30.50	–	–	2
R.P.Arnold	3	3	–	50	69	23.00	–	1	1
M.S.Atapattu	3	5	1	29	84	21.00	–	–	7
A.Ranatunga	3	4	2	19*	34	17.00	–	–	4
S.T.Jayasuriya	3	5	1	21*	57	14.25	–	–	1
R.S.Kaluwitharana	3	3	–	25	39	13.00	–	–	2/3
M.Muralitharan	3	2	1	7*	7	7.00	–	–	1
D.N.T.Zoysa	3	2	–	7	8	4.00	–	–	–

Also batted: (2 matches) R.Herath 3; (1 match) U.D.U.Chandana 12.

SRI LANKA – BOWLING

	O	*M*	*R*	*W*	*Avge*	*Best*	*5wI*	*10wM*
W.P.U.C.J.Vaas	63.4	17	143	10	14.30	4-54	–	–
M.Muralitharan	141.1	24	349	15	23.26	5-71	1	–
R.Herath	69.3	16	195	6	32.50	4-97	–	–
D.N.T.Zoysa	39	10	98	3	32.66	3-38	–	–

Also bowled: R.P.Arnold 7-4-3-1; U.D.U.Chandana 10.2-1-48-1; P.A.de Silva 3-0-5-0; S.T.Jayasuriya 27-4-41-0.

AUSTRALIA – BATTING AND FIELDING

	M	*I*	*NO*	*HS*	*Runs*	*Avge*	*100*	*50*	*Ct/St*
R.T.Ponting	3	4	1	105*	253	84.33	1	2	3
M.J.Slater	3	4	–	96	182	45.50	–	2	1
G.S.Blewett	3	4	–	70	146	36.50	–	2	2
D.W.Fleming	2	2	–	32	48	24.00	–	–	–
S.R.Waugh	3	3	–	19	52	17.33	–	–	1
G.D.McGrath	3	4	3	10*	14	14.00	–	–	1
J.L.Langer	3	4	–	32	51	12.75	–	–	1
M.E.Waugh	3	4	–	13	29	7.25	–	–	2
I.A.Healy	3	4	–	11	25	6.25	–	–	4
C.R.Miller	3	4	–	8	14	3.50	–	–	2
S.K.Warne	3	4	–	6	6	1.50	–	–	2

Played in one Test: J.N.Gillespie 41.

AUSTRALIA – BOWLING

	O	*M*	*R*	*W*	*Avge*	*Best*	*5wI*	*10wM*
S.K.Warne	56.1	20	115	8	14.37	5-52	1	–
D.W.Fleming	32.5	6	103	5	20.60	3-14	–	–
C.R.Miller	60.3	10	193	8	24.12	4-62	–	–
G.D.McGrath	68.5	19	214	6	35.66	3-81	–	–

Also bowled: G.S.Blewett 3-0-12-0; J.N.Gillespie 12-2-43-0; R.T.Ponting 4-1-7-0; M.E.Waugh 2-1-9-0.

INDIA v NEW ZEALAND (1st Test)

At Punjab C.A. Stadium, Mohali, Chandigarh, on 10, 11, 12, 13, 14 October 1999.
Toss: New Zealand. Result: **MATCH DRAWN**.
Debuts: India – R.V.Bharadwaj, D.J.Gandhi, M.S.K.Prasad.

INDIA

D.J.Gandhi	c Parore b Nash	0	lbw b Astle	75
S.Ramesh	b Nash	0	c and b Vettori	73
R.Dravid	c Astle b Cairns	1	b Vettori	144
*S.R.Tendulkar	b O'Connor	18	not out	126
S.C.Ganguly	b Nash	2	not out	64
R.V.Bharadwaj	c Parore b Cairns	0		
†M.S.K.Prasad	not out	16		
S.B.Joshi	c Spearman b O'Connor	0		
A.Kumble	c Spearman b Nash	7		
J.Srinath	c Astle b Nash	20		
B.K.V.Prasad	c Fleming b Nash	0		
Extras	(B 8, LB 5, NB 6)	19	(B 9, LB 7, NB 7)	23
Total		**83**	(3 wickets declared)	**505**

NEW ZEALAND

M.J.Horne	c Ganguly b Srinath	6	c Ganguly b Joshi	33
M.D.Bell	b Srinath	0	lbw b Srinath	7
C.M.Spearman	c and b Kumble	51	c Ganguly b Joshi	35
*S.P.Fleming	lbw b Srinath	43	c Ganguly b Kumble	73
N.J.Astle	c Kumble b Srinath	45	c M.S.K.Prasad b Srinath	34
C.D.McMillan	lbw b Joshi	22	c Ramesh b Kumble	18
†A.C.Parore	not out	13	c Gandhi b Kumble	7
C.L.Cairns	b B.K.V.Prasad	7	not out	0
D.J.Nash	c M.S.K.Prasad b Srinath	2		
D.L.Vettori	b Srinath	0		
S.B.O'Connor	c Gandhi b Bharadwaj	2		
Extras	(B 5, LB 11, NB 8)	24	(B 24, LB 15, NB 5)	44
Total		**215**	(7 wickets)	**251**

NEW ZEALAND	O	M	R	W		O	M	R	W
Cairns	9	4	23	2		24	3	76	0
Nash	11	3	27	6		37	16	79	0
O'Connor	7	1	20	2	(4)	18	3	73	0
Vettori					(3)	71	24	171	2
Astle						31	8	82	1
McMillan						2	0	8	0
INDIA									
Srinath	22	9	45	6		31	9	63	2
B.K.V.Prasad	19	6	56	1		16	7	24	0
Ganguly	1	0	1	0					
Kumble	18	3	49	1	(3)	41	19	42	3
Bharadwaj	14.1	4	26	1		13	3	34	0
Joshi	17	8	22	1	(4)	28	12	38	2
Tendulkar					(6)	6	2	11	0

FALL OF WICKETS

	I	NZ	I	NZ
Wkt	*1st*	*1st*	*2nd*	*2nd*
1st	2	7	137	24
2nd	3	8	181	95
3rd	7	99	410	108
4th	10	156	–	186
5th	22	179	–	227
6th	38	181	–	246
7th	38	199	–	251
8th	53	207	–	–
9th	83	212	–	–
10th	83	215	–	–

Umpires: P.T.Manuel (*Sri Lanka*) (5) and S.Venkataraghavan (33).
Referee: R.S.Madugalle (*Sri Lanka*) (19). **Test No. 1462/38 (I326/NZ272)**

INDIA v NEW ZEALAND (2nd Test)

At Green Park, Kanpur, on 22, 23, 24, 25 October 1999.
Toss: New Zealand. Result: **INDIA** won by eight wickets.
Debuts: None.

NEW ZEALAND

M.J.Horne	c Prasad b Ganguly	5		lbw b Kumble	3
M.D.Bell	lbw b Srinath	15		lbw b Kumble	7
C.M.Spearman	c Ramesh b Kumble	12	(4)	c Tendulkar b Harbhajan	1
*S.P.Fleming	b Srinath	2	(5)	c Dravid b Harbahjan	31
N.J.Astle	lbw b Srinath	39	(6)	c Bharadwaj b Kumble	0
C.D.McMillan	c Ramesh b Joshi	34	(8)	lbw b Kumble	31
†A.C.Parore	c Dravid b Kumble	35		b Harbhajan	48
C.L.Cairns	c Tendulkar b Kumble	53	(9)	b Joshi	2
D.J.Nash	not out	41	(3)	b Kumble	0
D.L.Vettori	c Bharadwaj b Harbhajan	0		not out	8
P.J.Wiseman	c Bharadwaj b Kumble	0		lbw b Kumble	0
Extras	(B 7, NB 13)	20		(B 5, LB 9, NB 10)	24
Total		**256**			**155**

INDIA

D.J.Gandhi	c Fleming b Astle	88	not out	31
S.Ramesh	c Parore b Astle	83	b Cairns	5
R.Dravid	c Parore b Vettori	48	lbw b Nash	1
*S.R.Tendulkar	c Astle b Vettori	15	not out	44
S.C.Ganguly	c and b Vettori	0		
R.V.Bharadwaj	c Spearman b Wiseman	22		
†M.S.K.Prasad	c Fleming b Vettori	19		
S.B.Joshi	c Bell b Vettori	19		
A.Kumble	st Parore b Vettori	5		
J.Srinath	c Astle b Wiseman	0		
Harbhajan Singh	not out	1		
Extras	(B 14, LB 6, NB 10)	30	(LB 1, NB 1)	2
Total		**330**	(2 wickets)	**83**

INDIA	O	M	R	W		O	M	R	W
Srinath	22	9	62	3		9	5	12	0
Ganguly	4	0	15	1		1	0	2	0
Kumble	32.5	12	67	4		26.5	5	67	6
Harbhajan Singh	17	6	30	1	(5)	15	3	33	3
Joshi	25	7	63	1	(4)	15	6	27	1
Bharadwaj	2	0	12	0					
NEW ZEALAND									
Cairns	16	8	34	0		3	1	10	1
Nash	22	10	41	0		4	1	11	1
Vettori	55.1	11	127	6		6.2	2	22	0
Wiseman	29	10	81	2		5	0	39	0
Astle	26	12	27	2					

FALL OF WICKETS

	NZ	I	NZ	I
Wkt	*1st*	*1st*	*2nd*	*2nd*
1st	7	162	16	5
2nd	33	214	16	7
3rd	40	243	17	–
4th	50	246	28	–
5th	112	255	33	–
6th	130	293	71	–
7th	172	311	128	–
8th	255	321	138	–
9th	255	326	150	–
10th	256	330	155	–

Umpires: D.J.Harper (*Australia*) (4) and A.V.Jayaprakash (3).
Referee: R.S.Madugalle (*Sri Lanka*) (20). **Test No. 1463/39 (I327/NZ273)**

INDIA v NEW ZEALAND (3rd Test)

At Sardar Patel Stadium, Motera, Ahmedabad, on 29, 30, 31 October, 1, 2 November 1999.
Toss: India. Result: **MATCH DRAWN**.
Debuts: None.

INDIA

D.J.Gandhi	c Parore b Cairns	6			
S.Ramesh	c Spearman b Harris	110	(1)	c Parore b Nash	16
R.Dravid	c Parore b Vettori	33		run out	12
*S.R.Tendulkar	c Nash b Vettori	217	(2)	b Cairns	15
S.C.Ganguly	c Nash b Astle	125	(4)	b Harris	53
A.Jadeja	b Vettori	13	(7)	not out	12
†M.S.K.Prasad	b Vettori	2	(5)	c Parore b Astle	17
A.Kumble	not out	27			
J.Srinath	not out	33	(6)	not out	19
B.K.V.Prasad					
Harbhajan Singh					
Extras	(B 4, LB 7, NB 6)	17		(LB 4)	4
Total	(7 wickets declared)	**583**		(5 wickets declared)	**148**

NEW ZEALAND

G.R.Stead	c Ganguly b Kumble	17	(2)	c M.S.K.Prasad b Harbhajan	78
M.J.Horne	c Dravid b Kumble	2	(1)	c sub (R.V.Bharadwaj) b Kumble	41
D.L.Vettori	c sub (R.V.Bharadwaj) b Kumble	3			
C.M.Spearman	c Ramesh b B.K.V.Prasad	17	(3)	not out	54
*S.P.Fleming	c M.S.K.Prasad b Srinath	48	(4)	not out	64
N.J.Astle	c Ganguly b B.K.V.Prasad	74			
†A.C.Parore	lbw b Kumble	11			
C.L.Cairns	b Kumble	72			
C.Z.Harris	c Ramesh b Srinath	12			
D.J.Nash	not out	14			
P.J.Wiseman	lbw b Harbhajan	3			
Extras	(B 8, LB 14, NB 13)	35		(B 1, LB 5, NB 9)	15
Total		**308**		(2 wickets)	**252**

NEW ZEALAND	O	M	R	W		O	M	R	W
Cairns	24	5	82	1		6	1	29	1
Nash	28	6	86	0		8	0	35	1
Vettori	57	5	200	4		2	0	23	0
Astle	17	2	55	1	(5)	5	0	13	1
Harris	17	3	64	1	(4)	11	0	44	1
Wiseman	24	2	85	0					
INDIA									
Srinath	35	11	72	2		15	3	59	0
B.K.V.Prasad	26	9	52	2		13	2	36	0
Kumble	48	21	82	5		31	16	57	1
Harbhajan Singh	30.4	8	78	1		26	8	55	1
Ganguly	2	1	2	0	(6)	4	0	20	0
Tendulkar					(5)	5	2	19	0
Dravid						1	1	0	0

FALL OF WICKETS

	I	NZ	I	NZ
Wkt	*1st*	*1st*	*2nd*	*2nd*
1st	20	13	21	131
2nd	102	29	35	131
3rd	182	33	68	–
4th	463	65	114	–
5th	502	135	122	–
6th	518	166	–	–
7th	521	231	–	–
8th	–	284	–	–
9th	–	294	–	–
10th	–	308	–	–

Umpires: R.E.Koertzen (*South Africa*) (15) and V.K.Ramaswamy (26).
Referee: R.S.Madugalle (*Sri Lanka*) (21). **Test No. 1464/40 (I328/NZ274)**

INDIA v NEW ZEALAND 1999-2000

INDIA – BATTING AND FIELDING

	M	*I*	*NO*	*HS*	*Runs*	*Avge*	*100*	*50*	*Ct/St*
S.R.Tendulkar	3	6	2	217	435	108.75	2	–	2
S.C.Ganguly	3	5	1	125	244	61.00	1	2	6
D.J.Gandhi	3	5	1	88	200	50.00	–	2	2
S.Ramesh	3	6	–	110	287	47.83	1	2	5
R.Dravid	3	6	–	144	239	39.83	1	–	3
J.Srinath	3	4	2	33*	72	36.00	–	–	–
A.Kumble	3	3	1	27*	39	19.50	–	–	2
M.S.K.Prasad	3	4	1	19	54	18.00	–	–	5
R.V.Bharadwaj	2	2	–	22	22	11.00	–	–	3
S.B.Joshi	2	2	–	19	19	9.50	–	–	–
B.K.V.Prasad	2	1	–	0	0	0.00	–	–	–
Harbhajan Singh	2	1	1	1*	1	–	–	–	–

Played in one Test: A.Jadeja 13, 12*.

INDIA – BOWLING

	O	*M*	*R*	*W*	*Avge*	*Best*	*5wI*	*10wM*
A.Kumble	197.4	76	364	20	18.20	6-67	2	1
J.Srinath	134	46	313	13	24.07	6-45	1	–
S.B.Joshi	85	33	150	5	30.00	2-38	–	–
Harbhajan Singh	88.4	25	196	6	32.66	3-33	–	–

Also bowled: R.V.Bharadwaj 29.1-7-72-1; R.Dravid 1-1-0-0; S.C.Ganguly 12-1-40-1; B.K.V.Prasad 74-24-168-3; S.R.Tendulkar 11-4-30-0.

NEW ZEALAND – BATTING AND FIELDING

	M	*I*	*NO*	*HS*	*Runs*	*Avge*	*100*	*50*	*Ct/St*
S.P.Fleming	3	6	1	73	261	52.20	–	2	3
N.J.Astle	3	5	–	74	192	38.40	–	1	4
C.M.Spearman	3	6	1	54*	170	34.00	–	2	4
C.L.Cairns	3	5	1	72	134	33.50	–	2	–
A.C.Parore	3	5	1	48	114	28.50	–	–	8/1
D.J.Nash	3	4	2	41*	57	28.50	–	–	2
C.D.McMillan	2	4	–	34	105	26.25	–	–	–
M.J.Horne	3	6	–	41	90	15.00	–	–	–
M.D.Bell	2	4	–	15	29	7.25	–	–	1
D.L.Vettori	3	4	1	8*	11	3.66	–	–	2
P.J.Wiseman	2	3	–	3	3	1.00	–	–	–

Played in one Test: C.Z.Harris 12; S.B.O'Connor 2; G.R.Stead 17, 78.

NEW ZEALAND – BOWLING

	O	*M*	*R*	*W*	*Avge*	*Best*	*5wI*	*10wM*
D.J.Nash	110	36	279	8	34.87	6- 27	1	–
N.J.Astle	79	22	177	5	35.40	2- 27	–	–
D.L.Vettori	191.3	42	543	12	45.25	6-127	1	–
C.L.Cairns	82	22	254	5	50.80	2- 23	–	–

Also bowled: C.Z.Harris 28-3-108-2; C.D.McMillan 2-0-8-0; S.B.O'Connor 25-4-93-2; P.J.Wiseman 58-12-205-2.

ZIMBABWE v AUSTRALIA (Only Test)

At Harare Sports Club on 14, 15, 16, 17 October 1999.
Toss: Zimbabwe. Result: **AUSTRALIA** won by ten wickets.
Debuts: Zimbabwe – T.R.Gripper.

ZIMBABWE

G.J.Rennie	c Ponting b McGrath	18	(4)	c McGrath b Miller	23
G.W.Flower	c Ponting b Fleming	1		lbw b McGrath	32
M.W.Goodwin	run out	0		c S.R.Waugh b Warne	91
*A.D.R.Campbell	c Slater b Fleming	5	(5)	run out	1
†A.Flower	c M.E.Waugh b McGrath	28	(6)	c Healy b McGrath	0
N.C.Johnson	c M.E.Waugh b McGrath	75	(7)	c M.E.Waugh b McGrath	5
T.R.Gripper	lbw b Warne	4	(1)	lbw b Miller	60
H.H.Streak	c M.E.Waugh b Warne	3	(9)	lbw b Warne	0
G.J.Whittall	c Healy b Warne	27	(8)	c M.E.Waugh b Warne	2
B.C.Strang	run out	17		c Langer b Miller	0
H.K.Olonga	not out	0		not out	0
Extras	(B 2, LB 4, NB 10)	16		(B 9, LB 2, W 1, NB 6)	18
Total		**194**			**232**

AUSTRALIA

M.J.Slater	c A.Flower b Strang	4	(2)	not out	0
G.S.Blewett	c Campbell b Streak	1	(1)	not out	4
J.L.Langer	run out	44			
M.E.Waugh	c and b G.W.Flower	90			
*S.R.Waugh	not out	151			
R.T.Ponting	c Johnson b Streak	31			
†I.A.Healy	c A.Flower b Strang	5			
S.K.Warne	b A.Flower b Streak	6			
D.W.Fleming	lbw b Streak	65			
C.R.Miller	c Johnson b Streak	2			
G.D.McGrath	c Johnson b Whittall	13			
Extras	(LB 5, W 4, NB 1)	10		(W 1)	1
Total		**422**		(0 wickets)	**5**

AUSTRALIA	O	M	R	W		O	M	R	W
McGrath	23	7	44	3		31	12	46	3
Fleming	15	6	22	2		21	6	31	0
Miller	19	6	36	0		34	10	66	3
Warne	23	2	69	3	(5)	30.1	11	68	3
Ponting	1	1	0	0	(4)	1	1	0	0
S.R.Waugh	4	1	17	0					
Blewett					(6)	5	1	10	0
ZIMBABWE									
Olonga	17	1	83	0					
Streak	34	8	93	5					
Strang	44	14	96	2	(1)	0.3	0	5	0
Johnson	2	0	14	0					
Whittall	21.4	3	74	1					
G.W.Flower	18	3	38	1					
Gripper	3	0	19	0					

FALL OF WICKETS

	Z	A	Z	A
Wkt	*1st*	*1st*	*2nd*	*2nd*
1st	6	6	56	–
2nd	6	7	154	–
3rd	22	96	200	–
4th	37	174	208	–
5th	107	253	211	–
6th	119	275	220	–
7th	125	282	227	–
8th	165	396	227	–
9th	190	398	232	–
10th	194	422	232	–

Umpires: I.D.Robinson (20) and G.Sharp (*England*) (10).
Referee: G.R.Viswanath (*India*) (1). **Test No. 1465/1 (Z34/A597)**

SOUTH AFRICA v ZIMBABWE (Only Test)

At Springbok Park, Bloemfontein, on 29, 30, 31 October, 1 November 1999.
Toss: South Africa. Result: **SOUTH AFRICA** won by an innings and 13 runs.
Debuts: South Africa – H.H.Dippenaar.

ZIMBABWE

G.W.Flower	lbw b Pollock	0	b Kallis	8
T.R.Gripper	run out	16	lbw b Kallis	11
M.W.Goodwin	c Boucher b Pollock	7	c Boucher b Kallis	0
*A.D.R.Campbell	c Klusener b Pollock	27	c Cronje b Pollock	33
†A.Flower	lbw b Pollock	13	lbw b Kallis	39
N.C.Johnson	c Boucher b Donald	6	lbw b Pollock	23
G.J.Rennie	c Cullinan b Kallis	14	c Boucher b Adams	10
G.J.Whittall	c Boucher b Kallis	85	b Adams	51
B.C.Strang	c Cronje b Pollock	9	lbw b Adams	0
H.K.Olonga	b Kallis	1	c Rhodes b Adams	24
M.Mbangwa	not out	0	not out	0
Extras	(LB 6, W 3, NB 5)	14	(LB 4, W 5, NB 4)	13
Total		**192**		**212**

SOUTH AFRICA

H.H.Dippenaar	lbw b Olonga	20
A.M.Bacher	c Goodwin b Mbangwa	42
J.H.Kallis	lbw b Whittall	64
D.J.Cullinan	c G.W.Flower b Whittall	27
*W.J.Cronje	c A.Flower b Mbangwa	64
J.N.Rhodes	lbw b Olonga	70
S.M.Pollock	c Campbell b Strang	8
L.Klusener	lbw b G.W.Flower	19
†M.V.Boucher	not out	55
A.Donald	b Olonga	2
P.R.Adams	c Gripper b Olonga	20
Extras	(LB 3, W 1, NB 22)	26
Total		**417**

SOUTH AFRICA	O	M	R	W		O	M	R	W
Donald	18	5	58	1		15	6	25	0
Pollock	21	6	39	5		19	5	62	2
Klusener	16	5	40	0	(4)	4	0	22	0
Kallis	17	4	44	3	(3)	21	3	68	4
Adams	3	1	5	0		12.1	5	31	4
ZIMBABWE									
Olonga	33.1	7	93	4					
Strang	27	6	99	1					
Johnson	2	0	8	0					
G.W.Flower	23	5	44	1					
Mbangwa	35	9	75	2					
Whittall	30	9	95	2					

FALL OF WICKETS

	Z	SA	Z
Wkt	*1st*	*1st*	*2nd*
1st	1	43	11
2nd	14	72	19
3rd	41	128	24
4th	63	218	77
5th	78	266	115
6th	79	278	123
7th	117	310	166
8th	140	342	166
9th	183	363	202
10th	192	417	212

Umpires: R.S.Dunne (*New Zealand*) (33) and D.L.Orchard (14).
Referee: J.L.Hendricks (*West Indies*) (9). **Test No. 1466/2 (SA234/Z35)**

AUSTRALIA v PAKISTAN (1st Test)

At Woolloongabba, Brisbane, on 5, 6, 7, 8, 9 November 1999.
Toss: Australia. Result: **AUSTRALIA** won by ten wickets.
Debuts: Australia – A.C.Gilchrist, S.A.Muller. Pakistan – Abdur Razzaq.

PAKISTAN

Saeed Anwar	c M.E.Waugh b Warne	61		c Gilchrist b McGrath	119
Mohammad Wasim	c Gilchrist b Fleming	18		lbw b Fleming	0
Ijaz Ahmed	c Warne b Fleming	0		c Gilchrist b McGrath	5
Inzamam-ul-Haq	lbw b McGrath	88		c Ponting b Fleming	12
Yousuf Youhana	c Gilchrist b Fleming	95		c M.E.Waugh b Muller	75
Azhar Mahmood	c Slater b McGrath	13	(8)	st Gilchrist b Warne	0
Mushtaq Ahmed	c Gilchrist b Fleming	0	(10)	not out	1
Abdur Razzaq	c M.E.Waugh b Muller	11	(6)	c Ponting b Warne	2
†Moin Khan	run out	61	(7)	c Muller b Fleming	17
*Wasim Akram	c and b Muller	9	(9)	b Fleming	28
Shoaib Akhtar	not out	0		b Fleming	5
Extras	(B 4, LB 2, NB 5)	11		(B 6, LB 6, NB 5)	17
Total		**367**			**281**

AUSTRALIA

M.J.Slater	c Youhana b Azhar	169	(2)	not out	32
G.S.Blewett	lbw b Mushtaq	89	(1)	not out	40
J.L.Langer	c Razzaq b Mushtaq	1			
M.E.Waugh	c Wasim Akram b Mushtaq	100			
*S.R.Waugh	c Moin b Shoaib	1			
R.T.Ponting	lbw b Shoaib	0			
†A.C.Gilchrist	b Shoaib	81			
S.K.Warne	c Mushtaq b Wasim Akram	86			
D.W.Fleming	lbw b Shoaib	0			
G.D.McGrath	c Youhana b Wasim Akram	1			
S.A.Muller	not out	6			
Extras	(B 3, LB 12, NB 26)	41		(LB 2)	2
Total		**575**			**74**

AUSTRALIA	O	M	R	W		O	M	R	W
McGrath	28	4	116	2		21	9	63	2
Fleming	31	5	65	4		14.1	2	59	5
Muller	19	4	72	2		10	1	55	1
Warne	28.1	11	73	1		25	8	80	2
Blewett	5	1	22	0					
Ponting	5	1	12	0	(5)	4	0	12	0
S.R.Waugh	1	0	1	0					
PAKISTAN									
Wasim Akram	31.1	6	87	2		4	0	14	0
Shoaib Akhtar	32	2	153	4		5	0	25	0
Abdur Razzaq	17	3	66	0					
Azhar Mahmood	19	2	52	1	(3)	3.2	0	13	0
Mushtaq Ahmed	38	3	194	3	(4)	2	0	20	0
Ijaz Ahmed	2	0	8	0					

FALL OF WICKETS

	P	A	P	A
Wkt	*1st*	*1st*	*2nd*	*2nd*
1st	42	269	3	–
2nd	42	272	8	–
3rd	113	311	37	–
4th	265	328	214	–
5th	280	342	223	–
6th	280	465	225	–
7th	288	485	227	–
8th	334	486	273	–
9th	356	489	276	–
10th	367	575	281	–

Umpires: D.J.Harper (5) and E.A.Nicholls (*West Indies*) (8).
Referee: J.R.Reid (*New Zealand*) (42). **Test No. 1467/44 (A598/P259)**

AUSTRALIA v PAKISTAN (2nd Test)

At Bellerive Oval, Hobart, on 18, 19, 20, 21, 22 November 1999.
Toss: Australia. Result: **AUSTRALIA** won by four wickets.
Debuts: None.

PAKISTAN

Saeed Anwar	c Warne b McGrath	0		b Warne	78
Mohammad Wasim	c Gilchrist b Muller	91		c McGrath b Muller	20
Ijaz Ahmed	c Slater b McGrath	6	(4)	c S.R.Waugh b McGrath	82
Inzamam-ul-Haq	b Muller	12	(5)	c M.E.Waugh b Warne	118
Yousuf Youhana	c M.E.Waugh b Fleming	17	(6)	c Ponting b Fleming	2
Azhar Mahmood	b Warne	27	(7)	lbw b Warne	28
†Moin Khan	c McGrath b Muller	1	(8)	c Gilchrist b Fleming	6
*Wasim Akram	c Gilchrist b Warne	29	(9)	c Blewett b Warne	31
Saqlain Mushtaq	lbw b Warne	3	(3)	lbw b Warne	8
Waqar Younis	not out	12		run out	0
Shoaib Akhtar	c Gilchrist b Fleming	5		not out	5
Extras	(B 10, LB 6, W 3)	19		(LB 6, W 1, NB 7)	14
Total		**222**			**392**

AUSTRALIA

M.J.Slater	c Ijaz b Saqlain	97	c Azhar b Shoaib	27
G.S.Blewett	c Moin b Azhar	35	c Moin b Azhar	29
J.L.Langer	c Mohammad Wasim b Saqlain	59	c Inzamam-ul-Haq b Saqlain	127
M.E.Waugh	lbw b Waqar	5	lbw b Azhar	0
*S.R.Waugh	c Ijaz b Wasim Akram	24	c and b Saqlain	28
R.T.Ponting	b Waqar	0	lbw b Wasim	0
†A.C.Gilchrist	st Moin b Saqlain	6	not out	149
S.K.Warne	b Saqlain	0	not out	0
D.W.Fleming	lbw b Saqlain	0		
G.D.McGrath	st Moin b Saqlain	7		
S.A.Muller	not out	0		
Extras	(B 2, LB 6, NB 5)	13	(B 1, LB 4, NB 4)	9
Total		**246**	(6 wickets)	**369**

AUSTRALIA	O	M	R	W		O	M	R	W
McGrath	18	8	34	2		27	8	87	1
Fleming	24.5	7	54	2		29	5	89	2
Muller	12	0	68	3	(4)	17	3	63	1
Warne	16	5	45	3	(3)	45.4	11	110	5
Blewett	2	1	5	0	(8)	2	0	5	0
S.R.Waugh					(5)	4	1	19	0
M.E.Waugh					(6)	2	0	6	0
Ponting					(7)	2	1	7	0
PAKISTAN									
Wasim Akram	20	4	51	1		18	1	68	1
Shoaib Akhtar	17	2	69	0	(3)	23	5	85	1
Waqar Younis	12	1	42	2	(2)	11	2	38	0
Saqlain Mushtaq	24	8	46	6		44.5	9	130	2
Azhar Mahmood	7	1	30	1		17	3	43	2

FALL OF WICKETS

	P	A	P	A
Wkt	*1st*	*1st*	*2nd*	*2nd*
1st	4	76	50	39
2nd	18	190	100	81
3rd	71	205	122	81
4th	120	205	258	125
5th	148	212	263	126
6th	153	236	320	364
7th	188	236	345	–
8th	198	236	357	–
9th	217	246	358	–
10th	222	246	392	–

Umpires: P.D.Parker (5) and P.Willey (*England*) (17).
Referee: J.R.Reid (*New Zealand*) (43).

Test No. 1468/45 (A599/P260)

AUSTRALIA v PAKISTAN (3rd Test)

At W.A.C.A. Ground, Perth, on 26, 27, 28 November 1999.
Toss: Pakistan. Result: **AUSTRALIA** won by an innings and 20 runs.
Debuts: None.

PAKISTAN

Saeed Anwar	c Ponting b McGrath	18		c Gilchrist b Fleming	6
Wajahatullah Wasti	c Ponting b McGrath	5		c Fleming b McGrath	7
Ijaz Ahmed	b Fleming	1		c Slater b Kasprowicz	115
Inzamam-ul-Haq	c S.R.Waugh b Kasprowicz	22	(5)	c M.E.Waugh b McGrath	8
Yousuf Youhana	c Gilchrist b McGrath	18	(6)	c S.R.Waugh b McGrath	0
Azhar Mahmood	c Warne b Fleming	39	(7)	b Warne	17
†Moin Khan	c and b Fleming	28	(8)	c Gilchrist b McGrath	26
*Wasim Akram	not out	5	(9)	c McGrath b Kasprowicz	52
Saqlain Mushtaq	c Blewett b Kasprowicz	7	(4)	lbw b Kasprowicz	12
Shoaib Akhtar	b Kasprowicz	0		c Warne b Fleming	8
Mohammad Akram	c M.E.Waugh b Kasprowicz	0		not out	10
Extras	(LB 4, NB 8)	12		(LB 6, NB 9)	15
Total		**155**			**276**

AUSTRALIA

M.J.Slater	lbw b Wasim	0
G.S.Blewett	c Inzamam b Mohammad Akram	11
J.L.Langer	c Moin b Shoaib	144
M.E.Waugh	c sub (Ghulam Ali) b Mohd Akram	0
*S.R.Waugh	c Youhana b Mohammad Akram	5
R.T.Ponting	c Ijaz b Azhar	197
†A.C.Gilchrist	c Mohammad Akram	28
S.K.Warne	c Moin b Saqlain	13
M.S.Kasprowicz	not out	9
D.W.Fleming	lbw b Saqlain	0
G.D.McGrath	c Azhar b Mohammad Akram	0
Extras	(B 9, LB 9, NB 26)	44
Total		**451**

AUSTRALIA	O	M	R	W	O	M	R	W
McGrath	19	4	44	4	21	5	49	4
Fleming	19	7	48	3	19.4	3	86	2
Kasprowicz	12	2	53	4	16	3	79	3
Warne	2	0	6	0	13	1	56	1
PAKISTAN								
Wasim Akram	17	2	55	1				
Mohammad Akram	27.5	1	138	5				
Shoaib Akhtar	16	2	74	1				
Azhar Mahmood	23	2	91	1				
Saqlain Mushtaq	26	7	75	2				
Wajahatullah Wasti	1	1	0	0				

FALL OF WICKETS

	P	A	P
Wkt	*1st*	*1st*	*2nd*
1st	18	0	15
2nd	26	28	25
3rd	26	48	53
4th	50	54	56
5th	83	381	114
6th	135	424	168
7th	142	424	230
8th	155	448	256
9th	155	450	261
10th	155	451	276

Umpires: D.B.Hair (30) and P.Willey (*England*) (18).
Referee: J.R.Reid (*Australia*) (44). **Test No. 1469/46 (A600/P261)**

AUSTRALIA v PAKISTAN 1999-2000

AUSTRALIA – BATTING AND FIELDING

	M	I	NO	HS	Runs	Avge	100	50	Ct/St
A.C.Gilchrist	3	4	1	149*	264	88.00	1	1	12/1
J.L.Langer	3	4	–	144	331	82.75	2	1	–
M.J.Slater	3	5	1	169	325	81.25	1	1	3
G.S.Blewett	3	5	1	89	204	51.00	–	1	2
R.T.Ponting	3	4	–	197	197	49.25	1	–	5
S.K.Warne	3	4	1	86	99	33.00	–	1	4
M.E.Waugh	3	4	–	100	105	26.25	1	–	7
S.R.Waugh	3	4	–	28	58	14.50	–	–	3
G.D.McGrath	3	3	–	7	8	2.66	–	–	3
D.W.Fleming	3	3	–	0	0	0.00	–	–	2
S.A.Muller	2	2	2	6*	6	–	–	–	2

Played in one Test: M.S.Kasprowicz 9*.

AUSTRALIA – BOWLING

	O	M	R	W	Avge	Best	5wI	10wM
M.S.Kasprowicz	28	5	132	7	18.85	4- 53	–	–
D.W.Fleming	137.4	29	401	18	22.27	5- 59	1	–
G.D.McGrath	134	38	393	14	28.07	4- 49	–	–
S.K.Warne	129.5	36	370	12	30.83	5-110	1	–
S.A.Muller	58	8	258	7	36.85	3- 68	–	–

Also bowled: G.S.Blewett 9-2-32-0; R.T.Ponting 11-2-31-0; M.E.Waugh 2-0-6-0; S.R.Waugh 5-1-20-0.

PAKISTAN – BATTING AND FIELDING

	M	I	NO	HS	Runs	Avge	100	50	Ct/St
Saeed Anwar	3	6	–	119	282	47.00	1	2	–
Inzamam-ul-Haq	3	6	–	118	260	43.33	1	1	2
Ijaz Ahmed	3	6	–	115	209	34.83	1	1	3
Yousuf Youhana	3	6	–	95	207	34.50	–	2	3
Mohammad Wasim	2	4	–	91	129	32.25	–	1	1
Wasim Akram	3	6	1	52	154	30.80	–	1	1
Moin Khan	3	6	–	61	139	23.16	–	1	5/ 2
Azhar Mahmood	3	6	–	39	124	20.66	–	–	2
Saqlain Mushtaq	2	4	–	12	30	7.50	–	–	1
Shoaib Akhtar	3	6	2	8	23	5.75	–	–	–

Played in one Test: Abdur Razzaq 11, 2 (1 ct); Mohammad Akram 0, 10*; Mushtaq Ahmed 0, 1* (1 ct); Wajahatullah Wasti 5, 7; Waqar Younis 12*, 0.

PAKISTAN – BOWLING

	O	M	R	W	Avge	Best	5wI	10wM
Saqlain Mushtaq	94.5	24	251	10	25.10	6- 46	1	–
Mohammad Akram	27.5	1	138	5	27.60	5-138	1	–
Azhar Mahmood	69.2	8	229	5	45.80	2- 43	–	–
Wasim Akram	90.1	13	275	5	55.00	2- 87	–	–
Shoaib Akhtar	93	11	406	6	67.66	4-153	–	–

Also bowled: Abdur Razzaq 17-3-66-0; Ijaz Ahmed 2-0-8-0; Mushtaq Ahmed 40-3-214-3; Wajahatullah Wasti 1-1-0-0; Waqar Younis 23-3-80-2.

ZIMBABWE v SOUTH AFRICA (Only Test)

At Harare Sports Club on 11, 12, 13, 14 November 1999.
Toss: South Africa. Result: **SOUTH AFRICA** won by an innings and 219 runs.
Debuts: None.

ZIMBABWE

G.Flower	c Kallis b Klusener	5	b Donald	0
T.R.Gripper	b Pollock	1	c Kallis b Cronje	18
M.W.Goodwin	c Cronje b Pollock	17	lbw b Pollock	7
N.C.Johnson	c Boucher b Pollock	20	c Boucher b Klusener	9
*†A.Flower	c Boucher b Pollock	8	b Donald	14
A.D.R.Campbell	c Pollock b Cronje	15	c Rhodes b Adams	25
G.J.Rennie	c Cullinan b Klusener	11	c Donald b Adams	34
G.J.Whittall	c Pollock b Klusener	3	c Dippenaar b Pollock	17
B.C.Strang	lbw b Cronje	11	lbw b Pollock	0
H.K.Olonga	c Boucher b Cronje	0	not out	4
M.Mbangwa	not out	1	lbw b Adams	3
Extras	(LB 7, NB 3)	10	(LB 4, W 2, NB 4)	10
Total		**102**		**141**

SOUTH AFRICA

A.M.Bacher	c A.Flower b Strang	8
H.H.Dippenaar	c Johnson b Olonga	33
J.H.Kallis	lbw b Strang	115
D.J.Cullinan	c A.Flower b Strang	0
*W.J.Cronje	c Rennie b Olonga	58
†M.V.Boucher	c Goodwin b Gripper	125
J.N.Rhodes	c G.W.Flower b Mbangwa	4
L.Klusener	c Olonga b Mbangwa	25
S.M.Pollock	c Campbell b Olonga	61
A.A.Donald	not out	17
P.R.Adams	not out	3
Extras	(LB 3, NB 10)	13
Total	(9 wickets, declared)	**462**

SOUTH AFRICA	O	M	R	W	O	M	R	W
Donald	10	5	10	0	9	2	25	2
Pollock	17	7	32	4	16	9	23	3
Klusener	12	3	39	3	9	1	29	1
Cronje	7.5	2	14	3	6	1	20	1
Adams					10.5	0	40	3
ZIMBABWE								
Olonga	33	7	107	3				
Strang	38	10	92	3				
Mbangwa	28	6	91	2				
Whittall	27	8	78	0				
G.W.Flower	18	3	52	0				
Goodwin	2	0	11	0				
Gripper	8	1	28	1				

FALL OF WICKETS

	Z	SA	Z
Wkt	*1st*	*1st*	*2nd*
1st	6	20	0
2nd	6	96	17
3rd	35	105	33
4th	59	205	37
5th	64	230	73
6th	79	237	83
7th	86	281	128
8th	101	429	128
9th	101	451	132
10th	102	–	141

Umpires: D.B.Hair (*Australia*) (29) and R.B.Tiffin (11).
Referee: J.L.Hendriks (*West Indies*) (10).

Test No. 1470/3 (Z36/SA235)

ZIMBABWE v SRI LANKA (1st Test)

At Queens Sports Club, Bulawayo, on 18, 19, 20, 21, 22 November 1999.
Toss: Sri Lanka. Result: **MATCH DRAWN**.
Debuts: Zimbabwe – G.B.Brent; Sri Lanka – S.I.de Saram, I.S.Gallage, T.M.Dilshan.

ZIMBABWE

G.W.Flower	c Arnold b Wickremasinghe	17	c Dilshan b Muralitharan	48
G.J.Rennie	lbw b Wickremasinghe	16	c Kaluwitharana b Vaas	2
M.W.Goodwin	c Arnold b Wickremasinghe	61	c Dilshan b Vaas	2
N.C.Johnson	c Arnold b Vaas	17	not out	52
*†A.Flower	c Muralitharan b Wickremasinghe	86	not out	15
A.D.R.Campbell	run out	0		
G.J.Whittall	run out	11		
G.B.Brent	c Jayawardena b Muralitharan	0		
B.C.Strang	c Kaluwitharana b Wickremasinghe	41		
A.R.Whittall	c Kaluwitharana b Wickremasinghe	8		
H.K.Olonga	not out	1		
Extras	(LB 5, NB 23)	28	(B 1, LB 4, NB 12)	17
Total		**286**	(3 wickets)	**136**

SRI LANKA

M.S.Atapattu	not out	216
*S.T.Jayasuriya	lbw b A.R.Whittall	49
R.P.Arnold	c A.Flower b Olonga	7
D.P.M.deS.Jayawardena	lbw b Brent	17
T.M.Dilshan	lbw b Olonga	9
†R.S.Kaluwitharana	c A.Flower b Olonga	30
S.I.de Saram	c A.Flower b Brent	39
W.P.U.C.J.Vaas	c Campbell b Strang	9
I.S.Gallage	c G.W.Flower b Strang	3
G.P.Wickremasinghe	c A.Flower b Strang	13
M.Muralitharan	c G.W.Flower b Olonga	6
Extras	(B 12, LB 11, W 1, NB 6)	30
Total		**428**

SRI LANKA	O	M	R	W	O	M	R	W
Vaas	28	3	88	1	13	4	27	2
Gallage	14	1	53	0	11	4	24	0
Wickremasinghe	21.2	6	60	6	8	1	20	0
Muralitharan	20	3	61	1	14	3	50	1
Arnold	6	3	8	0	2	0	9	0
Jayasuriya	7	1	11	0	1	0	1	0
ZIMBABWE								
Olonga	32	6	103	4				
Strang	30	9	91	3				
Brent	32	12	55	2				
A.R.Whittall	35	6	105	1				
G.J.Whittall	14	3	48	0				
G.W.Flower	4	2	3	0				

FALL OF WICKETS

	Z	SL	Z
Wkt	*1st*	*1st*	*2nd*
1st	37	85	8
2nd	38	98	27
3rd	68	141	72
4th	167	159	–
5th	167	238	–
6th	212	345	–
7th	214	372	–
8th	250	390	–
9th	275	417	–
10th	286	428	–

Umpires: K.C.Barbour (1) and E.A.Nicholls (*West Indies*) (9).
Referee: J.L.Hendriks (*West Indies*) (11). **Test No. 1471/8 (Z37/SL94)**

ZIMBABWE v SRI LANKA (2nd Test)

At Harare Sports Club on 26, 27, 28, 29, 30 November 1999.
Toss: Sri Lanka. Result: **SRI LANKA** won by six wickets.
Debuts: None.

ZIMBABWE

G.W.Flower	b Muralitharan	19		c Kaluwitharana b Muralitharan	13
T.R.Gripper	lbw b Zoysa	0		c Arnold b Vaas	4
M.W.Goodwin	c Kaluwitharana b Zoysa	0		run out	48
N.C.Johnson	lbw b Zoysa	0	(5)	c Atapattu b Zoysa	14
*†A.Flower	lbw b Vaas	74	(6)	c Atapattu b Jayasuriya	129
A.D.R.Campbell	lbw b Wickremasinghe	36	(7)	lbw b Muralitharan	5
G.J.Whittall	b Muralitharan	1	(8)	not out	53
G.B.Brent	c Kaluwitharana b Vaas	3	(9)	lbw b Jayasuriya	0
B.C.Strang	c Dilshan b Vaas	4	(10)	c Jayawardena b Jayasuriya	3
H.K.Olonga	not out	10	(11)	lbw b Jayasuriya	0
E.Z.Matambanadzo	c Jayawardena b Muralitharan	6	(4)	run out	0
Extras	(B 2, LB 8, NB 11)	21		(B 3, LB 15, NB 5)	23
Total		**174**			**292**

SRI LANKA

M.S.Atapattu	run out	37	run out	6
*S.T.Jayasuriya	c A.Flower b Olonga	6	c Gripper b Brent	7
R.P.Arnold	c Campbell b Strang	49	c A.Flower b Brent	1
D.P.M.deS.Jayawardena	c A.Flower b Strang	91	not out	6
T.M.Dilshan	not out	163	lbw b Brent	0
†R.S.Kaluwitharana	run out	19	not out	14
S.I.de Saram	c Goodwin b Matambanadzo	17		
W.P.U.C.J.Vaas	c Gripper b Matambanadzo	5		
G.P.Wickremasinghe	c A.Flower b Whittall	7		
M.Muralitharan	c G.W.Flower b Olonga	5		
D.N.T.Zoysa	c Gripper b G.W.Flower	5		
Extras	(B 1, LB 10, W 7, NB 10)	28	(LB 1, W 2, NB 1)	4
Total		**432**	(4 wickets)	**38**

SRI LANKA	O	M	R	W		O	M	R	W
Vaas	27	8	50	3		35	7	78	1
Zoysa	13	4	22	3		11	2	24	1
Wickremasinghe	18	7	31	1		28	10	51	0
Muralitharan	29.5	11	44	3		43	15	71	2
Jayasuriya	3	1	7	0		12.4	3	40	4
Arnold	5	2	10	0		1	0	3	0
Jayawardena						4	2	7	0
ZIMBABWE									
Olonga	30	5	88	2		5	1	14	0
Brent	22	4	68	0		7.2	3	21	3
Matambanadzo	31	6	95	2					
Strang	37	13	70	2	(3)	3	1	2	0
Gripper	1	0	6	0					
Whittall	19	2	60	1					
G.W.Flower	9.3	2	34	1					

FALL OF WICKETS

	Z	SL	Z	SL
Wkt	*1st*	*1st*	*2nd*	*2nd*
1st	0	17	5	10
2nd	0	97	28	15
3rd	0	105	28	19
4th	53	283	51	20
5th	133	323	152	–
6th	134	371	159	–
7th	152	381	284	–
8th	153	403	284	–
9th	161	408	292	–
10th	174	432	292	–

Umpires: S.A.Bucknor (*West Indies*) (46) and R.B.Tiffin (12).
Referee: J.L.Hendriks (*West Indies*) (12). **Test No. 1472/9 (Z38/SL95)**

ZIMBABWE v SRI LANKA (3rd Test)

At Harare Sports Club on 4, 5, 6, 7, 8 December 1999.
Toss: Sri Lanka. Result: **MATCH DRAWN**.
Debuts: Zimbabwe – R.W.Price.

ZIMBABWE

G.W.Flower	c Dilshan b Pushpakumara	13		c Dilshan b Vaas	13
C.B.Wishart	lbw b Vaas	1		b Vaas	9
M.W.Goodwin	b Pushpakumara	11		c Jayawardena b Muralitharan	38
N.C.Johnson	lbw b Wickremasinghe	70		c Dilshan b Wickremasinghe	9
*†A.Flower	c Arnold b Vaas	14		not out	70
A.D.R.Campbell	lbw b Pushpakumara	9		c Jayawardena b Vaas	27
G.J.Whittall	c Arnold b Pushpakumara	37		c Arnold b Muraltharan	9
R.W.Price	lbw b Pushpakumara	2		run out	4
E.A.Brandes	b Vaas	9		not out	1
B.C.Strang	c Atapattu b Vaas	28			
H.K.Olonga	not out	3			
Extras	(LB 4, W 2, NB 15)	21		(B 3, LB 5, NB 9)	17
Total		**218**		(7 wickets declared)	**197**

SRI LANKA

M.S.Atapattu	c Johnson b Olonga	0		c A.Flower b Brandes	6
R.P.Arnold	not out	104	(3)	not out	14
D.P.M.deS.Jayawardena	c Goodwin b Brandes	2			
*S.T.Jayasuriya	c A.Flower b Brandes	4	(2)	not out	16
T.M.Dilshan	c A.Flower b Strang	37			
†R.S.Kaluwitharana	c A.Flower b Whittall	7			
S.I.de Saram	c G.W.Flower b Whittall	38			
W.P.U.C.J.Vaas	c Campbell b Brandes	0			
K.R.Pushpakumara	lbw b Strang	7			
G.P.Wickremasinghe	c A.Flower b Olonga	18			
M.Muralitharan	b Olonga	5			
Extras	(LB 2, W 2, NB 5)	9			
Total		**231**		(1 wicket)	**36**

SRI LANKA	O	M	R	W		O	M	R	W
Vaas	29.4	10	56	4		22	5	48	3
Pushpakumara	25	5	56	5		21	5	39	0
Wickremasinghe	16	6	41	1		21	6	30	1
Muralitharan	24	6	51	0	(5)	35	12	52	2
Jayasuriya	4	1	10	0	(6)	8	4	8	0
Jayawardena					(4)	2	0	12	0
ZIMBABWE									
Olonga	22.4	2	54	3		4	1	11	0
Brandes	17	5	45	3		4	0	20	1
Strang	24	8	71	2		1	0	5	0
Whittall	17	9	37	2					
Price	8	3	22	0					

FALL OF WICKETS

	Z	SL	Z	SL
Wkt	*1st*	*1st*	*2nd*	*2nd*
1st	5	1	14	7
2nd	24	4	28	–
3rd	33	29	51	–
4th	67	82	93	–
5th	82	90	151	–
6th	143	158	174	–
7th	174	159	184	–
8th	175	178	–	–
9th	196	208	–	–
10th	218	231	–	–

Umpires: I.D.Robinson (21) and S.Venkataraghavan (*India*) (35).
Referee: J.L.Hendriks (*West Indies*) (13). **Test No. 1473/10 (Z39/SL96)**

ZIMBABWE v SRI LANKA 1999-2000

ZIMBABWE – BATTING AND FIELDING

	M	*I*	*NO*	*HS*	*Runs*	*Avge*	*100*	*50*	*Ct/St*
A.Flower	3	6	2	129	388	97.00	1	3	13
N.C.Johnson	3	6	1	70	162	32.40	–	2	1
G.J.Whittall	3	5	1	53*	111	27.75	–	1	–
M.W.Goodwin	3	6	–	61	160	26.66	–	1	2
G.W.Flower	3	6	–	48	123	20.50	–	–	4
B.C.Strang	3	4	–	41	76	19.00	–	–	–
A.D.R.Campbell	3	5	–	36	77	15.40	–	–	3
H.K.Olonga	3	4	3	10*	14	14.00	–	–	–
G.B.Brent	2	3	–	3	3	1.00	–	–	–

Played in one Test: E.A.Brandes 9, 1*; T.R.Gripper 0, 4 (3 ct); E.Z.Matambanadzo 6, 0; R.W.Price 2, 4; G.J.Rennie 16, 2; A.R.Whittall 8; C.B.Wishart 1, 9.

ZIMBABWE – BOWLING

	O	*M*	*R*	*W*	*Avge*	*Best*	*5wI*	*10wM*
E.A.Brandes	21	5	65	4	16.25	3- 45	–	–
G.B.Brent	61.2	19	144	5	28.80	3- 21	–	–
H.K.Olonga	93.4	15	270	9	30.00	4-103	–	–
B.C.Strang	95	31	239	7	34.14	3- 91	–	–

Also bowled: G.W.Flower 13.3-4-37-1; T.R.Gripper 1-0-6-0; E.Z.Matambanadzo 31-6-95-2; R.W.Price 8-3-22-0; A.R.Whittall 35-6-105-1; G.J.Whittall 50.4-14-145-3.

ŚRI LANKA – BATTING AND FIELDING

	M	*I*	*NO*	*HS*	*Runs*	*Avge*	*100*	*50*	*Ct/St*
T.M.Dilshan	3	4	1	163*	209	69.66	1	–	6
M.S.Atapattu	3	5	1	216*	265	66.25	1	–	3
R.P.Arnold	3	5	2	104*	175	58.33	1	–	7
D.P.M.deS.Jayawardena	3	4	1	91	116	38.66	–	1	5
S.I.de Saram	3	3	–	39	94	31.33	–	–	–
R.S.Kaluwitharana	3	4	1	30	70	23.33	–	–	6
S.T.Jayasuriya	3	5	1	49	82	20.50	–	–	–
G.P.Wickremasinghe	3	3	–	18	38	12.66	–	–	–
M.Muralitharan	3	3	–	6	16	5.33	–	–	1
W.P.U.C.J.Vaas	3	3	–	9	14	4.66	–	–	–

Played in one Test: I.S.Gallage 3; K.R.Pushpakumara 7; D.N.T.Zoysa 5.

SRI LANKA – BOWLING

	O	*M*	*R*	*W*	*Avge*	*Best*	*5wI*	*10wM*
D.N.T.Zoysa	24	6	46	4	11.50	3-22	–	–
S.T.Jayasuriya	32.4	9	70	4	17.50	4-40	–	–
K.R.Pushpakumara	46	10	95	5	19.00	5-56	1	–
W.P.U.C.J.Vaas	154.4	37	347	14	24.78	4-56	–	–
G.P.Wickremasinghe	112.2	36	233	9	25.88	6-60	1	–
M.Muralitharan	165.5	50	329	9	36.55	3-44	–	–

Also bowled: R.P.Arnold 14-5-30-0; I.S.Gallage 25-5-77-0; D.P.M.deS.Jayawardena 9-3-26-0.

SOUTH AFRICA v ENGLAND (1st Test)

At The Wanderers, Johannesburg, on 25, 26, 27, 28 November 1999.
Toss: South Africa. Result: **SOUTH AFRICA** won by an innings and 21 runs.
Debuts: England – C.J.Adams, G.M.Hamilton, M.P.Vaughan.

ENGLAND

M.A.Butcher	c Boucher b Donald	1	lbw b Donald	32
M.A.Atherton	b Donald	0	c Boucher b Pollock	0
*N.Hussain	c Klusener b Pollock	0	b Pollock	16
M.P.Vaughan	c Boucher b Pollock	33	lbw b Donald	5
†A.J.Stewart	lbw b Donald	0	c Rhodes b Donald	86
C.J.Adams	c Boucher b Donald	16	c Boucher b Donald	1
A.Flintoff	c Boucher b Pollock	38	c and b Adams	36
G.M.Hamilton	c Pollock b Donald	0	c Pollock b Donald	0
A.R.Caddick	c Boucher b Donald	4	b Pollock	48
D.Gough	not out	15	not out	16
A.D.Mullally	lbw b Pollock	10	c Kallis b Pollock	0
Extras	(LB 3, W 2)	5	(B 4, LB 10, W 6)	20
Total		**122**		**260**

SOUTH AFRICA

G.Kirsten	lbw b Mullally	13
H.H.Gibbs	b Mullally	85
J.H.Kallis	c Stewart b Gough	12
D.J.Cullinan	b Caddick	108
*W.J.Cronje	b Gough	44
J.N.Rhodes	lbw b Mullally	26
L.Klusener	b Gough	72
S.M.Pollock	c Stewart b Gough	2
†M.V.Boucher	not out	4
A.A.Donald	b Gough	0
P.R.Adams	not out	0
Extras	(B 7, LB 18, W 2, NB 10)	37
Total	(9 wickets declared)	**403**

SOUTH AFRICA	O	M	R	W		O	M	R	W
Donald	15	3	53	6		23	7	74	5
Pollock	14.4	6	16	4		24.4	11	64	4
Cronje	5	2	15	0	(5)	6	3	22	0
Klusener	6	1	30	0	(3)	19	3	55	0
Adams	1	0	5	0	(4)	11	1	31	1
ENGLAND									
Gough	30	8	70	5					
Caddick	34	12	81	1					
Mullally	34	7	80	3					
Flintoff	14	5	45	0					
Hamilton	15	1	63	0					
Vaughan	11	1	39	0					

FALL OF WICKETS

	E	SA	E
Wkt	*1st*	*1st*	*2nd*
1st	1	37	0
2nd	2	79	31
3rd	2	175	41
4th	2	284	145
5th	34	299	147
6th	90	378	166
7th	91	398	166
8th	91	403	218
9th	103	403	260
10th	122	–	260

Umpires: D.L.Orchard (15) and S.Venkataraghavan (*India*) (34).
Referee: B.N.Jarman (*Australia*) (17). **Test No. 1474/116 (SA236/E762)**

SOUTH AFRICA v ENGLAND (2nd Test)

At St George's Park, Port Elizabeth, on 9, 10, 11, 12, 13 December 1999.
Toss: England. Result: **MATCH DRAWN**.
Debuts: South Africa – M.Hayward.

SOUTH AFRICA

G.Kirsten	c Hussain b Caddick	15	c Vaughan b Gough	2
H.H.Gibbs	run out	48	c Flintoff b Caddick	10
J.H.Kallis	c Caddick b Silverwood	1	not out	85
D.J.Cullinan	st Stewart b Tufnell	58	b Caddick	18
*W.J.Cronje	c Flintoff b Tufnell	2	c Vaughan b Flintoff	27
J.N.Rhodes	c Atherton b Flintoff	50	not out	57
L.Klusener	c Adams b Gough	174		
S.M.Pollock	c Vaughan b Flintoff	7		
†M.V.Boucher	c Stewart b Tufnell	42		
A.A.Donald	c Hussain b Tufnell	9		
M.Hayward	not out	10		
Extras	(B 10, LB 5, W 1, NB 18)	34	(B 4, LB 11, W 1, NB 9)	25
Total		**450**	(4 wickets declared)	**224**

ENGLAND

M.A.Butcher	b Pollock	4	lbw b Hayward	1
M.A.Atherton	b Hayward	108	b Pollock	3
*N.Hussain	c Boucher b Donald	82	not out	70
M.P.Vaughan	b Hayward	21	c Boucher b Kallis	29
†A.J.Stewart	b Donald	15	lbw b Pollock	28
C.J.Adams	c Kallis b Pollock	25	c Rhodes b Cronje	1
A.Flintoff	b Pollock	42	c Boucher b Kallis	12
A.R.Caddick	b Hayward	35	not out	4
D.Gough	b Donald	6		
C.E.W.Silverwood	c Klusener b Hayward	6		
P.C.R.Tufnell	not out	7		
Extras	(B 1, LB 8, NB 13)	22	(LB 2, NB 3)	5
Total		**373**	(6 wickets)	**153**

ENGLAND	O	M	R	W		O	M	R	W
Gough	21.1	1	107	1		19	6	52	1
Caddick	31	5	100	1		18	4	29	2
Silverwood	24	4	57	1		10	1	24	0
Tufnell	42	9	124	4		35	9	71	0
Vaughan	3	0	16	0		2	0	9	0
Flintoff	7	0	31	2		8.5	2	24	1
SOUTH AFRICA									
Donald	34	9	109	3		13	4	37	0
Pollock	34	7	112	3		17	8	18	2
Hayward	28.1	7	75	4		20	8	55	1
Klusener	25	9	48	0	(5)	14	9	17	0
Cronje	16	5	20	0	(6)	6	4	2	1
Kallis					(4)	7	1	22	2

FALL OF WICKETS

	SA	E	SA	E
Wkt	*1st*	*1st*	*2nd*	*2nd*
1st	28	5	5	5
2nd	57	160	17	5
3rd	87	228	50	80
4th	91	229	98	125
5th	146	264	–	137
6th	252	281	–	149
7th	268	336	–	–
8th	387	349	–	–
9th	401	364	–	–
10th	450	373	–	–

Umpires: S.A.Bucknor (*West Indies*) (47) and R.E.Koertzen (16).
Referee: B.N.Jarman (*Australia*) (18). **Test No. 1475/117 (SA237/E763)**

SOUTH AFRICA v ENGLAND (3rd Test)

At Kingsmead, Durban, on 26, 27, 28, 29, 30 December 1999.
Toss: England. Result: **MATCH DRAWN**.
Debuts: None.

ENGLAND

M.A.Butcher	c Klusener b Adams	48
M.A.Atherton	b Hayward	1
*N.Hussain	not out	146
D.L.Maddy	c Adams b Donald	24
†A.J.Stewart	lbw b Hayward	95
C.J.Adams	b Adams	19
A.Flintoff	lbw b Cronje	5
A.R.Caddick	lbw b Cronje	0
D.Gough	c Klusener b Donald	9
C.E.W.Silverwood	c Boucher b Pollock	0
P.C.R.Tufnell	not out	0
Extras	(B 1, LB 14, W 3, NB 1)	19
Total	(9 wickets declared)	**366**

SOUTH AFRICA

G.Kirsten	c Stewart b Caddick	11		b Butcher	275
H.H.Gibbs	c Stewart b Caddick	2		c Maddy b Caddick	26
J.H.Kallis	c Stewart b Caddick	0		c Stewart b Gough	69
D.J.Cullinan	b Gough	20		c Stewart b Flintoff	16
*W.J.Cronje	c Stewart b Caddick	28		c Stewart b Flintoff	1
L.Klusener	c Maddy b Tufnell	15	(7)	b Butcher	45
S.M.Pollock	b Caddick	64	(8)	not out	7
†M.V.Boucher	b Caddick	0	(6)	c Stewart b Adams	108
A.A.Donald	c Atherton b Caddick	0			
P.R.Adams	c Silverwood b Gough	9			
M.Hayward	not out	0			
Extras	(B 4, LB 1, W 1, NB 1)	7		(B 5, LB 13, W 2, NB 5)	25
Total		**156**		(7 wickets)	**572**

SOUTH AFRICA	O	M	R	W		O	M	R	W
Donald	23.4	3	67	2					
Pollock	33	14	55	1					
Hayward	20	3	74	2					
Kallis	23	9	38	0					
Klusener	17	5	38	0					
Adams	43	17	74	2					
Cronje	7	5	5	2					
ENGLAND									
Gough	15.5	6	36	2	(3)	28	5	82	1
Caddick	16	5	46	7	(1)	36	12	70	1
Silverwood	6	1	38	0	(2)	30	6	89	0
Tufnell	10	1	24	1	(5)	45	6	117	0
Flintoff	3	0	7	0	(4)	30	9	67	2
Adams						13	3	42	1
Maddy						14	1	40	0
Butcher						8.2	0	32	2
Hussain						5	1	15	0

FALL OF WICKETS

	E	SA	SA
Wkt	*1st*	*1st*	*2nd*
1st	7	11	41
2nd	82	11	193
3rd	138	24	242
4th	294	57	244
5th	336	74	436
6th	345	84	537
7th	345	84	572
8th	362	84	–
9th	362	154	–
10th	–	156	–

Umpires: D.B.Cowie (*New Zealand*) (15) and D.L.Orchard (16).
Referee: B.N.Jarman (*Australia*) (19). **Test No. 1476/118 (SA238/E764)**

SOUTH AFRICA v ENGLAND (4th Test)

At Newlands, Cape Town, on 2, 3, 4, 5 January 2000.
Toss: England. Result: **SOUTH AFRICA** won by an innings and 37 runs.
Debuts: None.

ENGLAND

M.A.Butcher	c Kirsten b Donald	40		c Boucher b Pollock	4
M.A.Atherton	c Kirsten b Donald	71		c Cullinan b Pollock	35
*N.Hussain	c Boucher b Adams	15		lbw b Klusener	16
M.P.Vaughan	c Kirsten b Donald	42		c Boucher b Klusener	5
†A.J.Stewart	c Kirsten b Donald	40		b Adams	5
A.R.Caddick	c Cullinan b Donald	0	(7)	c Gibbs b Donald	14
C.J.Adams	c Pollock b Kallis	10	(6)	b Adams	31
A.Flintoff	c Rhodes b Klusener	22		absent hurt	–
D.Gough	c Boucher b Klusener	4	(8)	c Donald b Kallis	8
C.E.W.Silverwood	not out	1	(9)	not out	5
P.C.R.Tufnell	b Kallis	2	(10)	c Cullinan b Adams	0
Extras	(LB 6, W 2, NB 3)	11		(LB 3)	3
Total		**258**			**126**

SOUTH AFRICA

G.Kirsten	c Stewart b Silverwood	80
H.H.Gibbs	c Vaughan b Silverwood	29
J.H.Kallis	c Atherton b Gough	105
D.J.Cullinan	c Vaughan b Tufnell	120
*W.J.Cronje	c Vaughan b Caddick	0
J.N.Rhodes	c Adams b Silverwood	16
L.Klusener	b Gough	3
S.M.Pollock	c Adams b Caddick	4
†M.V.Boucher	lbw b Silverwood	36
A.A.Donald	c Adams b Silverwood	7
P.R.Adams	not out	3
Extras	(B 1, LB 7, NB 10)	18
Total		**421**

SOUTH AFRICA	O	M	R	W		O	M	R	W
Donald	26	13	47	5	(2)	10.4	2	35	1
Pollock	27	8	59	0	(3)	14	8	19	2
Kallis	20	4	61	2	(4)	9.2	2	19	1
Klusener	16	5	42	2	(5)	7	4	8	2
Cronje	3	2	5	0					
Adams	21	9	38	1	(1)	19.3	5	42	3
ENGLAND									
Gough	37	6	88	2					
Caddick	31	6	95	2					
Silverwood	32	6	91	5					
Flintoff	4	0	16	0					
Tufnell	39.4	10	97	1					
Butcher	3	0	9	0					
Adams	7	2	17	0					

FALL OF WICKETS

	E	SA	E
Wkt	*1st*	*1st*	*2nd*
1st	115	43	4
2nd	125	201	40
3rd	141	246	59
4th	213	247	62
5th	213	279	66
6th	218	290	105
7th	231	307	113
8th	253	397	125
9th	255	405	126
10th	258	421	–

Umpires: B.C.Cooray (*Sri Lanka*) (17) and C.J.Mitchley (26).
Referee: B.N.Jarman (*Australia*) (20). **Test No. 1477/119 (SA 239/E 765)**

SOUTH AFRICA v ENGLAND (5th Test)

At Centurion Park, (Verwoerdburg), Pretoria, on 14, 15‡, 16‡, 17‡, 18 January 2000.
Toss: England. Result: **ENGLAND** won by two wickets. ‡ (*no play*)
Debuts: South Africa – P.C.Strydom.

SOUTH AFRICA

G.Kirsten	c Adams b Gough	0	
H.H.Gibbs	c Adams b Caddick	3	
J.H.Kallis	b Caddick	25	
D.J.Cullinan	c and b Mullally	46	
*W.J.Cronje	c Maddy b Gough	0	
P.C.Strydom	c Stewart b Silverwood	30	
L.Klusener	not out	61	
S.M.Pollock	run out	30	
†M.V.Boucher	b Mullally	22	
P.R.Adams	not out	4	
M.Hayward			
Extras	(B 2, LB 11, W 3, NB 11)	27	
Total	(8 wickets declared)	**248**	(innings forfeited)

ENGLAND

M.A.Butcher			lbw b Klusener	36
M.A.Atherton			c Boucher b Pollock	7
*N.Hussain			c Gibbs b Pollock	25
†A.J.Stewart			c Boucher b Hayward	73
C.J.Adams			c Boucher b Hayward	1
M.P.Vaughan			b Hayward	69
D.L.Maddy			run out	3
A.R.Caddick			c Boucher b Pollock	0
D.Gough			not out	6
C.E.W.Silverwood			not out	7
A.D.Mullally				
Extras			(B 4, LB 9, W 4, NB 7)	24
Total	(innings forfeited)		(8 wickets)	**251**

ENGLAND	O	M	R	W	O	M	R	W
Gough	20	2	92	2				
Caddick	19	7	47	2				
Mullally	24	10	42	2				
Silverwood	7	1	45	1				
Vaughan	2	0	9	0				
SOUTH AFRICA								
Pollock					20	7	53	3
Hayward					17.1	3	61	3
Klusener					14	4	38	1
Kallis					13	2	44	0
Cronje					5	3	15	0
Strydom					6	0	27	0

FALL OF WICKETS

	SA	E	SA	E
Wkt	*1st*	*1st*	*2nd*	*2nd*
1st	1	–	–	28
2nd	15	–	–	67
3rd	50	–	–	90
4th	55	–	–	102
5th	102	–	–	228
6th	136	–	–	236
7th	196	–	–	236
8th	243	–	–	240
9th	–	–	–	–
10th	–	–	–	–

Umpires: D.B.Hair (*Australia*) (32) and R.E.Koertzen (17).
Referee: B.N.Jarman (*Australia*) (21). **Test No. 1478/120 (SA240/E766)**

SOUTH AFRICA v ENGLAND 1999-2000

SOUTH AFRICA – BATTING AND FIELDING

	M	I	NO	HS	Runs	Avge	100	50	Ct/St
L.Klusener	5	6	1	174	370	74.00	1	2	4
G.Kirsten	5	7	–	275	396	56.57	1	1	4
D.J.Cullinan	5	7	–	120	386	55.14	2	1	3
J.N.Rhodes	3	4	1	57*	149	49.66	–	2	3
J.H.Kallis	5	7	1	105	297	49.50	1	2	2
M.V.Boucher	5	6	1	108	212	42.40	1	–	19
H.H.Gibbs	5	7	–	85	203	29.00	–	1	2
S.M.Pollock	5	6	1	64	114	22.80	–	1	3
P.R.Adams	4	4	3	9	16	16.00	–	–	2
W.J.Cronje	5	7	–	44	102	14.57	–	–	–
A.A.Donald	4	4	–	9	16	4.00	–	–	1
M.Hayward	3	2	2	10*	10	–	–	–	–

Played in one Test: P.C.Strydom 30.

SOUTH AFRICA – BOWLING

	O	M	R	W	Avge	Best	5wI	10wM
A.A.Donald	145.2	41	422	22	19.18	6-53	3	1
S.M.Pollock	184.2	69	396	19	20.84	4-16	–	–
M.Hayward	85.2	21	265	10	26.50	4-75	–	–
P.R.Adams	95.3	32	190	7	27.14	3-42	–	–
J.H.Kallis	72.2	18	184	5	36.80	2-22	–	–
L.Klusener	118	40	276	5	55.20	2- 8	–	–

Also bowled: W.J.Cronje 48-24-84-3; P.C.Strydom 6-0-27-0.

ENGLAND – BATTING AND FIELDING

	M	I	NO	HS	Runs	Avge	100	50	Ct/St
N.Hussain	5	8	2	146*	370	61.66	1	2	2
A.J.Stewart	5	8	–	95	342	42.75	–	3	13/1
M.P.Vaughan	4	7	–	69	204	29.14	–	1	6
M.A.Atherton	5	8	–	108	225	28.12	1	1	3
A.Flintoff	4	6	–	42	155	25.83	–	–	2
M.A.Butcher	5	8	–	48	166	20.75	–	–	–
D.Gough	5	7	3	16*	64	16.00	–	–	–
A.R.Caddick	5	8	1	48	105	15.00	–	–	1
D.L.Maddy	2	2	–	24	27	13.50	–	–	3
C.J.Adams	5	8	–	31	104	13.00	–	–	6
C.E.W.Silverwood	4	5	3	7*	19	9.50	–	–	1
A.D.Mullally	2	2	–	10	10	5.00	–	–	1
P.C.R.Tufnell	3	4	2	7*	9	4.50	–	–	–

Played in one Test: G.M.Hamilton 0, 0.

ENGLAND – BOWLING

	O	M	R	W	Avge	Best	5wI	10wM
A.D.Mullally	58	17	122	5	24.40	3- 80	–	–
A.R.Caddick	185	51	468	16	29.25	7- 46	1	–
D.Gough	171	34	527	14	37.64	5- 70	1	–
A.Flintoff	66.5	16	190	5	38.00	2- 31	–	–
C.E.W.Silverwood	109	19	344	7	49.14	5- 91	1	–
P.C.R.Tufnell	171.4	35	433	6	72.16	4-124	–	–

Also bowled: C.J.Adams 20-5-59-1; M.A.Butcher 11.2-0-41-2; G.M.Hamilton 15-1-63-0; N.Hussain 5-1-15-0; D.L.Maddy 14-1-40-0; M.P.Vaughan 18-1-73-0.

AUSTRALIA v INDIA (1st Test)

At Adelaide Oval on 10, 11, 12, 13, 14 December 1999.
Toss: Australia. Result: **AUSTRALIA** won by 285 runs.
Debuts: None.

AUSTRALIA

G.S.Blewett	c M.S.K.Prasad b Srinath	4	(2)	b Agarkar	88
M.J.Slater	c Ramesh b Ganguly	28	(1)	c Ganguly b Srinath	0
J.L.Langer	lbw b B.K.V.Prasad	11		c Gandhi b Kumble	38
M.E.Waugh	c M.S.K.Prasad b B.K.V.Prasad	5		c Laxman b Agarkar	8
*S.R.Waugh	c M.S.K.Prasad b Agarkar	150		c M.S.K.Prasad b Agarkar	5
R.T.Ponting	run out	125		c M.S.K.Prasad b B.K.V.Prasad	21
†A.C.Gilchrist	c and b Agarkar	0		c Laxman b Srinath	43
S.K.Warne	lbw b Kumble	86		c Dravid b Srinath	0
M.S.Kasprowicz	b Kumble	4		not out	21
D.W.Fleming	not out	12			
G.D.McGrath	c M.S.K.Prasad b B.K.V.Prasad	4			
Extras	(B 1, LB 5, NB 6)	12		(B 3, LB 8, W 2, NB 2)	15
Total		**441**		(8 wickets declared)	**239**

INDIA

D.J.Gandhi	c Kasprowicz b McGrath	4	c Gilchrist b McGrath	0
S.Ramesh	run out	2	lbw b Warne	28
V.V.S.Laxman	c S.R.Waugh b McGrath	41	b Fleming	0
R.Dravid	c Langer b Warne	35	c Gilchrist b Warne	6
*S.R.Tendulkar	c Langer b Warne	61	lbw b McGrath	0
S.C.Ganguly	st Gilchrist b Warne	60	c Gilchrist b Fleming	43
†M.S.K.Prasad	b Warne	14	c Langer b Fleming	11
A.B.Agarkar	b Fleming	19	c S.R.Waugh b Fleming	0
J.Srinath	c S.R.Waugh b Fleming	11	c Slater b McGrath	11
A.Kumble	not out	17	b Fleming	3
B.K.V.Prasad	lbw b Fleming	0	not out	2
Extras	(LB 1, W 1, NB 19)	21	(LB 1, NB 5)	6
Total		**285**		**110**

INDIA	O	M	R	W		O	M	R	W
Srinath	29	3	117	1		21.5	4	64	3
Agarkar	26	5	86	2		18	6	43	3
B.K.V.Prasad	24.3	4	83	3		18	5	48	1
Ganguly	7	1	34	1					
Kumble	34	1	101	2	(4)	32	9	73	1
Tendulkar	2	0	12	0					
Laxman	3	1	2	0					
AUSTRALIA									
McGrath	30	13	49	2		12	2	35	3
Fleming	24.4	7	70	3		9.1	2	30	5
Kasprowicz	11	2	62	0	(4)	6	0	23	0
Warne	42	12	92	4	(3)	10	6	21	2
Blewett	6	1	11	0					
M.E.Waugh					(5)	1	1	0	0

FALL OF WICKETS

	A	I	A	I
Wkt	*1st*	*1st*	*2nd*	*2nd*
1st	8	7	1	0
2nd	29	9	65	3
3rd	45	90	95	24
4th	52	107	113	27
5th	291	215	153	48
6th	298	229	204	93
7th	406	240	205	93
8th	417	266	239	102
9th	424	275	–	108
10th	441	285	–	110

Umpires: R.S.Dunne (*New Zealand*) (34) and D.J.Harper (6).
Referee: R.S.Madugalle (*Sri Lanka*) (22). **Test No. 1479/55 (A601/I329)**

AUSTRALIA v INDIA (2nd Test)

At Melbourne Cricket Ground on 26, 27, 28, 29, 30 December 1999.
Toss: India. Result: **AUSTRALIA** won by 180 runs.
Debuts: Australia – B.Lee; India – H.H.Kanitkar.

AUSTRALIA

G.S.Blewett	b Srinath	2	(2)	c Ganguly b Kumble	31
M.J.Slater	c Srinath b B.K.V.Prasad	91	(1)	lbw b Agarkar	3
J.L.Langer	lbw b Srinath	8		c M.S.K.Prasad b Agarkar	9
M.E.Waugh	lbw b Agarkar	41	(5)	not out	51
*S.R.Waugh	c M.S.K.Prasad b B.K.V.Prasad	32	(6)	lbw b Agarkar	32
R.T.Ponting	lbw b Srinath	67	(7)	not out	21
†A.C.Gilchrist	c Ganguly b Agarkar	78	(4)	c Srinath b Kumble	55
S.K.Warne	c M.S.K.Prasad b Agarkar	2			
D.W.Fleming	not out	31			
B.Lee	c and b Srinath	27			
G.D.McGrath	run out	1			
Extras	(B 1, LB 9, W 1, NB 14)	25		(LB 2, W 1, NB 3)	6
Total		**405**		(5 wickets declared)	**208**

INDIA

V.V.S.Laxman	c M.E.Waugh b McGrath	5		c McGrath b Fleming	1
S.Ramesh	b Lee	4		retired hurt	26
R.Dravid	c Gilchrist b Lee	9		c Gilchrist b Lee	14
*S.Tendulkar	c Langer b Fleming	116		lbw b Warne	52
S.C.Ganguly	c M.E.Waugh b McGrath	31		b Blewett	17
H.H.Kanitkar	lbw b Warne	11		lbw b Fleming	45
†M.S.K.Prasad	b Lee	6		c Warne b M.E.Waugh	13
A.B.Agarkar	lbw b Lee	0		c Blewett b M.E.Waugh	0
J.Srinath	c M.E.Waugh b Lee	1	(10)	c Warne b Lee	1
A.Kumble	not out	28	(9)	run out	13
B.K.V.Prasad	c M.E.Waugh b McGrath	10		not out	6
Extras	(LB 8, NB 9)	17		(LB 4, NB 3)	7
Total		**238**			**195**

INDIA	O	M	R	W		O	M	R	W
Srinath	33.1	7	130	4		14	0	45	0
Agarkar	28	7	76	3		17	3	51	3
B.K.V.Prasad	26	6	101	2		10	0	38	0
Ganguly	2	0	10	0					
Kumble	29	3	78	0	(4)	18	3	72	2
AUSTRALIA									
McGrath	18.1	3	39	3		17	8	22	0
Fleming	15	0	62	1		21.3	7	46	2
Lee	18	2	47	5	(4)	19	6	31	2
Warne	24	5	77	1	(3)	26	7	63	1
M.E.Waugh	1	0	5	0	(6)	3	0	12	2
Blewett					(5)	3	1	17	1

FALL OF WICKETS

	A	I	A	I
Wkt	*1st*	*1st*	*2nd*	*2nd*
1st	4	11	5	5
2nd	28	11	32	72
3rd	123	31	91	110
4th	192	108	109	133
5th	197	138	167	162
6th	341	167	–	162
7th	343	167	–	184
8th	345	169	–	185
9th	404	212	–	195
10th	405	238	–	–

Umpires: S.J.Davis (3) and D.R.Shepherd (*England*) (49).
Referee: R.S.Madugalle (*Sri Lanka*) (23). **Test No. 1480/56 (A602/I330)**

AUSTRALIA v INDIA (3rd Test)

At Sydney Cricket Ground on 2, 3, 4 January 2000.
Toss: India. Result: **AUSTRALIA** won by an innings and 141 runs.
Debuts: None.

INDIA

†M.S.K.Prasad	c M.E.Waugh b McGrath	5	(2)	c M.E.Waugh b McGrath	3
V.V.S.Laxman	c Slater b Lee	7	(1)	c Gilchrist b Lee	167
R.Dravid	c Ponting b McGrath	29		c Warne b McGrath	0
*S.R.Tendulkar	lbw b McGrath	45		c Langer b Fleming	4
S.C.Ganguly	c S.R.Waugh b Blewett	1		c M.E.Waugh b McGrath	25
H.H.Kanitkar	c Gilchrist b Lee	10		c Slater b Lee	8
R.V.Bharadwaj	c Gilchrist b Lee	6		absent hurt	–
A.Kumble	c Langer b McGrath	26	(7)	c Ponting b McGrath	15
A.B.Agarkar	c M.E.Waugh b Lee	0	(8)	c Gilchrist b McGrath	0
J.Srinath	c Ponting b McGrath	3	(9)	not out	15
B.K.V.Prasad	not out	1	(10)	run out	3
Extras	(LB 12, W 1, NB 4)	17		(B 4, LB 2, W 1, NB 14)	21
Total		**150**			**261**

AUSTRALIA

G.S.Blewett	b B.K.V.Prasad	19
M.J.Slater	c M.S.K.Prasad b Srinath	1
J.L.Langer	c B.K.V.Prasad b Tendulkar	223
M.E.Waugh	b Ganguly	32
*S.R.Waugh	lbw b Srinath	57
R.T.Ponting	not out	141
†A.C.Gilchrist	not out	45
S.K.Warne		
D.W.Fleming		
B.Lee		
G.D.McGrath		
Extras	(B 2, LB 21, NB 11)	34
Total	(5 wickets declared)	**552**

AUSTRALIA	O	M	R	W		O	M	R	W
McGrath	18.5	7	48	5		17	1	55	5
Fleming	13	7	24	0		13	2	47	1
Lee	21	9	39	4		11	2	67	2
Warne	12	4	22	0	(5)	13	1	60	0
Blewett	3	2	5	1	(4)	2	0	16	0
Ponting						1	0	8	0
Slater						1	0	2	0
INDIA									
Srinath	28	4	105	2					
Agarkar	19	3	95	0					
B.K.V.Prasad	28	10	86	1					
Kumble	33.2	6	126	0					
Ganguly	12	1	46	1					
Bharadwaj	12	1	35	0					
Tendulkar	7	0	34	1					
Kanitkar	1	0	2	0					

FALL OF WICKETS

	I	A	I
Wkt	*1st*	*1st*	*2nd*
1st	10	9	22
2nd	27	49	26
3rd	68	146	33
4th	69	267	101
5th	95	457	145
6th	118	–	234
7th	119	–	234
8th	119	–	258
9th	126	–	261
10th	150	–	–

Umpires: D.B.Hair (31) and I.D.Robinson (*Zimbabwe*) (22).
Referee: R.S.Madugalle (*Sri Lanka*) (24). **Test No. 1481/57 (A 603/I 331)**

AUSTRALIA v INDIA 1999-2000

AUSTRALIA – BATTING AND FIELDING

	M	*I*	*NO*	*HS*	*Runs*	*Avge*	*100*	*50*	*Ct/St*
R.T.Ponting	3	5	2	141*	375	125.00	2	1	3
J.L.Langer	3	5	–	223	289	57.80	1	–	6
A.C.Gilchrist	3	5	1	78	221	55.25	–	2	9/1
S.R.Waugh	3	5	–	150	276	55.20	1	1	4
D.W.Fleming	3	2	2	31*	43	–	–	–	–
M.E.Waugh	3	5	1	51*	137	34.25	–	1	8
S.K.Warne	3	3	–	86	88	29.33	–	1	3
G.S.Blewett	3	5	–	88	144	28.80	–	1	1
B.Lee	2	1	–	27	27	27.00	–	–	–
M.J.Slater	3	5	–	91	123	24.60	–	1	3
G.D.McGrath	3	2	–	4	5	2.50	–	–	1

Played in one Test: M.S.Kasprowicz 4, 21* (1 ct).

AUSTRALIA – BOWLING

	O	*M*	*R*	*W*	*Avge*	*Best*	*5wI*	*10wM*
G.D.McGrath	113	34	248	18	13.77	5-48	2	1
B.Lee	69	19	184	13	14.15	5-47	1	–
D.W.Fleming	96.2	25	279	12	23.25	5-30	1	–
S.K.Warne	127	35	335	8	41.87	4-92	–	–

Also bowled: G.S.Blewett 14-4-49-2; M.S.Kasprowicz 17-2-85-0; R.T.Ponting 1-0-8-0; M.J.Slater 1-0-2-0; M.E.Waugh 5-1-17-2.

INDIA – BATTING AND FIELDING

	M	*I*	*NO*	*HS*	*Runs*	*Avge*	*100*	*50*	*Ct/St*
S.R.Tendulkar	3	6	–	116	278	46.33	1	2	–
V.V.S.Laxman	3	6	–	167	221	36.83	1	–	2
S.C.Ganguly	3	6	–	60	177	29.50	–	1	3
A.Kumble	3	6	2	28*	102	25.50	–	–	–
S.Ramesh	2	4	1	28	60	20.00	–	–	1
H.H.Kanitkar	2	4	–	45	74	18.50	–	–	–
R.Dravid	3	6	–	35	93	15.50	–	–	1
M.S.K.Prasad	3	6	–	14	52	8.66	–	–	10
J.Srinath	3	6	1	15*	42	8.40	–	–	3
B.K.V.Prasad	3	6	3	10	22	7.33	–	–	1
A.B.Agarkar	3	6	–	19	19	3.16	–	–	1

Played in one Test: R.V.Bharadwaj 6; D.J.Gandhi 4, 0 (1 ct).

INDIA – BOWLING

	O	*M*	*R*	*W*	*Avge*	*Best*	*5wI*	*10wM*
A.B.Agarkar	108	24	351	11	31.90	3- 43	–	–
J.Srinath	126	18	461	10	46.10	4-130	–	–
B.K.V.Prasad	106.3	25	356	7	50.85	3- 83	–	–
A.Kumble	146.2	22	450	5	90.00	2- 72	–	–

Also bowled: R.V.Bharadwaj 12-1-35-0; S.C.Ganguly 21-2-90-2; H.H.Kanitkar 1-0-2-0; V.V.S.Laxman 3-1-2-0; S.R.Tendulkar 9-0-46-1.

NEW ZEALAND v WEST INDIES (1st Test)

At Seddon Park, Hamilton, on 16, 17, 18, 19, 20 December 1999.
Toss: West Indies. Result: **NEW ZEALAND** won by nine wickets.
Debuts: West Indies – R.L.Powell.

WEST INDIES

A.F.G.Griffith	c Parore b Vettori	114		c Parore b Cairns	18
S.L.Campbell	c Parore b Nash	170		b Cairns	0
D.Ramnarine	c Parore b Cairns	8	(9)	c and b Cairns	0
S.Chanderpaul	c Fleming b Astle	14	(3)	c Parore b Cairns	0
*B.C.Lara	c Nash b Vettori	24	(4)	c Parore b Nash	1
R.L.Powell	c Wiseman b Cairns	0	(5)	c Spearman b Vettori	30
J.C.Adams	not out	17	(6)	c sub (S.B.O'Connor) b Cairns	25
†R.D.Jacobs	c Spearman b Vettori	5	(7)	run out	2
F.A.Rose	c Wiseman b Nash	4	(8)	lbw b Cairns	3
R.D.King	b Nash	1		lbw b Cairns	0
C.A.Walsh	b Vettori	0		not out	5
Extras	(LB 6, NB 2)	8		(B 7, LB 3, NB 3)	13
Total		**365**			**97**

NEW ZEALAND

G.R.Stead	b Walsh	22		b Walsh	16
M.J.Horne	c Rose b King	32		retired hurt	5
C.M.Spearman	b Ramnarine	27		not out	30
*S.P.Fleming	c Jacobs b Ramnarine	66			
D.L.Vettori	c Adams b King	29			
N.J.Astle	c Ramnarine b Walsh	48	(4)	not out	7
C.D.McMillan	c Jacobs b King	51			
C.L.Cairns	c Campbell b Ramnarine	72			
†A.C.Parore	run out	8			
D.J.Nash	c Powell b King	6			
P.J.Wiseman	not out	0			
Extras	(B 4, LB 9, W 3, NB 16)	32		(B 4, LB 1, NB 7)	12
Total		**393**		(1 wicket)	**70**

NEW ZEALAND	O	M	R	W		O	M	R	W
Cairns	31	11	73	3	(2)	22.5	10	27	7
Nash	28	12	63	2	(3)	7	1	37	1
Vettori	34.1	9	83	4	(1)	22	12	20	1
Astle	16	2	67	1					
Wiseman	22	10	51	0	(4)	2	0	3	0
McMillan	4	1	22	0					
WEST INDIES									
Walsh	29	4	81	2		8	1	33	1
Rose	27	4	103	0		6	0	28	0
Ramnarine	36	10	82	3		1	0	4	0
King	26.2	2	81	4					
Powell	5	2	13	0					
Adams	7	1	20	0					

FALL OF WICKETS

	WI	NZ	WI	NZ
Wkt	*1st*	*1st*	*2nd*	*2nd*
1st	276	61	0	59
2nd	289	67	0	–
3rd	311	107	1	–
4th	336	162	36	–
5th	336	215	78	–
6th	336	258	85	–
7th	345	374	90	–
8th	352	379	90	–
9th	362	388	90	–
10th	365	393	97	–

Umpires: D.B.Cowie (14) and D.R.Shepherd (*England*) (48).
Referee: R.Subba Row (*England*) (31). **Test No. 1482/29 (NZ275/WI353)**

NEW ZEALAND v WEST INDIES (2nd Test)

At Basin Reserve, Wellington, on 26, 27, 28, 29 December 1999.
Toss: West Indies. Result: **NEW ZEALAND** won by an innings and 105 runs.
Debuts: New Zealand – M.S.Sinclair.

NEW ZEALAND

C.M.Spearman	c Walsh b King	24
G.R.Stead	c Campbell b King	17
M.S.Sinclair	b King	214
*S.P.Fleming	c Adams b Chanderpaul	67
N.J.Astle	run out	93
C.D.McMillan	c Jacobs b King	31
C.L.Cairns	c Adams b Rose	31
†A.C.Parore	b Rose	5
D.J.Nash	not out	2
D.L.Vettori	c Campbell b Rose	2
S.B.O'Connor		
Extras	(B 5, LB 12, W 1, NB 14)	32
Total	(9 wickets declared)	**518**

WEST INDIES

A.F.G.Griffith	c Fleming b Nash	67		run out	45
S.L.Campbell	lbw b Cairns	0		lbw b Cairns	3
N.O.Perry	c Parore b Cairns	3	(7)	lbw b Astle	0
S.Chanderpaul	c Parore b Cairns	5	(3)	c Parore b Nash	70
*B.C.Lara	b Vettori	67	(4)	c Parore b Nash	75
J.C.Adams	c Stead b Vettori	8	(5)	c Parore b Nash	4
†R.D.Jacobs	not out	19	(6)	c Stead b Vettori	20
F.A.Rose	c Parore b Cairns	0		lbw b Cairns	10
R.D.King	run out	0	(10)	not out	4
C.A.Walsh	b Cairns	0	(9)	lbw b Nash	0
D.Ganga	absent hurt	–		absent hurt	–
Extras	(B 2, LB 4, W 2, NB 2)	10		(B 1, LB 1, W 1)	3
Total		**179**			**234**

WEST INDIES	O	M	R	W		O	M	R	W
Walsh	41	5	112	0					
King	36	11	96	4					
Rose	32.3	5	113	3					
Perry	32	5	120	0					
Adams	26	9	45	0					
Chanderpaul	6	1	15	1					
NEW ZEALAND									
Cairns	19	5	44	5	(4)	12.1	4	25	2
Nash	18	8	23	1	(3)	16	4	38	4
Vettori	31	9	69	2	(2)	32	8	86	1
O'Connor	19	8	25	0	(1)	16	3	50	0
Astle	4	1	12	0		7	0	33	1

FALL OF WICKETS

	NZ	WI	WI
Wkt	*1st*	*1st*	*2nd*
1st	33	1	8
2nd	76	5	83
3rd	240	17	148
4th	429	129	154
5th	456	141	189
6th	507	174	204
7th	507	175	225
8th	514	176	225
9th	518	179	234
10th	–	–	–

Umpires: R.B.Tiffin (*Zimbabwe*) (13) and E.A.Watkin (2).
Referee: R.Subba Row (*England*) (32). **Test No. 1483/30 (NZ276/WI354)**

NEW ZEALAND v WEST INDIES 1999-2000

NEW ZEALAND – BATTING AND FIELDING

	M	*I*	*NO*	*HS*	*Runs*	*Avge*	*100*	*50*	*Ct/St*
N.J.Astle	2	3	1	93	148	74.00	–	1	–
S.P.Fleming	2	2	–	67	133	66.50	–	2	2
C.L.Cairns	2	2	–	72	103	51.50	–	1	1
C.D.McMillan	2	2	–	51	82	41.00	–	1	–
C.M.Spearman	2	3	1	30*	81	40.50	–	–	2
G.R.Stead	2	3	–	22	55	18.33	–	–	2
D.L.Vettori	2	2	–	29	31	15.50	–	–	–
D.J.Nash	2	2	1	6	8	8.00	–	–	1
A.C.Parore	2	2	–	8	13	6.50	–	–	12

Played in one Test: M.J.Horne 32, 5*; S.B.O'Connor did not bat; M.S.Sinclair 214; P.J.Wiseman 0* (2 ct).

NEW ZEALAND – BOWLING

	O	*M*	*R*	*W*	*Avge*	*Best*	*5wI*	*10wM*
C.L.Cairns	85	30	169	17	9.94	7-27	2	1
D.J.Nash	69	25	161	8	20.12	4-38	–	–
D.L.Vettori	119.1	38	258	8	32.25	4-83	–	–

Also bowled: N.J.Astle 27-3-112-2; C.D.McMillan 4-1-22-0; S.B.O'Connor 35-11-75-0; P.J.Wiseman 24-10-54-0.

WEST INDIES – BATTING AND FIELDING

	M	*I*	*NO*	*HS*	*Runs*	*Avge*	*100*	*50*	*Ct/St*
A.F.G.Griffith	2	4	–	114	244	61.00	1	1	–
S.L.Campbell	2	4	–	170	173	43.25	1	–	3
B.C.Lara	2	4	–	75	167	41.75	–	2	–
S.Chanderpaul	2	4	–	70	89	22.25	–	1	–
J.C.Adams	2	4	1	25	54	18.00	–	–	3
R.D.Jacobs	2	4	1	20	46	15.33	–	–	3
F.A.Rose	2	4	–	10	17	4.25	–	–	1
C.A.Walsh	2	4	1	5*	5	1.66	–	–	1
R.D.King	2	4	1	4*	5	1.66	–	–	–

Played in one Test: D.Ganga did not bat; N.O.Perry 3, 0; R.L.Powell 0, 30 (1 ct); D.Ramnarine 8, 0 (1 ct).

WEST INDIES – BOWLING

	O	*M*	*R*	*W*	*Avge*	*Best*	*5wI*	*10wM*
R.D.King	62.2	13	177	8	22.12	4- 81	–	–
D.Ramnarine	37	10	86	3	28.66	3- 82	–	–
C.A.Walsh	78	10	226	3	75.33	2- 81	–	–
F.A.Rose	65.3	9	244	3	81.33	3-113	–	–

Also bowled: J.C.Adams 33-10-65-0; S.Chanderpaul 6-1-15-1; N.O.Perry 32-5-120-0; R.L.Powell 5-2-13-0.

SECOND XI FIXTURES 2000

No symbol	Second XI Championship	3 days
*	Second XI Championship	4 days
†	Aon Trophy	1 day

APRIL		
Wed 19	Ashford	Kent v Lancs
	Campbell Park	Northants v Notts
Tue 25	tbc	*Glam v Glos
	Old Trafford	*Lancs v Worcs
Wed 26	Riverside	Durham v Yorks
	Northampton	Northants v Middx
	The Oval	Surrey v Notts
	Hove	Sussex v Derbys
MAY		
Tue 2	Trent Bridge	*Notts v Durham
	Taunton	*Somerset v Kent
	Moseley	*Warwks v Hants
Wed 3	Derby	Derbys v Northants
	Horsham	Sussex v Yorks
	Worcester	Worcs v Glam
Mon 8	Duffield	†Derbys v Northants
Tue 9	Bristol	*Glos v Somerset
	Crosby	*Lancs v Yorks
Wed 10	Worksop CC	Notts v Derbys
	Stirlands CC	Sussex v Worcs
Thu 11	Swindon	†MCCA v Glam
Mon 15	Southampton	†Hants v Somerset
	Canterbury	*Kent v Leics
Tue 16	Ealing	*Middx v Notts
	Northampton	*Northants v Warwks
	Scarborough	*Yorks v Durham
Wed 17	Saffron Walden	Essex v Glos
	Southampton	Hants v Lancs
Fri 19	Dunstable	†MCCA v Leics
Mon 22	Darlington	*Durham v Derbys
	Worcester	†Worcs v Yorks
Tue 23	Hove	*Sussex v Somerset
	Studley CC	*Warwks v Yorks
	Kidderminster	*Worcs v Hants
Wed 24	Ashford	Kent v Glam
	Blackpool	Lancs v Middx
	Hinckley	Leics v Essex
	Cheam CC	Surrey v Northants
Thu 25	Sleaford	†MCCA v Notts
Fri 26	Farnsfield CC	†Notts v MCCA
Mon 29	Bristol	Glos v Worcs
Tue 30	Dunstall	*Derbys v Lancs
	Ammanford	Glam v Middx
	Maidstone	*Kent v Hants
	Northampton	*Northants v Durham
	Leamington	†Warwks v Yorks
Wed 31	Taunton	Somerset v Yorks
JUNE		
Thu 1	W Brom/Dartmouth	†Warwks v Worcs
Fri 2	Cardiff	†Glam v MCCA
Mon 5	Hinckley	†Leics v Glos
	Stowe S	†Northants v Derbys
Tue 6	So'ton (W End)	*Hants v Sussex
	Leicester	*Leics v Glos
	The Oval	*Surrey v Middx
Wed 7	Cheadle	Derbys v Somerset
	Coggeshall	Essex v Lancs
	Pontarddulais	Glam v Durham
	Worcester	Worcs v Notts
Mon 12	Chelmsford	†Essex v Kent
	Southampton	†Hants v MCC YC
	Ealing	†Middx v Northants
	Worksop C	†Notts v Glos
	Harrogate	Yorks v Leics
Tue 13	Derby	Derbys v Warwks
	Riverside	*Durham v Worcs
	Chelmsford	*Essex v Kent
	Finchampstead	Hants v Surrey
	Trent Bridge	Notts v Glos
	Taunton	*Somerset v Glam
Mon 19	Harrow	†Middx v Essex
	Taunton	†Somerset v MCC YC
Tue 20	Bristol	*Glos v Lancs
	So'ton (W End)	*Hants v Glam
	Canterbury	Kent v Notts
	Harrow	*Middx v Essex
	Todmorden	*Yorks v Northants
Wed 21	Hinckley	Leics v Worcs
	The Oval	Surrey v Durham
	Solihull	Warwks v Sussex
Mon 26	Billericay	†Essex v Northants
	Bristol	†Glos v Glam
	Hinckley	†Leics v Notts
	The Oval	†Surrey v Somerset
	Middleton	†Sussex v Hants
Tue 27	Canterbury	†Kent v Northants
	Welbeck Colliery	†Notts v Leics
	York	†Yorks v Worcs
Wed 28	Sunderland	†Durham v Warwks
	Nelson	†Lancs v Yorks
	Hinckley	†Leics v Glam
	The Oval	†Surrey v Hants
Thu 29	Derby	†Derbys v Middx
	Bolton	†Lancs v Durham
	Northampton	†Northants v Kent
	Collingham CC	†Notts v Glam
	Banbury CC	†MCCA v Glos
Fri 30	Derby	†Derbys v Kent
	Hinckley	†Leics v MCCA
	Isham	†Northants v Middx
	Taunton	†Somerset v Hants

	Worcester	†Worcs v Warwks
	Bingley	†Yorks v Durham
JULY		
Mon 3	Cardiff	†Glam v Glos
	So'ton (W End)	†Hants v Sussex
	Richmond	†Middx v Kent
	Campbell Park	†Northants v Essex
	Taunton	†Somerset v Surrey
	Edgbaston	†Warwks v Durham
	Worcester	†Worcs v Lancs
Tue 4	Newport	†Glam v Notts
	Manchester U	†Lancs v Warwks
	Taunton	†Somerset v Sussex
	Ombersley	†Worcs v Durham
Wed 5	Bristol U	†Glos v Notts
	Southampton	†Hants v Surrey
	Folkestone	†Kent v Derbys
Thu 6	Hartlepool	†Durham v Yorks
	Bristol U	†Glos v Leics
	Folkestone	†Kent v Essex
	Finchley	†Middx v Derbys
	Hove	†Sussex v Surrey
	Cov/N Warwick	†Warwks v Lancs
	Uxbridge CC	†MCC YC v Somerset
Fri 7	South Shields	†Durham v Worcs
	Saffron Walden	†Essex v Derbys
	Ebbw Vale	†Glam v Leics
	Hove	†Sussex v Somerset
	Uxbridge CC	†MCC YC v Surrey
Mon 10	Seaton Carew	†Durham v Lancs
	Old Brentwoods	†Essex v Middx
	Sutton CC	†Surrey v Sussex
	Harrogate	†Yorks v Warwks
	Uxbridge CC	†MCC YC v Hants
Tue 11	Chelmsford	*Essex v Surrey
	Castleford	†Yorks v Lancs
	Uxbridge CC	†MCC YC v Sussex
Wed 12	Cardiff	Glam v Derbys
	Stowe S	Northants v Glos
	Nottingham HS	Notts v Warwks
Thu 13	Canterbury	†Kent v Middx
	Radcliffe CC	†Lancs v Worcs
Fri 14	Hastings	†Sussex v MCC YC
Mon 17	The Oval	†Surrey v MCC YC
Tue 18	Hinckley	Leics v Lancs
	Uxbridge (Vine L)	*Middx v Derbys
	Northampton	*Northants v Hants
Wed 19	Stockton	Durham v Sussex
	Bristol	Glos v Warwks
	Canterbury	Kent v Yorks
	Taunton	Somerset v Notts
	Worcester	Worcs v Essex
Mon 24	Repton S	†Derbys v Essex
	Oakham S	*Leics v Sussex
Tue 25	Heanor	*Derbys v Essex
	Maidstone	*Kent v Northants

	Uxbridge (Vine L)	Middx v Yorks
	Stratford	*Warwks v Worcs
Wed 26	Panteg	Glam v Surrey
	Middleton	Lancs v Somerset
	Worksop C	Notts v Hants
Fri 28	Bristol	†Glos v MCCA
Mon 31	Chelmsford	*Essex v Yorks
	Hinckley	*Leics v Derbys
AUGUST		
Tue 1	Riverside	Durham v Kent
	Usk	*Glam v Warwks
	Unity Casuals	*Notts v Surrey
	Barnt Green	*Worcs v Northants
Wed 2	Bristol U	Glos v Sussex
	Clevedon	Somerset v Hants
Mon 7	**†Semi-Finals**	(*Reserve Tue 8*)
Wed 9	Halstead	Essex v Hants
	Southport	Lancs v Glam
	Harrow	Middx v Worcs
	Taunton	Somerset v Northants
	Wimbledon	Surrey v Leics
	Walmley CC	Warwks v Kent
	Rotherham	Yorks v Derbys
Mon 14	Caythorpe CC	*Notts v Leics
Tue 15	Riverside	*Durham v Lancs
	Bristol	*Glos v Middx
	Hastings	*Sussex v Kent
	Kidderminster	*Worcs v Somerset
Wed 16	Dunstable	Northants v Essex
	Leamington	Warwks v Surrey
Tue 22	Heanor	*Derbys v Notts
	So'ton (W End)	*Hants v Glos
	Old Trafford	*Lancs v Warwks
	Ealing	Middx v Kent
	North Perrot	*Somerset v Surrey
Wed 23	Gateshead Fell	Durham v Essex
	Campbell Park	Northants v Leics
	Harrogate	Yorks v Glam
Tue 29	Cardiff	*Glam v Leics
	Oxted	*Surrey v Sussex
	Kenilworth Wdns	*Warwks v Essex
	Middlesbrough	*Yorks v Notts
Wed 30	Bristol	Glos v Durham
	Bournemouth SC	Hants v Derbys
	Lytham	Lancs v Northants
SEPTEMBER		
Mon 4	**†Final**	(*Reserve Tue 5*)
Wed 6	Derby	Derbys v Glos
	Wickford	Essex v Somerset
	Ashford	Kent v Worcs
	Blackpool	Lancs v Surrey
	Southgate	Middx v Warwks
	N'ham (Boots)	Notts v Northants
	Headingley	Yorks v Hants
Tue 12	The Oval	*Surrey v Glam
	Hove	*Sussex v Middx

MINOR COUNTIES CHAMPIONSHIP FIXTURES 2000

	Venue	*Match*
MAY		
Sun 21	Hungerford	Berks v Wales
	Barrow	Cumb v Herts
	Colwall	Herefords v Dorset
	Bourne	Lincs v Staffs
	Shrewsbury	Salop v Oxon
Tue 23	Alderley Edge	Cheshire v Oxon
	Jesmond	Northumb v Herts
Sun 28	Finchampstead	Berks v Herefords
	Torquay	Devon v Dorset
	Sleaford	Lincs v Beds
	Westbury	Wilts v Wales
Wed 31	Sleaford	Lincs v Northumb
JUNE		
Sun 4	Flitwick	Beds v Northumb
	Wellington	Salop v Wilts
Mon 5	Netherfield	Cumb v Norfolk
Tue 6	Wisbech	Cambs v Northumb
Wed 7	Stone	Staffs v Norfolk
Sun 11	Bedford	Beds v Cumb
	Weymouth	Dorset v Salop
	Banbury CC	Oxon v Wales
	Warminster	Wilts v Berks
Mon 12	Truro	Cornwall v Cheshire
Tue 13	Cannock	Staffs v Bucks
Wed 14	Saffron Walden	Cambs v Suffolk
	Bovey Tracey	Devon v Cheshire
Sun 25	Kington	Herefords v Devon
Wed 28	March	Cambs v Staffs
JULY		
Sun 2	Hurst CC	Berks v Cornwall
	Beaconsfield	Bucks v Norfolk
	Long Marston	Herts v Suffolk
	Lincoln Lindum	Lincs v Cumb
	Colwyn Bay	Wales v Salop
Tue 4	Saffron Walden	Cambs v Cumb
	The Parks	Oxon v Cornwall
Sun 9	S Northumbland	Northumb v Staffs
Tue 11	Askam	Cumb v Staffs
Wed 12	Fenner's	Cambs v Bucks
Sun 16	Cheadle Hulme	Cheshire v Herefords
	Penzance	Cornwall v Dorset
	Bishop's Stortford	Herts v Bucks
	Grantham	Lincs v Cambs
	Ipswich School	Suffolk v Beds
	Marlborough	Wilts v Oxon
Sun 23	Marlow	Bucks v Beds
	Dean Park	Dorset v Berks
	Lakenham	Norfolk v Lincs

	Venue	*Match*
Sun 23	Christ Church	Oxon v Devon
	Whitchurch	Salop v Herefords
	Ransomes	Suffolk v Northumb
	Neath	Wales v Cornwall
	South Wilts CC	Wilts v Cheshire
Mon 24	Brewood	Staffs v Herts
Tue 25	Falkland CC	Berks v Devon
	Dean Park	Dorset v Cheshire
	Dales CC	Herefords v Cornwall
	Lakenham	Norfolk v Northumb
	Ransomes	Suffolk v Lincs
Sun 30	Dunstable	Beds v Herts
	Oxton	Cheshire v Wales
	Budleigh Salterton	Devon v Salop
	Dean Park	Dorset v Oxon
	Luctonians CC	Herefords v Wilts
Mon 31	Millom	Cumb v Suffolk
	Lakenham	Norfolk v Cambs
AUGUST		
Tue 1	Camborne	Cornwall v Salop
Wed 2	Lakenham	Norfolk v Herts
	Leek	Staffs v Suffolk
Sun 6	Wardown Park	Beds v Norfolk
	Milton Keynes	Bucks v Suffolk
	Exmouth	Devon v Wilts
	Radlett	Herts v Lincs
	Thame	Oxon v Herefords
	Ynysygerwn	Wales v Dorset
Sun 13	Southill Park	Beds v Cambs
	Neston	Cheshire v Berks
	Falmouth	Cornwall v Wilts
	Jesmond	Northumb v Bucks
	Pontarddulais	Wales v Devon
Tue 15	Carlisle	Cumb v Bucks
	Bridgnorth	Salop v Berks
Sun 20	Reading CC	Berks v Oxon
	High Wycombe	Bucks v Lincs
	Bowdon	Cheshire v Salop
	St Austell	Cornwall v Devon
	Brockhampton	Herefords v Wales
	Stevenage	Herts v Cambs
	Jesmond	Northumb v Cumb
	Walsall	Staffs v Beds
	Bury St Edmunds	Suffolk v Norfolk
	Corsham	Wilts v Dorset
SEPTEMBER		
Sun 10	tba	*CHAMPIONSHIP FINAL* (three days)

38 COUNTY COMPETITION FIXTURES 2000

	Venue	*Gp*	*Match*
MAY			
Sun 14	Bristol Optimists	1	Somerset v Wilts
	Mildenhall	3	Suffolk v Hunts
	St Georges	4	Salop v Herefords
Sun 21	Lakenham	5	Norfolk v Beds
	New Brighton	6	Cheshire v Derbys
Thu 25	Elland CC	8	Yorks v Lancs
Sun 28	North Perrott	1	Somerset v Cornwall
	Oswestry	4	Salop v Worcs
	Porthill Park	6	Staffs v Notts
Tue 30	Keswick	8	Cumb v Lancs
JUNE			
Sun 4	Sidmouth	1	Devon v Somerset
	Thatcham	2	Berks v Sussex
	Shenley Park	3	Middx v Herts
	King's Heath	4	Warwks v Wales
	Heanor Town	6	Derbys v Notts
	Wormsley	7	Bucks v Kent
Wed 7	Imber Court	7	Surrey v Oxon
Sun 11	St Just	1	Cornwall v Devon
	Hertford	3	Herts v Suffolk
	Chelmsford	3	Essex v Hunts
	Halesowen	4	Worcs v Herefords
	Raunds CC	5	Northants v Leics
	Wisbech	5	Cambs v Norfolk
	Heanor Town	6	Derbys v Staffs
	Boots Ground	6	Notts v Lincs
	Jesmond	8	Northumb v Yorks
Thu 15	Richmond	3	Middx v Essex
	Penrith	8	Cumb v Yorks
Sun 18	Corsham	1	Wilts v Devon
	Bristol U	1	Glos v Cornwall
	Horsham SC	2	Sussex v Berks
	Burridge	2	Hants v Dorset
	Luctonians CC	4	Herefords v Wales
	Stratford	4	Warwks v Salop
	Oakham School	5	Leics v Norfolk
	March	5	Cambs v Beds
	Longton	6	Staffs v Lincs
	Stockton	8	Durham v Northumb
Sun 25	Swindon	1	Wilts v Glos
	Finchampstead	2	Berks v Dorset
	Stirlands CC	2	Sussex v Hants
	Hertford	3	Herts v Essex
	Copdock CC	3	Suffolk v Middx
	Ynysygerwn	4	Wales v Worcs
	Bedford Town	5	Beds v Leics
	Lakenham	5	Norfolk v Northants
Sun 25	Grimsby	6	Lincs v Cheshire
	Christ Church	7	Oxon v Bucks
	Ashford	7	Kent v Surrey
	Tynemouth CC	8	Northumb v Cumb
Mon 26	Haslingden	8	Lancs v Durham
Tue 27	Stamford Br CC	8	Yorks v Durham
Thu 29	Banstead	7	Surrey v Bucks
JULY			
Sun 2	Bristol U	1	Glos v Somerset
	Dean Park	2	Dorset v Hants
	Ramsey	3	Hunts v Middx
	Raunds CC	5	Northants v Cambs
	Nantwich	6	Cheshire v Staffs
	Challow & Childrey	7	Oxon v Kent
	Ormskirk	8	Lancs v Northumb
Tue 4	Kidderminster	4	Worcs v Warwks
Sun 9	Helston	1	Cornwall v Wilts
	Instow	1	Devon v Glos
	Weymouth	2	Dorset v Sussex
	Liphook	2	Hants v Berks
	Warboys	3	Hunts v Herts
	Chelmsford	3	Essex v Suffolk
	Brockhampton	4	Herefords v Warwks
	St Fagans	4	Wales v Salop
	Dunstable	5	Beds v Northants
	Ratcliffe College	5	Leics v Cambs
	Boots Ground	6	Notts v Cheshire
	Cleethorpes	6	Lincs v Derbys
	Aylesbury	7	Bucks v Surrey
	Ropery Lane	8	Durham v Cumb
Tue 11	The Mote	7	Kent v Oxon
Wed 19			QUARTER-FINALS
	Match A		Winners of Group 1 v Winners of Group 4
	Match B		Winners of Group 6 v Winners of Group 8
	Match C		Winners of Group 5 v Winners of Group 7
	Match D		Winners of Group 3 v Winners of Group 2
AUGUST			
Thu 10			SEMI-FINALS (Reserve Day Fri 11)
	Match E		Winners of Match A v Winners of Match D
	Match F		Winners of Match C v Winners of Match B
Wed 30	Lord's		**FINAL**

PRINCIPAL FIXTURES 2000

BHC	Benson & Hedges Cup	NL1	CGU National League (1st Division)
CC1	PPP County Championship (1st Division)	NL2	CGU National League (2nd Division)
CC2	PPP County Championship (2nd Division)	NWT	NatWest Trophy
FCF	First-Class Friendly	TM	Cornhill Insurance Test Match
LOI	Limited-Overs International	VC	Vodaphone Challenge

F Floodlit

Fri 7 – Sun 9 April

FCF	Taunton	Somerset v Oxford U
FCF	Cambridge	Cambridge U v Lancashire

Tues 11 – Thurs 13 April

FCF	Nottingham	Notts v Cambridge U
FCF	Oxford	Oxford U v Hampshire

Sat 15 April

BHC	Derby	Derbyshire v Leics
BHC	Chester-le-St	Durham v Yorkshire
BHC	Chelmsford	Essex v Surrey
BHC	Cardiff	Glamorgan v Glos
BHC	Southampton	Hampshire v Middlesex
BHC	Canterbury	Kent v Sussex
BHC	Manchester	Lancashire v Notts
BHC	Northampton	Northants v Worcester
BHC	Birmingham	Warwks v Somerset

Sun 16 April

BHC	Bristol	Glos v Warwks
BHC	Leicester	Leics v Durham
BHC	Lord's	Middlesex v Essex
BHC	Nottingham	Notts v Derbyshire
BHC	Taunton	Somerset v Northants
BHC	The Oval	Surrey v Kent
BHC	Worcester	Worcs v Glamorgan
BHC	Leeds	Yorkshire v Lancashire

Tues 18 April

BHC	Chester-le-St	Durham v Lancashire
BHC	Canterbury	Kent v Essex
BHC	Hove	Sussex v Surrey
BHC	Birmingham	Warwks v Northants
BHC	Worcester	Worcs v Glos

Weds 19 April

BHC	Chelmsford	Essex v Hampshire
BHC	Taunton	Somerset v Glamorgan
BHC	Leeds	Yorkshire v Leics

Thurs 20 April

BHC	Derby	Derbyshire v Lancashire
BHC	Southampton	Hampshire v Kent
BHC	Lord's	Middlesex v Sussex
BHC	Northampton	Northants v Glos
BHC	Nottingham	Notts v Durham

Fri 21 April

BHC	Lord's	Middlesex v Surrey
BHC	Taunton	Somerset v Worcs

Sat 22 April

BHC	Derby	Derbyshire v Yorkshire
BHC	Cardiff	Glamorgan v Warwks
BHC	Leicester	Leics v Notts

Sun 23 April

BHC	Hove	Sussex v Hampshire

Mon 24 April

BHC	Chester-le-St	Durham v Derbyshire
BHC	Chelmsford	Essex v Sussex
BHC	Bristol	Glos v Somerset
BHC	Canterbury	Kent v Middlesex
BHC	Manchester	Lancashire v Leics
BHC	Northampton	Northants v Glamorgan
BHC	Nottingham	Notts v Yorkshire
BHC	The Oval	Surrey v Hampshire
BHC	Birmingham	Warwks v Worcs

Weds 26 – Fri 28 April

FCF	Cambridge	Cambridge U v Essex
FCF	Oxford	Oxford U v Warwks

Weds 26 – Sat 29 April

CC1	Derby	Derbyshire v Leics
CC2	Bristol	Glos v Sussex
CC1	Canterbury	Kent v Lancashire
CC2	Nottingham	Notts v Northants
CC1	Taunton	Somerset v Surrey
CC2	Worcester	Worcs v Glamorgan

Thurs 27 – Sun 30 April

VC	Southampton	Hampshire v Zimbabweans

Sun 30 April

NL2	Cardiff	Glamorgan v Surrey
NL1	Bristol	Glos v Sussex
NL1	Canterbury	Kent v Lancashire
NL2	Chelmsford†	Middlesex v Essex
NL2	Nottingham	Notts v Durham
NL1	Worcester	Worcs v Yorkshire

† *Home match for Middlesex*

Mon 1 May

NL2	Derby	Derbyshire v Middlesex
NL2	Southampton	Hampshire v Warwks
NL1	Canterbury	Kent v Northants
NL1	Leicester	Leics v Sussex
NL1	Taunton	Somerset v Glos

Tues 2 May

NWT Round 1 (*see p 286; reserve Weds 3 May*)

Tues 2 – Thurs 4 May

FCF	Cambridge	Cambridge U v Worcs

Tues 2 – Fri 5 May

CC1	Chester-le-St	Durham v Surrey

Weds 3 – Fri 5 May

FCF	Bristol	Glos v Oxford U

Weds 3 – Sat 6 May

CC2	Chelmsford	Essex v Notts
CC1	Southampton	Hampshire v Somerset
VC	Canterbury	Kent v Zimbabweans
CC1	Manchester	Lancashire v Leics
CC2	Lord's	Middlesex v Northants
CC2	Birmingham	Warwks v Glamorgan
CC1	Leeds	Yorkshire v Derbyshire

Sat 6 May

NL2	Chester-le-St	Durham v Surrey

Sun 7 May

NL2	Chelmsford	Essex v Notts
NL1	Manchester	Lancashire v Leics
NL2	Lord's	Middlesex v Hampshire
NL1	Northampton	Northants v Glos
	Hastings	Sussex v Zimbabweans
NL2	Birmingham	Warwks v Glamorgan
NL1	Leeds	Yorkshire v Worcs

Tues 9 May

BHC Quarter-Finals (*Reserve Weds 10 May*)

†Chelmsford/Hove/Canterbury/Oval — Essex/Sussex/Kent/Surrey v Zimbabweans

† Depending on BHC Quarter-Finalists

Thurs 11 – Sun 14 May

CC1	Chester-le-St	Durham v Lancashire
VC	Chelmsford	Essex v Zimbabweans
CC2	Cardiff	Glamorgan v Glos
CC1	Leicester	Leics v Somerset
CC2	Northampton	Northants v Notts
CC1	The Oval	Surrey v Kent
CC2	Hove	Sussex v Warwks
CC2	Worcester	Worcs v Middlesex

Fri 12 – Sun 14 May

FCF	Cambridge	Cambridge U v Derbyshire

Fri 12 – Mon 15 May

CC1	Leeds	Yorkshire v Hampshire

Tues 16 May

NWT Round 2 (*see p 286; reserve Weds 17 May*)

Tues 16 – Thurs 18 May

FCF	Cambridge	Cambridge U v Middlesex
FCF	Oxford	Oxford U v Glamorgan

Weds 17 May

NL1	Hove F	Sussex v Worcs

Weds 17 – Sat 20 May

CC1	Derby	Derbyshire v Yorkshire
CC1	Leicester	Leics v Hampshire
CC2	Nottingham	Notts v Glos
CC2	Birmingham	Warwks v Essex

Thurs 18 – Sun 21 May

CC2	Hove	Sussex v Worcs

Thurs 18 – Mon 22 May

TM1	**Lord's**	**England v Zimbabwe**

Sun 21 May

NL2	Chester-le-St	Durham v Glamorgan
NL1	Leicester	Leics v Kent
NL2	Nottingham	Notts v Derbyshire
NL1	Taunton	Somerset v Northants
NL2	The Oval	Surrey v Middlesex
NL2	Birmingham	Warwks v Hampshire
NL1	Leeds	Yorkshire v Glos

Tues 23 – Fri 26 May

CC2	Chelmsford	Essex v Sussex

Weds 24 – Sat 27 May

CC1	Chester-le-St	Durham v Leics
CC2	Cardiff	Glamorgan v Warwks
CC2	Bristol	Glos v Worcs
CC1	Southampton	Hampshire v Lancashire
CC1	Canterbury	Kent v Surrey
CC2	Northampton	Northants v Middlesex
CC1	Taunton	Somerset v Derbyshire
VC†	Leeds	Yorkshire v Zimbabweans

† Played 24-26 May if Yorkshire in BHC S-F

Sat 27 May

BHC First Semi-Final (*Reserve 28 May*)

Sun 28 May

BHC Second Semi-Final (*Reserve 29 May*)

NL2	Chester-le-St	Durham v Notts
NL2	Cardiff	Glamorgan v Derbyshire
NL1	Bristol	Glos v Lancashire
NL1	Tunbridge W	Kent v Sussex
NL2	The Oval	Surrey v Essex
NL1	Worcester	Worcs v Northants
	Castleford	MCC v Zimbabweans

Tues 30 May

NL2	The Oval F	Surrey v Hampshire

Weds 31 May

NL2	Birmingham F	Warwks v Notts

Weds 31 May – Sat 3 June

CC2	Ilford	Essex v Northants
CC1	Tunbridge W	Kent v Durham
CC1	Manchester	Lancashire v Derbyshire
CC2	Lord's	Middlesex v Glos
CC2	Hove	Sussex v Glamorgan
CC1	Leeds	Yorkshire v Leics

Thurs 1 – Sun 4 June

CC1	The Oval	Surrey v Hampshire

Thurs 1 – Mon 5 June

TM2	**Nottingham**	**England v Zimbabwe**

Fri 2 – Sun 4 June

VC	Worcester	Worcs v West Indians

Fri 2 – Mon 5 June

CC2	Birmingham	Warwks v Notts

Sun 4 June

NL2	Ilford	Essex v Durham
NL1	Tunbridge	Kent v Glos
NL2	Lord's	Middlesex v Glamorgan
NL1	Northampton	Northants v Lancashire
NL1	Bath	Somerset v Sussex
NL1	Leeds	Yorkshire v Leics

Tues 6 – Thurs 8 June

VC	Cardiff	Glamorgan v West Indians
FCF	Oxford	Oxford U v Northants

Tues 6 – Fri 9 June

CC1	Bath	Somerset v Kent

Weds 7 June

	Clontarf	Ireland v Zimbabwe

Weds 7 – Sat 10 June

CC1	Derby	Derbyshire v Surrey
CC1	Chester-le-St	Durham v Yorkshire
CC2	Bristol	Glos v Essex
CC1	Liverpool	Lancashire v Hampshire
CC2	Nottingham	Notts v Worcs
CC2	Horsham	Sussex v Middlesex

Thurs 8 June

	Clontarf	Ireland v Zimbabwe

Sat 10 June

BHC	**Lord's**	**FINAL** (*Reserve 11 June*)

Sat 10 – Mon 12 June

FCF	Arundel	West Indies v Zimbabwe

Sun 11 June

	Oxford	British U v New Zealand A
NL2	Derby	Derbyshire v Surrey
NL1	Manchester	Lancashire v Worcs
NL2	Nottingham	Notts v Hampshire
NL1	Taunton	Somerset v Kent
NL1	Horsham	Sussex v Leics

Tues 13 June

NL2	Cardiff F	Glamorgan v Essex

Tues 13 – Fri 16 June

FCF	Liverpool	Lancashire v New Zealand A

Weds 14 June

NL1	Worcester F	Worcs v Glos
	Beaconsfield	England Board XI v Zimbabweans

Weds 14 – Sat 17 June

CC1	Basingstoke	Hampshire v Durham
CC1	Leicester	Leics v Derbyshire
CC2	Lord's	Middlesex v Notts
CC2	Northampton	Northants v Warwks
CC1	The Oval	Surrey v Somerset
CC1	Leeds	Yorkshire v Kent

Thurs 15 – Sun 18 June

CC2	Cardiff	Glamorgan v Essex
CC2	Worcester	Worcs v Sussex

Thurs 15 – Mon 19 June

TM1	**Birmingham**	**England v West Indies**

Fri 16 – Mon 19 June

VC	Gloucester	Glos v Zimbabweans

Sun 18 June

NL2	Basingstoke	Hampshire v Durham
	Leicester	Leics v New Zealand A
NL2	Lord's	Middlesex v Derbyshire
NL1	Northampton	Northants v Somerset
NL1	Leeds	Yorkshire v Kent

Mon 19 June

	The Oval	Surrey v New Zealand A

Weds 21 June

NWT	Round 3 (*see p 286; reserve Thurs 22 June*)	

Weds 21 – Fri 23 June

FCF	Cambridge	British U v Zimbabweans

Weds 21 – Sat 24 June

FCF	Chelmsford	West Indians v New Zealand A

Fri 23 June

NL1	Manchester F	Lancashire v Northants
NL1	Hove F	Sussex v Kent
NL2	Birmingham F	Warwks v Surrey

Sat 24 June

NL2 Cardiff Glamorgan v Hampshire
NL1 Bristol Glos v Yorkshire
NL2 Nottingham Notts v Essex
NL1 Taunton Somerset v Worcs

Sun 25 June

NL2 Chester-le-St Durham v Middlesex
Southampton Hampshire v West Indians
NL1 Leicester Leics v Glos
Taunton Somerset v Zimbabweans
NL2 Birmingham Warwks v Essex
NL1 Leeds Yorkshire v Northants

Mon 26 June

NL2 Derby F Derbyshire v Notts
Worcester Worcs v New Zealand A

Tues 27 June

Chester-le-St Durham v Zimbabweans
NL2 Southampton Hampshire v Surrey
NL1 Manchester F Lancashire v Yorkshire

Weds 28 June – Sat 1 July

CC1 Darlington Durham v Derbyshire
CC2 Chelmsford Essex v Middlesex
CC2 Swansea Glamorgan v Worcs
CC1 Maidstone Kent v Somerset
Hove Sussex v New Zealand A
CC2 Birmingham Warwks v Glos

Thurs 29 June

Nottingham Notts v Zimbabweans

Thurs 29 June – Sun 2 July

CC1 Southampton Hampshire v Surrey
CC1 Manchester Lancashire v Yorkshire

Thurs 29 June – Mon 3 July

TM2 Lord's England v West Indies
The 100th Test Match at Lord's

Sat 1 July

Northampton Northants v Zimbabweans

Sun 2 July

NL2 Darlington Durham v Derbyshire
NL2 Chelmsford Essex v Middlesex
NL2 Swansea Glamorgan v Warwks
NL1 Maidstone Kent v Somerset
NL1 Northampton Northants v Sussex
NL1 Worcester Worcs v Leics

Mon 3 July

Bristol F Zimbabweans v NZ A

Tues 4 July

Bristol F West Indians v NZ A

Weds 5 July

NWT Round 4 (*see p 286; reserve Thurs 6 July*)

Thurs 6 July

LOI 1 Bristol F West Indies v Zimbabwe

Fri 7 – Mon 10 July

CC1 Derby Derbyshire v Lancashire
CC1 Oakham S Leics v Surrey
CC2 Southgate Middlesex v Worcs
CC2 Northampton Northants v Glamorgan
CC2 Nottingham Notts v Essex
CC1 Taunton Somerset v Hampshire
CC2 Birmingham Warwks v Sussex
CC1 Leeds Yorkshire v Durham
FCF Milton Keynes FCC Select v NZ A

Sat 8 July

LOI 2 The Oval England v Zimbabwe

Sun 9 July

LOI 3 Lord's England v West Indies

Tues 11 July

LOI 4 Canterbury West Indies v Zimbabwe

Tues 11 – Thurs 13 July

FCF Lord's Cambridge U v Oxford U

Weds 12 – Sat 15 July

CC1 Derby Derbyshire v Kent
CC2 Cheltenham Glos v Northants
Portsmouth Hampshire v N Zealand A
CC1 Leicester Leics v Durham
CC2 Southgate Middlesex v Glamorgan
CC1 Taunton Somerset v Lancashire
CC1 The Oval Surrey v Yorkshire
CC2 Arundel Sussex v Essex
CC2 Worcester Worcs v Notts

Thurs 13 July

LOI 5 Manchester F England v Zimbabwe

Sat 15 July

LOI 6 Chester-le-St England v West Indies

Sun 16 July

LOI 7 Chester-le-St West Indies v Zimbabwe

Sun 16 July

NL2 Derby Derbyshire v Warwks
NL1 Cheltenham Glos v Worcs
NL1 Leicester Leics v Northants
NL2 Southgate Middlesex v Durham
NL1 Taunton Somerset v Lancashire
NL2 The Oval Surrey v Glamorgan
NL1 Arundel Sussex v Yorkshire

Mon 17 July

Cheltenham Glos v New Zealand A

Tues 18 July

LOI 8 Birmingham F England v Zimbabwe

Tues 18 – Fri 21 July

FCF Oxford MCC v New Zealand A

Weds 19 – Sat 22 July

CC2	Chelmsford	Essex v Worcs
CC2	Cardiff	Glamorgan v Northants
CC2	Cheltenham	Glos v Warwks
CC1	Portsmouth	Hampshire v Kent
CC1	Manchester	Lancashire v Durham
CC1	Guildford	Surrey v Leics
CC2	Hove	Sussex v Notts
CC1	Scarborough	Yorkshire v Somerset

Thurs 20 July

LOI 9	**Nottingham**	**England v West Indies**

Sat 22 July

LOI 10	**LORD'S**	**FINAL** (*Reserve 23 July*)

Sun 23 July

NL2	Chelmsford	Essex v Derbyshire
NL1	Cheltenham	Glos v Kent
NL2	Portsmouth	Hampshire v Middlesex
NL1	Leicester	Leics v Lancashire
NL2	Guildford	Surrey v Notts
NL2	Birmingham	Warwks v Durham
NL1	Scarborough	Yorkshire v Somerset

Mon 24 – Weds 26 July

VC	N'ton/Leeds	Northants/Yorks v WI

Depending on NWT Quarter-Finalists

Tues 25[1] and Weds 26[2] July

NWT Quarter-Finals

[1] *Reserve 26, 27 July.* [2] *Reserve 27 July.*

Fri 28 – Sun 30 July

VC	Leicester	Leics v West Indians

Fri 28 – Mon 31 July

CC1	Chester-le-St	Durham v Somerset
CC1	Canterbury	Kent v Derbyshire
CC2	Southgate	Middlesex v Sussex
CC2	Birmingham	Warwks v Northants
CC2	Worcester	Worcs v Glos
CC1	Leeds	Yorkshire v Lancashire

Sun 30 July

NL2	Southampton	Hampshire v Essex

Tues 1 August

NL2	Nottingham **F**	Notts v Warwks

Weds 2 August

NL1	Northampton **F**	Northants v Worcs

Weds 2 – Sat 5 August

CC1	Derby	Derbyshire v Hampshire
CC2	Bristol	Glos v Glamorgan
CC1	Canterbury	Kent v Leics
CC2	Lord's	Middlesex v Essex
CC1	Taunton	Somerset v Yorkshire
CC1	The Oval	Surrey v Lancashire

Thurs 3 – Sun 6 August

CC2	Nottingham	Notts v Warwks

Thurs 3 – Mon 7 August

TM3	**Manchester**	**England v West Indies**

Fri 4 – Mon 7 August

CC2	Northampton	Northants v Worcs

Sun 6 August

NL2	Derby	Derbyshire v Hampshire
NL2	Cardiff	Glamorgan v Durham
NL1	Canterbury	Kent v Leics
NL2	Lord's	Middlesex v Surrey
NL1	Taunton	Somerset v Yorkshire

Mon 7 August

NL1	Hove **F**	Sussex v Lancashire

Weds 9 August

NL1	Bristol **F**	Glos v Somerset
NL2	Whitgift S	Surrey v Warwks
NL1	Leeds **F**	Yorkshire v Lancashire

Weds 9 – Fri 11 August

VC	Derby	Derbyshire v WI

Weds 9 – Sat 12 August

CC1	Chester-le-St	Durham v Kent
CC1	Southampton	Hampshire v Leics
CC2	Northampton	Northants v Sussex
CC2	Nottingham	Notts v Middlesex
CC2	Kidderminster	Worcs v Essex

Sat 12 August

NWT First Semi-Final (*Reserve 13 Aug*)

Sun 13 August

NWT Second Semi-Final (*Reserve 14 Aug*)

Titwood, Glasgow Scotland v West Indies

Sun 13 August

NL2	Derby	Derbyshire v Essex
NL2	Chester-le-St	Durham v Warwks
NL2	Southampton	Hampshire v Glamorgan
NL1	Manchester	Lancashire v Glos
NL1	Northampton	Northants v Leics
NL2	Nottingham	Notts v Middlesex
NL1	Worcester	Worcs v Sussex

Tues 15 August

NL1	Manchester **F**	Lancashire v Kent

Weds 16 August

NL2	Birmingham **F**	Warwks v Middlesex

Weds 16 – Sat 19 August

CC2	Colchester	Essex v Glos
CC2	Cardiff	Glamorgan v Notts
CC1	Leicester	Leics v Yorkshire
CC1	Taunton	Somerset v Durham
CC1	The Oval	Surrey v Derbyshire
CC2	Eastbourne	Sussex v Northants

Thurs 17 – Sun 20 August

CC1	Manchester	Lancashire v Kent
CC2	Birmingham	Warwks v Middlesex

Thurs 17 – Mon 21 August

TM4	**Leeds**	**England v West Indies**

Sun 20 August

NL2	Colchester	Essex v Hampshire
NL2	Colwyn Bay	Glamorgan v Notts
NL1	Leicester	Leics v Yorkshire
NL2	The Oval	Surrey v Derbyshire
NL1	Eastbourne	Sussex v Northants
NL1	Worcester	Worcs v Somerset

Tues 22 – Fri 25 August

CC1	Derby	Derbyshire v Durham
CC2	Colwyn Bay	Glamorgan v Sussex
CC2	Bristol	Glos v Middlesex
CC1	Canterbury	Kent v Hampshire
CC1	Leicester	Leics v Lancashire
CC2	Worcester	Worcs v Warwks

Weds 23 August

NL2	Colchester **F**	Essex v Surrey

Weds 23 – Sat 26 August

VC	N'ham/Taunton	Notts/Somerset v WI

Depending on NWT Finalists

Sat 26 August

NWT	**Lord's**	**FINAL** (*Reserve 27 Aug*)

Sun 27 August

NL2	Derby	Derbyshire v Glamorgan
NL2	Chester-le-St	Durham v Essex
NL1	Canterbury	Kent v Worcs

Mon 28 August

NL1	Bristol **F**	Glos v Leics
NL2	Richmond	Middlesex v Notts
NL1	Northampton	Northants v Yorkshire
NL1	Hove **F**	Sussex v Somerset

Tues 29 August

NL2	Chester-le-St **F**	Durham v Hampshire

Weds 30 August

NL1	Taunton **F**	Somerset v Leics

Weds 30 August – Sat 2 September

CC2	Southend	Essex v Glamorgan
CC2	Northampton	Northants v Glos
CC2	Nottingham	Notts v Sussex
CC2	Birmingham	Warwks v Worcs
CC1	Scarborough	Yorkshire v Surrey

Thurs 31 August – Sun 3 September

CC1	Chester-le-St	Durham v Hampshire

Thurs 31 August – Mon 4 September

TM5	**The Oval**	**England v West Indies**

Fri 1 – Mon 4 September

CC1	Taunton	Somerset v Leics

Sun 3 September

NL2	Southend	Essex v Glamorgan
NL1	Northampton	Northants v Kent
NL2	Nottingham	Notts v Surrey
NL2	Birmingham	Warwks v Derbyshire
NL1	Worcester	Worcs v Lancashire
NL1	Scarborough	Yorkshire v Sussex

Tues 5 September

NL1	Canterbury **F**	Kent v Yorkshire
NL1	Hove **F**	Sussex v Glos

Tues 5 – Fri 8 September

CC2	Lord's	Middlesex v Warwks

Weds 6 September

NL1	Manchester **F**	Lancashire v Somerset

Weds 6 – Sat 9 September

CC1	Southampton	Hampshire v Derbyshire
CC2	Northampton	Northants v Essex
CC2	Nottingham	Notts v Glamorgan
CC1	The Oval	Surrey v Durham
CC2	Hove	Sussex v Glos

Fri 8 September

NL1	Leicester **F**	Leics v Worcs

Fri 8 – Mon 11 September

CC1	Manchester	Lancashire v Somerset

Sat 9 September

NL2	Lord's	Middlesex v Warwks

Sun 10 September

NL2	Southampton	Hampshire v Derbyshire
NL2	Nottingham	Notts v Glamorgan
NL2	The Oval	Surrey v Durham

Weds 13 – Sat 16 September

CC1	Derby	Derbyshire v Somerset
CC2	Chelmsford	Essex v Warwks
CC2	Cardiff	Glamorgan v Middlesex
CC2	Bristol	Glos v Notts
CC1	Southampton	Hampshire v Yorkshire
CC1	Manchester	Lancashire v Surrey
CC1	Leicester	Leics v Kent
CC2	Worcester	Worcs v Northants

Sun 17 September

NL2	Derby	Derbyshire v Durham
NL2	Chelmsford	Essex v Warwks
NL2	Cardiff	Glamorgan v Middlesex
NL1	Bristol	Glos v Northants
NL2	Southampton	Hampshire v Notts
NL1	Manchester	Lancashire v Sussex
NL1	Leicester	Leics v Somerset
NL1	Worcester	Worcs v Kent

NATWEST TROPHY FIXTURES 2000

Round 1 – Tuesday 2 May

1	Herefordshire	v	Sussex Board
2	Northants Board	v	Northumberland
3	Hertfordshire	v	Cambridgeshire
4	Cheshire	v	Lincolnshire
5	Ireland	v	Shropshire
6	Worcs Board	v	Kent Board
7	Staffordshire	v	Somerset Board
8	Wiltshire	v	Scotland
9	Wales	v	Buckinghamshire
10	Glos Board	v	Notts Board
11	Durham Board	v	Leics Board
12	Suffolk	v	Lancs Board
13	Cornwall	v	Norfolk
14	Hants Board	v	Hunts Board

Round 2 – Tuesday 16 May

15	Winner # 1	v	Berks
16	Winner # 2	v	Beds
17	Winner # 3	v	Cumberland
18	Winner # 4	v	Holland
19	Winner # 5	v	Surrey Board
20	Warwks Board	v	Winner # 6
21	Devon	v	Winner # 7
22	Middx Board	v	Winner # 8
23	Winner # 9	v	Oxfordshire
24	Derbys Board	v	Winner # 10
25	Winner # 11	v	†Denmark
26	Essex Board	v	Winner # 12
27	Dorset	v	Winner # 13
28	Winner # 14	v	Yorks Board

Round 3 – Wednesday 21 June

29	Winner # 15	v	Durham
30	Winner # 16	v	Leicestershire
31	Winner # 17	v	Kent
32	Winner # 18	v	Lancashire
33	Winner # 19	v	Somerset
34	Winner # 20	v	Hampshire
35	Winner # 21	v	Surrey
36	Winner # 22	v	Sussex
37	Winner # 23	v	Essex
38	Winner # 24	v	Derbyshire
39	Winner # 25	v	Northamptonshire
40	Winner # 26	v	Warwickshire
41	Winner # 27	v	Glamorgan
42	Winner # 28	v	Yorkshire
43	Worcestershire	v	Gloucestershire
44	Middlesex	v	Nottinghamshire

Round 4 – Wednesday 5 July

45	Winner # 29	v	Winner # 34
46	Winner # 39	v	Winner # 42
47	Winner # 40	v	Winner # 38
48	Winner # 32	v	Winner # 37
49	Winner # 44	v	Winner # 33
50	Winner # 31	v	Winner # 41
51	Winner # 30	v	Winner # 43
52	Winner # 35	v	Winner # 36

Quarter-Finals Tues 25 and Wed 26 July
Semi-Finals Sat 12 and Sun 13 August
Final Sat 26 August

FIRST ROUND BYES: Bedfordshire, Berkshire, Cumberland, Derbyshire Board, Devon, Dorset, Essex Board, Denmark, Holland, Middlesex Board, Oxfordshire, Surrey Board, Warwickshire Board, Yorkshire Board. First-class counties enter in Round 3.

Board — Cricket Board 'recreational team'.
† — Denmark will play all matches away (grass pitch not approved for NWT).

ECB TOURS PROGRAMME

2000
Zimbabwe (2)/West Indies (5)
2000-01
Pakistan (3)/Sri Lanka (3)
2001
Pakistan (2)/Australia (5)
2001-02
†India (3)/†New Zealand (3)
2002
†Sri Lanka (2 or 3)/†India (4 or 5)
2002-03
Australia/World Cup (South Africa)

2003
South Africa/†New Zealand
2003-04
†West Indies
2004
Zimbabwe/Pakistan
2004-05
†South Africa
2005
Australia
2006
†West Indies

† *To be confirmed*
No of Tests in brackets (where confirmed)
Schedule subject to the possible introduction of a world championship of Test cricket.

FIELDING CHART

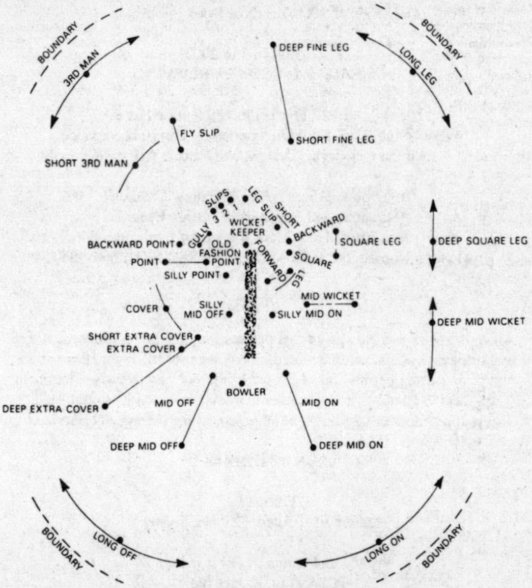

SCORING OF EXTRAS 2000

The confusing variations of penalties involved in scoring no-balls and wides in our international and county cricket remain unchanged from last season:

COMPETITION	NO-BALL PENALTY	WIDE PENALTY
Test Matches Limited-Overs Internationals	1 + other runs scored	1 + other runs scored
County Championship Second XI Championship Tourist Matches (First-Class) Tourist Matches (Limited-Overs)	2 + other runs scored	2 + other runs scored
Benson & Hedges Cup NatWest Trophy AON Trophy	2 + other runs scored	1 + other runs scored
CGU National League	2 + other runs scored + a free hit next ball	1 + other runs scored

First published in 2000
by HEADLINE BOOK PUBLISHING

Cover photographs: (*Front*) Andrew Caddick
(Somerset and England) © Patrick Eagar;
(*back*) Jack Russell and Mark Alleyne of Gloucestershire
celebrate winning the 1999 NatWest Trophy © PA Photo/EPA.

10 9 8 7 6 5 4 3 2 1

ISBN 0 7472 6448 1

Typeset by
Letterpart Limited, Reigate, Surrey

Printed and bound in Great Britain by
Clays Ltd, St Ives plc.

HEADLINE BOOK PUBLISHING
A division of the Hodder Headline Group
338 Euston Road
London NW1 3BH

www.headline.co.uk
www.hodderheadline.com